A BEER A DAY

366 beers to help you through the year

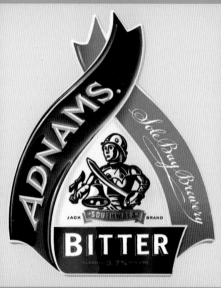

A BEER A DAY

366 beers to help you through the year

**CAMPAIGN
FOR
REAL ALE**

JEFF EVANS

Published by the Campaign for
Real Ale Ltd
230 Hatfield Road
St Albans
Herfordshire AL1 4LW

www.camra.org.uk/books

Text © Jeff Evans 2008
Design and layout © Campaign for Real
    Ale 2008

ISBN 978-1-85249-235-9

A CIP catalogue record for this book is
available from the British Library

Printed and bound in Singapore
by KHL Printing Co Pte Ltd

Managing Editor: Simon Hall
Project Editors: Katie Hunt; Debbie
    Williams
Editorial Assistance: Emma Haines
Copy Editor: Helen Ridge
Design/Typography: Alison Fenton
Picture Research: Sarah Airey (Nadine
    Bazar)
Senior Marketing Manager: Georgina
    Rudman

A Beer a Day

PICTURE CREDITS
The Publisher would like to thank the
breweries for their kind permission to
reproduce these photographs. All
photographs have been provided by
the breweries except:

8 Rex Features/Isopress; 9 Rex Features;
10 SuperStock/Hubertus Kanus; 12
SuperStock/Christie's Images; 14
SuperStock/age fotostock; 19 Rex
Features/Sedak Ozkomec; 20
Gettyimages/The Bridgeman Art Library;
25 Topfoto; 33 Topfoto/imageworks/Rob
Crandall; 34 Keith Airey; 36 Topfoto/
Roger-Viollet; 42 Vanessa Courtier; 44
SuperStock/age fotostock; 47 Vanessa
Courtier; 49 Topfoto/HIP; 52 Topfoto/
ARPL/HIP; 54 Topfoto/Caro; 56 Rex
Features/Dave Penman; 59 Rex Features/
Roger-Viollet; 61 Rex Features/SNAP;
62 Rex Features/Eye Ubiquitous; 74 Rex
Features/The Everett Collection; 76 Rex
Features/Ilpo Musto; 79 Rex Features/
Times Newspapers; 84 Rex Features/Sipa
Press; 86 Topfoto/ARPL/HIP; 88
Gettyimages; 91 The Art Archive/Culver
Pictures; 97 Topfoto; 102 Topfoto/Print
Collector/HIP; 106 Topfoto/Roger-Viollet;
111 Rex Features/SNAP; 114 Topfoto; 115
Gettyimages/AFP; 117 Rex Features/Sipa
Press; 126 MGM courtesy The Kobal
Collection; 128 Topfoto/Roger-Viollet;
130 akg-images; 133 Rex Features/
J Jacquemart; 134 Gettyimages; 140
Gettyimages; 144 Rex Features; 151
Gettyimages; 153 SuperStock; 159 Rex
Features/Nils Jorgensen; 160 Topfoto; 167
Topfoto/Roger-Viollet; 169 Rex Features/
Lindsay Parnaby; 172 Topfoto/British
Library/HIP; 175 Rex Features/John
Curtis; 176 Rex Features/The Everett
Collection; 180 Topfoto/English Heritage/
HIP; 183 Topfoto/Roger-Viollet; 184
Topfoto; 190 Topfoto; 191 Topfoto/Charles
Walker Collection; 193 Gettyimages; 198
Jeff Evans; 200 Topfoto/Alinari; 203 Rex
Features/Roger-Viollet; 208 SuperStock;
209 Topfoto/AP; 214 Rex Features/Lewis
Durham; 223 Rex Features/Nicolas Bailey;
226 Rex Features/Eye Ubiquitous; 231
Rex Features/Sam Morgan Moore; 235
Gettyimages/Time Life Pictures; 239

Topfoto; 242 Rex Features/Stephen
Meddle; 245 Gettyimages; 249
akg-images/Nelly Rou-Häring; 250
Gettyimages; 253 Rex Features/© New
Line/The Everett Collection; 263 Rex
Features/Jean Michel/Sunset; 267 Rex
Features/Patrick Frilet; 269 Gettyimages/
The Bridgeman Art Library; 270 Rex
Features/Brian Rasic; 273 Rex Features/
Andrew Aiken; 278 Gettyimages; 279 Rex
Features/Joe Pepler; 280 SuperStock/
Christie's Images; 281 Rex Features/
© Paramount/The Everett Collection;
282 Rex Features/Pekka Sakki; 288 Rex
Features/Geoff Wilkinson; 292 Rex
Features/Nils Jorgensen; 293 Rex
Features/Sipa Press; 295 Gettyimages;
297 Gettyimages; 299 Jeff Evans; 304
The Art Archive/Private Collection; 307
Rex Features/The Travel Library; 314 Rex
Features; 320 Rex Features/Roger-Viollet;
326 Rex Features; 329 Topfoto; 334 Rex
Features/Reg Wilson; 337 SuperStock;
341 Rex Features; 342 Gettyimages;
346 Rex Features; 351 Rex Features/Peter
Price; 354 Gettyimages/Gallo Images;
357 Rex Features/Adrian Wyld; 359 Rex
Features/Roger-Viollet; 363 Rex
Features/© Tavin/The Everett Collection;
371 Topfoto/AP; 373 Rex Features/
Roger-Viollet

Jeff Evans would like to thank all the
breweries that kindly helped with
the research for this book and provided
sample beers and product images.
Thanks also go to Nigel Stevenson of
beer importer James Clay for his
assistance, to mail order beer company
onlyfinebeer.com, and to Erwin de Cock
for help with a little research in Dutch.
Apologies go to anyone else whose
contribution has been inadvertently
overlooked – it's all gratefully appreciated!

Contents

ABOVE: THE BRITISH ARE COMING! RAISE A GLASS TO A HERO OF AMERICAN INDEPENDENCE ON 18 APRIL

Introduction

Welcome to a beer book with a difference. *A Beer a Day* is not just a catalogue of great beers: it is a celebration of high days, holidays and the otherwise gentle passing of the seasons as seen through the eyes of the world's greatest brewers. Major anniversaries, religious feasts and important birthdays come under the spotlight, along with commemorations, carnivals and some even more eccentric events. Whatever the occasion, there is always a beer for it, and there is no more fitting beverage with which to toast the unfolding of each day, week and month. Beer, you see, is not simply the ultimate party drink, brilliantly bringing people together, but one that itself has always danced to the tune of the seasons.

SEASONAL SPECIALS

In pre-industrial times, brewing in summer months in many parts of the world was impossible, due to the difficulty of controlling fermentation. Hence, brewers took to brewing beers in the winter that could be kept for enjoyment later. This is the origin of harvest ales in Britain, bières de garde in France, saisons in Belgium and of Märzen beers in Germany. It's also a major part of the story of lager: it was while needing to store beer for a long period in cold conditions to keep it fresh that monks discovered the benefits of lagering.

Today, there is a new seasonality to brewing. For most of the 20th century, British beers were pared back to two or three draughts per brewery, usually a mild, a bitter and a best bitter, with perhaps a stronger ale for winter. Since the introduction of the guest beer law in the early 1990s, with pubs clamouring for new and tempting beers with every delivery, breweries have re-introduced the concept of seasonals, so you'll find spring, summer and autumn ales to join the winter offering, and very often semi-seasonals dropped in between to celebrate events such as St Valentine's Day, Easter, May Day, Hallowe'en and Bonfire Night. The seasonal concept has been revived in the US, too, in the hands of the new legion of craft breweries that have brought such badly needed colour and quality to the American beer market. In other countries, such as Germany, Belgium and France, similar trends are emerging or have been long established.

A BEER ALMANAC

A Beer a Day selects some of the most interesting new seasonals and brings them together with other beers that do a terrific job in keeping alive the memories of historic events and great achievers. Looking for once behind the pump clips and labels, it unearths fine beers that vibrantly recall glorious and sometimes inglorious moments of history, beers that mark cultural highlights, and beers that have been inspired by religion and culture. What we have here, therefore, is a beer almanac, with a story for every beer and a beer for every story. The pages are arranged just like a calendar, with a major event, season or other commemoration featured on each day, together with an appropriate beer for the occasion. Room has been saved for saints and sinners, for beginnings and endings, for the famous and for the largely forgotten. Some of the events are deadly serious, others are frivolous and fun, and also included is a short sample of births, deaths and other events, to provide a flavour of what else has happened on each day of the year.

Most beers will be reasonably easy to get hold of, given the number of specialist beer shops that now exist and the additional facility of Internet mail order. Some will, undoubtedly, prove to be more elusive, but therein lies part of the purpose of a book such as this – to encourage the wider distribution of fine beers.

The overall message that I hope emerges from these pages is that few industries do more to preserve our heritage, honour our illustrious forebears and foster a sense of community than the brewing industry. Brewers are all too often attacked for fuelling what has become known as anti-social behaviour. I hope this book proves that, when enjoyed responsibly, beer actually has quite the opposite effect.

Jeff Evans

No. 1 Barley Wine

Source The White Shield Brewery, Burton-upon-Trent, Staffordshire **Strength** 10.5%
Website worthingtonswhiteshield.com

Whoever came up with a simple red triangle as the trademark for Bass Breweries could never have imagined how famous it would become. Not only did it go on to adorn thousands of pub signs, it also earned a place in history as Britain's first ever registered trademark.

It was on 1 January 1876 that the Bass logo set that legal precedent. A company employee waited all night outside a registration office to lodge the red triangle design as soon as the new Trademarks Registration Act came into force. It shows that the company was quick to recognize the importance of its image rights. Bass India Pale Ale was being exported all over the world at this time, as proved by Edouard Manet's famous 1882 painting of *Bar at the Folies-Bergère*, in which a doleful-looking barmaid stands guard over a selection of champagnes, liqueurs and, yes, bottles of Bass pale ale, complete with the telltale red triangle.

Back from the dead

What is not often remembered, however, is that Bass not only acquired the first trademark, but also the second, as the sleep-deprived operative handed over one more Bass logo, this time featuring a red diamond, for use on other ales from Burton. While not nearly as famous as its stablemate, the red diamond continues to this day, most recently appearing on the label of No. 1 Barley Wine, brewed at the White Shield Brewery in in Burton-upon-Trent.

The tiny brewery is now owned by Coors but brewer Steve Wellington, a long-time Bass employee, revels in the fun of re-creating defunct beers once brewed somewhere in the mighty Bass empire. No. 1 is just one beer that Steve has brought back from the dead. It's a magnificent, bottle-conditioned barley wine that owes its rich red colour to a 12-hour boil in the copper that caramelizes the abundant pale malt. Three charges of Fuggle and Golding hops ensure that this is no sweet, sickly offering. After primary fermentation, the beer is matured for up to a year before bottling.

At 10.5% ABV, it tastes rich and fruity, with warming fortified wine notes and a creamy finish, ideal for staving off the chills of early January, and – if New Year's Eve has not been too heavy – a full and satisfying way in which to kick off a year of tasting great beers.

Births Paul Revere (American patriot), 1735; EM Forster (novelist), 1879; J Edgar Hoover (FBI Director), 1895

Deaths Heinrich Hertz (physicist), 1894; Hank Williams (country singer), 1953; Maurice Chevalier (singer), 1972

Events Samuel Pepys begins his diary, 1660; the *Daily Universal Register* changes its name to *The Times*, 1788; the Euro adopted as currency by 12 European countries, 1999

Barley Wine

Brooklyn Lager

Source The Brooklyn Brewery, Brooklyn, New York **Strength** 5.1% **Website** brooklynbrewery.com

On this day in 1870, work began on one of the world's iconic bridges. The New York and Brooklyn Bridge, as it was originally called, now known simply as the Brooklyn Bridge, began to take shape as the ground was cleared ready for construction to commence.

Previously, a ferry linked these two parts of the city, a slow boat across the East River. It was while negotiating this tedious crossing that architect John Augustus Roebling came up with the idea for a bridge that would render the ferry redundant. He sold the scheme to the authorities, and his plans were accepted. After the first sod was broken on this day in 1870 (some sources claim a day later), work continued until 1883, when the bridge – the longest suspension bridge in the world at the time – opened for traffic.

Pre-Prohibition beer

Beer lovers have good reason to be grateful for the Brooklyn Bridge, in that it has allowed beer from Brooklyn to gain access to the wider world. The Brooklyn Brewery was founded in 1987 by Steve Hindy, a former foreign correspondent for the Associated Press, and his business partner, ex-bank official Tom Potter. With the help of brewer William M Moeller, they began to contract-brew at another New York brewery until finally opening their own brewhouse in Brooklyn itself. Today the brewmaster is Garrett Oliver, an internationally known beer personality, who is at the forefront of the movement to raise beer to gourmet levels. Under Garrett's

guidance, the Brooklyn Brewery has expanded its range of outstanding beers to include a weissbier, a brown ale and an IPA, as well as luxurious specials such as Black Chocolate Stout and the Belgian-inspired ale Local 1. However, its main brand, Brooklyn Lager, remains a stand-out, world classic, bottom-fermented beer broadly in the Vienna tradition, which means it is has a slightly darker, toastier malt profile. That said, it is the hops that really make the difference here. Whereas so many lagers – and particularly mass-produced American lagers – fight shy of a hop accent, Brooklyn is only too happy to espouse its wonders, even to the point where the beer is dry hopped during its long conditioning period at the brewery.

Pungent, resinous American hops fill the aroma, which is also slightly nutty and toasted, with a light citrus edge. In the crisp, clean taste, bold, tangy hops dominate over soft oranges and gentle toffee, with a little caramel on the swallow. The

finish is bitter, hoppy and quite dry with more orange character. The recipe is said to have been derived from the brewing books of William M Moeller's grandfather and, as the label with its 'pre-Prohibition beer' tagline explains, it takes us back to the days when all-malt, tasty lagers like this were all the rage in Brooklyn – and probably slaked the thirst of many a construction worker as the famous bridge slowly developed over the New York water.

Births James Wolfe (general), 1727; Isaac Asimov (writer), 1920; David Bailey (photographer), 1938

Deaths Tex Ritter (actor), 1974; Errol Garner (jazz musician), 1977; Cyril Fletcher (comedian), 2005

Events Russia launches *Luna 1*, the first spacecraft to fly close to the moon, 1959; Rupert Murdoch acquires his first Fleet Street newspaper, the *News of the World*, 1969

Vienna-style Lager

Alaskan Smoked Porter

Source Alaskan Brewing Company, Juneau, Alaska **Strength** 6.5% **Website** alaskanbeer.com

'**N**orth to the Future', that's the motto of America's wildest state, a motto adopted in 1967 with the aim of tapping into the growing aspiration around the world for a cleaner environment free from urban clutter. In a region as unspoilt as Alaska, man can be free, seems to be the suggestion.

The motto was acquired to mark the centenary of the purchase of Alaska by the US. Previously, the territory had been in Russian hands, but in the aftermath of the Crimean War, with resources stretched, the great Asian bear decided to withdraw back across the Bering Sea and concentrate on lands closer to home. The sum paid for the transaction was a princely $7,200,000. If only the Russians had known the value of the oil deposits. Once in US hands, Alaska was afforded department, district and, ultimately, territorial status until the Alaska Statehood Act was sanctioned by President Eisenhower. This allowed for the region to be formally included in the Union, as state number 49, which it duly was on 3 January 1959.

What Alaska did for us

So, what has Alaska brought to the party? Well, apart from some of the most stunning scenery and natural beauty on the planet, it's also offered up some talented brewers. Breweries have been operating here since gold miners worked the territory in the 1880s, but the best-known today only started production in 1986.

The Alaskan Brewing Company, based in state capital Juneau, has learned to deal with the limitations of transport – basically everything comes in and out by sea or air – to export its fine beers to mainland US and elsewhere in the world. A strong Alaskan Amber Ale, a robust Big Nugget barley wine and other fine beers, however, are rather overshadowed by the brewery's flagship, the magnificent Smoked Porter, an unusual take on the German rauchbier style that is available only in limited vintage batches. Five malts in all are used, including some that are locally smoked over alder wood.

Smoked Porter was first brewed in 1988, and at the 2006 Great American Beer Festival punters could queue up to try various vintages of this spectacular bottle-conditioned ale. Getting hold of earlier versions may prove tricky, but you can always create your own cellar and do similar comparisons in a few years' time. Meanwhile, just enjoy the complex smoky flavours, the underlying chocolate and coffee, and the almost-elusive fruitiness of this striking brew, and think that, even if it's a bit chilly outside on 3 January, it's nothing like as cold as it is in the 49th State of America.

Births Clement Attlee (politician), 1883; JRR Tolkien (writer), 1892; John Thaw (actor), 1942

Deaths Josiah Wedgwood (potter), 1795; Conrad Hilton (hotel magnate), 1979; Freddy Heineken (brewery executive), 2002

Events Sarcophagus of Tutankhamen discovered in Egypt by Howard Carter, 1924; first Open University broadcasts, 1971; Charles Schulz pens his last *Peanuts* comic strip, 2000

Smoked Porter

You are now Entering WORLD FAMOUS ALASKA HIGHWAY

ABOVE: FREEWHEELING IN ALASKA

Coniston Bluebird Bitter

Source Coniston Brewing Co., Coniston, Cumbria **Strength** 3.6% **Website** conistonbrewery.com

In the history of speed record attempts, two names stand out: Campbell and *Bluebird*. There were, in fact, two Campbells who etched their names into the record books. Sir Malcolm Campbell had achieved more than a dozen land and water speed records in the 1920s and '30s. His son, Donald, took up the family pastime with relish and soon notched up significant milestones in human transportation himself, also using the name of his father's craft, *Bluebird*, for his vehicle.

There wasn't, of course, just one *Bluebird*. Rather, the name was applied to a succession of custom-built craft, each geared to a different challenge. It was while testing *Bluebird K7* on 4 January 1967 that the Campbell story came to a tragic end.

Donald Campbell had already broken the water speed record on seven occasions. To this he added a land speed record in 1964, thus becoming the first and so far only person to achieve world land and water speed records in the same year. Now he returned to the water, looking to better his previous performances. It was during practice that Campbell ran into trouble. While he was aiming to push the boat to beyond 300mph, *Bluebird* flipped up, somersaulted and broke into two, killing the 45-year-old Campbell instantly and dropping to the lake bed, where it remained undiscovered and undisturbed for 34 years. In 2001, the vehicle was raised and Campbell given a family burial at Coniston Cemetery.

A simple tribute

The Campbell name lives on, of course. Records come and go, feats are achieved and surpassed, but, thanks in no small part to the brewing industry, the names of pioneers are never truly wiped from the slate. A tribute to Campbell was one of the first projects of the Coniston Brewing Company, set up in 1995. The ten-barrel brewery is based behind the Black Bull pub. The first beer it brewed was called simply Bluebird Bitter and the recipe was equally straightforward: pale malt for the fermentable sugars, a touch of crystal malt to deepen the golden colour, and just one hop, Challenger, to provide a crisp, orangey, peppery bitterness. It may have been simple but it was hugely effective: the beer won CAMRA's Champion Beer of Britain contest in 1998, earning national exposure for the name of *Bluebird* all over again.

Bluebird is still brewed at Coniston, but the bottled version (slightly stronger at 4.2%) is brewed for Coniston by Peter Scholey, former Brakspear head brewer. There's also an even stronger, export version called Bluebird XB (4.4%), showcasing American hops.

CONISTON BREWING CO.
Bluebird Bitter
TRADITIONAL HAND BREWED CASK & BOTTLE CONDITIONED
USING ONLY THE FINEST SELECTION OF HOPS & MALTS
CBC

"The Beauty of Hops"
• SUPREME CHAMPION 1999 •
The finest beer brewed using only English Hops

Births Sir Isaac Newton (scientist), 1643; Louis Braille (inventor of Braille writing system), 1809; Floyd Patterson (boxer), 1935

Deaths Albert Camus (writer), 1960; TS Eliot (poet), 1965; Phil Lynott (rock musician) 1986

Events Samuel Colt sells his first revolver to the US Government, 1847; *Billboard* magazine publishes first pop music chart, 1936; British Fifth Army launches attack on Monte Cassino in Italy, 1944

Bitter

Hook Norton Twelve Days

Source Hook Norton Brewery, Hook Norton, Oxfordshire **Strength** 5.5% **Website** hooknortonbrewery.co.uk

Strong Ale

According to tradition, tonight's the night when all Christmas decorations need to be taken down, in order to avoid bad luck throughout the coming year. If you fail to remove them before 5 January is out, then they should stay in place all year, as the date marks the end of the Christmas festivities. Historically, it was on this day that the yule log was allowed to burn out.

In religious terms, Twelfth Night is the eve of Epiphany, the day that commemorates the adoration of the magi. It is believed that, 12 days after the birth of Jesus, the three wise men from the East finally arrived at the cribside, bearing gifts of gold, frankincense and myrrh. For those confused as to why Twelfth Night should fall before Twelfth Day, the explanation comes from the belief in olden times that a day ended, and the next began, at sunset. So night preceded the day and sunset on the Twelfth Day would actually be the beginning of the Thirteenth Day.

Among the traditions of Twelfth Night are the performing of mummer's plays – which may explain the origin of Shakespeare's comedy of the same name – and the eating of a rich fruit cake. The cake contained various rogue items, which, when discovered, provided the inspiration for some fun and games. If a bean were found, the finder was declared king or queen and everyone else had to obey their orders. If a twig were discovered, the finder was a fool – and so on. It's probably the source of today's popular Christmas cake.

A beer for all seasons

A really good accompaniment for a slice of rich fruit cake such as this is a beer from Hook Norton Brewery in Oxfordshire that goes by the name of Twelve Days. It was added to the brewery's range of excellent ales in 1991 and is brewed from a grist of Maris Otter pale malt, chocolate malt and crystal malt, with Fuggle, Golding and Challenger hops adding a fruity, bitter twist.

It may be strong and dark, but this is really quite light bodied for a malty beer. Big chocolate notes fill the aroma – like the chocolate dusting on a sponge or a cappuccino – becoming nutty and toffeeish, too, with faint orange emerging. Nutty, chocolaty, toffeeish malt dominates the taste with a firm roasted grain edge and ripples of orange fruitiness running throughout. Nutty, grainy, roasted malt takes control of the dry, moderately bitter aftertaste.

Twelve Days is Hook Norton's Christmas ale on draught, and is served from the cask only in November and December, but it is available in bottle all through the year, so even when the decorations have been long put away, you can still enjoy a little Christmas treat.

Births Sam Phillips (record producer), 1923; King Juan Carlos of Spain, 1938; Diane Keaton (actress), 1946

Deaths Edward the Confessor, 1066; Ernest Shackleton (explorer), 1922; Amy Johnson (aviator), 1941; Brian Johnston (broadcaster), 1994

Events Captain Alfred Dreyfus sent to Devil's Island for life, beginning the notorious Dreyfus Affair in France, 1895; oil tanker *Braer* runs aground off Shetland, 1993

ABOVE: *TWELFTH NIGHT* BY WALTER H DEVERELL

Brakspear Bitter

Source Marston's, Witney, Oxfordshire **Strength** 3.4% **Website** brakspear-beers.co.uk

Detective Chief Inspector Morse, of the Thames Valley Police: a man who loves Wagnerian opera, cryptic crosswords and real ale. When he made his UK television debut on 6 January 1987, all lovers of good beer sat up and took notice. We were used to watching Jack the Lad cops, tearing around in sporty cars and knocking back the lagers. Now we found one of our own: a man of culture who cruised the dreaming-spired streets of Oxford in an elegant old Jaguar, always finding time to stop for a drop of quality ale during his busy working day.

Morse – faultlessly portrayed on screen by John Thaw – was the creation of Oxford academic Colin Dexter, who imbued the rather grouchy detective with a love of his own personal pastimes, including good beer. Dexter reveals that a drop of something special often helps release the muse when he sits down to write, in the same way that a pint or two of fine Oxfordshire ale oils the cogs of Morse's brilliant detective mind and helps him to crack the most baffling cases.

When Dexter's novels were brought to television, real Oxford pubs frequented by Morse became tourist attractions. Many of these boozers belonged to Morrells, a family brewery that, sadly, fell into the hands of city investors who sold the site, took the money and ran. Morrells is no more and its demise is a crime worthy of a Morse investigation.

Brewery location

One memorable episode of the long-running series was partly filmed at Brakspear's in Henley-on-Thames, sadly another brewery that has suffered the same fate as Morrells. The ownership there was blind to the fact that they owned one of the world's great drinking treasures and sold the brewery for property development. Thankfully, the Brakspear beers survive and are in good nick.

It's impossible to re-create a beer precisely when you move it to another brewery, but Refresh UK, a beer marketing business that owns Wychwood Brewery and which acquired the Brakspear brands, pulled out all the stops to make it right. They decided to rebuild the Brakspear fermenting rooms at Witney, and worked hard to get the flavours as close as possible, keeping faith with the original yeast strain, Maris Otter pale malt, and Fuggle and Golding hops. Even though Refresh was bought by Marston's in 2008, you can still enjoy Brakspear Bitter today and marvel at how a beer of such little strength can have such a moreish character and so full a taste.

The Oxfordshire drinking scene is much changed since Morse made his bow, but were he around today, I think he'd be more than happy to join us in a pint or two of Brakspear.

Births Joan of Arc (French patriot and martyr), 1412; Terry Venables (football coach), 1943; Rowan Atkinson (comedian and actor), 1955

Deaths Theodore Roosevelt (26th US President), 1919; Dizzy Gillespie (jazz musician), 1993; Rudolf Nureyev (dancer), 1993

Events King Henry VIII marries his fourth wife, Anne of Cleves, 1540; first public test of an electric telegraph system by Samuel Morse, 1838; first commercial round-the-world flight by Pan Am, 1942

Bitter

Russian Orthodox Christmas

Harvey's Imperial Extra Double Stout

Source Harvey & Son, Lewes, East Sussex **Strength** 9% **Website** harveysonline.co.uk

If you haven't indulged enough over the Christmas and New Year holidays, you can extend your celebrations by a week by marking the Russian Orthodox Christmas on 7 January (the Russian Orthodox Church still uses the Julian calendar, which is 13 days behind that used in the West).

Russians have revived their Christmas celebrations since the downfall of the Soviet Union and the collapse of Communist control. Under this previous regime, Christmas was banned and if citizens wanted to preserve any customs associated with the festival – decorating trees, swapping presents – they needed to transpose them to other times of the year (such as New Year). Once again, however, Christmas is being celebrated in the time-honoured fashion, beginning with a 12-course vegetarian feast on Christmas Eve (marking the end of a fasting period) and including the bearing of gifts for children by Grandfather Frost, a Santa Claus figure who is accompanied by his granddaughter, named Snowmaiden. Alternatively, Babushka, a grandmother figure, doles outs the presents.

Authentic re-creation

Given the traditional fondness for strong dark stouts in this part of the world, it would seem highly appropriate to mark the occasion with a glass or two of an Imperial Russian Stout. These rich, malty yet well-hopped beers were once shipped regularly from Britain across the icy Baltic to warm the cockles of Russian aristocrats, particularly those in the court of Empress Catherine the Great, about whom there is more later in this book (see 21 April). The best-known survivor was Courage's Imperial Russian Stout, but even that has disappeared now, having been last brewed at John Smith's in Tadcaster in 1993. But the demise of the Courage beer has at least prompted numerous smaller breweries in the UK to develop their own versions of these stouts. Some of these are mentioned on other pages, but possibly the most authentic comes from Harvey's in Sussex.

The Lewes brewery developed Imperial Extra Double Stout in 1999, largely for export to the US, where such big, bold beers are particularly appreciated. Brewer Miles Jenner took as his inspiration the work of one Albert Le Coq, a Belgian beer merchant who set up his own brewery in what is now Estonia to brew Russian stout and other beers for that part of the world. The Harvey's re-creation is a gem, but stout drinkers weaned on nitrogenated draught Guinness won't find it an easy taste to acquire. This is a beer with muscle, thick and strong, malty and vinous, with a coffeeish finish. It's surprisingly mellow, once you get the hang of it, but it's definitely one for special occasions rather than everyday drinking. A Russian Christmas would fit the bill.

Births Gerald Durrell (naturalist), 1925; David Caruso (actor), 1956; Nicolas Cage (actor), 1964

Deaths Catherine of Aragon (first wife of King Henry VIII), 1536; Trevor Howard (actor), 1988; Hirohito (Emperor of Japan), 1989

Events First telephone service between London and New York opens, 1927; Harlem Globetrotters basketball team plays its first game, 1927

Imperial Stout

ABOVE: ST BASIL'S CATHEDRAL, RED SQUARE, MOSCOW

St Austell Admiral's Ale

Source St Austell Brewery, St Austell, Cornwall **Strength** 5% **Website** staustellbrewery.co.uk

When a national hero breathes his last, it is unseemly for the funeral arrangements to be made in haste. The public demand the opportunity to pay their respects and that's what they were given on this day in 1806 when the body of the late Admiral Nelson made its way, amid great pomp and ceremony, to central London.

England's greatest naval hero was born in the Norfolk village of Burnham Thorpe in 1758, the son of the local rector. After schooling, he joined the Royal Navy when aged just 12, rapidly gaining seafaring experience through major expeditions around the globe. By the age of 20, Nelson was captain of his own ship. His later exploits against the Spanish and French saw him lose an eye and an arm in the call of duty, but underscored his considerable military prowess. He was not only promoted within the Navy but also aristocratically, becoming Baron Nelson of the Nile (after one of his most famous victories against Napoleon). His dramatic life came to an end on the day that saw the destruction of the French and Spanish fleets in the Battle of Trafalgar in 1805 (see 21 October). Mortally wounded in the conflict, Nelson died around three hours later. His body was brought back to England and, after lying in state at Greenwich, was given a lavish send-off with a ceremonial procession on 8 January, aboard a royal barge originally commissioned for King Charles II. The flotilla cortege slowly sailed up the River Thames to Westminster, where Nelson's coffin was disembarked and taken to the Admiralty building where it lay overnight before burial at St Paul's Cathedral.

Inventive beers

Our tribute beer for today takes us to southwest England. It's an inventive beer suitably called Admiral's Ale from St Austell Brewery. The inventive bit lies in the unique malt that is used. Whereas nearly all other beers – even dark ones – need a high percentage of pale malt in the mash tun, to ensure enough fermentable sugars are extracted, Admiral's Ale uses none. Instead, it is based on a new malt called Cornish Gold, created out of Cornish barley for St Austell by Tucker's Maltings in Devon. The malt has a darker hue but humidity in the malting process ensures that, unlike in conventional dark malts, vital sugars don't crystallize and become useless for brewing. When matched with Styrian Golding and Cascade hops, as in this case, it produces a delicious bronze-coloured beer that is full-bodied, malty, nutty and yet curiously fruity at the same time.

Admiral's Ale was first brewed for St Austell's annual Celtic Beer Festival in 2004 but it was then introduced commercially to tie in with the 200th anniversary of the Battle of Trafalgar a year later. It's available in cask and bottle conditioned, and has also been sold in Asda stores under the name of Smuggler's Ale – but I doubt if Nelson would ever have approved of that.

Births Elvis Presley (rock 'n' roll singer), 1935; Professor Stephen Hawking (physicist), 1942; David Bowie (rock musician), 1947

Deaths Galileo Galilei (scientist), 1642; Terry-Thomas (actor), 1990; François Mitterand (French President), 1996

Events Food rationing imposed in Britain, 1940; trial of seven men implicated in the Watergate Scandal begins, 1973; Kegworth air disaster, 1989

Strong Ale

15

Timothy Taylor's Landlord

Source Timothy Taylor, Keighley, West Yorkshire **Strength** 4.3% **Website** timothy-taylor.co.uk

Mention the name Landlord in pub circles these days and more than likely someone will tell you that it's Madonna's favourite beer. Yes, it's true that the pop diva is partial to a drop or two of this magnificent Yorkshire ale – she admitted that much on television to Jonathan Ross – and it's proof that a traditional British bitter can have appeal right across the age, gender and cultural divides, but there's more to Landlord than that.

It's a fitting drink to seek out on this particular day of the year, as 9 January marks the passing of Timothy Taylor, the man who founded the brewery that gave the world this champion ale. Timothy was born in 1826. He was initially a tailor by trade as well as name, but also became a maltster before starting to brew in Keighley in 1858. He expanded the business five years later, buying some land at auction for new premises in May 1863. The precise date when brewing started at the new site is not known but it was well established by the time Timothy died in 1898, making good use of the pure waters that provided its full name of the Knowle Spring Brewery.

One thing we can't credit the astute Mr Taylor for is the creation of Landlord itself. That came about in the 1950s. Early experiments on a new bottled beer took place in 1952, using the brewery's BB Superior Bitter Beer recipe as a template. A year later, the beer made its debut under the name of Competition Ale 1953. The competition invited local drinkers to suggest a more appropriate title, using the label from the bottle as an entry form. The prize of £500 was claimed by a club steward, who presumably looked in the mirror and came up with Landlord.

What Taylors created was a beer of astonishing drinkability, perfectly balancing Golden Promise pale malt, brewing sugar and three kinds of hops (Fuggle, Whitbread Golding Variety and aromatic Styrian Golding) to create a fruity, satisfying best bitter that has turned many more heads than Madonna's. The bottled version is filtered, pasteurized and a touch weaker than the draught at 4.1%. It has won several awards, but it is to the cask-conditioned version that the beer owes its exalted reputation. No fewer than four outright Champion Beer of Britain titles from CAMRA suggest that this is a beer that would have made the late Mr Taylor exceptionally proud.

TIMOTHY TAYLOR'S
LANDLORD
"could we meet at the bar?"

Births Gracie Fields (singer and actress), 1898; Richard Nixon (37th US President), 1913; Joan Baez (singer), 1941

Deaths Tommy Handley (comedian), 1949; Peter Cook (comedian), 1995

Events Introduction of income tax in Britain, 1799; Sir Anthony Eden resigns as Prime Minister because of ill health, 1957; liner *Queen Elizabeth* destroyed by fire in Hong Kong harbour, 1972

Best Bitter

Achouffe La Chouffe

Source Brasserie d'Achouffe, Achouffe　**Strength** 8%　**Website** achouffe.be

In the much-pondered list of famous Belgians, Tintin is way up there, alongside Eddy Merckx, Kim Clijsters and Plastic Bertrand. However, such has been the international appeal of the daring cub reporter that most British children grew up knowing nothing of his Belgian origins.

The creation of writer George Rémi, who wrote under the pen-name of Hergé, Tintin was first seen on 10 January 1929, in a cartoon strip in *Le Petit Vingtième*, the weekly youth supplement of a Belgian national newspaper. He went on to star in more than 20 books, sharing adventures like *The Crab with the Golden Claws* and *Red Rackham's Treasure* with his dog Snowy (Milou in the original French), the bearded Captain Haddock and the bowler-hatted Thompson Twins (from whom the '80s pop band acquired their name). But it wasn't the books or cartoon strips that influenced British youngsters so much as the television mini-serials in which Tintin appeared. With English-language narration, the tufty red-head became a latter-day Dick Barton, his adventures chopped up into breathless five-minute instalments with thrilling cliff-hanger endings. And no one can ever forget the beginning of each episode either, with the announcer bellowing out an invitation to join 'Hergé's Adventures of… TINTIN!'

Cartoon heritage

Belgium is also responsible for other cartoon creations that have graced the world stage, not least the rather nauseating Smurfs. Indeed, Brussels has its own comic strip museum, which makes a nice break while bar hopping. Cartoon characters have even found their way into Belgian beer culture, courtesy of the Achouffe brewery.

Achouffe (bless you!) was founded in the village of the same name by former telecoms engineer Chris Bauweraerts and his brother-in-law Pierre Gobron in 1982. It sits in a quiet valley in the beautiful Ardennes forest in the south of Belgium and made its name by producing spiced ales that owe a little to both Duvel and Hoegaarden. Chris grew up in the region in which Duvel is king, and so it is no surprise to see the brewery's main beer, La Chouffe, served in its own curvaceous, Duvel-shaped glass. Chris was also a huge admirer of Hoegaarden in its early days and so borrowed the idea of coriander spicing for his beer.

La Chouffe glows appealingly golden, and tastes bitter and fruity, with fragrant coriander notes. The cartoons come in to promote the beer. A family of cheeky little gnomes has become the brewery's trademark and can be seen dotted around the brewhouse, peering out from behind fermenting vessels and splashed all over the beer labels.

In 2006, with production booming, Achouffe was sold to Duvel-Moortgat. We hope they will retain the gnomes that have helped create Achouffe's identity and idiosyncrasy – and, in their own modest way, prolonged Belgium's cartoon heritage.

Births Barbara Hepworth (sculptor), 1903; Rod Stewart (singer), 1945; George Foreman (boxer), 1949

Deaths Samuel Colt (gunsmith), 1862; 'Buffalo Bill' Cody (frontiersman), 1917; 'Coco' Chanel (fashion designer), 1971

Events London Underground opens, 1863; first meeting of the League of Nations, 1920; Harold Macmillan becomes Prime Minister, 1957

Blonde Beer

Innis & Gunn Oak-Aged Beer

Source Innis & Gunn Brewing Co, Dufftown, Banffshire **Strength** 6.6% **Website** innisandgunn.com

There are few more arcane rituals than the Burning of the Clavie, which takes place every 11 January at Burghead, near Elgin, Scotland. This was the date of Hogmanay in the old calendar, and the ceremony remains a means of bestowing good luck for the year ahead on the local community.

It works as follows: a half-barrel nailed to a post is filled with wood and tar and set alight. The post is then hoisted on the shoulders of a local man who is joined by a small crew of neighbours on a clockwise tour of the town. After occasional pauses to offer a smouldering ember to selected households for luck, the group eventually pitches up at a stone altar and more wood is added to the barrel. When it all burns out, the embers are scattered over the hillside, ensuring a scramble for lucky cinders among the onlookers.

The origins of the festival are disputed. Some say it was Roman; others place the ritual in Pictish or Norse traditions. The barrel used at one time would have been rescued from the fishing industry, where it may have held herrings. These days it is usually a whisky cask.

Cask creativity

Whisky casks also do a fine job of creating one of Scotland's most interesting beers. It is said that Innis & Gunn's Oak Aged Beer was discovered by accident. Former Caledonian Brewery executive Dougal Sharp was asked to provide a beer that distiller William Grant's could use to provide a beer 'finish' to one of its whiskies. (It is common for whiskies to have port or sherry finishes, created by filling oak casks with fortified wine so that the wood absorbs the flavour and then passes it on to whisky when the cask is refilled.) Dougal's beer was mostly thrown away once it had served its purpose but some canny workers realized that the beer was not just drinkable, but also rather special, having acquired vanilla, toffee and citrus notes from the wood.

When told about this, Dougal set up Innis & Gunn to exploit the idea. He now has beer brewed under contract at an unnamed Scottish brewery. This is aged for 30 days in white oak casks originally intended for the Bourbon industry and is then blended with that from other oak casks in a marrying tun, where it sits for 47 days. The beer is then beautifully packaged and marketed as a quality product.

The vanilla and toffee notes certainly show through in both aroma and taste, along with gentle hints of lemon, before a warming, oaky finish. It would be just the job after a chilly January ramble around a fishing town in the north of Scotland.

Births Arthur Scargill (trade union leader), 1938; Bryan Robson (football manager), 1957

Deaths Georges-Eugène Haussman (town planner), 1891; Thomas Hardy (writer), 1928; Richmal Crompton (writer), 1969

Events Insulin first used successfully to treat diabetes, 1922; first Open University degrees awarded, 1973

Cask-aged Beer

Ellezelloise Hercule Stout

Source Brasserie Ellezelloise, Ellezelles **Strength** 8.4% **Website** brasserie-ellezelloise.be

She published 66 best-selling detective novels in her 56-year writing career. Her books have been filmed and televised time and time again, and with *The Mousetrap* she holds the record for a continuous run of a stage play. Nevertheless, there are some critics who carp at Agatha Christie's literary style. They point to her deliberately functional language and limited characterization and at the way in which she seems to hold back information that is vital to solving the crime. She's been getting away with murder for years, they say, but she is undoubtedly the Queen of Crime Fiction. The popularity of her work is second to none and has not diminished one iota since she died on this day in 1976.

Christie was born Agatha Miller in Torquay in 1890. She took up writing, using her first husband's surname, during World War I, when she worked as a drug dispenser at a hospital – fundamental research, it would seem, for the twist-in-the-tale stories of murder that she made her own. Her most prolific creation (and most popular, although Miss Marple fans may object) was Hercule Poirot, the dapper little Belgian detective with the waxed moustache and the egg-shaped head. He first appeared in a book called *The Mysterious Affair at Styles*, published in 1920, and went on to feature in more than 30 more.

Local hero

Poirot's distinctive image features on the label of a beer produced by the Ellezelloise brewery, based in the village of Ellezelles, between Brussels and Lille, in the French-speaking part of Belgium. Ellezelles claims to be Poirot's home town – well, it's one way of bringing in some tourists – and the beer that the local brewery has created in his honour is as clever and polished as its namesake.

Stylistically, Hercule is a stout, and a substantial, chunky one at that, with the spark of individuality and mystery that epitomizes a great Belgian beer. Smoky dark malts and plain chocolate are among the suspects in the aroma before an investigation of the bittersweet taste finds more chocolate, spiky pepper and also a little pruney fruit. The 8.4% alcohol is a red herring. Being bottle conditioned, this is no heavy, lumpy beer: the natural carbonation adds a welcome lightness to the body. The denouement, meanwhile, points the finger at dry, smoky, nutty, roasted grain. It's just the perfect beer for a lazy evening in with an easy-reading whodunit.

ABOVE: PORTRAIT OF AGATHA CHRISTIE WITH SOME OF HER DETECTIVE NOVELS

Births Jack London (writer), 1876; Des O'Connor (entertainer), 1932; Joe Frazier (boxer), 1944

Deaths Nevil Shute (writer), 1960; Stanley Unwin (comedian), 2002; Maurice Gibb (pop musician), 2003

Events The National Trust founded, 1895; Henry Cooper becomes British and Commonwealth heavyweight boxing champion, 1959

Imperial Stout

Rochefort 10

Source Brasserie Trappistes Rochefort, Rochefort **Strength** 11.3% **Website** trappistes-rochefort.com

Although his feast day is celebrated on 1 October, one of Christianity's most powerful early preachers can be remembered on 13 January, the day that he died, in 533.

St Remigius – or Remy – was born near Laon, France, into an aristocratic family. He was known for his tireless work ethic and his passion for learning, and he became so devout a follower of Christ that by the age of 22 he had been appointed Archbishop of Reims. Among his later achievements, the conversion of the Frankish king Clovis to the faith – one of the key moments in the history of Christianity in France – ranks highest.

However, Remigius's influence was felt beyond the boundaries of his native country, and he is remembered today in the name of one of Belgium's Trappist breweries. Notre-Dame de Saint-Remy is better known as Rochefort, after the Ardennes town just a couple of miles away from the abbey. The community here was founded around 1230, but at the time was a convent. The nuns later swapped homes with a body of monks, who have been here ever since – conflict and revolution permitting. The origins of the monastery's brewery lie in the 16th century but, like the abbey itself, it has been abandoned time and again as war has raged across Europe, and before the 1950s, its role was very low key. Then the brothers' farming interests declined and money was needed to maintain the abbey, so the brewery was given new prominence. It was then rebuilt in the 1960s, with new equipment added, and is today a veritable basilica of beer, its handsome copper vessels guarded by a cross and sparkling with light breaking through stained-glass windows.

Heavenly beers

The beers are truly heavenly. They are only produced in bottle-conditioned format and all three are variations on the same theme. From a malt-and-hops purist's viewpoint, they break a few rules, but, frankly, who cares, when the beer is this good? Along with pale and caramel malts, a small quantity of wheat starch is added, 'to help the yeast express itself', say the brewers. There are also white and brown sugars, and a little coriander helps the Hallertau and Styrian Golding hops with the seasoning. The range begins with Rochefort 6, a mere stripling at 7.5% ABV, and continues with Rochefort 8, an extravagant meal in a glass at 9.2%. The crowning glory, however, is the 11.3% ABV Rochefort 10, a truly stunning, nourishing, malty, fruity, peppery ale that underlines everything that is so special about monastic brewing.

Births Sophie Tucker (singer), 1884; Stephen Hendry (snooker player), 1969; Orlando Bloom (actor), 1977

Deaths Edmund Spenser (poet), 1599; Wyatt Earp (lawman), 1929; James Joyce (writer), 1941

Events Talks begin to found the National Geographic Society in Washington, DC, 1888; first meeting of the Independent Labour Party, 1893

Trappist Ale

ABOVE: MEDIEVAL ILLUMINATION SHOWING THE BAPTISM OF CLOVIS BY ST REMIGIUS

Harvey's Elizabethan Ale

Source Harvey & Son, Lewes, East Sussex **Strength** 8.1% **Website** harveysonline.co.uk

Following the death of her sister Queen Mary I in November 1558, Elizabeth, daughter of King Henry VIII and his second wife Anne Boleyn, acceded to the English throne. It was a tricky time to become monarch. Mary's firmly Catholic beliefs had driven a rift through the nation, which showed every sign of breaking apart. But the new queen was a Protestant, and there were hopes that she would reunite the people and stamp out religious intolerance. Shrewdly, Elizabeth built upon these aspirations right from the start, using her coronation on this day in 1559 as a launch pad for a hugely successful reign.

To set the tone for her monarchy, the ceremony was cleverly designed as a two-day festival. On 14 January, Elizabeth was paraded through the streets of London as part of a gaudy pageant designed to put a spin on what her reign was likely to bring. Much was made that the Queen was the granddaughter of King Henry VII and his wife, Elizabeth of York – the two parties that brought the Houses of Lancaster and York together and thus ended the bitter conflict known as the Wars of the Roses. Elizabeth – this message sent out – was a conciliator who could hold together the country. The next day, the formal crowning provided a clear example of how the Queen planned to rein back unpopular Catholic policies, but in a way that alienated as few supporters of Rome as possible: the coronation service was held in English as well as in Latin.

Hopes & fears

But while her accession certainly offered hope, there were also fears that another female monarch would prove too weak to hold together a divided country that was in economic trouble and under threat from foreign powers. However, over 45 years of rule, Elizabeth easily dispelled those worries and, while it was not without its difficulties – unrest over taxation, famine and the Spanish Armada, to name but a trio – her era has been classified by historians as a golden age, the time when England became a world power and embarked upon a cultural Renaissance epitomized by the works of Shakespeare.

One would imagine that many a quart of ale was quaffed during the festivities of 15 January 1559. The beer at that time would have been strong and heady: that's certainly what Harvey's of Lewes believed when they created a brew stylistically from that era to mark the coronation of the second Queen Elizabeth in 1953. Elizabethan Ale, as Harvey's called it, proved so popular that it has remained part of their bottled beer offering ever since. We'd call the style barley wine today and this is a magnificent example. The full, malty aroma has a creamy toffee note as well as suggestions of sherry and strawberry. More creamy toffee and strawberries can be found in the taste, along with dried fruits and liquorice. It's sweet at first before falling victim to a good balancing smack of bitterness, which also takes over the drying finish.

Elizabethan may roll out at 8.1% ABV, but just like the Virgin Queen with that clever, reconciliatory pageant ahead of her coronation, it disguises its strength brilliantly.

Births Albert Schweitzer (doctor and humanitarian), 1875; Warren Mitchell (actor), 1926; Richard Briers (actor), 1934

Deaths Lewis Carroll (writer), 1898; Humphrey Bogart (actor), 1957; Shelley Winters (actress), 2006

Events The hippie gathering known as the Human Be-in takes place in San Francisco, starting the 'Summer of Love', 1967; Sir Matt Busby announces his retirement as manager of Manchester United FC, 1969

Barley Wine

Goose Island Honker's Ale

Source Goose Island Beer Co., Chicago, Illinois **Strength** 4.3% **Website** gooseisland.com

In the US, it's the second biggest blow-out day of the year. More food and drink is consumed during the broadcast of American football's Super Bowl game than at any time except Thanksgiving. No wonder the major beer companies plough millions into advertising during this loud-and-proud sporting spectacle.

The first Super Bowl took place on 15 January 1967. It was seen as a way of bringing together the two conferences that controlled football in the US, the well-established NFL (National Football League) and the much younger AFL (American Football League). Teams in each conference didn't play each other, so the new end-of-season 'play-off' offered a chance to weigh up the merits of the respective champions. The first match was staged in Los Angeles and was won by the NFL champs Green Bay Packers from Wisconsin, who defeated the Kansas City Chiefs 35–10. The Packers won the second Super Bowl, too, and, when their revered coach Vince Lombardi died in 1970, a new trophy was awarded to the Super Bowl winners in his name. This is still the prize today.

The other prize is, of course, commercial exposure. US TV audiences of more than 90 million have been known to watch the Super Bowl, and 30-second commercials during the game can cost upwards of $2.5 million.

Beer cashes in

Beer and football go hand in hand in the US. It is generally the light lager sector, on which most American drinkers were weaned, that benefits most, with Budweiser, Miller and Coors rolling out the cans to keep their loyal customer base lubricated while they're yelling at their TV screens. But if you're looking for an American beer with a lot more flavour to wash down your pizza or hot dog, there are plenty of outstanding examples to be found in the UK. Many are mentioned, for other reasons, elsewhere in this book, so the one selected for today is Honker's Ale from Goose Island in Chicago, especially as its comes with a manageable strength.

Goose Island is a brewery that knows what to do with hops. Just take a sniff as you pour the beer into a glass and get a load of those sumptuous Styrian Goldings. It's just like rummaging around in a sack of hop leaves – fresh, resinous and fruity. Rich, earthy hop resins are immediately to the fore in the taste, with a tart fruitiness developing, all nicely balanced by malty sweetness. The finish takes a little time to build but is soon filled with tangy, almost nutty hops and biscuity grain. In all, this is a clean, ultra-fresh-tasting amber ale, loaded with flavour. It's said to have been inspired by a visit to an English pub, but it's considerably more hoppy than many British pale ales. And it's just the job for a late-night tipple while watching the big game from the other side of the Atlantic.

Births Molière (playwright), 1622; Ivor Novello (actor, writer and composer), 1893; Martin Luther King (civil rights campaigner), 1929

Deaths Sammy Cahn (songwriter), 1993; Harry Nilsson (rock musician), 1994

Events The British Museum opens, 1759; Aswan High Dam in Egypt officially opened, 1971

Pale Ale

Leffe Tripel

Source InBev **Strength** 8.5% **Website** leffe.com

Trappist and abbey beers: the same thing, aren't they? Not so. The basic difference between the two lies in whether the beer is brewed by monks, or whether it is produced commercially. If the latter is the case, then the Trappist name cannot be used on the label, and the term abbey has to be employed instead.

There are only seven Trappist breweries, found in Belgium and the Netherlands, but there are scores of beers with religious-sounding titles, or boasting the names of existing or defunct abbeys. Undoubtedly, the most influential of abbey beer brands is Leffe, thanks to its position within the mighty empire of InBev, the world's largest brewer. That this should be the case has much to do with events taking place on this day in 1950.

Leffe Abbey stands near the town of Dinant, in the south of Belgium. Like nearly all monasteries, it used to have a brewery at one time, but when the monastery was dissolved during the French Revolution, beer production ended. On 16 January 1950, however, the beer's fortunes changed. It was on this day that a new man was elected to take charge of the community. Father Cyrille Nys assumed the role of Father Abbot and it was under his auspices that production of Leffe beer began once more.

The Father Abbot, it seems, was rather concerned about the abbey's finances and discussed the situation with Albert Lootvoet, a brewer from nearby Overijse. Lootvoet agreed to produce beer bearing Leffe's name, with the proceeds shared between his business and the monastery. With the Father Abbot's blessing, Leffe rolled back into production in 1952. The brewery at Overijse was eventually taken over by Brasseries Artois, the forerunner of InBev, and then the production of most Leffe brands was transferred to the company's main base, at Leuven (home of Stella Artois).

Leffe beers are generally filtered but there remains one beer in the range, Leffe Tripel, which is naturally conditioned in the bottle. It has been brewed not at Leuven but at the Hoegaarden brewery and has picked up some interesting tricks along the way, most notably in the coriander spicing, as used by the famous wheat beer from the same brewery. Leffe Tripel comes over as a stronger, chunkier but rather fresher-tasting version of Leffe Blond, with the same tropical fruit notes but also a sweet bakers' spice character. It's the pick of the Leffe selection.

Births Ethel Merman (actress and singer), 1908; Dian Fossey (zoologist), 1932; John Carpenter (film director), 1948

Deaths Edward Gibbon (historian), 1794; Léo Delibes (composer), 1891; Carole Lombard (actress), 1942

Events Ivan the Terrible crowned Tsar of Russia, 1547; the Shah of Iran flees to Egypt, 1979

Tripel

23

Ballard's Wassail

Source Ballard's Brewery, Nyewood, Hampshire **Strength** 6% **Website** ballardsbrewery.org.uk

Wassailing is an old English celebration that takes place around New Year, often on Twelfth Night and in some places on 17 January. It's a time when the cider crop is lavished with attention and the spirits of the fruit trees are offered gifts to encourage a good harvest.

The term wassail roughly translates as 'be whole', and came to be used as a greeting for friends and neighbours at around this time of year. The tradition has its origins in Scandinavia and was adopted and adapted by the Anglo-Saxons. The drink served for the occasion was a strange concoction. Mulled ale was mixed with all manner of things, from spices and eggs to apples and cream, and served in a special wassail bowl. It is said that pieces of toast were bobbed in the drink – giving it the appearance and nickname of lambs' wool – and that it was lucky to find one in your drinking bowl, but that seems like an all-too-convenient source for the idea of drinking a toast.

Hampshire celebrations

Ballard's brewery, on the border of Hampshire and West Sussex, has been brewing has been brewing a beer called Wassail since 1980. There's no egg, cream or spices, just good old malt and hops (Fuggle and Golding), but it may be the sort of the beer that would provide a base for mulling, weighing in at a chunky 6% ABV. It's ruddy in colour, fruity, malty and strong, leaving a pleasant little tingle on the gums, and can be found in both cask- and bottle-conditioned forms, the latter with a label harking back to the roots of the tradition. It depicts Hengist, the 5th-century leader of the Jutes, who is seen toasting Vortigern, King of the Britons. Also seen is Rowena, daughter of Hengist, who had her wicked way with the king. Indeed, some say that the whole wassailing tradition began in England when Rowena offered Vortigern a bowl of wine.

An even better beer to consider mulling is the special strong ale that Ballard's issues at the start of December each year as part of its long-running 'Old Bounder' series. The name changes annually – recent topical offerings have included WMD, Pom's Delight and Thin Ice – as does the strength, but expect something around 9%, with the old bounder in question pictured in cartoon form on the label. Heat the beer gently, add a little sugar and throw in some nutmeg, cloves, ginger or other spices. That should keep out the cold while you're worshipping your apple trees.

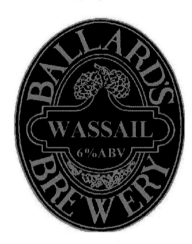

Births Benjamin Franklin (statesman and inventor), 1706; David Lloyd-George (Prime Minister), 1863; Muhammad Ali (boxer), 1942

Deaths Rutherford B Hayes (US President), 1893; Bobby Fischer (chess player), 2008

Events Cartoon strip sailor *Popeye* makes his debut, 1929; the BBC launches its breakfast television service, 1983

Strong Ale

Arkell's Bee's Organic Ale

Source Arkell's Brewery Ltd, Swindon, Wiltshire **Strength** 4.5% **Website** arkells.com

The misadventures of Winnie the Pooh, Christopher Robin, Piglet, Eeyore, Tigger and others have captivated children since the 1920s, so why not – when we live in a world that commemorates much darker events – establish a day when the lighter side of life can be revisited?

18 January 1882 was the birthday of Alan Alexander (AA) Milne, and some grateful person, identity unknown, has declared this day to be Winnie the Pooh Day. Milne came from a privileged background and enjoyed a public school education that led to studies at Cambridge. On graduating, he made literature his career, composing poems, writing novels and essays, and scripting plays, eventually becoming assistant editor of *Punch* magazine. It was in *Punch* that Milne's greatest creation, Winnie the Pooh, made his bow. He was called Teddy Bear at the time and featured in a poem. Three years later, in 1926, the bear moved to centre stage when Milne penned Winnie the Pooh, which enjoyed astonishing popularity, thanks in no small measure to magical illustrations by Ernest H Shepard. Other stories about 'the bear of very little brain' followed.

Milne based his tales on the nursery toys played with by his son, Christopher Robin Milne, and set the action in the Hundred Acre Wood, inspired by Ashdown Forest in Sussex, where Milne and his family lived. In the 1960s, Walt Disney broadened the appeal of Pooh even further with a perennially popular series of cartoons, but sadly Milne never saw them. He died in 1956.

Honey bunch

If Pooh has one obsession it is with getting some honey. One of his best-known mishaps comes about when he uses a party balloon to fly close to a bees' nest in the hope of stealing their honey. Like most Pooh tales, it ends uncomfortably, with the bees seeking revenge.

Honey when used in brewing adds a mellow softness, which is particularly noticeable on the swallow. It may also bring floral notes, depending on which plants the bees have been visiting. Perhaps it was a Pooh fan who brought honey back into brewing in recent times. In the 1990s, Vaux Brewery adventurously created a beer called Waggle Dance, which is now brewed by Wells & Young's. Fuller's has added Organic Honey Dew to its range, and many microbreweries have also begun to share Pooh's fascination with honey. Today's selection, however, is from Arkell's Brewery, the long-established Swindon family brewery.

Bee's Organic Ale was introduced in 2001 and is available in cask-conditioned form and also in bottle, where it is filtered but not pasteurized. Pale malt is joined by a little crystal malt and some wheat malt in the mash tun; the hops in the copper are First Gold, with Hallertauer from New Zealand added as the beer is strained through the hop back. The honey also goes in the copper. The result is a golden beer with a fresh and appealing aroma – spicy, malty, honeyed and floral, with suggestions of pineapple. On the palate, the beer is soft and velvety. The honey is obvious but doesn't destroy the balance, which falls just on the bitter side of bittersweet, with floral and pineapple notes floating around. Honeyed malt lingers after the swallow until bitter hops eventually take over, but this is a mellow finish, with no sting in the tail.

Births Peter Mark Roget (lexicographer), 1779; Oliver Hardy (comedian), 1892; Cary Grant (actor), 1904; Danny Kaye (actor), 1913

Deaths Rudyard Kipling (writer), 1936; Hugh Gaitskell (politician), 1963 Wilfrid Brambell (actor), 1985

Events Cook discovers the Sandwich Islands (now Hawaii), 1778; Versailles Peace Conference opens, 1919

Honey Beer

ABOVE: ILLUSTRATION FOR *WINNIE THE POOH* BY ERNEST H SHEPARD

Anchor Steam Beer

Source Anchor Brewing Company, San Francisco, California **Strength** 4.8% **Website** anchorbrewing.com

The influence of James Watt on beer production can't be underestimated. The Scots scientist is known as the inventor of the steam engine, a device that changed the way breweries operate. But Watt himself gained inspiration from the brewing industry first. When searching for a way to make primitive steam pumps more effective, he took a lesson from a brewery. Seeing how the kettles in the brewhouse were so stoutly built as to be able to hold vast quantities of liquid and deal with extremes of temperature gave Watt the idea of how to improve his pumps. Pumps up to that time had failed because they weren't able to maintain pressure. The strength of the brewing kettles revealed that it was possible to build a boiler that could do the job.

Watt's invention, however, more than repaid the brewers. His steam engine eventually made it possible for beers to be transported all around the country, while within the brewhouse the power generated by his equipment proved useful in all departments, from milling the malt to pumping the beer from vessel to vessel.

To mark Watt's birthday, in theory any beer from a modern brewery would fit nicely, as they all owe a massive debt to the Scots genius. But it's worth bringing in a beer that has steam in its name, if only to explain that, contrary to popular myth, on this occasion the inspiration wasn't actually the work of Watt.

California steaming

In the 19th century, warm and sunny California was a beacon to travellers from other regions of America. They came to join the Gold Rush and, after a day's hard toil, longed to slake their dusty thirst with a cold, refreshing lager. Unfortunately, California only brewed ale; in those days before refrigeration, local brewers simply couldn't bring temperatures down low enough to produce lager, as was possible in cooler parts of the country. But they did their best to please and came up with a compromise. They decided to make ale-type beers using pilsner yeast, cooling the beer as best they could, using shallow fermenting tanks that had a large surface area. The result was a beer with high natural carbonation that let off a steam-like hiss when casks were broached.

The most notable steam beer today is Anchor Steam Beer, produced in San Francisco. The brewery was rescued from closure in 1965 by Fritz Maytag, part of the Maytag washing machine dynasty. His actions in keeping the brewery open and then improving the quality and range of the beers on sale effectively signalled the birth of the craft brewing movement in the US. Anchor Steam is a dark amber beer with good malt character and a lacing of resins and fruit from Northern Brewer hops – all wrapped up in the well-rounded palate of lager. You'll struggle to find other examples, as Anchor has the steam appellation sewn up, but it's such a good beer that you won't even need to look.

Births Edgar Allan Poe (writer), 1809; Paul Cézanne (artist), 1839; Janis Joplin (rock singer), 1943; Dolly Parton (country singer), 1946

Deaths Carl Perkins (rock 'n' roll singer), 1998; Hedy Lamarr (actress), 2000; Wilson Pickett (soul singer), 2006

Events Indira Gandhi becomes Prime Minister of India, 1966

Steam Beer

Annoeullin L'Angelus

Source Brasserie d'Annoeullin, Annoeullin **Strength** 7% **Website** None

Unless you're a keen art viewer, it's easy to get lost among the Manets, Monets and Millets of French culture. Happily, there's a beer that provides a little insight into the work of one of this illustrious trio, which makes it the drink of the day for today. It was on 20 January 1875 that Jean François Millet died, bequeathing to the world a collection of distinctive rustic portraits that, as with many artists, only really found true appreciation after their creator's passing.

Millet was born in 1814 into Normandy farming stock. His upbringing, conditioned by the endless struggle of the local people to eke a living from the land, inevitably influenced the work that he produced after leaving the fields to study as a painter in Paris. Mere mention of the titles of his paintings exposes the nature of his output – *The Sower*, *Peasant Grafting a Tree* and *The Gleaners* are just three – and just one glance at his canvases reveals an empathy with the rural working class, and a recognition of the hardship and dignity that ran through their lives. Consequently, some critics have labelled Millet a socialist, although he himself rejected this description, claiming that it was the human side of art, not the political, that touched him most.

There is certainly humanity in Millet's most famous work. Entitled *L'Angelus*, the painting depicts a peasant couple alone in their fields, work temporarily set aside while their heads are bowed in prayer. The intriguing story about this work, however, is that it was commissioned by an American and initially entitled *Prayer for the Potato Crop*. When the buyer failed to take possession, Millet added a church steeple on the horizon and changed the title to something more religious. Even more fascinating is Salvador Dali's obsession with the painting. He believed that the peasants are actually praying over the grave of an infant and wrote a treatise on the matter. His theory was seemingly proved correct when x-rays of the artwork revealed a coffin-shaped item that had been painted over.

Droit de suite

On Millet's death in 1875, the painting was the subject of a bidding war and when it was finally sold for a then sensational 553,000 francs – many times the sum the artist had received for his efforts – it led to the concept of droit de suite being introduced to ensure that artists – or their estate if deceased – benefit financially from future sales of their works.

A reproduction of *L'Angelus* is now to be found on the label of a beer of the same name brewed by the Brasserie d'Annoeuillin, which was founded in 1905 in a corner of northern France halfway between Lens and Lille. The business, which is still family run, created this beer in 1985, after a rummage through old brewing books brought to light an intriguing recipe for a beer containing a high proportion of wheat. It was also a beer that matured over time at the brewery, in the local bière de garde tradition. Today, L'Angelus is an acknowledged classic, surprisingly delicate for its 7% ABV. On the palate, a lightly syrupy cereal base is overlaid with zesty, perfumed orange notes – the beer contains a secret spice mix as well as wheat – with a gentle tingle to reveal the subtle potency. Pouring gloriously golden into the glass, it appropriately reflects the warm glow that permeates much of Millet's work.

Births George Burns (comedian), 1896; Federico Fellini (film director), 1920; Tom Baker (actor), 1934

Deaths King George V, 1936; Audrey Hepburn (actress), 1993; Sir Matt Busby (football manager), 1994

Events John F Kennedy inaugurated as US President, 1961; Terry Waite kidnapped in Lebanon, 1987

Bière de Garde

Wye Valley Dorothy Goodbody's Wholesome Stout

Source Wye Valley Brewery, Stoke Lacy, Herefordshire **Strength** 4.6% **Website** wyevalleybrewery.co.uk

George Orwell was born Eric Arthur Blair in Bengal, India, in 1903. He was educated on a scholarship among the privileged at Eton, but his political leanings were socialist, as evidenced by his writing. His most famous books, *Animal Farm* and *1984*, reveal him to be a man of the people. There is another work, however, that shows not only his common touch but also attracts him to beer lovers. In 1946, Orwell penned a fictional pub review for the London *Evening Standard*. It described his favourite hostelry, the non-existent Moon under Water, and by focusing on its positives he highlighted the failings of so many real public houses.

What appeals to Orwell about this Utopian boozer is the fact that it is very much a local, free from rowdy outsiders. It has maintained its Victorian architecture and a multi-room layout that is able to accommodate all members of society. Games are sensibly confined to one area, and conversation is always possible, with music and other distractions mercifully rare. Food is limited but snacks can be bought, and there's a pleasant garden for summer months where families are welcome. Orwell wishes that children could be allowed inside the pub. The law against this is a law that 'deserves to be broken' in his view, so that pubs return to being family meeting places rather than merely drinking dens.

Stout revival

The beer provision at The Moon under Water is singled out for extra praise. It is one of the few pubs in London, Orwell says, that serve draught stout. 'Soft and creamy,' he describes it, and thinks 'it goes better in a pewter pot'. Things haven't changed much stout-wise since Orwell's time. Although keg Guinness and other Irish stouts are common now, the cask-conditioned, fresh-tasting stout has had a troubled 60 years. Thankfully, things are now on the mend. The new generation of microbreweries has taken stout to heart and there are some truly magnificent ones to be sought out.

I'm convinced Orwell would have found a soft spot for Dorothy Goodbody's Wholesome Stout, from Wye Valley Brewery in Herefordshire. Sadly, Dorothy Goodbody has never existed. She is as fictitious as Orwell's Moon under Water, a beautiful blonde bombshell simply created by computer to promote Wye Valley's range of seasonal beers. But Wholesome Stout is not seasonal any longer – it's too popular for that. The beer was created by brewery founder Peter Amor, a former Guinness employee, which partly explains the dry, roasted grain bitterness normally associated with Irish stouts. It may not be quite as soft and creamy as Orwell would have preferred, but he would surely have approved. The pewter pot remains optional.

Births Christian Dior (fashion designer), 1905; Benny Hill (comedian), 1924; Jack Nicklaus (golfer), 1940

Deaths Vladimir Ilyich Lenin (politician), 1924; Cecil B DeMille (film director), 1959; Jack Lord (actor), 1998

Events First Monte Carlo Rally, 1911; first commercial flights of Concorde, 1976; American hostages held in Tehran freed after 444 days, 1981

Stout

Pitfield 1837 India Pale Ale

Source Pitfield Brewery, Great Horkesley, Essex **Strength** 7% **Website** pitfieldbeershop.co.uk

The reign of Britain's longest-serving monarch came to an end on this day in 1901. Victoria's time on the throne lasted more than 60 years, and she presided over a dramatically changing world. Her era was the era of the Industrial Revolution, a time that saw massive changes in brewing as well as in other industries. Her days were also the heydays of the British Empire, when far-off countries like India became closely tied to Britain.

British influence in India had been considerable for some time. The East India Company, although basically a trading company, effectively ruled the country. However, after the Indian Mutiny of 1857, the company's days were numbered, and its interests passed into the hands of the Crown. Victoria herself became the first Empress of India in 1877.

On the sea

One of the great beer stories of her era also concerns India. British brewers had been shipping India pale ales to the British in residence there since the end of the 19th century, but it was during Victoria's lifetime that the trade really took off. The brewers, however, needed to be resourceful. In the days before the Suez Canal, all shipping had to take the long route, rounding the southern tip of Africa and crossing the Equator twice. It was a rough, tough journey involving searing heat and troubled waters. Not every beer would be able to survive in good order, hence the development of the India pale ale, or IPA, style. To withstand the travails of months on the sea, these beers were made strong, around 7% or more, so that the alcohol could fight off any infections developing in the beer. They were also made profusely hoppy, because hops, in addition to their many flavouring benefits, also act as a preservative.

Over the decades, the IPA genre has become watered down, quite literally. By the 1990s, there was hardly a genuine IPA to be found in the UK. Instead, a new generation of weak 'IPAs' had been created, no more than standard pale ales in essence, and the origins of the term IPA had been lost in time. Brewing historians and enthusiastic microbrewers have since helped put real IPA back on the map, and the suggested beer for today is a fine example of how a true Victorian IPA would have tasted.

Pitfield Brewery, a small operation set up in London in the 1980s as part of a specialist beer off-licence called The Beer Shop, is now located in rural Essex, but it continues to produce a fine range of bottled beers, including a small selection of historical re-creations. The recipe for this hugely hoppy, fruity strong ale comes from the research of a group of dedicated private brewers called the Durden Park Beer Circle. It's based on a beer that was produced in 1837 – the year that Victoria ascended the throne.

Births Sir Alf Ramsey (football manager), 1920; Sam Cooke (soul singer), 1931; John Hurt (actor), 1940

Deaths Lyndon B Johnson (36th US President), 1973; Herbert Sutcliffe (cricketer), 1978; Telly Savalas (actor), 1994

Events Battle of Rorke's Drift, 1879; Ramsay MacDonald elected first Labour Prime Minister, 1924

IPA

Robinson's Old Tom

Source Frederic Robinson, Stockport, Cheshire **Strength** 8.5% **Website** frederic-robinson.com

Cheer up. It can't get any worse, at least that's what a Cardiff University psychologist, Dr Cliff Arnall, reckons. He pored over data that revealed that 23 January is officially the saddest day of the year. Apparently, more working days are lost to illness and depression today than any other, as the exuberance of Christmas and New Year fades into memory, the January winds bite cold and it seems like an eternity until your next holiday. Surveying the long year ahead from this lowly position is a daunting prospect, especially when New Year resolutions have already been broken, and fitness regimes and diets lie in shreds by the roadside. Arnall's calculations were geared up for 2006, so this cheerless day may slip over onto another date in other years, but it's likely that 23 January is always going to be a bit grim.

Winter champion

While not usually one to suggest alcohol as the way to wipe out a depression – that's a slippery slope, for sure – it does seem to me that what may just lift this little cloud of misery is one of our great winter ales. CAMRA's Festival of Winter Ales is normally held around this time in Manchester, so you'd find plenty of cheer there if you can make it. Otherwise, I'd recommend a beer that has stolen the show at this event on more than one occasion.

Robinson's Old Tom is brewed in Stockport by one of Britain's great regional family breweries. It is a vinous ruby beer, with a chocolaty malt sweetness, along with red berries, pears and a splash of citrus fruit, plus a liquorice/aniseed note. The rich flavours blend handsomely on the tongue, a port wine note emerges, and the beer slips down a treat on a cold night. No wonder it has been voted Champion Winter Beer of Britain on two occasions. The strength should warn you to sip rather than sup, however: at 8.5% this is a classic barley wine to treat with respect.

They'll tell you at Robinson's that the beer is named after a brewery cat, sketched by brewer Alfred Munton on the day he brewed the first batch, which was, if records are correct, 1 November 1899. Some outsiders suggest that the cat had little to do with it, that Old Tom was just a fairly common name for beers at the time. Nevertheless, a cat still adorns the pump clip and bottle label, and certainly adds a bit of charm to the beer's history, so let's not concern ourselves too much with that. After all, we all have far more to worry about today, don't we?

Births Stendhal (writer), 1783; Edouard Manet (artist), 1832; Bob Paisley (football manager), 1919

Deaths William Pitt the Younger (politician), 1806; Salvador Dali (artist), 1989; Brian Redhead (broadcaster), 1994

Events House of Lords proceedings first televised, 1985; Madeleine Albright becomes first female US Secretary of State, 1997

Old Ale

Hop Back Summer Lightning

Source Hop Back Brewery Co., Downton, Wiltshire **Strength** 5% **Website** hopback.co.uk

A can of beer anyone? It's not an offer that discerning drinkers would normally accept. It may have something to do with the fact that usually it's only rather dull beers that are canned, and the fact that canned beers are filtered and pasteurized. There's also some truth in the assertion that beer in a can sometimes tastes rather metallic, with the container tainting the flavour of the liquid, although producers will always deny this, stating that technology has moved on since the early days.

Those early days date back to the 1930s. It was the New Jersey brewery Krueger that first managed to can beer successfully, working in conjunction with container specialist CanCo. Earlier experiments had seen cans burst or leak from the pressure of the beer. The breakthrough came on this day in 1935, when Krueger's beer went on sale in Richmond, Virginia. The move stole the thunder from an unlikely source. Tiny Felinfoel in West Wales was also looking to can beer, inspired by the local tin plate industry. In December that year, it succeeded and Europe had its first canned beer, too (see 3 December).

Party Seven

While cans have proved convenient, they have also proved controversial. Remember the giant-size Party Sevens introduced by Watney's in the late 1960s? Getting at the beer proved to be an exercise of Krypton Factor-like toughness, with anything from screwdrivers to chisels employed to puncture the container (in two

places, no less) to release the beer, which promptly re-emulsioned the ceiling or shampooed the carpet. In recent years, however, there's been a new confidence in canning in some quarters, with one or two American craft brewers canning beer again. But if you really want to celebrate the arrival of the world's first canned beer, I suggest the following route. See if your local brewery is now producing mini-casks. They look a bit like Party Sevens, only more shapely. More importantly, the beer inside is real. It's effectively cask beer in a smaller package.

The concept has been pioneered in the UK by Wells & Young's with its Bombardier mini-casks, but other breweries have followed suit, including Hop Back in Wiltshire, whose Summer Lightning, a trend-setting, strong golden ale with crisp citrus notes, can be enjoyed at home in the same format. The beer was first brewed for the CAMRA Salisbury Beer Festival in 1988, simply fashioned out of pale malt and Golding and Challenger hops. Founder John Gilbert named it after a PG Wodehouse novel.

Summer Lightning is now one of the UK's most famous ales, and, in its 5-litre mini-cask, is perfect for parties. What's more, you don't even need a screwdriver to get at it.

Births Desmond Morris (anthropologist), 1928; Neil Diamond (singer), 1941; Vic Reeves (comedian), 1959

Deaths Caligula (Roman emperor), 41; Lord Randolph Churchill (politician), 1895; Sir Winston Churchill (politician), 1965

Events Gold is discovered in California, prompting the Gold Rush, 1848; Apple Macintosh computers go on sale, 1984

Golden Ale

Traquair House Ale

Source Traquair House Brewery, Innerleithen, Borders **Strength** 10.5% **Website** traquair.co.uk

For Scots, 25 January is a special day. The date commemorates the birthday of their national poet Robert Burns (1759–1796), the author of the lyrics to 'Auld Lang Syne' and such famous lines as 'My luve's like a red, red rose'.

It is whisky, rather than beer, that is generally used for the toast at a traditional Burns Night supper, but maybe a beer with whisky connections would provide an interesting alternative. I'm thinking of the vanilla- and toffee-accented Innes & Gunn Oak Aged Beer, matured in casks that are used for whisky making. Or perhaps, Tuillibardine Blackford 1488, made by Bridge of Allan brewery, using the malt grist, water and distilling yeast from the Tuillibardine distillery, and then conditioning the beer in whisky casks.

Nevertheless, I'm tempted to avoid the whisky connection, as there is one beer that is as traditionally Scottish as

it gets and which would round off the celebratory Burns supper of haggis, neaps (swede) and tatties (potatoes) quite brilliantly. Strangely, it's a beer that's only just over 40 years old.

Brewing revival

It was in 1965 that Peter Maxwell-Stuart, the late laird of 12th-century Traquair House estate near Peebles, in the Scottish Borders, discovered an ancient brewery in an 18th-century wing of the building. In its day, the brewery's role had been to provide beer for the household and the estate workers. Maxwell-Stuart decided to breathe new life into the dusty equipment, and the beer he chose to re-commission it belonged to a disappearing style. It was strong and malty, deep and heady, a blast from Scotland's brewing past, akin to the type of ale that Burns – a poor farmer for most of his life – may have drawn upon to fire his poetic spirit.

Traquair House Ale, as the beer has become known, is brewed using the estate's own spring water and hopped with East Kent Goldings, though don't expect a bombardment of hops. This is a brew from a land that doesn't grow hops but instead has a glorious heritage of barley malt production. Malt, liquorice and toffee combine in the taste, although thankfully it's not particularly sticky or sweet. The beer is occasionally to be found on draught but, at a fulsome 7.2% ABV, it is better suited to the bottle.

At Traquair, they remain wedded to Scottish tradition and heritage. The famous Bear Gates on the estate were locked shut many years ago, and they won't be opened again until a Stuart once more sits atop the Scottish throne. Many Burns Night suppers will have been eaten before that time arrives – and many a glass of Traquair House Ale downed with pleasure.

Births Virginia Woolf (writer), 1882; Corazon Aquino (Philippines President), 1933; Eusébio (footballer), 1942

Deaths Al Capone (gangster), 1947; Ava Gardner (actress), 1990; Fanny Blankers-Koen (athlete), 2004

Events League of Nations founded, 1919; first Winter Olympic Games open in Chamonix, France, 1924; Idi Amin deposes Milton Obote to become Uganda's leader, 1971

Strong Ale

ABOVE: HISTORIC TRAQUAIR HOUSE

Coopers Sparkling Ale

Source Coopers, Regency Park, South Australia **Strength** 5.8% **Website** coopers.com.au

On 26 January 1788, Captain Arthur Phillip unfurled the British flag and formally laid claim to the colony of New South Wales, becoming its first governor. The day is now marked internationally as Australia Day, a vibrant celebration of all things Oz.

It doesn't take much to entice an Aussie into a bar, so imagine just how lively Australia Day can get among ex-pat communities around the globe. Inevitably, most of these festivities will be lubricated only by Australian lagers that have become international commodities. We shan't discuss them here. This is a book dedicated to good beer.

Sadly, because of these global brands, Australian beer doesn't have a great reputation, but you really don't have to dig too deep to find beers from the country that are not just drinkable but truly excellent. In recent years, Little Creatures Pale Ale – a bottle-conditioned, fresh and hoppy brew from an expanding Western Australia brewery – has made deep inroads in the UK and other countries. It could easily have been my selection for 26 January, but I've saved it for elsewhere in the book. I have instead opted for a brewery that has been flying the flag for fine Australian beer for much longer.

Family resistance

It was in 1862 that Yorkshireman Thomas Cooper started brewing in Adelaide, South Australia, and the business has remained in the hands of his descendents ever since, although rivals would like to have things differently. In 2006, the family bravely fought off an unwelcome take-over bid by Antipodean brewing giant Lion Nathan, owner of Castlemaine, Toohey's and other well-advertised products. It was a rare triumph of confidence and conviction over quick cash.

The brewery has moved to modern premises in recent years and some changes have taken place in the brewing process, but the jewel in the company's crown remains a traditional pale ale of the kind Thomas himself brewed 150 years or so ago. It's called simply Sparkling Ale and it's been knocking around the international stage for several decades now, buoyed by its uniqueness during most of this period as a bottle-conditioned Australian beer. Sparkling Ale (5.8%) is noted for its hazy appearance as the fine sediment infiltrates the beer in the glass. It's fresh, it's fruity – with spicy, peppery pear notes emerging from the fermentation process and the combination of Saaz and Pride of Ringwood hops – and it's very refreshing. Other beers from the Coopers stable are available, too. So, if you're thinking of raising a cork-dangling hat to the Australian nation, remember that discerning Aussie drinkers wouldn't give a XXXX for a glass of the 'Amber Nectar'. They'd be seeking out a Coopers.

Births Maria Von Trapp (singer), 1905; Stéphane Grappelli (violinist), 1908; Michael Bentine (comedian), 1922; Paul Newman (actor), 1925

Deaths Edward Jenner (scientist), 1823; Edward G Robinson (actor), 1973; Nelson Rockefeller (US Vice-President), 1979

Events India becomes a republic, 1950; Václav Havel elected President of the Czech Republic, 1993; US President Bill Clinton denies having 'sexual relations' with Monica Lewinsky, 1998

Pale Ale

Valhalla Island Bere

Source Valhalla Brewery, Unst, Shetland **Strength** 4.2% **Website** valhallabrewery.co.uk

Of all the Viking traditions that remain in the north of Britain, none is stronger than the annual festival of Up-Helly-Aa, celebrated in Shetland on the last Tuesday of January.

The Shetland Islands have a colourful Viking history. They were occupied by Norsemen for around 800 years from the ninth century. Up-Helly-Aa, which originated in the 19th century, is a vibrant remembrance of those times.

While there are smaller celebrations staged throughout the islands, the main Up-Helly-Aa event takes place in the Shetland capital, Lerwick, and involves a party of up to a thousand local men dressed for the part as Viking characters, complete with battleaxes and silver armour. The leader of the group adopts the guise of Jarl Sigurd Hlodvisson, a powerful ninth/tenth-century chieftain. Marching through the town, the men receive a church blessing and then take their flamboyant costume drama on to schools and old people's homes through the afternoon. But the revelry really begins when darkness falls and a torchlit procession takes to the streets. The centrepiece is the fiery destruction of a full-size replica longship, after which the participants split into groups to tour local halls and perform a little variety show, involving music, dance and comedy. Pubs see a roaring trade as partying continues until the following morning.

Viking barley

Enjoyed as part of the celebrations these days are beers from the local brewery. Valhalla Brewery was founded in 1997 by Sonny and Sylvia Priest, and takes its name from the mythical home of slain Viking warriors. The brewery is based on the island of Unst, making it the UK's most northerly.

Unique is a word that is used far too often and, on most occasions, quite inappropriately. However, Island Bere, the Valhalla beer selected for today, is clearly a unique product, and one that is particularly fitting for Up-Helly-Aa celebrations. It's the only beer currently being made using an ancient and rare type of barley, known as bere. It is thought that this grain may have been brought to Shetland and Orkney by the Vikings, but it fell out of favour with farmers during the last century. To revive its fortunes, Valhalla has joined with the Agronomy Institute of Orkney College to come up with a beer that makes commercial use of this heritage crop.

In order to soften the rather harsh properties of bere malt for modern palates, the grain is blended with Maris Otter pale malt in the mash tun. Cascade hops are used early in the copper, with Fuggles added later, which is the reverse of what you'd normally expect brewers to do. All this considered, the aroma and flavour of this orange/amber ale are very unusual. There's a distinct smoky note to the nose, which is otherwise creamy and malty. The bittersweet taste is also smoky, with nutty, creamy

malt and a lightly fruity hop edge. The same smoky, nutty notes continue into the dry finish, which also becomes rather bitter as the hops emerge more and more.

Island Bere was first launched at the Orkney Folk Festival in May 2006 and is now available in cask, locally, and to the wider world in bottle.

Births Wolfgang Amadeus Mozart (composer), 1756; Lewis Carroll (writer), 1832; Jerome Kern (composer), 1885

Deaths Giuseppe Verdi (composer), 1901; Mahalia Jackson (gospel singer), 1972

Events End of the German siege of Leningrad, 1944; *Apollo I* spacecraft bursts into flames during a test in Florida, killing astronauts Grissom, White and Chaffee, 1967

Bere Ale

Burton Bridge Tickle Brain

Source Burton Bridge Brewery, Burton-upon-Trent, Staffordshire
Strength 8% **Website** burtonbridgebrewery.co.uk

It is sometimes wondered why other countries – Belgium and Germany in particular – still have a strong tradition of monastic brewing, whereas the UK does not. The truth is that there was indeed plenty of beer brewed in British abbeys in centuries past, but most of it ran dry with the dissolution of the monasteries by King Henry VIII who died on this day in 1547.

Henry's beef with the Church resulted from his marriage trials. His first wife was Catherine of Aragon, the wife of his late elder brother Arthur. Special dispensation was needed from Rome to allow the marriage to take place. However, when Henry grew increasingly impatient about the fact Catherine could not bear him a healthy male heir, he pushed his luck too far with the Catholic Church by then asking for the marriage to be annulled. Permission was refused, Henry decided to ditch Catherine in favour of Anne Boleyn, and the Church excommunicated him accordingly. The king set up the Church of England, with himself as the head, and the split that survives to this day was created.

Henry soon exercised his new powers by closing down some of the smaller monasteries, cutting off their supply of funds to Rome and pocketing their revenue himself. He also sold monastery lands to wealthy citizens, further lining his own deep pockets. It wasn't long before the bigger abbeys were targeted, destroying most of the monastic culture in Britain. With it, Henry wiped out the tradition of monastic brewing.

Abbeys had long brewed beer, partly as a daily drink for the brethren at a time when drinking water was unsafe, and partly to serve the many pilgrims who enjoyed the shelter of the monasteries as they were travelling the country. The beer they would have brewed is likely to have been rich, strong and malty, with hops, a relative newcomer during Henry's era, perhaps still subdued. It is said that the king himself was not a fan of the hop and forbade its use by his court brewer.

One brewery that has taken a stab at how an abbey beer in Henry's time would have tasted is Burton Bridge. This small brewery in Burton-upon-Trent introduced such a beer in 1996. They called it Tickle Brain, a term plucked from the works of Shakespeare, and they put Henry VIII colourfully on the label. The beer is sweet and malty with a raspberryish fruitiness and just enough hop for balance. The mouth-numbing finish pleasingly confirms the strength. It's a beer fit for a king, or a monk.

Births Henry Morton Stanley (journalist and explorer), 1841; Ronnie Scott (jazz musician), 1927; Alan Alda (actor), 1936

Deaths Charlemagne (Holy Roman Emperor), 814; Sir Francis Drake (navigator), 1596; William Butler Yeats (poet), 1939

Events Elvis Presley makes his debut on American network television, 1956; Space Shuttle *Challenger* explodes on take-off, 1986

Strong Ale

Iceni Thomas Paine Porter

Source Iceni Brewery, Ickburgh, Norfolk **Strength** 4.2% **Website** icenibrewery.co.uk

'**N**oted author, revolutionary and man of reason,' says the label of Iceni's Thomas Paine Porter. It's a beer brewed in celebration of the life of a local boy come good, a man who was to have a major impact on world affairs.

Thomas Paine was born in Thetford – close to Iceni's home – in 1737, but his greatest achievements took place abroad. Paine established a friendship with Benjamin Franklin, who encouraged him to move to America, which he duly did in 1774. There, Paine worked as a journalist, writing material that helped him become an instrumental figure in the American Revolution, his publication *Common Sense* advocating the breaking of ties with the UK. He later became involved in the French Revolution, too, writing *The Rights of Man* in defence of the cause. This enraged the British monarchy and he fled to France, where he was elected to serve on the new governing body, the National Convention. He opposed Robespierre's Reign of Terror, however, and soon had to leave France as well.

All the while, Paine was a solid proponent of liberalism, an early supporter of social security and a fierce critic of religion, or at least the superstitions and supernatural side of it. Being a deist, he advocated only religious beliefs based on reason and human experience in the natural world. His work to this effect, *The Age of Reason*, made him many enemies in England. Consequently, Paine returned to America for his last days.

Ill health and poverty took their toll and he died at New Rochelle in 1809.

In Paine's later years, his accomplishments and clear thinking were largely forgotten, so it is welcome that they be recognized today. Harvey's in Sussex brews a beer in his honour, reflecting the fact that, before embarking on his world travels, Paine had worked as an excise man in Harvey's home town of Lewes and was also elected to the town council there. But the Iceni brew, being closer to his roots, seems a more fitting choice for today's beer.

Thomas Paine Porter is ruby in colour, thanks to the inclusion of roasted barley alongside the lighter malts. Fuggle and Challenger hops provide balance but overall this is a dry, coffeeish stout/porter in the Irish style, which is not surprising as brewery founder Brendan Moore is an Ulsterman. The beer is available in cask form and also as one of Iceni's many bottle-conditioned beers.

Births WC Fields (actor and comedian), 1879; Germaine Greer (feminist writer), 1939; Oprah Winfrey (TV presenter and executive), 1954

Deaths King George III, 1820; Alan Ladd (actor), 1964; Jimmy Durante (entertainer), 1980

Events The Victoria Cross instituted, 1856; radio series *Desert Island Discs* begins, 1942; Venetian opera house La Fenice destroyed by fire, 1996

Porter

ABOVE: THOMAS PAINE

St Austell HSD

Source St Austell Brewery, St Austell, Cornwall **Strength** 5% **Website** staustellbrewery.co.uk

Whether he was born on this day, or simply baptized, is not clear, but 30 January marks the first official record of the life of Walter Hicks, one of the Victorian age's great brewing entrepreneurs.

Hicks was Cornish through and through. He was born into a farming family and found his first vocation in the related industry of malting. But his dealings brought him into close contact with all the local brewers, which no doubt fuelled plans for an alternative future. With his appetite whetted for the licensed trade when his business expanded into wines and spirits trading, Walter eventually took the plunge and purchased a large hotel in the middle of St Austell that he saw was perfect for establishing a brewing business. The London Inn was transformed into its new guise in 1869.

What Hicks created there was a state-of-the-art brewery that was the envy of the county. His beers proved so popular that, within 20 years, he was forced to look for a new, larger site on which to expand. He found it on green fields on the hill above the town. This second brewery opened in 1893 and it is still home today to St Austell Brewery, which was how the company was renamed in the 1930s.

Progressive & exciting

Hicks died in 1916, aged 87, but his legacy lives on in the fifth generation of family members who run the business. The last decade has seen great changes at St Austell. Under the auspices of managing director James Staughton, Hicks's great-great grandson, the company has shaken off its mantle of sleepy Cornish giant and woken up to a new identity as a progressive, exciting regional brewery, with much to offer not only the Cornish locals but also beer drinkers in Britain as a whole. A number of new beers have arrived – the widely distributed Tribute, the golden, hoppy Proper Job and the nutty yet fruity Admiral's Ale, to name but three – revealing that St Austell perfectly combines the solid traditions of regional family brewing with a modern view of the beer market.

Walter Hicks's memory is also preserved in the name of one of St Austell's longest-established beers. HSD stands for Hicks Special Draught, although some drinkers have cheekily dubbed it High Speed Diesel. It's not really that strong, but at 5% does demand a certain respect. This is a complex malty ale with a nutty bittersweet flavour and traces of banana and raisin, Maris Otter pale, crystal and black malts in the mash tun, and good old Fuggle and Golding hops doing sterling work in the copper. While it's good to see modern tastes catered for, it's also good to see that some things don't change.

Births Franklin D Roosevelt (US President), 1882; Vanessa Redgrave (actress), 1937; Phil Collins (rock musician), 1951

Deaths King Charles I, 1649; Mahatma Gandhi (political activist and pacifist), 1948; Gerald Durrell (naturalist), 1995

Events State funeral of Sir Winston Churchill, 1965; the Beatles give their last live performance, on the roof of the Apple Corps building in London, 1969; Bloody Sunday sees the death of 13 civilian protestors in Northern Ireland, 1972

Strong Ale

Boon Oude Gueze

Source Brouwerij Boon, Lembeek   **Strength** 7%   **Website** boon.be

St Veronus is one of the lesser-known saints with connections to the brewing industry. His association is purely local to the town of Lembeek in Belgium, which is home of the lambic style of beer.

Veronus lived in the ninth century. It is said he was the grandson of Charlemagne, one of the most famous Holy Roman Emperors. But the high life was not for Veronus. When faced with marriage as a teenager, he left his family and went to work on a farm near Lembeek. While there, he performed a miracle by tapping on the ground with a stick, an action that caused a spring to issue forth. He died on 31 January 863.

The town of Lembeek still has a St Veronus Church, and his life is celebrated each Easter Monday with a religious procession through the town. The local brewers have adopted him as their patron saint.

Saint's protection

If there is one brewing region that may need a saint's care and protection, it is the area around Lembeek, lambic beer production being as unpredictable and open to the elements as brewing gets these days. This is Payottenland, the land of spontaneous fermentation, where wild yeasts from the atmosphere are invited to work their own miracles in turning sugars into alcohol and carbon dioxide. It's a rural patch to the southwest of Brussels, and you have to travel to it in order to find some of the most authentic examples of the lambic style. Of the more accessible purveyors Boon is well known.

Frank Boon entered the business in 1975, taking over an historic brewery whose owner was retiring. The company now has close connections with the Palm Rodenbach group but still maintains a fine list of lambic-style beers, including some luscious fruit beers. To mark St Veronus's Day, I would suggest a glass of Boon Oude Gueze. Gueuze (to give it its more common spelling) is a blend of old and young lambics with a pleasant effervescence. It's often been called the champagne of the beer world but, in truth, gueuze is far more challenging than champagne, particularly if you select one of the less commercial examples, such as this one from Boon. Expect an electrifying experience, a palate honed to razor-like sharpness by tart, dry, acidic, earthy, musky, almost cidery flavours. It's the sort of drink that after the first sip you will never want to try again, but by the time you've finished the glass, you are so intrigued that you will definitely call for another – if not immediately, then at least at some time in the future.

Births Franz Schubert (composer), 1797; Mario Lanza (singer), 1921; John Lydon (punk rocker), 1956

Deaths Guy Fawkes (conspirator), 1606; Bonnie Prince Charlie (Charles Edward Stuart, pretender), 1788; AA Milne (writer), 1956

Events Leon Trotsky exiled by the Soviet Union, 1929; McDonald's opens its first restaurant in Moscow, 1990

Oude Gueuze

O'Hanlon's Original Port Stout

Source O'Hanlon's Brewing Company Ltd, Whimple, Devon **Strength** 4.8% **Website** ohanlons.co.uk

One of the many saints popular among beer lovers has her feast day today. 1 February is the date that commemorates St Brigid, who, along with St Patrick and St Columba, is one of Ireland's saintly trinity.

Details of Brigid's life are sketchy to say the least and are clouded by contrary accounts of her background and work. Some claim she came from ordinary stock but others have it that Brigid was the illegitimate daughter of a chieftain named Dubhthach. It is thought she was born around the year 453 near Dundalk and that she devoted herself to God from an early age, with poverty one of her greatest inspirations. Indeed, she often angered her father (if we go with the chieftain story) by giving his possessions away to the poor. Eventually, her calling led her formally into the church and ultimately to founding monasteries and other religious institutions. It is thought she lived to be more than 70.

As part of her generosity of spirit, Brigid often provided food and drink for the hungry and thirsty. On one occasion, it is reported – in a new twist on the loaves-and-fishes concept – she produced a barrel of beer that didn't run dry until the congregations of 18 churches had had their fill. On another occasion, it is said she turned her bathwater into beer to give to a visiting cleric. Perhaps it is Brigid's influence that explains the great fondness for beer among the Irish.

Irish roots

Brigid's feast day calls for celebration with something that has Irish roots. The choice is O'Hanlon's Original Port Stout, a multi-award-winning dark beer whose crowns have included CAMRA Champion Bottled Beer in 2003 and 2007. It's not brewed on the Emerald Isle, but its background is authentic. It begins with John O'Hanlon, a rugby-mad Irishman running an Irish bar in Clerkenwell, London, in the 1990s. He decided to start his own brewery and this soon became the focus of attention. The pub was sold and, in 2000, O'Hanlon's decamped to the green, green grass of Devon, setting up home on a farm just east of Exeter. It's since gone from strength to strength, turning out an excellent range of cask and bottled beers, including the selection for today.

Original Port Stout is brewed from a grist of pale and crystal malt, caramalt and both roasted and flaked barley. The hops are Phoenix and Styrian Golding, but the intriguing ingredient is Ferreira port which is added to the brew just before bottling, at a ratio of two bottles for every brewer's barrel (36 gallons). This adds a touch of winey fruit to what is otherwise a satisfying, dry, bitter stout in the Irish style, packed with the flavours of dark chocolate and coffee.

Port Stout is also sold as a cask beer and was, in fact, one of O'Hanlon's earliest. John added the port to differentiate this brew from a keg stout that was also produced for the pub. He reveals that the inspiration was an Irish hangover cure, a mix of alcoholic drinks known colloquially as a 'corpse reviver'. St Brigid may have performed many miracles, but it's not clear if even she managed that particular feat.

Births Clark Gable (actor), 1901; Stanley Matthews (footballer), 1915; Terry Jones (writer and actor), 1942

Deaths Mary Shelley (writer), 1851; Buster Keaton (actor), 1966

Events Ayatollah Khomeini returns to Iran from exile, 1979; breakfast television arrives in the UK with the start of broadcasts by TV-am, 1983

Stout

Crouch Vale Brewers Gold

Source Crouch Vale Brewery, Chelmsford, Essex **Strength** 4% **Website** crouch-vale.co.uk

This day presents an occasion when religious and secular traditions collide. In the Christian calendar, 2 February is known as Candlemas, the day that marks the purification of the Virgin Mary after giving birth to Jesus. In Jewish tradition, child-bearing women were not allowed into the temple until 40 days had passed if the child had been a boy, and 60 days if a girl. The name Candlemas derives from the fact that it was on this day that all the candles in a church were blessed.

Candlemas also falls conveniently on one of the cross-quarter days of the year, marking the halfway point between the winter solstice and the spring equinox. It has always been used a marker, therefore, in the progress of winter and a guideline as to when spring will arrive. As the old saying put it:

> If Candlemas Day be fair and
>   bright,
> Winter will have another flight.
> If Candlemas Day brings cloud
>   and rain,
> Winter won't come again.

The principle has now been adopted for Groundhog Day, which, as anyone who has seen the 1993 film of the same name starring Bill Murray will know, takes place in a small town in Pennsylvania called Punxsutawney. There, each 2 February, a groundhog named Punxsutawney Phil is extracted from his burrow and, based on whether or not he sees his own shadow, forecasts the proximity of

spring. The ceremony dates back to 1886 and is an extension of a crude form of weather forecasting in which hibernating mammals were watched for their first appearance of the year.

As a result of the massive success of the film, Groundhog Day has taken on a new meaning. In the plot, Murray, as weather forecaster Phil Connors, finds himself trapped in the same recurring day. Every day, he goes through the same routine and meets the same people in the same places, and it looks as if this is what the rest of his life is going to be like.

Beer's own Groundhog Day took place on 1 August 2006. It wasn't in Punxsutawney but in Earl's Court, London. This is the time of year when CAMRA announces its Champion Beer of Britain winners. Judging takes place in the morning and at around 3pm in the afternoon the category winners and the overall supreme champion are announced to the

world. Very few beers have won the supreme title more than once. Until 2006, they were Thwaites Best Mild, Fuller's ESB and Timothy Taylor's Landlord, the last beer winning two titles in a row in 1982 and 1983. Amid great excitement, that remarkable feat was equalled when Brewers Gold from Crouch Vale Brewery in Essex was declared the judges' favourite again in 2006, having collected the top gong only a year earlier.

Brewers Gold is the most successful of the new breed of golden bitters. Crafted out of just lager malt and precisely seasoned with Brewers Gold hops, it is an easy-drinking, yet characterful beer, brimming with juicy citrus flavours, grapefruit in particular. The pump clip, with typical English reserve, describes the beer as 'a light thirst quenching brew', but its double success has meant that the brewery has rapidly expanded to cope with unprecedented demand. As it was for Bill Murray in the film, Groundhog Day has proved to be a life-changing experience for the guys at Crouch Vale.

Births Nell Gwynne (actress), 1650; James Joyce (writer), 1882; David Jason (actor), 1940

Deaths Boris Karloff (actor), 1969; Bertrand Russell (philosopher), 1970; Fred Perry (tennis player), 1995; Gene Kelly (dancer and actor), 1996

Events Funeral of Queen Victoria, 1901; opening of New York's Grand Central Station, 1913

Golden Ale

Bryncelyn Buddy Marvellous

Source Bryncelyn Brewery, Ystalyfera, Neath Port Talbot **Strength** 4% **Website** bryncelynbrewery.org.uk

On the third day of February 1959, rock star Buddy Holly lost his life. Tired of travelling by concert tour bus through the frozen American Midwest, Buddy and fellow rock stars Richie Valens and The Big Bopper chartered a small plane to take them from Clear Lake, Iowa, to Fargo, North Dakota, for their next gig. They never made it. In bad weather, the plane crashed just a few minutes' after take-off. All three were killed. For many, this day has become known as 'the day the music died', but for Will Hopton, a young man in the South Wales valleys, it was the day a lifelong obsession began.

'I was a fan of Buddy Holly before then, but not really in a big way,' he recalls. He'd not even taken the trouble to see Buddy when he made his only visit to Wales a year earlier. 'But after the crash, I grew to appreciate the music more and more. That's when I discovered some strange coincidences.' It turns out that Will was brought up in a house called Bryncelyn, which he didn't know translated from Welsh as 'Holly Hill'. Then, in 1963, he was married on 7 September, without realizing that it was also the date of Buddy's birthday, back in 1936. The Holly fascination has since grown and grown, to the point where Will has started a brewery and dedicated it to the late Texan singer.

Holly selection

Will has been the licensee of a pub called the Wern Fawr ('Big Alder'), in the Swansea valley village of Ystalyfera, since 1986. In 1999, he installed a tiny brewery in the cellar, producing enough beer to supply the bar and lounge upstairs, plus the odd beer festival, although not much beyond. He's named it, once again, Bryncelyn and it turns out a range of award-winning beers, all bearing a Buddy Holly connection in the name. The headliner brew is called Oh Boy. It's a golden ale at 4.5% with a beautiful fruit-cocktail fragrance. The backing group includes Rave On (5%), CHH (Charles Hardin Holley – Buddy's real name, 4.5%) and Peggy's Brew, a 4% beer for St David's Day. There are also seasonal beers such as May B Baby (4.5%) and a Christmas ale labelled That'll Be The Sleigh (7.1%). But the beer to savour today, perhaps with Buddy's *Greatest Hits* playing softly in the background, is Buddy Marvellous. This is a reddish, 4% mild that was deservedly voted CAMRA's Champion Beer of Wales in 2002. Only gently bitter, the beer has a complex fruit and malt flavour, and enough body to be totally satisfying. Like Will's other beers, it's a classy and respectful tribute to one of music's greats.

CHAMPION BEER OF WALES 2002-2003 Buddy Marvellous Brewed at THE WERN FAWR Ystalyfera

Births Felix Mendelssohn (composer), 1809; Norman Rockwell (artist), 1894; Val Doonican (entertainer), 1927

Deaths John of Gaunt (founder of House of Lancaster), 1399; Woodrow Wilson (28th US President), 1924; Joe Meek (record producer), 1967

Events Harold Macmillan criticizes apartheid in South Africa in his 'Wind of Change' speech, 1960; the Soviet Union's *Luna 9* probe makes the first controlled landing on the moon, 1966

Mild

Lion Stout

Source The Lion Brewery Ceylon Ltd, Biyagama **Strength** 8% **Website** lionbeer.com

The world of beer is full of surprises. One of the biggest is to travel to the Indian subcontinent and find that one of the most popular local brews is an 8%, black-as-yer-hat stout. What on Earth possessed the locals to create such a beer in such a fiery climate? The answer, as is so often the case, is the British.

The part of the subcontinent in question is Sri Lanka, the raindrop-shaped island that lies off India's most southerly point. Other countries had taken an interest in local affairs, including the Portuguese and the Dutch, but the island eventually fell into British hands in 1796, where it stayed until 1948 when the country finally gained independence. Not surprisingly, the Brits left a big impression, especially through the tea industry. In the days when the country was known as Ceylon, British workers founded the many tea plantations that still flourish on the island, and, to keep them happy in their resting hours, they called for British-style beers.

The Lion roars

In 1881, the Lion Brewery was established, brewing at altitude in the Sri Lankan mountains to keep the tea planters content. Today, Lion is the major purveyor of Sri Lankan stout to the world, although a certain amount of the romance was lost from the story when practical considerations forced the company to move production to Biyagama, about 24km (15 miles) from the country's capital Colombo.

Lion also produces the more predictable golden lagers, but its name has been built on this strong, dark beer style that pours deep and mysterious, with a creamy head. The taste offers chocolate and roasted notes, but this is something of a cross between the often-vinous imperial Russian stout styles and the weaker sweet stouts. There is some confusion whether the beer is bottle conditioned these days, but the importers tell me that this is certainly the case. In a constantly surprising beer world, where stout has come roaring back, Lion remains one of the kings of the jungle.

Births Charles Lindbergh (aviator), 1902; Norman Wisdom (comedian), 1915; Dan Quayle (US Vice-President), 1947; Alice Cooper (rock musician), 1948

Deaths Adolphe Sax (musical instrument maker), 1894; Karen Carpenter (singer), 1983; Liberace (musician), 1987

Events The Confederate States of America formed by six breakaway states, 1861; start of Yalta Conference, 1945; first colour supplement issued by *The Sunday Times*, 1962

Double Maxim

Source Frederic Robinson, Stockport, Cheshire **Strength** 4.7% **Website** dmbc.org.uk

On the face of it, there is little to celebrate in the birth of a man whose main achievement in life was to invent a highly destructive weapon, but heroes often go hand in hand with weapons, which is why today's recommended beer was brought into the world.

Hiram Maxim was born in Maine, USA, on this day in 1840. His father was a mechanic, and Hiram spent all his life dabbling with inventions. Among his creations were a mousetrap and a steam-driven aeroplane, but the device that most notably carried his name was the Maxim Machine Gun. It was in London in 1884 that Maxim came up with the idea for an automatic gun, recognizing that the recoil after a shot had been fired could be used to eject the spent cartridge and insert the next round. No external power was needed, meaning that the gun was relatively portable. With a possible output of 500 bullets a minute, the Maxim Gun had the fire power of around 100 conventional rifles. The British Army acquired his invention and it became standard issue during The Great War. Maxim, who had been knighted by Queen Victoria in 1901, died halfway through that conflict, in 1916.

Local hero

Maxim's achievement is commemorated in the brewing industry in a beer called Double Maxim. Once brewed by Vaux in Sunderland, which closed in 1998, the beer is now produced by Robinson's in Stockport for two former Vaux directors who operate under the name of the Double Maxim Beer Company. The beer's original title was simply Maxim Ale and it was created in 1901 to mark the return of local hero Major Ernest Vaux, commander of the Maxim Gun Detachment of the Northumberland Hussars, from the Boer War. Ernest Vaux was later closely involved in helping his friend, and former Boer War colleague, Robert Baden-Powell found the Scouting movement. The beer named in his honour was increased in strength in 1938, hence the current name of Double Maxim. Recipe tweaking in subsequent years has made it stronger still, at 4.7%.

The beer is a brown ale in the northeastern style and, before anyone suggests that it is a copycat of Newcastle Brown, I will add that it was first brewed 26 years before its rival. It is a bittersweet, fruity brew, with a creamy maltiness and a pleasant hoppy finish, attributes that certainly back up its advertising slogan of 'All Flavour, No Flannel'. It was once available in cask-conditioned form, but only the filtered bottle survives today.

Births Robert Peel (Prime Minister), 1788; John Dunlop (inventor), 1840; Sven-Göran Eriksson (football coach), 1948

Deaths Thomas Carlyle (historian), 1881; Joseph L Mankiewicz (film director), 1993

Events United Artists film company established by Mary Pickford, Charlie Chaplin, DW Griffith and Douglas Fairbanks, 1919; Greenwich Time Signal ('BBC pips') initiated, 1924; first Comic Relief 'Red Nose Day', 1988

Brown Ale

Williams Bros Kelpie

Source Williams Bros Brewing Co., Alloa, Clackmannanshire   **Strength** 4.4%   **Website** fraoch.com

It is indicative of the importance of the ocean to the economy and culture of Japan that the people celebrate an annual Seaweed Day on 6 February. Originally, the day was instituted to commemorate an ancient law that decreed that seaweed – a culinary delicacy – was a fitting tribute to offer the Emperor. These days, it's a good excuse to munch sushi and dark green laver, just as we in the UK opt for turkey at Christmas.

We don't eat much seaweed in the West, although the Welsh have always had a way with laver bread, and there has been a dollop of brittle fried shreds on many a Chinese restaurant plate in recent decades, but that's where we more or less draw the line. We don't sup much seaweed either or, rather, drinks that include seaweed. Judging from the taste of one Scottish beer that does include this maritime vegetable, we may be missing out.

The Williams Brothers, Bruce and Scott, have been digging up Scotland's brewing past since 1992. Heather Ale is their most celebrated re-creation (more about which on 13 November), and they've also fiddled about with convincing fruit beers. But seaweed? Now there's a challenge.

Back to the roots

The brothers hark back to the days, several hundreds of years ago, when coastal farmers in Scotland would fertilize their lands with seaweed, or even grow barley and other cereals in beds of seaweed. Inevitably, this unusual practice would have had an influence on the flavour of the crop and that is what the lads have tried to re-create. They've not gone back to the roots, so to speak, but have attempted to bring a little seaweed influence to bear by bunging some bladderwrack into the mash tun while making a dark, rich brew – Kelpie – from organic barley. It turns out at only 4.4% ABV, but it's a full-value beer that doesn't really taste much of the ocean or its produce, except for a dry, savoury note. Instead, it takes me back to my childhood when, as my teeth can testify, I ate far too many of the chewy sweets called Chocolate Toffee Rolls. If you remember these, you'll have no trouble with the taste of the beer, which also sees a little coffee breaking through in the finish.

A beer containing seaweed doesn't really sound too appealing, if we're honest, but take a leaf out of the Japanese book and give it a go. February 6 gives you an excuse.

Births Christopher Marlowe (playwright), 1564; Ronald Reagan (politician), 1911; François Truffaut (director), 1932

Deaths King Charles II, 1685; Lancelot 'Capability' Brown (landscape gardener), 1783; Arthur Ashe (tennis player), 1993

Events Women over 30 given right to vote in UK, 1918; Queen Elizabeth II succeeds her father, King George VI, as monarch, 1952; Manchester United football team suffers Munich air crash, 1958

Seaweed Ale

ABOVE: COLLECTING SEAWEED IN JAPAN

Mauldons Micawber's Mild

Source Mauldons The Black Adder Brewery, Sudbury, Suffolk **Strength** 3.5% **Website** mauldons.co.uk

The greatest storyteller of the 19th century was born on this day in 1812. Charles Dickens, it has been said countless times, captured the public imagination like no previous novelist, charming and entrancing Victorian readers (and millions since) with his shrewdly observed, colourful reflections on contemporary society.

Dickens's own early life was not especially happy. His father was imprisoned for debt, and Charles was forced to work in a rat-infested blacking warehouse, while aged only 12, before he turned rags to riches by becoming a writer. Such social injustice is reflected throughout his work, along with the merrier side of life, and pubs and beer – as you'd expect – play a notable hand in his oeuvre. Many a bustling, architecturally distinctive hostelry, vibrant with larger-than-life characters, is graphically depicted in his generous prose, with pubs like The Six Jolly Fellowship Porters in *Our Mutual Friend* becoming the Queen Vic or The Rovers Return of their day. For a closer inspection of Dickens's considerable fascination with the pubs of his time, readers should seek out Barrie Pepper's engaging book *The Inns of Dickens*, published by Heritage House Press, which has tracked down more than 150 fictional and real-life pubs that feature in his work.

Dickensian brewing

Breweries also feature in Dickens's world, where they are seen as places of great opportunity. One of his most famous characters, Wilkins Micawber, even tries to enter the brewing trade, as his long-suffering wife reveals in *David Copperfield*. 'I have long felt the Brewing business to be particularly adapted to Mr Micawber,' she says. 'Look at Barclay and Perkins! Look at Truman, Hanbury and Buxton! It is on that extensive footing that Mr Micawber, I know from my own knowledge of him, is calculated to shine; and the profits, I am told, are en-or-mous!' Sadly, the said brewers never reply to Micawber's letters of application and Copperfield's eccentric friend carries on waiting for 'something to turn up'.

There is one brewer that has taken on Micawber, however, and that is Mauldons in Sudbury. This Suffolk market town was immortalized in Dickens's *The Pickwick Papers* when, under the pseudonym of Eatanswill, it was the setting for a tale woven around a parliamentary election. Mauldons recognizes the close connection with a beer called Pickwick Bitter and, keeping its hat respectfully doffed to the maestro, also brews a Peggotty's Porter and even a summer ale simply called Dickens. But the beer selected for today's celebration is its Micawber's Mild. Although no stronger than 3.5%, this traditional dark beer is never short of flavour. It has a fair degree of bitterness for a mild, with slightly nutty, plain chocolate flavours overshadowing a gentle fruitiness in the taste. It might have been a touch weak for the inns of Dickens, but it's thoroughly enjoyable and worth seeking out today.

Births Gerald Davies (rugby player), 1945; Pete Postlethwaite (actor), 1945; Eddie Izzard (comedian), 1962

Deaths Harvey Firestone (tyre pioneer), 1938; Matt Monro (singer), 1985; King Hussein of Jordan, 1999

Events The Beatles begin their first tour of the US, 1964; Maastricht Treaty signed, 1992; Ellen MacArthur completes the fastest solo circumnavigation of the globe, 2005

Mild

45

Westmalle Dubbel

Source Brewery der Trappisten van Westmalle, Westmalle **Strength** 7% **Website** trappistwestmalle.be

Publicans all over the UK should raise a glass today to the *Morning Advertiser*, the national licensed trade publication, which was first issued on this day in 1794, priced 3½d.

The publication was founded by a group of licensed victuallers and soon became one of the major daily newspapers of the Victorian age, second only in circulation and in age to *The Times*. Licensed trade issues have dominated the content, although political and other stories have also featured. In the late 20th century, the paper became known for its extensive horse racing coverage but the *Morning Advertiser* has changed considerably over time, even in recent years. It is now published weekly and is owned by the William Reed group, which specializes in trade magazines, although it is published in association with The Licensed Trade Charity, a descendant of the organization that started things off.

It's not that easy to find a British beer that could have been supped while reading that first edition. Brewers such as Shepherd Neame and Young's, for instance, were certainly in operation at the time but to celebrate the first imprint I've opted to go to another institution that came into existence in the same year that the *Morning Advertiser* first appeared.

Double celebration

It takes us over to Belgium and to the founding of the Trappist monastery at Westmalle, to the north of Antwerp. The brotherhood here was initiated by a group of monks fleeing the French Revolution. Their intention was to sail to North America but they were persuaded to stay and set up a community on land donated by the Bishop of Antwerp. Today, Our Lady of the Sacred Heart, to give the monastery its proper name, is one of seven monasteries in Belgium and the Netherlands that still brew beer. Brewing started here in the 1830s, and beers were sold outside the abbey walls to local communities a few decades later, but commercial activity didn't really kick off until after World War I.

A fine Westmalle beer to sip on this cold February day is the Dubbel. This term is mostly applied to the darker beers in an abbey's collection, weighing in at around 7% ABV. Westmalle's is thought to be the original, with its roots in a beer first formulated in 1926. It shows a deep ruby colour and has traces of banana and spice in the chocolaty dark malt taste. The pale and darker malts and candy sugar in the recipe tend to caramelize in the direct-fired copper to add a toffeeish note throughout, while the hops remain restrained, just balancing the brew. The bottle-conditioned version is widely noted as being a touch drier than the draught.

Births John Ruskin (art critic), 1819; Jules Verne (writer), 1828; Jack Lemmon (actor), 1925; James Dean (actor), 1931

Deaths Mary, Queen of Scots, 1587; Del Shannon (singer), 1990; Iris Murdoch (writer), 1999

Events Elizabeth II proclaimed Queen on the death of King George VI, 1952; final mission aboard space station *Skylab* ends after 85 days, 1974; Derby-winning racehorse Shergar kidnapped and never seen again, 1983

Trappist Ale

Baltika No. 3 Classic

Source Baltika, St Petersburg **Strength** 5.1% **Website** baltikabeer.com

In post-Soviet Russia, beer has done rather well. Foreign investment in new breweries and equipment, the availability of better ingredients and, significantly perhaps, tax hikes on vodka, have conspired to raise beer drinking levels in recent years. However, as our date with history reveals, beer has always played an important part in Russian life.

We are given the opportunity to explore the local beer with the death of writer Fyodor Dostoevsky on this day in 1881. Dostoevsky was born in Moscow in 1821 and, after beginning his writing career, found his socialist leanings out of favour and was imprisoned in Siberia. On his release, he travelled throughout Europe, picking up experiences and influences that culminated in such masterpieces of literature as *Crime and Punishment*, *The Idiot* and *The Brothers Karamazov*.

Pleasurable shudder

It is in *Crime and Punishment* that the extent of beer drinking among the common people of 19th-century Russia is made clear. The lead character, Raskolnikov, is a man haunted by murders he has committed, and it is through beer that he finds some solace. The author says it brings a 'pleasurable shudder' to his spine. When his head is blazing with angry thoughts, beer proves to be a calming influence. Raskolnikov enters a tavern and orders a glass. Drinking it down in one, he feels immediately better. 'Only one glass of beer, a piece of dry bread, and in an instant the mind grows stronger, the thoughts clearer,

the intentions more resolute!', he explains to himself. Later in the novel, when a tormented Raskolnikov is ill, the ailment is diagnosed by an acquaintance who tells him he has not had 'enough beer and horseradish'.

The beer to serve with your horseradish today is undoubtedly the most successful beer ever to come out of Russia. Construction began on the Baltika brewery in St Petersburg, in 1978. In 1992, the company, now a division of Baltic Beverages Holding, introduced a number of new brands all simply designated by a number. No. 6 is a porter, No. 8 a wheat beer, for instance. No. 3 also goes by the name of Classic and is a pale lager, broadly in the style of a German hell. The company says it was the first post-Soviet beer in Russia and, in line with Russian law, declares the ABV to be 'not less than 4.8%' – for the UK, the strength is revealed to be 5.1%. Magnum is the bittering hop, topped off with an aroma hop that varies and has included Tradition, Aurora and Super Styrian. The beer is now made in ten different breweries in Russia, under licence at a brewery in the Ukraine, and at Camerons in the UK.

The aroma is spicy and lighty malty, with a hint of bubblegum. In the mouth, the taste is a pleasantly bitter, lightly nutty blend of malt and hops, with herbal notes, while the finish is dry and softly bitter, with hops building nicely. It's a very well-balanced, easy-drinking beer that aims for widespread appeal and achieves it. If you want something more demanding from the range, try Baltika No. 4 (see 4 November).

Births Carole King (singer-songwriter), 1942; Joe Pesci (actor), 1943; Glenn McGrath (cricketer), 1970

Deaths Bill Haley (rock 'n' roll musician), 1981; Yuri Andropov (Soviet premier), 1984; Ian Richardson (actor), 2007

Events The first star awarded on Hollywood's Walk of Fame goes to actress Joanne Woodward, 1960; Trevor Francis becomes Britain's first £1 million footballer, 1979

Pale Lager

Earl Soham Albert Ale

Source Earl Soham Brewery, Woodbridge, Suffolk **Strength** 4.4% **Website** earlsohambrewery.co.uk

Queen Victoria had been on the throne for three years by the time she married Prince Albert of Saxe-Coburg and Gotha, her Bavarian-born first cousin. The idea of their marriage was conceived even before Victoria became queen. Albert had visited the then Princess Victoria in 1836 and made a favourable impression on the young royal. Although there was no formal engagement at that time, there was an understanding that Albert should be groomed for the challenges of partnering a future monarch. In the end, it fell to the Queen to take the lead and propose marriage, knowing that taking on the role of her husband would involve considerable personal sacrifice for the handsome young aristocrat. Albert happily accepted.

The marriage took place in the Chapel Royal at St James's Palace in 1840. Albert became His Royal Highness and, later in life, Victoria bestowed a second title, that of Prince Consort, on her beloved husband, who proved to be a loyal and supportive companion. His sudden death from typhoid in 1861 shocked and deeply wounded Victoria. She remained in mourning (hence the familiar black outfits) until her own death 40 years later. In his memory, public monuments like London's Royal Albert Hall and Albert Memorial were constructed.

Royal ales

The names of Victoria and Albert also live on in the beers of a small Suffolk beer producer. Earl Soham Brewery is based in the country village of the same name, located about halfway between Stowmarket and Southwold. It began life in an old chicken shed behind a pub called The Victoria in 1984, hence the name of its popular Victoria Bitter (3.6%). In 2001, the brewery moved a few hundred yards along the main road to much larger premises in a former garage next to the village post office. Here, beers could be supplied more easily to other pubs, including the brewery's own second house, The Station, at nearby Framlingham, as well as in bottled form to the post office, which has its own delicatessen.

To accompany the golden-coloured Victoria Ale, Earl Soham found the ideal partner in Albert Ale, a darkish best bitter that was first brewed in 1985. Maris Otter pale malt, crystal malt and some darker influence from black malt provide a nutty, roasted grain base that is nicely balanced by Fuggle hops – a right royal marriage, you could say.

Brewed for Tastebuds by Earl Soham Brewery

Albert Ale

ABV 4.4%
500ml

Contact:
www.tastebudsfood.com

Tasting notes:
Nutty roasted grain is prominent. Strong hop balance, nutty, dark malt and hoppy finish.

An ale for the evening when there is time to savour it's subtleties.

Great with all casseroles and with game. Copper coloured with a malty and hoppy aroma.

JUG & BOTTLE

Ingredients:
Maris Otter and Optic pale malted barley. Crushed crystal and black malt. Whitbread Goldings Variety. Fuggles

Bottling date:

Best before:
3 months after bottling date. For best condition allow at least three weeks from the above date.

Births Harold Macmillan (Prime Minister), 1894; Larry Adler (harmonica player), 1914; Mark Spitz (swimmer), 1950; Greg Norman (golfer), 1955

Deaths Alexander Pushkin (writer), 1837; Edgar Wallace (writer), 1932; Arthur Miller (dramatist), 2005

Events Captured US pilot Francis Gary Powers exchanged for Russian spy Rudolph Abel, 1962; chess champion Gary Kasparov beaten by the Deep Blue computer, 1996

Best Bitter

Asahi Black

Source Ashai Breweries Ltd　**Strength** 5%　**Website** asahibeer.co.uk

Japan has a public holiday nearly every month of the year, but it is on 11 February that National Foundation Day is celebrated. The day commemorates the coronation of Jimmu as emperor in the year 660 BC, the event that established Japan as a country.

Jimmu was thought to have been a descendent of the sun goddess Amaterasu, and it was on a hereditary line from Jimmu that subsequent emperors based their claim to the throne. National Foundation Day was inaugurated in the 19th century but abandoned in the aftermath of World War II. It was reinstated in 1967, even though certain academics pulled holes in the mythology surrounding the event and argued that there was no accurate historical reason for celebrating this particular date.

If you're looking for a beer with which to join the Japanese in their celebration today, you'll find it's not easy to lay your hands on any native beer with real character. Most of the exports – and even beers brewed under licence in Europe – are of the bland, Asian lager type, good for wetting the whistle but not characterful enough to keep you interested for long. An excellent alternative, however, is Asahi Black.

Asahi was founded in 1899 as the Osaka Beer Brewing Company, with Asahi Beer – the name means 'Rising Sun' – launched three years later. There are now nine breweries in the group and Asahi products account for about 50 per cent of the Japanese domestic beer market. Although the packaging declares Asahi Black to be a 'Munich-type' beer, it is far more a schwarzbier in the East German tradition than a softer, fruitier dunkel from Bavaria, packed with the dry, heavily roasted flavours of three dark malts, which comfortably overshadow rice and maize in the cereal grist. It was introduced into the range in 1995 and is still brewed at Osaka, and not under licence. Coffee and chocolate feature in the aroma, while the taste is crisp and bittersweet, with faint caramel and liquorice flavours and a creamy coffee/chocolate maltiness, plus spicy alcohol notes that provide a little warmth. The dry finish is dominated by the flavour of well-roasted coffee beans.

If the black lager market continues to grow – as Czech brewers like Herold, Regent, Krusovice, Bernard, Budvar and Pilsner Urquell, as well as Köstritzer, Kaltenberg and other German brewers, step up their dark exports – then we are likely to see a lot more of Asahi Black.

Births Thomas Edison (inventor), 1847; Mary Quant (fashion designer), 1934; Sheryl Crow (singer-songwriter), 1962

Deaths René Descartes (philosopher), 1650; Peter Benchley (writer), 2006; Jackie Pallo (wrestler), 2006

Events The signing of the Lateran Treaty grants the Vatican City sovereign state rights within the city of Rome, 1929; Nelson Mandela freed after 27 years of imprisonment in South Africa, 1990

Dark Lager

ABOVE: JAPANESE GIRL IN TRADITIONAL DRESS

Darwin Rolling Hitch

Source Darwin Brewery Ltd, Sunderland, Tyne and Wear **Strength** 5.2% **Website** darwinbrewery.com

The world's perception of life and its origins began to change on this day in 1809, when Charles Darwin was born in Shropshire. Darwin dabbled in medicine and the Church early in life, but he became fascinated with botany, geology and natural history, and when given the chance to further his interests on a long sea voyage in 1831, he took it with both hands. The voyage was aboard HMS *Beagle* and it lasted five years. It took Darwin to South America, allowing him to witness natural phenomena at first hand and to begin to develop theories about natural selection and the way species develop. On his return, his findings brought him celebrity and he was able to work as an independent scientist. Eventually, in 1859, Darwin published his most famous work, known popularly as *The Origin of the Species*, in which he propounded his controversial theories of evolution and natural selection, contradicting the Creationist idea that God created all creatures in unrelated groups.

Brewing science

There's not just one beer that pays tribute to Darwin's work: there's a whole brewery. Darwin Brewery has its own origins in The University of Sunderland. It was here that the Brewlab brewing school and research centre took up residence in 1994 after leaving its initial home in London. The lab began brewing commercially, lifting its trading name from the University's Darwin Annexe and reflecting Darwin's work in the names of some of its beers, such as Evolution Ale and Extinction Ale. The one selected for today is called Rolling Hitch – after the well-known sailor's knot – with reference to the many years Darwin spent at sea. The beer is a traditional, full-bodied India Pale Ale, but is seasoned with American Amarillo hops, for a tangy, lemon-citrus accent. It was launched in 2004 and entered into a beer competition at Asda, justly taking the top honours.

One of the specialities of Darwin Brewery is the re-creation of old brewing styles and forgotten beers. Some recipes from the long-lost Hammonds Brewery in Bradford have been brought back to life, for instance, while Richmond Ale has been devised to emulate the sort of beer that would have been brewed at Richmond, North Yorkshire, in the late 19th century. There's also a notable beer called Flag Porter, brewed using yeast re-cultivated from bottles of porter found on the sea bed. Such work is not simply brewing: it's scientific research of the kind that would have fascinated Darwin himself.

Births Abraham Lincoln (16th US President), 1809; Anna Pavlova (ballerina), 1881; Franco Zeffirelli (film director), 1923

Deaths Lady Jane Grey (Queen of England), 1554; Lillie Langtry (actress), 1929; Jean Renoir (film director), 1979

Events Chile declares independence from Spain, 1818; US President Bill Clinton acquitted at the end of his impeachment trial, 1999

IPA

Fuller's Prize Old Ale

Source Fuller, Smith & Turner, Chiswick, London **Strength** 9% **Website** fullers.co.uk

Links between the Church and brewing are explored in various places in this book, but 13 February provides one of the more unusual connections. It comes through the death of Alexander Nowell, a prominent clergyman in Elizabethan times. Nowell was born in Lancashire, educated at Oxford, became a schoolmaster and was then elected Member of Parliament for Looe. Religion became increasingly important in his life and he eventually ended up as Dean of St Paul's.

It was while working in this capacity, it is said, that Nowell made a great discovery. Away from the office, he was a keen angler. The story has it that, while on one fishing trip near to Henley-on-Thames, Nowell tucked away a jar of ale to keep it cool. When he left for home, he accidentally left it behind. A week later, he returned to the same spot for some more fishing, rediscovered his beer and popped the cork. He found that the ale had gained carbonation and improved somewhat, the living yeast continuing to mature the beer in his absence. Now, fishermen are famous for their tall tales, so it would be foolish to set too much store by this account, but if Nowell was the first to proclaim the merits of 'bottle conditioning', he did brewers a fine service.

Prize acquisition

Bottle conditioning, if executed properly, provides one of the best beer experiences. The beer is left unpasteurized and contains living yeast, with plenty of sugars for the yeast to work on in maturing the beer. It's a process that particularly suits stronger beers. Old ales, porters, barley wines and such styles often ripen magnificently in the bottle. One particular beer that is brewed with this in mind is Prize Old Ale (9%). The beer was created at Gale's in Horndean, Hampshire, in the 1920s, by a new brewer from Yorkshire. Gale's continued to brew the beer up to the time that the company was sold to Fuller's and brewing ceased in 2006. Fuller's have since relaunched the beer.

Prize Old Ale is matured in tanks at the brewery for up to two years after fermentation, and acquires an acidic character along the way that adds to the drinkability of what is a very full but not particularly sweet beer, with dried fruit notes and a warming glow of alcohol. Bottle conditioning, in this case, is very much the key to success. So farewell, and thank you, Alexander Nowell.

Births Oliver Reed (actor), 1938; Jerry Springer (TV presenter), 1944; Robbie Williams (pop singer), 1974

Deaths Catherine Howard (fifth wife of King Henry VIII), 1542; Richard Wagner (composer), 1883; Waylon Jennings (country singer), 2002

Events William of Orange and his wife, Mary, proclaimed joint monarchs of Great Britain and Ireland, 1689; Konstantin Chernenko takes over from the deceased Yuri Andropov as Soviet premier, 1984

Old Ale

51

Harvey's Kiss

Source Harvey & Son, Lewes, East Sussex **Strength** 4.8% **Website** harveysonline.co.uk

Golden Ale

St Valentine's Day has to be one of the most widely celebrated of all saints' feast days, being an international event with no national allegiances. However, the saint commemorated today remains a bit of a mystery. It is suggested that there were three possible Valentines: an early Christian priest in Rome, a provincial bishop outside Rome and a martyr in Africa – all living in the third century. Quite how the name of any of these has become associated with the notion of heated romance is equally unclear, and may just have been an idea that grew up in the Middle Ages. Certainly, by Chaucer's time, the name of Valentine had become firmly associated with the concept of ardent love.

St Valentine's Day was formally dropped from the Christian calendar by the Vatican in 1969, during its purge of saints whose background was uncertain. But that hasn't stemmed the commercial activity that surrounds 14 February, even in the brewing industry. One of the many brewers producing a Valentine's Day beer is Harvey's in Sussex. But Harvey's beer is not a simple cash-in: it has its own romantic tale to tell that makes it a perfect choice for today.

Disgusted of Lewes

Harvey's Kiss was first brewed to celebrate an exhibition taking place in the brewery's home of Lewes. It also recalls a moment in the town's history when its conservative citizens were outraged by the presence in their midst of a piece of highly erotic, explicit artwork. The exhibition centred on Auguste Rodin's famous sculpture *The Kiss*. This was one of a series of works by Rodin depicting the same theme, the story of 13th-century lovers Paolo and Francesca, whose adulterous behaviour featured prominently in Dante's *Inferno*. The statue was commissioned by an American millionaire who owned a mansion at Lewes. He agreed to put it on show in the town in 1914.

Rodin's work graphically illustrates two naked bodies entwined, so graphically in fact that local headmistress Miss Kate Fowler-Tutt publicly objected to its presence. On the grounds that the work would prove distracting for the many young soldiers billeted in Lewes, she succeeded in having the steamy statue covered up and then removed from display. The work eventually ended up in the Tate Gallery in London, but in 1999 it was brought back to Lewes for a five-month visit to mark the arrival of the new millennium.

Harvey's Kiss has been brewed as a cask beer for St Valentine's Day ever since and is also available in bottle. Light-coloured malt is used as a base for the beer, with some malted pinhead oats for smoothness. The hops are Fuggle and Styrian Golding. The beer is golden in colour, with an aroma of pears and other cocktail fruit. The bittersweet taste has a mealy character from the oats and is slightly nutty, but perfumed floral notes and more pears dominate the palate, running on into the slightly warming, drying and gradually more bitter finish. It's the beer equivalent of a bouquet of St Valentine's Day flowers.

Births Jack Benny (comedian), 1894; Alan Parker (film director), 1944; Kevin Keegan (footballer and manager), 1951

Deaths James Cook (explorer), 1779; PG Wodehouse (writer), 1975; Frederick Loewe (composer), 1988

Events Chicago gangsters die in the 'St Valentine's Day Massacre', 1929; nationalization of the Bank of England, 1946

ABOVE: AMERICAN VALENTINE CARD SENT IN 1910

Castle Rock Hemlock

Source Castle Rock Brewery, Nottingham, Nottinghamshire **Strength** 4.1%
Website castlerockbrewery.co.uk

The truth is obscured by the mists of time, but it is believed that the father of Western philosophy met his end on 15 February. Socrates, well-known Athenian thinker, was an eccentric figure. By all accounts, he spent his life wandering the streets, talking to small groups of people, expounding his views on the world, listening to what the others had to say and then correcting faults in their arguments. He certainly had his admirers – Plato for one – but he had his enemies, too, particularly among the authorities who were worried that he was corrupting the city's youth. They eventually caught up with him, using his outspoken beliefs as ammunition to charge him with atheism and heresy. Found guilty, Socrates was given two options: leave Athens or take the poison he was offered. Being far too proud an Athenian to think of abandoning the city, he took the latter option, sinking a potion of hemlock and ending his 70-year-old life. They say he was a genius but, let's be honest, it's not the choice most rational thinkers would take.

It is largely through Socrates that the poison hemlock has gained its fame. The plant has a stem that is spotted purple, well-divided leaves, small white flowers and a noted 'mousey' aroma. The origins of its name are interesting: it actually means 'little hop', possibly because hops, like hemlock, are thought to have a sedative effect.

Brave brewery

All the same, it's a brave brewery that decides to give one of its beers the same name, but that's exactly what Castle Rock has done. The ingredients are entirely wholesome – pale and crystal malts, torrefied wheat and Fuggle and Golding hops – and the beer rolls out at 4.1% ABV, which makes it a satisfying best bitter, with a backdrop of dark malt flavours and fruity notes at all times. The beer is available both in cask and bottle-conditioned formats. But why Hemlock? The answer lies in a strange natural rock formation in a place called Bramcote, just outside Nottingham, where Castle Rock is based. The weird-shaped stone doesn't appear to take its name from the plant. It is thought to have been used in ceremonies by ancient druids, so the origin of the word might be cromlech, Welsh for a prehistoric stone. There are plenty of other suggestions for its existence, too, including that it was thrown down by the Devil or that it's the remains of a meteorite that tumbled from space, which means we know even less about its roots than we do the demise of Socrates.

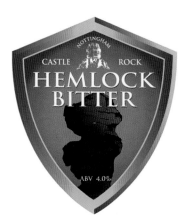

Births Galileo Galilei (scientist), 1564; Ernest Shackleton (explorer), 1874; Matt Groening (cartoonist), 1954

Deaths Herbert Asquith (Prime Minister), 1928; Nat King Cole (singer), 1965; Ethel Merman (singer and actress), 1984

Events British forces surrender Singapore in World War II, 1942; Britain switches to decimal currency, 1971; Soviet troops withdraw from Afghanistan after a nine-year occupation, 1989

Best Bitter

53

Svytyrus Ekstra

Source Svyturio, Klaipéda **Strength** 5.2% **Website** svyturys.lt/en

On 16 February 1918, Lithuania declared its independence from Russia – for the first time – and the country remained independent until the outbreak of World War II. Then, after a period of German domination, it fell once more into Russia's control as part of the Soviet Union, breaking free only after the fall of the Berlin Wall. Independence was reasserted in 1990, but only recognized by Russia in 1991. Russian troops finally left Lithuanian soil in 1993.

This constant struggle for freedom shows a great determination among the people of Lithuania, a country that had once held much influence in the Baltic and Black Sea regions. The small state has since moved quickly to firm up its new, free status by forging alliances with the West, joining both NATO and the EU, with one consequence being the large number of Lithuanian migrants who have transferred to the UK. It has also led to beers being imported from Lithuania to serve these ex-pats, beers that are now also interesting British drinkers.

Sea connections

The Svyturys brewery was founded in 1784 in the coastal town of Klaipéda, near the Polish border, by a merchant seaman whose family crest – featuring a sea eagle – remains on the brewery's logo to this day. After World War II, the brewery was reconstructed and continued to trade in state hands until independence, when the business was sold to its employees. Today,

Svyturys is part of Baltic Beverage Holdings, a division of Carlsberg.

The quality of the output is high. It includes clean-tasting lagers, both light and dark, some strong specials and a very good German-style weissbier called Baltas, but the most easily found is Svyturys Ekstra, a 5.2% premium lager that has been on sale in Wetherspoon pubs. The beer is based on the Dortmunder Export style, which makes it full and mellow, rather than exceptionally hoppy. It's got a pleasant herbal aroma and an enjoyable bittersweet lemon taste. You can also look out for Svyturys Ekstra Draught, which is the same beer – in bottle, confusingly

– but left unpasteurized. As an introduction to Lithuanian brewing, and as a way of celebrating the fighting spirit of this Baltic nation on its national day, they are all worthy beers.

Births Sonny Bono (singer and politician), 1935; John McEnroe (tennis player), 1959; Christopher Eccleston (actor), 1964

Deaths Leslie Hore-Belisha (road safety pioneer), 1957

Events Fidel Castro becomes leader of Cuba, 1959; US National Hockey League season cancelled over a labour dispute, 2005

Pale Lager

ABOVE: PILGRIMS ON THE HILL OF CROSSES, LITHUANIA

Kirin Ichiban

Source Wells & Young's Brewing Co., Bedford **Strength** 5% **Website** kirineurope.com

Opera, you'd think, was more of a champagne form of entertainment than beer, but today's date with history proves that even lager can have its day on the cultural stage. It all relates to Puccini's opera *Madame Butterfly,* which received its premiere at La Scala in Milan on this day in 1904. But the story begins about 40 years earlier with the founder of Japan's Kirin Brewery.

Madame Butterfly is set in Nagasaki. It is the tale of an American naval lieutenant named Pinkerton, who marries a young geisha girl named Butterfly during a tour of duty. He thinks it's merely a formality that he has to undergo to get his kicks while away from home; for the girl it is a life-changing experience, and she cuts all connections with her family to make this commitment to him. Inevitably, Pinkerton is called back to the US and ultimately runs out on the girl. When he gets wind of the fact that Butterfly has given birth to his child, he returns to Japan – not to do the honourable thing but to try to secure the child so it can be brought up in the US with his new American wife. Such caddish behaviour is sure to end in tears, and so it does when Butterfly, with typical Japanese dignity in such matters, takes her own life.

The real-life Pinkerton, it seems, may well have been Sir Thomas Blake Glover, a Scotsman known today as 'the father of Japanese brewing', thanks to his founding of Kirin (as the Japan Brewery Company) in 1885. Glover was married to his own Japanese lady, who went by the name of Butterfly. He also had a geisha mistress, with whom he had a son that he later adopted. The facts aren't quite the same, but there's enough similarity to lead us to conclude that this is where an American author named John Luther Long found the material to publish a short story in 1898 that, in turn, provided the basis for Puccini's opera. Not surprisingly, Kirin is now keen to develop the link between the musical masterpiece and its beer, sponsoring performances in the name of the company's most prestigious product, Kirin Ichiban.

Pure beer

Ichiban, which was first brewed in 1990, is a typical Asian lager in many respects. The recipe includes rice and maize as well as barley malt, while the hops are German Hallertauer and Czech Saaz, but the company is keen to stress one key difference, which is that only the first runnings from the cereals are used in the beer, unlike in other beers where the grist is sparged, or sprayed, to extract every last bit of fermentable sugar. They claim this method, known as the shibori process, produces a purer beer, and Ichiban is certainly crisp and well balanced.

In the UK, the beer has been brewed for Kirin since 1993 by Charles Wells (now Wells & Young's). Sweet, grainy cereal notes are evident in the aroma, along with a herbal hop note that gradually takes over. The taste is sweet at first, with a grainy texture, then herbal hops bring balance. There's also a little twist of lemon, while the finish is herbal, drying and increasingly bitter. Ichiban is not a heavy beer in any way, and that refreshing lightness makes it perfect for sipping with a traditional Japanese dish like sushi.

Births Ruth Rendell (writer), 1930; Barry Humphries (actor and comedian), 1934; Michael Jordan (basketball player), 1963

Deaths Molière (playwright), 1673; Geronimo (Native American leader), 1909; Thelonious Monk (jazz musician), 1982

Events St Clare of Assisi declared the patron saint of television by Pope Pius XII, 1958; start of the London Congestion Charge, 2003

Pale Lager

Palmers Tally Ho!

Source Palmers, Bridport, Dorset **Strength** 5.5% **Website** palmersbrewery.com

In 1949, the House of Commons debated two private members' bills to ban, or to restrict, hunting with dogs. Both failed to make it onto the statute book. It was a disappointment to animal rights campaigners who had hoped that the Labour Government's 1945 landslide majority would enable such a ban to come into force. Similar hopes were raised when Labour again swept into power with a three-figure majority in 1997, with promises to allow MPs a free vote on whether to ban hunting built into its manifesto. Nevertheless, it took eight years before legislation actually came into force as various bills bounced around Westminster until Commons Speaker Michael Martin used the Parliament Act to break the deadlock between MPs and the House of Lords and bring hunting to an end. On 18 February 2005, hunting with dogs was officially banned in England and Wales (it had already been banned in Scotland).

The hunting lobby predicted thousands of job losses in rural communities as a result of the ban and the destruction of even more redundant dogs, although, as packs switched to drag hunting and followed the allowable practice of using hounds to flush out a fox for other methods of extermination, these numbers were not realized. While calls for a repeal of the law remain strident, the status quo means that those who thrill to the sight of folk in red coats racing across country fields can continue to revel in this typically English eccentricity, with arguably a less cruel outcome.

A pub tradition

The licensed trade still relies heavily on the hunting tradition. There are, of course, thousands of pubs with names such as The Fox and Hounds or The Hare and Hounds. Furthermore, the traditional hunting cry of Tally Ho! can be heard even today in many bar rooms as drinkers ask for a pint of their favourite strong ale. It happens in Suffolk, for instance, where Adnams Tally Ho is available around Christmastime. And it happens in Dorset, where Palmers has been brewing Tally Ho! since the 1920s. Indeed, you could say that Palmers has been brewing it for even longer, as a member of the Palmer family was brewer at Adnams when Tally Ho started there.

Tally Ho! is probably the best-known ale in the Palmers portfolio, perhaps because it is also widely sold in bottle. Ruby in colour, the 5.5% old ale (5.2% in bottle) is made from Maris Otter pale and crystal malts, plus a touch of malt extract for colour, with whole-leaf English Goldings and Slovenian Styrian Goldings adding the bitterness and spice. The beer has a big, creamy, malty nose, with resin-like hops and soft banana notes. The same rich, deep maltiness acts as a base for more estery banana flavours in the taste, where a little warmth and spice nicely offset the creamy mouthfeel. The finish, meanwhile, is nutty and dry, with malt lingering and bitterness growing.

Even those who abhor the spectacle of the blood-thirsty pack in full cry can appreciate this particularly fine example of the brewers' art.

Births Queen Mary I, 1516; Bobby Robson (football manager), 1933; John Travolta (actor), 1954

Deaths Martin Luther (religious reformer), 1546; Michelangelo Buonarroti (artist), 1564; J Robert Oppenheimer (atomic physicist), 1967

Events Pluto discovered by astronomer Clyde Tombaugh, 1930; The Gambia achieves independence from the UK, 1965

Strong Ale

ABOVE: HUNTING WITH HOUNDS

Broughton Black Douglas

Source Broughton Ales Ltd, Broughton, Midlothian **Strength** 5.2% **Website** broughtonales.co.uk

Mention Scotland's historic fight for independence and the names Robert the Bruce and William Wallace come to mind. Their legacies are commemorated with beers later in this book. Today, however, one of the nation's lesser-known heroes is brought into focus, with Sir James Douglas remembered in a dark, chocolaty beer from Broughton Ales.

Douglas was a close ally of the aforementioned Robert the Bruce. He was born in 1286 and became a sworn enemy of the occupying English when his family's lands were confiscated. He met Bruce in 1306, as the self-proclaimed Scottish king was making his way to Scone for his coronation. Pledging himself to his service, Douglas worked closely with the rebel ruler to undermine the English position.

Outnumbered and out-resourced, the Scots developed a highly effective form of guerilla warfare, and Douglas was one of its leading tacticians. This is well illustrated by the events of 19 February 1314. On the evening of what was Shrove Tuesday, Douglas led his troops against one of the English bastions in Scotland. Roxburgh Castle, in the Borders, was well fortified and, knowing the Scots to be under-equipped, the English were more than a little lackadaisical with its defence. Shrewdly, Douglas drew up a plan that called for his men to crawl slowly to the walls under the cover of night, hidden beneath their cloaks. In the darkness, the English sentinels, perhaps more fixated with the celebrations that preceded Lent,

thought the slow, meandering movements to be just those of cows. Douglas's men were thus able to scale the walls, penetrate the castle and eject the complacent English.

Malty tribute

'Black Douglas' later fought alongside Bruce in the Battle of Bannockburn and then became a scourge of northern England, executing numerous raids on border towns. Always close to Bruce, he accepted one final request from the dying king, to take his heart to the Holy Sepulchre in Jerusalem for burial. Douglas never fulfilled his mission – he was killed in battle en route in August 1330.

Broughton Ales was founded in Peeblesshire in 1979, just a few miles along the Tweed Valley from the spot where Douglas and Bruce first met. Its tribute beer, Black Douglas, bears the portrait of James on the label and is brewed from Optic pale malt, crystal malt and black malt. The hops are Challenger and First Gold, although it is the malt that has the greater say.

In the glass, the beer is not actually black at all, rather a bright 'cherryade' red, but the dark malts still have plenty of impact. The nose is full of chocolate and toffee aromas, and the taste is also chocolaty and sweet. Hops are light and the body is fairly slender for the strength, giving a pleasant crispness. The finish is dry, malty and bitter, with a gentle lingering sweetness, making the overall effect akin to a porter, although not so full and with a more bitter finish. Try it from the cask or from the bottle.

Births Nicolaus Copernicus (astronomer), 1473; Smokey Robinson (soul musician), 1940; Prince Andrew, Duke of York, 1960

Deaths Anthony Crosland (politician), 1977; Derek Jarman (film director), 1994; Deng Xiaoping (politician), 1997

Events Thomas Edison patents the phonograph, 1878; the first episode of soap opera *EastEnders* broadcast, 1985

Scottish Ale

Flying Dog Gonzo Imperial Porter

Source Flying Dog Brewery, Denver, Colorado **Strength** 9% **Website** flyingdogales.com

Every now and then a writer comes along who throws the rulebook out of the window and sets a fashion for others to follow. Hunter S Thompson was one. Born in Kentucky in 1937, Thompson was always a rebel, from his teenage trouble years to his early discharge from the US Air Force. At least the military afforded him a new career. By working as editor of an Air Force sports magazine, he gained a ticket into the world of journalism, where his approach crashed through established barriers, culminating in what came to be termed the Gonzo style. This involves blurring the distinction between reality and fiction, and allowing personal input to influence the story.

Drugs & politics

In the 1960s, Thompson was part of the hippie scene in San Francisco, where drugs, particularly LSD, became interwoven in his life and work. His most famous book is *Fear and Loathing in Las Vegas*, a graphic account of a drug-crazed, hedonistic weekend in America's gambling capital in the early 1970s, but he also penned a book about Hell's Angels, after infiltrating the movement and suffering a beating for his trouble. He was later political correspondent for *Rolling Stone* magazine, famously unleashing his venom on President Richard Nixon. For his last years, he holed up on his ranch in Aspen, Colorado, where he once ran for sheriff – promising drug liberation – and narrowly lost. It was here that he took his own life in 2005, aged 67.

Thompson became a hero to many who enjoyed his acerbic approach to US culture and authority, and his name is remembered in a clutch of beers from the Flying Dog brewery, based in Denver, Colorado. This is more than just a collection of tribute brews, however. Thompson was an old friend and beer buddy of brewery co-founder George Stranahan. Their association eventually created the first 'Gonzo beer', with labels drawn by Thompson's long-term illustrator Ralph Steadman and graced with the Thompson quote that 'good people drink good beer'. The Gonzo Imperial Porter is probably the easiest to track down, a mighty 9% brew in the style of the dark, rich, hoppy stouts and porters that once crossed the icy Baltic from Britain to Russia. In true Gonzo style, it offers its own eccentric interpretation, of course, and like Thompson is bold and outspoken, belting out 80 units of bitterness. According to Flying Dog, the beer is 'dry hopped with a shit load of Cascade hops' and should be drunk 'wherever fear and loathing strike'.

Births Sidney Poitier (actor), 1927; Jimmy Greaves (footballer), 1940; Gordon Brown (politician), 1951

Deaths Robert Peary (explorer), 1920; Sandra Dee (actress), 2005

Events Coronation of King Edward VI, 1547; Lord Mountbatten becomes last viceroy of India, 1947; FA Premier League formed, 1992

Bartrams Comrade Bill Bartrams Egalitarian Anti Imperialist Soviet Stout

Source Bartrams Brewery, Rougham, Suffolk **Strength** 6.9% **Website** bartramsbrewery.co.uk

What was to become the 20th century's greatest political conflict took shape on this day in 1848 when Karl Marx and Friedrich Engels published their *Communist Manifesto*. The two philosophers had for some time been at the forefront of radical thinking in Europe and jointly organized the Communist League, a body of like-minded people, in 1847. What such a movement needed, however, was a written document that crystallized all that it stood for.

'A spectre is haunting Europe – the spectre of Communism,' the *Manifesto* declares, highlighting both the rise of communist feeling and the fear that it engendered in the ruling classes. The document moves on to expose the power imbalance between the bourgeoisie and the proletariat, and advocate methods of eradicating injustice in labour and society. It also inspired the leaders of the Bolshevik Revolution in Russia in 1917, and elements of Marx and Engels's work became the blueprint for establishing the Soviet Union, sweeping aside centuries of rule by the Czars and their aristocratic cronies.

One for the workers

A small Suffolk brewery offers a humorous take on this dramatic transition in Russian society. Bartrams Brewery, based on a disued airfield near Bury St Edmunds, Suffolk, was set up by Marc Bartram in 1999. Marc's beer range is ever increasing, and most of his ales are also bottled

as well as being sold in cask form. The interesting beer for today is a strong stout in the style that has become known as Imperial Russian because of the favour it found in the Russian royal court in the 19th century. Marc, however, has given a revolutionary twist to its name, which may well be the longest currently bestowed on a beer.

Comrade Bill Bartrams Egalitarian Anti Imperialist Soviet Stout was first brewed in 2004, and Marc's own image appears on the label, suitably hatted for the brutal Russian winter. The ingredients are officially declared as being 'the blood of the bourgeoisie, the sweat of the proletariat and the tears of the capitalists', although this has already drawn a complaint from

Trading Standards officers! The actual components are pale, crystal, dark crystal and chocolate malts, roasted barley and Golding and Galena hops. This is a big, nourishing beer, bright ruby in colour when held to the light. The aroma is appealingly malty, with plain chocolate and hints of Malteser, plus a little tart fruit – red berries, perhaps? Being bottle conditioned, the beer has wonderful, airy texture in the mouth, where bitter chocolate dominates other roasted grain flavours, and peppery alcohol adds a warming touch. The long-lasting, dry, bitter finish has more chocolate, along with coffee notes.

Not surprisingly, this beer has already won several major awards, which, in theory, really should be shared with every other brewer, don't you think?

Births WH Auden (writer and poet), 1907; Sam Peckinpah (film director), 1925; Kelsey Grammer (actor), 1955

Deaths Malcolm X (black nationalist leader), 1965; John Thaw (actor), 2002; John Charles (footballer), 2004

Events Start of the Battle of Verdun in World War I, 1916; identity cards abolished in the UK, 1952

Imperial Stout

ABOVE: THE *COMMUNIST MANIFESTO*, WRITTEN BY MARX AND ENGELS

Früh Kölsch

Source Cölner Hofbräu Früh, Cologne **Strength** 4.8% **Website** frueh.de

Anyone who believes that there are only four seasons in the year should pay a visit to Cologne. The locals there celebrate five.

The 'Fifth Season' is the name people give to the period of merriment that begins on 11 November. It is, in fact, a long, drawn-out prelude to Easter, and it comes to a head with the world-famous Cologne Carnival. Being tied to the religious festival, the date of the Carnival changes yearly, but it generally falls around this time in February.

After the November launch, things quieten down somewhat until the approach of Lent, when the city erupts in what are known as the 'Crazy Days'. These kick off on a Thursday, with fancy dress and masked balls. Partying continues over the weekend, with pubs and bars open way beyond their regular hours, and then reaches its zenith on Rose Monday (the day before Shrove Tuesday). This is when the big official procession takes to the streets, headed by the leading Carnival figures of the Prince, the Peasant and the Maiden.

Floral, fruity & fun

Beer, as in most areas of German life, plays an important role in the Fifth Season and in the Cologne Carnival. The city, with its environs, is home to around 20 breweries or brewpubs, and has its own particular beer style, called Kölsch, after the local name for the city, Köln. This is characterized, generally, as being an ale that is given a long lagering period at low temperatures. What emerges is a clean, spritzy, golden beer, often brimful of flowery, fruity aromas and flavours. It is traditionally served in small tubular glasses, which help accentuate the perfumed aromas.

If you make it to Cologne for the Carnival, you'll have to battle with the crowds, but you'll be able to try plenty of examples of this unique beer style. If you're looking to re-create a touch of the atmosphere at home, then there are a number that are widely exported. One of the best is Früh Kölsch. It comes from a brewery founded in 1904 by Peter Josef Früh. The beers are now produced in a new brewery outside of town but the heart of the business remains where Peter Josef placed it, in a bustling tavern near the magnificent cathedral. Beer labels prominently display three crowns – an allusion to the heritage of this cathedral, which houses what are said to be the relics of the Magi, the Three Kings who attended the baby Jesus. Früh Kölsch has a very pale golden colour, which belies its flavour-packed taste. Typically lively on the palate, the beer is pleasantly bitter with a smooth malt backdrop and lemon and spicy-herbal notes from the hops. The finish is moreishly hoppy. Floral, fruity and fun – it's all a Kölsch is meant to be.

The city, quite rightly, is proud of its indigenous beer style and has secured a trademark on the use of the name. This means that outside brewers should not call any of their beers Kölsch. But that doesn't stop them producing some very fine replicas of the Cologne style – handy fallbacks in case you can't lay hands on originals. In the UK, Meantime Brewing creates Cologne-Style Lager for Sainsbury's Taste the Difference range of quality goods, for instance, while in the US, St Arnold Brewery in Houston, Texas, offers the strangely named, but highly effective, Fancy Lawnmower.

Births George Washington (US President), 1732; Luis Buñuel (film director), 1900; Bruce Forsyth (entertainer), 1928

Deaths Amerigo Vespucci (explorer), 1512; Adrian Boult (conductor), 1983; Andy Warhol (artist), 1987

Events Frank Woolworth opens his first store, in Utica, New York, 1879; Dolly, the cloned sheep, unveiled to the world, 1997

Ulverston Another Fine Mess

Source Ulverston Brewing Co., Ulverston, Cumbria **Strength** 4% **Website** ulverstonbrewing.co.uk

Golden celebration

Celebrating, quite rightly, the local Stan Laurel connections is Ulverston's newest brewery. Set up in 2006, the brewery is run by former hairdresser Anita Garnett and her partner Paul Swann, and the range of beers includes such tribute titles as Lonesome Pine (after the song in the film *Way Out West*), Desert Son (inspired by the 1933 film *Sons of the Desert*) and Laughing Gravy (in honour of Laurel and Hardy's dog in the 1931 film of the same title). The beer they call Another Fine Mess is anything but. As a tribute to the golden age of comedy, and one of Cumbria's golden sons, it's an appropriately golden beer, gleaming in the glass and delivering a wonderfully fresh and appealing hoppy aroma. Juicy, fruity hops dominate the delightfully bittersweet taste. It would be well worth seeking out a pint before visiting Ulverston's own Laurel and Hardy museum and enjoying a chuckle at one of the duo's films that are screened throughout the day.

It may come as a surprise to some to learn that one of Hollywood's all-time greats was born in a small Cumbrian town. While his outsize partner Oliver Hardy hailed from Georgia, weedy Stan Laurel was from Ulverston, on the fringe of the Lake District, otherwise famous for its Hartleys brewery, sadly closed by Robinson's in 1991.

Laurel was born Arthur Stanley Jefferson on 16 June 1890, the son of a theatre manager. He learned his comic skills on the British music-hall stage before touring America with the Fred Karno troupe. There he was drawn into the movie industry. He first appeared with Ollie in a film called *The Lucky Dog* around 1919, but it was another seven years or so before they embarked on their on-screen partnership. Together they starred in more than 80 films, moving seamlessly from silent film shorts to feature-length talkies, and adding verbal humour to their already well-honed physical slapstick comedy. As their new career developed, so did character traits and catchphrases, best known of the latter being Hardy's huffy, 'Well, that's another fine mess you've gotten us into.' It became so well known that 'Another Fine Mess' became the title of one of their films.

Births Samuel Pepys (diarist), 1633; George Frederick Handel (composer), 1684; Bernard Cornwell (writer), 1944

Deaths John Keats (poet), 1821; LS Lowry (artist), 1976; Stanley Matthews (footballer), 2000

Events Cato Street Conspiracy to kill British Cabinet ministers exposed, 1820; siege of the Alamo, Texas, begins, 1836; Mussolini forms Italy's Fascist Party, 1919

ABOVE: STAN LAUREL

Golden Ale

A Le Coq Porter

Source A. Le Coq, Tartu **Strength** 6.5% **Website** alecoq.ee

Imperial Porter

On 16 February, we marked the national holiday in Lithuania, noting the date the country declared its independence in 1918. Eight days later, Lithuania's near neighbour, Estonia, did the same. 'Never in the course of centuries have the Estonian people lost their ardent desire for Independence,' the proclamation began, going on to describe the 'rotten foundations of the Russian Tsarist Empire' from which it wished to break free. After falling back into Soviet (and for a time German) hands as a consequence of World War II, Estonia regained its independence in 1991 and Russian troops finally left the country in 1994. Like Lithuania, Estonia has since joined NATO and the EU. It's even won the Eurovision Song Contest.

Cheesy songs apart, one of the country's most acclaimed exports is a beer from a brewery that has its roots in London. In 1807, a Belgian merchant by the name of Albert Le Coq set up a business to export strong stouts to the Baltic region. His company was very successful, helped by the fact that during the Russian-Japanese War in 1904–5, it donated supplies of beer to the wounded in Russian military hospitals, a gesture that earned favouritism within the Russian court. Its beer became so well regarded that fraudsters tried to pass off their inferior products as Le Coq's, even using his trademark. To combat this underhand trade, and also to avoid import tariffs, the company decided to open its own brewery closer to the action.

Soviets & Finns

In 1913, it acquired a brewery in Tartu, Estonia, that had been founded in 1826 but rebuilt in 1898. The brewery was later nationalized under the Soviet Union, but it is back in private hands today, indeed owned by a Finnish group. Its beer selection is extensive and varied, taking in such styles as pilsner, stout, double bock and even an English ale. The most notable beer it offers is, fittingly, a strong porter, although not quite as strong as the beers that Le Coq would have exported originally (for more on these, see 7 January).

The beer pours a deep ruby colour and presents a full malty aroma, with hints of caramel and a light fruity edge. More malt and caramel feature in the bittersweet taste, making this a smooth and easy-drinking beer for its strength.

Births Denis Law (footballer), 1940; George Harrison (pop musician), 1943; Dennis Waterman (actor), 1948; Alain Prost (racing driver), 1955

Deaths Joseph Rowntree (chocolate executive and philanthropist), 1925; Bobby Moore (footballer), 1993; Dennis Weaver (actor), 2006

Events Juan Perón becomes President of Argentina, 1946; Prince Charles and Lady Diana Spencer announce their marriage plans, 1981

ABOVE: TOWN HALL SQUARE, TALLINN, ESTONIA

Wells Banana Bread Beer

Source Wells & Young's Brewing Co., Bedford **Strength** 5.2% **Website** wellsandyoungs.co.uk

It's hard to believe in this time of plenty that food was not only rationed during World War II, but also that some of it was impossible to get hold of at all. Fruit, for instance, was scarce and truly seasonal. Apples, pears and other British produce were available, if it was the right time of year, while more exotic fruits stayed in the far-flung corners of the world where they grew. The banana was the prime example. 'Yes, we have no bananas' was a popular wartime song, based on shoppers' experience. Many children grew up never having seen a banana until the war was over. They may have been given an inkling of what one tasted like, however, as mothers were known to boil up parsnips, mash them down and add banana essence to create a substitute, but it wasn't until this day in 1946 that they would have been able to sample the real thing – it was on 25 February that the first post-war shipment of bananas arrived in Britain.

Comfortable bedfellows

Bananas and beer are not such unlikely bedfellows as some people might think. When beers are fermented to around 5% ABV and above, the yeast does wondrous things in the fermenting vessel. As well as turning sugars into alcohol and carbon dioxide, it starts to produce chemical compounds known as esters. These compounds have typically fruity aromas and flavours, of which banana is certainly one. This explains why some strong ales have a whiff of

banana about them, and why German weissbiers have such a strong banana character. Why not harness this attribute and make more of it?, was a question raised by Charles Wells Brewery in Bedford, but in taking up the challenge, they went a step further and actually put bananas into the brew.

What Wells achieved with Banana Bread Beer was an ale with wide appeal, especially to drinkers who normally find beer too bitter or hoppy. From a beer purist's point of view, however, it is important to note that the banana flavours are full and enjoyable, but not overbearing. This is still a rich, toffeeish, malty ale at heart, with an appealing dried banana chip character.

The beer is available as a seasonal offering in cask at 4.5%, and all-year-round filtered in bottles at 5.2%. A splendid accompaniment to toffee desserts, even though not especially sweet itself, it has one other feather in its cap, too: the bananas used are Fairtrade, making this an ethical as well as thoroughly enjoyable beer.

Births Pierre-Auguste Renoir (artist), 1841; Enrico Caruso (singer), 1873; Tom Courtenay (actor), 1937

Deaths Sir Christopher Wren (architect), 1723; Tennessee Williams (dramatist), 1983; Sir Donald Bradman (cricketer), 2001

Events Cassius Clay (later Muhammad Ali) defeats Sonny Lister to win world heavyweight boxing crown, 1964; Corazon Aquino replaces Ferdinand Marcos as President of the Philippines, 1986

Strong Ale

Fuller's ESB

Source Fuller, Smith & Turner, Chiswick, London **Strength** 5.5% **Website** fullers.co.uk

The world's most famous horse race, the Grand National, took place for the first time on 26 February, 1839. It was a Tuesday, which seems surprising now, but what is not so surprising in retrospect is that the winner should be named Lottery. Anyone who has laid a few quid on one of the hopefuls will know how lucky you have to be to choose a horse that actually gets round, let alone wins the race.

There are many memorable races in the history of the event: Foinavon winning at 100/1 in 1967 when most of the other horses fell; Red Rum claiming an unparalleled three victories in the 1970s; Bob Champion and Aldaniti both returning from life-threatening sickness to stride home in 1981; Esha Ness winning the 'race that never was' after a false start in 1993 – but there is one race that makes the choice of beer for today very easy.

In 1956, future best-selling crime novelist Dick Francis was aboard the Queen Mother's horse, Devon Lock, which seemed certain to romp home. Heading into the final furlong comfortably in front, the horse inexplicably spreadeagled itself, allowing rival jockey Dave Dick to take his horse into the record books instead. The name of that winning horse? It was ESB.

Champion & inspiration

The beer called ESB is just as much a champion as the best horses the Grand National has ever seen. One of the jewels in the sparkling Fuller's crown of London ales, the beer was launched in 1971 and then reformulated a few years ago to make it more quaffable for its strength. The strength of the cask version remains at 5.5%, but the bottled version has a little more oomph, at 5.9%, to compensate for filtration. Although the hop mix also contains Challenger, Target and Northdown, it is the Goldings that shine through, countering the full malty body and adding a distinctive orange marmalade note throughout. Not surprisingly, the beer has won countless awards, including CAMRA's Champion Beer of Britain no fewer than three times. It's proved an inspiration to other brewers, too, especially in the US where they've created a whole beer style around the beer and do their best to emulate it. If they're skilful, they may do justice to the beer's full name: Extra Special Bitter – three words that say it all.

Births Victor Hugo (writer), 1802; Buffalo Bill Cody (frontiersman), 1846; Fats Domino (rock 'n' roll singer), 1928; Johnny Cash (country singer), 1932

Deaths Lou Costello (actor and comedian), 1959; Bill Hicks (comedian), 1994

Events Napoleon escapes from exile on Elba, 1815; Church of England Synod votes to allow ordination of women priests, 1987

Strong Ale

The Shipyard Longfellow Winter Ale

Source Shipyard Brewing Co., Portland, Maine **Strength** 5.8% **Website** shipyard.com

In the established tradition of breweries paying tribute to local heroes, The Shipyard in Portland, Maine, brews a beer in honour of Henry Wadsworth Longfellow, one of the major poets of the 19th century, who was born on this day in 1807.

Longfellow was a child of Portland, and his boyhood home in the harbour city is now a museum. The young man had a gift for languages, and he studied at the local Bowdoin College, where he also later taught. His most fruitful years, however, were as a professor at Harvard University, where many of his most acclaimed poems were composed. They include *Hyperion*, which was inspired by the tragic loss of his first wife while travelling in Holland; *Ballads and Other Poems*; and *Tales of a Wayside Inn*. Undoubtedly, his best-known work, however, is the captivating *The Song of Hiawatha*, an epic tale of love among Native Americans, seemingly constructed to the beat of a tom-tom. Longfellow died in 1882. Such was his international renown that a sculptured bust of him was placed in Westminster Abbey's Poets' Corner.

Almost a hybrid

Longfellow Winter Ale was first brewed in 1995 and is described by brewer Alan Pugsley as 'almost a hybrid between a porter and a Scottish ale'. It is dark enough for both, although the colour is cherry-red rather than brown. Alan is an ex-pat British brewer, who once worked at Ringwood Brewery. Indeed, he has secured a licence to brew Ringwood's Old Thumper at Shipyard, which he founded in 1994 on Portland's historic waterfront. It is now the largest brewery in Maine and one of the top 20 biggest craft breweries in the US. The business was partly owned by Miller for four years, but Pugsley and his partner, Fred Forsley, re-acquired sole ownership in 2000.

Longfellow is built on a base of pale, crystal and chocolate malts, with roasted barley and torrefied wheat. The hops are Cascade, Tettnang, Warrior and East Kent Goldings. For the bottle, it is coarse filtered but not pasteurized.

The aroma has dusty chocolate notes and caramel hints from the rich, nutty malt, and the same characteristics appeal to the drinker on the palate. Fairly sweet overall, it tastes malty and nutty with bitter chocolate notes and just a suggestion of apple from the esters created by fermentation. Smoky roasted grains take over the drying finish, with yet more bitter chocolate, nuts and traces of coffee. It's a fresh-tasting, big, rewarding ale that makes a classy tribute to one of literature's all-time greats.

Births Elizabeth Taylor (actress), 1932; Paddy Ashdown (politician), 1941; Timothy Spall (actor), 1957

Deaths Lillian Gish (actress), 1993; Spike Milligan (comedian), 2002; Linda Smith (comedian), 2006

Events The Labour Representation Committee, forerunner of the Labour Party, founded, 1900; Rowan Williams enthroned as Archbishop of Canterbury, 2003

Strong Ale

Carib Royal Extra Stout

Source Carib Brewery (Trinidad) Ltd, Champs Fleurs **Strength** 6.6% **Website** caribbeer.com

Six days ago, the beginning of Lent in Germany provided us with our beer selection. For today, pre-Easter celebrations in a more sultry part of the world are our inspiration.

In the UK, the day before Ash Wednesday (the official start of Lent) is known as Shrove Tuesday. More popularly, it's called Pancake Day, as pancakes are the traditional food eaten on that day – a means of using up fatty ingredients not permitted during Lent. In many other parts of the world, of course, the day is known as Mardi Gras, or Fat Tuesday, and nowhere – not even New Orleans – lays on a more extravagant festival than Trinidad and Tobago.

In this multi-island state, the pre-Lent carnival takes over local life. Preparations for what the organizing committee describes as 'our gift to the world' begin even before Christmas. Initially, the boisterous celebrations were enjoyed only by the working classes, but gradually the whole of island society has come aboard. The date varies because Lent always begins 40 days before Easter, which falls differently every year, but the lively activities fill two manic days, beginning with J'ouvert (from the French for open day) on the Monday.

The art of having fun here is known as 'playing mas', which means joining one of the carnival's masquerade bands and wearing an appropriately creative and colourful costume. But even observers get carried away with the processions and partying. Steel and soca bands provide the pulsating beat, and the calypso shimmies its way through the streets. Sleep suddenly seems superfluous. It's a vibrant, feel-good send off to the days of excess, as the austere run-up to Easter lurks around the corner.

Thirsty work

You'd expect a beer or two to feature prominently in the high jinks – all that dancing is thirsty work. Trinidad's major brewer, Carib, certainly does well out of the occasion. The company was founded in 1947, and later acquired the island's earlier brewery, Walters'. Its best-selling beer, also simply called Carib, is a typical Caribbean light lager, introduced in 1950. It is suitably quenching under the West Indian sun, but lacks the character to really hit the spot when away from its home patch. Happily, there is a beer in the stable that does have more to offer. It's a strong, sweet stout, akin to the beers selected for 4 February and 6 August, in Sri Lanka and Jamaica, respectively.

A relic from the Walters' days, the beer is called Royal Extra Stout and pours a deep ruby colour with a honey-brown head. The aroma is particularly complex, packed with buttery malt, bitter chocolate, caramel, some winey dried fruit and hints of both liquorice and polished leather. The taste isn't so complicated, thanks to the predominant sweetness, but there's still coffee, chocolate and traces of liquorice to enjoy, as well as more than a little citrus zest. Similar flavours run on into the finish, which leaves a sugary taste in the mouth, and that, of course, makes it just perfect as a dessert beer.

The obvious pudding that comes to mind today is the pancake, and there can be few beers that wash down a chocolate pancake as well as this sweet Caribbean creation.

Births Stephen Spender (poet), 1909; Harry H Corbett (actor), 1925; Stephanie Beacham (actress), 1947

Deaths Henry James (writer), 1916; Dermot Morgan (actor and comedian), 1998; Chris Brasher (athlete), 2003

Events Last episode of the comedy series *M*A*S*H* broadcast in the US, 1983; the Gulf War ends, 1991

Sweet Stout

Batemans Salem Porter

Source Batemans Brewery, Wainfleet, Lincolnshire **Strength** 4.7% **Website** bateman.co.uk

One of the most infamous incidents in American history began on this day in 1692. In the small Massachusetts village of Salem, the young daughter of the local vicar Samuel Parris and some of her friends had been taken ill. They suffered fits, complained of sharp pains and were generally unruly. They even blocked their ears to the vicar's sermons, which wasn't a good sign. At a time of great superstition and fear, when fledgling communities like Salem were struggling to survive in a hostile environment, it was declared by a bemused doctor that the children had been possessed by witchcraft.

Three women were initially suspected of putting the children under a curse. Sarah Good, a beggar, Sarah Osbourne, a sick old woman, and Parris's own servant, Tituba, were the suspects – all three of them notably defenceless people – and it was on Leap Year Day that they were arrested, to be put on trial. Events then spiralled out of control, with more men and women accused and drawn into the controversy. By the time the outrage had come to an end, 14 women and six men had been executed, most convicted on 'spectral evidence' – claims by the afflicted of being able to see the shapes of their tormentors. The shameful trials later provided the inspiration for Arthur Miller's acclaimed play *The Crucible*.

Salem today respectfully trades on the tragic events of more than 300 years ago, attracting more than a million tourists a year, but hoping the experience will send them away imbued with the virtues of tolerance and understanding. The city appears to have no connection with Batemans' Salem Bridge Brewery in Wainfleet, Lincolnshire, where a beer called Salem Porter is brewed. A witch on a broomstick features on the pump clip, but I'm told the origin of the name Salem in this case is 'safe home', Wainfleet once operating as a port.

A magical beer?

Salem Porter, an award-winning dark brew of 4.7%, is certainly dark and mysterious, but is it magical? Some drinkers think so. Pale and crystal malts are joined by roasted barley in the mash tun to provide the deep colour and rich body, while Golding and Liberty hops supply the balance. The beer is grainy and nutty, with lots of malt flavour but a good counter bitterness, too. It was CAMRA's Champion Stout/Porter in 2005, which does rather suggest that it must indeed have a rather beguiling character.

Births Gioacchino Rossini (composer), 1792; Jimmy Dorsey (bandleader), 1904; Joss Ackland (actor), 1928

Deaths Patrick Hamilton (religious reformer), 1528; John Whitgift (Archbishop of Canterbury) 1604

Events Thousands die in an earthquake at Agadir, Morocco, 1960; *The Lord of the Rings: The Return of the King* wins 11 Oscars, 2004

Porter

Breconshire Red Dragon

Source The Breconshire Brewery, Brecon, Powys **Strength** 4.7% **Website** breconshirebrewery.com

It seems a little odd to reach for a glass of beer to celebrate the feast day of a saint who instructed his followers never to take alcohol, but St David's Day has become more than a tribute to an influential preacher. 1 March is the day that Wales calls its own, when schoolchildren don traditional costumes and most adults won't venture outside without a leek or a daffodil pinned to their lapel. It's a day to celebrate being Welsh.

What we know about David, or Dewi, to give him his Welsh title, is a mixture of fact and legend. We are told he was born around the year 500 and died around 589 – on 1 March. It is said his mother gave birth on a clifftop during a raging storm. Despite these inauspicious beginnings, David enjoyed a good education and used his knowledge to travel around Wales and other Celtic regions of Britain, preaching the Lord's work. He founded a monastery on the site of what is today St David's Cathedral, in the little West Wales settlement that bears his name, and he advocated the most rigid of lifestyles. His brethren were strict vegetarians and were even forbidden from using farm animals to plough their fields. The only recommended drink was water.

Beer revival

That wouldn't do for much of today's population in Wales. They like their beer, although it is only in relatively recent times that the real ale revival has reached here, with new microbreweries now opening all over the principality. There are still far too many good-beer deserts, but there are heartlands of cask ale, too, such as the capital city of Cardiff, well served by the long-established Brains brewery. Brains presents a commemorative ale for St David's Day, as do other Welsh brewers, including Breconshire Brewery, a small producer founded in 2002 in the lee of the wild and windy Brecon Beacons National Park. Sadly, the St David's Day specials tend to be available on draught only, and only for a short period, which would make them rather difficult to acquire outside of Wales. So the selection for today is another Breconshire beer, a beer that takes as its name that other great symbol of Wales, the Red Dragon.

Red Dragon is sold in cask and bottle forms and is true to its name in terms of colour – brewer Buster Grant employs dark crystal malt as well as ordinary crystal malt to generate the ruddy hue. Chocolate notes from these grains emerge in the aroma and taste, but the hops are not shy either, with Pioneer, Golding and First Gold all having an impact in balancing the beer. At 4.7%, Red Dragon is robust enough to provide a glow in this still wintry time of year and it makes a good companion to strong Welsh cheeses – even if St David wouldn't have approved.

Births Sandro Botticelli (artist), 1445; Frédéric Chopin (composer), 1810; Glenn Miller (bandleader), 1904; Yitzhak Rabin (politician), 1922

Deaths Gabriele D'Annunzio (writer), 1938; Peter Osgood (footballer), 2006; Jack Wild (actor), 2006

Events World's first National Park established at Yellowstone, Wyoming, 1872; radioactivity discovered by Henri Becquerel, 1896; Charlie Chaplin's coffin stolen from a cemetery in Switzerland, 1978

Strong Ale

Daleside Morocco Ale

Source Daleside Brewery Ltd, Harrogate, North Yorkshire **Strength** 5.5% **Website** dalesidebrewery.co.uk

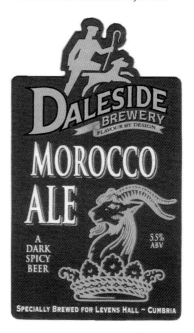

Lying just a stone's throw away from the Spanish shore, Morocco is Africa's closest country to Europe. Not surprisingly, it was considered suitable colonial territory for the Western powers and eventually ended up in the hands of the French. In 1956, however, everything changed when Morocco decided to go it alone, parting peacefully from its French masters and becoming an independent sultanate, transforming into a kingdom a year later.

In line with other Arabic and African lands, Morocco does not enjoy a great indigenous beer culture. You'll mostly find non-descript lagers if you wander into a bar in Casablanca, Rabat or any of the other main cities, so that leaves us scratching our heads a little to find a suitable partner for this important day in the country's history. Luckily, there is a beer called Morocco Ale, brewed by Daleside Brewery in North Yorkshire – rather a long way, it has to be said, from the African desertlands. It's not so much Sahara as Saharrogate.

Enigmatic brew

There is much mystery in the making of this beer. Morocco Ale's origins date back hundreds of years and involve a stately home in Cumbria called Levens Hall. The beer's name may derive from the marriage of King Charles II to Catherine of Braganza. As part of her dowry, Catherine brought with her the Moroccan port of Tangiers. It is not clear how this ties in with an earlier story of the recipe being buried under evergreens in the Levens Hall gardens during the Civil War, but the legend continues with the report that, every May until 1877, Morocco Ale was served at a great feast held in those gardens. For the privilege of a taste of this ale – matured for 21 years – guests were required to stand on one leg and empty in one draught a tall glass, at the same time wishing luck to the old hall.

Secrets persist in the making of Morocco Ale. It's not matured for 21 years anymore. In fact, it's hardly matured at all, but that doesn't mean it lacks character. Black malt and roasted barley in the mash tun ensure a deep ruby colour, with balance presented by Northern Brewer and Golding hops. Today's mystery really lies in the spicing, which is mainly with ginger but also involves selected North African ingredients. These aromatic spices lead throughout, warming and perfumed at all times, but, with its treacle toffee underbelly, this is a surprisingly drinkable ale and especially interesting with spicy food. It's Daleside's most successful beer in award terms, so, with its dash of Moroccan exoticism, it certainly has the pedigree to do justice to the occasion.

Births Mikhail Gorbachev (President of the Soviet Union), 1931; Lou Reed (rock musician), 1942; Ian Woosnam (golfer), 1958

Deaths John Wesley (religious reformer), 1791; DH Lawrence (writer), 1930; Dusty Springfield (singer), 1999

Events First test flight of supersonic airliner *Concorde*, 1969; Rhodesia declared a republic by Prime Minister Ian Smith, 1970

Spiced Ale

69

Van Steenburge Celis White

Source Brewery Van Steenburge, Ertvelde **Strength** 5% **Website** vansteenberge.com

Consolidation in the brewing industry is hardly ever a cause for celebration and the events of 3 March 2004 are certainly not, but the significance of this day in the industry cannot be ignored. What we're talking about here is the creation of the world's largest brewing company, when Interbrew of Belgium, at the time the third largest beer producer, merged its assets with AmBev of Brazil, number five in the pecking order. The new business, dubbed InBev, soared past Anheuser-Busch to become the biggest of the big boys.

Interbrew started life as a merger between the Artois and Piedboeuf breweries in Belgium, but grew through internal and external expansion, swallowing up Belgian rivals and then taking over the likes of Bass in the UK and Beck's in Germany. AmBev was the market leader in Latin America, its most famous brand being Brahma lager. The size of the new organization was immediately daunting, and consumer and employee concerns were swiftly realized as the company began rationalizing its business. Labatts in Toronto and Boddingtons in Manchester were soon closed as an indication of what was to come. The Hoegaarden Brewery was also slated for the scrap heap, but a massive backlash from the public forced InBev to rethink.

Hoegaarden had been opened by Pierre Celis in the 1960s, as a small brewery specializing in re-creating the old white beer style of Belgium, a type of beer that had disappeared from bars. His spiced wheat beer, laced with coriander and curaçao bitter orange peel, was an instant hit and saw the business grow rapidly. Artois stepped in with some financial assistance when a fire forced a rebuild at Hoegaarden, and it was to the successor of Artois, Interbrew, that Celis eventually sold his business.

Insensitive plans

Interbrew/InBev then marketed Hoegaarden forcefully, making it, along with Leffe, the driving force behind its speciality beer range. Production increased and InBev decided that the brewery at Hoegaarden was no longer big enough. They planned to close it, put dozens of people out of work, drain the lifeblood out of the town and move production elsewhere in the InBev empire – insensitively to the French-speaking part of Belgium. Thankfully, in September 2007, after global condemnation, local industrial action and a spirited campaign by Hoegaarden townsfolk, the company was forced to backtrack. Hoegaarden would remain open, with new investment to enable it to be a specialist white beer production centre.

So there can be life after InBev, it seems. Indeed, the beer selected for today underlines this. For this we go back to Pierre Celis. He may have sold his original brewery, but he has continued to brew outstanding white beers. For a while, he ran a brewery in Austin, Texas, until this was bought (and closed!) by Miller Brewing, but the beer he created there is now brewed in two centres – firstly, at Michigan Brewery in the US, and secondly, by the Van Steenberge brewery in Belgium.

A 50-50 mix of barley malt and unmalted wheat, seasoned with American Willamette and Cascade hops, plus coriander and orange peel, Celis White is Pierre's vision of a white beer for Americans. It pours a hazy yellow-gold and, also like Hoegaarden, has a fruity, bready character. But it's a richer beer than Hoegaarden, with a toffee accent, bittersweet lemon notes and a gentler hand with the spices. Raise a glass today to those who stand up to the power of big business.

Births Alexander Graham Bell (inventor), 1847; Jean Harlow (actress), 1911; Ronan Keating (singer), 1977

Deaths Lou Costello (comedian), 1959; Hergé (cartoonist), 1983; Danny Kaye (actor), 1987

Events *Time* magazine first published, 1923; Saudi Arabia discovers oil, 1938; Steve Fossett becomes first man to fly solo around the world without stopping or refuelling, 2005

White Beer

Victory Hop Devil India Pale Ale

Source Victory Brewing Company, Downingtown, Pennsylvania **Strength** 6.7% **Website** victorybeer.com

This day in 1681 was a big one for religious tolerance: King Charles II granted land in America to Quaker William Penn, so that he could set up a colony where his particular brand of Christianity would be free of persecution.

Penn was born in London in 1644, the son of Admiral William Penn. Unusually for a man of his social standing, Penn was a religious renegade. Rather than join the Catholic-Protestant battle in the country, he opted to follow the Society of Friends, a movement of people who held idiosyncratic views on religion, shunning ritual and rote, rejecting war and preferring a simple mode of dress and speech. Their unconventional approach to life inevitably drew hostility from other religions, but, in Penn, with his friends in high places, the movement had a valuable spokesman.

Penn fought for the Quakers, as the Friends became known, but, ultimately, he recognized that religious tolerance was unlikely to be achieved in England. Thus he talked the king into providing a safe haven in the New World. On 4 March 1681, Charles signed the papers, handing over a stretch of land west of the River Delaware and north of Maryland. In April, the grant became law and the first settlers left for their new life.

Brotherly love

Penn did not travel with them, but arrived a year later to establish the constitution and then governed the colony for two years. He called it Pennsylvania, after his father and the landscape of the region, the name meaning 'Forests of Penn'. The place where Penn landed in 1682 he dubbed Philadelphia, after the Greek for 'city of brotherly love'.

To mark this blow for freedom and what is effectively Pennsylvania's birthday, some excellent local beers can be found at Victory Brewing, based in the town of Downingtown, just west of Philadelphia. The business was founded by two old friends, who dreamt up the idea while still at school. Time passed, education was completed and ill-judged career paths abandoned before Bill Covaleski and Ron Barchet eventually became professional brewers. In 1996, they set up on their own and now produce a range of outstanding beers, packed with character and flavour. One of the most popular is Hop Devil India Pale Ale. Interestingly, for a hoppy ale, there is plenty of malt in the taste, with dark toffee notes and suggestions of chocolate. Then the hops kick in, adding sharpness and fruitiness through a rainbow of citrus and dried fruit flavours. The finish is extravagantly hoppy and tangy, drying and tingling the palate.

Hop Devil may be a provocative name for a beer with which to celebrate religious freedom, but it's a splendid example of how American brewers have recently found a freedom of a different sort – freedom to push the bounds of flavour to new levels.

Births Antonio Vivaldi (composer), 1678; Kenny Dalgliesh (footballer), 1951; Chris Rea (rock singer), 1951

Deaths Saladin (Muslim leader), 1193; John Candy (comedian and actor), 1994; Ian Wooldridge (sports journalist), 2007

Events First electric trams run in London, 1882; the Forth railway bridge officially opened by the future King Edward VII, 1890

IPA

71

Skinner's St Piran's Ale

Source Skinner's Brewing Co., Truro, Cornwall **Strength** 4.5% **Website** skinnersbrewery.com

While St Petroc and St Michael may also lay claim to being the patron saint of Cornwall, the honour is generally bestowed upon St Piran, an early Christian who is celebrated in the name of a popular ale from Skinner's Brewery in Truro.

Piran was born in Ireland. His background remains vague but he is thought to be the same saint the Irish call Ciarán of Saighir, who lived in the first part of the sixth century. Piran travelled abroad and furthered his religious studies in Rome before returning to Ireland, where, like many early missionaries, he suffered at the hands of those he tried to convert. His legend reveals that, for his pains, he was strapped to a millstone by his heathen enemies and rolled into a tempestuous sea. Miraculously, the sea calmed, the stone floated and the saint survived, eventually washing up on the beach near what is today Perranporth in Cornwall. There he continued his beneficent work, also becoming the patron saint of tin-miners. It is said that it was Piran who rediscovered the long-lost art of tin smelting, when a lump of tin ore he was using as a hearth stone began to ooze the valuable metal.

Early Beach Boy

Piran's feast day of 5 March is celebrated with a parade through the city of Truro and a re-enactment of his life and death on Perranporth beach. However, the beer brewed in his honour is available all year-round and pours a dark golden colour. Hops are the main feature, with Northdown and, particularly, Styrian Goldings bringing a resin-like bitterness and lots of powerful fruit and floral flavours. Piran is comically depicted on the artwork, cruising the waves on his millstone like an early Beach Boy. Britain's first ever surfer, the label calls him, and goes on to say that he lived until the improbable age of 206. Above his head unfurls his personal flag: black with a white cross – apparently the shape formed by the smelting tin in Piran's hearth stone.

St Piran's Ale is filtered for the bottle but you can also try it in cask-conditioned form when it is sold as Cornish Knocker. This time the name comes from the 'knockers', or mischievous tin-mine pixies that Skinner's has used in most of its colourful artwork since it was founded by Steve and Sarah Skinner in 1997.

1998 SUPREME SKINNER'S CHAMPION W

ST PIRAN'S ALE

ALC 4.5% VOL

GOLDEN ALE • HAND CRAFTED IN CORNWALL • G

Births Rex Harrison (actor), 1908; Pier Paolo Pasolini (film director), 1922; Matt Lucas (comedian), 1974

Deaths Sergei Prokofiev (composer), 1953; Josef Stalin (politician), 1953; Patsy Cline (country singer), 1963

Events Winston Churchill coins the term 'Iron Curtain' in a speech in Missouri, 1946; Elvis Presley makes his TV debut on *The Louisiana Hayride*, 1955

Golden Ale

Rodenbach Grand Cru

Source Brouwerij Rodenbach, Roeselare **Strength** 6% **Website** rodenbach.be

Most drinkers have now sampled Leffe Blonde and Hoegaarden. Maybe they've even ventured as far as a Duvel and a Grimbergen. Their toes have been dipped in the water of Belgian brewing, but they really are in the shallow end. This is a country that offers around 120 breweries. Between them they create well over a thousand beers in dozens of different styles, and only a visit to the country gives a true flavour of what it's all about. Even then, however, time is against you, as there are only so many beers you can take in one session – especially at Belgian strength.

If you're looking for the ideal opportunity to gather as much information about the local brewing scene, then the first weekend of March provides it. This is when the largest Belgian beer festival takes place. It's hosted by Zythos, the Belgian equivalent of CAMRA, and is staged in the town of St-Niklaas, 24km (15 miles) west of Antwerp. The great benefit of the event is that beers are sold in small samples, so you can stroll around the room tasting Belgium in a day.

When you arrive at the venue, you'll be confronted by a mind-boggling selection of more than 200 Belgian beers, supplied by around 60 breweries. A scan down a typical beer list for the event reveals some familiar names – Achouffe, Palm, Westmalle, perhaps – but not many foreign drinkers will have heard of Blaugies, Saint Monon or Van den Bossche, for example. The added bonus is that

beers are often served by the brewers themselves, so you can chat to the makers about their products.

World's most refreshing

We can't all make it to St-Niklaas, so here's a giant on the Belgian stage that will provide plenty of consolation comfort. The Rodenbach brewery in Roeselare, West Flanders, was founded in the 1820s, by the astonishingly versatile and influential Rodenbach family, Rhineland immigrants who, in no small degree, helped shape the emerging Belgian nation. Its speciality has always been oak-aged sour red beers, which were once described by Michael Jackson as 'the world's most refreshing'. In 1998, Rodenbach was acquired by Palm Breweries, Belgium's fourth largest brewing group, and a brand new brewhouse has been installed.

Rodenbach's famous red beer is produced using a mix of three different malts, a sizeable proportion of maize, and hop pellets from the Belgian hop gardens of Poperinge. These are low in bitterness, and deliberately not used fresh so that their flavour is minimized. But what makes this beer a classic is not the brewing but the maturation in massive oak tuns, some dating back to 1830. Row after row of these giant casks – 300 in all – line the cellars, where the beer rests at around 15ºC (59ºF) for up to two years. During this time, the beer is infiltrated by wild yeasts and micro-organisms that live in the old oak, feeding off oxygen that the wood allows through.

Beer drawn directly from the tun tastes fruity, earthy and highly acidic. It's also rather flat, so, before bottling, the beer is blended. The 'standard' Rodenbach (5%) is a mix of this old beer with fresh, lively young beer, at a ratio of 1:3. Rodenbach Grand Cru (6%) is 100% old beer, but sweetened and carbonated.

Whenever I go to Belgium, Rodenbach is often the first beer I call for, its tart fruit flavours and acetic bite sharpening the palate and setting me up for some of the heavier beers to come. Its idiosyncrasy is typical of the Belgian brewing industry as a whole.

Births Michelangelo Buonarroti (artist), 1475; Dave Gilmour (rock musician), 1946; Alan Davies (comedian and actor), 1966

Deaths Louisa May Alcott (writer), 1888; Ivor Novello (musician and actor), 1951; George Formby (singer and comedian), 1961

Events The Battle of the Alamo, Texas, 1836; the *Herald of Free Enterprise* ferry disaster at Zeebrugge, 1987

Sour Red Ale

Orkney Red MacGregor

Source The Orkney Brewery, Stromness, Orkney **Strength** 4% **Website** orkneybrewery.co.uk

I n our bibulous almanac, 7 March belongs to Orkney Brewery and its tribute to a folk hero baptized on this day in 1671. Rob Roy, probably born sometime in February that year, is one of those figures most people have heard of but know very little about. In brutal summary, he was a cattle rustler, blackmailer and extortionist, which, grouped together, doesn't make him the sort of fellow you'd want to celebrate in the name of a beer or anywhere else for that matter. But a better understanding comes with a little exploration into the Scotland in which he lived.

Robert MacGregor was born into one of the country's oldest clans, the MacGregors, but they were constantly undermined by their rivals, the Campbells, who often had the King on their side. Over time, the MacGregor lands were lost to the Campbells, and they were forced to become tenants of their bitter rivals. In desperation, the MacGregors took to rustling cattle and poaching, a move that sadly reduced them to a criminal underclass. Use of the name MacGregor was actually outlawed in 1603.

Personal feud

Although Robert was well educated, he was forced to eke out a meagre living from the land, which, like his forbears, he supplemented with a spot of cattle rustling, blackmail and protectionism. A key incident in his life came with a financial dispute with the Duke of Montrose, in which Robert may have been wholly innocent. It saw Robert evicted from his home, which was torched by his adversaries, and his wife badly abused. The feud, understandably, intensified but, after numerous dramatic instances of pursuit, capture and escape, Robert was pardoned and allowed to live out his days quietly in his own part of the Scottish Highlands, where he died in 1734. During his final years, Robert's personal economy operated in the same fluctuating manner as before, although he did enjoy a reputation as something of a Robin Hood figure, for the help he gave to the locally disadvantaged. It was perhaps this that encouraged both Daniel Defoe and Sir Walter Scott to pen romantic tales about this colourful brigand.

'Rob Roy' is the anglicized version of the Gaelic 'Raibert Ruadh', which translates as 'Red Robert', a nickname gained from the auburn colour of Robert's hair. Orkney Brewery acknowledges this in naming a beer in his honour. Red MacGregor, as you'd expect, is appropriately ruddy in colour, thanks to the use of crystal and chocolate malts in the mash tun, which also provide the rich, biscuity character of the aroma and taste. Like Rob Roy, this is something of a bittersweet creation, however, with a healthy dose of hops bringing a fruity acidity and a crisp dryness to the taste, before a very dry, hoppy and spicy finish.

Births Ranulph Fiennes (explorer), 1944; Viv Richards (cricketer), 1952; Rik Mayall (comedian and actor), 1958

Deaths Thomas Aquinas (philosopher), 1274; Stanley Kubrick (film director), 1999; John Junkin (comedian, actor and writer), 2006

Events Roald Amundsen announces that his team reached the South Pole the previous December, 1912; Indian Sunil Gavaskar becomes first batsman to reach 10,000 runs in Test cricket, 1987

Scottish Ale

ABOVE: LIAM NEESON IN THE 1995 FILM *ROB ROY*

Whittingtons Cats Whiskers

Source Whittingtons Brewery, Newent, Gloucestershire **Strength** 4.2% **Website** whittingtonbrewery.co.uk

The true story of Richard 'Dick' Whittington has been fogged by time. It is claimed in folklore and thigh-slapping pantomime exuberance that he became Lord Mayor of London with the help of his cat. The story has it that, having failed initially to find his fortune in the city, Whittington was leaving London for good but, on hearing the ringing of Bow bells, was encouraged to return and give life in the capital one more go. 'Turn again, Whittington,' they seemed to say, promising him three outings as the Lord Mayor of London.

In rural Gloucestershire, the Three Choirs Vineyard has been growing and pressing grapes since 1975. In 2003, the business looked to expand by tagging on a brewery. They called it Whittingtons Brewery, after Dick, who, in real life, was born locally in the 1350s, the son of the squire of Pauntley Court. Being the younger son of the family, and therefore lacking an inheritance, young Richard set out in search of his fortune. He took an apprenticeship in the textiles trade and became a wealthy businessman, with dealings with the court of King Richard II. In 1397, the king appointed Whittington mayor, a position to which he was re-elected three times. When he died, he left much of his wealth for the betterment of London, establishing an almshouse, a library and other public institutions.

Purrfect pints

The cat's major role in the story of Dick's success is entirely fanciful. Nevertheless, Whittingtons makes full use of the feline connection in the names of its beers, trading under the slogan of 'Purveyors of the purrfect pint'. The session ale (3.6%) is called Nine Lives, but more widely available, because it is also bottled, is Cats Whiskers, which was voted Gloucestershire Beer of the Year by the local CAMRA branch in 2004. A malt grist of Maris Otter pale malt, crystal malt and chocolate malt is spiced up by First Gold and Cascade hops. Prise the cap from a bottle and you're greeted with a nutty, chocolaty aroma that turns fruity and floral as the hops kick in. It's bittersweet to taste, and quite dry, with more nut, hop and lemon, wrapped up by a bitter finish. The beer is sold at the vineyard's shop and restaurant, and also further afield. With the help of national exposure in Sainsbury's supermarkets in 2006, the beer has followed in Dick's historic footsteps, setting out from Gloucestershire to find its fortune.

Births Kenneth Grahame (writer), 1859; Lynn Redgrave (actress), 1943; Mickey Dolenz (actor and singer), 1945

Deaths Harold Lloyd (silent film actor), 1971; Joe DiMaggio (baseball player), 1999; Adam Faith (singer and actor), 2003

Events International Women's Day inaugurated, 1911; Charles de Gaulle Airport opens, 1974; first part of *The Hitchhiker's Guide to the Galaxy* broadcast on BBC Radio, 1978

Best Bitter

Orval

Source Brasserie d'Orval, Villers-devant-Orval **Strength** 8% **Website** orval.be

There is no beer in the world like Orval. It's such a delicate blend of malt, hop and assertive, acidic dryness that anyone attempting to re-create the magic is sure to slip up somewhere along the way.

The beer is brewed by the brothers at Orval abbey, a religious settlement in Belgium's Ardennes forest, close to the borders of both France and Luxembourg. The origins of the site date back to the 11th century, when monks from southern Italy made a base here. In 1076, a visiting countess, Mathilda of Tuscany, lost her wedding ring in a gushing spring in the grounds. She prayed to the Virgin Mary for its safe return, only to find a trout rising to the surface carrying the ring in its mouth. Her jubilation led her to declare the site 'a golden valley' ('orval') and to offer funds for the betterment of the community. For some unknown reason, the original monks fled not long after, leaving control of the abbey to local church workers. They fell into financial distress and applied to the Cistercian body of friars for assistance. They were accepted into the order and, on 9 March 1132, seven monks arrived to refashion the church for community living.

Turbulent times

For Orval, like most religious settlements, the following centuries proved turbulent. Times of prosperity alternated with times of desperation as war raged across Europe. The abbey burned down and was rebuilt, but after further destruction during the French Revolution, it remained in ruins until its resurrection and reconstruction, with the help of a wealthy local family, from 1926. The abbey now belongs to the Trappist branch of the Cistercian movement, which is based on the strictest observance of the rules of founder St Benedict.

Orval's brewery was re-established in 1931. It brews only one beer for commercial sale, although there is a weaker version for the monks that can also be enjoyed at the hostelry just outside the abbey walls – Orval (6.2%), which is a true classic.

Water comes from Matilda's original spring and is used to mash pale and caramel malts. Candy sugar adds to the fermentability, without filling out the body, and Hallertau and Styrian Golding hops provide the seasoning. The beer enjoys a bottle fermentation but, before that, also has two fermentations at the brewery, the second in horizontal tanks in which more of the same hops are added. Crucially at this stage, a small dosage of brettanomyces yeast is also introduced. This is the yeast that gives lambic beers their lactic tartness and which endows Orval with its remarkable dry, acidic character. Combined with that notable second hopping, it gives Orval a uniqueness in world brewing – and a saintly status among beer lovers.

Births Amerigo Vespucci (navigator), 1454; Yuri Gagarin (cosmonaut), 1934; Bobby Fischer (chess player), 1943

Deaths Menachem Begin (politician), 1992; George Burns (comedian), 1996; John Profumo (politician), 2006

Events Napoleon marries Joséphine de Beauharnais, 1796; Inter Milan football club is founded, 1908; the Barbie doll is launched at a New York toy fair, 1959

Trappist Ale

Abita Bock

Source Abita Brewery, Abita Springs, Louisiana **Strength** 6.1% **Website** abita.com

A key event in the development of the United States of America took place on this day in 1804. The fledgling country, not even 30 years independent, was still struggling to find its feet, sharing the North American continent with the colonial interests of Britain, Spain and France. In one fell swoop, however, President Thomas Jefferson managed to simplify the situation and in doing so safeguard the viability of his country. It was a move that has become known as the Louisiana Purchase.

One of the key factors for the development of the US was the ability to navigate the mighty Mississippi River, the vast stretch of water that linked territories in the centre of the land mass. The river flowed through Spanish land, but a deal was put in place to allow access to the water and, crucially, its port at New Orleans. However, when Napoleon forced Spain to cede its North American colonies to France, the US was once again at the mercy of a foreign power.

Jefferson sent envoys to France to negotiate a purchase of New Orleans, to guarantee at least an outlet to the sea, but he received something that he hadn't quite bargained for. Napoleon, militarily and financially stretched, had been persuaded by a close advisor to concentrate his efforts on Europe and to take the opportunity to get out of North America. So it was that Jefferson found his negotiators buying not only New Orleans but the whole of the Louisiana Territory, which covered not just most of the state of Louisiana but also what today breaks down into the states of Arkansas, Iowa, Kansas, Missouri, Nebraska and Oklahoma, plus large tracts of Colorado, Minnesota, Montana, North and South Dakotas and Wyoming, and parts of New Mexico and Texas. For the cost of around $15 million, the size of the US had been virtually doubled overnight and vital commercial infrastructure had been preserved. The deal was signed in April 1803 and formally put into place through a ceremony in St Louis, Missouri, on 10 March 1804.

Strong survivor

New Orleans and Louisiana have, of course, suffered horribly in recent years, thanks to Hurricane Katrina. A great survivor, however, is Abita Brewery, which was founded in 1986 in a woodland area some 48 km (30 miles) north of the city. Despite the traumas of recent years, the brewery continues to grow and its range of beers is ever expanding. The beer chosen to mark the anniversary of the Louisiana Purchase is its version of a German strong lager, created from pale and caramel malts and seasoned with Perle hops. Abita Bock is only a seasonal beer on draught, brewed between January and March, but, crucially, available over Mardi Gras season when it is the tipple of choice of many party animals. In bottle, it is sold all year.

The label doesn't look especially inspiring but don't be fooled by modest appearances. This is a full-bodied, flavoursome bock with an appealing golden colour. Big, grainy, nutty malt dominates the aroma, followed by a rich and pleasantly bittersweet taste with lots of smooth, sticky, very nutty malt overshadowing a soft, hoppy bite. Gently warming at all times, the beer ends dry, nutty and increasingly tangy, hoppy and bitter. Make it your Louisiana purchase today.

Births Bix Beiderbecke (jazz musician), 1903; Sharon Stone (actress), 1958; Prince Edward, 1964

Deaths Ray Milland (actor), 1986; Barry Sheene (motorcyclist), 2003; Dave Allen (comedian), 2005

Events Alexander Graham Bell makes his first telephone call, 1876; syzygy takes place, with all nine planets in alignment, 1982

Bock

77

Freeminer Co-op Organic Premium Ale

Source Freeminer Brewery Ltd, Cinderford, Forest of Dean, Gloucestershire
Strength 5% **Website** freeminer.com

The Fairtrade movement has done wonders in improving the lives of Third World food producers. Its declared aims are to ensure that producers receive a price for their goods that will enable them to make a decent living if they are small holders, or to reward their employees properly if they are larger concerns. The premium charged for Fairtrade goods also covers investment in sustainable production and workers' welfare, and manufacturers and distributors are asked to sign contracts with suppliers to allow for long-term planning.

The Fairtrade Foundation in the UK was established by a collection of aid charities in 1992. Today, there are more than 1,500 available items, the most common being bananas, coffee and tea, but other products such as spices, rice, flowers and even sports balls are also sold. To raise the profile of this worthy initiative, Fairtrade Fortnight now takes place in late February and early March (the dates vary annually). More precisely for today, it was on 11 March 2003 that Mayor Ken Livingstone committed London to work towards Fairtrade City status. Both occasions give us good reason for looking more closely into Fairtrade beer.

Brewers play fair

The biggest-selling Fairtrade beer is BeeWyched, from Wychwood Brewery in Oxfordshire. This incorporates Fairtrade honey sourced from the foot of the Andes in Chile. It has a rival in the form of Bumble Bee, another Fairtrade honey beer, this time brewed exclusively for the Co-op supermarket chain. It comes from Freeminer Brewery in the Forest of Dean, Gloucestershire. In 2007, Freeminer introduced another Fairtrade beer for the Co-op. It goes by the name of Organic Premium Ale, and, along with other organic ingredients, including malt from Warminster Maltings in Wiltshire, features Fairtrade demerara sugar, sourced from producers in Malawi. This adds a lightness and a sweetness to the beer, which is rare considering how hoppy and bitter Freeminer's other ales tend to be. That's not to say that this beer is shy of hops. German Hallertauer Tradition is the variety used and it adds a pleasant fruity balance to the sugar.

The beer pours a clear golden colour and offers an aroma that is both spicy and hoppy. There's good malt balance but also pleasant background fruit – faint melon, apricot and zesty orange – which slowly becomes more obvious. Despite the sugar, the taste is actually not too sweet. It's also nicely fruity, with more oranges and apricots, and just the faintest suggestion of pineapple. Sappy hop resins add another dimension and run on into the dry finish, gradually overpowering fruity sweetness. What's more, there's a delightful moreish quality to the aftertaste, which makes you want to reach for another bottle – and, of course, make another worthy contribution to the Fairtrade cause.

Births Harold Wilson (Prime Minister), 1916; Douglas Adams (writer), 1952; Alex Kingston (actress), 1963

Deaths Alexander Fleming (scientist), 1955; John Wyndham (writer), 1969; Erle Stanley Gardner (writer), 1970

Events Mikhail Gorbachev becomes Soviet premier, 1985; the £1 note ceases to be legal tender in the UK, 1988

Golden Ale

Buntingford Britannia

Source Buntingford Brewery Co. Ltd, Royston, Hertfordshire **Strength** 4.4%
Website buntingford-brewery.co.uk

Everyone knows the rousing refrain *Rule Britannia*, but many a pub quiz team has been stumped when asked who composed it. Today provides the answer.

12 March was the birthday in 1710 of one Thomas Augustine Arne. In keeping with his rather grandiose name, Arne grew up in a somewhat privileged position in London. His father had made money in the upholstering business, enough to send his son to Eton where he furthered his musical interests among other academia. His dad wasn't initially keen that Thomas made music his livelihood, and tried to channel him into law, but the Muse will out, they say, and Arne went on to compose a number of operas and shorter works, including *The Masque of Alfred*. This particular piece, based on the life of Alfred the Great, featured *Rule Britannia* as part of its score. The work was first performed in 1740 at Cliveden, the palatial Buckinghamshire country house that was later the scene of John Profumo's first encounter with Christine Keeler, but at the time belonged to Frederick, Prince of Wales, whose patronage Arne enjoyed. *Rule Britannia* was easily the pick of the tunes on offer that night and went on to be staged in its own right at other locations, most notably, of course, in recent decades during the Last Night of the Proms, when union flags are waved with a vigour that will deter any alien invader. As Arne sternly lectures foreign tyrants in his lyrics, Britons never will be slaves.

Waving the flag

Also cloaked in the gaudy stripes and crosses of the national flag is a beer called Britannia from the Buntingford brewery, based near Royston, Hertfordshire. The *Good Beer Guide* has described Britannia succinctly as 'a light brown bitter', which may be accurate but definitely underplays its merits. The beer is brewed from a mix of five different malts and a generous helping of Bramling Cross hops. The Bramling Cross is known as one of Britain's fruitiest hops and it certainly lives up to that reputation in this beer. Juicy red apple notes lead the way, quickly countered by a resin-like hoppy edge, which leads into a dry, hoppy finish. It's all shored up by 4.4% alcohol and a full malty body to guarantee happy drinking, as judges in the Society of Brewers' regional beer competition agreed, when they hung a bronze medal around its neck in 2007.

Thomas Arne's later works included setting Shakespeare to music but, although these were well received during his lifetime, nothing – for posterity – was to reach the giddy heights of his super-patriotic anthem.

Births Vaslav Nijinsky (ballet dancer), 1890; Jack Kerouac (writer), 1922; James Taylor (singer-songwriter), 1948

Deaths Cesare Borgia (soldier and cleric), 1507; Charlie Parker (jazz musician), 1955; Yehudi Menuhin (violinist), 1999

Events Paul McCartney marries Linda Eastman, 1969; UK miners' strike begins, 1984; the Church of England ordains its first female priest, 1994

Best Bitter

ABOVE: SINGING AND FLAG WAVING AT THE LAST NIGHT OF THE PROMS

Van Eecke Poperings Hommelbier

Source Van Eecke, Poperinge-Watou   **Strength** 7.5%   **Website** brouwerijvaneecke.tk

If you've only ever considered the hop as being useful for adding bitterness to a beer, think again. Hops give a lot more to beer than that, in terms of a rainbow of flavours – from herbal, tangy and grassy to floral, peppery and fruity – as well as acting as an important preservative, keeping beer fresh. But the humble hop is rather a magical plant. Medical researchers keep finding new ways in which its properties can help in the fight against certain diseases and ailments, and now gourmets are discovering the concept of hop shoots as part of a fine dining experience.

Chef Rick Stein has eaten them on his TV series, and Booths supermarket chain has rushed them fresh from Kent into their chiller cabinets, but the appreciation of hop shoots has been around longer than there have been middle-class viewers and shoppers to seek out these expensive little luxuries. The Romans, apparently, savoured their tender, asparagus-like texture, and the Belgians, probably the most underrated gastronomes in Europe, have known what to do with them in the kitchen for centuries.

Hopping around

As a celebration of the culinary delights of the hop plant, there's even an annual Hop-Shoot Festival staged around this time in March every year. This is the season for these delicacies: by the time we get to May, they've become too tough and bitter. The festival takes place at Poperinge, close to the French border, at the heart of the Belgian hop gardens. Guided visits to hop farms are included in the fun, along with a visit to the local hop museum and a gastronomic lunch held in the well-known Hommelhof beer restaurant at Watou, with opportunities to sample hop-shoot cuisine.

The simplest way to serve hop shoots is simply by steaming or boiling them and sprinkling them with lemon or butter, but, in Belgium, they make more of an effort, perhaps whipping up a creamy onion sauce to raise them to new levels of flavour. This is no cookery book, so I'll leave you to devise appropriate methods of preparing your own dishes, but, if you're looking for the ideal beer to marry with them, surely it must come from the same part of the world where they enjoy the fruit of the bine in so many ways.

Produced by the Van Eecke brewery, which has been based in Watou since 1862, Poperings Hommelbier (literally 'hop beer') is the essence of the Belgian hop fields distilled into a glass. It's strong and full bodied but, because of the skilful balance of three different hops, it is by no means a daunting drink. Grassy, fruity hops take control and dominate the palate, handsomely offsetting the sweetness of the malt and bringing a sappy, apricot and orange fruitiness to the tongue. The hops linger on through the dry, tangy finish. Understandably, there are quite a few glasses of this splendid ale supped during hop-shoot weekend – another reason for making the trip.

Births Joseph Priestley (scientist), 1733; Percival Lowell (astronomer), 1855; Neil Sedaka (singer-songwriter), 1939

Deaths Benjamin Harrison (US President), 1901; Frank Worrell (cricketer), 1967; Jimmy Johnstone (footballer), 2006

Events The planet Uranus discovered by William Herschel, 1781; the discovery of planet Pluto by Clyde Tombaugh announced, 1930

Strong Ale

Hepworth Iron Horse

Source Hepworth & Co., Horsham, West Sussex **Strength** 4.8% **Website** hepworthbrewery.co.uk

Television in the 1960s. Who can forget the endless Saturday morning repeats of *Casey Jones*, that rousing, all-action adventure series set on an American railroad line? But how many of us knew that the programme was based on a real person? On screen, as personified by the cheerful Alan Hale Jr, Casey Jones is the man behind the throttle of the famous *Cannonball Express*. Supported by his fireman, Wallie Simms, and conductor, Red Rock, Casey never lets his passengers down, even as disaster after disaster befalls his pioneering railroad. The films may have been made in black-and-white but they were vividly colourful to us kids.

Yes, Casey Jones really did exist, but this fact has become somewhat forgotten over time, thanks to a rather mournful ballad that was composed in his honour and which has turned him into something of a folklore legend. The song relates how Casey was tragically killed in the line of duty in 1900, bringing to an end an eventful life that began on this day in 1863.

Fateful day

John Luther Jones was born in Missouri but later moved to the town of Cayce in Kentucky (hence his nickname). A lifelong obsession with the railroad led eventually to a job in the business and to his recognition as one of the leading engineers of his day. He was handed the *Cannonball* route, which ran from Chicago to New Orleans, in 1900.

On one fateful day, Jones was heading rapidly north to regain lost time when the *Cannonball* collided with a freight car that was jutting onto the line from a siding. With the collision imminent, Jones told his fireman to jump to safety but remained on the train himself, to try to slow the vehicle. Although he managed to save the lives of all the passengers, Casey himself was killed in the accident.

In those days, when the heroic Jones was 'steaming and a-rolling' – to quote the memorable TV theme song – the railroad system in America was still in its infancy. As the new engines powered their way across the West, they gained the nickname of Iron Horse. The name Iron Horse was also adopted by Cornish engineer Richard Trevithick for one of his engines – indeed the world's first railway engine when it went into service in 1804. It is depicted – from an artist's impression – on the label of Iron Horse from Hepworth & Co. in Horsham. This is a fine British strong amber bitter of 4.8% ABV, with plenty of Admiral hops for bitterness and Goldings added late for aroma. It tastes rich and hoppy, with a lightly chocolaty and nutty malt background. Just the job, I would imagine, after a hot dusty day on the footplate.

Births Albert Einstein (physicist), 1879; Michael Caine (actor), 1933; Jasper Carrott (comedian), 1945

Deaths Karl Marx (philosopher), 1883; George Eastman (photography pioneer), 1932; Busby Berkeley (choreographer), 1976

Events Eli Whitney patents the cotton gin, 1794; first performance of Gilbert and Sullivan's *The Mikado*, 1885

Strong Ale

Van Honsebrouck Bacchus

Source Van Honesbrouck, Ingelmunster **Strength** 4.5% **Website** vanhonsebrouck.be

'**B**eware the Ides of March!'. When Shakespeare's Soothsayer utters this warning to the soon-to-be-dispatched Julius Caesar, it is only a matter of time before the dagger strikes and Caesar falls, pointing a knowing finger at his murderers. Thanks, therefore, to the great bard, the unluckiest day in March is now well known to the world.

In the time of Caesar, the Romans were comfortably off for public festivals. Each year saw dozens celebrated, including the Ides of each month, a special day dedicated to the supreme god, Jupiter. On most occasions, the Ides fell on the 13th day, but for March and three other months, it was noted on the 15th. Although one Roman met his grisly end on this fateful day, others were ready to party, as the Ides of March became the prelude to the beginning of a gluttonous, boozy festival dedicated to Bacchus, the god of wine.

By the time of Caesar's assassination in 44 BC, the original raucous festivals – known as Bacchanalia – had been cleaned up somewhat. These clandestine orgies started out as Sodom and Gomorrah-type spectacles, grotesque, no-holds-barred sessions of perversity and indulgence. They were finally outlawed in 186 BC, leaving in place a markedly toned-down event known as the Liberalia, which kicked off each year on 16 March.

Beer with a wine taste

We can hardly let such a celebration of good drink go unnoticed, hence today's selection, a fascinating Belgian ale called Bacchus. It comes from the Van Honesbrouck brewery, based at Ingelmunster, near Kortrijk (see 28 October), and the label, somewhat fittingly, declares it to be a beer 'met wijnsmaak' – with a wine taste. If you're familiar with the oak-aged, highly acetic, red ale called Rodenbach, then Bacchus will not take you by surprise. From the first sniff, you realize that there is something wild and intriguing about this beer. It is tart, acidic and musty, with subtle cherry notes. In the mouth, the beer demands your full attention, switching between vinous fruit, soft malt and dry acidity, with a tart, lambic-like funkiness thrown in for good measure.

Bacchus is a thinner beer than Rodenbach, and not quite as electric on the tongue, but it's certainly refreshing, coming over as a cross between the Rodenbach style of aged red ales and the wild-yeast-inspired lambic culture. You wouldn't want to party on it all night, but it would certainly sharpen the palate if you felt a little jaded at one point.

Births Andrew Jackson (US President), 1767; Lightnin' Hopkins (blues musician), 1912; Frank Dobson (politician), 1940

Deaths Aristotle Onassis (shipping magnate), 1975; Benjamin Spock (paediatrician), 1998; Thora Hird (actress), 2003

Events Selfridge's department store opens in Oxford Street, London, 1909; the Liberal Party gains a famous victory in the Orpington parliamentary by-election, 1962

Sour Red Ale

Cox & Holbrook Goodcock's Winner

Source Cox & Holbrook, Buxhall, Suffolk **Strength** 5% **Website** None

Picture the scene. It's a tense day at the end of the long 1933–4 football season. All eyes are on the Billingham North End versus Stockton United match. Billingham need to win to secure the championship but it's all square. Then up steps Archie Goodcock to hammer home the winner. He's an instant hero.

Sadly, Archie never existed. His on-the-pitch heroics are just as fictitious as those of the legendary Roy of the Rovers. Archie is just a character created by Suffolk brewer David Cox to give a name and a story to Goodcock's Winner, his russet-coloured strong ale featuring Fuggle hops. The beer has a deliciously fruity, sweetish taste and a dry, bittersweet finish. It's a beer I selected as the winner of an East Anglian bottled beer competition several years ago, and it's frustrating not to find it in bottle so often these days. Still, it is available in cask form and is well worth seeking out to mark this notable day in footballing history.

Real-life heroics

It was on 16 March 1872, that the first FA Cup final took place, bringing with it more than 130 years of fantastic real-life stories worthy of *Boys' Own* comic. Feats of giant-killing by lower-league sides such as Sunderland over Leeds in 1973; human interest such as Manchester City goalkeeper Bert Trautmann completing the 1956 final with a broken neck; last-gasp winners and equalizers such as Alan Sunderland's for Arsenal against Manchester United in 1979. The antics of Archie Goodcock and Billingham North End would have been perfectly at home on this stage.

The very first FA Cup final had more than its share of quirks. Held at the Kennington Oval, now one of England's cricket test match arenas, the match was won by the Wanderers, a team mostly comprised of public school old boys, who defeated the Royal Engineers 1–0. Only 12 teams took part in the competition, and the Wanderers' own Archie Goodcock, Morton Peto Betts – who also played first-class cricket for Kent and Middlesex and who bizarrely played in the final under the pseudonym of AH Chequer because he had already registered for another team – tucked away the only goal. The next season, Wanderers, being the holders, were given a bye to the final – the only team ever to defend the 'Challenge Cup' as its full name reads – where they defeated Oxford University.

Such warm-hearted tales clearly belong to a world that has more in common with Goodcock's Winner than today's hyped-up world of extravagantly paid players, multi-million-pound sponsorships and intense supporter rivalries. Which do we prefer?

Births Jerry Lewis (comedian), 1926; Bernardo Bertolucci (film director), 1940; Jimmy Nail (actor), 1954

Deaths Tiberius (Roman Emperor), 37; Judge Roy Bean (Texan lawman), 1903

Events Harold Wilson resigns as Prime Minister, 1976; oil tanker *Amoco Cadiz* runs aground off Brittany, 1978

Strong Ale

Hilden Molly Malone Single X

Source Hilden Brewing Co., Lisburn, Co. Antrim **Strength** 4.6% **Website** hildenbrewery.co.uk

It's 17 March and hordes of youths are wandering the streets of the capital. St Patrick's Day celebrations are well underway and the bars are packed to the gills with revellers. It's not an unusual scenario, you might think, for Ireland. Except that this is not Dublin. This is Prague.

That's the thing about St Patrick's Day: it's become an international event, a global excuse for a party. Fake Irish bars all over the world push the boat out for this celebratory occasion, serving up pint after pint of creamy keg Guinness. One wonders what the man whose life started it off would think of it all.

St Patrick wasn't even Irish, not by birth at any rate. He was born in the fifth century somewhere in Britain (some say Cumbria, others say Wales or Scotland) and was captured while a teenager and sent into slavery in Ireland. He later escaped and fled back home, finding his vocation in the Church. He then returned to the Emerald Isle to practise Christianity and was largely responsible, it is said, for converting the locals to the faith. The exact dates of when he was born and died have been lost somewhere over the Irish Sea (although there is a good chance that he died on 17 March). Also uncertain is the truth about whether he really did expel all the snakes from Ireland. Theologians suggest that this is a metaphor: the snakes were the pagan beliefs he drove away.

Real character

I doubt whether any of the drunken revellers I bumped into in Prague knew anything at all about St Patrick, or even if any of them were Irish, which somewhat undervalues the occasion, I think. To restore a bit of class and dignity to St Patrick's Day, I would forgo a pint of ubiquitous Guinness and choose a beer brewed in Ireland that still has real character. The Hilden Brewery in Lisburn, County Antrim, has been in operation since 1981, for many of those years flying the flag alone on the island for cask-conditioned ale. Among its selection of beers is Molly Malone Single X, sold in both cask and bottle-conditioned form, so there's none of the nitrogen gas dispense, which sweetens beer, robs it of character and makes it flabby. This is real ale, fresh and flavoursome, with a gentle natural effervescence. Molly Malone pours a ruby-red colour and has a dry, vinous taste of gentle roasted malt. It's an unadulterated pleasure on what has become an increasingly adulterated day.

Births Gottlieb Daimler (motor car pioneer), 1834; Nat 'King' Cole (singer), 1919; Rudolph Nureyev (ballet dancer), 1938

Deaths Marcus Aurelius (Roman emperor), 180; Luchino Visconti (film director), 1976; Rod Hull (comedian), 1999

Events First rubber bands patented, 1845; Golda Meir becomes Prime Minister of Israel, 1969

Porter

ABOVE: ST PATRICK'S DAY CELEBRATIONS, NEW YORK STYLE

Woodforde's Norfolk Nog

Source Woodforde's Norfolk Ales, Woodbastwick, Norfolk **Strength** 4.6% **Website** woodfordes.co.uk

A turbulent and record-breaking political career came to an end on this day in 1745, with the death of the man who has become known as Britain's first Prime Minister.

Robert Walpole was born in Houghton, Norfolk, in 1676. He came from a large family but was very well educated, studying at both Eton and Cambridge. He entered politics when he inherited a country estate, which gave him the independent wealth with which to pursue his ambitions. As Whig member for Castle Rising, Norfolk, Walpole quickly made a name for himself at Westminster, soon climbing to Cabinet position. His career hit a rocky patch when he was imprisoned in the Tower of London for six months, for taking an illegal payment, but on his release, and the Whigs' return to power, Walpole swiftly rose to the top, becoming First Lord of the Treasury and Chancellor of the Exchequer. It was a position he regained some years later, filling it out into the role that we now know as Prime Minister (initially, the title Prime Minister was simply a term of abuse, and it was only formally recognized as the official title for the leader of the Government in 1905). Walpole remained at the top until he resigned in 1741, nearly 21 years later, which makes him not only the first PM but also the longest serving.

Brewing pastime

It's hard to believe that Walpole would have had much time for interests outside politics, but apparently brewing beer was one. Dark beers would have been all the rage during his time in power so, bearing in mind his origins, Woodforde's Norfolk Nog would seem a nice little beer to remember him by. Woodforde's produces a fine range of cask- and bottle-conditioned ales, with Norfolk Nog slotting in sort of halfway along the strength spectrum at 4.6%. It is a strong mild or old ale crafted from pale, crystal and chocolate malts, and laced with Golding and Styrian Golding hops. What all this provides is a fine, orange-fruity, malty, sweetish ale with hints of plain chocolate, good enough to be voted CAMRA's Champion Beer of Britain in 1992.

As for the name 'Nog', apparently this was a term applied in East Anglia to a stock ale, a beer that would have been set aside to age for months after brewing. I'd suggest drinking Norfolk Nog sooner rather than later for freshness, and today is as good a day as any.

Births Neville Chamberlain (Prime Minister), 1869; Alex 'Hurricane' Higgins (snooker player), 1949; Courtney Pine (jazz musician), 1964

Deaths Laurence Stern (writer), 1768; Percy Thrower (TV gardener), 1988

Events Tolpuddle Martyrs sentenced to transportation to Australia, for forming a trade union, 1834; Alexei Leonov becomes first man to walk in space, 1965; oil tanker *Torrey Canyon* runs aground off Cornwall, 1967

Old Ale

Adnams Explorer

Source Adnams plc, Southwold, Suffolk **Strength** 5.5% **Website** adnams.co.uk

The 19th century was the great age of exploration. Although most corners of the world had been reached in earlier centuries, it wasn't until the 1800s that in-depth reports came back to the Western world of mysterious continents, most notably Africa. One of the most fascinating figures of the age was the explorer David Livingstone, who was born on this day in 1813, in Blantyre, South Lanarkshire, Scotland.

Coming from a poor family, Livingstone worked initially in a cotton mill from the age of ten, taking his education by night. He later studied in Glasgow and then became a minister, hoping to travel and use the medical and religious knowledge he had acquired as a student. He made his first visit to Africa in 1840. In the 1850s, he delved deeper into the interior of the Dark Continent, becoming the first European to see the Mosi-o-Tunya cascade, which he re-dubbed Victoria Falls for his monarch back home. In seeking to open up routes for commerce and Christianity, which together, he believed, would bring civilization, Livingstone travelled throughout Central Africa, but a later expedition to chart the progress of the Zambezi river proved disastrous, with his wife, Mary, dying from malaria en route.

Missing in action

Livingstone returned to Africa to seek the source of the Nile, but this time became ill himself. All contact with the outside world was lost for some six years and it wasn't until

an American journalist named Henry Morton Stanley was dispatched to find him as a publicity stunt that Livingstone was tracked down. The two men met at Ujiji, on Lake Tanganyika, in 1871, when Stanley is said to have uttered the famous words: 'Dr Livingstone, I presume.' They travelled together for a time, but after a while Livingstone continued alone. He died in 1873, and his body was eventually returned for burial at Westminster Abbey.

Such was the lot of the brave, sometimes arrogant, occasionally foolhardy explorers of that age. Their ideas were big and their plans were ambitious. What they brought back to Britain was often exciting and valuable, and they deserve to be remembered. For Livingstone's birthday, therefore, I would draw your attention to Adnams Explorer, a strong golden ale introduced in

2005. Produced using American hops (Chinook and Columbus), there's an appropriate touch of the New World about it, and it makes a most refreshing beer on summer days, with its zesty grapefruit flavours and fine, hoppy finish. That said, it carries enough clout (5.5% ABV) to add a little warmth in March, too.

Births Wyatt Earp (lawman), 1848; Tommy Cooper (comedian), 1921; Glenn Close (actress), 1947; Bruce Willis (actor), 1955

Deaths Arthur Balfour (Prime Minister), 1930; Edgar Rice Burroughs (writer), 1950; Paul Kossoff (rock musician), 1976

Events Sydney Harbour Bridge opens, 1932; Academy Awards ceremony first televised, 1953; Argentinians land on South Georgia, the first act in the Falklands War, 1982

Golden Ale

ABOVE: DAVID LIVINGSTONE ARRIVING AT LAKE NGAMI, BOTSWANA

Durham St Cuthbert

Source The Durham Brewery, Bowburn, Co. Durham **Strength** 6.5% **Website** durham-brewery.co.uk

Today is the feast day of the patron saint of Northumbria. St Cuthbert was born around the year 634, in what these days would be termed the Scottish Borders. He is said to have given his life to God after seeing St Aidan, Bishop of Lindisfarne, being transported to Heaven in a blaze of light. Thereafter, Cuthbert travelled the region and further afield, preaching and helping the disadvantaged. He was himself appointed Bishop of Lindisfarne but much preferred a hermit's existence, and many of his years were spent in solitude on the Farne Islands, which is where he died on 20 March 687. After his death, the monks that he had inspired fled with his body and finally settled in what is now the city of Durham. It is said they were led there by a vision.

Medieval mysticism

St Cuthbert's remains still lie in the awesome, dimly lit cathedral in Durham, and his name is celebrated in a top-quality beer from a local brewery. Durham Brewery was founded in 1994 by former music teachers Steve and Christine Gibbs, who left education when it looked likely that funding cuts could make them redundant. Their brewery now produces a wide range of excellent beers, some named after Durham and its religious connections. The names are evocative of medieval mysticism: Cloister, Silver Chalice, Benedictus, Magus and Black Abbot are just some to conjure with. The beer called St Cuthbert was the brewery's first ever

bottled beer, setting a trend that was to culminate in another of Durham's beers, Evensong, which won CAMRA's Champion Bottled Beer of Britain title in 2005.

St Cuthbert was originally named Millennium City, highlighting the fact that Durham was celebrating its 1,000th year as a city at the turn of the millennium. However, with the millennium festivities out of the way, Steve renamed this special ale in honour of the local saint. The beer is an IPA in style, light amber in colour and with a full aroma of orange and toffeeish malt, thanks to a recipe that includes crystal and wheat malts, and no fewer than five different strains of hop. Challenger, Target, Columbus, Golding and Saaz combine with the malt to produce a bittersweet, citrus taste, with pear drop notes pointing to the considerable strength (6.5%), before a soft, bitter finish.

Durham also produces a cask-conditioned beer called Cuthbert's Cross, which is named after a cross kept in Durham Cathedral. The same cross features on all Durham Brewery's labels.

Births Henrik Ibsen (writer), 1828; Vera Lynn (singer), 1917; Spike Lee (film director), 1957

Deaths King Henry IV, 1413; Sir Isaac Newton (scientist), 1727; Lev Yashin (footballer), 1990

Events Harriet Beecher Stowe's anti-slavery novel, *Uncle Tom's Cabin*, published, 1852; football World Cup stolen in London, 1966; John Lennon marries Yoko Ono, 1969

IPA

Paulaner Salvator

Source Paulaner, Munich **Strength** 7.5% **Website** paulaner.de

If you're tempted to visit the Oktoberfest (see 12 October) but are daunted by the crowds and lack of hotel space, then maybe March in Munich is a better option. Beginning on St Joseph's Day, 19 March, the city marks the end of winter with a strong beer season, known as the Starkbierzeit. Just be warned that the beer widely consumed at this time of year kicks off at about 7.5% ABV!

The origins of the Starkbierzeit lie with the monks who founded what is today Paulaner Brewery. Followers of St Francis of Paula (see 2 April) set up base in Munich in the 17th century and brewed beer largely for their own consumption. When Napoleon took over all the monasteries and sold them into private ownership, the beer became more widely available, including a strong beer that the monks had specifically fashioned for sustenance during Lent, when solid food was prohibited.

The beer was known by a number of religious names but eventually settled down under the title of Salvator, or saviour. When this strong lager went on sale to the public, it proved extremely popular, and other breweries clamoured to make their own versions. The brewery finally took out a trademark on the name Salvator in 1896, but rival brewers continued to pay homage to the original by giving their beers names that also ended in the suffix 'ator'. These included Ayinger (Celebrator), Spaten (Optimator), Löwenbräu (Triumphator) and Augustiner (Maximator).

Meal in a glass

The style created by Salvator has become known as doppelbock. Bock is a strong lager in Bavaria and so the 'double' version, while never actually twice the strength, is more potent again. Salvator pours a welcoming russet colour and brings a cleanness to the palate that only a long lagering period can achieve. It is steeped in sweet, raisin-fruity malt and hop flavours with a light toffee undercurrent. As the monks who brewed it first knew only too well, it is a meal in a glass, somewhat belying its 7.5% alcohol.

On 19 March each year, celebrities and politicians gather for the ceremonial opening of Starkbierzeit in Paulaner's bier keller on top of Munich's highest hill. A cask of Salvator is tapped amid great festivity, and the locals, foaming jugs in hand, toast the fact that the hard Bavarian winter is hopefully behind them and the green buds of spring are on their way. Don't worry if you can't make it to Munich on that very day. The event runs for a couple of weeks afterwards and other local breweries continue the celebrations in their own pubs, with their own 'ator' beers. You don't even have to be in Munich to join in the fun. A glass of Salvator will take the chill off a March day anywhere in the world.

Births Johann Sebastian Bach (composer), 1685; Michael Heseltine (politician); 1933; Brian Clough (footballer and manager), 1935

Deaths Robert Southey (poet), 1843; Leo Fender (guitar manufacturer), 1991; Ernie Wise (comedian), 1999

Events Alcatraz prison in San Francisco Bay closes, 1963; Martin Luther King leads more than 3,000 civil rights campaigners on a successful march from Selma to Montgomery, Alabama, 1965

Bock

ABOVE: SATIRICAL COMEDY DURING MUNICH'S STARKBIERZEIT

Köstritzer Schwarzbier

Source Köstritzer Brewery, Bad Köstritz　**Strength** 4.8%　**Website** koestritzer.de

While Italy has Dante, and Britain has Shakespeare, for the Germans the great literary figurehead is Johann Wolfgang von Goethe. Goethe was born in Frankfurt in 1749 and initially trained to be a lawyer. It was while practising law that he began to write – poetry, novels and dramas – his most famous work being *Faust*, the story of a scholar who makes a pact with the Devil. But Goethe was more than just an inspirational writer: he was also active and successful in other fields. He was a state official in the little principality of Weimar and he even dabbled in science, questioning some of Newton's work and proving inspirational to Charles Darwin through his study of anatomy.

Goethe's last years were spent in Weimar, which today is part of the German state of Thuringia. It became famous as the place where the new German constitution was signed after World War I; the Weimar Republic, as that time in German history became known, lasted until the rise of Hitler in 1933. From the end of World War II until the collapse of the Berlin Wall, the town was part of the German Democratic Republic and it is probably to the Communist regime that one of Germany's great beers owes its survival.

Communist control

The Köstritzer brewery in the town of Bad Köstritz, near Weimar, was founded in the 1500s, with a new brewhouse built in the early 20th century. The business was nationalized during the Communist years, which proved to be a mixed blessing. While there was no great investment in the brewery, there was little attempt to rationalize beers either, so the brewery's Schwarzbier ('black beer') remained in production, despite being in much less demand than pale lagers. With the end of state control, the brewery was bought by the Simon family, owners of West Germany's Bitburger brewery, in 1991. Seeing potential in Schwarzbier, they invested in the plant and modified the beer's recipe. They made it stronger, too, taking it from 3.5% to 4.8% – strong enough to compete in the wider world.

The beer is visually stunning – as black as the ace of spades. Being well lagered, it has a crisp bitterness to offset the mellow coffee and bitter chocolate flavours that come from the dark malts in the grist. Sales have nearly doubled in ten years, and the beer is now available in the UK through Adnams.

Because of the recipe changes, the beer is clearly not quite the same as would have been available during Goethe's time, but the great man was apparently a fan of this type of beer. It is said that he drank rather a lot of Schwarzbier during his final years, which came to an end on this day in 1832.

Births Chico Marx (comedian), 1887; Marcel Marceau (mime artist), 1923; Andrew Lloyd Webber (composer), 1948

Deaths Thomas Hughes (writer), 1896; William Hanna (animator), 2001; Terry Lloyd (journalist), 2003

Events Football League formed, 1888; Arab League founded, 1945; the Beatles' first album, *Please Please Me*, released, 1963

Dark Lager

Humpty Dumpty Railway Sleeper

Source Humpty Dumpty Brewery, Reedham, Norfolk **Strength** 5% **Website** humptydumpty.typepad.com

There have been few people (criminals and tyrants excepted) who have been more vilified in recent decades than Richard Beeching. Dr Beeching, as he became known, was the man who famously advocated sweeping cuts to Britain's rail network, but since his death on this day in 1985, attempts have been made to put his work into proper context and to restore his tarnished reputation.

Beeching was born in Kent in 1913 and gained a First Class degree in Physics from Imperial College, London. Much of his working life was devoted to high-profile jobs with chemical giant ICI, but it was when he was asked to join a panel looking into the state of the UK's railways in 1960 that he stepped into the public eye. Beeching was asked for his input because of his reputation as a great analyst. He could absorb data quickly and draw swift and clear conclusions. A year later, he was appointed chairman of the British Transport Commission and was charged with drawing up a plan for the future of the rail network. Faced with a system that was haemorrhaging money, Beeching advocated a radical overhaul, closing underused branch lines and reducing staffing costs. His plans were welcomed by both Conservative and Labour governments, at a time when road building was seen as the way forward. When they were implemented, 2,128 stations closed and nearly 70,000 jobs were lost. With his plans largely accepted, Beeching returned to ICI.

End of the line

Beeching's supporters claim that he actually saved the rail network rather than ruined it, by making the tough decisions necessary to keep it afloat. They point to significant improvements in certain sectors, especially freight handling. Nevertheless, as the nostalgic TV sitcom *Oh Doctor Beeching!* revealed in the 1990s, it was indeed the end of the line for the heyday of British railways.

Of course, railways never die for some people. The number of preserved steam engine lines run by volunteers is impressive and evocative, and there is a very firm crossover between enthusiasts of steam and real ale. Tapping into this is the Humpty Dumpty Brewery in Reedham, Norfolk, where classes of old locomotive and other railway connections are remembered in the names of its beers (Humpty Dumpty itself is a type of forgotten steam engine). In the collection is Railway Sleeper, a 5% red-amber ale with a light lemony note from the First Gold hops, the single variety used in the beer. It is available in both cask- and bottle-conditioned forms and is perhaps a fitting drink today for those who dream that the age of the train will one day return.

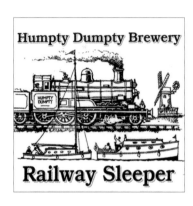

Births Joan Crawford (actress), 1904; Roger Bannister (athlete), 1929; Damon Albarn (rock musician), 1968

Deaths Stendhal (writer), 1842; Peter Lorre (actor), 1964; Ben Hollioake (cricketer), 2002

Events Pakistan becomes an independent Muslim republic, 1956; US President Reagan announces plans for the 'Star Wars' space defence system, 1983; Conservative government launches the Citizens' Charter, 1991

Strong Ale

Erdinger Weissbier

Source Erdinger Weissbrau, Erding   **Strength** 5.3%   **Website** erdinger.com

Forget David Blaine, Derren Brown and all today's illusionists, there is one man whose reputation is second to none in the history of magic and escapology and that is Harry Houdini. Houdini was born in Budapest on this day in 1874, although his family emigrated to the US while he was only a toddler. The young Houdini developed an interest in magic, and turned this into a profession as a teenager, working in music halls, a funfair and a circus. Escapology entered his repertoire, his well-practised acrobatic skills coming into their own as he began to slip free of handcuffs, chains and other bondage. As he attracted more and more attention, publicity stunts made sure his name was on everyone's lips, and supreme showmanship ensured that audiences were always stunned by his feats. Strangely, it was beer that nearly brought about his downfall.

Struggles with beer

One of Harry's most popular stunts was his immersion in an oversized milk churn filled with water. Normally, he would free himself quickly and then wait behind a curtain for several minutes to make the audience anxious. When touring Britain, however, Houdini allowed the container to be filled with beer rather than water. He began to struggle and needed to be rescued by an assistant. Not being used to alcohol, it seems that the teetotal Houdini was overcome by the vapours from the beer. This, coupled with the lively carbonation that reduced the oxygen in the container, disorientated him and he nearly drowned. It was a rare failure. Although Houdini never readily used beer again in his act, he relented in 1915, when issued with a challenge by Standard Brewing of Scranton, Pennsylvania. They suggested that Houdini be sealed inside a barrel of the company's Tru-Age, a beer that was matured for nine months. Houdini accepted, and this time proved successful.

So what beer could be recommended to reward the thrills and excitement this genius brought to the world? Standard Brewing and Tru-Age no longer exist, so we have to look elsewhere. As Houdini never drank beer, there are none of his favourites to recall either. It's a bit cheeky, but I've opted for Erdinger Weissbier (5.3%), one of the most easily accessible German wheat beers, in terms of both availability and taste. It comes from a dedicated wheat beer brewery in a small town just east of Munich and has a refreshing, subdued fruitiness, with pear, banana and lemon floating around the palate, supported by lightly warming spices. It's a great beer to enjoy on any day but in a way fits here once you are aware of Houdini's real name. He grew up as Ehrich Weiss, so a weissbier it has to be!

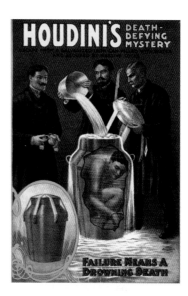

Births John Harrison (clockmaker), 1693; Clyde Barrow (criminal), 1909; Steve McQueen (actor), 1930

Deaths Queen Elizabeth I, 1603; John Harrison (clockmaker), 1776; Henry Wadsworth Longfellow (poet), 1882

Events 80 Allied servicemen tunnel out of Stalag Luft III prison camp, 1944; oil tanker *Exxon Valdez* runs aground off Alaska, 1989

ABOVE: POSTER ADVERTISING ONE OF HOUDINI'S MOST POPULAR STUNTS

Wheat Beer

Three Floyds Robert the Bruce

Source Three Floyds Brewing Co., Munster, Indiana **Strength** 6.5% **Website** threefloyds.com

One of the iconic figures of Scottish history – Robert the Bruce – takes centre stage today. It is the anniversary of the day that he became King Robert I of Scotland.

The story most people know about Robert is the one of his hiding in a cave while on the run from his enemies, only to be enlightened by the sight of a spider patiently and relentlessly building a web in the most difficult of circumstances. Perseverance was the message, and Robert took it to heart by emerging from his hideout and defiantly reclaiming the throne of Scotland.

The tale is apocryphal, and it may not even have been Robert but a colleague who witnessed the spider 'try and try again'. Nevertheless, Bruce used the lesson well in his long-running battle against his English and Scottish enemies.

Coronation & comeback

Robert was born in 1274, a member of the powerful Bruce clan, a family that had contested the right to rule Scotland for decades with their arch-rivals, the Comyns.

However, it was only after murdering his contemporary, John Comyn, at the Church of the Grey Friars in Dumfries in 1306 that Robert really pushed on with his claim to the throne, much against the wishes of the ruling English under King Edward I. His efforts were rewarded with a coronation at Scone but Robert still faced battle at every turn, with both the Comyns and King Edward on his tail. After his army was routed in summer 1306, Bruce fled to an island off the coast of Northern Ireland where he lived for a while in a cave. From there – spider-inspired – he returned to the battlefield to eventually subdue the English at the Battle of Bannockburn in 1314. It wasn't a conclusive victory, however, and cross-border hostilities continued for another 14 years, until a treaty was finally agreed that recognized Scotland's sovereignty over its own affairs. Bruce died just over a year later, in 1329.

Surprisingly, there is not a Scottish beer (at the time of writing) that directly honours this local hero, but there is an ale from the US that does just that. Three Floyds Brewing was founded in 1996 and is based in Munster, Indiana. It has won numerous awards for the quality of its beers, with Robert the Bruce (6.5%) rightly collecting a sizeable share. It's a red beer with a typically malty character (for what is described as a 'Scottish style ale'), but also a burst of orange-citrus to counter the lightly roasted cereal and mildly savoury edge. With a satisfying, dry and bitter, roasted-malt finish, it's a flavour-packed, quite excellent beer with which to toast the life of the man who secured the independence of the Scottish nation.

Births David Lean (film director), 1908; Aretha Franklin (soul singer), 1942; Elton John (rock musician), 1947

Deaths Claude Debussy (composer), 1918; Billy Cotton (bandleader), 1969; Kenneth Wolstenholme (football commentator), 2002

Events The European Economic Community created through the signing of the Treaty of Rome, 1957; Cambridge sinks in the University Boat Race, 1978

Scottish Ale

Lovibonds Henley Amber

Source Lovibonds Brewery Ltd, Henley-on-Thames, Oxfordshire **Strength** 3.4% **Website** lovibonds.com

Unless you're a keen rower or part of the social circuit that flits between 'must do' events like Royal Ascot and Wimbledon in the early summer, it's best to avoid Henley-on-Thames in early July. At that time, the attractive Oxfordshire river town is a nightmare to negotiate, unless you're heading for the world-famous Royal Regatta. It wasn't always like this, however. The very first Henley Regatta took place in June, 1839, having been conceived at a public meeting in Henley Town Hall on 26 March that year. The first event only lasted one afternoon. It was also a much more open affair, with amusements of all kinds laid on for townsfolk. Today's five-day event has a rather more exclusive air, sadly, but it certainly lives up to its reputation as a magnet for the world's best rowers.

Brewing heritage lost

While Henley still trades handsomely on its rowing heritage, its other great cultural asset, the Brakspear Brewery, was thrown into a redevelopment skip in 2002. The rather ramshackle old brewery buildings that once provided one of the beer world's greatest creations, Brakspear Bitter, have given way to luxury apartments and a hotel that is no doubt greatly appreciated by the Pimm's brigade who tend to dominate the Regatta. The irony of the hotel's name will probably be lost on most of them, but not on the ale lover: it's part of the Hotel du Vin chain.

Thankfully, Brakspear Bitter has been revived elsewhere (see 6 January), and equally thankfully

Henley is once again home to a brewery. Lovibonds was set up by Jeff Rosenmeier in 2005. The name relates to a brewery that operated in the town between 1916 and 1959, and also to a method of grading the colour of malt, which was developed by a member of the Lovibond family.

Beers for the new Lovibonds were initially produced elsewhere under contract but the business planned to start production in the town, pending planning permission. Most beers are filtered but some cask-conditioned ale has been produced for beer festivals, and Lovibonds has attempted to fill the gap in local drinking by introducing its own, highly quaffable 'ordinary' bitter at the Brakspear Bitter strength of 3.4%. Henley Amber, as it's suitably titled, is also sold in bottle and pours a dark copper colour. There are three hop varieties in the beer but the predominant flavours are malt and chocolate on the nose and pronounced nuttiness in the taste and the dry finish. As such it doesn't taste anything like Brakspear Bitter, but it certainly does the job of bringing local colour back to a town that became a few shades greyer on the day that Brakspear's brewed its last beer.

Births Tennessee Williams (playwright), 1911; Diana Ross (singer), 1944; William Hague (politician), 1961

Deaths Ludwig van Beethoven (composer), 1827; David Lloyd-George (politician), 1945; Noel Coward (actor and writer), 1973; James Callaghan (politician), 2005

Events Israel and Egypt reach peace deal at Camp David, 1979; SDP launched by 'Gang of Four' UK politicians, 1981; Vladimir Putin elected President of Russia, 2000

Pale Ale

Verhaeghe Duchesse de Bourgogne

Source Brouwerij Verhaeghe, Vichte **Strength** 6.2% **Website** proximedia.com/web/breweryverhaeghe.html

Whenever the subject of Flemish red ales is raised, one beer dominates the conversation. Rodenbach is without doubt the best known of this peculiar style of soured beer and is such an outstanding product that it deserves its pre-eminence. But this book, with its emphasis on events and real lives, gives us the opportunity to shine a light on one of Rodenbach's lesser-known rivals, a beer called Duchesse de Bourgogne from the Verhaeghe brewery in a West Flanders town named Vichte, near Kortrijk.

It is the enigmatic portrait of the said duchess on the label that draws us to this beer. Who was she? Why is she thus honoured? We only ask such questions because we are ignorant foreigners. In Belgium, her history is far better known. The lady of the label is, in fact, Mary of Burgundy, the daughter of Charles the Bold, Duke of Burgundy, and heiress to his lands in France and the Low Countries. On his death in 1477, Mary was pressured into marrying the Dauphin of France, so that the Burgundy lands in the Low Countries would be absorbed into French rule. But she resisted. To strengthen her position in the Netherlands, Mary returned to her citizens the civil rights abolished by her ancestors, in a gesture known as the Great Privilege. This bought her time and she finally snubbed the French well and truly by opting to marry Archduke Maximilian of Austria (later Emperor Maximilian I). That resulted in the region being ruled by the Hapsburgs and, as such, proved to be an event of the greatest significance in the history of continental Europe, stoking the intense rivalry between the Austrians and the French. Mary died on this day in 1482, after a fall from her horse while indulging in her hobby of falconry. The falcon can be seen with her on the bottle label, while her tomb can be viewed in the Church of Our Lady in Brugge.

Sweet & sour

The beer that bears her image is brewed with a mix of roasted malts and wheat, and lightly seasoned with hops that bring very little bitterness to the beer. Their role is largely as a preservative. After two fermentations, the beer is then racked into oak casks, where it sits for around 18 months, picking up fruity, sour qualities from the wood and the micro-organisms within it. When it is deemed ready, the beer is blended with a younger beer, only eight months old.

Presumably the beer is also sweetened, as there's a full, sugary note upfront that can be a little off-putting but never fully obscures the delightfully tart, acetic notes of the base beer. There's a good malt presence, too, bringing a bright red colour, with balsamic notes and dried fruit also in the mix. Duchesse finishes off sweet and sugary but drying all the time and laced with a soft acetic tartness.

It's one of those beers that makes a wonderful, palate-sharpening appetizer to a long evening in a Belgian bar.

Births James Callaghan (Prime Minster), 1912; Michael Jackson (beer writer), 1942; Quentin Tarantino (film maker), 1963

Deaths King James I, 1625; Yuri Gagarin (cosmonaut), 1968; Ian Dury (rock musician), 2000

Events Marconi transmits the first radio signal across the English Channel, 1899; the Beeching Report on the future of Britain's rail network published, 1963

Sour Red Ale

Rogue Kells Irish Lager

Source Rogue Brewery, Newport, Oregon **Strength** 5% **Website** rogue.com

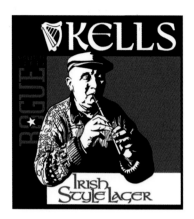

Today, 28 March, was the birthday of one of America's great beer pioneers. Frederick Pabst was born in 1836 in Saxony, Germany, and emigrated to Chicago in 1848. He found his first vocation as a steamship captain on Lake Michigan, through which he met and married the daughter of the owner of a brewery in Milwaukee. Frederick became a partner in the firm, and eventually sole owner, when the business name was changed to Pabst Brewing Company.

Under Pabst, the brewery grew dramatically, with its most famous beer, Blue Ribbon, added to the range in the 1880s. Pabst died in 1904. His name lives on, but probably not as he would have envisaged. From being the biggest brewing company in the US, Pabst now owns no breweries, and its beers are contract brewed by Miller.

Today, strangely, was also the birthday in 1899 of August 'Gussie' Anheuser Busch, grandson of Adolphus Busch, co-founder of the Budweiser giant Anheuser-Busch. During Gussie's time in charge of the business, A-B became the biggest brewer in the world. As a sideline, he also rode to the rescue of the St Louis Cardinals baseball team, leading them to new heights. Busch died in 1989 but his legacy for beer lovers was not as benign as it was for his baseball buddies. He left a beer market heavily dominated by massive breweries like his own.

American lagers

I suppose the appropriate beer for a double commemoration like today's would have to be an American light lager, perhaps even Pabst Blue Ribbon or the 'King of Beers' itself. Sadly, neither is likely to light fires for readers of this book, so thoughts turn to other popular American lagers. Both Samuel Adams Boston Lager and Brooklyn Lager are featured on other pages, which leaves room here for Kells Irish Lager, brewed by Rogue Ales in Oregon. The tall (unpasteurized) Rogue bottles have occasionally found their way across the Atlantic, and it is to be hoped that they do so again very soon, for the brewery produces some of the tastiest beer in the US. Even Kells Irish Lager, which, frankly, doesn't sound as if it's going to be anything special, is highly enjoyable.

The beer was first brewed for a small chain of Irish pubs on the West Coast of America but has gone on to experience wider circulation and win numerous awards. The malts are pale, crystal and wheat, along with acidulated malts – malts treated with lactic acid – that are added to produce a sharp, green-apple note in the finished beer. The hops are Sterling, the beer is fermented with a Czech pilsner yeast and there is a long period of cold conditioning in true lager tradition.

Kells pours a rich golden colour, with a clean aroma of malt and herbal hops. The taste is bittersweet and herbal, with lime-like notes, which may be my interpretation of the green-apple sharpness the brewers are aiming for. It's ultra-smooth on the palate and rounds off with a drying hoppy-herbal finish. Loyal fans of Pabst and Bud may disagree, but to my mind this is what American lager for everyday quaffing should taste like.

Births Michael Parkinson (journalist and broadcaster), 1935; Neil Kinnock (politician), 1942; Nasser Hussain (cricketer), 1968

Deaths Virginia Woolf (writer), 1941; Dwight D Eisenhower (US President), 1969; Peter Ustinov (actor), 2004

Events The Crimean War begins, when Britain and France declare war on Russia, 1854; a nuclear power plant at Three Mile Island, Pennsylvania, suffers a major radiation leak, 1979

Premium Lager

Fuller's Discovery

Source Fuller, Smith & Turner, Chiswick, London **Strength** 3.9% **Website** fullers.co.uk

With heroism, tragedy sadly very often goes hand in hand. It was certainly the case with Robert Falcon Scott and his team of Antarctic explorers.

Scott was born near Plymouth in 1868 and took the Navy as his profession in 1881. He made his first trip to the Antarctic in 1901, joining the ship *Discovery* which spent two years navigating the frozen southern wastes. Scott was promoted to captain on his return. The lure of the South Pole proved too strong to keep Scott employed in other naval activities, however, and in 1910 he set sail again, on this occasion in the ship *Terra Nova*. The aim was to reach the South Pole itself, and the expedition set out from its icy southern camp in November 1911. Five members of the original party were selected to make the journey all the way. Alongside Scott were Captain Lawrence Oates, Lt. Henry Bowers, Dr Edward Wilson and Petty Officer Edgar Evans. The quintet battled through and made it to their destination on 17 January 1912, but only to find that the Norwegian explorer Roald Amundsen and his crew had beaten them to it by a month.

The return journey was never going to be easy – now it was a crestfallen party that fought the elements to return to their ship. They never made it. The last entry in Scott's diary was made on 29 March, and their bodies were retrieved by a search party eight months later, just 18km (11 miles) from the safety of one of their supply depots.

Inspiration in defeat

One of Scott's diary pages predicted the tragic outcome, reading: 'Had we lived I should have had a tale to tell of the hardihood, endurance and courage of my companions which would have stirred the heart of every Englishman.' On that account, at least, Scott needed to have few fears. The commitment and effort of Scott and his men have inspired countless others to take on the elements in the search of adventure. To reach the South Pole in those days, without modern equipment and technology, was a remarkable achievement and deserves to be commemorated.

There is one beer that has a Scott connection. In 2005, Fuller's introduced a beer that bears the same name as Scott's first vessel. Discovery (3.9%) is an easy-drinking blond ale. There is some malted wheat alongside the pale malt in the mash tun, to add a little crispness to the beer, and Saaz pilsner hops are joined in the copper by the more citrus character of Liberty hops, for a zesty sharpness. If golden Discovery, which is designed to be served at a lower temperature, encourages lager drinkers to be a little more adventurous and cross the great beer divide, it will certainly live up to its name.

Births William Walton (composer), 1902; Eric Idle (comedian and actor), 1943; John Major (Prime Minster), 1943

Deaths J Arthur Rank (film executive), 1972; Carl Orff (composer), 1982

Events Queen Victoria opens the Royal Albert Hall, 1871; London Marathon first run, 1981; Republic of Ireland bans smoking in all workplaces, 2004

Golden Ale

Young's Special

Source Wells & Young's Brewing Company, Bedford **Strength** 4.5% **Website** wellsandyoungs.co.uk

When Royalty pays a ceremonial visit to a pub, you don't expect it to nip behind the bar and start pulling a pint. But that's what happened when Queen Elizabeth, the Queen Mother, attended a function at The Queen's Head pub in Stepney in 1987. It was a memorable moment in the history of Young's, which owned the pub, and they recorded it in a famous photograph that found its way onto the walls of other pubs in the brewery's estate. The lady also set a precedent for her family. Both the Prince of Wales and the Earl of Wessex were called upon to pull a pint themselves on subsequent visits to Young's hostelries.

Elizabeth Bowes-Lyon was born in London in 1900, the ninth of ten children of Claude George Bowes-Lyon, Lord Glamis, and his wife, Lady Cecilia Nina Cavendish-Bentinck. Despite such a background, she was considered a commoner, which made it unusual for her to be accepted as the wife of a possible heir to the throne. That man was Prince Albert, who, with Elizabeth as his consort, became King George VI on the abdication of his brother, King Edward VIII, in 1936. On his own death in 1952, he was succeeded by their daughter, Elizabeth, with his wife taking on the title and position of Queen Mother.

National celebration

It was a role Elizabeth (senior) played to perfection, judging from the fondness with which she was regarded by the British people. They admired her common touch and remembered her support for ordinary people during the war. Her 100th birthday was a cause for national celebration, and when she died, peacefully in her sleep on this day in 2002, the nation mourned.

In light of her relationship with the people of Britain, it is appropriate that the beer she has become associated with is called Special. It has long been one of the jewels in Young's own crown. A few years ago, the recipe was tweaked to give it broader appeal, a move that didn't go down well with die-hard Young's drinkers, although their fury then was as nothing compared to the uproar when Young's closed its Wandsworth site in 2006 and transferred all beer production to a joint venture with Charles Wells in Bedford, called Wells & Young's. Special is still one of the great British bitters, however, with a fine balance between malt and hops, and a dry, bitter aftertaste. The malts are Maris Otter pale and crystal, and the hops are Fuggle and Golding. In this respect it's about as traditional a British beer as you can find, and a good choice with which to remember a popular lady.

ABOVE: THE QUEEN MOTHER'S COFFIN

Births Paul Verlaine (poet), 1844; Vincent van Gogh (artist), 1853; Rolf Harris (entertainer), 1930; Eric Clapton (rock musician), 1945

Deaths Beau Brummell (dandy), 1840; James Cagney (actor), 1986; Alistair Cooke (journalist), 2004

Events Thomas Cranmer becomes Archbishop of Canterbury, 1533; America buys Alaska from Russia for $7.2 million, 1867; US President Ronald Reagan shot by a would-be assassin, 1981

Best Bitter

Oldershaw Alchemy

Source Oldershaw Brewery, Grantham, Lincolnshire **Strength** 5.3% **Website** oldershawbrewery.com

This day in history saw the passing of one of the greatest scientific minds the human race has ever created. When Sir Isaac Newton left this world on 31 March 1727, he bequeathed a whole new understanding of a wide range of scientific issues, making sense of matters previously misunderstood and laying down the basis for future understanding as his work was built on by other great thinkers.

Newton was born in Woolsthorpe, Lincolnshire, in 1643, a sickly child to a single mother. It was through her insistence that, after local schooling, he went to Cambridge as a poor scholar, paying his way by doing chores for the academics. Although Newton passed his degree with few problems, his work in mathematics showed little distinction at the time and it wasn't until he returned home and began experimenting with light – making serious advances in the construction of telescopes – that his brilliance began to shine forth. Newton also closely studied the heavens and worked out the mechanics of the planetary and star systems, while his work on gravity – allegedly inspired by a falling apple – has become his best-known legacy. In his later years, Newton – by this time renowned throughout Europe – lectured at Cambridge and was a Member of Parliament and Master of the Mint. He was knighted in 1705.

Golden tribute

Just a few miles away from Newton's birthplace is the town of Grantham, where his memory is celebrated by, among other things, a selection of beers from the local microbrewery. Gary and Diane Oldershaw founded Oldershaw Brewery in 1996, after Gary was made redundant from his job with BT. He'd been brewing at home since he was a teenager and was so convinced by the quality of his beers that he decided to invest his redundancy cheque in a brewery and make them available to the public. He now pays tribute to the local genius in beers named Isaac's Gold, Newton's Drop and the beer selected for today, Alchemy.

It is not so well known that Newton was also a dedicated alchemist, endeavouring to turn base metals into gold. He devoted many years to his fascination with this arcane science, writing numerous texts about his work and discoveries, but these have always been downplayed in favour of his more successful and spectacular scientific work. Oldershaw's Alchemy is a full-bodied and robust, strong blonde ale, with plenty of smooth malt crisped up by tangy, citrus hops. It displays its strength right through to the chunky, tangy, dry finish that has hints of bitter orange marmalade from the First Gold hops at the heart of the recipe. Alchemy is mostly sold in cask form, but occasionally it can be discovered bottle conditioned. Although Newton never managed to create gold, Oldershaw has come pretty close with this beer.

Births Andrew Marvell (poet), 1621; David Steel (politician), 1938; Al Gore (politician), 1948

Deaths John Constable (artist), 1837; Charlotte Brontë (writer), 1855; Jesse Owens (athlete), 1980

Events The Eiffel Tower officially opened, 1889; the Dalai Lama flees Tibet and occupying Chinese forces, 1959

Golden Ale

North Yorkshire Fools Gold

Source North Yorkshire Brewing Co., Guisborough, North Yorkshire **Strength** 4.6%
Website nybrewery.co.uk

According to Mark Twain, 1 April is 'the day upon which we are reminded of what we are on the other three hundred and sixty-four'. It's a typically pithy Twain take on what is a rather odd tradition.

Quite how the idea of playing tricks and jokes on people on this day came into being is a mystery, but it dates back centuries. Chaucer, for instance, in his *Nun's Priest's Tale*, sets the action 32 days after the beginning of March (i.e. 1 April) and involves a foolish fox and a rooster. This predates by two centuries a popular explanation of the custom placed in France in 1582, the year when the Julian calendar gave way to the Gregorian, and the date of New Year festivities was switched from 1 April to 1 January. Only fools, it was said, continued to celebrate the New Year on the old date.

The idea of presenting a huge hoax on 1 April has become so over-used that it's a wonder anyone still falls for it. *Panorama*'s 'spaghetti harvest' edition in 1957 is regularly pulled out of the archives to show how 'wacky' serious TV programmes can become. Beer, too, has fallen foul of the prankster. Apparently, in Singapore an advertisement was aired celebrating the arrival of a new beer called XO. They claimed it was so strong that it could only be consumed lying down and invited punters to a hotel to try it for themselves. Then there was the San Diego radio station KFMB-AM that broadcast news of a beer tanker that had jack-knifed. The only way it could be shifted was if the contents were removed, so volunteers were requested to drink the tanker dry. More than 100 thirsty people turned up.

All in jest

Keeping the spirit of foolery alive is North Yorkshire brewery. The business was founded in Middlesbrough in 1989 and moved to a new home in historic Pinchingthorpe Hall, near Guisborough, in 1998. Here the beer range was expanded to accommodate names and traditions from the Hall's noble past. One of the new ales was Fools Gold, harking back to the days when grand houses and aristocratic families would employ jesters, or fools, to provide entertainment. It's a shiny golden ale made, like all the brewery's products, only from organic ingredients. Pale malt and First Gold hops are the only constituents, apart from water and yeast, of course. As you might expect from the colour, delicate pale malty sweetness is well to the fore, balanced out by melony fruit and a bitterness that takes over, especially in the finish. Of course, if this doesn't appeal, you can always try that new Tibetan beer brewed from wild grass and seasoned with yak droppings and cheese.

Births William Harvey (physician), 1578; Lon Chaney (actor), 1883; David Gower (cricketer), 1957

Deaths Eleanor of Aquitaine (wife of Henry II), 1204; Scott Joplin (composer), 1917; Marvin Gaye (singer), 1984

Events Royal Air Force formed, 1918; Apple Computer Inc. founded, 1976; Iran becomes an Islamic republic, 1979

Golden Ale

Paulaner Original Münchner Hell

Source Paulaner, Munich   **Strength** 4.9%   **Website** paulaner.de

Evidence of the brewing traditions of religious orders is plentiful – in the form of the seven Trappist monasteries that still brew in Belgium and Holland for a start. It is also apparent in the existence of the Paulaner brewery in Munich, which, although a thoroughly commercial operation today, began life as the brewing arm of a local abbey.

The abbey was founded in 1627, in the Bavarian village of Au, by followers of St Francis of Paola, the saint whose life is celebrated on 2 April. Francis grew up in the town of Paola, in Calabria, Italy, and in his youth became a hermit, a close adherent to the principles of the earlier St Francis of Assisi. He soon attracted a large band of followers and laid down a particularly austere rule for them to abide by, based on humility, penance and charity, with vegetarianism thrown in for good measure. His brotherhood, later known as the Franciscan Order of Minim Friars, was officially sanctioned by the Pope. He died in France, on Good Friday 1519, and was canonized seven years later. As we've seen, his religious order continued to expand throughout the continent.

Monks' legacy

The Paulaner monks (as they became known) eventually left the abbey at Au in 1799, beaten by the tide of secularism sweeping across Europe, but the brewery was taken over by the Bavarian state, and then fell into private hands. It is now one of Munich's big breweries, with a strong presence at the Oktoberfest every year and a decent selection of beers. The pick of the bunch is Salvator, discussed in more detail on 21 March, but extremely popular is the beer labelled Original Münchner Hell.

Hell beer, rather than being a blasphemous contradiction of the origins of the brewery, simply translates as pale beer. It is the 'ordinary' everyday drinking beer of Munich, at its best a well-lagered, clean, refreshing golden beer with a fine balance of malt and hops. Paulaner's version of this style is clearly better drunk fresh in one of the city's beer gardens or pubs, but even in bottle it illustrates how enjoyable this kind of beer can be.

Spicy, herbal hop notes sing out in the aroma, which also has a touch of sweetcorn and some toasted grains in the mix. In the bittersweet taste, sharp lemony hops lead the way over a peppery graininess and delicate pale malt, and the beer rounds off dry, hoppy and firmly bitter. It's a lasting finish that means you don't rush to empty the glass, as there's plenty to savour.

If you were in a German tavern, you'd probably tear apart a big, soft, twisted pretzel, crunch the salt crystals on top and let this wonderfully balanced beer wash away the thirst generated by the pretzel. That would make a simple but appropriate little feast for this important saint's remembrance day.

Births Hans Christian Andersen (writer), 1805; Emile Zola (writer), 1840; Alec Guinness (actor), 1914; Marvin Gaye (soul musician), 1939

Deaths Samuel Morse (communications pioneer), 1872; Buddy Rich (jazz musician), 1987; Pope John Paul II, 2005

Events Red Rum wins his record-breaking third Grand National, 1977; Argentina invades the Falkland Islands, 1982

Pale Lager

Greene King Strong Suffolk

Source Greene King, Bury St Edmunds, Suffolk **Strength** 6% **Website** greeneking.co.uk

*B*righton Rock, *The Power and the Glory*, *The Heart of the Matter*, *The End of the Affair*, *Our Man in Havana*, *The Third Man* and *The Honorary Consul* – some of the best-known works of 20th-century literature, and all from the pen of Graham Greene, who died this day in 1991.

Greene was born in Berkhamsted, Hertfordshire, in 1904, and was educated at Oxford. He later became a Catholic, a conversion that was to shine through much of his writing. One of Graham's brothers was Hugh Carleton Greene, celebrated Director General of the BBC during its golden age in the 1960s.

Greene's connection with the beer world is also through his family – the Greene part of Greene King, so it is fitting to choose one of the company's beers for this occasion. While the brewery is currently flooding the market with its middle-of-the-road IPA, it also has a few gems in its portfolio that don't receive as much exposure as they should. The most intriguing is Strong Suffolk (Olde Suffolk for the US), a beer that offers both echoes of ancient porter making and the Flemish tradition of ageing beers in wood.

Classic blend

The beer is, in fact, a blend of two brews. The first is a strong old ale called Old 5X that is aged for a year or more in wooden casks at the Bury St Edmunds brewery. It packs around 12% alcohol, has the smooth taste of a dry sherry, with just a faint tartness and a touch of wood, and is never sold in its pure form. The second is a young beer of 5% ABV called simply BPA (Best Pale Ale), a malty brew whose only purpose is to combine with 5X to produce Strong Suffolk.

The concept of blending young and aged beers lies at the origins of porter, when London publicans used to fill mugs from three separate casks, one containing aged beer, one containing young pale beer and the third containing brown ale. The idea of maturing beer in wood is most popularly exhibited today by the Belgian brewer Rodenbach, whose sour, acidic ales are remarkably refreshing, if a little daunting for a novice. In Strong Suffolk, we have a combination of both practices, which results in a complex dark, fruity, malty, oaky ale with gentle sour notes. It's not often found in cask form, which is a great pity, and it would be fascinating if the beer were allowed to condition naturally in the bottle, but even in its pasteurized state it is still a beer to savour.

Births Marlon Brando (actor), 1924; Tony Benn (politician), 1925; Helmut Kohl (German Chancellor), 1930; Eddie Murphy (actor), 1961

Deaths Jesse James (outlaw), 1882; Johannes Brahms (composer), 1897; Kurt Weill (composer), 1950

Events Coronation of King Edward the Confessor, 1042; first successful Pony Express run, from Missouri to California, 1860; Grand National declared void after two false starts, 1993

Old Ale

Coastal Golden Hinde

Source Coastal Brewery, Redruth, Cornwall **Strength** 4.3% **Website** coastalbrewery.co.uk

One man's naval hero is sometimes no more than another man's pirate, and certainly that's the case with Sir Francis Drake. A favourite of Queen Elizabeth I, Drake clearly had maritime skills aplenty. Although he was born in Devon, he moved with his family to Kent at a young age and acquired his sailing credentials on the turbulent North Sea. By his early twenties, Drake had already sailed the Atlantic, bringing himself to the attention of the monarch, who then commissioned him to sail west yet again, to raid Spanish territories in the Americas. His journey of plunder and exploration eventually led to a circumnavigation of the globe, and he claimed the honour of being the first Englishman to do so, with only the Portuguese Magellan beating him to the feat. On 4 April 1581, the Queen came aboard Drake's flagship, the *Golden Hind*, and knighted her hero for his efforts. Drake was later to excel, of course, in the defeat of the Spanish Armada, and he carried on with his voyages until he was in his fifties, when he died of dysentery off Porto Bello in the Caribbean in 1596.

Cornish tribute

Drake's flagship for the round-the-world voyage was a vessel called the *Pelican* but he renamed it the *Golden Hind* just as he was entering the notoriously difficult Magellan Straits, in honour of his friend Christopher Hatton, whose emblem featured a hind, or deer. A replica of the ship has sat in the harbour at Brixham, Devon, since 1963, offering an insight into life at sea during those swashbuckling days. Further down the West Country is Coastal Brewery, based in Redruth. The brewer is Alan Hinde, a former Cheshire publican, who has mingled his own surname with that of Drake's ship to create a beer he calls Golden Hinde. Alan's beer is a suitably straw-coloured best bitter at 4.3%. He uses Challenger hops for bitterness and then two aroma hops, Brewers Gold and Styrian Goldings, which combine to produce a fragrant hop character throughout the beer. There's only pale malt in the mash tun, but a hint of dry, almost roasted maltiness joins the hops in the finish.

The brewery has been running only since the end of 2006 and its capacity is a mere five barrels, so it's unlikely that Coastal's beers will be circumnavigating the globe for a while yet, but it's a very promising start.

Births Linus Yale (lockmaker), 1821; Anthony Perkins (actor), 1932; David Blaine (illusionist), 1973

Deaths Oliver Goldsmith (writer), 1774; Karl Benz (car manufacturer), 1924; Kenny Everett (broadcaster), 1995

Events Robert Walpole effectively becomes first UK Prime Minister, 1721; Martin Luther King assassinated in Memphis, 1968

Golden Ale

ABOVE: *QUEEN ELIZABETH I KNIGHTING FRANCIS DRAKE* BY WS BAGDATOPULOS

Strangford Lough St Patrick's Ale

Source Strangford Lough Brewing Co. Ltd, Killyleagh, Co. Down   **Strength** 6%   **Website** slbc.ie

It's strange how, when mystery enshrouds so much of the past, somehow a precise date can sometimes be pinpointed. That's the case with the life of St Patrick. Earlier, on 17 March, I suggested that there was little known factually about Ireland's patron saint, and yet some sources can actually relate actions in his life to specific, individual days. So it is with 5 April, the date it is said that Patrick really began his missionary work in Ireland.

Patrick had already embraced the Church while living in Britain and Europe, and now he set out to evangelize the country where he had been held for six years as a slave. He landed in the north of the island around 433 AD (or it could be 456) and the given date of 5 April is believed to have been the day when Patrick fulfilled his first public baptism. It has henceforth been known as the day that the baptism of Ireland, as a whole, began.

Story on a bottle

Patrick's story is told on the labels of beers from the Strangford Lough Brewing Company. It's important to note that Strangford doesn't call itself a brewery – it's not. The company was founded by two bright men who decided there was a market to be tapped for quality beers with an Irish connection and who realized they could make this happen without running to the expense of building a brewery. The beers were initially produced under contract in Britain, but there have been plans to transfer production to a site closer to the company's headquarters in County Down, Northern Ireland. Whitewater Brewery would appear to be in the picture. In the US, the beers are brewed at St Stan's Brewery in California.

Strangford Lough's base is at Killyleagh, near Downpatrick, the place where St Patrick died, some reckon, in 461 – others claim 493. The company offers three beers bearing his name, all of which are bottle conditioned. The first is a session ale called St Patrick's Best (3.8%), and the second a wheat beer called St Patrick's Gold (4.8%). The third is St Patrick's Ale (6%), which is the one to pop open today. With crystal and black malts in the mash tun, along with pale malt, this is a copper-red beer laced with three types of hops: Golding, Progress and Challenger. Accordingly, there is some citrus fruit in the nose, but the taste has a firm liquorice note, plenty of malt and a dash of almond.

Call it an evangelical beer. After all, in this age it's quite possible that more people will learn about Ireland's patron saint from the back of this bottle than by going to church.

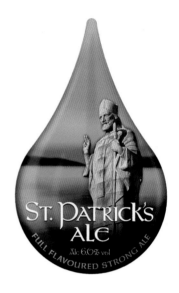

Births Joseph Lister (surgeon), 1827; Bette Davis (actress), 1908; Colin Powell (politician), 1937

Deaths Howard Hughes (millionaire aviator), 1976; Kurt Cobain (rock musician), 1994; Gene Pitney (singer), 2006

Events Native American Pocahontas marries English colonist John Rolfe, 1614; Winston Churchill resigns as Prime Minster, 1955; James Callaghan takes over as Prime Minister, 1976

Strong Ale

Belvoir Melton Red

Source The Belvoir Brewery, Old Dalby, Leicestershire **Strength** 4.3% **Website** belvoirbrewery.co.uk

On 6 April 1837, the Marquis of Waterford enjoyed a drunken day out at Croxton Park racecourse in Leicestershire. Not one to know when he'd taken a drop too much, the Marquis then led his coterie of sycophants back to the town of Melton Mowbray where he was staying for the night. Chaos ensued as the drunken toffs ran amok in the streets, fighting, singing and generally making a nuisance of themselves. The highlight of their evening was the acquisition of some red paint, which they proceeded to daub over the buildings of the town. When the night was over, a good time had been had by all – locals apart – and the Marquis and his louts had become the first people to 'paint the town red'.

So is this really the origin of that well-worn phrase? Well, the event, it seems, really did take place. The third Marquis of Waterford – Henry de la Poer Beresford, to give him his full name – lived between 1811 and 1859,

and was a notorious troublemaker, always seeking pleasure by bullying or breaking the law. When such a rabble-rouser gets together with a bunch of similarly minded hotheads, anything can happen, so it's entirely feasible that they did run riot in the streets of Melton. There's even evidence of this in a contemporary painting, which shows the men, in red hunting jackets, causing mayhem in the town. The epigraph that accompanies it, however, gives no mention to the phrase 'painting the town red', which some say dates back instead to Roman times, when gleeful legionnaires would celebrate a famous victory by daubing victims' blood over the walls of a newly vanquished town.

Truth, not porkies
Melton locals still cling to the fame, however, and when buildings were refurbished in the town in the 1980s, and ancient red paint was discovered beneath the surface plaster, it was

claimed as further evidence that this Leicestershire town had even more to offer the world than its already celebrated pork pies.

Using the tale to good effect is Belvoir Brewery, which was founded in 1995 by former Shipstone's and Theakston's brewer Colin Brown. The brewery is located in the village of Old Dalby, between Melton Mowbray and Loughborough, in the beautiful Vale of Belvoir (pronounced 'beaver'), and in autumn 2007 it moved into purpose-built new premises in the same location. Melton Red is one of its newer beers, introduced in 2002, but it already enjoys pride of place by having its artwork emblazoned over the back of the brewery's dray. The beer itself is amber in colour – the result of combining pale and crystal malts, plus a little torrefied wheat – and has a dry, malty, bitter flavour with a toffee note, a little orchard fruit and some herbal hop character, courtesy of a complex mix of five hops – Target, Bramling Cross, Progress, Golding and Styrian Golding. It's not available in cask form, only in bottle.

Births Raphael (artist), 1483; Ian Paisley (clergyman and politician), 1926; Paul Daniels (illusionist), 1938

Deaths Raphael (artist), 1520; Albrecht Dürer (artist), 1528; Isaac Asimov (writer), 1992

Events First modern Olympic Games begin, 1896; Anthony Eden becomes Prime Minister, 1955; Abba win Eurovision Song Contest at odds of 20/1, 1974

Best Bitter

Buntingford Highwayman IPA

Source Buntingford Brewery Co. Ltd, Royston, Hertfordshire **Strength** 3.6%
Website buntingford-brewery.co.uk

Forget thrilling tales of life on the road, of athletic masked men thundering through the night on a dark steed, plundering the wealth of hapless, deserving nobles and winning the hearts of fair maidens. The truth behind some of the most notorious highwaymen is more low-key and far grubbier. It's certainly the case with the most celebrated highwayman of all, Dick Turpin, who swung for his crimes on York's Knavesmire on this day in 1739.

Far from being a dashing anti-hero, Turpin was no more than a petty crook whose chief weapon was torture. He was born in Essex in 1705 and became a member of a local gang whose speciality lay in rustling, smuggling and attacking isolated farmhouses. For the stranded, terrified victims, such raids meant handing over the family riches or enduring the cruellest treatment at the hands of Turpin and his cronies. Later, Turpin took to attacking travellers, but ended his days in hiding in Yorkshire. Sadly for him, he couldn't stay out of trouble and, once his true identity had been revealed, he was sentenced to hang. Only at the end did Turpin apparently reveal any of the bravado with which his reputation has since been endowed, swaggering his way to the gallows and calmly chatting to his executioners before making the drop.

Roads to success

Coach House Brewery in Cheshire has a cask ale that bears Turpin's name, but the beer selected for today comes from the criminal's own territory. Buntingford Brewery, near Royston in Hertfordshire, stands close to the A1 and A10, major coaching routes that villains like Turpin saw as theirs to pillage. For the brewers, therefore, Highwayman seemed like too good a name to let slip, but it took them a couple of years to find the right beer to go with it. It was in spring 2007 that the two were put together, with the suffix IPA tagged on, not because it's a genuine IPA – at 3.6% it's certainly not that – but in order to hijack some sales that otherwise would go to Greene King's omnipresent IPA of the same strength.

The beer glimmers deeply golden in the glass and has a sherbety hop aroma, thanks to the inclusion of Progress and – somewhat appropriately – Bullion hops. With Bullion stocks now low, it may be that a different strain will be used in future. And this beer does have a future. It's crisp, clean and delightfully easy-drinking, with plenty of taste for its modest strength and an enjoyably dry, hoppy finish. As session beers go, this one certainly stands and delivers.

Births William Wordsworth (poet), 1770; Billie Holiday (blues singer), 1915; Sir David Frost (broadcaster), 1939; Francis Ford Coppola (film director), 1939

Deaths El Greco (artist), 1614; PT Barnum (circus pioneer), 1891; Jim Clark (racing driver), 1968

Events Eruption of Mount Vesuvius, 1906; inventor Clive Sinclair sells his computer business to Amstrad, 1986

Bitter

Jenlain Ambrée

Source Brasserie Duyck, Jenlain **Strength** 6.5% **Website** duyck.com

You'd never believe it if you were a regular reader of the British tabloids, but the UK and France are the best of friends. Yes, it's true. On this day in 1904 it was even set out in black and white.

The Entente Cordiale is a document that recognizes the close relationship between Britain and its nearest continental neighbour. Literally translated as 'friendly understanding', it sought to bring to an end the sporadic wars between the two parties that had plagued previous centuries and, in a colonial world, to ensure that both countries recognized each others' imperial and trading interests. The agreement was promoted by King Edward VII and was signed by British Foreign Secretary Lord Lansdowne and the French Ambassador Paul Cambon.

One hopes that the signatories sealed their day's business by sharing a beer afterwards – there is, after all, nothing that quite brings people together like a glass of good beer, but I doubt if that were the case. One beer that is certainly forging good relations between Britain and France is Jenlain Ambrée. This is probably the best known of all the bières de gardes produced in Northern France.

Farmhouse tradition

Bière de garde comes from a farmhouse tradition, from the days when farmers used to brew beer in the winter and store ('*garde*') it for drinking by their workers at warmer times of the year when brewing was too difficult. Generally, such beers are strong and malty, with an interesting spicy character from the yeast. That's definitely the case with Jenlain, which looks to the unsuspecting for all the world like a pint of British best bitter, in all its deep amber finery. It's top fermented just like best bitter, which ensures a complex fruity character typical of an ale, as opposed to bottom-fermented lager, and is matured for 40 days at the brewery. When you drink it, it is filtered but not pasteurized, and weighs in at a hearty 6.5% ABV.

Jenlain comes from a fourth-generation family brewery (Brasserie Duyck) based in the village of Jenlain near the Belgian border. It was first brewed in 1922 and was originally available only on draught, until the family started packaging it in old champagne bottles. There are other bières de garde that are now available in the UK – Ch'ti and Trois Monts are the most widely seen – but Jenlain has been knocking around for many years, sometimes appearing on supermarket shelves, sometimes not, and it's been joined of late by a blonde version and also a newer, equally golden beer called Jenlain Six. The Ambrée remains the star of the show, but they'd all do rather nicely if you want to raise a glass to prolonged cordiality with our good friends across the Channel.

Births Mary Pickford (actress), 1893; Jacques Brel (singer-songwriter), 1929; Kofi Annan (UN Secretary General), 1938

Deaths Caracalla (Roman emperor), 217; Vaslav Nijinsky (ballet dancer), 1950; Pablo Picasso (artist), 1973

Events Venus de Milo discovered on a Greek island, 1820; Clint Eastwood becomes Mayor of Carmel, California, 1986

Bière de Garde

ABOVE: COMMEMORATIVE ENTENTE CORDIALE POSTCARD

Butcombe Brunel IPA

Source Butcombe Brewery, Wrington, Bristol, Somerset **Strength** 5% **Website** butcombe.com

When the BBC ran a national poll to find the greatest ever Briton in 2002, the overall runner-up – second only to Winston Churchill – was Isambard Kingdom Brunel. Championed on screen by motoring presenter Jeremy Clarkson, Brunel saw off challenges to the number two spot from the likes of William Shakespeare, Isaac Newton and Horatio Nelson, with a little further down the list Robbie Williams, Boy George and David Beckham (although in the interests of credibility, the last three should perhaps be ignored on this occasion). While the persuasiveness of Clarkson's presentation will have helped sway the voting public, there is no doubt that Brunel and his remarkable achievements truly deserved such a high position in the voting.

Brunel was born in Portsmouth on 9 April 1806, the son of French engineer Marc Brunel. Learning his trade from his father, he went on to score numerous engineering successes and gain a reputation for his inventive genius and audacity. At the age of only 20, he was placed in charge of the project to build the tunnel under the Thames at Rotherhithe. From there Brunel went on to design the Clifton Suspension Bridge in Bristol – the longest single-span road bridge in the world. He also turned his hand to navigation, building steamships like the *Great Western* (the first steamship to go into regular use across the Atlantic), the *Great Briton* (the first iron-hulled passenger liner) and the *Great Eastern* (the biggest ship of its time by some distance). As engineer to the Great Western Railway, Brunel was responsible for installing the main line from London to the West Country – just another example of how his work was at the forefront of the civil engineering changes that helped Britain become the crucible of the Industrial Revolution. Throw in a selection of docks, tunnels and viaducts and you have the astonishing portfolio of a remarkable man. Brunel died in 1859, the same year that his railway bridge over the River Tamar at Saltash was opened, and which still carries rail traffic into Cornwall.

Celebrating 200
Four years after the BBC poll, Brunel hit the headlines again, when the 200th anniversary of his birth was

celebrated. True to form, brewers played a notable role in the festivities, with companies such as Archers, Cottage, Downton and Wickwar all creating special Brunel beers for the occasion. Some of these are still in circulation, as is a beer from Butcombe Brewery in Somerset. To play its part, Butcombe opted for a traditional India pale ale. They pitched it on the weaker side of what a 19th-century IPA would have been, at 5%, but certainly didn't stint on the powerful IPA flavours, especially hoppiness. Maris Otter pale malt is joined by some crystal malt in the mash tun, while in the copper the hops are purely Golding. The aroma is full of zesty, bitter oranges and floral peachy notes, while the taste is packed with bitter citrus fruits and earthy hop resins, with just a hint of nut in the background malt sweetness. Not surprisingly, the dry finish is also hoppy and bitter, with a dash of roasted malt. A rare photograph of the great man is featured on the dark green label.

Births Paul Robeson (singer), 1898; Seve Ballesteros (golfer), 1957; Robbie Fowler (footballer), 1975

Deaths Francis Bacon (philosopher and statesman), 1626; Dante Gabriel Rossetti (poet and artist), 1882; Frank Lloyd Wright (architect), 1959

Events The Conservative Party wins its fourth consecutive UK general election, 1992; Prince Charles marries Camilla Parker-Bowles, 2005

Negra Modelo

Source Grupo Modelo, Mexico City **Strength** 5.3% **Website** gmodelo.com.mx

On the face of it, it seems quite bizarre that a beer style originating in Europe can have all but died out in its home city yet still be alive and kicking half a world away. And all because of three tumultuous years in the middle of the 19th century.

The beer style in question is the Vienna, named after the Austrian capital where it was first developed by brewer Anton Dreher in the year 1841. These were the days before it was technically possible to create the subtle pale malts that produce golden pilsner, but advances had been made in malting, and Dreher was able to acquire a lightly kilned malt, which was far subtler than the smoky dark malts everyone else was using at the time. Thus his beer appeared red-brown in the glass and had an unusual, nutty, malty taste.

Puppet emperor

Visit Austria today and you struggle to find a glass of Vienna. But hop on a plane to Central America, and you'll see plenty gushing from the taps. It's all the fault of one man. His name was Maximilian and he was the second son of Archduke Franz Karl of Austria. In rather unfortunate circumstances, the Hapsburg prince was persuaded to accept the offer of the throne of Mexico by Napoleon III of France, whose troops occupied the country. Sadly, Maximilian hadn't bargained for Mexican displeasure at this colonialism and, only three years after he had been crowned Emperor, on this day in 1864, he was driven from power and executed, on the orders of his arch-rival, the rebel Benito Juárez. Austrian rule had come to a quick and sudden end when Napoleon deserted his puppet ruler, but the country's influence hung around a lot longer. It seems the locals had fallen for Central European music – the rhythms of the polka and the jaunty sway of the accordion – and they allowed it to slip into their national culture. They also took a shine to the beer that came over with the Austrians. That's why the pilsner became so prevalent down Mexico way, and also why the nutty, reddish-brown Vienna remained in circulation, long after the Viennese themselves had given it the boot.

Probably the best-known example of the Mexican Vienna is Dos Equis, which means two crosses, from the Moctezuma brewery, now part of InBev. However, a tastier example comes from Grupo Modelo and is called Negra Modelo. This was first brewed in 1926. The parent company also produces the Corona and Pacifico brands, so by association you'll be expecting subtlety rather than big flavours, and Negra Modelo, it has to be said, is not the most aggressive of dark beers. Nevertheless, it is crisp, clean and far more interesting than the average Mexican lager, with a creamy, nutty aroma, followed by a malty, nutty, lightly chocolaty, smooth taste, with a hoppy tang for balance. It's a good illustration of what the Vienna style is all about and is just perfect for washing down rice and refried beans, or some of the more exotic dishes on a cantina menu, such as chocolate mole.

Births Joseph Pulitzer (journalist), 1847; Omar Sharif (actor), 1932; Lesley Garrett (opera singer), 1955

Deaths Emiliano Zapata (revolutionary), 1919; Evelyn Waugh (writer), 1966; Peter Jones (actor), 2000

Events Paul McCartney quits the Beatles, 1970; the Good Friday Agreement for peace in Northern Ireland achieved, 1998

Vienna-style Lager

Cropton King Billy Bitter

Source Cropton Brewery, Pickering, North Yorkshire **Strength** 3.6% **Website** croptonbrewery.com

Outside the King William pub in Hull stands an impressive equestrian statue of the monarch of the same name, William III to be precise, who, from this day in 1689, shared the role of joint ruler with his wife, Mary. Inside the pub, they sell a beer called King Billy Bitter, a quaffable session ale with a dry, hoppy taste of bitter oranges, a beer that was created for the pub by Cropton Brewery in North Yorkshire. The landlord of the King William had asked Cropton for a beer that his regulars could 'drink all day and not become excitable'. King Billy was the result and now, in bottle-conditioned form as well as draught, it is one of the mainstays of the Cropton Brewery range.

Glorious Revolution

The coronation of William and Mary was similarly contrived, albeit on a much grander scale. English Protestants, unsettled by the reign of King James II, a Catholic, promulgated the idea of removing him from the throne, and replacing him with his own daughter, Mary,

who was married to William, Prince of Orange, a Protestant Dutch nobleman. William, himself a nephew of James, was not averse to becoming King of England. Indeed, he thought it wise to acquire it, if only to secure his wife's inheritance, which was under threat. But he played a canny game, ostensibly only calling for a free parliament and the restoration of liberties taken away by James.

With the support of senior English noblemen, the royal duo set sail for Britain, landing with a Dutch army at Brixham on 5 November, 1688. As they progressed through the country, support among influential Protestants grew and their installation as monarchs became unstoppable. The Glorious Revolution, as this has become known, saw King James at first trying to fight back, then negotiating and finally fleeing the country.

While only Mary was truly eligible to take the throne, she refused to rule without her husband being given equal status, and thus a period of joint monarchy began that was to last five years, and be extended by a further eight when William ruled alone after his wife's death.

The gilded statue of William in Hull was erected in 1734. Its significance lies in the fact that Hull was one of the first places in the country to declare for the Dutch invader after his forces had landed in Devon – echoing the city's earlier prompt support for Oliver Cromwell in his battle against King Charles I.

Births Bob Harris (broadcaster), 1946; Lisa Stansfield (singer), 1966; Ian Bell (cricketer), 1982

Deaths Llewelyn the Great (Welsh prince), 1240; Joseph Merrick (the 'Elephant Man'), 1890; Harry Secombe (comedian and singer), 2001

Events First pillar boxes (green) erected in London, 1855; Singapore wins self-rule from Britain, 1957; major riot in Brixton, 1981

Bitter

Young's Double Chocolate Stout

Source Wells & Young's Brewing Company, Bedford **Strength** 5.2% **Website** wellsandyoungs.co.uk

Easter is, literally, a movable feast. Because it is tied to the first full moon on or after the spring equinox, the religious festival can fall any time between 22 March and 25 April. 12 April would seem as good a date as any to note its presence in this book, especially as the brewing industry now widely celebrates Easter through its seasonal offerings.

Easter, of course, commemorates the crucifixion of Christ on Good Friday, and His resurrection on Easter Sunday. But, as earlier entries have confirmed, the road to Easter is a long one, with the 40 days of Lent following on from Mardi Gras, or Shrove Tuesday. The austerities of the Lent period come to an end on Holy Saturday – the day before Easter Sunday – when once again all foods are permitted. That may be one reason why festive treats such as simnel cake and hot cross buns have traditionally been welcomed at this time – although, such is the commercial world we live in today that the latter tend to be in the shops even before the mince pies of Christmas have left the shelves. Another increasingly early arrival is the Easter egg, a symbol of new life, tied in with the rebirth of Christ.

Tailor-made treat

So Easter has become the season of chocolate, which makes it rather easy to find a beer that slots into the occasion. While there are numerous beers in circulation drawing on other Easter traditions – Oakleaf Bunny's Delight and Wood's Hopping Mad,

for instance – there is one beer that seems tailor-made for the modern-day interpretation of the festival and that is Young's Double Chocolate Stout.

Take a look at the label before you even open the bottle. The regal purple wrapping and swirly writing are very reminiscent of the packaging of Cadbury's chocolate, so there's no excuse for not knowing what this beer's all about. Young's introduced Double Chocolate in 1997. It was revolutionary at the time in actually containing chocolate. There are a number of other chocolate-infused beers around now, including Samuel Adams Chocolate Bock, Rogue Chocolate Stout and Meantime's Chocolate, but Young's has proved the most successful, the winner of numerous industry awards.

The base beer is a nutty, chocolaty stout, created from pale, crystal and chocolate malts, some brewing sugars, and Fuggle and Golding hops, but dark chocolate and chocolate essence are added during the brewing process. The result is a sumptuously chocolaty beer, with a fudgy flavour, a hint of pear and a velvety texture, yet also the restraining character of a good stout to ensure it doesn't just appeal to chocoholics and deter lovers of beer. As the brewery itself declares, it's decadent but not too sweet.

Births Alan Ayckbourn (playwright), 1939; Bobby Moore (footballer), 1941; David Cassidy (actor and singer), 1950

Deaths Franklin D Roosevelt (US President), 1945; Joe Louis (boxer), 1981; Sugar Ray Robinson (boxer), 1989

Events The first space shuttle, *Columbia*, blasts into orbit, 1981; opening of Disneyland Paris, 1992

Stout

110

Tipples Moon Rocket

Source Tipples Brewery, Norwich   **Strength** 5%   **Website** tipplesbrewery.com

Triskaidekaphobiacs look out. This is not a day to take lightly, as the brave astronauts of *Apollo XIII* discovered to their cost. Anyone with a fear of the number 13 would have thought twice about joining this particular space mission, and quite rightly it seems.

The American moon landings had begun with *Apollo XI*, so *Apollo XIII* was planned to be the third mission to the lunar surface. Even though man had only walked on the moon for the first time less than a year before, such a journey was beginning to sound routine – that was until the third day of the mission, the 13th day of April, 1970.

As Ron Howard's absorbing film *Apollo 13* about the disaster reveals, when the spacecraft was 322,000km (200,000 miles) from Earth, an explosion rocked its oxygen tanks. From aiming to be lunar heroes, the men inside were immediately locked into a struggle for survival. With a team of NASA scientists working flat out at Mission Control in Houston to find ways of bringing the stricken vehicle back to Earth, the trio of Jim Lovell, John Swigert and Fred Haise, decamped to the tiny lunar landing craft attached to the command module. This they used effectively as a lifeboat. It allowed them to shut down power on the main craft that would be needed to see them back into Earth's atmosphere, if they managed to get that far. Defying icy temperatures and overcoming numerous crises that could have meant the end for all three, they did reach home safely, but 13 is not a number they take lightly any longer in NASA circles.

Brewer by name

There's a happier story behind the Moon Rocket chosen for today. It is brewed by Tipples Brewery, whose proprietor, Jason Tipple, has clearly fallen into the right line of work. That said, he took a while to realize the message in his name, working previously in the financial services and food industries before starting his little brewery in Acle, Norfolk, in autumn 2004. Moon Rocket is a beer with a 5% thrust. Brewed from Maris Otter pale malt and crystal malt, it pours an enticing orange-gold in the glass. The blend of Bramling Cross, Golding and Cascade hops sounds fruity on paper, and they don't disappoint in the beer, balancing the sweetness of the malt and adding sappy resin-like notes to the taste and finish. You could say it's a star performer.

Oh, one more thing, for the superstitious among us. I forgot to mention that *Apollo XIII* was actually launched at 13.13 hours, Houston time.

Births Guy Fawkes (conspirator), 1570; Richard Trevithick (engineer), 1771; Samuel Beckett (writer), 1906

Deaths Boris Godunov (Russian Tsar), 1605; Muriel Spark (writer), 2006

Events John Dryden becomes first Poet Laureate, 1668; Sidney Poitier becomes first black actor to win an Oscar, 1964; Neil Kinnock resigns as leader of the Labour Party, 1992

ABOVE: A STILL FROM THE FILM *APOLLO 13*, STARRING BILL PAXTON, KEVIN BACON AND TOM HANKS

Golden Ale

Titanic Stout

Source Titanic Brewery, Stoke-on-Trent, Staffordshire **Strength** 4.5% **Website** titanicbrewery.co.uk

With a certain degree of understatement, the 1958 film about the sinking of the *Titanic* was called *A Night to Remember*. That night began on 14 April, when the world's newest and most luxurious passenger liner struck an iceberg and began its painful descent into the North Atlantic. It took two hours and 40 minutes for the ship to disappear beneath the waves, taking with it the lives of around 1,500 passengers and crew.

Apart from being new and luxurious, the ship was also widely believed to be unsinkable. It had been constructed for the White Star line at the Harland and Wolff shipyard in Belfast, where engineers followed a new design that included watertight compartments and electronic watertight doors. It was ironic, to say the least, that the system proved ineffective on its first voyage.

The captain of the *Titanic* was Edward Smith, a Stoke-on-Trent man who was himself lost in the disaster and whose misfortune has been remembered by the local brewery. Titanic Brewery was set up in 1985 and produces some of the most sought-after beers in the Midlands. Several of the company's ales have won awards, most notably Titanic Stout, which was CAMRA's Champion Bottled Beer of Britain in 2004.

The beer is fashioned from pale malt, wheat malt and roasted barley, which gives an indication of the deep ruby colour and biscuity roasted grain flavours to follow. In a stout, the hops generally play second fiddle, usually just adding a little bitterness and balancing out the sweetness in the malt, and that is mostly the case here, with just a little fruitiness from the mix of Fuggle, Northdown and Golding hops to provide some contrast in the mouth. The finish is full of smoky coffee notes, with nuts and more roasted bitterness. In all, it is a very fine stout, with plenty of flavour for its 4.5% ABV.

The success of Stout, and a whole selection of *Titanic*-inspired ales such as Steerage, Lifeboat, Anchor, Iceberg, White Star and Captain Smith's, has seen the brewery grow and grow, with new premises required in 2002, and a major expansion in brewing capacity going ahead in 2005. It was perhaps tempting fate to name a business after such a calamitous real-life event, but it's good to see that the word Titanic is no longer just associated with a disaster story.

Births John Gielgud (actor), 1904; Rod Steiger (actor), 1925; Gerry Anderson (TV producer), 1929; Julie Christie (actress), 1941

Deaths George Frederick Handel (composer), 1759; Ernest Bevin (trade unionist), 1951; Anthony Newley (actor and singer), 1999

Events Webster's *American Dictionary of the English Language* first published, 1828; first UK *Highway Code* published, 1931; first edition of *The Eagle* comic, 1950

Stout

Farsons Cisk

Source Simonds Farsons Cisk plc, Mriehel **Strength** 4.2% **Website** farsons.com

The Victoria Cross is the highest award that can be bestowed by the UK for heroism among the military. Its civilian counterpart is the George Cross, created in 1940 to recognize the bravery of citizens during the war. The medal is normally only awarded to individuals but, on this day in 1942, the whole island of Malta was afforded the highly prestigious honour.

Malta has long been an important base for British forces in the Mediterranean. Lying just off Sicily, and close to North Africa, the island's harbours have conveniently sheltered many Royal Navy vessels over the centuries. However, World War II placed the island in greater peril than ever before. Hitler noted the strategic importance of the island for Allied troops and determined to 'neutralize' the country. From 1940 to 1942, Malta was subject to a vicious bombing campaign, with Messerschmitt fighters also raking the ground with machine gun fire in an attempt to weaken the resolve of the loyal Maltese people. Sheltering in caves carved out of the island's distinctive soft, yellow limestone, the Maltese remained defiant, despite a desperate shortage of food that caused severe malnutrition, and the Germans were denied. It was a feat that truly echoed the George Cross citation, 'for acts of the greatest heroism or of the most conspicuous courage in circumstances of extreme danger'.

Foreign influences

British influence in Malta over the years has extended to more than just military. English is the language of business on the island, and familiar high street names like Marks & Spencer have a foothold. Cars still drive on the left, and thousands of British tourists take their annual holiday in this little patch of Mediterranean sunshine. There's even British-style beer to quench their thirsts.

In 1880, Simonds Brewery of Reading began exporting its ales to Malta, and eventually became a partner with a local producer, Farrugia & Sons – or Farsons – in a brewery. Farsons remains the island's main brewer and still turns out popular British ales, but the company also has a continental connection. Shortly after its new brewery was constructed in the immediate post-war years, the business merged with another island brewer. Malta Export Brewery had been founded with the help of Munich's Augustiner brewery, so its focus was on quality lager. Farsons has kept this alive alongside its British-style ales.

There are two main lagers in the Farsons portfolio. Both are called Cisk, after the local word for 'cheque' – the founding family of the Malta Export Brewery were bankers. Cisk Export, at 5%, was introduced as a less bitter alternative for young Maltese drinkers who found the longer-established Cisk Lager, at 4.2%, to be too hoppy, but it is the latter that is recommended for today.

Cisk is a delicate beer, as indicated by its pale, almost watery, golden colour, but it's tasty, refreshing and by no means short of character. The aroma has grainy malt and grassy, herbal notes, with tart lemon emerging. In the mouth, it is crisp and fully hopped, with bitter, herbal flavours and a gentle, sweet lemon accent. In the very dry finish, the hops really kick in, bringing an increasing bitterness.

Farsons has been toying with the idea of producing its own special George Cross Ale to celebrate the remarkable wartime heroics. If that happens, it will, of course, drop nicely into our beery calendar for today. In the meantime, we can respectfully mark the bravery of the Maltese with a refreshing glass of Cisk.

Births Leonardo da Vinci (artist), 1452; Joe Davis (snooker player), 1901; Emma Thompson (actress), 1959

Deaths Abraham Lincoln (US President), 1865; Jean-Paul Sartre (philosopher and writer), 1980; Tommy Cooper (comedian), 1984; Kenneth Williams (actor and comedian), 1988

Events Dr Johnson publishes his *Dictionary of the English Language*, 1755; Hillsborough football stadium disaster, 1989

Pale Lager

Traquair Jacobite Ale

Source Traquair House Brewery, Innerleithen, Peeblesshire **Strength** 8% **Website** traquair.co.uk

The story of Traquair House, its brewery and its connections to the House of Stuart have already been covered in the entry for 25 January. 16 April now gives us the opportunity to explore a second beer from this country house brewery.

Jacobite Ale is a celebration of the Jacobite cause, the rebellion of the followers of the Stuarts in the 17th and 18th century, when they attempted to restore a member of the family to the British throne. Leader of the most famous uprising was Charles Edward Stuart, otherwise known as Bonnie Prince Charlie, grandson of the deposed King James II of England. James had been the last Catholic king, and had been replaced by his Protestant daughter, Mary, and her husband, William, in the so-called Glorious Revolution of 1688.

Bonnie Prince Charlie decided to retake the throne by force. From exile in Italy, he assembled an army and invaded England. His support came largely from the Highlands, where the clan system saw him guaranteed plenty of supporters. After a foray into England, the forces were made to turn back and, eventually, the adventure came to an end on this day in 1746, when the Jacobite Rebellion was snuffed out in a brief but bloody battle at Culloden, near Inverness. After just over an hour's fighting, around 1,200 men lay dead. Charlie's under-prepared forces were easily overrun by the well-stocked, technologically superior English forces, led by the Duke of Cumberland, son of King George II. The aftermath was just as brutal. Cumberland showed little magnanimity in victory, taking out his wrath on the innocent people of the Highlands, destroying the clan system and leaving the area a wasteland.

Romance lingers on

Bonnie Prince Charlie unceremoniously fled the scene, never to return, although the romance of Stuarts lingers still in places such as Traquair. The house had played host to Charles when he arrived in 1745, and its Bear Gates were locked shut after he left, never to open again until a Stuart once more sits on the throne. The Jacobite Ale they brew is sweet and malty in the Scottish tradition, but not heavy, in spite of its 8% strength, with a soft spiciness. It is brewed from an 18th-century recipe, laced with coriander, and makes a far better case for the Stuarts and their cause than any amount of pointless bloodshed.

Births Charlie Chaplin (actor), 1889; Spike Milligan (comedian), 1918; Peter Ustinov (actor), 1921; Dusty Springfield (singer), 1939

Deaths Marie Tussaud (waxworks pioneer), 1850; Arthur Chevrolet (racing driver and car maker), 1946; David Lean (film director), 1991

Events Harriet Quimby becomes first woman to fly the Atlantic, 1912; royal yacht *Britannia* launched, 1953

Spiced Ale

ABOVE: MODERN-DAY CLANSMAN RE-ENACT THEIR FOREFATHERS' LAST STAND

Hop Back Taiphoon

Source Hop Back Brewery, Sailsbury, Wiltshire **Strength** 4.2% **Website** hopback.co.uk

Although, officially, New Year in Thailand is celebrated on 1 January, as in most of the world, the country still hangs on to its traditional 'New Year' celebrations that take place in mid-April. The festival of Songkran, as it is known, has its origins in the solar calendar, marking the point when the sun moves into the zodiac sign Aries, and – on a more down-to-earth level – highlighting the start of a new farming cycle. In most places, celebrations begin on 13 April and last three days, but the festival can start later and run on until 18 April or beyond. It's a time when gifts are exchanged, city workers return to their homes in the country, and friends liberally douse each other in water, as a symbol of cleansing and purification. For this reason, Songkran is also known as the Water Festival, and strangers are also likely to get soaked – quite refreshing considering the local heat at this time of year. Food plays a major role in the whole shebang, with traditional Thai specialities such as spicy fish, curries and fragrant rice dishes served up in abundance.

Exotic ingredients

If you're thinking of joining our Thai friends in making an occasion out of the often-uneventful middle of April, perhaps by ordering a meal from your local Thai take-away, then you'll be hunting for a beer to wash it all down. You could try a native lager, such as Singha or Chang, but I would point you in the direction of a beer brewed in Britain specifically for such occasions. Look no further than Hop Back's Taiphoon, a crisp, golden, bottle-conditioned ale from Wiltshire, primed with coriander and lemongrass, two exotic ingredients that also figure prominently in the cuisine of old Siam. The aroma immediately reveals the oriental influence. It's delicately malty but also peppery and spicy, with a distinctly perfumed note. The same spiciness continues on the palate but with plenty of sweetness as a counterbalance and with satisfying bitterness in the scented finish. The flavours marry wonderfully with the spices in Thai cooking but even if you're not thinking of an oriental meal and just fancy something suitable for this time of the year, Taiphoon is enough of a drink to enjoy on its own. It's refreshing, too – not as refreshing as bucket of water over the head, that's true, but certainly in a quenching sort of way.

Births James Last (band leader), 1929; Nick Hornby (writer), 1957; Sean Bean (actor), 1959

Deaths Benjamin Franklin (politician and inventor), 1790; Eddie Cochran (rock 'n' roll singer), 1960; Linda McCartney (photographer), 1998

Events American-backed invaders attempt to overthrow Cuba's Fidel Castro at the Bay of Pigs, 1961; journalist John McCarthy kidnapped in Lebanon, 1986

ABOVE: THAI NEW YEAR CELEBRATIONS

Spiced Ale

Anchor Liberty Ale

Source Anchor Brewing Company, San Francisco, California **Strength** 5.9% **Website** anchorbrewing.com

In the struggle for American independence from Britain, the name of Paul Revere stands tall. Revere was a Boston silversmith, a patriot and a republican who took part in protests against British rule. He was one of the instigators of the Boston Tea Party, which, by throwing chests of tea from ships into Boston Harbour, made a stand against punitive taxation. He was also a major player in the battle to remove British forces that were sent to quieten dissent.

Probably his biggest contribution, however, came in the creation of an early warning network, which could be used to alert militias in towns across New England of any advances by British troops, and it is by being a part of the network himself that he owes his lasting fame.

On the night of 18 April 1775, Revere was given a signal that indicated that the British were on the march and heading to confront rebels in the towns of Lexington and Concord. Revere jumped on a horse and rode through the darkness to get the message to the local militias, giving them enough advantage to win the subsequent battles. Revere's later involvement in the War of Independence is chequered, thanks to a disastrous expedition to drive out British forces from Penobscot Bay in Maine. He was court-martialled for his actions there but exonerated. After pioneering work as an industrialist later in his life, Revere died in Boston in 1818, aged 83.

Poetic fame

In truth, Revere was but one of three riders sent out that fateful night, but his name is the one that everyone remembers, his heroic 'midnight ride' becoming part of American folklore and legend. It was immortalized in a poem by Henry Wadsworth Longfellow, and is celebrated in an outstanding beer from San Francisco's Anchor Brewery.

Liberty Ale was first brewed in 1975 to mark the 200th anniversary of Revere's bravery and quick thinking. Lush tropical and citrus fruits fill the aroma and taste, with grapefruit and lime to the fore over full, smooth malt, before a robust, bitter, dry and hoppy finish. This pale ale – a showcase for American Cascade hops – has long been recognized as one of America's greatest beers, belying its strength with immense drinkability. Predating the birth of the craft brewing movement in the States, it is very much one of the heroes of the American beer revolution.

Births Hayley Mills (actress), 1946; Malcolm Marshall (cricketer), 1958; David Tennant (actor), 1971

Deaths Albert Einstein (scientist), 1955; Thor Heyerdahl (explorer), 2002

Events League of Nations dissolved, 1946; Chancellor of the Exchequer Harold Macmillan introduces the premium bond, 1956

Pale Ale

Weihenstephaner Hefeweissbier

Source Bavarian State Brewery, Freising **Strength** 5.4% **Website** brauerei-weihenstephan.de

The election of the German Joseph Ratzinger as Pope Benedict XVI prompted a number of important questions. What sort of Pope would Benedict be? Would the Church's position on contraception change? What could he deliver for the world of beer?

Okay, the last question wasn't asked by quite so many as the others, but it was an interesting point to debate. Ratzinger's predecessor, John Paul II, was born in Poland, a beer-drinking nation but with clearly not as strong a beer culture as the new pontiff's homeland. Before John Paul, four centuries of Italian-born popes ensured that beer gained short shrift at the Vatican table. Could it be that Ratzinger's elevation would place beer on a more heavenly footing in the Holy See and thus in the wider world?

The omens were good, not least in the new pope's choice of name. St Benedict was the founder of the Benedictine order of monks, the rule of which is observed by today's Trappist monks who are famous for brewing beer. Furthermore, being born in Bavaria and serving as the Archbishop of Munich, it is inevitable that Ratzinger would have grown up with the tradition that places beer at the heart of everyday life.

Weissbier connections

It is also intriguing that, when Ratzinger was ordained into the priesthood, the ceremony took place in Freising, just north of Munich. Freising is an important ecclesiastical settlement, with an abbey from the

eighth century. But it is also a major brewing town, home to Weihenstephan, which claims to be the oldest brewery in the world, established by monks in 1040. As Ratzinger also worked at Freising's university, I find it hard to believe that he never enjoyed a glass of Weihenstephan's famous Hefeweissbier. This is one of the classic Bavarian wheat beers – bready, lightly spicy and tartly fruity, attributes that make this such a refreshing style of beer. It would be a wholesome drink with which to celebrate a new papacy.

Shortly after Benedict's election, I spoke to a friend in Bavaria, who reported that only hours after white smoke had issued from the Vatican's chimney, the first shipment of weissbier was already on its way to Rome. For whose consumption he couldn't say, although he does recall seeing photographs of a pre-papal Ratzinger with a mug of beer in his hand.

When it comes to religious drinks, beer tends to be overlooked. Wine is used at Communion, and even strange liqueurs produced by some monasteries are more famous than beers brewed in abbeys. According to Benjamin Franklin, 'Beer is living proof that God loves us and wants to see us happy.' A pope who understands the benefits of beer could help extend that message.

Births Dickie Bird (cricket umpire), 1933; Jayne Mansfield (actress), 1933; Dudley Moore (comedian, actor and musician), 1935; Trevor Francis (football manager), 1954

Deaths Benjamin Disraeli (Prime Minister), 1881; Pierre Curie (scientist), 1906; Frankie Howerd (comedian), 1992

Events Sir Francis Drake destroys the Spanish fleet in Cadiz harbour, 1587; first *Miss World* contest staged, 1951; Prince Rainier of Monaco marries actress Grace Kelly, 1956

Wheat Beer

ABOVE: POPE BENEDICT XVI GREETS THE CROWDS IN ST PETER'S SQUARE

Coors Worthington's White Shield

Source The White Shield Brewery, Burton-upon-Trent, Staffordshire **Strength** 5.6%
Website worthingtonswhiteshield.com

On 20 April 1862, the great French scientist Louis Pasteur and his colleague Claude Bernard conducted the first test into pasteurization. The aim was to find a way to kill off organisms in food that would otherwise spoil the product. They discovered that by heating milk, for instance, to a high temperature for a short period of time, they could eradicate unwanted organisms and stop the milk going off quickly.

In subsequent decades, the same principle was widely applied to beer. Brewers began filtering and pasteurizing their products, stripping out life-giving yeast and blasting beer with heat to wipe out anything that might change its taste once it left the brewery. Sadly, a lot of the character and complexity was removed from the beer as well, but that didn't daunt most brewers. Instead of pursuing greater hygiene at the brewery, which would have achieved the same preservative effect, they opted for the easier route of pasteurization. Consistency was the key, and taste became secondary.

Consumer backlash

A consumer backlash eventually followed. The Campaign for Real Ale (CAMRA) was founded in 1971 to fight back against the widespread pasteurization of draught beer but, by this time, the situation for unpasteurized bottled beers was already grave. Only five unpasteurized, unfiltered bottled beers remained in regular production in the UK. The rest of the market was given over to pasteurized beer, which not only lacks complexity and freshness, but can often have a nasty 'wet paper' staleness, caused by oxygen being cooked into the beer during the heat treatment.

One of these famous five unpasteurized beers was Worthington's White Shield, first brewed in the 1820s. It came from Burton-upon-Trent and was an IPA by style. While other bottled beers lost their charms to the pasteurizer, White Shield remained pure, fermenting naturally in the bottle. As draught beer became progressively less interesting, White Shield became a reliable stand-by in many a pub.

White Shield is now owned by Coors, and is brewed at the tiny White Shield Brewery in Burton. It is great to see that it is still a very impressive brew – loaded with sweet, nutty malt and balanced by a good smack of bitterness from the tropical-fruity hops – well worthy of the Champion Bottled Beer of Britain award it collected from CAMRA in 2006.

The number of living bottled beers has thankfully swollen in recent years, as drinkers recognize the benefits of naturally conditioned beer. White Shield is a great survivor, constantly outshining the many pasteurized beers that are on sale and proving all the time that, as long as the production process is hygienic and the bottling regime scrupulously clean, there is no need to pasteurize beer.

Births Adolf Hitler (dictator), 1889; Jessica Lange (actress), 1949; Nicholas Lyndhurst (actor), 1961

Deaths Bram Stoker (writer), 1912; Steve Marriott (rock musician), 1991; Benny Hill (comedian), 1992

Events Launch of BBC 2, 1964; Enoch Powell makes his 'Rivers of Blood' speech, concerning immigration, 1968

IPA

Teignworthy Empress Russian Porter

Source Teignworthy Brewery, Newton Abbot, Devon **Strength** 10.5% **Website** teignworthybrewery.com

Catherine the Great, Empress of Russia, was born this day in 1729, the daughter of a German prince. Her passage to power began with marriage to a cousin who became Russian Emperor Peter III. When Peter proved to be weak, Catherine ruthlessly removed him from the throne, seizing power for herself. He was murdered soon afterwards, with Catherine – a notorious adulteress – possibly the instigator.

Catherine ruled Russia autocratically for 34 years, and her intelligence and determination could have ensured her a glorious legacy. Under her control, Russia's empire expanded. She boosted its industrial base and valued its culture. However, her close association with the nobility meant that she was no friend to the poor, despite early ambitions to improve life for the servile classes.

To her redemption, however, rides the fact that Catherine was a noted lover of beer and in particular Imperial Russian Stout. This dark, malty, yet profoundly hoppy, strong beer was brewed to withstand a journey across the icy, choppy waters of the Baltic and to warm the hearts of frost-bitten Russians when it got there. Catherine developed a taste for the beer, which did British exports no harm whatsoever.

Russian renaissance

Sadly, the trade in Russian stouts diminished in the 20th century, to the point where there was only one true example in regular production in the UK. That was Courage's version, but even that trickled to a stop in 1993. This left beer aficionados frustrated.

Down in Devon, Tucker's Maltings is a working, traditional floor maltings that offers tours to holidaymakers. It also houses a specialist bottled beer shop. When manager Brian Gates found he could no longer get supplies of Courage Imperial Russian Stout, he set about creating his own to meet demand from his customers. Luckily, the Maltings is also home to Teignworthy Brewery. It is run as a separate business but the two companies work hand in hand, even to the point where Teignworthy brews a range of bottled beers specifically for the Tucker's shop. Charged with re-creating the Russian stout style, brewer John Lawton came up with Empress Russian Porter, a dark mysterious brew with a don't-mess-with-me ABV of 10.5%. That was in 1998 and the beer has been brewed intermittently since, the most recent batch issuing in 2006.

The recipe blends pale malt with crystal malt, chocolate malt and wheat malt, all spiced up with a generous helping of Challenger hops. Expect to taste thick, creamy malt, chocolate and toffee, backed with the bitterness of an espresso coffee. There may be some citrus-fruit acidity, too. It's almost a meal in itself, just the job for a chilly April evening in Devon, if not a full-blown Russian winter.

Births Charlotte Brontë (writer), 1816; Anthony Quinn (actor), 1915; Alistair MacLean (writer), 1922; Queen Elizabeth II, 1926

Deaths Mark Twain (writer), 1910; Manfred von Richthofen (fighter pilot), 1918; John Maynard Keynes (economist), 1946

Events In legend, Rome founded by Romulus and Remus, 753 BC; Russian Army begins advance on Berlin, 1945

Imperial Porter

Westmalle Tripel

Source Brewery der Trappisten van Westmalle, Westmalle **Strength** 9.5% **Website** trappistwestmalle.be

The entry for 8 February discusses the founding of the abbey at Westmalle, near Antwerp, Belgium, by a group of monks running away from the turmoil of the French Revolution. On this day, 22 April 1836, the abbey officially became part of the Trappist order, which – apart from strict considerations regarding prayer, study and work – meant that the brothers were able to drink local beer with their meals. Their own brewery was installed the same year, and a glass of the first beer brewed on the premises was served with lunch on 10 December. However, the wider world needed to wait a bit longer to appreciate their brewing prowess.

It was only in the 1920s that the community began to supply beer commercially. Production, even today, is limited, with just enough beer released to bring in funds for the upkeep of the abbey and to support local good causes. Three types of beer are now produced: the Dubbel mentioned on 8 February; Westmalle Extra – brewed only a couple of times a year and purely for the monks and their guests; and Westmalle Tripel.

The original tripel

Tripel was first brewed in 1934 and is widely recognized as the original tripel. Setting the standard for other beers with the same title, Westmalle's beer is a warm orange colour – thanks to the use of just pilsner malt – and packs quite a punch at 9.5% alcohol. The aroma is heady and spicy, with lemon and other citrus notes from the hops – a blend of several strains about which

the monks maintain a Trappist silence. The beer can be dry and herbal in the mouth, but it doesn't lack sweetness. There are more citrus notes, and the alcohol adds a pleasant glow. Dryness takes over in the hoppy, bitter finish with fruit lingering on. These flavours will, of course, change in time, as the beer is presented in bottle-conditioned form. As months and years pass, and the living yeast ferments and matures the beer, the flavour becomes less hoppy and fruit subsides, allowing malt to have a greater say. The effect even depends on which size of bottle you buy. The brothers believe that the larger 750 ml bottle matures the beer differently from the smaller 330 ml. They say the aroma is softer and that the beer picks up a hint of vanilla in

the bigger bottle. But that's the joy of living beer. If you want the same taste time and again, go for a dull pasteurized beer. Thankfully, the Trappists at Westmalle are happy for nature to take its course.

Births Henry Fielding (writer), 1707; Yehudi Menuhin (violinist), 1916; Jack Nicholson (actor), 1937

Deaths Sir Henry Campbell-Bannerman (Prime Minister), 1908; François 'Papa Doc' Duvalier (dictator), 1971; Richard Nixon (US President), 1994

Events Pedro Cabral discovers Brazil, 1500; Henry VIII becomes King, 1509; first edition of Russian Communist newspaper *Pravda* published, 1912

Trappist Ale

ABOVE: HOPS BEING ADDED TO ONE OF WESTMALLE'S COPPER KETTLES

Hook Norton 303 AD

Source Hook Norton Brewery, Hook Norton, Oxfordshire **Strength** 4% **Website** hooknortonbrewery.co.uk

It's infuriating for English patriots. They witness the Welsh, Irish and Scots take great pride in their national saints' days, but see only apathy at home when it comes to celebrating the day dedicated to St George. They'd like it to be declared officially a public holiday, but surveys repeatedly show that many English people don't even know the date of their saint's day, let alone feel the urge to use it as way of bonding as a nation.

You can't blame the brewing industry for this, however. Brewers never forget 23 April. Perhaps recognizing the commercial benefits of St Patrick's Day, when Irish folk all over the world take boozy indulgence to new levels, they've been competing for some time to produce a pint that can form a centrepiece to national festivities. Charles Wells' Bombardier (see 23 December) shouts louder than most, declaring itself to be the 'drink of England', while numerous other breweries produce beers with St George connections that they hope can savour at least a little of the success that Guinness enjoys every 17 March. The beer selected for today has a more subtle affiliation with the saint than others. It's called 303 AD, a name derived from the year in which St George became a Christian martyr.

George's story begins around the year 270 with his birth in the Cappadocia region of Turkey. Not much is known about George, except that he was raised as a Christian and became a Roman soldier. When the pagan Emperor Diocletian stepped up his persecution of Christians, George rebelled, declared his faith and was beheaded for his frankness. The legend of his slaying a dragon is even more obscure, and is probably just a metaphor for good – in the form of the steadfast George – defeating evil, in the shape of the fiery monster.

The generation game

George subsequently became patron saint of numerous countries, including Lithuania, Georgia and Portugal. His English connections date back to a visit he is supposed to have made while on Roman duty, but his position in English society was considerably strengthened when King Richard I adopted St George's emblem of a red cross on a white background during the Crusades. George then replaced Edward the Confessor as the country's patron saint in the 14th century.

303 AD, the beer, began life in 1997 under the name of Generation, to celebrate the birth of another George, the first son of Hook Norton's managing director, James Clarke. The name was changed in 2005, bringing the two Georges together as the Oxfordshire regional made its pitch for a share of the patriotic beer market. Maris Otter pale malt ensures that the beer has a saintly golden glow, with some amber malt adding a dry note, especially in the finish. Fuggle and Golding hops go into the copper early, with the dwarf hop First Gold added halfway through the boil to exaggerate the fruity character. Consequently, 303 is crisp and surprisingly dry to taste, with delicate but smooth, vaguely chocolaty malt notes, a hop resin bite and light, orange-citrus marmalade-like flavours. It's available in cask or in bottle, at an easy-drinking 4% ABV.

Births Max Planck (physicist), 1858; Shirley Temple (actress and politician), 1928; Michael Moore (film maker), 1954

Deaths William Wordsworth (poet), 1850; Rupert Brooke (poet), 1915; John Mills (actor), 2005

Events Coronation of King Charles II, 1661; the UK's first decimal coins go into circulation, 1968

Golden Ale

Otter Head

Source Otter Brewery, Honiton, Devon **Strength** 5.8% **Website** otterbrewery.com

Anthony Trollope is one of the more unconventional Victorian authors. He may be widely known for a series of romantic and political novels but writing was, for him, just a sideline for much of his life. His main job was as a civil servant. He spent 33 years as an employee of the Post Office and, as well as being the negotiator of numerous important postal treaties, had the unlikely distinction of being the inventor of the pillar box.

To fit all this into a busy life, it is said that Trollope – who also once stood as a Liberal Party candidate for Parliament – disciplined himself into writing a set number of words each morning – starting at 5am – before heading off to work. He must have had considerable self-control: during his lifetime, he penned no fewer than 47 novels, the highlights including *The Warden*, *Barchester Towers* and his collection of novels about the Palliser family.

Trollope's most famous works concern the well-observed residents of Barsetshire (somewhere in southwest England), who pop in and out of a sequence of tales, but it is one of his lesser-known novels that gives us our lead for today. In *Rachel Ray*, written in 1863, Trollope takes us to the fictional Devon town of Baslehurst. Here, events revolve around the future control of the town's brewery, a small concern by the rather fitting name of Bungall and Tappitt. Looking to take charge is young Luke Rowan, a legal clerk from London who has inherited a third of the company. However, his life is complicated by his courtship of the eponymous heroine, who keeps company with the Tappitt girls whom Rowan is lodged with and expected to woo.

A sour & muddy stream

Victorian romance has its followers but it is the brewery side that interests us most here. When Rowan arrives in Baslehurst, Bungall and Tappitt is not in very rude health. Indeed, the author openly questions how it makes any money. 'It was to be found at no respectable inn. It was admitted at no private gentleman's table,' he reveals, having already informed us of the reason why. 'It was a sour and muddy stream that flowed from their vats; a beverage disagreeable to the palate, and very cold and uncomfortable to the stomach.'

Thankfully, Devon is much better served by breweries these days. Indeed, the county is a veritable hot bed of brewing activity and has been since Blackawton Brewery opened up in 1977, heralding a new generation of microbreweries to take the place of many of the long-established, local businesses like Heavitree and St Anne's Well that had disappeared over the 20th century. Joining the influx in 1990 was Otter Brewery. This is a modern-day family affair, run from an old farm near Honiton by the McCaig clan. Its beers now travel far and wide, as well as serving a dedicated audience in Devon, and they include the beer chosen for today's tribute to Trollope.

Otter Head is a deep amber-coloured ale with juicy fruit dominating both the aroma and taste, courtesy of its blend of Challenger, Northern Brewer and Fuggle hops. Thanks to its abundant Maris Otter pale malt (with just a little chocolate malt, too), the beer falls on the sweet side, but it is very nicely balanced, with the body, strength and character to have more than pleased the Victorian drinkers of Trollope's novels. It's the sort of beer that would have turned around the fortunes of a struggling business like Bungall and Tappitt. Respectable inns clamour for it, and this is one private gentleman who would always be glad to see it on his table.

Births Clement Freud (writer and politician), 1924; Barbra Streisand (actress and singer), 1942; Stuart Pearce (footballer), 1962

Deaths Bud Abbot (comedian), 1974; Wallis Simpson, Duchess of Windsor, 1986; Estée Lauder (cosmetics entrepreneur), 2004

Events Start of the Easter Rising in Ireland, 1916; Winston Churchill knighted by Queen Elizabeth II, 1953; Joseph Ratzinger inaugurated as Pope Benedict XVI, 2005

Strong Ale

Little Creatures Pale Ale

Source Little Creatures Brewing, Fremantle **Strength** 5.2% **Website** littlecreatures.com.au

The 25th day of April is ANZAC Day, when the citizens of Australia and New Zealand pay tribute to their compatriots who have died in war. It is a solemn and respectful occasion, one in which the people of the two countries take great pride.

The roots of the day can be found in World War I, when Australian and New Zealand forces worked together to play their part in defeating Germany (ANZAC is an acronym for Australia and New Zealand Army Corps). On 25 April 1915, the ANZACs spearheaded a mission to capture Constantinople (now Istanbul) and open up access to the Black Sea. Their bridgehead was a beach at Gallipoli, and the aim was a quick, pre-emptive strike that would catch the Turks, allies of the Germans, unawares. Things didn't go to plan, however. Turkish resistance was fierce, and the campaign waged for eight months before the ANZACs withdrew, thousands of men having lost their lives in the conflict.

Commemorations

ANZAC Day is commemorated with a number of remembrance services for the men who died in the Gallipoli campaign, and also in later wars. Consequently, if a glass is to be raised in respect and memory, then it needs to be filled with something special. That something special could be Little Creatures Pale Ale.

Little Creatures comes from a brewery and pub founded in 2000 in a converted boatshed on the harbour at Fremantle, Western Australia. The brewery also produces a pilsner and an amber ale called Rogers, but it is the pale ale that rightly attracts all the attention. What lifts the beer out of the ordinary is the use of American whole-leaf hops. They don't go into the copper – the bittering job is done by hop pellets. Instead, they sit in a giant 'tea bag' in the hop back – the container through which the hopped wort is strained before being cooled – so the big floral, fruity flavours from the Cascade and Chinook hops soak into the beer just before fermentation begins. The beer is also bottle conditioned, which means that those fragrant hop notes are not tarnished by pasteurization and there's a good, clean freshness to the whole drink. Tangy, peppery hops feature prominently in the taste, along with spritzy grapefruit notes and other citrus fruit.

Little Creatures has proved to be such a hit in Australia and the wider world that they've now had to expand the brewery.

Births Oliver Cromwell (Lord Protector of England), 1599; Guglielmo Marconi (scientist), 1874; Johann Cruyff (football manager), 1947

Deaths Carol Reed (film director), 1976; Ginger Rogers (dancer), 1995; Lisa 'Left Eye' Lopes (rap artist), 2002

Events Daniel Defoe's *Robinson Crusoe* published, 1719; Hitler's diaries (later proved fake) first published in German *Stern* magazine, 1983

Pale Ale

Rogue Shakespeare Stout

Source Rogue Brewery, Newport, Oregon **Strength** 6.3% **Website** rogue.com

It is generally assumed that, rather uncannily, William Shakespeare was born and also died on the same date, 23 April. However, with no records to support the fact that he was actually born on that day, we can only truly celebrate his arrival on the day he was baptized, which was 26 April 1564.

Shakespeare's connections with the world of beer are numerous. In his writing he shows his love of a good beer on more than one occasion. Autolycus in *The Winter's Tale* sings the praises of a decent brew when he claims 'a quart of ale is a dish fit for a king'. There are similar sentiments in *Henry VI, Part II*, when rebel Jack Cade declares that, given his chance to reform society, he would not only ensure that seven halfpenny loaves would be sold for a penny but also that 'I will make it a felony to drink small beer,' referring to the weaker beer often made from the second run-off from the malt after a strong beer has been brewed.

Another of the Bard's famous beer quotes can be read above the door of a pub in the West Midlands. 'Blessing of your heart, you brew good ale', originates in *The Two Gentlemen of Verona* but is now emblazoned across the facade of The Vine in Brierley Hill. The pub is more commonly known as The Bull & Bladder, and is the brewery tap of Batham's Brewery, so perhaps a pint of their sweetish, refreshing Bitter would make a good choice for today's beer. The quote also features on the label of Samuel Smith's Winter Welcome, but that is unlikely to be available at the end of April.

Name games

Shakespeare's image appears on the livery of Flowers beers. Flowers was a brewery in Stratford-upon-Avon, until it was closed by Whitbread in 1968. Flowers IPA and Original are still available, owned by InBev and brewed under contract by Badger Brewery in Dorset. They are available in cask-conditioned form, but frankly aren't the most exciting of beers.

A better option would be to choose a beer from a brewery named after the great man himself. Shakespeare's Brewery opened near Stratford in 2005, and has a selection of cask and bottled beers with names like Noble Fool, Taming of the Brew, The Scottish Ale and The Tempest. However, it's hard to ignore an American beer that borrows Shakespeare's name. Shakespeare Stout from Rogue Ales in Oregon is such a good beer that it can't be overlooked. It's a crisp, tasty stout perfectly marrying malt, roasted grain and lightly fruity hops to provide bags of flavour without too much body. Bitterness lingers with burnt grain and coffee in the aftertaste and, like all Rogue's unpasteurized beers, it has a fantastically fresh taste. Just be careful: it's all too drinkable for its strength.

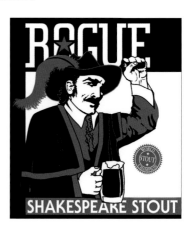

Births Marcus Aurelius (Roman Emperor), 121; Eugène Delacroix (artist), 1798; Duane Eddy (guitarist), 1938

Deaths Sid James (actor), 1976; Count Basie (jazz musician), 1984; Lucille Ball (actress), 1989

Events Town of Guernica bombed by the Germans in the Spanish Civil War, 1937; accident at Chernobyl nuclear power plant leads to disaster, 1986

Stout

Teignworthy Spring Tide

Source Teignworthy Brewery, Newton Abbot, Devon **Strength** 4.3% **Website** teignworthybrewery.com

*Spring, the sweet spring, is the
    year's pleasant king;
Then blooms each thing, then
    maids dance in a ring.
Cold doth not sting, the pretty
    birds do sing*

In these few lines, 16th-century poet Thomas Nashe puts his finger on the air of renewal that pervades this season, with the winter hopefully behind us and the promise of summer ahead as the evenings start to lengthen. Maids may not dance so readily these days but it's still a sweet time of year.

Brewers, traditionally, have welcomed the new season with some distinctive beers, most notably in Germany where the strong lager known as bock goes on sale (see 21 March and 13 May). US craft brewers now provide their own spin on the bock style, too. In Britain, the tendency has been to produce light, fruity beers to match the change of mood in the seasons. Look for such offerings as Spring Breeze from Batemans, Spring Equinox from Dark Star, and Spring Fever from Harviestoun. Some beers hang onto the coat tails of Easter, such as Hopping Hare, a fine, suitably hoppy, bitter from Hall & Woodhouse, while others pin their hopes on other seasonal associations, Mauldons' Cuckoo, for example. Possibly the most unusual spring beer comes from Stonehenge Brewery in Wiltshire, where Danish brewer Stig Anker Andersen annually releases a light green-coloured beer called Sign of Spring.

High water mark

Our selected beer for the season is now produced all year, in both cask- and bottle-conditioned formats. It is brewed by Teignworthy Brewery, which occupies part of the historic Tucker's Maltings at Newton Abbot in Devon. Teignworthy was founded by former Oakhill and Ringwood brewer John Lawton in 1994, when Tucker's was delighted to welcome a working brewery on board to add a new dimension to its daily tours for visitors. Thousands of Devon holiday-makers have now taken the trip through the malting process and wound up with a glass of John's excellent ale in the tasting room. It is, after all, the end product of the work the maltings initiates.

The Teignworthy beer that stands out for today is called Spring Tide. It is a 4.3% ale, brewed from Maris Otter pale malt, with some crystal malt added to the mash tun to darken the golden colour. The hops are Fuggle, Golding, Bramling Cross and Challenger. When it reaches the glass, the beer is nutty and nicely bitter, with a complex fruitiness that brings in both citrus and orchard fruits. There are herbal hop notes, too, and then, in the finish, suggestions of orange.

The beer takes its name from the high waters that wash up the estuary of the River Teign, close to the maltings, but of course the title also offers a nice little play on words for the time of year.

Births Samuel Morse (inventor), 1791; Ulysses S Grant (US President), 1822; Cecil Day-Lewis (Poet Laureate), 1904

Deaths Ferdinand Magellan (explorer), 1521; Ralph Waldo Emerson (writer), 1882; Ed Murrow (journalist), 1965

Events Betty Boothroyd becomes the first female Speaker of the House of Commons, 1992; first flight of the super passenger aircraft, the Airbus A380, 2005

Bitter

125

Rebellion Mutiny

Source Rebellion Beer Co., Marlow, Buckinghamshire **Strength** 4.5% **Website** rebellionbeer.co.uk

In 1987, Whitbread caused outrage among lovers of cask ale when it closed the popular Wethered brewery in Marlow. Thankfully, that wasn't the end of brewing in the town. A few years later, a couple of local men decided to give Marlow a brand new brewery of its own. Raising two fingers to the Whitbread accountants, Rebellion was born.

The brewery offers a wide range of beers, including a Belgian-style white beer, a red ale and some fine traditional bitters. One of these, a 4.5% dark bitter, is called Mutiny, rather appropriately for today's major event in history, as it was on 28 April that the infamous mutiny on the *Bounty* took place.

In search of breadfruit

The *Bounty*, under the command of Lt William Bligh, was pursuing a long expedition to the South Pacific. Its mission was to visit Tahiti and collect breadfruit plants, which it would then take to the Caribbean for cultivation. Breadfruit, a starchy and versatile fruit, was seen as a cheap and useful food with which to feed slaves. After a troublesome, weather-delayed outward journey that took ten months, the *Bounty* finally arrived at Tahiti, where it harboured for five months. Bligh allowed his men to live on the island, where many developed relationships with the locals, to the point where, when it came to returning home, there was understandably some resentment in the ranks. It is possibly that this precipitated one of the most notorious actions in the history of the Royal Navy. On this day in 1789, Bligh was confronted by his Master's Mate, Fletcher Christian, and 18 followers, who took control of the ship. Bligh, along with 22 loyal seamen, was set adrift in the ship's launch. There was no bloodshed, but prospects for the stranded men on the open sea looked poor. However, Bligh's seamanship saw them find their way to Timor and safety. The mutineers later revisited Tahiti, kidnapping local men and women, and taking them on to a new base on Pitcairn Island, where the *Bounty* was burned.

Bligh returned home and was promoted to Captain. He even undertook a second (and successful) mission to gather breadfruit plants, and was eventually appointed Governor of New South Wales. As for Christian, it is believed he was killed on Pitcairn, which eventually became a British colony, populated by descendants of the mutineers.

Rebellion's Mutiny is not such an awkward customer. It is eminently drinkable, with dark malts adding a touch of nut in the mouth, and lots of fruity notes stemming from the hops. It does not – to my limited knowledge – taste of breadfruit, and that's probably a good thing.

Births Lionel Barrymore (actor), 1878; Oskar Schindler (industrialist and war hero), 1908; Harper Lee (writer), 1926; Terry Pratchett (writer), 1948

Deaths Benito Mussolini (dictator), 1945; Francis Bacon (artist), 1992; Sir Alf Ramsey (football manager), 1999

Events Thor Heyerdahl sets sail on the raft *Kon-Tiki* to cross the Pacific, 1947; Charles de Gaulle resigns as President of France, 1969; billionaire Dennis Tito becomes the first space tourist, paying $20 million for his trip, 2001

Best Bitter

ABOVE: MARLON BRANDO AS FLETCHER CHRISTIAN IN THE 1962 FILM *MUTINY ON THE BOUNTY*

Cains Double Bock

Source Robert Cain Brewery, Liverpool, Merseyside **Strength** 8% **Website** cainsbeer.com

At Cains in Liverpool, they are happy to draw parallels with their operation today and the way in which the brewery was founded. They like to think that the spirit of Robert Cain lives on at a time when ambitious plans are being pursued for the brewery's future.

Robert Cain was born on this day in 1826 in Cork, Ireland. Having worked at sea, he landed on Merseyside and set about involving himself in the pub and brewing trade. After six years in Liverpool, and at the age of just 24, he bought his first pub and began brewing.

Industrious to a fault, Cain clocked up the hours standing over his mash tun and copper, desperate to see his business succeed. That it did, to the point where it was eventually forced to move to a new site – one that was previously occupied by a failed brewery – where Robert was to build a new brewhouse in 1887. Up went the terracotta palace that is home to Cains today, a Victorian gem, steaming and rattling to quench the thirst of the sweaty dockers servicing the vessels moored on the river just down the hill.

By the time Robert died in 1907, the self-made man had 'arrived'. The title of Lord Brocket had been bestowed upon him (he was the great-great grandfather of the current Lord Brocket, of celebrity TV fame), and his brewery was a fundamental part of the character of Liverpool.

Sadly, shortly after his demise, the company was merged with Peter Walker, and production was moved to Warrington. In 1923, the Liverpool brewery was sold to Higson's, who brewed there until 1990, when the business was closed by Whitbread. That wasn't the end of the story, however. A beer canning company re-opened the site and it later fell into the hands of the Danish Brewery Group (brewers of Faxe), who revived the Cains name. Then, in 2002, the business was acquired by two entrepreneurs of Indian origin, and the great Cains revival really gathered pace.

Ambitious plans

Brothers Ajmail and Sudarghara Dusanj have much in common with Robert Cain. Second-generation immigrants themselves, they recognized the way in which the Irish brewery founder worked hard to establish himself and his business in a foreign land. By building up their father's fish and chip business in Kent, the brothers did a similar thing themselves. Now they're putting in the hours and figuratively standing over the mash tun and copper to raise the profile of Cains even higher.

In 2007, they announced a reverse take-over of the Honeycombe Leisure pub group, to build an estate of more than 100 pubs, and the same year homed in on their goal of building a strong portfolio of world-class beers by brewing Cains Double Bock to celebrate the 800th anniversary of Liverpool's city charter.

A dark amber homage to the German style of strong lagers that were traditionally brewed for spring,

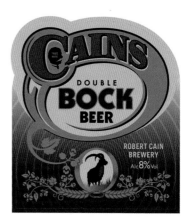

it's a bold beer for a British brewery to develop but it's a real gem – richly sweet, malty and creamy, with gentle nut and dried fruit flavours that ensure it's exceptionally easy to drink for its strength. It's probably not the sort of beer that Robert Cain would ever have conceived of brewing, but he'd surely recognize the endeavour that has led to its creation and the positive direction that the brewery is determined to follow.

Births William Randolph Hearst (media magnate), 1863; 'Duke' Ellington (jazz musician), 1899; Phil Tufnell (cricketer), 1966

Deaths St Catherine of Siena, 1380; Alfred Hitchcock (film director), 1980; Mick Ronson (rock musician), 1993

Events Joan of Arc enters Orléans and defeats the English, 1429; Muhammad Ali stripped of his world heavyweight boxing crown after refusing to serve in the US Army, 1967

Jacobsen Saaz Blonde

Source Carlsberg, Jacobsen Brewhouse, Valby **Strength** 7.1% **Website** jacobsenbeer.com

One of the most important men in the entire history of brewing passed away on this day in 1887, bringing to an end a life that changed the way in which beer was brewed throughout the world.

Jacob Christian Jacobsen was born in 1811, the son of a Jutland father who had moved to Copenhagen and opened a brewery. True to the times, Jacobsen senior brewed top-fermenting beers. Young JC, however, was fascinated by the new lager beers that were coming out of Bavaria and he tried to re-create them. He soon established that it was the yeast that made all the difference, and paid visits to Germany to find out more. There, he acquired a supply of yeast from renowned brewer Gabriel Sedlmayr and somehow managed to take it back home in viable condition.

The yeast did the trick, and it wasn't long before Jacobsen produced Denmark's first commercial bottom-fermented beer. On the back of his success, Jacobsen opened a new brewery in 1847 to concentrate on this novel beer style. He built it on a hill on the outskirts of Copenhagen and named it after his son, Carl, so giving rise to the empire that is now known as Carlsberg.

Discovering how to brew lager was but one of Jacobsen's achievements, however. He also established a state-of-the-art laboratory that proved to be at the heart of another major brewing breakthrough, when scientist Emil Christian Hansen established there that yeast came in several strains, and only some were good for brewing – the bad ones turned the beer sour. It's hard to underplay the significance of this discovery, and hard to imagine how much sour beer there must have been in circulation until that time.

Great philanthropist

Jacobsen was also a great philanthropist. Profits from his brewery were diverted into the Carlsberg Foundation, which benefited the arts and sciences. Jacobsen's son, Carl, followed him into the trade and promoted culture himself, using money generated by his own New Carlsberg brewery, built next door to the old. The two eventually merged, with New Carlsberg taking over as the production centre, and the old brewery turned into a museum.

In 2005, however, brewing returned to the old brewery when a microbrewery was built there as part of the visitors' centre, preserving the heritage of the business and the name of its founder. Here, at the Jacobsen Brewery, some of Carlsberg's most interesting beers are brewed. The beer selected for today is one.

Jacobsen's Saaz Blonde is a very suppable, hybrid beer, drawing on the strong Belgian blonde ale tradition and adding a Czech twist through the choice of Saaz hops. Pilsner malt creates the golden colour, darkened a touch by a little caramel malt. There's also some extract of angelica, which, the brewery claims, introduces a hint of juniper to the beer.

Saaz Blonde has a powerful aroma of mellow tropical fruits, especially pineapple and banana, plus bubblegum. The taste is bittersweet, smooth and rich, with a pleasant moussey texture and more pineapple, as well as citrus fruit and a peppery warmth from the alcohol. The hops in the beer's name finally squeeze through in a tangy, clove-like, fruity finish. It's a big, satisfying beer and, along with the other experimental beers emerging from the Jacobsen brewery, is a nice tribute to the illustrious founder of the business.

Births Dickie Davies (broadcaster), 1933; Willie Nelson (country musician), 1933; Bobby Vee (pop singer), 1943

Deaths Edouard Manet (artist), 1883; Muddy Waters (blues musician), 1983; Sergio Leone (film director), 1989

Events George Washington inaugurated as first US President, 1789; Prince Charles opens London Underground's Jubilee Line, 1979

Blonde Beer

ABOVE: JACOB CHRISTIAN JACOBSEN

Oakleaf Maypole Mild

Source The Oakleaf Brewing Co. Ltd, Gosport, Hampshire **Strength** 3.8% **Website** oakleafbrewing.co.uk

In the northern hemisphere, 1 May marks the halfway point between the vernal equinox and the summer solstice, and therefore has always had a cultural significance. In pagan times, and still in some Celtic circles, the date was honoured as Beltane, a festival that ushers in warmer weather as cattle are taken outdoors and springtime fertility is celebrated. Dancing around a dressed maypole is just one of the rituals we have inherited from Beltane.

In British brewing circles, May has now become recognized as Mild Month, thanks to the efforts of the Campaign for Real Ale in using this month to highlight and preserve a fast-fading beer style. Mild used to be Britain's most popular beer, right up to the turn of the 1960s, but a decline in industry and heavy labour saw workers no longer needing the nutritiously sugary top-up that mild provided at the end of the working day, and the national preference changed to bitter. The growth of standard lager further consigned mild to the past during the '60s and '70s.

CAMRA's move to place mild back on the map in more places than its last surviving hotbeds in the Midlands and northern England has proved hugely successful. Dozens of small brewers now produce a mild during May, and many of them carry their milds forward through the rest of the year, having seen how popular the beer has become. Some major brewers like Batemans, Fuller's, Theakston's and Wadworth have also contributed to the resurgence.

Still, however, mild faces a struggle to compete in a busy beer marketplace, so May as Mild Month needs to continue, but we can at least enjoy a pint of this mellow, malty, less bitter beer much more easily these days. One mild that is available all year round in cask- and bottle-conditioned format is Maypole Mild from Oakleaf Brewery. The brewery stands in a small industrial area on the edge of Gosport harbour, not exactly a place where you'd expect to find maypoles and May Day celebrations, but many of the pubs that the brewery serves are located in just the sort of inland rural setting where you can imagine dancers revelling at this time of year. The beer itself has won a Society of Independent Brewers gold medal and has heaps of dark malt flavour – smoky, chocolaty-sweet with a hint of caramel and the nutty bitterness of roasted grain. At 3.8%, it's a tad stronger than milds have generally become, but it's a fine drink with which to put the winter days behind you and look forward to the brighter days of summer.

Births Arthur Wellesley, Duke of Wellington (soldier and politician), 1769; Judy Collins (singer), 1939; Joanna Lumley (actress), 1946

Deaths David Livingstone (explorer and missionary), 1873; Antonin Dvorak (composer), 1904; Ayrton Senna (racing driver), 1994

Events Betting shops become legal in the UK, 1961; Elvis Presley marries Priscilla Beaulieu, 1967; Labour Party wins general election, 1997

Mild

Shepherd Neame Early Bird Spring Hop Ale

Source Shepherd Neame, Faversham, Kent **Strength** 4.3% **Website** shepherdneame.co.uk

The age of satellite television really began on this day in 1965. The most famous of man-made satellites up to this time had been *Telstar*, launched in 1962 and immortalized in music by the instrumental group The Tornados. *Telstar*, however, was only partially effective. Being placed in a random orbit, it was available only for carrying signals at certain times of the day. What was required for full-time coverage was a geostationary satellite, one that would orbit Earth at the same speed as the planet turned, thereby maintaining a fixed position in the heavens. In 1965, the first such satellite for communications use was introduced. Its proper name was *Intelsat I*, but it became popularly known as *Early Bird*.

The satellite was launched from Cape Kennedy, Florida, on 6 April and went into full commercial service on 28 June. However, it was on 2 May that *Early Bird* carried its first transatlantic TV pictures, thereby heralding a new dawn in global broadcasting. From a position 35,888km (22,300 miles) above the Equator, the tiny satellite – just under 60cm (2ft) and just over 60cm (2ft) in diameter – offered a direct link between North America and Europe, and during its short lifetime was put to use ferrying telephone, fax and telegraph traffic, as well as television. *Early Bird* was eventually decommissioned in 1969.

Farmer's choice

The name Early Bird clearly refers to the satellite's ground-breaking status and is said to have been derived from the proverb about early birds catching worms. One hopes that the type of hop also known as Early Bird doesn't suffer the same fate. Aromatically fruity, the Early Bird – or Amos's Early Bird, to give it its full name – is said to have been cultivated by farmer Alfred Amos of Wye, Kent, who selected it out of a garden of Bramling hops in 1887. Although, therefore, a derivative of the Bramling strain, it is today considered to be part of the Golding family. It gets its name from the fact that it ripens early and its charms are used to full effect by Kent brewer Shepherd Neame, which is well known for its dedication to the local hop gardens. In its cask form, Early Bird Spring Hop Ale is brewed seasonally, going on sale in February and running through until the end of May, but the beer is also bottled for year-round enjoyment. It's a delicate, finely balanced bitter with an ABV of 4.3%. Subtle malt and spritzy hops are the key features, leaving a dry, hoppy and pleasantly subtle finish. A good telly-watching beer perhaps?

Births Benjamin Spock (paediatrician), 1903; David Suchet (actor), 1946; Brian Lara (cricketer), 1969; David Beckham (footballer), 1975

Deaths Leonardo da Vinci (artist and inventor), 1519; Nancy Astor (politician), 1964; Oliver Reed (actor), 1999

Events Argentinian battleship *General Belgrano* sunk during the Falklands conflict, 1982; Nelson Mandela's ANC party wins South Africa's first all-race elections, 1994; Tony Blair becomes Prime Minister, 1997

Golden Ale

ABOVE: PRE-LAUNCH TESTS ON THE *EARLY BIRD* SATELLITE

Cantillon Rosé de Gambrinus

Source Cantillon Brewery, Brussels **Strength** 5% **Website** cantillon.be

'The King of Beer' died this day, so the story has it, when Jan, Duke of Brabant, drew his last breath in 1294. A skilful warrior, Jan is thought to have led a colourful life, with a particular fondness for beer way up there among his personal pastimes. It's all a bit vague, to be honest, and it may be that Jan has simply been latched onto by historians desperate to find an origin for the legendary beer king, Gambrinus. While there are other suggestions as to where Gambrinus stems from, the most popular is certainly from the corruption of the Duke's name, Jan Primus (Jan the First). Whatever the source, Gambrinus is a name that is celebrated and used the world over for connections with good beer. In America, Gambrinus is a beer marketing business that owns Shiner Brewery in Texas, Bridgeport Brewery in Oregon and the Pete's Wicked

brands. One of the most popular beers in the Czech Republic is also called Gambrinus. It was once next-door-neighbour of the famous Pilsner Urquell, but both are now part of the SABMiller stable. Any of these products would have slotted nicely into today's commemoration, but it's probably more appropriate to return to Belgium and settle on a beer that still bears the Gambrinus name.

Fit for a king

The Cantillon brewery, tucked in the backstreets behind Brussels's Midi station, specializes in lambic beers. This form of production, in which wild yeasts soaked in from the atmosphere ferment the beer as it lies in dusty wooden casks, results in beers that are acidic, dry and rather sour-tasting. Cantillon's beers are about as sour as they come. You can pop in for a tour, see the

lambic process at work and round off your visit with a tasting of the brewery's beers. But be prepared: they still come as a shock after years of sampling. If you're lucky, you may get a swig of Rosé de Gambrinus, Cantillon's take on the framboise (raspberry) beer style. Don't expect the vibrant red hue or the sweet commerciality of many framboises on the market today. Here, the raspberries merely add a blush to the beer's complexion and a subtle fruitiness to do battle with the tart dryness of the aged, wild beer. The fruit is steeped into two-year-old lambic for up to six months, with a good proportion of young lambic added late to stimulate a further fermentation in the bottle.

Lambic is one of the last connections we have to the age of pre-industrial brewing and is therefore probably close in style and unpredictability to the beers that Jan Primus would have savoured all those centuries ago. If he could indeed drink gallons of demanding beers like this, he richly deserves to be known as the King.

Framboise

Brains SA Gold

Source S A Brain & Co. Ltd, Cardiff **Strength** 4.7% **Website** sabrain.com

It's impossible to visit the capital of Wales without noticing that the city is home to a major brewery. Nearly every pub displays its unusual name, and, where one doesn't, billboards and buses fill in the gap. Now talk of Brains is spreading throughout the principality, as what used to be simply Cardiff's regional brewer is rapidly becoming a national icon.

Brains Brewery has its origins in this day in 1850, with the birth of co-founder Samuel Arthur Brain into a commercially minded family. The Brains were involved in both the mining and banking industries in the west of England, and soon spread their wings over the River Severn. Samuel Arthur arrived in Cardiff in the early 1860s and trained as a brewer at the local Phoenix Brewery, which was later purchased by Hancock's. He was keen, however, to plough his own furrow. In 1882, Samuel drew on the financial assistance of his uncle, Joseph Benjamin Brain, to acquire Cardiff's Old Brewery – which had been established, it seems, for at least 60 years – from his brother-in-law, John Griffen Thomas. With SA Brain at the helm, the business flourished, and five years later a new brewhouse was constructed on the same site. Brain himself became a notable figure in local society, as a city councillor and later Mayor of Cardiff. He died in 1903, at the age of only 52, but the Brain family is still at the helm of the brewery, which in recent years has expanded by moving into the much larger Cardiff brewery vacated by Bass in 1999.

Golden future

A pint of Brains has always been a highlight for visiting rugby fans, so it wasn't a surprise to see the name of the company finally emblazoned on the red shirts of the national team, thanks to the securing of a major sponsorship deal in 2004. A year later, Wales won the Six Nations Grand Slam, for the first time in 27 years, and Brains was the name – and increasingly the beer – on everyone's lips.

The company now runs more than 250 pubs and produces a wide range of beers. The perennial favourite has always been the beer named simply SA, in honour of the founder. Although the initials have irreverently been interpreted by hung-over drinkers as 'Skull Attack', SA is only a best bitter in terms of style, with a malty, yet bitter, profile. The SA brand was extended in April 2006, with the creation of a new blonde ale called SA Gold. This is a beer with a more modern image, cashing in on the trend for straw-coloured beers, and also latching onto the current preference for more hop, in a bid to steal more of the UK guest beer market. It's SA Gold that is today's selection, as it conveniently links the long history of the company with the dynamism and foresight shown by the present management. They've turned the local drink of Cardiff into the national beer of Wales and that's no mean achievement.

Births John Hanning Speke (explorer), 1827; Eric Sykes (comedian), 1923; Audrey Hepburn (actress), 1929

Deaths Marshal Tito (politician), 1980; Diana Dors (actress), 1984; Paul Butterfield (blues musician), 1987

Events The first Epsom Derby, 1780; Margaret Thatcher becomes the UK's first female Prime Minister, 1979; Ken Livingstone becomes Mayor of London, 2000

Golden Ale

Gouden Carolus Classic

Source Brouwerij Het Anker, Mechelen **Strength** 8.5% **Website** hetanker.be

Anyone who has visited Belgium for a beer break will vouch for the country's impressive rail network. The trains may look big, clumsy and rather scruffy, but they do their job and, indeed, have done so since 5 May 1835. That was the momentous day when the country's first commercial rail service began, with a journey from Brussels to Mechelen (about halfway towards Antwerp).

Using steam engines designed by George Stephenson, which had been imported from Britain, the rail pioneers not only took Belgium into a new age but dragged continental Europe with them, the journey being the first of its kind on the European mainland. The Belgian rail network developed rapidly after that and, with its efficiency, affordability and comprehensive coverage, in several respects puts the UK system to shame.

Beer halt

If beer travellers were to make the same journey today, they'd find Mechelen is still a railway hub. The outskirts are urban and unattractive, but the old centre is more than pleasant, with the cathedral and some fine old buildings having survived the destruction of World War II. Another reason for taking the ride is to seek out the beers from the Anker brewery, even if its name implies a closer association with ships than trains.

Anker is one of the most respected breweries in Belgium. The origins date back to the 14th century, or even before, and the brewery has remained in the Van Breedam family since 1873. There's been plenty of investment in recent years to push it in the right direction and even to add peripheral attractions, such as a hotel. Refurbishment of the 19th-century brewhouse has helped keep the beers in fine order, and has extended the fame of the Gouden Carolus range.

This group of beers is named after Holy Roman Emperor Charles V, who was raised in Mechelen, and more specifically the golden coins minted during his 16th-century reign. The range has gradually extended to include Ambrio (amber) and Tripel, plus Christmas and Easter specials, but the original, Gouden Carolus Classic, is the one to hop aboard today. This is a deep ruby-coloured ale that matures well in the bottle. It is packed with darker malts to give a sweet, mellow, toffeeish, raisiny flavour, and there's a spicy alcoholic bite – well, it is 8.5%. Importantly, there's also a crisp bitterness for balance. The beer enjoys international fame, and rightly so.

The term classic is too easily banded about in beer circles, but this is one brew that certainly deserves the title.

Births Karl Marx (philosopher), 1818; Michael Palin (comedian and actor), 1943; Craig David (singer), 1981

Deaths Napoleon Bonaparte (French Emperor), 1821; Walter Sisulu (anti-apartheid campaigner), 2003

Events Amy Johnson begins her record-breaking flight to Australia, 1930; Council of Europe founded, 1949; Alan Shepard becomes the first American in space, 1961

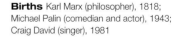

ABOVE: SOUTH STATION IN BRUSSELS, PART OF THE IMPRESSIVE BELGIAN RAIL NETWORK

Strong Ale

Hampshire Penny Black

Source Hampshire Brewery Ltd, Romsey, Hampshire **Strength** 4.5% **Website** hampshirebrewery.com

The world's most famous postage stamp came into use on this day in 1840. Everyone has heard of the Penny Black, but it's not a particularly rare stamp or very valuable. Its significance lies in the fact that it was the first adhesive stamp to come into service, establishing the idea of pre-paid postage at a standard rate that could be simply affixed to letters.

The stamp was the brainchild of Worcestershire-born teacher and social reformer Rowland Hill, who identified problems in the existing postal service in which weight and distance were taken into account to work out the cost of postage, which the receiver paid – or refused to do so, thereby costing the post office time and money.

If you come across any Penny Blacks with a postage date of before 6 May, that's because the stamps were issued to the public on 1 May and some were used, unofficially, before the launch day.

Simplicity reigns

Simplicity won through when the layout of the stamp was revealed. An engraved profile of the reigning monarch, Queen Victoria, was chosen, setting a precedent for the monarch's head to feature on all UK stamps. The stamps were issued in a sheet, but without perforations, which meant that scissors were needed to separate them. The Penny Black remained in circulation for only a year. It was found that red cancellation ink didn't work very well

over the black colour, so the stamp was changed to a Penny Red in 1841, with black cancellation ink introduced to reveal whether the stamp had been used or not. Rowland Hill was later knighted for his services to the Empire and is buried at Westminster Abbey.

Hampshire Brewery has adopted the name Penny Black for its porter. The porter is part of a range of monthly special beers and normally comes out in winter. This means that you are unlikely to find the beer on draught to mark this particular occasion in May. There is, however, a good chance of finding the beer in bottle, as Hampshire tends to bottle condition most of its seasonal and monthly brews so they stick around a fair bit longer.

Penny Black is actually a deep ruby-coloured beer. The roasted malts combine to produce a rich, smoky coffee taste, but there's also good countering malty sweetness and a light, airy body. In all, it's a full-flavoured, good-value porter – a beer, you could say, that takes some licking.

Births Sigmund Freud (psychoanalyst), 1856; Rudolph Valentino (actor), 1895; Orson Welles (actor and film director), 1915

Deaths King Edward VII, 1910; Marlene Dietrich (actress and singer), 1992

Events German zeppelin *Hindenberg* bursts into flames, 1937; Roger Bannister runs the first four-minute mile, 1954; Channel Tunnel officially opened, 1994

Porter

ABOVE: PENNY BLACK STAMPS

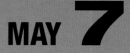

Schlösser Alt

Source Brauerei Brinkhoff, Dortmund　**Strength** 4.8%　**Website** schloesser.de

Brahms and Liszt: two giants of the classical music world cruelly reduced by Cockney rhyming slang to a euphemism for over-indulgence. We're probably not helping the situation here, either, by exploring the life of one of these composers through the bottom of a beer glass, but the birth of Brahms on this day in 1833 does give us a chance to tap into one of the world's great beer styles.

Johannes Brahms was born in Hamburg, the son of an orchestra musician. Such was his precocious talent that, while barely a teenager, he was topping up the family income by playing music in pubs. His abilities soon brought him into contact with other musical giants, of which the young man was in considerable awe. He eventually became a great friend of Robert Schumann – and particularly of Schumann's wife, Clara, after the composer's death – but there's a rather entertaining story about how, having impressed the couple on their first meeting in October 1853, he was invited back to lunch at their home in Düsseldorf the next day, only to be too nervous to attend. When he didn't show up, Clara was dispatched to search the city's taverns. Happily, she found him and, in part due to the Schumanns' patronage and support, Brahms went on to compose some of the most memorable German music of the 19th century.

But perhaps it wasn't shyness that caused Brahms to miss that lunch date. He was known to like a good beer and it is certainly hard to prise yourself away from the old inns that line the cobbled heart of historic Düsseldorf, especially as the city has managed to hold on to its own distinctive style of brewing, in defiance of the pale lagers that have washed over much of Germany.

Old beer

The style here is called Alt. It means old, which tells you that it was here before pilsner began its national conquest. The style has more in common with British ales, in fact, brewed with top-fermenting yeast and featuring a malt grist that favours darker malts alongside pale malt for a nuttier note. Where Alt leans back towards its compatriot beer styles is in the conditioning, enjoying several weeks of slow maturation at low temperatures. What you get in the glass is a beer with the look and flavour of a malty best bitter but the crispness and cleanness of a well-matured lager.

A good example is Schlösser Alt, a brand now owned by the Oetker group, and sadly brewed not in Düsseldorf any longer, but in Dortmund. It pours a bright chestnut colour in the glass and offers up a nutty, slightly chocolaty malt aroma. The same nut and chocolate notes lead the way in the bittersweet, smooth taste, with hops – as perhaps Brahms might have annotated – playing second fiddle. The brewery has been in operation since 1873 – some time after Brahms lived in Düsseldorf – but it's likely that the Liszt-less young composer may have been comforting himself with a stein of something similar during that awkward lunchtime absence.

Births Robert Browning (poet), 1812; Pyotr Ilyich Tchaikovsky (composer), 1840; Eva Peron (actress and politician), 1919

Deaths Antonio Salieri (composer), 1825; Douglas Fairbanks Jr (actor), 2000

Events Passenger liner *Lusitania* sunk by a German U-boat, 1915; Germany signs unconditional surrender in World War II, 1945

Alt

Batemans Victory Ale

Source Batemans Brewery, Wainfleet, Lincolnshire **Strength** 6% **Website** bateman.co.uk

This day, 8 May 1945, will for ever just be known as VE Day. After nearly six years of warfare, Nazi Germany was finally defeated and Victory in Europe was declared. It was understandably a day for enormous celebration, a jubilation that has since mellowed into chequered memories of dread and deprivation and a quiet respect for those that fell during the conflict, as we mark the event more than 60 years on.

Savouring a glass of beer named Victory is clearly an appropriate way to note the occasion, although the beer selected here was actually brewed for quite a different success. It's one of the award-winning ales that flow from the fermenters at Batemans Brewery at Wainfleet, Lincolnshire. The label currently depicts Admiral Nelson and his flagship, also of course called *Victory*, but the beer was created for events rather closer to home than war in Europe or battles on the high seas.

Family split

In the mid-1980s, Batemans entered a period of great instability. To the despair of beer lovers, it looked very much as if the brewery was going to be sold. Shares of the company were split between Chairman George Bateman, who held 40%, and his brother, John, and sister, Helen, who held 40% and 20%, respectively. When John and Helen announced that they wanted to sell the brewery and cash in their shares, George was appalled. As grandson of the original George Bateman, founder of the company in 1874, he had no intention

of relinquishing his birthright. Although he was in a minority on the board, the brewery would stay open if he had anything to do with it.

Support was forthcoming from employees, customers and CAMRA members but money needed to be found in order to keep the company independent. After many fraught months, George was able to raise the funds to buy out his siblings. So Batemans remained in brewing, with George and his immediate family – wife Pat, son Stuart and daughter Jaclyn – at the helm, and to celebrate their success in a battle for independence, the Batemans created Victory Ale in October 1987.

At 6% ABV, Victory is an ale to respect. Brewed from Maris Otter pale malt, some crystal malt and Fuggle and Golding hops, it's a firmly British ale, full-bodied and malty, with plenty of hop character and the Batemans trademark banana-like yeastiness. It's available only in cask form in the autumn these days, but you can always find it in bottle.

Sadly, both George and Pat Bateman are no longer with us, but they have left many happy memories for beer lovers, not least when, in 1987, this beer allowed George to figuratively raise two fingers in triumphant salute, just like Winston Churchill 40 years earlier. The battle may have been on a completely different scale, of course, but this was also a victory worth winning.

Births Harry S Truman (US President), 1884; David Attenborough (naturalist and broadcaster), 1926; Peter Benchley (writer), 1940

Deaths Gustave Flaubert (writer), 1880; Paul Gauguin (artist), 1903; Dirk Bogarde (actor), 1999

Events Coca-Cola first goes on sale, 1886; the DUP's Ian Paisley and Sinn Féin's Martin McGuinness become First Minister and Deputy First Minister, respectively, of Northern Ireland, 2007

Strong Ale

Christoffel Bier

Source Brouwerij St Christoffel, Roermond **Strength** 6% **Website** christoffelbier.nl

St Christopher is the patron saint of travellers: in pub parlance you could say he was the original Traveller's Friend. His day is celebrated on two days. In the Western world, it falls on 25 July; in Greece, from where it seems his name originates, it falls on 9 May.

Officially, however, Christopher doesn't actually have a feast day. His name was removed from the Catholic calendar in 1969 because it was impossible to verify his story. There are, in fact, several versions of the life of this man, which place his birth in different parts of the world, and even allocate him different names. The most common is that he was a third-century Roman giant by the name of Reprobus, who made his contribution to the world by ferrying people, on his shoulders, across a fast-flowing river. One day a small child asked for a crossing. Reprobus obliged but found that the child was almost unbearably heavy and struggled to make it to the other bank. It was then revealed to him that the child was Jesus Christ and the burden was so great because all the sins of the world were being carried with Him. Christ then baptized Reprobus and his name was changed to Christopher, from the Greek for 'Christ bearer'. He was later martyred for his faith.

Aloof pilsner

Despite the Vatican's downgrading of his status, Christopher remains sanctified and is the patron saint not only of travellers but also of numerous towns and cities, one of which is the former coal-mining town of Roermond in The Netherlands, home of the Christoffel brewery.

Christoffel was founded in 1986 and its main beer is an unfiltered, unpasteurized pilsner. It has never called it that, however, preferring the names Christoffel Bier or Christoffel Blond to keep the product nicely aloof from the often debased term pilsner. You can understand why when you taste it. The beer comes in swing-stoppered bottles – short and stubby for the small version, and tall and jug-like for the larger, 2-litre package – and, because it is unfiltered, pours with a slightly hazy golden hue. The beer is produced in accordance with Germany's Reinheitsgebot beer purity law, which means the only ingredients are water, yeast, malt and, as is perfectly obvious from this particular beer, hops. It is fermented in open vessels before being transferred to more conventional lagering tanks.

The aroma has a musty yeast note and lots of sticky pale malt, along with spicy tropical fruits and a hit of hops. In the taste, those hops really take over. There's some light citrus fruit but the real flavour is tangy and resin-like, with a smooth, malty sweetness in the background. The dry finish goes on for ever, loaded with increasingly bitter hops. Thoroughly enjoyable, it's definitely a beer worth travelling for.

Births John Brown (abolitionist), 1800; Howard Carter (archaeologist), 1873; Glenda Jackson (actress and politician), 1936

Deaths Tenzing Norgay (mountaineer), 1985; Alice Faye (actress), 1998

Events Columbus sets sail from Cádiz on his final voyage, 1502; impeachment hearings begin against President Richard Nixon, 1974

Pilsner

Westerham British Bulldog

Source Westerham Brewing Co. Ltd, Edenbridge, Kent **Strength** 4.3% **Website** westerhambrewery.co.uk

Once described as 'the greatest living Englishman', and posthumously voted number one Great Briton in a BBC Television poll, Winston Churchill needs little introduction. Without Churchill, it is widely acknowledged, we may never have emerged from World War II victorious. His leadership during the conflict proved decisive: his military skills were influential, his diplomacy effective, his rhetoric inspirational to the common man. But it could so easily have not turned out that way. While Nazi Germany was re-arming itself in the 1930s and Fascism was building a bridgehead on the continent, Churchill was a sad and isolated figure, an outcast from Government. Disagreements with his Conservative colleagues, not least over their inability to see the looming threat across the water, meant that a man who had served in the past in high Cabinet positions was just a voice in the wilderness. When war was finally declared in 1939, Churchill could be ignored no longer. He was restored to the leadership of the Admiralty but, with Prime Minister Neville Chamberlain's position untenable, it was only a matter of months before he secured the top job, which, at one point, had seemed well beyond his grasp.

Brewing revival

One brewery that celebrates Churchill's life and influence is Westerham in Kent. The brewery is housed in a barn on a National Trust farm, very close to Sir Winston's country retreat, Chartwell. It has revived brewing in an area where the last producer – Black Eagle – closed in 1965, strangely the same year that Churchill died. All the Westerham pump clips and labels have an appropriately 1940s aura. Its beers may be 21st century, but homage is certainly being paid to the war years in terms of typefaces and styling. The concept emerges most clearly with a beer called British Bulldog, which is available in both cask- and bottle-conditioned formats.

British Bulldog is a robust best bitter at 4.3% ABV. It's made from Maris Otter pale malt and crystal malt, and hopped with Northdowns and Goldings. It pours a rich copper colour, with wafts of smoky hop and juicy fruit lifting from the glass. Brewery founder Robert Wicks talks a lot about supporting local hop growers, and his fine words are backed up in practice, as proved by Bulldog's taste, with citrus fruit and a firm bitterness leading the way. Barley notes linger in the full finish, but the hops have their say to the bitter end. It's a good, solid British ale that more than does justice to Churchill's timely promotion to the Premiership – a fine tribute to the original British Bulldog.

Births Fred Astaire (dancer and actor), 1899; Donovan Leitch (pop musician), 1946; Maureen Lipman (actress), 1946; Bono (rock musician), 1960

Deaths Leonhard Fuchs (botanist), 1566; Thomas 'Stonewall' Jackson (US Confederate leader), 1863; Joan Crawford (actress), 1977

Events London's National Gallery opens, 1824; first Mother's Day held, 1908

Best Bitter

Brasserie Nationale Hausbéier

Source Bofferding, Bascharage **Strength** 5.2% **Website** bofferding.lu

When, for so many years, you've been traded as a pawn in a protracted game of real-life chess, to be granted independence finally over your own affairs is certainly a reason to celebrate. You can therefore imagine the excitement of being a Luxembourg citizen on 11 May 1867.

The area now known as Luxembourg was first populated by Celtic tribes and then occupied during Roman times, when its strategic position between Paris and the Roman outpost at Trier was recognized. By the 14th century, Luxembourg had developed into a Duchy, with land that stretched right up to Limburg in what is today The Netherlands. But invaders came and went, and the land became subject to the rule of the Spanish, the Burgundians, the Dutch and the Austrians before, in the aftermath of the Napoleon empire, it settled down as a Grand Duchy linked to the Netherlands. The independence it was gradually asserting was noted in the first Treaty of London in 1839, but it took another 28 years for autonomy to be granted permanently, as part of a second Treaty of London in 1867. Apart from yet more invasion during World Wars I and II, Luxembourg has enjoyed self-government now for more than 140 years.

Brewing minnow

The country today is but a fraction of its former size, with a large tract of its land seceded to the newly created Belgian state in 1830. It, unfortunately, also lies in the shadow of its northern neighbour in beer terms, with Germany to the east also helping to cast the little country as a brewing minnow. But look carefully, as I've done in choosing today's tipple, and you can find a few gems among the locally produced beers.

To share the Luxembourger's appreciation of independence, I suggest you consider a brewery that goes by the dual name of Brasserie Nationale or Bofferding, the latter being the name under which it was founded in 1842. One of the most popular beers in its repertoire is called simply Hausbéier, or 'house beer', which surely underplays its quality.

This is a golden pilsner-type beer presented, Grolsch-style, in a swing-stoppered bottle. The aroma is softly fruity and floral, with delicate, sticky pale malt, light lemon notes and some herbal hops. The taste falls on the bitter side of bittersweet and is reasonably hoppy but with a buttery malt character throughout and a pleasant peppery spiciness. The finish is a touch on the thick side but is nicely bitter and hoppy. It lasts well, adding considerably more depth to a brew that can conveniently add another flag to your collection of 'done that' beer countries.

Births Irving Berlin (composer), 1888; Salvador Dalí (artist), 1904; John Parrott (snooker player), 1964

Deaths William Pitt, the Elder (politician), 1778; Bob Marley (reggae musician), 1981; Douglas Adams (writer), 2001

Events Siam officially changes its name to Thailand, 1949; the Academy of Motion Picture Arts and Sciences, which awards the annual Oscars, is founded, 1927

Pilsner

Draught Bass

Source InBev **Strength** 4.4% **Website** inbev.com

Edward Lear, who was born this day in 1812, enjoys a reputation for being the king of nonsense verse. Unfortunately, I doubt if even he would claim that the rhymes he penned involving beer are among his best. Take this one as an example:

> There was an Old Man of
>   Columbia,
> Who was thirsty, and called out
>   for some beer,
> But they brought it quite hot,
> In a small copper pot,
> Which disgusted that Man of
>   Columbia.

Or perhaps this one:

> There was an old person of
>   Sheen,
> Whose expression was calm
>   and serene;
> He sate in the water, and drank
>   bottled porter,
> That placid old person of Sheen.

Could do better, you might say.

Lear was born in London, the 20th child of a stockbroker's gargantuan family. He worked first as a zoological artist and, indeed, tried in later life to make his name as a serious painter, travelling around Europe and further afield, and eventually passing away in San Remo, Italy, in 1888. The nonsense verse came about through a close relationship with the Earl of Derby, for whose grandchildren Lear put together these little bits of frivolity. *The Owl and the Pussycat* and *The Jumblies* are his two masterpieces.

They far outshine all the beery rhymes he devised, but one of these at least has some interest as a sign of the times in which Lear lived:

> It is a virtue in ingenuous youth
> To leave off lying and return to
>   truth,
> For well it's known that all
>   religious morals
> Are caused by Bass's Ale and
>   South Atlantic Corals.

The South Atlantic Corals reference remains a mystery but the fact that Bass features in a poem such as this reveals just how big a brand it was during the 19th century. Sadly, Bass no longer exists as a company. Its brewing interests were sold in 2000 to Interbrew (now InBev). The crying shame of the company's last days was the neglect shown to Draught Bass, the cask-conditioned diamond in the brewery's crown. 'The Rolls-Royce of cask ales', as it was at times described, was a satisfying, complex beer that kept you interested to the last drop – malty, fruity and hoppy. Sadly, Bass put all its eggs into the Carling lager basket and starved Draught Bass of promotion. The country's best-selling real ale was allowed to dwindle away to almost nothing, with poor quality control in pubs also impacting on its reputation.

As it no longer owns any breweries in Bass's home town of Burton-upon-Trent, InBev has switched production of Draught Bass to Marston's. A fine brewery, Marston's can certainly revive this classic ale, given the right

encouragement and resources from the top. Seek out a pint today – if you can find one – and see how well it's faring. Given its illustrious heritage, one can only hope that the days of nonsense are over and that it's once again a religiously moral experience.

Births Florence Nightingale (nursing reformer), 1820; Katharine Hepburn (actress), 1907; Tony Hancock (comedian), 1924

Deaths John Masefield (poet), 1967; John Smith (politician), 1994; Perry Como (singer), 2001

Events General Strike ends after nine days, 1926; coronation of King George VI, 1937; Mick Jagger marries Bianca de Macias, 1971

Best Bitter

Hofbräu Maibock

Source Staatliches Hofbräuhaus München, Munich **Strength** 7.2% **Website** hofbraeu-muenchen.de

The entry for 21 March focuses on Bavaria's Starkbierzeit, or strong beer season. At that time of year, Munich goes crazy for doppelbocks, bottom-fermenting, well-lagered beers such as Paulaner's Salvator that are so full, rich and warming that they stave off the last of the winter's chills. Two months later, the same German drinkers, with a true zest for living, bring out another fine beer to lead them on through the year.

The Bavarians consider Maytime to offer the last vestiges of spring. To see out the season and to welcome the impending arrival of warmer weather, they break open a celebratory beer that they call maibock. Maibock is generally lighter in colour than doppelbock, and has a notably malty profile. Brewers retaining this style include Ayinger and Paulaner, with many US craft brewers also joining in the fun. The maibock highlighted for today, however, comes from the Hofbräu Brewery, which claims to have created the style.

Saviour of the city

Hofbräu is a business with history. Its origins lie in the year 1589, when Wilhelm V, Duke of Bavaria, decided to build his own brewery. Under Wilhelm's successor, Maximilian I, the brewery transferred from the royal palace to the centre of Munich and began to specialize in weissbiers, over which the Bavarian court held a profitable monopoly. It then diversified by emulating the strong beers of the northern trading city of Einbeck. From the name Einbeck comes the term 'bock'. The first maibock was produced in 1614 and, it is said, proved to be the saviour of the city. Eighteen years later, when Swedish troops invaded Munich, they were bought off with 344 pails of Hofbräu Maibock.

The brewery later opened its own in-house tavern – the famous Hofbräuhaus – but brewing then moved to a new site, leaving the pub to stand alone. The Hofbräuhaus was badly damaged by World War II bombs, but has been grandly restored and is now a major tourist attraction. The brewery itself moved to its fourth site, a state-of-the-art complex on the outskirts of the city in 1988. The business is presently owned by the Bavarian state.

Hofbräu Maibock – not surprisingly, given the above history – is described by the brewery as Munich's oldest bock beer. Its orange-golden glow perhaps anticipates the sunny days that are just around the corner, while its big foaming head murmurs the last echo of winter snows. Once you penetrate the deep froth, the aroma is richly malty, full of creamy toffee notes. In the mouth, the beer is full bodied and, again, very malty. There's yet more creamy toffee here, along with some nut and raisin fruitiness, plus a gentle hop balance. The taste is fairly sweet, as you'd expect, but crisply drinkable, considering the hefty 7.2% ABV. Malt lingers long into the aftertaste, which is otherwise dry, peppery and with a little hop bite that slowly develops into pleasant bitterness. The only downside is that the beer is available only on draught for this one month of the year, but that's really what makes it so special. As a consolation, you can still find it in bottle at other times.

Births Joe Brown (singer), 1941; Zoë Wanamaker (actress), 1949; Stevie Wonder (soul musician), 1950

Deaths John Nash (architect), 1835; Gary Cooper (actor), 1961; Gene Sarazen (golfer), 1999

Events The first convict ships leave Britain for a penal colony in Australia, 1787; the Royal Flying Corps, forerunner of the Royal Air Force, formed, 1912

Maibock

141

St Austell Proper Job

Source St Austell Brewery, St Austell, Cornwall **Strength** 5.5% **Website** staustellbrewery.co.uk

The commemoration for 14 May takes us back to the era of the British Empire and, more particularly, to the turbulent days of the Indian Mutiny of 1857. It had been one hundred years since the British had taken control of India, and resentment at the foreign presence was growing. Rejecting evangelical attempts to convert them to Christianity, locals began to assert their religious independence. An unfortunate dispute over the greasing of gun cartridges with pork or beef fat led to unrest among the Hindu and Muslim natives serving in the British army. Gradually the mood developed: the insensitive British needed to be ejected from the subcontinent. This sentiment was also fostered by the Indian aristocracy, who had seen their pre-eminence eroded by the invaders.

One of the main flashpoints came in the northern city of Lucknow. There, the British residency came under prolonged attack. Luckily, the base had been well fortified but the result was a siege that lasted four months. Central to the defence of the base was the 32nd (Cornwall) Regiment. These men fought manfully to keep out the Indians, and held on until help finally arrived. Their contribution was recognized in a message sent to them by Queen Victoria on 14 May 1858. It accorded the regiment the new status of Light Infantry, 'in consideration of the enduring gallantry displayed in the defence of Lucknow' – recognition, if you like, of the 'proper job' the Cornish soldiers had done in

protecting British interests. Four members of the regiment were each awarded a Victoria Cross.

Proper heroes

The heroics of the soldiers are also recognized in a relatively new beer from St Austell, Cornwall's oldest brewery. Proper Job is, appropriately, an India pale ale, with a full alcoholic strength and plenty of hops, as befits a beer of this style. The difference lies in the selection of hops. Inspired by American beers that St Austell head brewer Roger Ryman experienced while on secondment at Bridgeport Brewery in the US, this is an IPA with a funky, transatlantic twist. Golden in colour, thanks to the use of only pale Maris Otter malt, the beer is laced with US Cascade, Chinook and Willamette hops, making it quenching yet delicate, and bouncing with the zest of orange peel, lime and grapefruit. It is sold both in cask form and as a bottle-conditioned beer.

It has been reported that the doughty Cornish defenders always refused to take down the Union flag at sunset each day, as would have been the military norm, thus demonstrating to the surrounding enemy that their little piece of Britain would never surrender. The flag and its loyal soldiers are now depicted on the label of the beer.

Births Eric Morecambe (comedian), 1926; George Lucas (film director), 1944; Cate Blanchett (actress), 1969

Deaths Henry Rider Haggard (writer), 1925; Rita Hayworth (actress), 1987; Frank Sinatra (actor and singer), 1998

Events English colony established at Jamestown, Virginia, 1607; founding of the children's charity NSPCC, 1889; Eastern European Communist states sign the Warsaw Pact, 1955

IPA

Springhead The Leveller

Source Springhead Fine Ales, Sutton-on-Trent, Nottinghamshire **Strength** 4.8% **Website** springhead.co.uk

For anyone not well versed in English history, Springhead Brewery's The Leveller seems a strange name for a beer. But put into the context of other beers produced by the same Nottinghamshire brewery – Oliver's Army, Puritans Porter and Roundheads' Gold, for instance – the name begins to make more sense. The origin, it becomes clear, lies in the English Civil War.

The Levellers were soldiers fighting on the side of Parliament. However, they stood out from their comrades in arms by their forward-thinking views on equality, justice, personal liberty, democracy and religion. At the forefront of the movement was John Lilburne, a lieutentant-colonel in Cromwell's army. Lilburne had a reputation as an agitator, publishing pamphlets on injustice in society that brought him many supporters but earned him enemies among the Establishment. In 1649, he produced a document called Agreement of the People, which proposed a written constitution for the country, based on a set of rights and freedoms that ranged from wider suffrage and equality before the law to proportionate taxation and freedom from religious persecution.

The document became the unofficial manifesto of the Levellers, many of them stowing a copy under their hatbands. As the first English Civil War drew to a close, however, they found that suspicion and resentment was building towards their cause, and it all erupted in May 1649 in a quiet Oxfordshire town.

Liberal legacy

Although it seemed that their duty had been done in England, some Roundhead soldiers now faced a new commission – to fight in Ireland. If they refused, they stood to lose the pay they had already earned in the service of Parliament. Levellers of various regiments took a stand and combined in a show of strength. Marching through the Thames Valley, they boarded for the night of 14 May in Burford, Gloucestershire, but their sleep was soon disturbed. Cromwell's officers seized the opportunity to take the rebels unawares. Many fled, but more than 300 were rounded up and imprisoned in Burford church. Two days later, three of the 'ringleaders' were hauled before a firing squad and executed in front of their captured colleagues. It spelled the end for the Leveller movement, which never had the same influence again, but it was certainly not the end for the principles established by this short-lived collection of radical thinkers. A century and a half later, many of the liberal values they espoused proved central to the new constitutions of France and the US, and the legacy of the Levellers has been remembered each year in Burford since 1975 with a rally and concert that has drawn speakers such as Tony Benn and Billy Bragg.

Springhead's The Leveller is, like Roaring Meg (see 31 July), the result of brewery founder Alan Gill's fascination with the Civil War era. Alan is no longer involved at Springhead but he based this beer stylistically on the strong, dark and malty beers called dubbels, produced by Trappist and abbey breweries in Belgium and Holland. It is brewed with pale malt, amber malt and roasted malt, and spiced with Northdown hops. Not surprisingly, smoky, dark malt flavours dominate the aroma and palate, with roasted grain pushing through to linger long in the bitter finish.

A strange name, perhaps, but a fine beer all the same.

Births James Mason (actor), 1909; Mike Oldfield (musician), 1953; Andy Murray (tennis player), 1987

Deaths Edmund Kean (actor), 1833; Eric Porter (actor), 1995

Events Attempted assassination of US Presidential Election hopeful George Wallace, 1972; Soviet troops begin withdrawal from Afghanistan after eight years of occupation, 1988

Dubbel

Thwaites Lancaster Bomber

Source Thwaites Brewery, Blackburn, Lancashire **Strength** 4.4% **Website** thwaitesbeers.co.uk

Peace dividend

Although eight aircraft were damaged or lost during the raid, the reputation of the Avro Lancaster Bomber was cemented during the operation, and the plane is now celebrated more peacefully in the name of a popular premium bitter from Daniel Thwaites in Blackburn.

Lancaster Bomber actually began life in Lancaster itself, when it was created by Mitchell's Brewery. Sadly, Mitchell's decided it preferred running pubs to running a brewery, and ceased production in 1999. Thwaites spotted the potential for Lancaster Bomber and brought it into its own portfolio. The beer is available pasteurized in bottles but is better fresh in cask form. Thanks to its malty and lightly toffeeish profile, it is very quaffable, especially with a pronounced resin-like hop note for balance. The beer has been promoted in recent years by Lancashire and England cricketing star Andrew Flintoff.

Operation Chastise, one of the most celebrated military missions during World War II, began on the evening of 16 May 1943. At RAF Scampton in Lincolnshire, Wing Commander Guy Gibson readied his brave crewmen for an audacious raid over German airspace. The aim: to severely damage the enemy's industrial infrastructure. Taking to the skies, 617 Squadron, soon to become known as 'The Dam Busters', headed for Germany's powerhouse, the Ruhr Valley, in their sights massive dams on the Rivers Möhne, Sorpe and Eder.

As we now know from the 1954 Richard Todd film *The Dam Busters*, the mission proved tense and at first indecisive. Armed with Barnes Wallis's novel 'bouncing bomb', the squadron's modified Lancaster Bomber aircraft needed to fly low over the water so that their payloads, when released, would skim across the surface and explode close to the dam walls. It took several runs before the dam on the Möhne was breached. The Eder dam was also fractured, and both reservoirs poured torrents of water down their respective valleys, flooding factories and homes. The Sorpe dam, however, remained intact. Nevertheless, the crews returned home heroes. Gibson was awarded a Victoria Cross, and the whole operation was a great fillip for the Allied war effort.

In strategic terms, however, the raids did not achieve all they had hoped to. Germany's industry was soon back in action and, of course, as with every wartime offensive, the casualties were horrific. It is estimated that more than 500 civilians died that night, as well as around 750 Ukrainian prisoners of war being held close to the Eder dam. Fifty-three of Gibson's men also lost their lives.

Births Henry Fonda (actor), 1905; Roy Hudd (actor and comedian), 1936; Olga Korbut (gymnast), 1955

Deaths Eliot Ness (US federal agent), 1957; Sammy Davis Jr (singer), 1990; Jim Henson (puppeteer), 1990

Events Joan of Arc canonized, 1920; first Academy Award ceremony, 1929; Women's Voluntary Service (WVS) founded, 1938

Best Bitter

ABOVE: ILLUSTRATION OF A LANCASTER BOMBER FROM 617 SQUADRON BOMBING THE MÖHNE DAM

Fine Ale Club
Against the Grain

Source The Fine Ale Club, Colchester, Essex
Strength 4.5%
Website ale4home.co.uk

St Peter's G-Free

Source St Peter's Brewery Co. Ltd, Bungay, Suffolk
Strength 4.2%
Website stpetersbrewery.co.uk

This part of May has been designated Coeliac Awareness Week by Coeliac UK, the charity that aims to support sufferers from coeliac disease and to raise its profile among the general public.

The success of the organization means that most people are now conscious of the fact that coeliac sufferers have an intolerance to gluten. But on a more detailed level, coeliac disease is not an allergy. In Coeliac UK's own words: 'It is an auto-immune disease, which means that the body produces antibodies that attack its own tissues. For people with coeliac disease, this attack is triggered by gluten.' Among the problems the ailment causes are bloating, diarrhoea, nausea, anaemia, tiredness, headaches, depression and joint pain. Consequently, sufferers can't eat or drink anything that introduces gluten to the diet, and most commonly that is food based on cereals such as wheat, rye or barley. A big problem, then, if you like a glass of beer.

Thankfully, there are a number of gluten-free beers now available, although, from personal tasting experience, some are significantly more pleasurable than others. The problem for brewers is matching the flavours of barley malt. While the sweetness is not difficult, that malty silkiness and character are often elusive.

Double solution

There are two beers in particular that I have discovered come closest to true beer flavours. The first is called Against the Grain. This is a 4.5%, bottle-conditioned ale produced for the mail-order company the Fine Ale Club and is hardly distinguishable from the full malty. Hops, of course, can be given free rein as far as coeliac sufferers are concerned, and this beer takes full advantage of that freedom, packing the aroma and taste with peppery, spicy, grapefruit-accented resins that come from Brewer's Gold hops. The fermentable cereal used is maize, and gluten content is certified at 5.1 ppm (parts per million), which is well under the 'safe' level (for many sufferers) of 200ppm. The beer was brewed for the Fine Ale Club by Oulton Brewery when I tasted it. More recent batches have come from Wold Top Brewery, with a slight tweaking of the recipe.

Likely to be more widely available is a beer launched in August 2007 by St Peter's Brewery. It's called G-Free. Again, there's a citrus hoppiness, but also this time the taste is characterized by a sugariness that you'd otherwise associate with boiled sweets. It comes from the use of sorghum as the cereal, with Challenger hops added for bitterness and Amarillo hops for that citrus aroma and taste. Initial sweetness after swallowing soon gives way to a dry, bitter and nicely hoppy finish.

Sufferers from coeliac disease are never going to be able to enjoy the full range of beer flavours that the rest of us take for granted, but at least now there are some more-than-drinkable alternatives on the market for them.

Births Edward Jenner (medical pioneer), 1749; Dennis Potter (playwright), 1935; Sugar Ray Leonard (boxer), 1956

Deaths Sandro Botticelli (artist), 1510; Frank Gorshin (actor), 2005

Events Relief of Mafeking during the Boer War, 1900; Jacques Chirac sworn in as President of France, 1995

Bitter & Golden Ale

145

Schneider Weisse

Source G. Schneider & Sohn, Kelheim **Strength** 5.4% **Website** schneider-weisse.de

This is a story about one brewery and one style of beer. It begins on this day in 1817 with the birth of the brewery founder, Georg Schneider, who, early in his life, worked as a brewer to the King of Bavaria. It was an unusual position, one that provided Georg with an important insight into the production of that most idiosyncratic of beer styles, the weissbier, or wheat beer.

For a couple of centuries, the royal court had held a monopoly on the production of such beers. It seems an odd prerogative to retain but, either the royals liked to keep refined, crisp, quenching beers made from wheat to themselves and away from the hoi-polloi, for whom darker beers made out of barley were good enough, or, as seems more likely, they made a lot of money out of selling their wheat beer to the public. Whatever the reason, by the 19th century, the Bavarian royals had finally decided to relinquish their special right – probably because wheat beer sales were in decline – and a licence to brew wheat beer was extended to commoners.

Commoner's licence

It is claimed that Georg Schneider held the first commoner's licence. Having been released from his job at the royal brewhouse, he turned to what he knew best and began producing his own wheat beer in a brewery he purchased in Munich in 1872. In 1927, his company acquired a second brewhouse, this time in the town of Kelheim, on the banks of the River Danube in northern Bavaria. This is now the brewery's single home, the Munich brewhouse having been destroyed by Allied bombs during World War II.

Schneider didn't just hold a licence to brew wheat beer, he made the style his speciality, and it's the only type of beer that's brewed at Schneider to this day.

The business is now in the hands of Georg Schneider VI, the founder's great-great-grandson. It produces numerous interpretations of the Bavarian wheat beer style, including a blonde version, a crystal-clear version, an alcohol-free version and the magnificent strong version called Aventinus, which is featured elsewhere in this book. However, the flagship beer is Schneider Weisse, the beer that the original Georg created back in 1872. It's darker and a touch sourer than many of today's Bavarian wheat beers, but aficionados of the style will tell you that this is the classic example of what a wheat beer should be like. The aroma is alive with a mix of fruit and bakers' spices. Banana, pear, marzipan and bubblegum all feature in the nose before a somewhat more restrained taste of gentle spices with the tartness of green apple and lemon. Cloves mark the dry, bready finish. Presented chilled and appropriately cloudy, in its own tall, bulbous glass, with a deep foamy head, this is one of the world's great beer drinking experiences.

Happy birthday Georg – and thanks for the legacy.

Births Margot Fonteyn (ballerina), 1919; Pope John Paul II, 1920; Nobby Stiles (footballer), 1942

Deaths Gustav Mahler (composer), 1911; Elizabeth Montgomery (actress), 1995

Events Volcano Mount St Helens erupts in Washington State, US, 1980; Helen Sharman becomes the first Briton in space, 1991

Wheat Beer

Hall & Woodhouse Stinger

Source Hall & Woodhouse, Blandford St Mary, Dorset **Strength** 4.5% **Website** hall-woodhouse.co.uk

It's sounds like a joke but the people behind Be Nice to Nettles Week are deadly serious. The dark green, prolific weed that clusters along our fences and riverbanks has a bad reputation, largely due to its irritating sting. Everyone wincingly remembers throbbing bumps across arms and legs after an unfortunate childhood encounter with a clump. But the nettle is a force for good, says CONE, a division of Blythe Council in North-East England that was set up to protect and cherish local nature. The movement has had success way beyond its Northumberland heartland, and Be Nice to Nettles Week – held annually in mid-May – is now finding support across the UK.

So what is it about the nettle that we should treasure? Well, firstly, it provides a perfect habitat for wildlife. Certain types of butterfly would struggle to survive without the nettle to feed their caterpillars, and ladybirds, the scourge of the aphid, also make the nettle their home. Additionally, the nettle has beneficial properties when used in compost and it has more direct uses for man, too. In centuries past, it was harvested for food, with the nutritious shoots providing a good alternative to spinach when used in soup, and the leaves making a herbal tea. It was also turned into fibre and spun into cloth, and its health-improving qualities have been noted as well, with gout and arthritis just two ailments thought to benefit from nettle medication.

Tongue tingler

Nettles were also used in brewing in the past, in the days before hops arrived in the UK. Along with other greenery, brewers added them to their boil to provide a sappy counterbalance to the sweetness of the malt. In 2005, Hall & Woodhouse revived this tradition when it launched Stinger, an organic premium ale conceived with the help of Dorset TV chef Hugh Fearnley-Whittingstall, whose River Cottage logo adorns every label. The organic nettles included are hand-picked (let's hope the gloves are thick) at River Cottage itself. They join the Admiral and Golding hops in the copper and they have a rather weird impact on the taste.

The pale and crystal malts at the heart of the beer provide a bright golden colour and an appealing, soft sweetness. The hops then contribute melon, lemon and possibly even gooseberry notes, plus a light bitterness, leaving the nettles to add their own influence, most notably in the form of a grassy aroma and a sappy, tongue-tingling taste. It really does feel as though your mouth is being ever-so-gently stung.

The beer is available in cask form from May to July, and in filtered bottles throughout the year. Today's a perfect day to seek it out and put past prejudices about nettles behind you.

Births Nellie Melba (opera singer), 1861; Malcolm X (civil rights campaigner), 1925; Victoria Wood (comedian and writer), 1953

Deaths William Gladstone (Prime Minister), 1898; John Betjeman (Poet Laureate), 1984; Freddie Garrity (pop musician), 2006

Events Execution of Anne Boleyn, 1536; Valéry Giscard d'Estaing becomes President of France, 1974

Spiced Ale

Oakham JHB

Source Oakham Ales, Peterborough, Cambridgeshire **Strength** 3.8% **Website** oakhamales.com

While other celebrated poets have reached for opium and other fashionable drugs to assuage their tortured minds, John Clare was a man of the people. His distraction lay in beer and he couldn't get enough of it.

Clare was born in Helpstone, Northamptonshire, in 1793, and he was forever in thrall to his deeply rural background. Never one to aspire to lofty language, Clare used the vernacular he grew up with and in verse told tales of country customs and simple pleasures. Sadly, his life was ravaged by mental instability and he spent many years in asylums where, it is said, he wrote poetry in exchange for beer. He certainly enjoyed a good pint, as evidenced by his poem *The Toper's Rant*, which celebrates a hearty session. Of course, beer often prevented Clare from being as assiduous as he should have been with his work, and one publisher, it is said, insisted he stay dry for a year in order to fulfil his contract.

Rather confusingly when it comes to discussing 'the Northamptonshire Poet', Clare's home village of Helpston is now part of Cambridgeshire, although it very nearly falls into Lincolnshire and Rutland as well. The nearest big town is Peterborough, which is home to the highly successful Oakham Brewery.

Initial success

Being of firmly rustic mindset, Clare may have been disturbed at how this young brewery has grown and developed, but he would surely have approved of its ales. The business started out in Rutland in 1993 and moved to Peterborough to find its fortune. It has achieved this thanks to an excellent range of interesting beers, of which the mainstay is a pale golden beer called JHB. The letters stand for Jeffrey Hudson Bitter, after an Oakham man who became a favourite courtier of King Charles I and his wife, Queen Henrietta Maria. What amused the Queen about Hudson was that he was a dwarf, introducing himself first by leaping out of a large pie. Hudson proved himself to be a daring companion, fighting with the Royalists in the Civil War but finally blotting his copybook with the Queen by shooting a rival dead in a duel.

The beer named after him has also proved to be a favourite, winning CAMRA's Champion Beer of Britain contest in 2001 among numerous awards. With its American-style, proud citrus flavours, it bombards the tastebuds from the first sip but there's plenty of malt for support, sweetness for balance and a dryness in the finish. At 3.8% on draught, and 4.2% in the bottle, it may have been a little underpowered for our friend John Clare, who, it is said, quaffed strong nut brown ale by the quart, but there's no doubt he would have been impressed by the quality.

Births Honoré de Balzac, 1799; James Stewart (actor), 1908; Cher (singer and actress), 1946

Deaths Christopher Columbus (navigator), 1506; Barbara Hepworth (sculptor), 1975; Jon Pertwee (actor), 1996

Events Explorer Vasco da Gama arrives in India, 1498; Tony Blair is first Prime Minister to become a father while in office for more than 150 years, 2000

Golden Ale

Princetown Jail Ale

Source Princetown Breweries Ltd, Princetown, Devon **Strength** 4.8% **Website** princetownbreweries.co.uk

Prison reform remains a lively issue. There are those who say that prisoners have life too easy on the inside and that prison is no longer a deterrent against future re-offending. Others claim that prisoners should be treated humanely as part of the process of rehabilitating them for return to society. This debate will, no doubt, continue – it's already been raging for nearly 200 years, thanks largely to the intervention of Elizabeth Fry, who was born today in 1780.

Fry was born Elizabeth Gurney in Norwich. Her family were Quakers, and she grew up with an interest in social welfare. Her married name reveals a connection to a famous chocolate manufacturer. It was a visit to Newgate Prison in 1813 that sparked her interest in improving prison standards. Fry was appalled at the conditions in which hundreds of women and children were living, some of whom had never even been tried for any crime. Crammed into small cells, where they cooked and fended for themselves, the inmates lived a life of extreme misery. It was some time before Fry was able to commit herself fully to their cause – she had 11 children of her own to care for – but when she did, she did so with a passion. She set up schools for the imprisoned children and encouraged the women to acquire new skills. She published a report into the prison situation, spoke to a House of Commons committee and even received audiences with Queen Victoria. Her actions made life more bearable for thousands of inmates.

Austere prison

There is no beer that directly celebrates Fry's life or her legacy, but there is a very fine beer that shares a connection with one of Britain's most famous prisons. Built in 1809, Dartmoor Prison at Princetown, Devon, was first used to house French and American prisoners of war. It became a criminal jail in 1850 and suffered a reputation for being a particularly austere place in which to serve time. As Fry would have hoped, much has been done in recent years to change this image.

Just along the road from the prison, a brewery was set up in 1994, although, as far as is known, the inmates have no access to its produce! Princetown Breweries' star performer over the years has been Jail Ale, which in its bottled form has won several notable awards. It pours an enticing dark golden colour and offers clean, bittersweet, fruity, floral flavours, thanks to the generous seasoning of Challenger and Progress hops.

I doubt if Princetown ever had Elizabeth Fry in mind when it devised the beer, but the names of those hops are certainly appropriate when it comes to remembering her life and her influence.

Births Fats Waller (jazz musician), 1904; Raymond Burr (actor), 1917; Leo Sayer (singer), 1948

Deaths Rajiv Gandhi (politician), 1991; Dame Barbara Cartland (writer), 2000; Sir John Gielgud (actor), 2000

Events Amelia Earhart becomes first woman to fly the Atlantic solo, 1932; boxer Cassius Clay (later Muhammad Ali) defeats Britain's Henry Cooper in the world heavyweight championship, 1966

Golden Ale

149

Samuel Smith Oatmeal Stout

Source Samuel Smith's Brewery, Tadcaster, North Yorkshire **Strength** 5% **Website** None

It was with the Battle of St Albans, on this day in 1455, that one of Britain's ugliest periods of history began, when the forces of King Henry VI came face to face with the army of his rival, Richard, Duke of York, in a vicious struggle for the English crown.

The series of battles that followed over the next 30 years has become known as the Wars of the Roses. They centred on the legitimacy of the king's right to the throne and Richard's counterclaim, and they were inflamed by Henry's bouts of mental illness that saw Richard taking over as regent and wreaking vengeance on his enemies. It was only when Henry Tudor, Henry's successor as head of the House of Lancaster, defeated Richard's son, King Richard III, at Bosworth Field in 1485 that the row was finally settled, the country uniting behind the new King Henry VII and his Tudor monarchy.

The Wars of the Roses take their name from the emblems of both sides, even though it seems that these emblems were not in place at the time. The symbol of the House of Lancaster was the red rose, while the House of York favoured the white rose. When it comes to selecting a beer that fits nicely into today's theme, it is tempting to opt for a beer from the Red Rose Brewery, near Blackburn, but, as Lancaster was the ultimate winner in this grotesque civil war, it seems more generous to offer the beer choice to the side of York. There isn't a White Rose Brewery at the time of writing, but there is a very well-known brewery that uses the white rose as its own emblem.

Old for new

Samuel Smith is based in Tadcaster, North Yorkshire, with its home in the town's 'old brewery', vacated by John Smith's when it decamped to a new brewery next door in 1884. Sam was John's nephew, and his company remains a private family business, with the emphasis firmly on 'private'. The brewery has little time for the media or extravagant sales campaigns, preferring the quality of its beers to do the talking for it, and the quality certainly does sing the brewery's praises, with one fine cask beer, Old Brewery Bitter, and an excellent range of bottled beers on offer.

The beer chosen for today is Oatmeal Stout, a deep ruby ale with a truly complex flavour that is filled with dark malt character and is both vinous and woody. There's a smack of liquorice, too, and an underpinning iron-like bite. It's a full-bodied, smooth and handsome beer with which to celebrate the fact that Henry's final victory brought a welcome degree of peace to very troubled times.

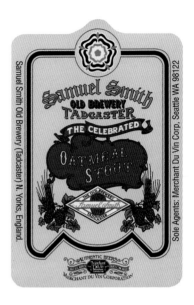

Births Richard Wagner (composer), 1813; Arthur Conan Doyle (writer), 1859; Laurence Olivier (actor), 1907; George Best (footballer), 1946

Deaths Victor Hugo (writer), 1885; Cecil Day-Lewis (poet), 1972; Margaret Rutherford (actress), 1972

Events Ceylon becomes Sri Lanka, 1972; Microsoft releases Windows 3.0 operating system, 1990

Stout

Van Steenberge Piraat

Source Brewery Van Steenberge, Ertvelde **Strength** 10.5% **Website** vansteenberge.com

The best-known beer from the family-run Van Steenberge brewery in Ertvelde, Belgium, is called Piraat, or pirate. It's an appropriate choice of drink for 23 May, as this was the day that one of the most notorious pirates finally met his maker.

William Kidd was born in Scotland, around 1645, but moved to America with his family while still a young boy. Much of his seafaring career appears to have been respectable, and perhaps it was only through circumstance that he lost his way. Kidd applied to the Royal Navy for a commission but was turned down. Instead, he was granted a licence as a privateer, a role that allowed him to intercept richly cargoed ships belonging to the enemies of Britain – i.e. France and pirates – with the proceeds of the haul shared with the Crown.

Unfortunately, to pursue this risky venture, Kidd was forced to recruit a gang of men from New York whose reliability and honesty were far from certain. Out on the ocean, he faced an attempt at mutiny, when the plunderous crew realized that he planned to ignore vessels belonging to friendly countries, even though they had bounty to spare. To keep his rebellious men on side, it seems, Kidd fell into the ways of a common pirate, and was denounced as such by the authorities. He attempted to bribe his way back into favour in the American colonies, but was captured and transported back to London for trial. He was sent to the gallows on this day in 1701, vainly protesting his innocence and promising, if released, to retrieve a secret haul of treasure he had hidden and give it to the government. The treasure has never been found.

Golden treasure

Van Steenberge's Piraat follows in the long tradition of strong beers that were brewed to be taken out to sea, according to the company's website. They claim it has 'a high nutritional value, keeps well for years and strengthens the body and morale of pirates and other seafarers', giving them 'the courage to face the rough weather… and the many other dangers, such as the boarding of another ship'. The beer actually comes in two forms, a stronger version at 10.5% and the more common 9%, which belongs to the school of potent golden ales of which Duvel is the market leader. Most commonly, it is found in bottle-conditioned form, although draught versions can be encountered in its native Belgium.

I would imagine that pirates would opt for the higher-strength version, which certainly doesn't pull any punches. To achieve such a percentage of alcohol without adding to the body of the beer, rice and sugar join pilsner malt among the fermentables. The dual hopping is courtesy of Saaz from the Czech Republic, and Hallertau from Germany. The perfumed aroma is filled with cutlass-sharp, zesty orange notes, which pop up again in the crisp taste, along with light herbal notes. The finish is drying, bittersweet, perfumed, hoppy and as warming as a daily ration of grog.

Births Joan Collins (actress), 1933; Marvin Hagler (boxer), 1954; Graeme Hick (cricketer), 1966

Deaths Girolamo Savonarola (religious reformer), 1498; Henrik Ibsen (writer), 1906; Bonnie Parker and Clyde Barrow (outlaws), 1934

Events King Henry VIII's marriage to Catherine of Aragon annulled, 1533; political leaders welcome the 'yes' vote in a referendum on the Good Friday Agreement for peace in Northern Ireland, 1998

Golden Ale

ABOVE: CONTEMPORARY DRAWING OF WILLIAM 'CAPTAIN' KIDD

Marston's Old Empire

Source Marston's, Burton-upon-Trent **Strength** 5.7% **Website** marstonsdontcompromise.co.uk

Colonialism is no longer something to be proud of. While some observers insist that the British Empire was a source for good – an educational and civilizing influence on less advanced quarters of the world – the overwhelming view today is that the idea of marching into a foreign country and dictating how it should be run is quite abhorrent. That's why it sounds odd that a celebration called Empire Day should have run for so long.

Instituted by the Earl of Meath in 1904 and staged on 24 May each year (the date of the late Queen Victoria's birthday), Empire Day ran for more than half a century and was the catalyst for schoolchildren to take pride in the achievements of Britain and its colonies, which accounted for around a quarter of the world's population at one time. Amid much waving of the Union flag, patriotic songs were sung, and stories of great heroism from the founding of the Empire were related as inspiration. Inevitably, in the post-war years, as political views changed and the Empire faded into the Commonwealth – a seemingly more equal foundation of countries that once used to be under British control – Empire Day changed, too. In 1958, it was renamed British Commonwealth Day (later simply Commonwealth Day) and then temporarily moved to 10 June, the official birthday of Queen Elizabeth II. Since 1977, however, Commonwealth Day has been celebrated on the second Monday in March, although it is much lower key than its earlier

incarnation, the high spot being a multi-faith service at Westminster Abbey attended by The Queen.

For those who still yearn for the good old days when Britannia ruled the waves and most countries in school atlases were coloured red, there is at least a beer that conjures up the spirit of those times. Old Empire was created by Marston's in 2003, in a bid to develop an authentic India pale ale, such as those that once rolled out of Marston's home town of Burton-upon-Trent and were shipped around the world to give the colonies a taste of British beer. Beer writer Roger Protz was taken on board as a consultant and he counselled, 'More hops!' on more than one occasion as the beer progressed from trial to trial. When it was finally released, Old Empire was immediately popular, with many drinkers delighted that such a large brewery was keen to add a strong, hoppy beer to its portfolio.

The beer is brewed from Optic pale malt only, hence its attractive golden glow. The hops in the copper are the British traditional favourites, Fuggle and Golding, with a spritzier twist added late through a dose of American Cascades. Sweet malt leads in the nose, which has a floral/citrus hoppiness and, typically for Marston's, a touch of lingering sulphur. Juicy malt in the taste is offset by tangy, floral hop resins that also bring a dash of lime, and the finish is dry and hoppy, resonant and lingering, with limes still in evidence. Overall, it's wonderfully balanced and very quaffable for its considerable strength.

Births Queen Victoria, 1819; Bob Dylan (singer-songwriter), 1941; Jim Broadbent (actor), 1949

Deaths Nicolaus Copernicus (astronomer), 1543; 'Duke' Ellington (jazz musician), 1974; Harold Wilson (Prime Minister), 1995

Events First Eurovision Song Contest staged, 1956; Birmingham's 'Spaghetti Junction' motorway interchange opened, 1972

IPA

Cropton Endeavour

Source Cropton Brewery, Pickering, North Yorkshire **Strength** 3.6% **Website** croptonbrewery.com

It was on 25 May 1768 that James Cook received his commission as commander of *HM Bark Endeavour*, the ship in which he was to make his first journey to the southern hemisphere. As is generally known, it proved to be a hugely significant voyage of discovery, charting lands in far-off oceans previously unknown to European seafarers.

Cook was born near Middlesbrough in 1728 and had found his sea legs as a youth in the merchant navy, before joining the Royal Navy in 1755. His early military expeditions took him to North America, where he successfully mapped the Canadian coastline and caught the attention of his superiors. Lieutenant Cook – as he was at the time – was then placed in charge of *Endeavour*, which was to become his most famous vessel.

Heading south

The *Endeavour* was a converted coal ship that was built in the Yorkshire port of Whitby in 1764. Only about 30m (100ft) long, it was home to a crew of just under one hundred when it set sail, so life aboard was rather cramped. Its mission was to head to Tahiti to observe a transit of Venus across the sun, and thereafter to explore the mysterious Great Southern Continent. This proved not to exist and, instead, after fulfilling his Tahiti task, Cook journeyed to New Zealand, charting its shoreline. He then explored the eastern and northern coasts of Australia. The voyage lasted three years and was but the first of three such expeditions that Cook was to undertake, although it was the only one aboard the *Endeavour*.

The original *Endeavour* has been lost at sea, but a smaller copy is now harboured at Whitby, plying the local coastline in summer for the benefit of tourists and offering an insight into maritime life in Cook's day. In celebration of the arrival of the new *Endeavour* in 2002, Cropton Brewery, which is based behind a pub called The New Inn on the Yorkshire Moors, brewed a popular quaffing ale of the same name. It's a simple recipe, ending up at just 3.6% ABV and based on pale malt seasoned with Challenger and Golding hops, which provide a refreshing bitter orange flavour. The beer is also available in bottle-conditioned form, with the ship depicted on the label, and is just one of a large series of bottled beers from this successful little pub brewery.

Births Richard Dimbleby (broadcaster), 1913; Miles Davis (jazz musician), 1926; Jonny Wilkinson (rugby player), 1979

Deaths Samuel Pepys (diarist), 1703; Gustav Holst (composer), 1934; Desmond Dekker (reggae musician), 2005

Events The original *Star Wars* film released, 1977; the 'Race against Time' charity run takes place globally, 1986

Bitter

ABOVE: *LANDING OF CAPTAIN COOK AT BOTANY BAY* BY E PHILLIPS FOX

Wickwar BOB

Source Wickwar Brewing Co., Wickwar, Gloucestershire **Strength** 4% **Website** wickwarbrewing.co.uk

The greetings card industry – now there's a licence to print money. There are 365, sometimes 366, birthdays to be celebrated in a year, as well as Christmas and numerous other religious festivals to milk, plus the likes of Mother's Day, Father's Day, Valentine's Day, engagements, weddings, births, christenings, retirements, 'get well soons', 'good lucks' and the more sombre 'sympathies'. In recent times, we've seen the promotion of Grandparents' Day, even Nurses' Day. Now it seems the industry is being encouraged to push ahead and make every day a celebration, and for the flimsiest of excuses.

Some of the ideas being bandied about for e-cards and, who knows, possibly even printed ones, are bizarre to say the least. If you happen to be reading this on 2 August, do make the most of it, as this is Tennis Ball Day. 31 March is Bunsen Burner Day, of course, and 18 February is Thumb Appreciation Day, which will tie in well with 29 June, Remote Control Day. Then there are some saccharine-sweet days clearly designed to lead us into a better world filled with the milk of human kindness. They include National Hugging Day on 21 January, Cheer Up Day on 11 July and Meet a Friend for Lunch Day on 9 October. Tavern Day on 4 March sounds good, but 23 November, Paranoia Day, has me worried.

Hello Bob

When it comes to 26 May, we find ourselves flying off on another tangent. Don't ask how or why, but today is Bob Day. I think you're meant to send a card to everyone you know whose name is Bob, but that's not made particularly obvious. And why Bob and not Jack, Tim or Derek? On the other hand, having a Bob Day is rather convenient, as we also have a beer called Bob, and there isn't a beer called Jack, Tim or Derek. So, if you know someone named Bob, send them a bottle of Bob beer. You can get it from Wickwar Brewery, just north of Bristol, and it's a fine bottle-conditioned ale of 4% ABV. They brew it with a little crystal malt and some black malt to darken the colour, and Fuggle and Challenger hops to provide a fruity bitterness, all in all creating a very suppable pint. The name really should be spelled in capital letters, as it's an acronym for the original full name of Brand Oak Bitter – derived from the name of the cottage where one of the brewery's founders was living when the beer was created in 1990.

Bob is also sold at times under the name of Dog's Hair, but that doesn't tie in so well. Dog's Hair Day is not in the calendar – yet.

Births Al Jolson (singer), 1886; John Wayne (actor), 1907; Peter Cushing (actor), 1913

Deaths Augustine, first Archbishop of Canterbury, 604; Samuel Pepys (diarist), 1703

Events American Civil War ends, 1865; Manchester United win the UEFA Champions League final with two late goals, 1999

Bitter

Thornbridge Saint Petersburg

Source Thornbridge Brewery, Ashford in the Water, Derbyshire   **Strength** 7.7%
Website thornbridgebrewery.co.uk

St Petersburg, the former capital of Russia, is a city of many names. When it was founded in 1703, as a fortress town to keep out the enemy Swedes, it was given the title of St Petersburg by Tsar Peter the Great. In 1914, with the outbreak of World War I, the city abandoned its German-sounding name in favour of its Russian equivalent, Petrograd, and ten years later it became Leningrad, after the late leader of the Russian Revolution. The city reverted to its original name in 1991, following the collapse of the Soviet Union.

St Petersburg is also known as 'the Venice of the North', thanks to its position on a series of islands at the mouth of the River Neva, on the edge of the Baltic Sea. As well as being a strategic site, it's a cultural centre, thanks to Peter the Great and his successors indulging their westernizing instincts and assembling a fine collection of Baroque buildings and now-priceless artworks. However, the city has known some terrible times. It has not only had to deal with the harshest of winters, but has been on the front line of German assaults on Russia. In World War II, it endured a brutal siege that lasted 900 days, and saw up to 800,000 citizens die of cold and starvation. Happily, St Petersburg is bouncing back as industry and tourism pick up in the aftermath of the Cold War.

Linen heritage

One little pleasure that the people of St Petersburg were able to enjoy in times past (at least, the wealthiest of them) was rich, warming, strong and heady stout imported from Britain. The history of the trade in what became known as imperial Russian stout is covered on other pages in this book, but now the city of St Petersburg has been nominally associated with this type of beer, thanks to a small brewery in a stately home in Derbyshire.

Thornbridge Hall Brewery, deep in the glorious Peak District, opened in 2004. The house had been acquired by one John Morewood in 1790, using money he had made from selling linen to St Petersburg, hence the interest in creating this particular beer. Saint Petersburg pours thick and ruby-coloured. Fifty-five days of maturation are allowed before bottling, and then a second fermentation is encouraged in the bottle. There's plenty of alcohol – 7.7% – and hops galore. The end result is a beer with a smooth, malty taste, notably bitter roasted grain, a tang of liquorice and, surprisingly, lots of juicy tropical fruit character from Galena and Bramling Cross hops.

It's a typically nourishing and warming drink with which to raise a glass to the brave and hardy people of the Russian city with many names.

Births 'Wild Bill' Hickok (frontiersman), 1837; Vincent Price (actor), 1911; Christopher Lee (actor), 1922; Henry Kissinger (politician), 1923

Deaths John Calvin (religious reformer), 1564; Niccolò Paganini (composer), 1840

Events San Francisco's Golden Gate Bridge opens, 1937; German battleship *Bismarck* sunk, 1941

Imperial Stout

Adnams Broadside

Source Adnams plc, Southwold, Suffolk **Strength** 4.7% **Website** adnams.co.uk

During the reign of King Charles II, maritime rivalry with the Netherlands culminated in three major conflicts. The third of these kicked off with the Battle of Sole Bay on this day in 1672.

Disputes with the Dutch over fishing waters and trade routes had escalated in the 17th century and came to a head in 1652–4, with the first Anglo-Dutch War. Peace was short-lived, however, and the second Anglo-Dutch War followed in 1664–7. As part of these hostilities, the English acquired New Amsterdam – now New York – from their enemy. The third conflict eventually ran from today in 1672 until 1674 and, ironically, saw the English doing battle with Prince William of Orange, the man who was to become their king only a decade later.

On this occasion, the English were, for once, allied with the French, and, at the outset, had assembled their joint fleet in the harbour at Sole Bay, off the town of Southwold, Suffolk, in preparation for a blockade of Dutch ports. The Dutch were ahead of the game, however, and sailed to attack the English and French at anchor. A brutal battle followed, with heavy losses on both sides. When the bloody day was over, neither side could claim victory, although the Dutch had at least succeeded in thwarting their enemies' plans.

Tradition & innovation

Sole Bay today is a somewhat calmer stretch of water. Southwold behind it is equally relaxed, an unspoilt, traditional English town that seems to be trapped in a time bubble. Its heart and soul is Adnams Brewery, a company that manages to look determinedly to the future while preserving the best of the past. There has been considerable expansion in recent years, but always with an eye on maintaining the special character of Southwold. For instance, in 2006, the company opened a new ecologically-friendly distribution centre, just outside town.

Adnams beers also marry tradition with innovation. One of the brewery's most famous ales is Broadside, which is now rapidly becoming a national brand in the guest beer market. Its name, of course, derives from those dramatic events taking place on this day in 1672 – the date appears on the pump clip – and particularly the naval practice of turning a ship sideways in order to aim its cannons at the opposition.

Broadside, the beer, packs plenty of ammunition. At 4.7% ABV, it has a full and rewarding taste of juicy, sweet, nutty malt and tangy, fruity Golding, First Gold and Fuggle hops, glowing an appealing dark amber colour in the glass. In bottle, the beer (filtered) is even stronger, pounding out at 6.3%. Either way it's a satisfying, comforting beer, worthy of marking this momentous day in Southwold's history.

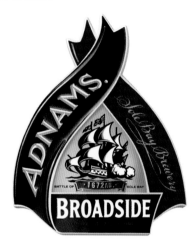

Births William Pitt, the Younger (politician), 1759; Ian Fleming (writer), 1908; Thora Hird (actress), 1911

Deaths Duke of Windsor (formerly King Edward VIII), 1972; Eric Morecambe (comedian), 1984

Events Radio's *Goon Show* first broadcast (as *Crazy People*), 1951; Sir Francis Chichester completes his single-handed voyage around the world, 1967

Strong Ale

O'Hanlon's Royal Oak

Source O'Hanlons Brewing Company Ltd, Whimple, Devon **Strength** 5% **Website** ohanlons.co.uk

It's a well-known tale that, following defeat at the Battle of Worcester in 1651, King Charles II fled to Boscobel House, Shropshire, and hid himself in an oak tree to avoid capture by Roundhead soldiers. From there, he made his way to France, returning to reclaim the throne in 1660. To mark the restoration of the monarchy, and his return to power, he then declared 29 May to be a holiday. This was not the date of his lucky escape, but actually his birthday, but thus Royal Oak Day, or Oak Apple Day, as it is more commonly known these days, was born.

Although this holiday was officially abolished in 1859, the occasion is still celebrated all over the UK, with traditional customs. At Great Wishford in Wiltshire, for instance, residents collect an oak bough from the woods and display it in the local church. At the Royal Hospital in Chelsea, founded by Charles II, the famous Pensioners are reviewed by a member of the royal family and celebrate with beer and plum pudding.

Pubs & beer

The story has given rise to hundreds of pubs called The Royal Oak, and also a famous beer, first brewed by Eldridge Pope in Dorset in 1896. At one time, the beer was advertised in pubs with a certificate citing the heritage of the beer but, sadly, Eldridge Pope didn't even take that seriously itself and gave up brewing in 1996, after nearly 160 years. Royal Oak was brewed under licence at the same site for a while but the Dorchester brewery finally closed its gates in 2003 and the 5%, big, fruity ale seemed to be lost for ever. Happily, rights to the beer were then acquired by Phoenix Imports, a company that specializes in importing beers into the US. They also acquired Thomas Hardy's Ale (see 2 June), and asked O'Hanlon's Brewery in Devon to re-create both brews. It may be that O'Hanlon's Royal Oak is not quite as sweet as the old version, or perhaps the memory is playing tricks to this effect, but the new beer nevertheless has been warmly welcomed back.

Pale and crystal malts are joined in the mash tun by a little torrefied wheat, and then the malty extract is spiced up by Challenger, Northdown and Golding hops in the copper. The beer is sold in cask form and also in bottle-conditioned format, which is a version that Eldridge Pope itself never produced. It's robust, malty and hoppy all at once, with some pleasant apricot fruitiness. Even committed republicans should be happy to raise a glass of this historic ale today.

Births Bob Hope (comedian), 1903; John F Kennedy (US President), 1917; Noel Gallagher (rock musician), 1967

Deaths Humphry Davy (scientist), 1829; William S Gilbert (librettist), 1911; Jeff Buckley (singer-songwriter), 1997

Events America's Hoover Dam on the Colorado river completed, 1935; Edmund Hillary and Tenzing Norgay climb Mount Everest, 1953

Strong Ale

157

Okells Elixir

Source Okells Ltd, Douglas **Strength** 6.1% **Website** okells.co.uk

For motorcyclists, it's the big one, a crazy fortnight covering the last week of May and the first week of June, when fans of two-wheeled racing crowd onto the Isle of Man for the annual Tourist Trophy (TT) races. These famous races are not staged on a track. Instead, the course takes in just over 59km (37 miles) of the island's public roads. Consequently, it's one of the world's toughest circuits and has proved to be a magnet for many greats from the world of motor sport, including John Surtees, Mike Hailwood, Carl Fogarty and the late, great Joey Dunlop, who claimed the TT title no fewer than 26 times.

The event began early in the life of the motorcycle. Bike pioneers were keen to show off their speed and skill but found that they weren't allowed to do so on the public roads of Britain. Happily, in 1904, the authorities on the Isle of Man decreed that part of the island's road network could be sectioned off, and so the race-hungry bikers decamped there. The first event took place in May 1907, following the St John's Course, an almost-26km (16-mile) circuit in the west of the island. In later years, the longer and more rigorous Mountain Course became the main circuit, and this remains a challenge for the best riders to this day.

One hundred up

The centenary of the first races was celebrated enthusiastically in 2007 and, as part of the occasion, local brewer Okells released a special ale. It was labelled 1907 but was, in fact, a re-badged beer first produced in January that year when it was called Elixir. 1907 is no longer in production, but Elixir is, both as a cask-conditioned winter ale and as a year-round bottled beer, and that's the obvious selection for today.

Elixir is a strong beer that, despite its full body, manages to offer all the flavours of a spritzy golden ale. Only Maris Otter pale malt features in the mash tun, but the hop regime is far more complicated. Fuggle and First Gold go into the copper early, joined later in the boil by Willamette from the US, and Saaz from the Czech Republic. The final hopping stage is in the whirlpool, while the boiled wort is being filtered ready for fermentation. Here, more American hops – Cascade and Amarillo – add the finishing touch. Notable citrus aromas, with little bursts of juicy orange, dominate the nose as a result, with clean and unobtrusive malt support. The taste is robust, crisp and hoppy, with a lemon-citrus lightness and, again, sweet, malty support.

This is a gently warming beer that happily doesn't drift off into the floral, tropical notes associated with many beers of this strength, and finishes dry, bitter and lipsmackingly hoppy.

Births Howard Hawks (film director), 1896; Benny Goodman (bandleader), 1909; Harry Enfield (comedian), 1961

Deaths Joan of Arc (French patriot), 1431; Voltaire (philosopher), 1778; Ted Drake (footballer), 1995

Events King Henry VIII marries Jane Seymour, 1536; first Indianapolis 500 motor race, 1911

Golden Ale

Warwickshire Lady Godiva

Source The Warwickshire Beer Co., Cubbington, Warwickshire   **Strength** 4.2%
Website warwickshirebeer.co.uk

Today this book suggests that you raise a glass to an event that almost certainly never took place. But it's a good tale anyway.

Back in the 11th century, beautiful Godiva was the wife of Leofric, Earl of Mercia. Being rather closer to the people than her husband, Godiva was concerned at the harsh taxes ordinary citizens were expected to pay, and raised the issue with her other half. His response, allegedly, was that he would lower taxes if she rode through the streets of Coventry naked. Surprisingly, she agreed and, wearing nothing but her birthday suit, Godiva climbed aboard her horse and proceeded through the city.

A later version of the tale adds a new character. Part of the deal, it is said, was that people had to remain indoors, with their windows shuttered, while the naked lady rode past. However, one mischievous lad named Tom had the audacity to bore a hole in his shutters through which he could see the entire show, so to speak. Thus the original Peeping Tom was born.

Drunk on duty

It's highly unlikely that any of the above happened. There is more evidence, however, that on 31 May 1678, the people of Coventry latched onto the legend by instigating a lively Godiva procession. The event became very popular, especially in the 19th century, when Godiva's route took in many of the city's pubs, leading to accusations that the lovely lady was often drunk on duty. The procession still takes place today and has led to a full-blown Godiva festival, a major occasion for free music of all kinds and other family entertainment, staged every summer.

One of the local breweries also plays its part in keeping the myth alive. Warwickshire Beer Company can be found housed in a former bakery in the village of Cubbington, near Leamington Spa. It's been in operation since 1998, although an earlier Warwickshire Brewery ran for a couple of years in the mid-1990s, producing some beers with the same name. These include Kingmaker, after Richard Neville, 15th-century Earl of Warwick, who played an important role in the Wars of the Roses. Alongside Kingmaker in the range is Lady Godiva, a 4.2% dark golden ale, available in both cask- and bottle-conditioned versions. It is brewed from Maris Otter pale malt with amber malt and some torrefied wheat. Cascade and Styrian Golding hops provide the citrus accent that characterizes the beer, which is otherwise mostly bitter with a dry finish. The fair maiden, naked but for the long, blonde hair that preserves her modesty, features on the colourful label.

Births Clint Eastwood (actor and film director), 1930; John Prescott (politician), 1938; Terry Waite (humanitarian), 1939

Deaths Tintoretto (artist), 1594; Franz Josef Haydn (composer), 1809; Joseph Grimaldi (clown), 1837

Events Launch of the liner *Titanic*, 1911; South Africa becomes a republic, 1961

Golden Ale

ABOVE: MODERN-DAY LADY GODIVA RIDING NAKED THROUGH COVENTRY

159

Spire Sgt Pepper Stout

Source Spire Brewery, Chesterfield, Derbyshire **Strength** 5.5% **Website** spirebrewery.co.uk

Arts critic Kenneth Tynan described it at the time as 'a decisive moment in the history of Western civilization'. That's a bit over the top, perhaps, but when the Beatles' eagerly awaited pop masterpiece *Sgt Pepper's Lonely Hearts Club Band* went on sale on this day in 1967, its impact was immediate and stunning.

It's hard to believe that what plays today like a pastiche of music hall and circus tunes in places, and in others as a swooning psychedelic trip, should be seen as revolutionary, but the flurry of excitement that surrounded the album's arrival has never been equalled in that sphere of entertainment.

The album marks a watershed in the group's career. The Beatles had given up touring a year before and with it consigned the days of hand holding and yeah, yeah, yeah to history. Their previous album, *Revolver*, had already turned them in a new direction and, if insider reports were anything to go by, it was clear that something unusual and exciting was going on at Abbey Road Studios.

In hindsight, the album is a mixed bag. Who would get excited about *With a Little Help from My Friends* or *When I'm 64* today, chirpy little songs though they are? And there are plenty of better tunes in the band's repertoire than *Lovely Rita* and *Good Morning, Good Morning*. On the other hand, the mournfully melodic *She's Leaving Home* remains one of Paul McCartney's finest ballads, and *Lucy in the Sky with Diamonds* and *A Day in the Life* – not to forget George Harrison's sitar-sodden *Within You Without You* – were clearly musical style leaders at a time when mind-expanding drugs were all the rage. And that's really the point about *Sgt Pepper*. It broke new ground, yes. It was musically adventurous and inspiring, true. But its real value lies perhaps in that it captures in music that strange, dreamy year of 1967.

Getting bitter

Relaxants of various kinds seem to imbue the work of the world's most influential rock band, and *Sgt Pepper* in particular, but beer, strangely, is always given the cold shoulder. The band were never big lovers of ale or lager and it shows in their works. Not one song they wrote and recorded together even mentions the drink. *There's no Lucy in the Sky with Double Diamond* or even a *Getting Bitter*. Thankfully, the brewing industry is no harbourer of cheap grudges, as one Derbyshire micro is happy to prove.

Spire Brewery was founded in Chesterfield in 2006. The town's famously twisted church spire is the source of the company name, and features on its pump clips and bottle labels. Then the brewers came up with another twist, this time on the theme of a stout. First, they pumped in enough Maris Otter pale malt to raise the ABV to a chunky 5.5%, with plenty of amber and pale chocolate malt to bring those aromatic roasted grain notes. Then they laced it with Northern Brewer and Fuggle hops before throwing in a distinctive but novel ingredient – freshly ground black pepper. There's no hiding it, either. It shows through in both the aroma and the taste, which is mostly sweet but warming on two fronts – from the strength and from the spice.

Of course, having created something novel, revolutionary and head-turning, they then needed to find a suitable name for the beer. They really didn't have to look far.

Births Marilyn Monroe (actress), 1926; Bob Monkhouse (comedian), 1928; Justine Henin (tennis player), 1982

Deaths Helen Keller (disability campaigner), 1968; Richard Greene (actor), 1985; Hansie Cronje (cricketer), 2002

Events Driving tests become compulsory in the UK, 1935; first Premium Bond draw, 1957; Lester Piggott rides his ninth Derby winner, *Teenoso*, 1983

ABOVE: THE ALBUM COVER FOR THE BEATLES' *SGT PEPPER'S LONELY HEARTS CLUB BAND*

O'Hanlon's Thomas Hardy's Ale

Source O'Hanlons Brewing Company Ltd, Whimple, Devon **Strength** 11.7% **Website** ohanlons.co.uk

The greatness of a man is often not fully recognized until his death. When you see who shows up for the funeral, then you properly understand what he has achieved in life. If Thomas Hardy's funeral was such an indicator, then greatness was certainly his. After the novelist and poet died in 1928, his service was staged at Westminster Abbey, with Rudyard Kipling, JM Barrie, John Galsworthy, AE Housman and George Bernard Shaw among the pallbearers. Now that's what's called peer recognition.

Fittingly for a man who enjoyed his ale, Hardy – who was born on this day in 1840 – was also recognized by the brewing industry. It took 40 years for that to happen, but it was well worth the wait. In 1968, Eldridge Pope, the brewer in Dorchester, a town reinvented by Hardy in his Wessex novels as Casterbridge, released a special commemorative ale inspired by a quotation from Hardy's novel *The Trumpet-Major*. The quote describes a beer that Hardy clearly relished tasting. 'It was of the most beautiful colour that the eye of an artist in beer could desire: full in body, yet brisk as a volcano; piquant, yet without a twang; luminous as an autumn sunset; free from streakiness of taste but, finally, rather heady.'

The brewers came up with a recipe for a beer that would mature in the bottle over several years. At around 12%, Thomas Hardy's Ale was rich and luxurious, pale malts and whole-leaf hops combining to create a drink of real complexity, warming, winey, sweet, fruity and gum-tingling.

Overnight, they created a world classic. Every brew from then on was given a vintage date, so comparative tastings could be carried out to see how the beer developed with age, but over time the number of bottles sold diminished, not helped by the fact that the beer was never promoted, apart from with a rather self-fulfilling slogan that described it as 'the rarest ale in Britain'.

From the ashes

When Eldridge Pope decided to pack in brewing, the beer continued to be brewed under contract at its original home for a while, until in 1999, whatever pride had once inspired the company to celebrate its associations with Hardy evaporated, and the plug was pulled.

Thankfully, Thomas Hardy's Ale is too good a beer to die. A company called Phoenix Imports recognized the market for it in the US and bought up the rights. They offered O'Hanlon's brewery in Devon the chance to re-create the brew and, after extensive research into how the beer used to be made, O'Hanlon's proudly presented Hardy's Ale again to the world in 2003. They've clearly got the beer spot on, as it's now regularly winning major awards.

There's no finer companion when flicking through the pages of a good book on a cold January night, as Hardy would have known very well.

Births Edward Elgar (composer), 1857; Johnny Weissmuller (swimmer and actor), 1904; Charlie Watts (rock musician), 1941

Deaths Giuseppe Garibaldi (revolutionary), 1882; Bruce McLaren (racing driver and car designer), 1970; Rex Harrison (actor), 1990

Events Italy votes to become a republic, 1946; coronation of Queen Elizabeth II, 1953; English soccer clubs banned from European competitions after repeated fan trouble, 1985

Barley Wine

Eggenberg Urbock 23°

Source Brauerei Schloss Eggenberg, Vorchdorf **Strength** 9.6% **Website** schlosseggenberg.at

If there's one family that has shaped the world's perception of Austrian society in the 19th century, it is the Strauss family. Headed by Johann Strauss Sr, a largely self-taught master musician with a flair for the waltz, the clan dominated local culture, and their sweeping music is still widely played as the soundtrack to Viennese travelogues.

Johann Strauss was a class act, and a hard one to follow – not least because he forbade his three sons to emulate him and take up a musical career. Nevertheless, they did just that, with foremost among the trio being Johann Strauss Jr, a composer of such brilliance that he even surpassed the achievements of his father. Strauss Jr is remembered today as it was on 3 June 1899 that he died.

The younger Johann was encouraged by his mother to make the most of what were extraordinary talents. He learned the violin in secret and composed his first waltz at the age of six. Over his 74-year lifespan, Johann scored more than 400 waltzes and other pieces of music. His legacy includes classics such as the operettas *Die Fledermaus* and *The Gypsy Baron*, and, of course, the majestic *Blue Danube* waltz. He deserves a glass raised in his memory, and an excellent option is a special lager from his native country.

Austrian dynasties

Housed in a chateau in an area of lakeland and mountain between Salzburg and Vienna, the Eggenberg brewery has origins dating back to the 14th century and has been in the hands of the Forstinger-Stöhr family since 1803. A highly modern brewhouse extension was added in spring 2000. Although it produces a fine pilsner, Eggenberg has built up a reputation as a brewer of stronger beers, most notably the mighty Christmas beer, Samichlaus (see 6 December). Eggenberg was able to take on Samichlaus because of the experience it had gained producing other potent lagers, and in particular a beer called Urbock 23° that it introduced in the 1970s primarily for the export market.

Don't be put off by the ominous 23° in the beer's name: it's not 23% ABV. That figure relates to the amount of sugars in the brew before fermentation. All the same, you need to take it steady with Urbock, as it does pack a hefty 9.6% alcohol. As ever, though, it's not size that matters but what you do with it. Eggenberg could easily just have created a beer that did the business on a park bench, but instead has fashioned a fine golden brew that is conditioned in the chateau's cellars for nine months before going on sale. Joining pilsner malt in the beer are four strains of hops. Hallertauer Magnum provides most of the bitterness and then Saaz, Tettnanger and an Austrian hop called Muehlviertler combine for aroma. When the beer is young, you can detect floral, resin-like hop notes but as the beer matures – which it does rather well – the hop character becomes less pronounced. Otherwise, the predominant feature is a syrupy, malty,

creamy taste with a light bitterness for balance, that develops sweet, fruity, sherry-like notes over time.

Urbock is a full-bodied, heady beer that glides along the palate like a dancer round a Viennese dance floor, and it proves that there's more than one Austrian dynasty that has helped make this stunning alpine country what it is today.

Births King George V, 1865; Tony Curtis (actor), 1925; Suzi Quatro (rock musician and actress), 1950

Deaths Georges Bizet (composer), 1875; Franz Kafka (writer), 1924; Anthony Quinn (actor), 2001

Events Ed White becomes the first American to walk in space, 1965; ill-fated racehorse *Shergar* wins the Derby, 1981

Okocim Mocne

Source Okocim, Warsaw **Strength** 7% **Website** okocim.com.pl

The scenes were remarkable. It was August 1980, with the Soviet Union seemingly a long way from disintegration, and a group of workers was openly defying the ruling Communists in Poland. Pictures transmitted around the world showed protests at the important Lenin shipyard in Gdansk, and revealed how the Polish authorities were having to give way to some of the workers' demands. Political and economic concessions were wrung from the powers that be, and a month later the workers formalized their activities by forming a new trade union that they called Solidarity. Soon its charismatic leader, electrician Lech Walesa, had become an international figure that the authorities had trouble containing.

The Polish government eventually clamped down on the protests but Solidarity was far from over. Despite being outlawed, it remained a significant force in Polish politics and, eventually, with the economy on the brink of collapse, the rulers had to bring the union to the conference table. As part of its price for collaboration, Solidarity secured (almost) free elections. On 4 June 1989, Poland went to the polls, knowing that the ruling Communists would remain in charge because only one third of the seats was to be freely contested. The vast majority of those free seats, however, were won by Solidarity candidates – a minority landslide, if there could be such a thing. Outmanoeuvred, the writing was on the wall for the Communists and, finally, the country's President

Jaruzelski was forced to invite Solidarity to form a government. Walesa was elected President a year later. The Soviet Union was in decline, and Solidarity had done more than most to make that happen.

The Beer Party

In subsequent years, Solidarity as a political entity broke up. Elements of it remained active in politics but, otherwise, it returned to being a trade union. As democracy cast its sunny rays and drew Poland out from beneath the totalitarian shadows, other political parties broke onto the scene, including the Polska Partia Przyjaciól Piwa. The PPPP, or Polish Beer Lovers' Party, was a movement that began in the pubs of Poland, where heated discussions about the economy and society would rage. The PPPP, surprisingly, secured 16 seats in Parliament in 1991 before it, too, splintered and went back to the bar. But its brief success shows the close affinity the Poles have with beer, something that is underscored by the number of Polish beers that can now be found in other countries, to cater for the influx of immigrant workers.

One of the best Polish imports comes from the Okocim brewery, which was founded in 1845 and is today part of the Carlsberg empire. This full-bodied golden lager is similar to other Polish creations like Tyskie, Lech and Zywiec, but the beer with which to toast the democratization of Poland is Okocim Mocne. Mocne (meaning strong) is also pale in colour but packs even more of a punch. It

seems rather fruity for a lager but is well balanced and has plenty of body. Sweetness is just about tempered by a lemony hop character, and fermentation flavours emerge, with pineapple notes particularly pushing through. The finish is bittersweet and lemony, with hops building.

It's a warming, tasty, potent beer, and one can only imagine how many litres of beer like this were drunk in celebration on the night of 4 June 1989.

Births Christopher Cockerell (inventor), 1910; Bob Champion (jockey), 1948; Angelina Jolie (actress), 1975

Deaths Giacomo Casanova (adventurer), 1798; Ronnie Lane (rock musician), 1997

Events Suffragette Emily Davison fatally trampled by the King's horse in the Derby, 1913; peaceful Tiananmen Square protests violently suppressed by the Chinese government, 1989

Strong Lager

Pitfield Eco Warrior

Source Pitfield Brewery, Great Horkesley, Essex **Strength** 4.5% **Website** pitfieldbeershop.co.uk

With the world only recently waking up to the threat of global warming and other environmental concerns, it's surprising to learn that the first World Environment Day was staged as long ago as 1972. The event is organized by the United Nations and was inaugurated during a related conference in Stockholm.

Therefore, 5 June is the day to make peace with the planet. A different city hosts the main event every year, with Beirut, Barcelona, Algiers and San Francisco some of the venues in recent years. Concerts, rallies, cycle rides, school festivities, clean-up campaigns, recycling initiatives and tree plantings are used to 'give a human face to environmental issues', according to the UN.

The world of beer has made great strides towards sustainability in the last decade. Breweries are now being designed to be energy-efficient, with significantly lower gas, electricity and water usage. Smaller brewers trade heavily on the 'food miles' argument, which explains the folly of having beer made in large factories and then trucking it hundreds of miles to go on sale. Local producers mean less traffic congestion and lower carbon emissions, they say. The same issue relates to the supply of the main raw ingredient, with more and more breweries looking to source barley grown in their own backyards. Some breweries have gone an extra mile and started producing organic beers. There are now several wholly organic breweries in the UK, such as Marble in Manchester, Organic Brewhouse in Cornwall, and Butts in Berkshire, and numerous others that produce at least one organic beer.

From city to country

Pitfield Brewery has been at the forefront of organic beer development. The company was founded in London in the early 1980s, largely to supply a specialist off-licence called The Beer Shop. The shop now only trades online, and the brewery has decamped to rural Essex where its organic credentials sit rather more comfortably than in the exhaust-choked capital.

Not all of Pitfield's beers are organic, but the majority are, including the pioneering Eco Warrior. First brewed in 1998, this premium golden ale has always been a step ahead of the organic game. It quickly found itself a market in health food shops and other green environments, but is more than just a gimmicky brew. Pale malt and Hallertau hops are the main ingredients, conjuring between them a delicate sweetness overlaid by soft orangey-peachy fruit that becomes gradually more bitter. The beer is sold in both cask- and bottle-conditioned versions.

Births Adam Smith (economist), 1723; John Maynard Keynes (economist), 1883

Deaths Lord Horatio Kitchener (soldier), 1916; Mel Tormé (singer), 1999; Ronald Reagan (US President), 2004

Events John Profumo resigns from the Cabinet over a sex scandal, 1963; Six Day War between Israel and Arab states begins, 1967

Golden Ale

Suthwyk Liberation

Source Suthwyk Ales, Fareham, Hampshire **Strength** 4.2% **Website** suthwykales.com

It is 1944 and war has been raging across Europe for nearly five years. Rationing is taking its toll, nights are blacked out and the threat of Nazism lies just across the Channel. Dark days indeed – especially when all the radio has to offer is *The Brains Trust* and Vera Lynn. In desperation, you pick up your gasmask and head for the pub. Having spent your shilling on a gravity-reduced pint of mild, you make for your favourite corner only to find it occupied by a couple of off-duty chaps from the local military base. They seem rather familiar. A few swigs of ale later and recognition comes with a shock. That fellow with the clipped speech looks and sounds strangely like British army hero Field Marshal Montgomery. Even more surprisingly, his American companion bears an uncanny resemblance to General Eisenhower, commander of Allied forces in Europe.

It must have turned a few heads when, in the run up to 6 June 1944 – D-day – these military giants turned up in the local boozer for a leisurely drink, but that's what happened at The Golden Lion in Southwick, a pretty little village just inland from Portsmouth. Plans for the Allied invasion were being finalized at nearby Southwick House and, to ease their mental muscles, the main men repaired to the local pub in the evening. It must have helped because Operation Overlord, as the D-day landings on Normandy beaches were codenamed, proved a great, if extremely bloody, success, paving the way for the routing of the Germans from France.

Farmer's ale

On the hills around Southwick, farmer Martin Bazeley grows barley for brewing. A few years ago, he decided to re-establish the field-to-table concept by having some of his barley malted and turned into his own beer. Suthwyk Ales was founded to market his first brew, a golden ale called Skew Sunshine Ale. A second beer, Bloomfields, followed soon after and, to mark the 60th anniversary of D-day in 2004, a third beer, Liberation, was introduced. All are brewed for Martin by Oakleaf in Gosport, with bottle-conditioned versions supplied by Hepworth & Co. in Horsham.

Liberation is the one that obviously concerns us today. It's a wonderfully balanced golden beer with a fresh hoppy nose that has intriguing hints of blackcurrants, thanks to the highly appropriate Liberty hops that season it. The same fruitiness emerges in the bittersweet, lightly perfumed taste, before a hoppy, drying finish.

Monty and Eisenhower now appear on the bottle's label, examining a bottle of this highly enjoyable ale – a worthy commemorative beer for one of the most significant days in the history of the world.

Births Alexander Pushkin (writer), 1799; Robert Falcon Scott (explorer), 1868; Björn Borg (tennis player), 1956

Deaths Robert Kennedy (politician), 1968; J Paul Getty (industrialist and art collector), 1976; Billy Preston (musician), 2006

Events Oxford's Ashmolean Museum opens, 1683; YMCA founded, 1844; the Beatles make their first recordings at Abbey Road Studios, 1962

Golden Ale

165

Meantime Union

Source The Meantime Brewing Co. Ltd, London **Strength** 4.9% **Website** meantimebrewing.com

Today is the birthday of one of the most significant brewers of the 19th century. Anton Dreher was born on 7 June 1810, the son of Austrian brewer Franz Anton Dreher. Anton took over the family brewery in the Vienna suburb of Schwechat in 1837 and expanded its reach, opening breweries in Bohemia, Budapest and Trieste. But it is Anton's behind-the-scenes work that is the most interesting.

With his colleague Gabriel Sedlmayr from Spaten Brewery in Munich, Dreher helped revolutionize the world of beer production, switching from top-fermenting ale to bottom-fermenting lagers and discovering the value of refrigeration in keeping beer fresh. Dreher and Sedlmayr travelled extensively together, visiting technically advanced breweries in Belgium and Britain and, it appears, stealing a few ideas along the way. When they returned to their home breweries, they put the information they had acquired into action, making beers that were cleaner, crisper and more reliable than before.

Red revival

The work of the two brewers predates the development of the first golden lager, made in Pilsen in 1842, so their products were definitely on the darker side. Whereas Sedlmayr dealt in the sort of beers that would be described as dunkels in Germany today, Dreher offered a more delicate touch by using malt that was not so heavily roasted. His beer was more of an amber-red in colour than deep brown, and it probably tasted nutty and crisp. It was a style of beer that became known as the Vienna red, a style that disappeared from most of the world during the 20th century. Not even in Vienna itself was it easy to find a typical example and perhaps the best place to look – if seemingly the most unlikely – was in Mexico, which had once been part of the Austrian empire and persisted with dark amber lagers such as Dos Equis and Negro Modelo.

Happily, the Vienna style has begun to resurface in recent years. In the US, Samuel Adams Boston Lager and Brooklyn Lager are variations on the theme. In the UK, look no further than a beer called Union, from Meantime Brewing. This 4.9% brew is lagered for 28 days and includes Perle, Spalter and Cascade hops, but it is the malt character that interests most. Constructed from pilsner, pale ale, crystal and Munich malts, it shows through in the aroma, which is nutty with a pleasant floral hop note and just a twist of citrus fruit, and in the taste, which is gently bitter and crispbread-nutty with a good hop presence and restrained floral/citrus flavours. Malt again makes its presence known in the dry, nutty, bitter finish, along with a lingering floral hop note. It is tasty, quaffable and well balanced.

Union was one of the first beers Meantime brewed. The label features a striking but rather odd portrait of a man in a striped jumper. It was provided by Ray Richardson, an artist friend of the brewery's founder, Alastair Hook. Alastair said to him: 'You paint a great picture and I'll brew a great beer.' And that's what they did.

Births Dean Martin (actor and singer), 1917; Tom Jones (singer), 1940; Prince (pop musician), 1958

Deaths Robert the Bruce (Scottish king), 1329; EM Forster (writer), 1970; Dennis Potter (dramatist), 1994

Events Resumption of the BBC's television service after World War II, 1946; celebrations for the Queen's Silver Jubilee get underway in Britain, 1977

Vienna-style Lager

Pilgrim Crusader

Source The Pligrim Brewery, Reigate, Surrey **Strength** 4.9% **Website** pilgrim.co.uk

Bloody disputes between East and West may be the headline story of the 21st century so far but, as historians know only too well, there is nothing actually new in this. The series of violent conflicts known as the Crusades reveals that hostility between faiths dates back a thousand years.

Today's entry, therefore, is certainly no celebration, merely a historical landmark. It notes the day when King Richard I landed with his troops at Acre, a coastal town in modern-day Israel, so launching the latest bid on behalf of the Christian church to free Jerusalem from Muslim control. Richard had decided to fight on the side of the cross ('crusade' is derived from 'croix' – French for cross) to ensure the Christian pilgrims had free and untroubled access to the holy shrines of Jerusalem. The city had been taken by the Muslims in 1076, and recaptured by Christians during the First Crusade. With the Muslims under Saladin now back in control of a city that they also recognized as holy, travellers from the West, it was claimed, were unable to visit the most sacred place in the Christian world.

Pilgrim's Way

After Richard's successful capture of Acre, progress was slowly made towards Jerusalem, but the conditions were hard and the killing was brutal. Ultimately, all the suffering proved to be in vain, as Richard realized he didn't have the strength to take the city and was forced to agree a truce with Saladin, which was designed to allow pilgrims access to the treasures of Christianity. Richard returned home, only to be taken hostage en route by his old rival Leopold of Austria and held prisoner for two years. He arrived back in England in 1194.

The beer that bears the name of Crusader, and respectfully recalls that troubled era, comes from a small brewery in Reigate, Surrey, that was founded by former civil servant David Roberts in 1982. David called his business Pilgrim, after the local Pilgrim's Way long-distance footpath, and his beer list has been largely unchanged for several years. It includes beers with other Pilgrim connections, including Progress, a sweet and malty best bitter, and Talisman, a stronger, darker, maltier ale, named after the religious trinkets worn by travelling Christians.

Crusader was introduced in 1985 and is a dark golden beer with plenty of malt and suggestions of chocolate in the aroma, along with some piney hops. The taste is gently bitter and fruity, with a light, barley sugar base, hints of pear drop, and a drying, soft hop character. The mild bitterness is also a feature of the dry, fruity finish.

Births Robert Schumann (composer), 1810; Frank Lloyd Wright (architect), 1867; Kim Clijsters (tennis player), 1983

Deaths Muhammad (founder of Islam), 632; Edward, the Black Prince, 1376; Thomas Paine (writer), 1809

Events Publication of George Orwell's novel *1984*, 1949

Golden Ale

Goddards Fuggle-Dee-Dum

Source Goddards Brewery, Ryde, Isle of Wight   **Strength** 4.8%
Website goddards-brewery.co.uk

In August 1970, Jimi Hendrix's wailing guitar ripped through the tranquil air of the Isle of Wight, sending seagulls and outraged yacht club members running for cover. It was one of rock's seminal moments. Ten days later, Hendrix was dead and the island's major music event died with him.

Happily, however, the Isle of Wight Festival is back. It was revived in 2002. The event now takes place in Newport in the early half of June each year, and artists that have featured since the renaissance include Paul Weller, Stereophonics, The Who, David Bowie, Razorlight, REM, The Rolling Stones and Keane. Other music events are staged on the island for around two weeks before and after the big weekend, and that gives rock fans plenty of time to become beer buffs as they take in a different kind of Isle of Wight festival, courtesy of the island's three fine breweries.

There's no set-piece beer event, but to have three breweries on such a compact, easily accessible island effectively means that you can effortlessly create your own local beer festival over the course of a few days.

The best known of the island's breweries is Ventnor, housed on the ground floor of the former Burts Brewery on the south coast. Among their main beers are the malty sweet Golden Bitter, the amber bitter, Sunfire, and the light and floral Pistol Knight. They also produce a well-known Oyster Stout that is brewed using real fresh oysters.

It was at Burts that Dave Yates learned his trade. He now has his own Yates' Brewery, tucked alongside The Inn at St Lawrence, near Ventnor. Dave's beers range from the bittersweet, lemony Undercliff Experience, through the coriander-infused and Cascade-hopped Holy Joe to the golden, fruity YSD (Yates Special Draught). Both Ventnor and Yates' also bottle their beers.

Cardboard cutout

The longest-established brewery, however, is Goddards, set up in 1993. Local businessman Anthony Goddard discovered a run-down farm on the outskirts of Ryde and turned it into an impressive home, with the barns refurbished to house not only a brewery, but offices and a large warehouse, from where he operates a wholesale drinks service for the island. The brewery was the latest in a run of ventures that, at one time, also included a vineyard, but this was sold following a financially disastrous time (Anthony was a Lloyd's 'name'), and this period is reflected now in the name of one of Goddards' seasonal brews. Crossword addicts will have fun unravelling the anagram in Duck's Folly.

Goddards' main choices are Special Bitter, a dry, bitter, lemony, quaffing ale, and the award-winning Fuggle-Dee-Dum, which marries English Fuggle hops with their American counterparts from Oregon. Amber in colour, the latter has a nutty, creamy malt aroma, with a herbal hop

note. The taste is clean, nutty and bittersweet, with plenty of tangy hops, while the finish is dry, nutty and hoppy. Fuggle-Dee-Dum is our beer for today, as it's also available in bottled form, allowing you to taste a little of the Wight spirit without ever boarding a ferry. The beer is filtered but not pasteurized, as head brewer Chris Coleman is at pains to stress: 'We won't have anything to do with pasteurization. We tried it once and the beer just tasted of cardboard.' Larger brewers, please note.

Births Cole Porter (composer), 1891; Michael J Fox (actor), 1961; Johnny Depp (actor), 1963

Deaths Nero (Emperor of Rome), 68; Charles Dickens (writer), 1870; Robert Donat (actor), 1958

Events Donald Duck makes his screen debut in *Wise Little Hen*, 1934; Margaret Thatcher wins her second UK general election, 1983

City of Cambridge Boathouse Bitter

Source City of Cambridge Brewery Co. Ltd, Cambridge, Cambridgeshire **Strength** 3.8%
Website cambridge-brewery.co.uk

On 12 March 1829, a challenge was issued by Cambridge University to its academic rival at Oxford to take part in a rowing contest. The idea was the brainchild of two old Harrovian schoolfriends, one named Charles Merivale, who was a student at Cambridge, and the other a nephew of William Wordsworth, named Charles Wordsworth, who was at Oxford. The challenge was accepted and three months later the two crews lined up for the start of the first University Boat Race, with the Dark Blues of Oxford the eventual easy winner.

That first contest was staged at Henley-on-Thames in Oxfordshire. Media reports suggest that 20,000 people turned up to watch, which prompted the town's rowers to stage their own racing programme in subsequent years that evolved into the world-famous Henley Regatta. The university race switched to the Thames at Westminster for its second running seven years later and, in 1845, relocated upstream to a quieter stretch of water, so developing today's 4 mile, 374 yard-course that begins at Putney, arcs around a major bend in the river and ends at Mortlake. The race became an annual event in 1856, with the exception of breaks for the two World Wars, and today attracts about 250,000 spectators in person and a worldwide television audience of many millions. With the Light Blues of Cambridge now just leading overall in the number of victories, it is fair to offer that city the selection of a beer to commemorate the first event.

Varsity selection

City of Cambridge Brewery – now located just north of Cambridge on the road to Ely – trades positively on its varsity connections. Founded in 1997, the brewery includes beers named after the university terms (Trinity, Mich'aelmas) in its portfolio, as well as a very quaffable, session ale called, appropriately, Boathouse Bitter. Despite its modest strength (3.8%), the beer has plenty of depth and character. A little crystal malt helps provide a rich amber hue and a hint of chocolate in the nose and taste, although, like most of City of Cambridge's beers, the dominant flavours are malt and fruit, in this case pineapple notes from the Cascade and First Gold hops. Being bottle conditioned as well as sold in cask, it is a super beer for quaffing on a riverbank on a hot, still June afternoon.

ABOVE: UNIVERSITY BOAT RACE, 2003

Births Prince Philip, Duke of Edinburgh, 1921; Judy Garland (actress), 1922; Robert Maxwell (newspaper baron), 1923

Deaths Spencer Tracy (actor), 1967; Les Dawson (comedian), 1993; Ray Charles (musician), 2004

Events London's Crystal Palace opens, 1854; Lazlo Biró files for a patent for his ballpoint pen, 1943

Bitter

Meantime London Porter

Source The Meantime Brewing Co. Ltd, London   **Strength** 6.5%   **Website** meantimebrewing.com

The reputation of Whitbread among beer drinkers has taken a turn for the worse in the last half century. Bland keg beers and a trail of brewery closures have proved to be the company's lasting sour legacy. It is even more regrettable that, with such an illustrious heritage, the brewery is no longer even involved in the industry. In 2000, Whitbread decided to sell its remaining brewing interests to Interbrew, now called InBev and the world's largest brewer. What the business's founder would have said about it all is probably best not even considered.

Samuel Whitbread was born near Bedford in 1720. Although his family was comfortably off, he was one of several children and faced an uncertain future. But, fortunately, funding was released for him to take an apprenticeship as a brewer in London, and Samuel made the most of it. Hard-working, he soon – together with business partners – founded his own brewery, seeking to capitalize on the expanding beer market and, in particular, on the increase in porter consumption.

Porter revival

This dark brown, malty beer style had been growing in popularity for some time in the capital but what made porter highly profitable for Whitbread was the recognition that it was an ideal beer to produce in bulk. It stored well – indeed, it improved with age – and economies of scale brought big savings throughout the process. Whitbread's business was a success,

which led to the opening of a new, much larger and more efficient brewery in Chiswell Street, where there was the space to house many vast casks of maturing porter. By the time of his death on this day in 1796, Samuel Whitbread was said to have been worth millions, and the name of his company was known throughout the world.

Whitbread stopped brewing porter several decades ago. Indeed, this style of beer had virtually disappeared until it was resurrected by some enterprising microbreweries during the 1980s. Now porter has roared back, with various interpretations available. One of the most authentic being brewed today comes from the Meantime Brewery in Greenwich. Not only is it a true London beer, but it is also the result of archive research into what genuine porters would have tasted like in the days of Samuel Whitbread.

Meantime London Porter comes packaged in large, champagne-like bottles, complete with cork and cradle, but in this case there is substance to match the style. Seven different malts are involved, and old and young beers are blended to make the final product. Sweet, biscuity malt, plain chocolate and coffee feature on the palate, along with a hint of liquorice and a light spiciness. The beer is also bottle conditioned, which gives it an airy lightness to offset the fullness of the malt. It is an exceptional beer, perfect for celebrating the heritage of London brewers such as Samuel Whitbread.

Births Ben Jonson (playwright), 1572; John Constable (artist), 1776; Jacques Cousteau (oceanographer), 1910; Hugh Laurie (actor and comedian), 1959

Deaths John Wayne (actor), 1979; Catherine Cookson (writer), 1998

Events King Henry VIII marries his first wife Catherine of Aragon, 1509; Cook's ship *Endeavour* runs aground on the Great Barrier Reef, 1770

Porter

Chiltern John Hampden's Ale

Source The Chiltern Brewery, Terrick, Buckinghamshire **Strength** 4.8% **Website** chilternbrewery.co.uk

While nowhere near as famous as his cousin Oliver Cromwell, or distant descendant Winston Churchill, John Hampden remains one of the iconic figures of British history. In standing up to the arbitrary government and financial recklessness of King Charles I, it was Hampden who helped assert the power of Parliament and defend the rights of the citizen.

Hampden was born in 1594 into a well-established Buckinghamshire family with close connections to the royal court. After studying at Oxford, he entered Parliament as the Member for Grampound in Cornwall (later becoming MP for Wendover in Buckinghamshire). Concerned at Charles I's flagrant disregard for Parliament over tax-raising matters, Hampden made a stand. He was imprisoned briefly in 1627 for refusing to agree to a forced loan that the King demanded in order to finance his war plans, but his greatest moment came seven years later, when he opposed the so-called 'ship money' that Charles wanted every citizen to pay in order to fund his navy. Previously, the cost of coastal defence was borne only by those who lived by the sea; now Charles wanted everyone to pay. Hampden's refusal to comply led to a trial, during which – on this day in 1637 – ship money was declared legal.

Moral victory

The judges may have sided with the King, but the moral victory proved to be Hampden's. The groundswell of support it precipitated eventually led to Charles recalling Parliament after an absence of 11 years and, ultimately, when that failed to rein in the King's abuse of power, to the onset of the English Civil War. Hampden – by this time known as Pater Patriae ('Father of the People') because of his confrontations with Charles – fought during the hostilities but his contribution was shortlived. In 1643, he was wounded in a battle at Chalgrove, Oxfordshire, and died shortly afterwards at Thame. 'He was a gallant man, an honest man, an able man,' wrote his friend Arthur Goodwin.

A more recent tribute has been paid by Chiltern Brewery, run by the enthusiastically patriotic Jenkinson family near Aylesbury. To celebrate the 15th anniversary of the founding of the brewery in 1980, they created a special beer that they named in Hampden's honour. Miles Hobart-Hampden, Earl of Buckinghamshire, mashed in the first brew and signed the portrait of his noble ancestor that adorns the label.

John Hampden's Ale is a single-varietal hop beer, using just the great British bittering hop Fuggle married with Maris Otter pale malt. It's a wholesome beer, packed with ripe, juicy malt and clean barley flavours, and punctuated with bursts of earthy hoppy bitterness. Spicy and gently warming, it leaves a firm, dry and hoppy finish.

Births Charles Kingsley (writer), 1819; Anthony Eden (politician), 1897; George Bush (US President), 1924

Deaths Billy Butlin (holiday camp pioneer), 1980; Marie Rambert (ballet dancer), 1982; Gregory Peck (actor), 2003

Events Three men escape from Alcatraz prison using tools made from spoons, 1962; Nelson Mandela sentenced to life imprisonment in South Africa, 1964

Strong Ale

Itchen Valley Wat Tyler

Source Itchen Valley Brewery, New Alresford, Hampshire **Strength** 5% **Website** None

June 1381 saw some turbulent days. England was under the rule of 14-year-old King Richard II and his unpopular advisors, and trouble was brewing among the masses.

Some time before, the Black Death had changed the status quo. Landowners had seen their workers killed by the disease and needed new help on their estates. Peasant labourers had been able to ask more for their services, as demand exceeded supply. Now, 35 years later, everything was settling down, and it seemed that the peasants would once again be under the yoke. When King Richard imposed a new poll tax of 12d on each citizen to pay for the Hundred Years' War against France, it proved to be a breaking point. The workers rose up and said no.

The rebellion began in Essex, when the villagers of Fobbing defied tax collectors. It spread to Kent, and a band of peasants – although not exclusively peasants – began marching on London, aided by a priest named John Ball. The leader of the revolt was one Walter, or Wat, Tyler.

The King listens

The men arrived at Blackheath on 12 June, where they were spurred on by an inspirational sermon from Ball. On 13 June, they marched into London, trashing notable buildings and making it inevitable that the King would meet them the following day. Richard heard the men's grievances at Mile End and agreed to many of their demands. Still, however, the peasants were restless, and more violence followed as drunkenness set in. On 15 June, the King again met the leaders, this time at Smithfield. Wat Tyler, who had been sent to speak with the monarch, was stabbed to death, the King's army surrounded the rebels and the revolt was quickly crushed. The beaten men returned home to tend their farms, only to find that, within weeks, the King had reneged on his promises and they were no better off. The Peasants' Revolt, as it has become known, had failed in its immediate aims, although there is evidence to suggest that the action did ultimately lead to a reform of the feudal system and the betterment of the lowest classes.

Wat Tyler's name proved to be a rallying cry in future rebellions and today it adorns the label of a beer from Itchen Valley Brewery, based at Alresford in Hampshire. The bottle label also describes its contents as 'a strong real ale winter warmer', although it is available in bottle all year round. It's made with pale malt, crystal malt and Progress hops, which together produce a fine red-brown ale with a bitter, but balanced, taste of smooth malt and hops, rounded off by a dry, bitter, hoppy finish. 'A rebel of a beer', Itchen Valley calls it.

Births William Butler Yeats (poet), 1865; Malcolm McDowell (actor), 1943; Peter Scudamore (jockey), 1958

Deaths Benny Goodman (bandleader), 1986; Charles Haughey (politician), 2006

Events First V-1 flying bomb lands on London, 1944; outer-planetary probe *Pioneer 10* exits our solar system, 1983

Strong Ale

ABOVE: ILLUMINATED MANUSCRIPT DEPICTING THE DEATH OF WAT TYLER AT SMITHFIELD, LONDON, IN 1381

West Berkshire Old Father Thames

Source The West Berkshire Brewery Co., Yattendon, Berkshire **Strength** 3.4% **Website** wbbrew.co.uk

If there's one book that sums up the majesty of the River Thames, it's Jerome K Jerome's *Three Men in a Boat*. It's a serendipitous tale of three Victorian chums – and their dog Montmorency – who decide to step out of their normal London lives and take an adventure on the water. Their excursion is not without mishap as the author – who died on this day in 1927 – whimsically explains in the first person, 'J' being one of the hapless trio struggling to find their river legs. The book was written at a time when Londoners were just beginning to discover the Thames as a pleasure ground, so the tale that Jerome weaves should be seen very much as part of a late 19th-century fad. The events are claimed to be true, but are inevitably embroidered and probably drawn from a variety of sources rather than one specific journey.

A fishy tale

The three men's voyage of discovery takes them rowing upstream from Kingston to Oxford, with a glass of beer or two keeping them in good humour along the way. One little story concerns a night spent at Streatley, on the Berkshire-Oxfordshire border. J and his chum George go for a walk to Wallingford and, on the way back, call into a riverside inn to wet their whistles. Their eyes alight on an enormous stuffed trout set in a presentation case on the wall. During the course of the evening, various locals come and go, and each spins the strangers a yarn about how it was they who had, with great effort, managed to land that fish. Eventually, the rowers corner the landlord who finds it hilarious that all of his regulars should claim the honour for the catch when it was he who had brought it ashore. Not long afterwards, when left alone in the parlour, J and George climb up for a closer inspection of the prize exhibit, only to bring it down with a crash and see it smashed into a thousand pieces of plaster of Paris.

Just the other side of the Berkshire Downs from Streatley, you can find the West Berkshire Brewery, founded by Dave and Helen Maggs in 1995. When Brakspear's Brewery in Henley-on-Thames was scandalously closed to be redeveloped into a hotel and luxury apartments in 2002, Dave decided to fill the void left by the transfer of Brakspear's wonderful Bitter out of the Thames Valley by brewing his own highly quaffable session beer of the same strength. Old Father Thames, as Dave named it, is by no means a clone of Brakspear Bitter, which is now back on form in a new home (see 6 January), but it does have the same drinkability and a remarkably full flavour for a beer of this strength. Fruity toffee in the nose leads to a sweeter taste than you'll find in Brakspear's before a delightfully floral, drying hop finish. It's the sort of beer that would admirably slake the thirst of any weary rower or teller of tall stories.

Births Harriet Beecher Stowe (writer), 1811; Che Guevara (revolutionary), 1928; Boy George (pop singer), 1961

Deaths John Logie Baird (TV pioneer), 1946; Dame Peggy Ashcroft (actress), 1991; Henry Mancini (composer), 1994

Events US adopts Stars and Stripes as its flag, 1777; first Henley Regatta, 1939; Falklands War ends, 1982

Bitter

Cropton Two Pints

Source Cropton Brewery, Pickering, North Yorkshire **Strength** 4% **Website** croptonbrewery.com

'**D**oes Magna Carta mean nothing to you? Did she die in vain?', demanded stony-faced Tony Hancock in a famous episode of *Hancock's Half Hour*. However, Hancock's mock ignorance of what Magna Carta entails is but an echo of how little most people know about the significant events of 15 June 1215.

As depicted in most of the film and television portrayals of his life, the king at that time, John, was not a popular man. Richard the Lionheart's younger brother was very much the sort to rub people up the wrong way, especially when it came to demanding ever more taxes. Much of the money he squeezed out of his subjects was squandered fighting a vain war to keep hold of territories in France and, when he came back for more, those who stood to lose most, the barons, made a stand. Putting together an armed force, they took London and forced the King to try his hand at conciliation. In June 1215, the two sides met at Runnymede, a meadow on the banks of the Thames between Windsor and Staines, and thrashed out their differences. In order to restore calm, John had to make numerous concessions and introduce safeguards to curb his behaviour. He did this by way of a written 'Great Charter', or Magna Carta, signed on 15 June.

The charter bound the King to certain guarantees, declared freedom for the Church and also ensured liberties for the nobles, stipulating certain freedoms that henceforward would form part of the fabric of English life. In doing so, it set an important precedent that the monarch's authority over the people could be limited by law and also laid the foundations for democracy as we know it today.

Ale standard

Among the less important guarantees offered by Magna Carta was a standard measure for wine, corn and ale. The measure was to be 'the London quart'. I doubt if many pubs have served a quart – or a quarter of a gallon – measure for many years (except perhaps in jugs for sharing or taking away), but one way of ordering a quart and getting to drink it all yourself is by asking for Cropton's Two Pints.

Cropton Brewery in North Yorkshire has been brewing this 4% ale since 1984, the year that it started production, and it's still the biggest seller. Whether from the cask or the bottle, it has a pronounced bitter orange character, courtesy of the fruity Challenger and Golding hops that are loaded into the copper. The name, the brewers say rather confidently, is derived from the belief that a pint of this beer is worth two of any other. Toast Magna Carta with it today and don't let her die in vain.

Births Edvard Grieg (composer), 1843; Waylon Jennings (country singer), 1937; Noddy Holder (rock musician), 1946

Deaths Wat Tyler (poll tax rebel), 1381; James Hunt (racing driver), 1993; Ella Fitzgerald (singer), 1996

Events Alcock and Brown complete first non-stop transatlantic flight, 1919; European football body UEFA formed in Switzerland, 1954

Bitter

Butts Barbus Barbus

Source Butts Brewery Ltd, Great Shefford, Berkshire **Strength** 4.6% **Website** buttsbrewery.com

Izaak Walton proclaimed the joys of it more than 350 years ago, and, today, angling is one of the UK's top participation sports. Some people fish for specimens, trying to catch the 'big one'; others battle it out in organized competitions, where the total weight of catches is the decisive factor. But most prefer the simple, leisurely approach, passing long, lazy hours on the riverbank, enjoying the fresh air and the tranquillity of the countryside, not to mention some important, reflective time in their own company.

By the time 16 June comes around, Britain's anglers are champing at the bit. Since 15 March in the UK, freshwater fishing has been illegal, except on lakes, reservoirs, ponds and other still waters. Now, the rivers

are open again, and as the longest day of the year approaches, the bright early mornings and warm, lingering twilights are put to the fullest use by our fishermen friends.

A perfect beer to take to the riverbank is Barbus Barbus from Butts Brewery in Berkshire. Founder Chris Butt is himself a very keen fisherman and, when he's not indulging his other great passion – cricket – can be found fiddling with his bait on stretches of the local waterways. Barbus Barbus was one of Chris's first ever beers and remains his flagship brand, a very popular premium ale at 4.6%. The odd name reflects his love of angling, *Barbus barbus* being the official Latin species name for the barbel fish, one of the

coarse fish – along with pike, roach, bream, tench and others – that become 'legal' at this time of the year. The barbel's name actually comes from the Latin for beard and reflects the two hair-like feelers that can be found near its mouth.

Trade secrets

Many anglers have their little secrets, tricks of the trade that help them outshine their rivals, and so it is with some brewers. Chris is notoriously silent when it comes to providing information about his beers, so the ingredients of Barbus Barbus remain a mystery to the outside world, except for the fact that the beer is organic and includes three different strains of hop. The hops certainly do their job, giving Barbus Barbus a wonderfully robust, hoppy, orange-fruity character. The bottled version – as with all of Butts's beers – is bottle conditioned. If you've never tried the beer before, today's your chance. It's very likely that you'll be hooked.

Births Geronimo (Native American leader), 1829; Stan Laurel (comedian), 1890; Enoch Powell (politician), 1912

Deaths Margaret Bondfield (politician), 1953; Lord John Reith (broadcasting pioneer), 1971; David 'Screaming Lord' Sutch (musician and politician), 1999

Events Wars of the Roses end at Stoke, 1487; Russian dancer Rudolf Nureyev defects to the West, 1961; Valentina Tereshkova becomes the first woman in space, 1963

ABOVE: FRESHWATER FISHING ON THE RIVER MOLE IN SURREY

Best Bitter

Eggenberg Mac Queen's Nessie

Source Brauerei Schloss Eggenberg, Vorchdorf **Strength** 7.3% **Website** schlosseggenberg.at

The Himalayas have their yeti, North America has its Big Foot, and Scotland has its Loch Ness Monster. The search for lost species and missing links continues, despite the best scientific efforts to explain unusual 'sightings' rationally.

Thirty-seven kilometres (23 miles) long, Loch Ness is a narrow but very deep, freshwater lake running south from Inverness in the Scottish Highlands. It's been the source of some unusual activity for centuries – or at least reports of unusual activity, with the 229m (750ft) depth of murky water declared to be home to at least one member of a long-forgotten species of water creature.

Eyewitnesses to the creature's behaviour describe it in various ways, but, generally, the impression created is one of a 9–12m (30–40ft) serpent-like creature with at least one hump, a small head and a maned neck. Various scientific expeditions have probed the waters of Loch Ness, with mixed results. Using sonar, some have declared the presence of large but unknown aquatic animals, while others have categorically ruled out any unusual creatures in the deep. But the sightings have continued. Indeed, on 17 June 1993, three separate sightings of 'Nessie' were reported, by four different people. One of the witnesses, Edna MacInnes, even claimed she ran along the shore to keep up with the swimming beast, always in fear that she might be caught by the heavy wash it was generating.

Global fame

If nothing else, the legend of the monster makes for fabulous tourism opportunities. Thousands flock to the lake every year from all over the world, and one of the small lochside towns, Drumnadrochit, is now home to a visitor centre. The creature's global fame is underscored by the fact that its name has also been borrowed by a brewery in Austria for one of its beers.

Mac Queen's Nessie has been brewed since the early 1980s by the family-run Eggenberg Brewery, which sits in its own stunning lakeland between Salzburg and Vienna. The name seems appropriate for an unusual brew created, in part, out of Highland malt that is normally reserved for whisky making. The result is a dark golden, smoky-peaty ale of 7.3% ABV that fools you into thinking it's considerably weaker. It's fairly sweet and has a toffee note over a background of whisky and lemon. It certainly takes the chill off the air on an Austrian winter's day and would be a fine alternative to a warming dram during a night-time vigil at the side of Scotland's most famous watercourse.

Births John Wesley (evangelist), 1703; Igor Stravinsky (composer), 1882; Barry Manilow (singer-songwriter), 1943; Ken Livingstone (politician), 1945

Deaths Joseph Addison (writer and politician), 1719

Events Battle of Bunker Hill, American War of Independence, 1775; Iceland becomes a republic, 1944

Strong Lager

ABOVE: A SIGHTING OF 'NESSIE'?

Berliner Kindl Weisse

Source Berliner Kindl Brauerei AG, Berlin **Strength** 3% **Website** berliner-kindl.de

It may have been only three years after World War II ended, but June 1948 was close to witnessing the start of yet another global conflict.

Tensions were rising in occupied Germany. In the west, restructuring of the country was in the hands of the UK, the US and France. In the east, former Ally the Soviet Union was in charge and looking to impose its Communist ideals. The city of Berlin lay as an island in the Soviet sector, split into regions controlled by the four former partners and, when the western Allies decided to boost the German economy by introducing a new currency, the Deutschmark, on this day in 1948, the city became a pawn in a very dangerous political game.

With the Soviets wanting no part of a new capitalist Germany, the eastern power imposed its own currency within its sphere of influence and, to force the other Allies to relinquish their stake in Berlin, immediately began interfering with the flow of traffic in and out of the city. By 24 June, the Red Army had imposed a complete blockade, cutting off the city by all land routes. In response, the Allies launched a massive airlift of goods to keep the city afloat and its people fed. Eventually, the Soviets gave way and the blockade was lifted in May 1949.

Challenging survivor

The political impasse that continued for the next 40 years clearly did little to help Berlin's own particular beer style to survive but, thankfully, it did

– just. Berliner Weisse contains a high percentage of wheat alongside barley malt in the grist, but do not confuse it with wheat beers from Bavaria. Firstly, it's a lot weaker, generally around 3% ABV. This is because it's designed to be a quick refresher. And refreshing it certainly is, as the Berliner Weisse is one of the most tart beers in the world, courtesy of lactobacillus bacteria that are added to the wort to develop a trademark acidity before the beer is fermented with an ale yeast. The tartness is similar to that seen in lambic beers in Belgium and it makes Berliner Weisse so demanding that most locals only drink it with a shot of syrup.

There are two types of syrup offered. One is based on raspberries and is red; the other is based on a herb called woodruff and is green. Only the bravest souls go for neither, as you'll find if you sample today's beer selection. This comes from the Berliner Kindl brewery, the largest remaining producer of the style. The company is part of the Oetker food group.

Berliner Kindl Weisse pours a delicate pale golden colour with a big, foaming head. There are none of the banana, bubblegum, apple or clove notes you'd associate with the other sort of German wheat beer. Instead, the nose is musty, yeasty and lemon-sharp. The first sip is like a squeeze of pure lemon juice on the tongue but, surprisingly, you can get used to it, especially when the finish mellows and dries.

Most drinkers, however, find it too challenging and, even for those who persevere, it's a real shock to the palate. But all beer lovers need to open a bottle at least once in their lives – not just for the taste experience but also to celebrate the fact that the bitter divide between East and West never quite managed to eradicate this fascinating part of Berlin's heritage and culture.

Births Sammy Cahn (composer), 1913; Ian Carmichael (actor), 1920; Paul McCartney (rock musician), 1942

Deaths William Cobbett (writer), 1835; Samuel Butler (writer), 1902; Roald Amundsen (explorer), 1928

Events Battle of Waterloo, 1815; Space shuttle astronaut Sally Ride becomes the first American female in space, 1983

Wheat Beer

RCH Old Slug Porter

Source RCH Brewery, Weston-super-Mare, Somerset **Strength** 4.5% **Website** rchbrewery.com

If this book proves nothing else, it's that people celebrate the strangest things. Today, our attention turns to the Pacific North West of America, to Northwest Trek Wildlife Park, to be precise, where, at this time in June every year, they make slugs the centre of attention.

Northwest Trek Wildlife Park, south of Seattle in Washington State, is one of those awesome natural paradises, with more than 700 acres of lakes, meadows, paths and trails. More than 30 species of animal call the park their home, including elk, black and brown bears and wild dogs. It's also where the rare, bright yellow banana slug lays its hat, a fact that has prompted annual Slug Fest activities for more than a quarter of a century. The event is largely an educational programme for families, with videos, games, dressing up, treasure hunts and other such stuff. There are also human slug races, tips for keeping slugs out of the garden and the chance to learn more about what the park describes as 'the Pacific Northwest's most valuable and misunderstood mollusk'. It's not the sort of event I'd imagine you'd fly half-way around the world to attend, but it's probably a bit of fun if you're in the area.

Don't be squeamish

The other reason this particular event caught my eye was because it provides a great opportunity to mention one of my favourite beers. Although it has the rather unedifying name of Old Slug Porter, this beer has enough awards under its belt to convince even squeamish customers to cast aside their worries and pick up a bottle.

The beer is brewed by RCH Brewery, based in an old cider mill, just outside Weston-super-Mare. RCH stands for Royal Clarence Hotel, the Burham-on-Sea establishment where Old Slug started life back in 1982. There, the brewers had a spot of trouble with the sandy soil, as it was the perfect habitat for our friend the slug. Keeping them out of the brewhouse was always a bit of a headache. When the team then came up with a dark beer that left a smooth, lacy trail down the side of the glass as you drank it, they couldn't resist naming it after their pesky pests.

Old Slug is brewed from pale, crystal and black malts, for a deep ruby colour, with Fuggle and Golding hops providing balance for the sweeter elements of the grist and also adding a hint of dark fruit. The aroma is packed with biscuity malt and mellow coffee, while the taste, appropriately for a porter, is complex but not too heavy. Bitter coffee comes to the fore, with nuts and hops. There's some residual sweetness, too, before a big, dry finish full of bitter coffee and plain chocolate. Available in both cask- and bottle-conditioned versions, it slips down a treat.

Births King James I, 1566; Charlie Drake (comedian), 1925; Kathleen Turner (actress), 1954

Deaths JM Barrie (writer), 1937; William Golding (writer), 1993

Events Kuwait becomes independent of the UK, 1961; William Hague becomes leader of the Conservative Party, 1997

Porter

RCH Pitchfork

Source RCH Brewery, Weston-super-Mare, Somerset **Strength** 4.3% **Website** rchbrewery.com

It wasn't easy being an English Protestant in the 17th century. With the Stuarts back on the throne, the threat of the Papacy taking control of religion was again a real one, after all the struggles of the Civil War. You could put up with King Charles II, as long as he didn't lean too far to the Catholic side, but having his brother, James II, on the throne seemed to promise an early slide towards Rome. Not surprisingly, Protestants looked for a saviour and some thought they had found it in James Scott, Duke of Monmouth, an illegitimate (some say legitimate) son of Charles, who pressed his claim for the monarchy ahead of James. It wasn't to be, however. Charles ratified James as his heir, and Monmouth sloped off to live in exile in Protestant Holland. But Monmouth was a military man – one-time commander of the English army – and, when Charles died, he decided to use force to claim what he saw as his birthright. His army arrived in Lyme Regis on 11 June 1685 and was joined by a core of local Protestants, some of them country folk and farm labourers, armed only with rudimentary weapons. The Pitchfork Rebellion had begun. Monmouth and his men decided not to march immediately upon London, but headed first to Somerset to try to capture Bristol, England's second city at the time. It was on 20 June (alternative sources give 18 June), at Taunton, that he declared himself king, but to no avail. James had been alerted of the uprising and his troops rode to meet the challenge. At the Battle of Sedgemoor, Monmouth was defeated, and the Protestants were forced to lie low once again until the arrival of a new claimant to the throne, William of Orange, three years later.

Bitter finish

Commemorating the events of early summer 1685 is a beer from the local RCH Brewery. As mentioned in yesterday's entry, RCH began life in the early 1980s at the Royal Clarence Hotel in Burnham-on-Sea (hence the name). In 1993, it moved to a new site just outside Weston-super-Mare. Sedgemoor lies about 20 miles to the south, so this is very much Monmouth territory. The beer takes the name of Pitchfork, after the rebellion. In its cask-conditioned form, it claimed the title of CAMRA's Champion Best Bitter in 1998, and the bottle-conditioned version has also won many fans. It's a soft and fruity golden ale with a juicy, fresh aroma. Fuggle and Golding hops contrive to introduce an orangey bitterness in the mouth and leave a dry, bitter finish – happily not as bitter a finish as that endured by Monmouth, who lost his head for treason, or the rebels, many of whom were tried by the notorious Judge Jeffreys and suffered cruelly for their actions.

Births Catherine Cookson (writer), 1906; Errol Flynn (actor), 1909; Brian Wilson (pop musician), 1942

Deaths Willem Barents (navigator), 1597; King William IV, 1837

Events *Savannah*, the first steam ship to cross the Atlantic, arrives in Liverpool, 1819; Queen Victoria ascends to the throne, 1837

Golden Ale

Stonehenge Heel Stone

Source Stonehenge Ales, Netheravon, Wiltshire **Strength** 4.3% **Website** stonehengeales.co.uk

In the northern hemisphere, 21 June marks the summer solstice, the day when the sun is at its most northerly and highest point in the sky, and the hours of daylight reach their peak. As we shall see in the entry for 23 June, it is a time of year when pre-Christian religions are celebrated in great style. The tradition of lighting bonfires to strengthen the sun as it begins its slow but steady decline from midsummer into winter continues in many parts of the world.

In the UK, most attention during the summer solstice focuses on Stonehenge. This prehistoric collection of stones – a World Heritage Site – has confused analysts for centuries, as to how it got there and the purpose it served. The consensus is that the giant bluestones, which form the major part of the construction, were brought over land and sea from West Wales, with the even bigger sarsen stones, which apparently arrived later, being local to Wiltshire. There are still disputes over the specific purpose of the construction, with one of the most fascinating theories relating to its use as an astronomical clock. What points to this conclusion is the fact that every summer solstice, the sun, as it rises, climbs directly above the so-called Heel Stone, a single sarsen block that sits outside the main circle of stones. Clearly, whoever planned Stonehenge had the mathematical knowledge to work out exactly where the Heel Stone should be positioned. The cleverness of the work, and the mysticism that surrounds it, means that thousands of people now descend on Stonehenge for the summer solstice to witness this rare dawn spectacle.

Striking the friar

There are numerous theories as to the origin of the name Heel Stone. At their most literal, they refer to an occasion when the Devil threw the stone at a friar, hitting him on the heel. The Heel Stone is also celebrated in the name, and on the pump clip, of a cask beer from Stonehenge Brewery. This microbrewery was founded in 1984 by Tony Bunce and, as Bunces

Brewery, traded from its picturesque watermill home in the village of Netheravon until 1993, when it was acquired by Danish brewer Stig Anker Andersen. Stig renamed it Stonehenge in honour of the stone circle just a few miles to the south.

Heel Stone is a light-bodied, copper-coloured best bitter. It has a malty, spicy nose that is followed in the mouth by a sweet spiciness from the hops over a clean, malty foundation. The finish is dry, malty, hoppy and decidedly moreish. Pale malt, crystal malt and wheat malt form the grist, while the hops are First Gold, Willamette and Bramling Cross, which may introduce a hint of blackcurrant to the aroma and taste. Unfortunately, the beer is not yet available in bottle, but Heel Stone can be found outside its normal Wiltshire trading area in summer, courtesy of wholesalers and beer festivals. And, of course, if you do join the early morning throngs hoping to catch a glimpse of the sun as it rises above the Heel Stone, there can be no more pertinent beer to seek out for a lunchtime pint afterwards.

Births Jean-Paul Sartre (writer and philosopher), 1905; Ray Davies (rock musician), 1944; Michel Platini (footballer), 1955

Deaths Niccolò Machiavelli (writer), 1527; Inigo Jones (architect), 1652; John Lee Hooker (blues musician), 2001

Events Golfer Tony Jacklin wins the US Open, 1970; premiere of the musical *Evita* in London, 1978

Best Bitter

ABOVE: SUNSET OVER STONEHENGE

Leatherbritches Ale Conner's Porter

Source Leatherbritches Brewery, Ashbourne, Derbyshire **Strength** 5.4% **Website** None

The name of King Richard II has been blackened elsewhere in this book for his duplicitous role in the Peasants' Revolt, but it can be redeemed somewhat here, for it seems that the young king may have been a friend to beer drinkers. Richard came to the throne on this day in 1377. He was the son of Edward, the Black Prince, and inherited the monarchy when his grandfather, King Edward III, died. He was only ten when he acceded to the throne and was inevitably at the mercy of many, not always scrupulous, advisors, which perhaps explains his dark dealings with the peasants. However, one law that he decided to introduce was more generous to the working man. In 1393, he declared that signs should be erected outside pubs so that they could be easily identified by ale conners, the local officials charged with ensuring that the quality of beer being sold was good. Of course, Richard didn't invent the pub sign – that honour goes to the Romans who displayed bushes or other greenery outside their taverns to show when wine was on sale – but he did standardize its use. Not surprisingly, Richard's own emblem, the White Hart, was soon to feature outside many a drinking establishment.

Sticking to the job

The title of ale conner, where it still exists today, is ceremonial. In past centuries, however, it was a job that was taken very seriously. Shakespeare's father was one. There is a fanciful tale still told about the clothes these dedicated officials wore for work – leather trousers that were put to good use when the ale conner poured a little ale onto his bench and then sat down. How well the leather garments stuck to the seat revealed how malty the beer was and therefore whether or not it was up to scratch. It is more realistic to expect that the ale conners actually employed rather more pertinent tests when going about their business – drinking the beer would seem a lot more appropriate – but the legend of these diligent men and their leather trousers is still celebrated in the name of a Derbyshire microbrewery.

Leatherbritches Brewery is housed in a small outhouse just behind the Bentley Brook Inn, a large pub on the edge of the Peak District. For years, both the pub and the brewery were owned by the Allingham family, but the pub was sold in 2005 and the brewery moved to The Green Man & Black's Head Royal Hotel in Ashbourne in 2008. Three of their beers have been bottled with the 'Ale Conner's' name, and a good selection for today would be Ale Conner's Porter. It's a gently creamy, bottle-conditioned porter, built around pale, crystal and dark chocolate malts, with a sweetish, biscuity taste and pleasantly soft roasted malt notes. The hops are Progress and, fittingly for a beer of this style, keep themselves nicely discreet.

Births Kris Kristofferson (singer and songwriter), 1936; Esther Rantzen (TV presenter), 1940; Meryl Streep (actress), 1949

Deaths David O Selznick (film producer), 1965; Judy Garland (actress and singer), 1969

Events First flight for Virgin Atlantic, 1984; Maradona's 'hand of God' goal helps defeat England in Mexico World Cup Finals, 1986

Porter

181

Sinebrychoff Porter

Source Sinebrychoff Brewery, Helsinki **Strength** 7.2% **Website** koff.net

Origins of the festival of Midsummer date back to pre-Christian times. They relate to the pagan lighting of fires to ward off evil spirits and to strengthen the sun, which was heading into its annual decline. Hopes for a good harvest also played a part. Today, Scandinavia, with its midnight-sun summers, still makes the most of the occasion, and it is in Finland that the festivities are at their peak. Midsummer's Eve, 23 June, is even a public holiday there.

On this day, Finnish families get together and head for their country cabins or lakeside second homes, and feast on herrings and new potatoes, with strawberries the preferred pudding, and schnapps or beer the liquid accompaniment. Parties and bonfire ceremonies follow, and, as the next day, Midsummer's Day, coincides with Finland's flag day, it's an occasion to confirm national identity and pride. The Finnish term for the whole festival, Juhunnus, relates to St John the Baptist, whose feast day falls on 24 June.

Finnish star

What probably goes down rather well at many a midsummer feast is a glass of one of Finland's most famous beers, a handsome reminder of the somewhat forgotten Baltic porter tradition. Sinebrychoff is the oldest brewery in Finland, founded by Nikolai Sinebrychoff in 1819. Today, it's a major drinks producer, part of the Carlsberg group, but it hasn't forgotten its beer origins. Much of the company's production is geared to golden lager but its star offering, known as Koff Porter, or simply Porter, is a dark ruby beer packing a hefty 7.2% ABV.

Based on the warming, dark beers that once staved off the bitter Baltic winters, Porter was added to the company's beer list in the 1950s. It's a quality, unfiltered product, with a truly complex, yet welcoming, aroma of peppery chocolate, treacly malt and a pinch of liquorice, thanks largely to the Munich malt used in the mash tun. Dark chocolate and toffee lead in the bitter, peppery taste, which gently tingles the tongue and, again, has a suggestion of liquorice, before a dry, bitter, dark chocolate finish that offers a toffeeish sweet note for balance.

You'd perhaps expect something lighter and more quenching for the apex of summer, but when it comes to washing down pickled fish, you certainly need a bit more character. It's a treat with strawberries, too, or just nicely chilled as a sipping beer with which to watch the long, slow slide of the bountiful sun into the distant horizon.

Births Colin Montgomerie (golfer), 1963; Zinedine Zidane (footballer), 1972; KT Tunstall (singer-songwriter), 1975

Deaths Jonas Salk (immunologist), 1995; Buster Merryfield (actor), 1999; Aaron Spelling (TV producer), 2006

Events King Edward VII establishes the Order of Merit, 1902; Pope John Paul II meets Lech Walesa, leader of Poland's banned trade union Solidarity, 1983

Farmer's Puck's Folly

Source The Maldon Brewing Co. Ltd, Maldon, Essex **Strength** 4.2% **Website** maldonbrewing.co.uk

Although it no longer marks the longest day in the year (in the northern hemisphere), thanks to calendar changes, 24 June is still celebrated as Midsummer's Day. Surviving traditions related to the occasion include the lighting of bonfires – to celebrate the sun or perhaps even strengthen it as it begins its decline into winter – but most of the more esoteric customs have not surprisingly faded away. You don't see many folk wandering naked through the midsummer dew these days in order to ensure their fertility in the year ahead. On the other hand, the double association of this day as St John the Baptist's Day, does still have a bearing, certainly in the alternative medicine world. The word was that the plant known as St John's wort was particularly effective if picked on Midsummer's Day, and had the power to ward off evil spirits. Its ancient name was 'chase devil'. Many people still swear by this plant as an aid to overcoming depression and sleeping disorders.

Magic in the air

All this just gives a flavour of the air of mysticism that hangs about this date. Some of it comes from the belief that the barrier between our world and the spiritual world on this day was particularly thin, and that supernatural beings were abroad and at work. The idea was underscored by Shakespeare in his *A Midsummer Night's Dream*, in which fairies interfere in the lives of mere mortals. Chief mischief maker in Shakespeare's opus is Puck, a practical joker even among imps, who enjoys entangling the love lives of his unfortunate victims. His name is celebrated in today's beer, a brew from Farmer's Ales in Maldon, Essex.

Nigel Farmer is the owner/brewer of this little enterprise and, in converted stables behind a historic coaching inn called The Blue Boar, he turns out an interesting selection of draught and bottle-conditioned ales. Puck's Folly is directly inspired by *A Midsummer Night's Dream*. Nigel was watching an amateur performance of the play after quaffing a pint of refreshing Polly's Folly from Buffy's Brewery in Norfolk. He decided to create a similar ale but simply using lager malt and Golding hops. The end result is a full-flavoured, blond best bitter featuring sappy, resin-like hops laid over delicate, honeyed sweetness. And the magic of it is that you can enjoy it all year, not just in midsummer.

Births WH Smith (bookseller), 1825; Brian Johnston (broadcaster), 1912; Jeff Beck (rock musician), 1944

Deaths Lucrezia Borgia (Italian aristocrat), 1519; Tony Hancock (comedian), 1968

Events Battle of Bannockburn, 1314; coronation of King Henry VIII, 1509; Soviet Union begins blockade of West Berlin, 1948

Golden Ale

Jever Pilsener

Source Friesisches Brauhaus zu Jever, Jever **Strength** 4.9% **Website** jever.de

Friesland is an area of northern Europe that is noted for its unspoilt beauty, an arcing shoreline of islands, sand dunes and grasslands divided, politically, between The Netherlands and Germany. It's relatively unknown even today, but it would have been even more obscure had it not been for a man whose birthday fell on this day in 1870.

Robert Erskine Childers was born in London and, after an education at Cambridge, became a civil servant. He worked at the House of Commons, where long holidays allowed him time to indulge his great passion for sailing. One of his numerous yachting expeditions he recaptured in a book, published in 1903. *The Riddle of the Sand*s revealed the barren beauty of Friesland to the world as the setting for a tale of two British yachtsmen who stumble upon secret German plans to invade Britain. Apart from its geographical importance, the book has a literary pre-eminence. It is widely recognized as being the first ever spy novel, and was realistic enough to have prompted British Intelligence to step up its surveillance of the area.

Erskine Childers's life itself became the stuff of literature in later years. He served with the Royal Navy during World War I, earning himself a Distinguished Service Cross in the process, but also took an interest in Irish republicanism, smuggling weapons to rebels, supporting the Easter Rising of 1916 and being considered a traitor. Caught in possession of a small revolver, Childers was sentenced to death. He was executed by firing squad in Dublin, in 1922. His son, Erskine Hamilton Childers, later became President of Ireland.

Friesland Dry

Spreading the word about Friesland today is a beer from one of the area's main towns, Jever. Jever Pilsener is brewed using local soft water, which, the brewers claim, allows them to throw in even more hops. The beer is certainly hoppy and has a remarkable dryness in the finish – the label warns you of this with its strapline, Friesisch Herb (Friesland Dry). It's a crisp and absorbing pilsner that has appeal way beyond the average lager drinker.

Friesland's brewing heritage however predates the Jever brewery by many years. When the company was set up in 1848, there were already more than 20 breweries in the area. The brewery – owned today by the Oetker food group – has grown into one of the landmark features of the town, its modern brewhouse very much part of its identity and economy, with Jever Pilsener a flagbearer for the whole region. As the brewery puts it: 'A single sip of this beer and the drinker is reminded of the unmistakable Friesian landscape that is its home.'

Births George Orwell (writer), 1903; Ricky Gervais (comedian), 1961; George Michael (pop musician), 1963

Deaths George Armstrong Custer (soldier), 1876; Johnny Mercer (composer), 1976; Jacques Cousteau (oceanographer), 1997

Events Battle of the Little Big Horn, 1876; the Beatles perform *All You Need Is Love* on Our World, a globally broadcast celebration of satellite technology, 1967

Pilsner

ABOVE: ERSKINE CHILDERS (LEFT) AT AN UNLOADING OF SMUGGLED ARMS FROM HIS YACHT *ASGARD*, 1914

Triple fff Gilbert White

Source The Triple fff Brewery, Alton, Hampshire　**Strength** 6%　**Website** triplefff.com

Today marks the passing of a modest, 18th-century clergyman, a man who lived a quiet life in the Hampshire countryside but left us a legacy that gave us all a better understanding of the natural world.

Gilbert White was born in Selborne, near Alton, in 1720. He studied at Oriel College, Oxford, but later joined the ranks of the clergy (a family tradition), returning home to become curate of the local church. It is not his religious teachings, however, that have bequeathed his name to posterity but his hobby of closely monitoring the flora and fauna that existed in his garden.

White kept scrupulously detailed notes of the fruits, flowers and vegetables that he planted, and of the animals that took up residence in his garden, or which even briefly passed through. He systematically observed the relationships between various species, and as such was the first person to properly explore the concept that all life on this planet is inter-connected and inter-dependent. His lifetime's work was collated for publication as *The Natural History of Selborne* in 1788, just five years before he died. This was no dry scientific volume, however. White's accessibility and lightness of touch not only drew readers into the wonders of natural history, they also won him admirers among the romantic poets of the time. As testimony to the greatness of his work, the book has never been out of print and is one of the best-selling texts in the English language.

Smoky re-creation

White's legacy is trumpeted by the Triple fff brewery, based just a few miles from White's Selborne home in Four Marks. The beer it has created in his honour is a strong, dark golden ale based on a recipe created by the great man himself, who was a keen brewer and, just as with his wildlife watching, kept close notes on the beers his manservant produced.

The recipe was discovered in the loft of Gilbert's house (now a museum) and was passed to Triple fff to see if it could be re-created. The key ingredient is malt that has been smoked over beech wood, and this joins pale malt in the mash. East Kent Golding hops provide balance. The aroma is very unusual. It is richly malty, smoky and nutty, with toffee notes and a honeyed accent. Smoked malt leads the way in the fairly sweet taste, but without overwhelming other characteristics, as this forceful ingredient can all too often do. Here, it allows breathing space for other, smooth malty flavours, including nut and toffee, all backed by a honeyed softness. The finish is dry, malty, smoky and bitter, with roasted malt poking through.

Triple fff's Graham Trott describes the beer in Marmite terms: you either love it or you hate it, and he is now thinking of reining back the smokiness a little to make it more widely popular. But if it's not quite your tipple, keep an eye open for a second Gilbert White beer. Another recipe has been discovered and the brewery is hoping to re-create that, too.

Births Peter Lorre (actor), 1904; Laurie Lee (writer), 1914; Georgie Fame (pop and blues musician), 1943

Deaths Denis Thatcher (businessman), 2003; Richard Whiteley (TV presenter), 2005

Events The charter of the United Nations signed, 1945; John F Kennedy declares 'Ich bin ein Berliner' on a visit to Berlin, 1963; Bertie Ahern becomes Taoiseach of Ireland, 1997

Smoked Beer

Isle of Skye Black Cuillin

Source The Isle of Skye Brewing Co., Uig, Isle of Skye **Strength** 4.5% **Website** skyebrewery.co.uk

The entry for 16 April in this book recounts the bloody events of the Battle of Culloden and its gory aftermath. The defeat of the Young Pretender, Charles Edward Stuart, during his attempt to return his family to the British throne, saw his supporters suffer brutally at the hands of the King's forces. Bonnie Prince Charlie, however, slipped through the net. As soon as the battle was lost, Charlie was away, scurrying into the wilderness of the Scottish Highlands and Islands where, he knew, lay his best hope of survival. But his enemies were always in pursuit, which brings us forward a couple of months to the highly romanticized legend of Flora MacDonald, the girl who helped the Prince escape from under the noses of the redcoats.

Speed bonnie boat

Flora was the foster daughter of the leader of Government troops on the island of Benbecula in the Outer Hebrides – an unlikely ally of the refugee prince, to say the least, especially when you throw in the fact that her boyfriend, Allan MacDonald, was also a redcoat officer. However, when it was discovered Charles was on the island and about to be arrested, she was persuaded to help him escape, probably as a way of avoiding reprisals for the locals who had harboured him. Her plan was simple but surprisingly effective, and involved dressing Charles up as her maidservant 'Betty Burke'. Despite his rather ungainly, angular looks, Charles and Flora deceived the enemy guards.

Stepping aboard their 'bonnie boat', they sped their way over to the island of Skye, from where Charles would eventually complete his escape back to the continent. Tales of how love blossomed during their hair-raising ordeal have added a rosy flourish to this daring deed, but the truth is that Flora and Charles spent barely a week in each other's company. She went on to marry Allan MacDonald and never saw Charles again.

To commemorate the flight of the defeated prince, Isle of Skye Brewery produces a beer called Young Pretender, a golden hoppy beer of 4% ABV. It's not available in bottle, however, so far easier to obtain is the brewery's Black Cuillin, which takes its name from the jagged but majestic Cuillin Hills on Skye, below which Charles later hid from his pursuers. You can still visit a cave in the lee of the mountains where, it is claimed, he took refuge.

Black Cuillin is a ruby-hued, almost stout-like ale that includes both oats and honey in the recipe for a pleasantly soft texture. The dark malts that give rise to the deep colour also bring lots of treacle toffee, chocolate and molasses to the aroma and taste, but this is not a sweet beer, especially when you hit the finish where roasted grain rears up immediately after the swallow, and coffee flavours linger long and bitter. In that respect, too, it's a fitting brew. Although Charles may have arrived in Scotland full of ambition and bravado, his brief, disastrous incursion left a bitter taste in many mouths for centuries to come.

Births Helen Keller (disability activist), 1880; Michael Ball (singer), 1962; Kevin Pietersen (cricketer), 1980

Deaths 'Cubby' Broccoli (film producer), 1996; Jack Lemmon (actor), 2001; John Entwistle (rock musician), 2002

Events Barclays Bank unveils the world's first 'hole-in-the-wall' cash machine in Enfield, 1967; Tony Blair resigns as Prime Minister, 2007

Scottish Ale

Hoegaarden De Verboden Vrucht

Source Brouwerij de Hoegaarden, Hoegaarden **Strength** 8.5% **Website** hoegaarden.com

Today would have been the birthday of one of the most influential painters of the 17th century. Peter Paul Rubens was born to Flemish parents in Siegen, Germany, but the town had close affiliations to the Belgian city of Antwerp, where he was educated and, later, became a court painter. His work is heavily influenced by Italian Renaissance masters, such as Michelangelo, Raphael and Titian, although Rubens's own style was later an inspiration to many others as he toured Europe working for kings and aristocrats, as both a painter and a diplomat. His busy life ended in 1640. His talents had been recognized by two monarchs, with knighthoods from both Charles I of England and Philip IV of Spain.

Original sin

The artist's close associations with Belgium are highlighted in a beer produced by InBev. De Verboden Vrucht, also labelled in French as Le Fruit Défendu, was created by Pierre Celis, the man who founded Hoegaarden. The beer is still brewed at that brewery, and while some say the beer is no longer as subtle and complex as it was in Celis's day, it's still bottle conditioned, rather enjoyable and worth tapping into today because of its colourful label. On this, you'll find a reproduction of one of Rubens's better-known works, *Adam and Eve in Paradise*. The original can be viewed in the Rubenshuis, a museum dedicated to the artist, based in his former home and studio in Antwerp. For marketing fun, the brewers have taken a little liberty with the artwork, cheekily inserting a glass of beer into the hands of the characters. The usual take on the original sin story is that Eve tempted Adam with an apple, but here it looks as if Adam is the tempter. 'Go on,' he seems to say, 'have a swig of this.'

If you're tempted to try it, you'll find it's a beer with a deep amber colour, packing a mighty 8.5% ABV, although this is a touch lower than it used to be. The aroma is quite modest for a beer of such magnitude, but eventually estery berry fruits and a hint of liquorice can be coaxed out, along with a slight sharpness and a gentle grassy note. In the mouth, the beer is warming, peppery and gently bitter – Pierre Celis's penchant for spices again shining through. There's malt aplenty, but also good hop balance, with citrus and berry fruits languishing in the background. The finish is fruity and drying, with lingering malt, but it is also firmly bitter with a pleasant, mildly citrus hop tang.

Births King Henry VIII, 1491; Jean Jacques Rousseau (philosopher), 1712; Mel Brooks (actor and film director), 1926

Deaths Archduke Franz Ferdinand of Austria, 1914; Stanley Baker (actor), 1976; Joan Sims (actress), 2001

Events Coronation of Queen Victoria, 1838; Treaty of Versailles signed, formally ending World War I, 1919

Spiced Ale

St Peter's Cream Stout

Source St Peter's Brewery Co. Ltd, Bungay, Suffolk **Strength** 6.5% **Website** stpetersbrewery.co.uk

Today is the feast day of two of the Catholic Church's most significant saints. One is St Paul; the other is St Peter. St Peter is the one who has greater bearing on the world of brewing, thanks to the way in which his name has been honoured in the 2,000 years since his death.

A Galilee fisherman, Peter was introduced to the teachings of Christ by his brother Andrew, but he quickly became an invaluable ally of the new messiah. Indeed, the importance of his support for Jesus saw his name changed from the original Simon to Peter, which means rock. After Christ's death, Peter was charged with carrying on the work, and was installed as the first ever pope. The next time you walk into a pub called The Cross Keys, bear this in mind. The name specifically relates to St Peter's own emblem and the legend that it was he who held the keys to the Kingdom of Heaven. On a more prosaic level, St Peter has now gained an even more prominent association with the world of beer, thanks to a small but enterprising brewery based in Suffolk.

Hall with potential

In 1996, John Murphy, founder of the marketing agency Interbrand, decided to branch out into brewing. His country bolt hole was in East Anglia, and he spotted the potential offered by a run-down old house called St Peter's Hall. The building, in part, dates back to around 1280. It's an impressive sight when approached along the driveway, with lush green surroundings and a small moat. There is a distinctly clerical air when you step over the threshold and explore the well-restored rooms and connecting corridors. Heavy flagstones feel solid beneath the feet, and leaded windows battle to filter in the daylight, while arched doorways lead you into quarters furnished with wood panelling and tapestries. Today, the hall is divided into a bar and a restaurant, both serving beers brewed in a more functional barn just behind the main house.

The brewery's output is extensive, ranging from traditional bitters to organic ales and beers flavoured with fruits and spices. Most are bottled for the export market, and the US, Russia and Japan are just a few of the territories in which the brewery's distinctive oval bottle – a replica of an 18th-century flask used in colonial America – has caught the eye. One of the most successful creations is Cream Stout, twice a gold medallist in the International Beer Challenge run by trade magazine *Off Licence News*. In awarding the medals, judges commented on the fine roasted grain character and underlying creamy, malty sweetness, plus the fact that, despite weighing in at 6.5% ABV, this is a remarkably easy stout to drink. It's an outstanding beer that has become a rock in the St Peter's selection.

Births Nelson Eddy (singer), 1901; Amanda Donohoe (actress), 1962; Katherine Jenkins (opera singer), 1980

Deaths Elizabeth Barrett Browning (poet), 1861; Jayne Mansfield (actress), 1967; Katharine Hepburn (actress), 2003

Events London's Globe Theatre destroyed by fire, 1613; first edition of *The Daily Telegraph*, 1855; Arthur Miller marries Marilyn Monroe, 1956

Stout

Deschutes Bachelor ESB

Source Deschutes Brewery, Bend, Oregon **Strength** 5.3% **Website** deschutesbrewery.com

Little is known about the saint whose feast day falls on 30 June. What is understood is that St Theobald was born into a noble family at Provins, near Champagne, France, in the year 1017, and that in 1054 he unexpectedly abandoned a military career, left the family fold and went to become a hermit with his close friend, Walter. The two continued a life of piety, eventually settling at Trier, Germany, from where they launched pilgrimages to Rome and Santiago de Compostela. It was while venturing on a journey to Palestine that Walter became ill and they were forced to set up a new base near Vicenza, Italy. Walter died two years later, but Theobald attracted many followers there and, it is said, performed numerous miracles. He died on this day in 1066. He was canonized seven years later and has become the patron saint of charcoal burners, probably because, to fund their life of devotion, Theobald and Walter once worked at maintaining fires in a forge.

Bachelor party

For more obvious reasons, Theobald is also the patron saint of bachelors, which allows us to tie in an outstanding beer from the US. The Deschutes Brewery, based in the graphically-named town of Bend, Oregon, was established (initially as a brewpub) in 1988, and named after a local river. It produces an excellent range of beers, many of them bottle conditioned and therefore conveniently available a long way from home. Bachelor ESB is one of the most lauded.

Taking its lead from the classic Fuller's ale of the same name, the ESB (Extra Special Bitter) style has many followers on the American West Coast and has been emulated by scores of brewers. The Deschutes example is among the very best. It's amber in colour and offers a full and balanced mix of rich malt, light toffee and a strong, tea-like hoppiness from the aroma through to the dry, full finish. It's a beer with more awards than you can shake a sheaf of barley at, with wins at the Great American Beer Festival and in the International Beer Challenge among its credits.

The name, inconveniently, has nothing to do with our featured saint or his lifestyle. It is taken from Mount Bachelor, a 2743-m (9,000-ft) dormant Oregon volcano, a picture of which features on the beer's label.

Births Winston Graham (writer), 1908; Susan Hayward (actress), 1917; Michael Phelps (swimmer), 1985

Deaths Montezuma II (Atzec emperor), 1520; Chet Atkins (guitarist), 2001

Events Official opening of London's Tower Bridge, 1894; the British sixpence goes out of circulation, 1980

Strong Ale

Unibroue Blanche de Chambly

Source Unibroue Inc., Chambly, Quebec **Strength** 5% **Website** unibroue.com

It may be seen by some as the US's quieter neighbour, but Canada is no second-class citizen, as the people of the country will loudly tell you, especially on this day, its national day.

Canada's history dates back to Asian tribes that crossed the frozen Bering Strait to colonize this area of outstanding natural beauty. They were joined by Vikings around the year 1000, but these soon beat a hasty retreat. European influence had to wait until the arrival of the French in the 15th century, followed by the British. While, at first, both countries existed amicably, the Seven Years' War between them spilled over into their North American territories and soured relationships. Britain seized control of the country after the Battle of Quebec City in 1759, but the two parties continued to feud until the establishment of the US focused their attention on cooperation for mutual benefit. In 1867, the Governor General gave the land a new start, when all territories were joined together under a federal government. On 1 July, the British dominion of Canada was established – the source of the celebrations known initially as Dominion Day but since 1982 as Canada Day.

Belgian influence

The French-speaking contingent of Canadians is still based in the province of Quebec. Here, one of the country's best-known and most highly regarded breweries also has its home. Unibroue was founded only in the early 1990s but quickly made a name for itself by producing high-quality, bottle-conditioned beers in the Belgian style. The company was acquired by rival Sleeman in 2004, and this, in turn, was swallowed up by Sapporo, the Japanese giant, in 2006. So far, there has been little to concern beer drinkers, as Unibroue's excellent range has been preserved. Any one of these beers is a worthy drink to savour for a taste of Canada today, but I've opted for Blanche de Chambly.

Chambly is the name of the Montreal suburb where the brewery is based and, in the fashion of Belgian ales, its Blanche is a cloudy wheat beer. The beer contains both malted and raw wheat, alongside barley malt, and, true to style, is only lightly hopped, leaving the character to emerge from the selection of secret spices that flavour the brew.

The beer may be called 'white', but it pours a pale golden colour. The aroma is fresh and appealing, slightly bready and laced with lemon-citrus notes. The same citrus accent is obvious in the taste, which is bittersweet and lemon-sharp with a suggestion of malty toffee behind. More of the same flavours run into the dry, bready finish. Blanche de Chambly is a highly quaffable, refreshing drink that is dedicated to a band of volunteer militiamen who lost their lives defending the territory of Lower Canada (Quebec) in the War of 1812 – a two-year conflict in which the US tried to claim Canadian lands.

Births Amy Johnson (aviator), 1903; Deborah Harry (pop musician), 1945; Diana, Princess of Wales, 1961

Deaths Marlon Brando (actor), 2004; Luther Vandross (soul musician), 2005; Fred Trueman (cricketer), 2006

Events Investiture of Prince Charles as Prince of Wales, 1969; Britain returns Hong Kong to Chinese rule, 1997; smoking banned in public places in England, 2007

Wheat Beer

ABOVE: CANADIAN MOUNTIES

Caracole Nostradamus

Source Brasserie Caracole, Falmignoul **Strength** 9.5% **Website** brasserie-caracole.be

The Great Fire of London, the rise of Adolf Hitler, the 9/11 attacks on New York – all these world-changing events were predicted by the 16th-century French mystic and astrologer Nostradamus – if you listen to his biggest fans. Sceptics, however, will tell you otherwise, but there's no denying that the alleged prophet, who died on this day in 1566, was one of the most intriguing figures of his time.

Michel de Notredame was born in St Rémy, near Avignon, in 1503. In his early life, he worked as an apothecary but soon began dabbling in the occult. Adopting the Latinized version of his name, he began publishing almanacs and then, in 1555, he released his most famous work. Called *Les Prophéties*, this was a collection of four-line verses that aimed to predict momentous events over future centuries. His work became known in high places, and he was summoned to Paris to become an adviser to King Henry II.

Academics argue that all Nostradamus did in this work was to draw on older prophecies made in ancient texts like the Bible and combine them with his knowledge of history and the work of classical scholars. That doesn't stop believers from making bold assertions about his clairvoyance, although a close analysis of Nostradamus's original text proves it to be sufficiently vague as to be open to many interpretations, some of which, inevitably, will sound promising. The clinching factor, according to the sceptics, is that no one has been able to predict *future* events accurately using Nostradamus's work. After the event, it is possible to twist his words to fit the circumstances, but therein lies the benefit of hindsight.

Future perfect

It is said that Nostradamus's last prediction came before the night he died, when he told his secretary that he wouldn't be alive by sunrise. He certainly got that one right. It's not clear whether he ever foresaw that one day there would be a beer named after him, but I predict that, if you try it, you'll be back for more. The beer comes from the Caracole brewery in southern Belgium. The brewery's emblem is a snail, but the business has not been slow to take off. Founded only in the early 1990s, it has rapidly built up a discerning following, and has moved from its original home in Namur to a larger base in the village of Falmignoul, near Dinant, on the northern fringe of the Ardennes.

Nostradamus is a classy, strong brown ale that was originally brewed in 1991 as a New Year beer. It proved so popular that it was extended to the rest of the year and given a new name. That was in 2000, when there was much speculation as to what the new millennium was to hold, making Nostradamus an easy choice of title. The beer comprises five different malts, with Hallertau the main hop. There are no spices but there's a distinct herbal character to this heady, winey, flame-red brew. Liquorice and celery notes emerge on the palate, ensuring the beer is bittersweet rather than sugary, despite the abundant malt, and, with melon and red berry flavours also present, this is a complex, understandably warming ale that leaves an increasingly bitter and moreish finish.

Births Alec Douglas-Home (Prime Minister), 1903; Larry David (actor and TV producer), 1947; Peter Kay (comedian), 1973

Deaths Jean Jacques Rousseau (philosopher), 1778; Ernest Hemingway (writer), 1961; James Stewart (actor), 1997

Events William Booth addresses the meeting that leads to the foundation of the Salvation Army, 1865; Live 8 concerts staged around the world to 'Make Poverty History', 2005

Strong Ale

ABOVE: NOSTRADAMUS, THE 16TH-CENTURY FRENCH MYSTIC AND ASTROLOGER

Daleside Crack Shot

Source Daleside Brewery Ltd, Harrogate, North Yorkshire **Strength** 5.5% **Website** dalesidebrewery.co.uk

Several years ago, I received a phone call from Daleside Brewery. They had produced a new beer and wanted to know my thoughts about the proposed name. Did I think that 'Trooper Jane' would set the beer world alight? I had to tell them that it probably wouldn't and, thankfully, they came up with a far sexier title. They called the beer Crack Shot, but the reference to Trooper Jane remained prominent, ensuring that the inspiration for the beer was not betrayed by its marketing.

'Trooper' Jane Ingilby was a prominent Royalist during the English Civil War. She lived at Ripley Castle, near Harrogate, Yorkshire, with her brother, Sir William Ingilby, and it is said that she fought in the nearby Battle of Marston Moor – which took place on 2 July 1644 – disguised as a male trooper. Alas, for the Ingilbys, the battle was won by the Roundheads, and they were forced to retreat. With the enemy in the form of Oliver Cromwell looking to use Ripley Castle for overnight accommodation, Sir William promptly disappeared into a priest hole to avoid capture, but Jane stood firm, drawing two pistols and standing guard over her brother's hiding place throughout the night. Keeping the surprised Cromwell in her sights, she ensured that Sir William survived and was one opponent who managed to thwart Cromwell during the bloody 17th-century hostilities.

Historic recipe

The beer that Daleside created in her honour is derived from a recipe book written in the 17th century by the head housekeeper of Ripley Castle, Elizabeth Eden. Brewer Craig Whitty needed to adapt the recipe for today's brewing process, translating quaint measurements such as 'handfuls' into more precise units, but he stuck to the basics of the Ripley brew. Thus, malted oats join barley malt in the mash tun, providing a wonderfully smooth and buttery barley sugar flavour that is perfectly countered by a mellow liquorice note from the Fuggle and Golding hops. Malt lingers in the finish as hops and bitterness grow to finish off what is a brilliantly rounded strong ale. It's a shame they sell it in clear glass bottles, which are notoriously poor at protecting beer from the effects of light, but, like Jane Ingilby, it's still a winner.

Births Ken Russell (film director), 1927; Tom Stoppard (playwright), 1937; Tom Cruise (actor), 1962

Deaths Brian Jones (rock musician), 1969; Jim Morrison (rock musician), 1971; Lew Hoad (tennis player), 1994

Events The Battle of Gettysburg, in the American Civil War, ends, 1863; Algerian War of Independence against France ends, 1962

Strong Ale

Rogue Younger's Special Bitter

Source Rogue Brewery, Newport, Oregon **Strength** 4.8% **Website** rogue.com

In a flurry of patriotic red, white and blue razzmatazz, the US celebrates its independence from Britain on 4 July. The day marks the anniversary of the adoption of the Declaration of Independence in 1776. A federal holiday in the US, it is a time for families and for picnics, parades, bands and barbecues.

In the UK, a different sort of independence was celebrated in July for many years by CAMRA, the Campaign for Real Ale. It started in the 1980s, when 4 July was declared Independents' Day, to highlight the threat to stand-alone breweries at a time when take-overs and mergers were wrecking the brewing industry. It was used to boost the new wave of microbreweries that had opened since the late 1970s. In later years, the event was widened to make July 'Independents' Month', but the buoyancy of the sector has meant that a formal campaign like this every summer is no longer needed.

So, for a choice of beer for today, we return to the US, and to one of the most successful independent breweries that have sprung up in the last two decades. Rogue Ales was founded in 1988 by former Nike executive Jack Joyce and two corporate colleagues. Initially, its home was a brewpub at Ashland, Oregon, but the business expanded rapidly and is now based in the coastal town of Newport in the same state.

English inspiration

Rogue beers are distinguished by their tall, colourful bottles and also

their big, beautifully balanced flavours. Products such as American Amber, Brutal Bitter, Mocha Porter, XS Imperial Stout and the Halloween-associated Dead Guy Ale have been seen on the world stage for a number of years and, being unpasteurized, have wowed drinkers with their clean, fresh, full flavours.

One of Rogue's finest ales, Shakespeare Stout, is featured on 26 April, but when the beers are this good we need to find room for another, and today gives us the perfect opportunity. The selection is Younger's Special Bitter, a satisfying premium ale named in honour of Bill Younger, brother of Don Younger, the proprietor of the Horsebrass Pub in Portland, Oregon, one of the US's best and longest-established specialist beer bars. It is brewed from pale and crystal malts, and laced with Willamette and East Kent Golding hops.

The beer opens up with abundant aromas of buttery, toffeeish malt, bitter oranges, tangy, spicy hop resins and

sultanas. It continues with a taste that is bursting with citrus fruitiness from the US hops, with zesty bitter oranges and grapefruit leading the way over smooth, buttery malt, and it rounds off with a long-lasting, defiantly hoppy, tangy finish.

Ironically, perhaps, for today, the bottle describes this as 'a classic English special bitter', but there aren't many English beers as bold and hoppy as this. Still, it's nice to know that the US still needs to call on the UK for inspiration occasionally.

Births Calvin Coolidge (US President), 1872; Gina Lollobrigida (actress), 1927; Colin Welland (actor and playwright), 1934

Deaths Thomas Jefferson (US President), 1826; Marie Curie (physicist), 1934; Barry White (soul musician), 2003

Events Food rationing ends in Britain, 1954; Israeli commandos break a siege at Entebbe airport, Uganda, rescuing 100 hostages, 1976

ABOVE: FOURTH OF JULY PARADE, ATLANTA, GEORGIA

Strong Ale

Okell's Mac Lir

Source Okells Ltd, Douglas **Strength** 4.4% **Website** okells.co.uk

Because of its geography, language, currency and general way of life, it's commonly assumed that the Isle of Man is a part of the United Kingdom. It's not. It's not even a part of the European Union. While the British monarch is officially the head of state of this island – 53km (33 miles) long by 21km (13 miles) wide, halfway between Lancashire and Northern Ireland – it is, in fact, an independent kingdom, something that is celebrated every 5 July.

On this day, the Tynwald, or Manx parliament, rises from its normal debating house in the capital, Douglas, and holds a ceremonial open-air session on Tynwald Hill, a terraced, circular mound in the village of St John's. Bills that have passed through the legislature are promulgated on this occasion, petitions are received, and the opportunity is taken to swear in important officials. It is a day to celebrate being a Manxman – perhaps with a glass of local beer.

Local brews

The island is home to three breweries: the Bushy's and Old Laxey microbreweries, and the well-established Okells. Okells was founded by Dr William Okell in 1850, and later merged with a wine merchant called Heron & Brearley, which is now the parent company. Diversification is the name of the game on such a small island, so H&B also has irons in other fires, including cellar services, refrigeration, security and road haulage. In the 1980s, the company took over and closed the rival Castletown Brewery, relocating all production to the Okells Falcon Brewery in Douglas. That itself closed after 120 years in 1994, when a state-of-the-art brewhouse was opened just outside the town, funded, in part, through a deal with Labatts to contract-brew lager. The Labatts arrangement was terminated by Okells four years later, leaving behind a modern, computerized brewing centre, geared up for either lager or ale production.

Now the range of ales is on the increase, as eyes have been turned to the export (i.e. English) market. One of the newer creations is a wheat beer called Mac Lir, which – as its name unintentionally suggests – pours bright rather than cloudy. It's actually named after Mannanan Mac Lir, a Norse god of the sea, who once was said to be a protector of the island. He is depicted in the swirling artwork on the bottle label. The beer contains 50% barley malt and 50% wheat malt. Wheat was something previously prohibited under the terms of the famous Manx Pure Beer Act (see 7 July), which meant that Okells needed to apply to the Tynwald for permission for its use. The resultant beer is broadly in the style of a Belgian witbier, golden in colour and laced with abundant peppery, bitter, zesty lime-like flavours that make it so refreshing, especially on a warm July day.

Births PT Barnum (showman), 1810; Cecil Rhodes (colonial statesman), 1853; Gianfranco Zola (footballer), 1966

Deaths Sir Stamford Raffles (colonial statesman), 1826; Walter Gropius (architect), 1969

Events The National Heath Service inaugurated, 1948; Arthur Ashe wins Wimbledon, 1975; Dolly, the cloned sheep, born, 1996

Wheat Beer

Marston's Owd Rodger

Source Marston's, Burton-upon-Trent **Strength** 7.6% **Website** marstonsdontcompromise.co.uk

Anyone who enjoys a life of leisure will be heartened by Kenneth Grahame's words of support in his short essay entitled *Loafing*. In this poetic little celebration of an idle life, Grahame extols the virtues of taking it easy, letting others hurry about their work while one, personally, takes things at a steady pace. There is one moment however, says Grahame, where even The Loafer must break with his languid approach to life, and that is when his thirst becomes too demanding. 'So, with a sigh half of regret, half of anticipation, he bends his solitary steps to the nearest inn,' he reports. 'Tobacco for one is good; to commune with oneself and be still is truest wisdom; but beer is a thing of deity – beer is divine.'

Kenneth Grahame was born in Edinburgh in 1859 and worked for a bank while penning his most famous literary work, *The Wind in the Willows*. He died on this day in 1932. So what beer should we raise to commemorate his life and appreciation of decent ale, and to celebrate the joy that he's brought to generations of young bookworms? One of the *Willows'* characters has a good suggestion.

Forgotten style

In the much-loved story, when Rat and Mole rediscover Mole's forgotten little home, it is revealed that the few things they can rustle up to eat and drink are a tin of sardines, a box of biscuits, a German sausage and several bottles of beer. To Mole, it doesn't sound like much of a feast but Rat makes the best of it, and even

allows himself a burst of excitement on examining the label on one of the bottles. '"I perceive this to be Old Burton," he remarked approvingly. "Sensible Mole! The very thing! Now we shall be able to mull some ale!"'

Old Burton refers to the style of beer that was developed in Burton-upon-Trent in the 19th century as an alternative to the pale ales for which the Staffordshire town was world famous. Burton was darker and maltier than pale ale, and often given longer to mature. The style, once very popular, has sadly fallen away, with perhaps the best surviving example of this style being Young's Winter Warmer, albeit rather weaker. In keeping with the spirit of strong Burton-brewed ale, however, and the idea of a beer that could be used for mulling – if not, perhaps, at this time of year – Marston's Owd Rodger offers a fine alternative.

Marston's likes to call this potent brew 'an old style country ale' but, like the old Burtons, it does have a rich ruby colour and plenty of malt character. What really shines through here, however, is fruit – sticky sultanas and juicy berries – with the obvious initial sweetness well countered by tangy hops, a spicy warmth and just a suggestion of liquorice. A glass or two would seem like an excellent way to top off even the most indulgent day of loafing.

Births Bill Haley (rock 'n' roll musician), 1925; Dave Allen (comedian), 1936; George W Bush (US President), 1946

Deaths King Edward VI, 1553; Aneurin Bevan (politician), 1960; Louis Armstrong (jazz musician), 1971

Events John Lennon meets Paul McCartney, 1957; Piper Alpha oil platform disaster, 1988; 2012 Olympic Games awarded to London, 2005

Old Ale

Bushy's 1874 Ruby Mild

Source Mount Murray Brewing Co., Braddan **Strength** 3.5% **Website** bushys.com

Germany, with its celebrated Reinheitsgebot, is not the only part of the world that can boast a law guaranteeing the purity of beer brewed locally. The Isle of Man has had such legislation since 1874, and it was on this day that the act that brought it in obtained its Royal Assent, having been previously passed by the Manx parliament on 19 June.

The Manx Pure Beer Act sought to criminalize the use of inferior or dangerous ingredients in beer production. Among its targets were such oddities as grains of paradise, guinea pepper, nux vomica and even opium. Anyone found breaching the strictures of the act was liable to a £300 fine and the confiscation of all their beer and brewing equipment.

The law is still in force today so, not surprisingly, as reported in the entry for 5 July, local brewer Okells was keen to clear the use of wheat as an ingredient with the authorities when it developed its new beer called Mac Lir. While the modest fine would have not disturbed the accountants too much, there's no way they would have wanted to risk the confiscation of a modern, computerized, 20,000-barrel brewhouse.

Extra pure

Brewing at a much smaller scale on the island is Bushy's. The business started out as a brewpub in 1986 but moved to larger premises in 1990, as demand for its beers grew. The company now runs four pubs on the island and prides itself on out-purifying even the Manx Beer Purity Law by not including sugar in its recipes. Several of Bushy's beers celebrate Manx landmarks and the world-famous TT motorcycle races that are held on the Isle of Man every summer, but one beer in particular relates specifically to the events of this day all those years ago. It's an easy-drinking, cask-conditioned dark mild, lightly seasoned with Fuggle and Challenger hops. Fruity sweetness leads up front, followed by a pronounced dry roasted malt flavour that continues pleasantly into the finish.

The beer goes by the simple title of 1874 Ruby Mild. Once again, as we've seen elsewhere in this book, by investigating an obscure date in the name of a beer you can discover so much.

Births Gustav Mahler (composer), 1860; Jon Pertwee (actor), 1919; Ringo Starr (pop musician), 1940

Deaths King Edward I, 1307; Richard Brinsley Sheridan (playwright), 1816; Sir Arthur Conan Doyle (writer), 1930

Events First Farnborough air display, 1950; Boris Becker wins Wimbledon, aged 17, 1985

Mild

Harpoon UFO Raspberry Hefeweizen

Source The Harpoon Brewery, Boston, Massachusetts **Strength** 4.7% **Website** harpoonbrewery.com

There are few things more likely to intrigue the American public than reports of a sighting of alien spacecraft. Imagine, then, the reaction on this day in 1947 when the news broke that an unidentified flying object had been recovered by the US military from a ranch near Roswell, New Mexico.

The Roswell incident is now the stuff of legend – the subject of countless articles, books, films, television programmes and internet sites. But what is fascinating about this particular 'close encounter' is that the US authorities at first confirmed its veracity and then promptly denied it. When the *Roswell Daily Record* broke the news on 8 July, sources at Roswell Army Air Field acknowledged the story. The next day, the newspaper ran a contrary one, with the military declaring that it had all been a mistake.

It was farmer Mack Brazel who allegedly discovered the debris of a crash on his land. Strangely, Brazel changed his story soon after being taken in for questionning by the authorities. He wasn't alone in reporting alien activity, however. Other local residents claimed they were eyewitnesses to the crash. Some later reported how they had handled the unusual debris or how the authorities had dramatically tightened up security in the area. There were also rumours that alien bodies had been retrieved and subjected to autopsies. In 1994, the Office of the Secretary of the Air Force issued its final word on the matter. In a 'case closed' report, it determined that the strange aircraft were high-altitude research balloons and the 'aliens' no more than humanoid test dummies.

Genuine UFOs

So was the incident and its confused reporting a cock up or a cover up? Were there really aliens in New Mexico, or was the US military up to some nefarious activity that it struggled to obscure in the aftermath of the crash? It's a story that will keep conspiracy theorists happy for centuries, probably until the real aliens finally turn up to look for their ancestors. And, whatever the truth, it's been good for Roswell, generating a very healthy tourist industry.

If you want to spot a genuine UFO, grab a bottle of today's beer. It comes from the Harpoon Brewery, founded in Boston, Massachusetts, in 1986. There are, in fact, two UFOs in the brewery's range. The first is a cloudy wheat beer, with a delicate, crisp, lemony character. Despite the space-age label, the name comes from the fact that it is an 'unfiltered offering'. The second beer is the same brew with added natural raspberry flavour, and it's UFO Raspberry Hefeweizen that I've plumped for.

This is a clean and very refreshing, unpasteurized beer, first produced in 2006, with appeal way beyond the regular beer drinker. It is brewed from pale and wheat malts, with Nugget the (restrained) hop. In the glass, it presents an attractive blush-pink colour and a generous raspberry aroma. In the mouth, it is crisp and light-bodied, with plenty of sweet raspberry flavours but also a pleasant tartness that stops it from cloying. Raspberry notes become creamy in the marginally bitter, dry finish. It's just a perfect beer for summer parties when you want to welcome your guests with a glass of something that is, if not totally alien, at least a little bit unusual.

Births John D Rockefeller (industrialist), 1839; Louis Jordan (jazz musician), 1908; Marty Feldman (comedian and writer), 1933

Deaths Percy Bysshe Shelley (poet), 1822; Vivien Leigh (actress), 1967; Wilfred Rhodes (cricketer), 1973

Events The London Society for the Prevention of Cruelty to Children (forerunner of the NSPCC) founded, 1884; first edition of the *Wall Street Journal* published, 1889

Wheat Beer

New Belgium Fat Tire Amber Ale

Source New Belgium Brewing Company, Fort Collins, Colorado **Strength** 5.3% **Website** newbelgium.com

Recent drug scandals may have taken a little of the shine off the Tour de France, but July's cycle-fest remains one of the big, colourful events of the European summer. This gruelling test of speed and stamina has its origins in 1903, when journalist Géo Lefèvre suggested to his boss at *L'Auto* magazine that a race covering the entire country – a round trip of around 2,500km (1,553 miles) – would be great fun. The first event pushed off on 1 July that year.

Le Tour has grown into the most celebrated test of cycling strength and skill, now extending to some 3,500km (2,175 miles) over three weeks, and throwing up legendary names such as Eddie Merckx, Bernard Hinault, Miguel Indurain and Texan Lance Armstrong, who claimed seven consecutive titles at the turn of the 21st century. The race enjoys festival status in France, with workers taking days off so they can cheer the leaders through their home towns. As the circuit changes every year, it is an honour for a community to find itself on the route, and a carnival atmosphere prevails.

Amber & green

For a beer with which to join in the fun, I'm not going to France but heading over to the US. It's a beer that was itself inspired by a cycling tour, but this time of Belgium, and a rather more leisurely one than followed by the professionals. The story concerns former electrical engineer and keen home-brewer Jeff Lebesch, who, in 1986, took to two wheels for a glimpse of Belgium's

brewing magic. He was impressed, so much so that he started brewing his own Belgian-style beers when he returned home. In 1991, he and his wife, Kim Jordan, decided to go commercial, founding New Belgium brewery at Fort Collins, about an hour's drive north of Denver. New Belgium has since had to relocate twice to meet demand, and the latest home, built in 2002, is a handsome and ever-expanding site, with hugely impressive green credentials.

The company now has an astonishing range of beers in its stable – including a pilsner, an abbey beer and some wood-aged beers – but the main brand is a malty, biscuity, easy-drinking amber ale called Fat Tire. There's a crisp, hoppy edge to this popular 5.3% brew, but predominantly it's the malt that calls the tune. The off-beat name takes us back to Jeff's original Belgian cycling

trip, but it also underlines that the bicycle is king here. After a year's employment, all staff are given a New Belgium bike on which to cycle to work. It's just one way of staying in harmony with nature, part of a package of ecological measures that make New Belgium an environmental leader among breweries. Renewable energies power the brewhouse. Some 15% comes from methane collected through waste-water treatment; the rest is bought from a windfarm in Wyoming. That's impressive when you consider that New Belgium – after Samuel Adams and Sierra Nevada – is now the third largest craft brewery in the US and by definition the second largest ale brewery in American history.

It shows that big doesn't necessarily need to be bad. Other brewers now need to get on their bikes and follow this shining example.

500

NEW BELGIUM BREWING

Births Edward Heath (Prime Minister), 1916; Tom Hanks (actor), 1956; Jim Kerr (rock musician), 1959

Deaths Zachary Taylor (US President), 1850; King Gillette (inventor), 1932; Rod Steiger (actor), 2002

Events First Wimbledon tennis tournament, 1877; York Minster struck by lightning, 1984

Strong Ale

ABOVE: NEW BELGIUM'S FORT COLLINS BREWERY

City of Cambridge New Model Ale

Source City of Cambridge Brewery Co. Ltd, Cambridge, Cambridgeshire **Strength** 4.4%
Website cambridge-brewery.co.uk

Just in case you were inclined to think this beer had something to do with cars or catwalks, the Roundhead helmet on the label puts you straight. City of Cambridge has named this beer in memory of Parliament's New Model Army, the body of highly trained soldiers that was created in February 1645 to ensure the Parliamentarians could give the Royalists a hard time. It turned out to be the military unit that won the Civil War for the King's opponents.

The important thing about the New Model Army was that its authority was based on merit and not privilege. Whereas, up to this point, the nobility held all the keys to the officers' mess, now even a humble blacksmith or a butcher's boy, if he showed military acumen, could rise through the ranks. A certain Thomas Pride, for instance, was a brewer who became a colonel. Consequently, it was a well-motivated army of all the talents that proved to be the keystone of its success. Renowned commander Thomas Fairfax (see 12 November) was placed in overall charge of the army, supported on the cavalry side by Oliver Cromwell. They ensured the unit was well disciplined, with training tough and tactics well considered.

Convincing winners

The New Model Army was first engaged with a crucial victory at the Battle of Naseby on June 1645, but on 10 July the same year, the unit proved its worth convincingly at the Battle of Langport, with decisive consequences for the entire war. Here, Fairfax and Cromwell advanced their troops against the last major Royalist force, an army commanded by Lord George Goring in the West of England. Goring himself had chosen the battlefield, on open countryside near the village of Langport in Somerset, and had time to set out his defence, but the skill and determination of the New Model Army were too great, and Parliament ran out convincing winners. It is said that some 2,000 Royalist men were captured, and morale on the King's side was fatally weakened. The end of the first Civil War was in sight.

New Model Ale recalls Cambridgeshire's historic links with Oliver Cromwell. It is a premium bitter, with the brewery's trademark fruity hop notes. In the glass, it shows a deep amber-red, lifting up an aroma that combines malt, nuts, floral notes and orchard fruits. The same fruity, floweriness is evident on the palate, with a touch of roasted malt in the background, before a drying, hoppy, bitter finish with lingering fruit. It is available in both cask- and bottle-conditioned versions.

Births Marcel Proust (writer), 1871; Virginia Wade (tennis player), 1945; John Simm (actor), 1970

Deaths El Cid (soldier and politician), 1099; George Stubbs (artist), 1806; Joe Davis (snooker player), 1978

Events Lady Jane Grey proclaimed Queen of England, 1553; *Telstar* communications satellite launched, 1962

Best Bitter

199

La Trappe Dubbel

Source Bierbrouwerij de Koningshoeven, Berkel-Enschot **Strength** 6.5% **Website** latrappe.nl

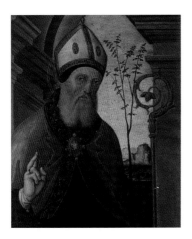

This book features a number of saints with close affiliations to the world of beer. None, however, has such a connection to our favourite drink as St Benedict, whose day is celebrated on 11 July.

Benedict was born in the Umbrian town of Nursia (now called Norcia) around 480 AD. His family was wealthy and he was raised in Rome but, having completed his education, he turned his back on the comfortable life and dedicated himself to God. He went away to live as a hermit but his piety was so renowned that he was encouraged to become the new abbot of a local monastery. It didn't work out. The monks were not devout enough for him, so he left. He did, however, later form new monasteries, which became the backbone of a movement that spread throughout Europe. Followers of Benedict, and his powerful 'Rule' – a set of principles monks should abide by – established thousands of abbeys across the continent in the centuries after his death, which was around 547.

The Benedictine movement transformed itself over time, with some groups adopting tougher discipline than others. One offshoot was the Cistercian order, and a scion of this is the Trappists, a 'Strict Observance' section that was created in the 17th century at the abbey of Grand Trappe in Normandy. Today, the Trappists are widely known for two things: their vow of silence and their brewing of beer.

It's not actually the case that Trappist monks never speak. They, rather wisely some would argue, simply avoid frivolous conversation and save their breath for things that really matter. In a similar fashion, they don't waste time brewing beer of little consequence. The Trappist beer range is characterized as being potent and nourishing, a selection of beers that may differ in terms of colour or actual strength, but which are united in being beers of quality.

Back in the fold

The seven Trappist monasteries that brew in northern Europe today include one in The Netherlands. The brothers of the Koningshoeven abbey, in the rural suburbs of Tilburg, have been brewing since 1884. In the late 1990s, they lost the right to call their beers Trappist, as it was deemed that the brothers' association with Dutch brewing giant Bavaria was too close, and that they were not sufficiently hands-on in the production of beer to meet the tight criteria of the Trappist

trademark. Happily, the impasse has been resolved, and La Trappe beers – under which Koningshoeven's products are marketed – are once more fully recognized.

The abbey produces an impressive range of regular beers, including Witte (5.5%), Blond (6.5%), Bockbier (7%), Tripel (8%) and Quadrupel (10%). Most commonly found, and absolutely sumptuous, is La Trappe Dubbel (6.5%). The porcelain-effect container, which became a trademark over the years, has gone, and Dubbel is now packaged in a conventional, but smart, little glass bottle. The contents are bottle conditioned, of course, and as reliable and enjoyable as ever – ruby-red, smooth, rich and sweet, with toffee notes from the abundant malt, plus raisins, pears and a pleasant tingling warmth.

Under the Rule of Benedict, the brethren are allowed to consume one beer a day (originally, it was one glass of wine per day, Benedict being an Italian). On that basis, some of us could never be monks. We wouldn't have the willpower to stick to just one.

Births Robert the Bruce (King of Scotland), 1274; John Quincy Adams (US President), 1767; Yul Brynner (actor), 1915

Deaths George Gershwin (composer), 1937; Laurence Olivier (actor), 1989; Robert Runcie (Archbishop of Canterbury), 2000

Events Harper Lee's novel *To Kill a Mockingbird* published, 1960; *Skylab* space station falls back to Earth after six years in orbit, 1979

Trappist Ale

Kaltenberg König Ludwig Weissbier Dunkel

Source König Ludwig Schlossbrauerei, Kaltenberg **Strength** 5.5% **Website** kaltenberg.de

They don't have kings in Bavaria any longer, but they do still have a prince, and he's a handy person to know because he also runs a brewery.

That brewery is Kaltenberg. It operates from two sites. One is a functional modern brewery in the town of Fürstenfeldbruck, around 32km (20 miles) west of Munich; the other is an altogether more fanciful creation, a little further to the south. Schloss Kaltenberg is one of those elaborate German castles that simply exude Wagnerian opera, or for the less high-minded, Walt Disney fantasy. This was where Prince Luitpold, great-grandson of the last Bavarian king, grew up. The Bavarian royal family gave up their throne after World War I (see 7 November), but they held on to their brewery. Luitpold inherited control from his father in the mid-1970s, and has since transformed its fortunes.

The castle is not merely a brewery or the home of a prince, however: it's quite an enterprise, catering for tourists with a pub, restaurant and gift shop, and drawing in the crowds every summer, when an impressive stadium stages a medieval jousting tournament. The Ritterturnier, as it is known, is, in some respects, Prince Luitpold's response to the Oktoberfest. His brewery is excluded from Munich's big event because it doesn't sit within the city limits. This seems an injustice, as the Oktoberfest was originally the wedding party of his great-great grandfather, King Ludwig I. The Prince is not sure why he is being excluded but rules have been changed on a regular basis to thwart his inventive attempts to gain access. Once, the Prince even walked from Kaltenberg to Munich carrying a litre of beer, with 2,000 supporters in tow, to make a point.

Medieval spectacle

Now, instead, he allows the Ritterturnier to make his point for him. The event's been running for more than 30 years – on the first three weekends in July – and is the biggest jousting tournament of its kind in Europe. Around 120,000 spectators flock to the castle to see an eight-hour programme acted out on seven stages. Stunt shows involving daring horseback deeds catch the eye, while 'medieval' market traders ply their wares at a series of colourful stalls. Accompanying the daily knights' tournament are a number of 'jesters' nights', more subdued and romantic evenings lit by flaming torch. At all times, typically robust Bavarian food is on offer, washed down by litres of Kaltenberg's own fine beer, including a special Ritterbock.

One of the other beers that has helped Luitpold restore the brewery's fortunes is König Ludwig Weissbier, which is imported into the UK by Thwaites. This was an obvious beer to promote when restructuring the company's portfolio, as the Bavarian royal family has held a profitable monopoly on weissbier production for around 200 years from the late 16th century. There is also a dark version, which is even more delicious. König Ludwig Weissbier Dunkel pours a hazy ruddy brown with a typically foaming wheat beer head. The aroma is spicy, with vanilla and creamy banana, as you'd often expect from this style of beer, but also light, smoky chocolate from the dark malts in the mash tun. Similar flavours pop up in the sweetish taste, which is crisp and quite light in body for the strength, rounding off nicely dry, bittersweet and chocolaty. With beers like this at the castle, the Oktoberfest's loss is surely the Ritterturnier's gain.

Births Josiah Wedgwood (potter), 1730; Bill Cosby (actor and comedian), 1937; Gareth Edwards (rugby player), 1947

Deaths Richard Cromwell (Lord Protector of England), 1712; Lon Chaney Jr (actor), 1973; Bill Owen (actor), 1999

Events King Henry VIII marries Catherine Parr, his last wife, 1543; Battle of the Boyne, 1690

Wheat Beer

Everards Tiger

Source Everards Brewery Ltd, Narborough, Leicestershire **Strength** 4.2% **Website** everards.co.uk

It would have been a great pleasure to include more brewing anniversaries in this book but, sadly, precise dates for brewery openings, the launch of new beers and even founders' birthdays seem to have been all too often lost in the steam billowing out of the mash tuns and coppers. One brewery that we can focus on with some certainty, however, is Everards in Leicester, whose founding father entered the world on this day in 1821.

The third of six sons born to a farming family, William Everard was a child of the industrial age. Although agriculture, as for his forebears, was his early business, he perceptively decided to broaden his horizons, forming a partnership with maltster Thomas Hull to take over Wilmot & Co.'s brewery in Leicester in 1849.

William was alert to the changes being introduced by the Industrial Revolution. Leicester, like other cities, was bursting with new arrivals seeking work in the hosiery and footwear factories. After a hard day's toil, thirsts needed quenching, and Hull & Everard's ales and porters were just the ticket. Indeed, they were so popular that, by the 1870s, a new, bigger brewery was needed.

Everards' second brewery was a state-of-the-art tower affair designed by William's nephew, John Everard. To help along the flow of beer, the company also began investing in a pub estate, acquiring the freeholds or leases of more than 70 pubs by the turn of the century.

Modern times

William died in 1892 and control of the brewery was bequeathed to his son, Thomas, who took the company solely into the family's hands. Everards continued to be popular, and a further brewery was opened in Burton to cope with demand. Today, Everards is centred entirely on Leicester again. Its impressive home is a modern brewhouse opened on the edge of the city in the 1980s.

Mention the name Everards and most drinkers will come back with the word Tiger. Although the company produces other fine beers, including Beacon Bitter and Original, it is its 4.2% best bitter for which it is widely known. The name is derived from the brewery's Leicester connections. The Leicestershire Regiment is known as the Tigers because of its years of service in India, and Leicester Rugby Club also shares the nickname.

Tiger has an appealing dark golden glow and an aroma that is malty, with a touch of toffee and some juicy raisin fruit. Juicy raisins continue in the mouth, along with plenty of malt and some balancing background hop, with the finish rounding off dry, bitter and hoppy with lingering malt sweetness. It's a well-balanced, easy-drinking beer that started life as a keg product, during the bleak days of pasteurized, pressurized beer in the early 1970s, but became a cask-conditioned ale when Everards returned to the real ale fold a few years later. It is also available filtered for the bottle.

Births Patrick Stewart (actor), 1940; Harrison Ford (actor), 1942; Ian Hislop (writer and broadcaster), 1960

Deaths Jean-Paul Marat (French revolutionary), 1793; Tom Simpson (cyclist), 1967

Events Queen Victoria becomes the first British monarch to reside at Buckingham Palace, 1837; Live Aid charity rock concerts take place around the world, 1985

Best Bitter

Castelain Ch'ti Blonde

Source Brasserie Castelain, Bénifontaine **Strength** 6.4% **Website** chti.com

It's time for the old joke to be wheeled out, I'm afraid. I've dusted it down and squirted on some Three-in-One but it still creaks and squeaks in all the wrong places. Nevertheless, here we go. Around 220 years ago today, the French were revolting.

Yes, it was on 14 July that the bold citizens of Paris finally told the King what they thought of him by ransacking the most important symbol of his authority. Around 1,000 invaders marched on the Bastille, the 14th-century fortress on the east side of Paris that the French monarchy had been using as a prison. Anyone who displeased the king was liable to be arrested and, without trial, thrown inside. Only seven prisoners were actually freed on the day of the rebellion, but, by giving the Bastille a good kicking, the mob sent a message to King Louis XVI that his days were numbered. Soon the Revolution was in full steam, the guillotine slicing away the power of the royalty and the associated aristocracy, and the French republic born.

Bastille Day, as outsiders call it, or Fête National as it is known in France, was officially declared a holiday in 1880 and is still celebrated with gusto. There's a military parade up the Champs-Elysées, firework displays staged from Calais to Cannes, and a glass or two of vin dispatched as part of the fun. Even beer gets a look in, which is as it should be in a country that may major on wine but has a brewing industry that is well worth shouting about.

Seductive northerner

The heartland of French beer production is in the north of the country, in the regions bordering Belgium and the English Channel, and it is here that we turn for an appropriate glass of beer. The Castelain brewery can be found in the village of Bénifontaine, in coal-mining territory near Lens. It has been run by the same family since 1926 and markets most of its beers under the Ch'ti name, which is local slang for a northerner. Today's beer, Ch'ti Blonde, is a glorious golden ale, introduced in 1979 after being trialled as a Christmas special. At the time, the beer was, you could say, revolutionary, breaking away from Castelain's traditional market among the miners and attempting to seduce the wider world with its sultry looks and fuller body. It succeeded.

Ch'ti Blonde has a distinctively herbal aroma. The taste is also herbal, with pleasing sour/tart notes, which mean it's not as sweet as expected. The texture is slightly moussey and, with its respectable 6.4% ABV, it's a touch warming, too, finishing up with a dry, lightly bitter, herbal aftertaste. In true bière de garde tradition, a period of conditioning (in this case at least six weeks) is allowed at the brewery before filtration and packaging. It's a big satisfying beer and, because it can easily be found in generous 750ml bottles, there's enough to share on a festive day like today.

Births Emmeline Pankhurst (suffragette), 1857; Terry-Thomas (actor), 1911; Ingmar Bergman (film director), 1918

Deaths Billy the Kid (outlaw), 1881; Dick McDonald (fast food pioneer), 1998

Events The belltower of St Mark's Cathedral in Venice collapses, 1902; all political parties, except the Nazi Party, banned in Germany, 1933

ABOVE: THE STORMING OF THE BASTILLE BY THE CITIZENS OF PARIS

Bière de Garde

Itchen Valley Pure Gold

Source Itchen Valley Brewery, New Alresford, Hampshire **Strength** 4.8% **Website** None

Some saints are known for their good works, others for their dedication to the faith or their courage in the face of adversity. Then there's a further band celebrated for the strangest of reasons, even though we know practically nothing about them or their lives. Take St Swithin, for instance, whose feast day is today. Most people will have heard the old saying that relates that if St Swithin's Day is wet, it will continue to rain for the next 40 days; and, if it is dry, then good weather will ensue. It's a bold prophesy that begs two rather obvious questions. First, when this forecast is proved wrong year after year, why do people still regurgitate it every July? And, second, who on Earth was St Swithin?

Swithin, we are told, was a Bishop of Winchester at some time during the ninth century, and the weather adage probably derives from events after his death. On his passing in 862, Swithin's admirable modesty and self-effacement were taken to a new level with his request that, being an unworthy soul, he be buried not inside his church but outside its walls. Those who thought he deserved better tried later to move his remains indoors, but they were thwarted when it rained for 40 days – an expression, it was said, of the saint's displeasure. Sadly, that is about all we know of this obviously great man. There's not even a beer named after him. The closest association we have is with a brewery just a few miles outside the city of which Swithin was chief cleric.

It's raining hops

Itchen Valley Brewery was founded in 1997 and from its base in New Alresford makes a play of its proximity to the ancient capital of England in some of its beer names. Winchester Ale, for instance, is one of the seasonal offerings, while Wykehams Glory has connections to famous Winchester College. Out of its fermenters also runs an unusual blonde beer called Pure Gold. We'll take the 'pure' bit as relating to St Swithin and use it to celebrate his largely forgotten life.

What's peculiar about this beer is the fact that hops are added not only in the copper as the wort is boiled, but also in the fermenter while the yeast is performing miracles of its own. The main, rather gentle, hops used for a spicy bitterness are Czech Saazs, but in the fermenter go notoriously citrus Cascades from America, so expect a Starburst-like drenching of juicy grapefruit and pineapple flavours from aroma to finish. The beer is available in both cask- and bottle-conditioned forms, so if the sun is shining, you can drink one on tap today, and if it's looking a bit grim outside, you can put a bottle – or 40 – aside for a rainy day.

Births Inigo Jones (architect), 1573; Rembrandt (artist), 1606; Iris Murdoch (writer), 1919

Deaths Anton Chekov (writer), 1904; Gianni Versace (fashion designer), 1997

Events Rosetta Stone, which helped crack the code of hieroglyphics, discovered in Egypt, 1799

Golden Ale

204

King Red River Ale

Source WJ King & Co. (Brewers), Horsham, West Sussex **Strength** 5%
Website kingfamilybrewers.co.uk

Most people know Hilaire Belloc for his children's nonsense verse. Humorous works like *The Bad Child's Book of Beasts* and *Cautionary Tales* come to mind and bring back nostalgic memories of infant school times. Beer lovers respect him for another reason, a simple quotation that has been used far and wide to illustrate the threat to our great institution, the British pub. 'When you have lost your inns,' Belloc once said, 'drown your empty selves, for you will have lost the last of England.'

Belloc was born in St Cloud, near Paris, in 1870. His prosperous family brought him to England during the Franco-Prussian War, and he became a British citizen. He studied at Oxford, where he was voted President of the Union and claimed a first-class degree. To earn a living, he turned to journalism and lecture tours, and was even a Member of Parliament for four years. In his writings, the subjects were many and various. Travel was one joy, but he also wrote about history, religion and politics, as well as biography, literary criticism and novels. Clearly a good pint was also well up his list of priorities, as revealed in verse he composed around 1910:

They sell good Beer at
    Haslemere
And under Guildford Hill.
At Little Cowfold, as I've
    been told,
A beggar may drink his fill:
There is a good brew in
    Amberley too,

And by the bridge also;
But the swipes they take in
    at Washington Inn
Is the very best Beer I know,
    the very best Beer I know.

The lines come from Belloc's *West Sussex Drinking Song*. Sussex was where the author settled down, and his love of the county is obvious from this and other texts. No doubt in his time in the area he would have sunk a few pints of Harvey's excellent beer from Lewes, and perhaps the odd glass of King & Barnes, the Horsham brewery that closed after more than 200 years in 2000, when it was acquired by Hall & Woodhouse.

Back to basics

The legacy of K&B lives on, however, in the form of WJ King & Co., a microbrewery founded by Bill King, latterly chairman and managing director of the closed regional. Bill's operation is obviously much smaller than he was used to, and his job considerably different. He's left the boardroom to get back to brewing basics, which even means digging out spent grains from the mash tun from time to time.

King operates from an industrial unit on the edge of Horsham, and produces a good variety of cask- and bottle-conditioned ales. I'd imagine the beer they call Red River would have appealed to Belloc. It's a strong, light ruby-coloured ale with plenty of malt character – sweet, nutty and smoky – with fruity notes supplied by Challenger, Golding and Whitbread Golding Variety hops. The aroma is also fruity and malty, while the finish is more bitter and roasted. It's not a million miles away from King & Barnes's old Festive Ale, which was first produced to celebrate the Festival of Britain in 1951 – just two years before Hilaire Belloc died. It's quite possible, when you consider this, that Festive may have been one of Belloc's final pints – his 'last of England', if you like.

Births Roald Amundsen (explorer), 1872; Ginger Rogers (dancer and actress), 1911; Shaun Pollock (cricketer), 1973

Deaths Anne of Cleves (fourth wife of King Henry VIII), 1557; Herbert von Karajan (conductor), 1989; Stephen Spender (poet), 1995

Events Opening of the Mont Blanc Tunnel between France and Italy, 1965; launch of *Apollo XI*, the first manned lunar rocket, 1969

Strong Ale

205

Vale Black Swan Dark Mild

Source Vale Brewery, Brill, Buckinghamshire **Strength** 3.3% **Website** valebrewery.co.uk

Ever wondered why some pubs have the rather frightening name of The Swan with Two Necks? Actually, it's a linguistic corruption. It should read The Swan with Two Nicks, but I doubt if most people are any the wiser for that. The answer lies in an event that takes place in the third week of July every year, a ceremonial river trawl that goes by the rather dubious title of Swan Upping.

In simple terms, Swan Upping is a census of swans on the River Thames. Tradition has it that all mute swans on the river belong to the Crown, an issue that dates back nine centuries to the days when swans were status symbols as well as prized table birds. The only exception to this royal prerogative is that two of the City of London's guilds – the Worshipful Company of Dyers and the Worshipful Company of Vintners – also have an entitlement to some birds. So it is that on or around 17 July each year, three teams of flannelled, blazered and flag-bearing swan uppers set out from Sunbury to row upstream to Abingdon in Oxfordshire. Their mission: to catch and identify every swan on the water so that cygnets can be marked with the same ownership as their parents. Swans belonging to the Dyers have one ring placed around a leg; those apportioned to the Vintners have rings placed on both legs. The sovereign's own swans are left unringed.

Useful survey

All this may seem a rather distressing business for the birds, but pomp and ceremony are hard obstacles to overcome, and anyway the RSPB suggests that, despite being mostly symbolic, the event provides a useful survey of the health of the swan population. Also, while the rings-on-the-legs ordeal may sound a bit cruel, it's nothing compared to the former way of establishing ownership of a swan. That was by marking each bird's beak with either one or two nicks from a sharp knife – hence the origin of that intriguing pub name.

One swan always worth trapping is produced by the Vale Brewery in Brill, Buckinghamshire. Black Swan Dark Mild is actually ruby in colour, thanks to the inclusion of crystal and black malts alongside pale malt. The hops are Fuggle and Golding, although, as befits a traditional mild, their presence is kept nicely in check, just adding a light fruitiness and gentle bitterness to marry with the sweetness of the malt. The beer's name actually comes from the emblem of Buckinghamshire, with the white swan on the county's crest darkened to match the nature of the beer. Served cool, it's as refreshing as any beer on a July afternoon.

Births James Cagney (actor), 1899; Camilla, Duchess of Cornwall, 1947; Angela Merkel (German Chancellor), 1954

Deaths Adam Smith (economist), 1790; John Coltrane (jazz musician), 1967; Edward Heath (politician), 2005

Events King George V adopts Windsor as the Royal Family's house and surname, 1917; Disneyland, California, opens, 1955; Humber Bridge formally opened, 1981

Mild

Saint Arnold Elissa IPA

Source Saint Arnold Brewing Co., Houston, Texas **Strength** 6.6% **Website** saintarnold.com

There are two St Arnolds with connections to beer. The second we shall meet on 14 August, but here the attention swings to St Arnold, or Arnulf, of Metz, a 6th-/7th-century nobleman born near Nancy, France, who became an influential member of the court of the Frankish king Theodebert. His claim to fame is that he was appointed Bishop of Metz at the age of around 30, even though he was only a layman at the time. On his retirement, he became a recluse and died in 640 in the Vosges mountains in northeastern France. It is said that his pallbearers stopped for refreshment on the way to the funeral service, but only one mug of beer could be found to serve them. Miraculously, the mug proved to be bottomless, and all thirsts were duly quenched. Thus, Arnold became one of brewing's patron saints and is often depicted with a bishop's mitre in one hand and a mashing fork in the other (although some attribute this image to the other St Arnold).

Lone Star saint

Arnold's name has been adopted by the oldest microbrewery in Texas. Saint Arnold was set up in 1994 and, whereas other craft brewers and brewpubs have come and gone in the Lone Star State, this Houston-based business has proved resilient in a tough market place. 'We aim for drinkability,' says brewer Dave Fougeron, which explains why Saint Arnold's beers are not as strident as those of many US micros. The recognition is that people need to come back for more and not simply give in after overloading their tastebuds on the first pint. That doesn't mean that the beers lack flavour: on the contrary. There's a fine portfolio of brews – from the malty, nutty Spring Bock to the strangely named Kölsch copy, Fancy Lawnmower – any of which would have done justice to today's celebration, but I've plumped for one called Elissa. Named after a restored, 19th-century tall ship moored on Galveston Island, Elissa is an IPA with just a touch more of a malt accent than a hoppy one, for a change, thanks to a generous helping of British Maris Otter pale malt and a little crystal malt in the mash tun, plus a steady hand with the citrus Cascade hops in the copper.

The brewery was founded by entrepreneur Brock Wagner, who came up with the idea while home-brewing as a student in the 1980s. Brock's family has German roots and he lived for a while in Brussels, so he's well aware of European brewing heritage and the story of St Arnold, which is recited on his beer labels.

Saint Arnold's beers may be tricky to track down, but the business is growing fast and some bottles may well cross the Atlantic before too long as interest in the US craft brewing movement continues to grow in the UK.

Births WG Grace (cricketer), 1848; Richard Branson (entrepreneur), 1950; Nick Faldo (golfer), 1957

Deaths Jane Austen (writer), 1817; Thomas Cook (tourism pioneer), 1892; Paul Foot (journalist), 2004

Events Adolf Hitler publishes his *Mein Kampf* manifesto, 1925; Romanian gymnast Nadia Comaneci scores the first perfect 10 at the Montreal Olympic Games, 1976

IPA

Harvey's Armada Ale

Source Harvey & Son, Lewes, East Sussex **Strength** 4.5% **Website** harveysonline.co.uk

One of the most notorious sea battles of all time effectively began on this day in 1588, when the Spanish Armada was sighted in the English Channel. The Armada was dispatched by King Philip II, who was determined to put the English Protestants in their place and ensure his fellow Catholics suffered no more at the hands of the Reformists. The fact that his ships in the Caribbean had been attacked and plundered by Sir Francis Drake also rubbed him up the wrong way, so he sent off an enormous fleet of 130 ships to teach the English a lesson and, hopefully, secure himself the English throne at the same time. As we now all know, the Spanish were roundly beaten by Drake, who even had time to finish his game of bowls before leading his crews out to sea. The English Navy trapped the Armada in the English Channel and forced it to undertake a long journey around the coasts of Ireland and Scotland to get home, a journey for which it was hopelessly ill prepared. With the help of stormy weather, the Armada was seen off, and the Protestants under Queen Elizabeth I remained in charge in England.

400th anniversary ale

Remembering times when Johnny Foreigner has been given a damn good whipping is the stuff that British celebratory beers are made of, and the rout of the Armada has been commemorated by beers from a number of breweries. The longest surviving is Armada Ale from Harvey's in Lewes, East Sussex. Like most of Harvey's fine beers, this 4.5% brew is a traditional British bitter in style, golden in colour, full bodied and totally delicious. Fuggle, Golding and Progress hops are joined in the copper by Bramling Cross for a fruity boost, and the beer is then dry-hopped with Styrian Goldings. As a result, there's a rich hop-resin character throughout – as if you've just rummaged in a brewery hop store – with a silky, delicate malt sweetness nicely in support.

Armada Ale was first brewed for the bottle, to be sold at the National Maritime Museum in Greenwich at the time of the 400th anniversary of the defeat of the Armada in 1988, but it is now also available in cask-conditioned form, justifiably earning itself a silver medal at the Great British Beer Festival in 1992.

Births Samuel Colt (gun pioneer), 1814; Ilie Nastase (tennis player), 1946; Brian May (rock musician), 1947

Deaths Petrarch (poet), 1374; Jack Warden (actor), 2006

Events Lady Jane Grey deposed as English monarch by Mary I, after just nine days on the throne, 1553; IRA announces its ceasefire, 1997

Pale Ale

ABOVE: ENGLISH SHIPS AND THE SPANISH ARMADA BATTLING IN THE ENGLISH CHANNEL

Triple fff Moondance

Source The Triple fff Brewery, Alton, Hampshire **Strength** 4.2% **Website** triplefff.com

W ell, if it was a hoax, it was a damn good one. On 20 July 1969, four days after blasting off from Cape Canaveral, Neil Armstrong and Buzz Aldrin set foot on the moon. The world watched as one, in awe of man's first steps on another galactic rock. The estimated television audience numbered around 500 million. No doubt a few beers were sunk in celebration.

Of course, the cynics insist it never really happened, that the whole thing was cooked up in a film studio somewhere in the deserts of the western US. But as an event of such enormous magnitude, it must feature in any book of days, and there are any number of lunar-themed liquids with which it could be partnered. For me, however, the one that takes all the beating is Moondance from Triple fff, a microbrewery based near Alton in Hampshire.

Moon rock

Whoever gave the brewery a name like Triple fff must have been a little spaced out, so there's a further appropriateness to the selection, although I doubt whether it was *Apollo XI* that inspired this particular brew. A glance through Triple fff's brewing books reveals such ales as Stairway to Heaven, and Dazed and Confused, both paying homage to the loud and proud antics of the band Led Zeppelin. There's also Comfortably Numb (Pink Floyd) and Pressed Rat and Warthog, which, true rock connoisseurs will inform you, is a track from Cream's 1968 album *Wheels of Fire*. So it seems that this Moondance would have more to do with the jaunty, jazzy track by Van Morrison than extraterrestrial activity.

The beer was one of Triple fff's early brews when it first fired up its copper in 1997. The clever blending of three hops – the solid bitterness of Northdown, the versatility of the fruity hedgerow strain First Gold and the assertive citrus notes of Cascade – has proved a winning combination. Moondance now has a couple of Champion Beer of Britain medals to its name, having won the Best Bitter category in 2002 and finishing third overall in 2006. Full and fruity, with a resonant bitterness, it's a fine way to mark any occasion – whether it actually happened or not.

Births Lord Reith (broadcasting pioneer), 1889; Sir Edmund Hillary (mountaineer), 1919; Diana Rigg (actress) 1938; Wendy Richard (actress), 1943

Deaths Guglielmo Marconi (radio pioneer), 1937; Bruce Lee (actor), 1973

Events Sri Lanka's Sirimavo Bandaranaike becomes the world's first female Prime Minister, 1960; Turkey invades Cyprus, 1974

Best Bitter

ABOVE: NEIL ARMSTRONG AND BUZZ ALDRIN WALKING ON THE MOON

De Koninck

Source Brouwerij De Koninck NV, Antwerp
Strength 5%
Website dekoninck.be

Bush Ambrée

Source Brouwerij Dubuisson, Pipaix
Strength 12%
Website br-dubuisson.com

Births Ernest Hemingway (writer), 1899; Yusuf Islam (singer-songwriter), 1947; Robin Williams (comedian and actor), 1951

Deaths Robert Burns (poet), 1796; Basil Rathbone (actor), 1967; Long John Baldry (blues singer), 2005

Events Official opening of the Tate Gallery in London, 1897; the final Harry Potter novel, *Harry Potter and the Deathly Hallows*, published, 2007

Hurray! It's Belgium's National Day. While the future of this endearing little country is now in some doubt, as its increasingly diverse Dutch- and French-speaking regions push to go their separate ways, it's nonetheless a day for celebration – especially if you are a beer lover.

Belgium has only been around as a country in its own right since 1830. Its previous history was one of pillar and post, with a group of neighbouring territories pushed unceremoniously between the two. The Austrians, Spanish and French all took control at one time or another, and inevitably they brought with them language, religious and other cultural conflicts. After the French under Napoleon were finally booted out, today's Belgium was subsumed into a greater Netherlands in which the Flemish people in the north found themselves second-class citizens to the Dutch, and the French-speaking Walloons in the south even more distant. It was the British who came up with a solution, which involved divorcing the Flems and Walloons from the Netherlands and setting up a new independent state called Belgium. Under King Leopold I, the country was quickly established, but gradually over the years, and particularly in recent times, the bonds holding together the Flemish- and French-speaking parts have weakened, with some parties calling for an amicable divorce. Perhaps some heed should be paid to the country's motto, 'Strength lies in unity'.

Double celebration

Should a split happen, it will hopefully be peaceful. Belgium, the cockpit of Europe, has seen enough blood shed on its lands over the centuries. Until then, 21 July remains the national day, marking the date when Leopold took the constitutional oath that made him king in 1831. To do justice to both communities, it seems right to select two beers to mark the occasion, one from the Flemish side and one from Wallonia.

The first choice is De Koninck ('The King'). Brewed by an independent family brewery in Antwerp, this easily found amber ale has a world reputation for its character and quality, even if outsiders snigger a little when it is revealed that the goblet used for serving the beer locally is known as a bolleke. De Koninck has a lightly toasted malt flavour, a hint of spice and an orangey-citrus note, all rounded off by a dryingly moreish, fruity, malty, gently bitter and delicately hoppy finish.

Our second beer comes from Wallonia. It is another amber ale, but this one is considerably stronger than De Koninck. The brewery is Dubuisson, based at Pipaix, about 24km (15 miles) east of Tournai. It was founded as a farm brewery as long ago as 1769. The beer, which was created in 1933, is called Bush in Belgium but, as a result of a rather unnecessary legal intervention by US giant Anheuser-Busch, goes by the name of Scaldis in other parts of the world. Bush/Scaldis is a big malty, sweet beer, with a fruity flavour and a peppery hop bitterness. The caramel malt used in the recipe brings a caramel tinge to the taste, too.

Try one or both beers today and be doubly glad that, despite internal frictions, Belgium remains united in its love of great beer.

Old Chimneys Black Rat

Source Old Chimneys Brewery, Market Weston, Diss, Norfolk **Strength** 4.5%
Website oldchimneysbrewery.com

Pest controllers of the world unite. If you work for Rentokil, ask for a day off. Join with your colleagues, have a pest-free party or stage some kind of rodent carnival, for 22 July is Ratcatcher's Day.

The origin of this peculiar celebration is the legend of the Pied Piper of Hamelin, as recited by Robert Browning in his famous poem of the same name. Browning jauntily relates how the northern German city was plagued with rats that 'fought the dogs and killed the cats/And bit the babies in the cradles'. Nothing could rid the city of this vermin until a strange figure in garish clothing arrived and offered to cleanse the streets in return for a thousand guilders. In desperation, the mayor and council accepted the offer and witnessed the stranger pick up his pipe and charm the rats out of the houses and into the River Weser, where they drowned. When the piper requested his fee, however, the duplicitous councillors reneged on the deal. In response, the piper raised his pipe once more and this time charmed the children of the city, leading them to a hidden cave from which they never returned. Only one child, who was lame and couldn't keep up with the crowd, was left behind. The date of this event, according to Browning, was 22 July 1376.

It's a good, if disturbing, tale, no doubt based on some truth but clearly elaborated over the centuries. There's speculation that it may refer to a mass migration of children, who left Hamelin to found a new settlement in Eastern Europe, or to a disease that, borne by rats, claimed the lives of the youngest citizens, but the sources of these stories are somewhat vague.

The rat to catch

The decision to celebrate Ratcatcher's Day is equally puzzling. Still, it provides an opportunity to draw attention to another fine beer. I suggest opening a bottle of Black Rat Stout from the small Old Chimneys Brewery in Norfolk. The brewery is run by former Greene King and Broughton brewer Alan Thomson, and his selection of bottle-conditioned ales is second to none. Black Rat slots mid-way into his range, strength-wise, and has all the hallmarks of a classic milk stout – a sweet stout that contains lactose, or milk sugar (see 9 December). At 4.5% ABV, it's a little stronger than two other examples of the style featured in this book – Mackeson and Farsons Lacto – but it's a deeply satisfying beer. The colour is dark ruby, and the biscuity nose has a gentle sourness behind its bitter chocolate aroma. The taste is also chocolaty with the same, pleasant milky sourness, before rounding off with a dry, creamy, coffeeish finish.

If you're going to catch a rat today, make it this one.

Births Bob Dole (politician), 1923; Don Henley (rock musician), 1947; Lasse Viren (athlete), 1949

Deaths John Dillinger (outlaw), 1934; Sacha Distel (singer), 2004

Events The Battle of Falkirk, 1298; Alec Douglas Home stands down as leader of the Conservative Party, 1965

Milk Stout

Saison Dupont

Source Brasserie Dupont Sprl, Tourpes **Strength** 6.5% **Website** brasserie-dupont.com

A quiet day on the anniversary front gives us an ideal opportunity to explore the tradition of brewing summer beers in that most idiosyncratic of brewing countries, Belgium.

Our attention is drawn specifically to the French-speaking south of the country, or Wallonia, to give it its true title. This part of the world shares brewing traditions with its neighbours across the border in France, where the bière de garde concept, explored elsewhere in this book, was developed. The idea is one of farmhouse breweries creating beer for their workers. Because brewing in warm weather was hugely unreliable before the age of refrigeration, these farmer-brewers brewed up until spring and then set aside special beers that their employees could quaff when summer arrived. In order to survive the long periods of storage, these beers needed to be strong and notably hoppy, as both alcohol and hops act as a preservative in beer.

The name that the Walloons gave to the concept was saison. It means, simply, season, but the season in question is summer, although some claim that the term refers to the season in which the beer was traditionally brewed, i.e. late winter/early spring. Today's saisons are a mixed bunch. They vary in strength and flavour, so it's not easy to band them into a general flavour profile. However, the most prominent and successful has been the one produced by the Dupont brewery, which was established on a farm at Tourpes, about 16km (10 miles) east of the city of Tournai, in 1844. The Dupont family acquired the business in 1920 and, today, it's still a family-run enterprise, reaffirming its farming roots with a cheese dairy on site.

Sappy quencher

Saison Dupont is a chunky golden ale of 6.5% ABV. When poured, it raises a moussey foam to the rim of the glass. The aroma is full of yeasty spice – the beer is bottle conditioned – with a hay-like freshness and juicy fruit notes that combine elements of orange, pineapple and apricot. In the mouth, the alcohol is certainly apparent through the gentle, spicy warmth. Bitter orange is backed by other fruit flavours, but the key feature is a sappy, herbal hoppiness, which continues into the dry, bitter aftertaste, bringing an almost liquorice-like note. Despite its strength, this is a quenching beer, just as the farm workers toiling the land would have demanded. It is also sold in a slightly weaker (5.5% ABV), organic version, known as Saison Dupont Biologique. Both versions are no longer seasonal and can be enjoyed all year round.

Births Michael Foot (politician), 1913; David Essex (singer and actor), 1947; Graham Gooch (cricketer), 1953

Deaths Ulysses S Grant (US President), 1885; DW Griffith (film director), 1948; Leo McKern (actor), 2002

Events End of military rule in Greece, 1974; Prince Andrew marries Sarah Ferguson, 1986

Saison

Meantime Coffee

Source The Meantime Brewing Co. Ltd, London **Strength** 6% **Website** meantimebrewing.com

I don't know who dreams up these events, but it seems that every vested interest is catered for in the American thematic calendar. Elsewhere in this book, we uncover the delights of Elephant Appreciation Day, Winnie the Pooh Day and Bob Day. Now, for 24 July, be prepared to celebrate the humble coffee bean. Today is Coffee Day!

Actually, this is Coffee Week, according to some 'experts', but I am not at all sure that coffee needs a day or a week. Isn't there enough of the stuff being drunk in the US anyway? For the health of the nation, you'd have hoped they'd have launched a No-coffee Day, but that wouldn't be very capitalist, I suppose.

So how can we do our bit to celebrate this important occasion? Easy, really. There are a number of beers out there that actually contain coffee. The Great American Beer Festival even judges beers in a 'Coffee Flavored Beer' category. If you can get your hands on them, try these award-winners for size: Java Porter from Blind Tiger Brewery in Kansas; Pipeline Porter from Hawaii; Arctic Rhino Coffee Porter from Midnight Sun Brewing in Alaska; or the 2007 GABF winner Coffee Bender, from the wonderfully named Surly Brewing Company in Minnesota. For my money, however, one of the best coffee beers comes from London.

Gold blend

It was back in 2004 that Meantime Brewing first dabbled in the cult of coffee. Using Fairtrade Arabica Bourbon beans from Rwanda, the brewery put together a 4% beer that was based on a porter recipe, the aim being for the dark roasted flavours of the malt to marry with the similar characteristics of the coffee. It was a beer that divided opinion and, eventually, Meantime decided to have another crack at it. The result was a much stronger beer, as it was recognized that the beer needed to be a bit heftier in order to fight its corner against the coffee. Opinions were not divided this time around. The beer was a big hit, engaging enough to strike gold at the World Beer Cup in 2006 and in the International Beer Challenge in 2007.

Deep garnet in colour, Meantime Coffee is a triumph, with an enticing aroma that always reminds me of a walk past the door of my local Starbucks. In the complex grist, you'll find pale malt, brown malt, chocolate malt, black malt and other undeclared malts, with Fuggles providing the underplayed hop. Consequently, malty sweetness and coffee bitterness are brilliantly balanced in the creamy taste, leaving a mildly bitter coffee finish. Be warned, however. The beer contains real coffee so watch out for the hit of caffeine.

Births Amelia Earhart (aviator), 1897; Zaheer Abbas (cricketer), 1947; Jennifer Lopez (singer and actress), 1969

Deaths James Chadwick (physicist), 1974; Peter Sellers (comedian and actor), 1980

Events *Apollo XI* returns safely to Earth after the first manned moon landing, 1969; Lance Armstrong wins the Tour de France cycle race for a record seventh time, 2005

Porter

213

Ventnor Oyster Stout

Source Ventnor Brewery, Ventnor, Isle of Wight **Strength** 4.5% **Website** ventnorbrewery.co.uk

The feast day of St James, one of the original disciples, falls on 25 July. James travelled to Spain to preach the gospel, and, on his return to the Holy Land, was martyred. It is said that his remains, whether by spiritual means or more mundane, were then transported back to the town of Compostela in Galicia, where they became a focus for pilgrimages among the devoted. As a badge of identity, those making the long trek to the place now known as Santiago de Compostela took to wearing a scallop shell. Quite why this item has been linked to James is not clearly known, and, while there are some suggestions floating around, they all seem a bit too tenuous to dwell on here.

Oyster fishers have adopted St James as their patron, linking the scallop to their own particular catch. Consequently, the saint's day is celebrated in grand style in England's most famous oyster port. The Whitstable Oyster Festival runs for a week around 25 July. It trumpets the Kent town's 1,000-year association with fishing, and oysters in particular, and also the revival of the industry here following its demise in the early part of the 20th century. Well-attended events include a blessing of the waters, regatta, firework display, street procession and even a beer festival.

Cheap gourmet treat

Oysters have long held a close association with beer. Before over-fishing and pollution reaped their bitter harvest, oysters in the Thames estuary were plentiful and therefore cheap. When combined with porter – the everyday beer of the 18th and 19th centuries – they offered even the poorest of the working classes a gourmet treat that today is beyond the pocket of most people.

But it wasn't just the hoi polloi who 'made do' with oysters. It was reported that Disraeli once dined heartily on Guinness and oysters after a long day in the House of Commons, which illustrates again the close affinity between the salty shellfish and the dry, roasted character of a stout or porter. Some breweries have even produced beers called oyster stouts – including Kent's own Whitstable Brewery – although only a few have had the temerity to actually include oysters in the beer in recent times. The best-known example comes from Ventnor, on the Isle of Wight.

Ventnor's Oyster Stout contains a small quantity of fresh oysters ('enough to make a difference', says brewer Xavier Baker), which are placed in a net and dropped into the copper as the wort is boiling. The net is then transferred with the beer into the fermenting vessel, so that the oyster character has longer to build. That said, the finished beer is not especially 'fishy'. It has just a light whiff of the ocean about it, plus an appealing silkiness and dryness. And plenty of chocolaty roasted malt flavours mean you don't just have to drink it with seafood.

Births Arthur Balfour (politician), 1848; Johnny Hodges (jazz musician), 1906; Matt LeBlanc (actor), 1967

Deaths Samuel Taylor Coleridge (poet), 1834; Charles Macintosh (inventor), 1843; Ben Hogan (golfer), 1997

Events Coronation of King James I, 1603; Louise Brown, first test tube baby, born, 1978

ABOVE: FISH SLAPPERS PERFORM A FERTILITY DANCE TO LAUNCH THE WHITSTABLE OYSTER FESTIVAL

Woodlands Oak Beauty

Source Woodlands Brewing Co., Wrenbury, Cheshire **Strength** 4.2% **Website** woodlandsbrewery.co.uk

If you've never heard of George Borrow, perhaps a fair description would place him as the Bill Bryson of his day. Born in Norfolk in 1803, Borrow was an endlessly inquisitive man for whom a training in law was not demanding enough. Literature became his profession instead, and he used his speedy grasp of languages to travel the world and pen a series of travelogues. He visited Spain, Portugal, Russia, France, Germany and other countries, bringing back tales of alien lifestyles and chance encounters, genially blending fact with a hefty dose of fiction.

Always a man for his ale, Borrow punctuated his traveller's tales with accounts of visits to numerous inns and taverns. His love of beer is manifested particularly in his work *Lavengro*, when he excitedly declaims 'Oh, genial and gladdening is the power of good ale, the true and proper drink of Englishmen!', going on to declare that 'He is not deserving of the name of Englishman who speaketh against ale.' For this he should be allocated CAMRA membership card number one.

Ale & cheese troubles

Among the places Borrow visited, however, there is one city of which he doesn't speak well, certainly as far as its beer is concerned. In his 1862 work *Wild Wales*, he mentions a most unsatisfactory encounter in a Chester inn. Past experience led him not to expect much in the way of drink provision, and he was not disappointed. 'My wife and daughter ordered tea and its accompaniments, and I ordered ale, and that which always should accompany it, cheese,' he relates. '"The ale I shall find bad", said I; Chester ale had a villainous character in the time of old Sion Tudor… and it has scarcely improved since.' As it turned out, the cheese proved to be inedible, and the ale just as rank. 'I took a little of the ale into my mouth, and instantly going to the window, spirted it out after the cheese,' he says, going on to recite fellow beer critic Sion Tudor's derogatory rhyme about the local beer.

> Chester ale, Chester ale! I could
>   ne'er get it down,
> 'Tis made of ground-ivy, of dirt,
>   and of bran,
> 'Tis as thick as a river below a
>   huge town !
> 'Tis not lap for a dog, far less
>   drink for a man…

A century and a half later, Borrow would have been delighted in the turnaround in fortune's for Cheshire's ale drinkers. The county as a whole is now home to around a dozen microbreweries and, to prove things have got better, I can recommend a glass of one of their beers to mark this day in 1881, on which Borrow died.

Woodlands Brewery provides an excellent example of raised standards. Based near Nantwich, it is a family concern. We could opt for its very popular Midnight Stout or citrus-fragrant Gold Brew, but instead – in hoping to pick out a beer that George would have really appreciated – the selection is Oak Beauty. This is a best bitter thankfully made not from ground-ivy, dirt or bran but from four different malts, with four varieties of hop for seasoning: Northdown, Cascade, Golding and Fuggle. The outcome is an amber ale with light toffee flavours and a very pleasant citrus fruit accent. It's a shame George can't pay another visit and revise his opinion of the local beer. He'd have been impressed.

Births George Bernard Shaw (writer), 1856; Carl Jung (psychologist), 1875; Mick Jagger (rock singer), 1943; Helen Mirren (actress), 1945

Deaths Offa, King of Mercia, 796; Eva Perón (actress and politician), 1952

Events Forerunner of the US Federal Bureau of Investigation (FBI) inaugurated, 1908

Best Bitter

Alcazar Devout Stout

Source Alcazar Brewery, Old Basford, Nottinghamshire **Strength** 8% **Website** alcazarbrewery.co.uk

Douglas Fairbanks, Errol Flynn, Richard Greene, Michael Praed, Sean Connery, Kevin Costner and Jonas Armstrong – just a handful of the actors who have brought to life the mysterious character of Robin Hood. Today, the outlaw of Sherwood Forest is a perennially popular cinematic man of action, fighting injustice in lawless times, and constantly being reinvented for a new generation of film-goers and television viewers. It's great news, of course, for the county of Nottinghamshire, which benefits richly from Robin Hood tourism, and which does its own bit to keep alive the memory of this dashing figure with a week-long Robin Hood Festival, held at this time of the year.

Theories abound about the life of the man in Lincoln green, but with no firm conclusion about his true identity. Evidence from later ballads and stories dates him to the 13th century, but little more is known about him or his band of Merry Men. They, of course, feature as characters in the annual festival staged in Sherwood Forest, which is free to attend and attracts around 70,000 visitors a year, with its entertaining mix of jesters, jousters and other medieval japes designed to entertain adults and children alike.

In 2003, Nottingham's Alcazar Brewery wisely decided to pay its own tribute to the county's most famous figure by launching a range of Sherwood Forest Ales. These are mostly sold in bottle, but are occasionally seen in cask form. Bowman's Bounty is an IPA celebrating Robin's prowess at archery; Gaoler's Ale, an amber ale in memory of Robin's arch-enemy, the Sheriff of Nottingham; Little John's Myth, a porter referring to the alleged height of John Little; Scarlet Fervour, a strong bitter in honour of Robin's red-clothed cousin, Will Gamewell; and Maiden's Magic, a honeyed brown ale named after Robin's girlfriend, Maid Marian. The beer chosen here to mark festival week is Devout Stout.

Secret recipe

This is a beer belonging to the imperial stout style, a successor, perhaps, to the secret dark beer that Friar Tuck was alleged to have brewed for his outlaw associates and which, according to Alcazar, was based on a recipe from a monastery in Europe. The beer pours a deep ruby/rich brown in colour, more than hinting at the dark malt flavours awaiting in the aroma and taste, courtesy of a grist that includes Maris Otter pale malt, crystal malt, chocolate malt and roasted barley. There is certainly dark malt in the nose, which is slightly honeyed, giving the impression of liquid Crunchie bars. The same sweetish note recurs in the taste, which is smooth, complex and interesting, with traces of liquorice, caramel and tropical fruit, and a pleasant vinous tartness. It's a little bit oaky on the swallow, and the finish is drying, biscuity and progressively bitter, with more liquorice. The hops, overshadowed to some degree, are Target and Golding.

Overall, this is a beautifully balanced stout that, at 8% ABV, may seem a little strong for this time of year. But, in my mind, there's never a wrong time for a great beer and this one, just like Robin's straight and true arrows, always hits the spot.

Births Shirley Williams (politician), 1930; Allan Border (cricketer), 1955; Christopher Dean (ice dancer), 1958

Deaths Gertrude Stein (writer), 1946; James Mason (actor), 1984; Bob Hope (comedian), 2003

Events Foundation of the Bank of England, 1694; the Korean War ends, 1953

Imperial Stout

La Choulette Bière des Sans Culottes

The name 'Beer for Those without Shorts' seems strange for a drink, more French farce than French Revolution. But when you look into the history behind the name, you will find that it conceals a most disturbing period of French history.

The so-called 'Sans Culottes' were the ordinary working people of France, the class of traders and labourers whose budgets didn't run to fancy trousers like those worn by the privileged. Culottes, specifically, refers to knee-britches – all the rage, apparently, in the early 1790s. The impoverished Sans Culottes preferred full-length trousers. But this lack of sartorial elegance became a badge of honour as the Revolution, which had broken out in 1789, turned ever more bloody under the control of Maximilien Robespierre. Those on the wrong side of the Revolutionary fence felt the cruel edge of Madame Guillotine's bloodthirsty blade, and the footsoldiers in Robespierre's relentless army were the Sans Culottes.

It was in July 1793 that Robespierre surged to a position of great influence in the National Convention – the body that ruled France – and, from September that year, those who opposed or dared criticize the Revolution or its leaders were purged from society. But, with thousands of citizens falling victim to his murderous policy every month, the bloodshed became too onerous for his colleagues in the Convention to bear and his power began to wane. On 27 July 1794, Robespierre was forced to flee for his life. He was quickly captured, however, and executed a day later, thus bringing the Reign of Terror to an end.

Fancy pants beer

It is the La Choulette brewery that brews Sans Culottes beer. It may have a quirky name but it's a serious beer reflecting a serious time in French history. The brewery is based at Hordain, near Cambrai, just over 160km (100 miles) northeast of Paris, and its story is recounted in more detail in the entry for 4 September. The beer itself belongs to the bière de garde tradition, typically matured for weeks at the brewery before being bottled. 'Golden, round and perfumed', is how the brewery describes the beer, which was banned in the US state of Missouri in 2000 because its label was deemed obscene. It featured a reproduction of a work by Delacroix that showed Lady Liberty, bare-breasted, on the front line of the Revolutionary struggle.

La Bière des Sans Culottes is a richly malty golden ale. The aroma brings immediate memories of a mug of Ovaltine at bedtime, but with light toffee notes and hop resins. The same Ovaltine maltiness runs through the taste, which is sweet, smooth and full bodied. Perfumed herbal notes from the hops increase gradually for a better balance, and there is some light bitter citrus in the background. The finish is bittersweet with lingering malt and herbal hops that slowly take control.

Births Beatrix Potter (writer), 1866; Jacqueline Kennedy Onassis (US First Lady), 1929; Garfield Sobers (cricketer), 1936

Deaths Cyrano de Bergerac (poet), 1655; Antonio Vivaldi (composer), 1741; Johann Sebastian Bach (composer), 1750

Events Paddy Ashdown becomes leader of the Liberal Democrats, 1988; the IRA declares its armed struggle to be over, 2005

Bière de Garde

Westerham William Wilberforce Freedom Ale

Source Westerham Brewing Co. Ltd, Edenbridge, Kent **Strength** 4.8% **Website** westerhambrewery.co.uk

Robert Wicks, founder of Westerham Brewery in Kent, is a devoted Christian. This doesn't mean, he says, that he 'goes around wearing "Jesus Saves" badges', but it does indicate that ethics play a large part in his business. The two fishes in the brewery's logo may be an allusion to Christ, but it is through good deeds and not simple imagery that Robert practises his faith.

Take, for example, Christmas. Like many breweries, Westerham produces a festive ale at this time. It even has a humorous title. They call it God's Wallop. Unlike other Christmas creations, however, this one is no mere cash-in. A percentage of the revenue from each sale is channelled into a Christian charity.

It was no surprise, therefore, to find that, in 2007, Robert produced a beer that again epitomized his Christian spirit. In March that year, commemorations took place for the 200th anniversary of the abolition of slavery in the UK. For the occasion, Westerham created a beer that not only recognized this landmark event but also highlighted the evil of modern-day slavery, in the form of people trafficking. Robert called the beer William Wilberforce Freedom Ale, after the man who pushed through the bill that outlawed this iniquitous practice in the early 19th century.

Parliamentary success

William Wilberforce was born in Hull in 1759. After studying at Cambridge, he became Member of Parliament for his home city. His political driving force turned out to be his evangelical Christianity. It led him to investigate inequalities in the labour market, to promote education for children and, most significantly, to expose the miseries of slavery. For 18 years, he campaigned in Parliament for its abolition, finally finding success in 1807, when the trade was outlawed. The battle was not over, however, as people already held in slavery were not immediately set free. That was eventually achieved in 1833, the year in which Wilberforce died on 29 July.

William Wilberforce Freedom Ale is brewed from floor-malted Maris Otter pale malt and crystal malt, with Kentish Northdown and Golding hops providing the bitterness and balance. A high percentage of Fairtrade demerara sugar from a smallholder's plantation in Malawi also forms part of the mix. Lively citrus fruit, gentle hop resins and light, biscuity malt fill the aroma, which is followed by full, smooth malt in the mouth, layered with tart fruit and bitter hops. The finish is dry, tangy, hoppy and notably bitter.

For every pint sold, a contribution is made to an organization called Stop the Traffik, a multinational body set up to raise public awareness of today's slave trade, and dedicated to practical action that will hopefully stamp out this hideous, devastatingly inhuman activity. Buy a bottle today and give them your support.

Births Clara Bow (actress), 1905; Nellie Kim (gymnast), 1957; Graham Poll (football referee), 1963

Deaths Vincent Van Gogh (artist), 1890; John Barbirolli (orchestral conductor), 1970; Luis Buñuel (film director), 1983

Events Launch of the BBC Light Programme radio network, 1945; Prince Charles marries Lady Diana Spencer, 1981

Strong Ale

Old Bear Duke of Bronte Capstan F.S.

Source Old Bear Brewery, Keighley, West Yorkshire **Strength** 12.5% **Website** oldbearbrewery.co.uk

The 30th day of July was the birthday of 19th-century novelist and poet Emily Brontë, but the date gives us an opportunity to broaden the picture and celebrate the lives of the hugely talented Brontë family as a whole, and to discover an unusual beer that pays tribute to them.

The family's tale begins with Patrick Brunty, born in County Down, Ireland, on St Patrick's Day, 1777. Patrick was largely self-educated and secured himself a place at Cambridge University, where he changed his surname from Brunty to the more noble and exotic Brontë. He was inspired, it seems, by the title of the Duke of Brontë that had been afforded to Lord Nelson by the King of Naples. Patrick Brontë then embarked on a career as a clergyman, eventually settling in 1820 at Haworth, on the outskirts of Keighley, where he established a family. His wife, Maria Branwell, and two daughters, Maria and Elizabeth, died young, leaving four children in the fold. There were three girls, Emily, Charlotte and Anne, and one boy, Branwell.

Their childhood days in the parsonage seem to have been rather isolated, but no doubt fuelled their imagination and creativity, culminating in the novels that the girls published. Anne's most famous work was *The Tenant of Wildfell Hall*. Charlotte created the classic *Jane Eyre*, while Emily's *Wuthering Heights* is one of the all-time great English romances, inspired by the many hours she spent on the wild and windswept Yorkshire moors close to her home. Emily's own tale is as tragic as that of her famous characters Cathy and Heathcliff. She died of tuberculosis in 1848, just a few months after Branwell had suffered the same fate. Within a year, Anne died, too. Charlotte survived only another seven years, meaning all the family was outlived by father Patrick.

Brontë beers

The Brontë heritage has been celebrated in ale for a number of years through a beer called Brontë Bitter, brewed by Goose Eye Brewery in Keighley. Keighley, of course, is also famous as the home of Timothy Taylor, but there is a third brewery in the town and it is from here that today's beer originates. Old Bear Brewery was founded in Cross Hills in 1993 and moved to Keighley in 2005. Its Brontë beer is intriguing in that it doesn't dwell on obvious images of romantic literature but on the strange decision of Patrick Brunty to change his name in emulation of Lord Nelson.

The orange-gold beer was first produced in February 2007 for a beer festival at the Flowerpot pub in Derby. It is an adventurous brew, broadly along the lines of an imperial IPA, the super-strong, highly hopped style that has emerged in the US in recent years. It weighs in at a potent 12.5% ABV and is bottle conditioned. The malt is simply pale malt, augmented by flaked barley and torrefied wheat. The hops are Golding and Pioneer, and it's a beer that is simply loaded with taste.

Smoky malt notes are the dominant feature, but with those ample hops working hard to counter the abundant sweetness in both taste and gum-tingling finish, bringing tangy, fruity flavours. Some drinkers have identified tobacco as part of the profile. Having never smoked or chewed tobacco, I can't confirm this finding, but it's interesting that the beer has the subtitle of Capstan F.S., the letters standing for 'Full Strength', after a brand of strong cigarettes once popular in the UK.

Births Henry Moore (sculptor), 1898; Kate Bush (singer-songwriter), 1958; Daley Thompson (athlete), 1958

Deaths William Penn (Quaker), 1718; Michelangelo Antonioni (film director), 2007; Ingmar Bergman (film director), 2007

Events England wins the football World Cup, 1966; last regular edition of *Top of the Pops* broadcast, 2006

Imperial IPA

Springhead Roaring Meg

Source Springhead Fine Ales, Sutton-on-Trent, Nottinghamshire **Strength** 5.5% **Website** springhead.co.uk

Big blonde

Springhead Brewery was founded in Sutton-on-Trent, Nottinghamshire, in 1991. There have been changes in ownership and management over the years, but it was original brewer Alan Gill who created the beer that is named after Birch's formidable cannon. Alan is a Civil War enthusiast. Thus the Springhead portfolio is loaded with beers with connections to that turbulent era – beers such as Roundhead's Gold, Cromwell's Hat and even one called Goodrich Castle. Roaring Meg has proved to be the most successful. It's available in cask-conditioned form and also in bottle. It used to be bottle-conditioned and is now filtered, but it maintains its silky, honeyed malt smoothness and sweetness, and a crisp bitter edge. Like its namesake, this rich, golden ale is a heavyweight. The brewers call it 'The Big Blonde' and, at 5.5% ABV, it packs plenty of power and body. Sadly, there's no explanation of the origin of the name on the label.

It's 1646 and the fag end of the first period of the English Civil War. Royalist strongholds are now few as Parliamentarians continue their rout of the supporters of King Charles. In the Welsh Marches, one of the last bastions is Goodrich Castle, near Monmouth, a fortress with origins in Norman times. Holed up inside are Royalist Sir John Lingen and around 200 local supporters; closing in on him and his troops is the Parliamentarian Governor of Hereford, Colonel John Birch. A siege is inevitable.

In June, Birch marches his men to the castle and mounts a blockade that is to last six, long weeks. Finally, to resolve the situation, Birch unveils what he hopes will bring down the solid walls of the sternly defended castle. It's called Roaring Meg. Smelted in the nearby Forest of Dean, she's the queen of all cannons, a massive instrument that dispatches cannon balls weighing 90kg (200lb) or more. Meg's effect is immediate and the battle concludes on this day, 31 July, when the Royalists raise the white flag. It isn't the end for Roaring Meg, however. In the hands of General Fairfax, she goes on to bludgeon the defenders of Raglan Castle a month later. Today, this early weapon of mass destruction can be seen back at the site of her finest hour, amid the ruins of Goodrich Castle.

Births Milton Friedman (economist), 1912; Wesley Snipes (actor), 1962; JK Rowling (writer), 1965

Deaths Ignatius Loyola (theologian), 1556; Franz Liszt (composer), 1886; Jim Reeves (country singer), 1964

Events The world's second-highest mountain, K2, climbed for the first time, 1954; Jim Laker completes 19 wickets in a test match at Old Trafford, 1956

Golden Ale

Saltaire Challenger Special

Source Saltaire Brewery Ltd, Shipley, West Yorkshire **Strength** 4.8% **Website** saltairebrewery.co.uk

Is there a region of the United Kingdom that is so fiercely self-confident as Yorkshire? There's certainly no other area that has the front to declare itself 'God's Own Country' – not without some justification, it has to be said, when you consider the beauty of its countryside and the down-to-earth warmth of the people.

Yorkshire pride reaches its zenith on 1 August with Yorkshire Day, the origins of which lie in the reorganization of historic counties in 1974. Like many old parts of Britain, Yorkshire was dismembered in the local government reshuffle. Whereas the giant county used to be broken down into three Ridings – North, West and East – the new Yorkshire that took its place on the map of Britain was carved up many ways. In came the separate counties of West, North and South Yorkshire, and bits of the historic territory were hived off into the artificial local authority areas of Humberside and Cleveland. Traditionalists loathed the idea and set up the Yorkshire Ridings Society to express their protest. The designation of a Yorkshire Day, starting in 1975, was one means of raising their unhappiness.

The date of 1 August was chosen because it was on this day in 1759 that Yorkshire soldiers, leaving the Battle of Minden in Germany, stopped and collected white roses as a tribute to their fallen colleagues. The white rose has remained the county's emblem ever since. Yorkshire Day is marked throughout the county with a celebration of local culture, be it brass band concerts, Yorkshire pudding suppers, church services or an eager quaffing of the fine local ale.

Special ale

What is it about Yorkshire ale that makes it so special? That was one of the questions posed at a thought-provoking seminar hosted by former British Guild of Beer Writers Chairman Barrie Pepper in February 2007. There was discussion of fermenting vessels, yeast, hops and water, as well as historic industrial patterns. The session also analyzed assorted beers from around the county but failed to define a distinct, unifying Yorkshire beer style. In the end, participants just settled on the fact that the local ale was good and left it at that. As Barrie himself concluded: 'Just look at the number of awards won by Yorkshire brewers and ask yourself why Yorkshire folk don't go very far on their holidays.'

Which leaves me with an open field when selecting a typical Yorkshire ale for today's celebrations. I've opted for one of the excellent beers from Saltaire Brewery, based in an old tram power station in Shipley, just north of Bradford. Its beers are beautifully presented, with both pump clips and bottle labels making exemplary use of space to describe the beer properly. The one I've selected is Challenger Special, which, like all Saltaire's beers, does what it says on the label, in true, plain-speaking Yorkshire fashion.

Challenger is the main hop in this special ale, with Fuggle in support. The grist is comprised of pale malt and dark crystal malt, with some crystal rye and roasted barley, which immediately suggests that this is going to have a rich, nutty character. That's what emerges in the taste, with hints of liquorice, molasses and tropical fruit, all excellently balanced by bitterness from both the roasted grain and the generous hopping. It's a robust, forthright, good-value beer – a fine, beery manifestation, perhaps, of the proud and defiant Yorkshire temperament.

Births Herman Melville (writer), 1819; Yves Saint-Laurent (fashion designer), 1936; Jerry Garcia (rock musician), 1942

Deaths Cosimo de' Medici (banker and politician), 1464; Queen Anne, 1714

Events Nelson wins the Battle of the Nile, 1798; major bridge over the Mississippi River in Minneapolis collapses during rush hour, 2007

Strong Ale

221

1648 Lammas Ale

Source 1648 Brewing Co. Ltd, East Hoathly, East Sussex **Strength** 4.2% **Website** 1648brewing.co.uk

The first day of August was traditionally celebrated by the Church to mark the miraculous release of St Peter from imprisonment in Jerusalem. Under the orders of Herod Agrippa, the disciple had been placed under heavy guard and bound with chains. His execution was imminent. Instead, an angel arrived during the night, cast off the chains and engineered his release.

The festival is also called Lammas, after a pagan commemoration that takes place at this time of year. In such circles, the start of August was welcomed as a celebration of the new wheat harvest (the name is a derivation of 'loaf-mass'), and, in pagan belief, the occasion marks one of the four cross-quarter days of the year (1 August is still an official quarter day in Scotland). As traditions collided, the Church absorbed elements of the pagan concept. Parishioners annually baked loaves of bread from the new wheat, and delivered them to their local place of worship.

Lammas celebrations often extended into 2 August, indeed throughout the first part of the month. In some circles, 6 August is the day associated with the festival. Some parts of Britain still hold Lammas fairs around this time, including St Andrews in Scotland and Exeter in Devon, although one of the biggest now is staged in Eastbourne. This Sussex event was conceived in 2001, initially against the wishes of the local council and some Church groups. However, a change in local authority leadership has seen the festival welcomed more widely by the community, and growing by the year. Today, it is a two-day sequence of folk music concerts, morris dancing displays and colourful parades, with profits going to support the RNLI. A local brewery has even created a beer to mark the event.

The bounty of summer

Lammas Ale is produced by the 1648 Brewery, which is based in East Hoathly, near Lewes. The brewery's name relates to the deposition of King Charles I – brewing takes place in the old stables behind The King's Head pub in the village – and Lammas Ale is now available in summer every year. Appropriately, this is a blend of barley and wheat malts, seasoned with locally grown hops. It pours a dark golden colour and has a fresh, fruity, floral aroma. Sappy hop resins and juicy fruit, reminiscent of cantaloupe melons, lead the way on the palate, before a dry, hoppy, earthy but gentle finish. It's a quenching, tasty beer that certainly encaptures the luscious bounty of summer.

Births Carroll O'Connor (actor), 1924; Alan Whicker (journalist), 1925; Peter O'Toole (actor), 1932

Deaths King William II, 1100; 'Wild Bill' Hickok (lawman), 1876; Alexander Graham Bell (inventor), 1922

Events Adolf Hitler assumes complete power in Germany after the death of President von Hindenburg, 1934; Iraq invades Kuwait, leading to the first Gulf War, 1990

Golden Ale

Three Bs Shuttle Ale

Source Three Bs Brewery, Blackburn, Lancashire **Strength** 5.2% **Website** threebsbrewery.co.uk

Industrial heritage is something that beer does very well. You can always rely on a brewery to rekindle memories of bygone local trades and professions, and so it is in Blackburn, Lancashire, where the Three Bs Brewery first fired up its mash tun in 2001. The inspiration for the names of brewer Robert Bell's beers lies in the local cotton industry. In Robert's selection of ales, you can find Tackler's Tipple, named in honour of the fitter who worked in a weaving shed; Doff Cocker, after a person employed to remove waste from a weaving machine; and Knocker Up, remembering the man who rapped on workers' doors to rouse them from their slumbers ready for another hard day at the mill.

Another beer Robert produces is a little more transparent in its title. Called simply Shuttle Ale, it refers to a vital tool in weaving that passes 'weft' yarn horizontally through the lengthwise 'warp' yarn to create material. Robert's strong beer has its own warp – the full, rounded toffeeish flavours of pale and crystal malts, with which a weft of blackcurrant-like fruitiness from Fuggle hops is interlaced to produce a fine liquid fabric. It's an ideal beer with which to mark the life of one of the most influential people in the development of Britain's cotton trade.

Spinning a yarn

Richard Arkwright was born in Preston in 1732. He trained first as a barber, specializing in making wigs and touring Britain collecting discarded human hair for the purpose. His travels brought him into close contact with the textiles industry and prompted him to look closely at a way of streamlining the process of spinning cotton. Using his finances to support the work of inventor John Kay, Arkwright developed a piece of kit that became known as the spinning frame. This was an advance on the earlier spinning jenny, created by James Hargreaves, which was in itself revolutionary in allowing several spindles to be run off one wheel. Arkwright's machine took the development further by mechanically producing stronger yarn while using less human labour.

The spinning frame simplified life in the cotton mill and made the business more efficient and profitable, but there was a down side, too. Fewer workers were needed as a result of Arkwright's invention, which inevitably led to unrest. Arkwright, like his employer contemporaries, also saw fit to employ child labour, although it is said in his defence that at least he did not expect children to start work until they were aged six. There were even accusations that Arkwright had stolen his most successful invention. Indeed, his patents on the spinning frame were successfully challenged in 1785, seven years before his death. Nevertheless, he remains one of the influential figures of the 18th century and, through his development of automation, one of the founding fathers of the Industrial Revolution.

Births Rupert Brooke (poet), 1887; PD James (writer), 1920; Terry Wogan (broadcaster), 1938

Deaths Joseph Conrad (writer), 1924; Lenny Bruce (comedian), 1966; Arthur Lee (rock musician), 2006

Events La Scala opera house in Milan opens, 1778; Paul McCartney reveals his new, post-Beatles, band, Wings, 1971

ABOVE: RICHARD ARKWRIGHT'S MILL IN MATLOCK BATH, DERBYSHIRE

Strong Ale

Eisenbahn Lust

Source Cervejaria Sudbrack Ltda, Blumenau SC **Strength** 11.5% **Website** eisenbahn.com.br

The drinks' world is full of myth and legend, none more widely promulgated than that of Benedictine monk Dom Pérignon and his invention of champagne. According to some sources, this took place on 4 August 1693. Although the story is now largely discredited, Pérignon was influential in the development of quality bubbly, overseeing improvements in the technique of producing sparkling wine from his abbey in Champagne. However, those who have developed his role to new heights put a romantic gloss on his work by relating a story about the day he visited his cellar only to find that wine had refermented in the bottle. 'I can taste the stars,' he is alleged to have shrieked when sampling the surprisingly fizzy drink.

The key to producing champagne lies in a secondary fermentation in the bottle. The wine is bottled with a little added sugar and fresh yeast. Bottles then age on their sides until the wine is deemed ready. It then undergoes *remuage*, a process that sees the bottles turned upside down and revolved to encourage the sediment to collect in the neck. The neck is then frozen, the crown cap is removed and the frozen sediment pops out. This is known as *dégorgement*. The bottle is then topped up with more of the same wine and quickly corked to keep in the generous natural carbonation.

Bubbly beers

In recent years, several brewers have aimed to create beers using this complex process. The most notable are Bosteel's Deus and Malheur's Bière Brut from Belgium, but just as unusual is a Brazilian beer called Lust. Lust is a product of an adventurous microbrewery called Eisenbahn. It was set up in 2002 by a group of enthusiasts who recognized the poverty of the local beer scene. Employing a brewer trained at the famous Weihenstephan brewing school in Munich, they have launched some excellent beers based on styles from all over the world, including a weissbier, a dunkel and a Belgian ale. Lust is the top of the range.

Lust is brewed from pilsner malt and Saaz hops. After primary top fermentation, using a Belgian yeast strain, it is shipped to a local winery for three months of fermentation in the bottle, with wine yeast the active

partner. It is then treated just like champagne, jumping through the hoops of *remuage* and *dégorgement* to produce a bottle-fermented beer that has all its yeast removed but still packs plenty of natural carbonation. It's not the sort of beer you'd want to order on a busy darts night at The Nag's Head, but it's definitely one to consider for special occasions, when otherwise sparkling wine would hold a monopoly. Served chilled in champagne flutes, it's a revelation. The beer foams noisily as you unwind the wire cradle, pop the cork and pour, and then settles down into a lively, sweet, warming taste of mellow melon and pineapple, with CO_2 bubbles bouncing incessantly around the mouth. The finish is only softly bitter, but quite appropriate, with gentle hops adding to the dryness and the same tropical fruits lingering.

Because of the complicated production technique, Lust doesn't come cheap. That said, this luxury beer still retails at a fraction of the cost of a half-decent champagne.

Births Percy Bysshe Shelley (poet), 1792; Queen Elizabeth, the Queen Mother, 1900; Louis Armstrong (jazz musician), 1901

Deaths Hans Christian Andersen (writer), 1875; Geoff Hamilton (gardener and broadcaster), 1996; Victor Mature (actor), 1999

Events Britain declares war on Germany, 1914; Anne Frank and her family discovered by the Nazis, 1944

Champagne-style Beer

Harviestoun Bitter & Twisted

Source Harviestoun Brewery, Alva, Clackmannanshire **Strength** 3.8% **Website** harviestounbrewery.co.uk

The first week of August has now gained hallowed status among beer connoisseurs. There's only one place to be at this time of year and that's in London, joining more than 60,000 like-minded people in celebrating the wonderful world of beer at CAMRA's Great British Beer Festival.

The festival has its origins in a much more modest event staged at Covent Garden in 1975. This was CAMRA's first attempt to put on an extended showcase of real ales for the general public. It was a dramatic success, attracting more than 40,000 people. In 1977, the first Great British Beer Festival was held at London's Alexandra Palace and over the years, the GBBF has grown in size and status. It moved to Leeds, Birmingham and Brighton, before returning to London in 1991, when the venue was the Docklands Arena. A year later, Kensington Olympia took over as host. In 2006, the GBBF transferred to Olympia's bigger brother, Earl's Court, with its better travel connections, proved an instant hit, with attendance numbers rocketing.

If you've never been to the GBBF, you've certainly missed out. Where else on the planet will you ever find more than 450 traditional British real ales on sale in one place? There is also a bottled beer bar, a real cider bar, and a bar serving foreign beers. Live entertainment is provided at every session, and there are plenty of other distractions in the form of pub games and food stalls of all kinds. The festival kicks off on the Tuesday, when the highlight is the announcement of the annual Champion Beer of Britain awards, which follows a busy morning of judging by CAMRA members and outside experts. The category winners are soon in hot demand over the bars and, for the brewer of the overall Champion Beer of Britain, life will never be the same again, as the phone immediately starts ringing with urgent orders from desperate publicans.

Scottish stars

Such was the story on 5 August 2003, when Harviestoun Brewery claimed the top award with its Bitter & Twisted. It was the second year running that Scotland had stolen the show, with Caledonian's Deuchars IPA the previous title holder. Harviestoun founder Ken Brooker sold the business in 2006, but it was Ken who was responsible for Bitter & Twisted, including its strange name, bestowed on the beer when he was in a bad mood after receiving a driving ban for speeding.

Pale and crystal malts are joined in the mash tun by wheat malt and also malted oats, to give a bit more body than its 3.8% ABV would normally suggest (the bottled version rolls out a bit stronger, at 4.2%). But it is with the hops that this beer gains its character, with Hersbrucker and Challenger employed for bitterness, and Styrian Golding for that aromatic twist. Zingy grapefruit and lemon notes fill the nose, with honey and light butterscotch behind. The taste is bittersweet and similarly packed with grapefruit and orange zest, before a dry and increasingly bitter finish with lots of pithy orange flavours.

It would come as no surprise to see Bitter & Twisted take the Champion Beer crown again in future, but as any visitor to the GBBF can tell you, there will always be plenty of competition.

Births John Huston (film director), 1906; Robert Taylor (actor), 1911; Neil Armstrong (astronaut), 1930

Deaths Marilyn Monroe (actress), 1962; Richard Burton (actor), 1984; Alec Guinness (actor), 2000

Events Formation of Welsh nationalist party Plaid Cymru, 1925; Nelson Mandela begins his 27-year imprisonment in South Africa, 1962

Golden Ale

Red Stripe Dragon Stout

Source Desnoes & Geddes plc, Kingston   **Strength** 7.5%   **Website** jamaicadrinks.com

Stout friends

Thomas Hargreaves Geddes and Eugene Desnoes first met as young men – the company's website describes an almost Stanley and Livingstone encounter that was to change both their lives. They each separately formed their own drinks companies but, in 1918, came together to create a business that produced beer, as well as soft drinks. Undoubtedly, the most intriguing beer in the portfolio is Dragon Stout, a style of beer that was brought here during the days of the British Empire. There's a similar beer from the Carib Brewery on Trinidad. My immediate thoughts on sipping Dragon Stout were that it would make a fantastic pudding beer – it's that sweet and strong. There's a creamy, smooth texture throughout and tons of rich malty flavours with some raisiny fruit, too. It's only in the finish that the roasted grain contrives to throw in some bitterness. Just like the Lion Stout from Sri Lanka (see 4 February), it goes to show that, even in the hottest climates, bland lager is not the only drink in town.

No one parties like the people of the Caribbean, so you can imagine the fun to be had every August when Jamaica celebrates its independence from the UK.

This stunning island, one of the jewels of the West Indies, was first colonized by natives of South America, but they were largely pushed out by the Spanish in the 15th and 16th centuries. In turn, Spain was forced to relinquish Jamaica when Admiral William Penn (father of William Penn, see 4 March) claimed the land for Britain in 1655. In subsequent centuries, the British, true to form, exploited the island to the full, reaping its bountiful sugar harvest with the use of slaves torn away from their African homelands. It wasn't until 1834 that slavery was abolished in Jamaica and the island was allowed to find its own way gradually in the world. Increasingly self-confident, Jamaica claimed the right to independence on 6 August 1962, but it remains part of the Commonwealth, with Queen Elizabeth still the head of state.

Each year, on the anniversary of independence, the island swings into party mode. There's a gala parade through the capital, Kingston, dancing to calypso and reggae, and the national colours of green, black and gold (signifiying the bounty of the land, the durability and creativity of the people, and the blessing of sunshine) are worn by many citizens in a show of national pride. Beneath the blazing sun, a fair few beers are downed, too, plenty of them Jamaica's best-known beer export, Red Stripe, which is brewed under licence in the UK by Wells & Young's. The beer was created by the Desnoes & Geddes brewery in Kingston in 1928, but the company is now owned by Diageo and operates under the Red Stripe name.

Births Alexander Fleming (scientist), 1881; Andy Warhol (artist), 1928; Barbara Windsor (actress), 1937

Deaths Ben Jonson (writer), 1637; Pope Paul VI, 1978; Robin Cook (politician), 2005

Events First atomic bomb dropped, on Hiroshima, 1945; the World Wide Web goes online, 1991

Sweet Stout

ABOVE: NEGRIL BEACH IN JAMAICA

Unibroue Raftman

Source Unibroue Inc., Chambly, Quebec   **Strength** 5.5%   **Website** unibroue.com

It's amazing the lengths that some people will go to just to win an argument. Today's commemoration recalls one such feat. It concerns Norwegian scientist Thor Heyerdahl, who had long reasoned that the natives of South America must have had some way of reaching the islands of Polynesia, way out west across the Pacific Ocean. The evidence seemed to point in the opposite direction, however, suggesting that the first outsiders to have reached these islands would have been from Asia in the east. In the end, it all boiled down to whether the South Americans had a craft that was seaworthy enough to take them there. As their vessel of choice seemed to have been the simple balsa wood raft – that was not only rather flimsy but also dangerously absorbent – it seemed unlikely.

So Heyerdahl decided to put it to the test. Lashing together nine trunks of balsa, each 60cm (2ft) thick and extending up to 14m (45ft) in length, he knocked up a typical Peruvian raft that he named *Kon-Tiki*, after a pre-Inca sun king who is said to have migrated across the Pacific. This raft he had towed out from shore off Callao, Peru, on 28 April 1947, and deposited in the natural Humbolt Current. There, with but a simple square sail for propulsion in the strong trade wind, and a long oar for steerage, he laid himself and his six-strong crew at the mercy of the waves.

Coral sheen

The Norwegian's conviction proved correct. After 101 days at sea, during which time the raft floated 6,920km (4,300 miles) westward, storms were bravely negotiated, and fish were plundered to feed the crew, *Kon-Tiki* ran aground on the Raroia coral reef near Tahiti. Heyerdahl had physically shown that it had been possible – indeed, likely – that native Americans would have had the resources to journey across the Pacific and influence the cultures of other lands.

Heyerdahl, who died in 2002, is remembered with great reverence in Norway, where *Kon-Tiki* and other vessels he employed in subsequent missions are housed in a dedicated museum on the outskirts of Oslo.

Raftman from Unibroue in Canada would be the perfect tribute beer for him, even though a glance at the label reveals that the rafts after which it is named are the ones used to bring timber down the snowy rivers of Canada, rather than the fragile balsa floats of the balmy Pacific. It's a fine, bottle-conditioned beer. The interesting ingredient is whisky malt, but this is nicely subdued in the taste, adding a light smoky character without dominating the otherwise bittersweet, slightly lemony, malty flavour. Appropriately, considering where *Kon-Tiki* concluded its voyage, the brewery describes the colour of Raftman as 'coral sheen'.

Births Greg Chappell (cricketer), 1948; Alexei Sayle (comedian), 1952; David Duchovny (actor), 1960

Deaths Oliver Hardy (actor and comedian), 1957; Red Adair (firefighter), 2004

Events First edition of game show *It's a Knockout* broadcast, 1966; American Lynne Cox becomes the first person to swim from the US to Russia, across the Bering Strait, 1987

Smoked Beer

Mont Blanc Blonde du Mont Blanc

Source Brasserie Distillerie du Mont-Blanc, Les Houches **Strength** 5.8%
Website brasserie-montblanc.com

Today in history arguably marks the birth of the sport of mountaineering. It was on 8 August 1786 that Western Europe's highest mountain was scaled for the first time, thus encouraging a legion of adventurers to gather up their ice picks and reach for the stars.

It was a Swiss scientist Horace-Bénédict de Saussure who kick-started the craze of alpinism. A famous naturalist, he wanted to find a way of getting to the top himself so he could conduct important experiments. He sponsored a competition with a prize for the first person to discover a successful route to the highest peak in the Alps.

A local doctor, Michel-Gabriel Paccard, took the bait. He monitored the slopes for three years to work out the best method of getting to the top, and recruited a local crystal hunter, Jacques Balmat, to help him on his ascent. On the morning of 7 August, the two men set out, taking a radically different path from that favoured by previous unsuccessful climbers. A day and a half later, they arrived on top of the mountain, clearly visible to onlookers in the valley below. It proved to be an exhausting and life-threatening experience, but Paccard and Balmat had proved that Mont Blanc – the great White Mountain on the border of Italy and France – could indeed be climbed, and others rushed to follow suit.

These days, around 20,000 people make the ascent every year, but that is not to say that the enterprise is without hazard. Many fail and need emergency rescue. Scaling an ice-crowned peak, 4,800m (16,000ft) above sea level, clearly presents significant dangers.

Brewery revival

Win or lose, you wouldn't half fancy a glass of beer at the end of all that effort and, luckily, there is a brewery not far away. The Mont Blanc microbrewery was opened in 1997 by two local businesses (from the liqueur and delicatessen trades) that joined together to revive brewing in the Savoy region of France. Inspired by the discovery of a spring disgorging exceptionally pure waters from the Mont Blanc glacier, they pooled their resources and, using contacts they had with brewers in Belgium, set up the Brasserie de Mont Blanc.

Production of liqueurs now takes place alongside brewing at the brewhouse in the town of Chambéry, between Grenoble and Annecy. On the brewing side, there's a small selection of beers, including a Belgian-style blanche (witbier). The most popular, however, seems to be Blonde, a strong, top-fermented golden beer, made with Mont Blanc water and pilsner malt, and seasoned with two different hops (primarily Czech Saaz), as well as some secret spices. The recipe was developed in 1999 by a brewer who, in a long career, had once worked at both Leffe and Hoegaarden. The beer is said to be bottle conditioned (although sediment is very low). It pours a bright golden colour and lifts a perfumed, notably lemony, herbal aroma to the nose. In the mouth, the beer is predominantly sweet and scented, with more lemon and herbal hop notes developing. Sweetness and lemon notes continue into the finish, with just a mild hoppiness emerging. Above all, this blonde is crisp and clean. It may be the marketing talk having an undue influence, but it really does seem to have that icy, pure and fresh quality. You can almost taste the alpine air.

Births Dustin Hoffman (actor), 1937; Nigel Mansell (racing driver), 1953; Roger Federer (tennis player), 1981

Deaths Frank W Woolworth (retailer), 1919; Fay Wray (actress), 2004; Barbara Bel Geddes (actress), 2006

Events The Great Train Robbery takes place in Buckinghamshire, 1963; Beirut hostage John McCarthy set free, 1991

Blonde Beer

Conwy Telford Porter

Source Conwy Brewery, Conwy **Strength** 5.6% **Website** conwybrewery.co.uk

In the pantheon of inspirational civil engineers, Thomas Telford stands right up there with Isambard Kingdom Brunel. Born on this day in 1757, in Westerkirk, Scotland, Telford found his first trade as a stone mason. This took him to London and Portsmouth before he settled in Shropshire as a surveyor of public works. By this time, his prowess as an engineer had been noted and he was placed in charge of numerous road and waterway schemes, including a bridge over the River Severn, and a canal connecting the heavy industries of North Wales to Shropshire and Cheshire, which involved the construction of the astonishing Pontcysyllte Aqueduct – 'the waterway in the sky' – over the steep-sided River Dee valley. He then returned to his homeland to build the Caledonian Canal, and work on major harbour schemes, and he was also responsible for Sweden's Göta Canal. Probably his greatest achievement, however, was the Menai Suspension Bridge, linking the mainland to the island of Anglesey over the hazardous Menai Strait.

Telford – the 'Colossus of Roads' – died in 1834 and, as befits a man of his brilliance, is buried among the greats in Westminster Abbey. With much of his finest works centred in the North Wales area, it is appropriate that he is remembered in the name of one of the region's beers.

Local tribute

Gwynne Thomas opened Conwy Brewery in the town of the same name in 2003. His beers are sold with bilingual labels, addressing both the Welsh- and English-speaking markets. Telford Porter was added to the list in 2005 as a new beer for Conwy's Feast, a food and drink festival. It is now a permanent part of the range and Gwynne's personal favourite among his bottled beers.

Today's bottle reproduces a silhouette of Thomas Telford over a sketch of the suspension bridge he built over the River Conwy, which opened in 1826, the same year as his more famous Menai crossing. The beer inside is brewed from Maris Otter pale malt, crystal malt and roasted barley, with Pioneer, Challenger and Golding hops going into the copper. What emerges is a porter that is rather different from most porters on the market today. It's very light in colour for a start, glowing a bright red in the glass. Then the aroma shows little in the way of the expected roasted grains. Indeed, malt is very subtle here, giving way to orchard fruitiness instead. It's a similar story in the sweetish taste, where more orchard fruit contrasts with a light malty body. There are subtle chocolate notes and a slightly chalky texture, but none of the dry roasted grains normally found in a beer of this type. It is only in the finish that the darker malts really assert themselves, with their bitterness enhanced as hops begin to break through.

Understandably, there was considerable interest in this beer in 2007, with commemorations of the 250th anniversary of Telford's birth.

Births Philip Larkin (poet), 1922; Rod Laver (tennis player), 1938; Whitney Houston (actress and singer), 1963

Deaths Joe Orton (playwright), 1967; Jerry Garcia (rock musician), 1995; Frank Whittle (aviation pioneer), 1996

Events Coronation of King Edward VII, 1902; Richard Nixon resigns as US President after the Watergate Scandal, 1974

Porter

229

Aecht Schlenkerla Rauchbier

Source Schlenkerla, Bamberg **Strength** 5.1% **Website** schlenkerla.de

Excruciating deaths were not uncommon among the early Christian saints, but the way in which St Lawrence met his end must have been one of the most painful.

Lawrence was born in Huesca, northeast Spain, but after climbing his way up the clerical ladder, worked in Rome for Pope Sixtus II, for whom he was a deacon and administrator. However, like the pontiff, Lawrence fell victim to the purges of the anti-Christian Emperor Valerian and was sentenced to death by being roasted alive in 258. Anecdotes circulate about how the future saint kept his composure throughout the ordeal, even suggesting that his tormentors 'turn him over' as he was already cooked on one side.

St Lawrence has been associated with fire ever since. Strangely, and not a little perversely you might think, he's been declared a patron saint of cooks and of firemen, and comedians also lay claim to his patronage. Lawrence is also one of the brewing world's patrons, which seems equally bizarre. The reasoning, it seems, is that in a profession where fiery accidents were all too common in early times, brewers needed the protection of a saint who knew the danger of flames.

It is in northern Bavaria that the closest links between St Lawrence and brewers were forged. The Franconian Brewers' Guild adopted the saint as their spiritual guide and, even today, there's a beer named in his honour. Laurentius is an unfiltered 'kellerbier', brewed by the Wernecker brewery in the town of Werneck, near Würzburg. That's not so easy to get hold of, so a better option for noting the saint's affiliation to our brewing brethren is another Franconian beer, in fact probably the best-known beer from the region.

Smoke town

Aecht Schlenkerla Rauchbier comes from Bamberg, a stunning old town in the heart of Franconia that still has ten breweries to call its own. Aecht means 'original', and the Schlenkerla is a tavern in the centre of town, in the shadow of the cathedral. Here, steins of foaming rauchbier are dispensed from wooden kegs, although the beer is now brewed elsewhere in town.

The distinguishing feature of rauchbier is that it is made from malt smoked over beechwood. Used clumsily, this is an ingredient that can quickly turn drinkers off, bringing an unwanted medicinal tang to the beer. But used judiciously, as they have learned to do over the centuries in Bamberg, it adds a delicious new dimension, and makes beer even more versatile when paired with food, particularly, of course, smoked meats or fish. Schlenkerla's rauchbier is wonderfully balanced, with a woody, bacony smokiness leading the way but never overpowering the full malty sweetness that lies beneath. It's a world classic and worthy of pride of place on this saint's feast day.

Births Herbert Hoover (US President), 1874; Roy Keane (footballer), 1971; Lawrence Dallaglio (rugby player), 1972

Deaths Rin Tin Tin (canine film star), 1932; Tony Wilson (music executive), 2007

Events Ferdinand Magellan sets sail to circumnavigate the globe, 1519; Henry Wood conducts the first Promenade Concert, 1895

St Austell Tribute

Source St Austell Brewery, St Austell, Cornwall **Strength** 4.2% **Website** staustellbrewery.co.uk

The total solar eclipse of 1999 was a much-anticipated event, and it wasn't just keen astronomers, photographers and hardened eclipse chasers who were revved up for the occasion. The UK went sun mad in the run-up to 11 August, the day that the extraordinary celestial phenomenon was due to take place.

Caused by the moon completely obliterating the sun's sphere, a total eclipse is a rare event. The last to be seen from British shores took place in 1927, and the 1999 event was only to be fully visible in Cornwall and southern Devon. Further north, only partial eclipses were on offer. That didn't stop the whole country from downing tools when the long-awaited moment arrived. At around 11am, factories emptied, children ran out into gardens and drivers pulled over to ready themselves for the rare moment. Those really keen made the journey to Cornwall. Hotels, b&bs and campsites were fully booked months in advance, and roads were jammed as the influx of tourists began.

On Tuesday 10 August, the sun rose high in the crystal-blue sky and the mercury soared. On Thursday 12 August, weather conditions were again outstanding for eclipse viewing. Sadly, on the day in between, when it all happened, the weather was lousy. Thick, grey cloud filled the heavens, and rain did its best to dampen proceedings. Breaks in the leaden canopy gave occasional rise to optimism, but by the magical hour of 11.10 am, very little was to be seen

of the sun. What everyone did notice was a remarkable loss of daylight for around two minutes and a fall in temperature as the eclipse achieved totality, with birds and other wildlife momentarily confused by the early onset of twilight. The next total eclipse visible in the UK will not take place until 2090, so there was understandably considerable disappointment at missing this once-in-a-lifetime show.

Daylight robbery

There was at least some beery consolation. For the occasion, St Austell created the cleverly titled Daylight Robbery. The only problem with names like this is that when the event is over – in this case at lunchtime on 11 August – they cease to be relevant. For St Austell, this posed a little problem, as their beer proved to be exceptionally popular and they wanted to keep it going. Hence the new title: Tribute.

Tribute is a golden ale brewed with Maris Otter pale malt and a darker malt called Cornish Gold, specially created for St Austell by Tucker's Maltings in Newton Abbot. The hops are Fuggle, Styrian Golding and Willamette, and together they provide a splendid lime and grapefruit zestiness that makes this beer so refreshing. St Austell have capitalized on the success of the beer by making it their contribution to the national guest beer market, so now you may find it anywhere from John O'Groats back down to Land's End, as well as (filtered) in bottle.

Births Enid Blyton (writer), 1897; Pervez Musharraf (President of Pakistan), 1943; 'Hulk' Hogan (wrestler), 1953

Deaths Andrew Carnegie (industrialist and philanthropist), 1919; Jackson Pollock (artist), 1956; Peter Cushing (actor), 1994

Events The Eiger mountain first climbed, 1858; last steam passenger train service in Britain, 1968

Golden Ale

ABOVE: THE 1999 SOLAR ECLIPSE AS SEEN FROM TOWAN BEACH, NEWQUAY

Theakston Grouse Beater

Source T&R Theakston Ltd, Masham, North Yorkshire **Strength** 4.2% **Website** theakstons.co.uk

Glorious or grotesque? 12 August is the day that the season for shooting red grouse opens. Attitudes to this high summer day have changed somewhat over the years, as the animal welfare lobby has increased in size and strength, but fighting the traditionalist corner are the shooters and beaters, for whom today is the highlight of the year.

While it may be hard for many people to understand how shooting live birds can in any way be justified as a sport, for those raised on country matters it is exactly that and – given the speed of the birds on the wing – one of the most exhilarating. That's why parties of tweedy toffs, checked-shirt businessmen and others with the right connections and deep pockets take to the moors of Northern England and Scotland at this time of year. With hotels, pubs and restaurants enjoying the spin-off trade, and locals employed as beaters to chase the birds into the air or as pickers-up to collect the fallen prey, the benefits to the economy should not be overlooked, supporters claim. The upkeep of the moorland by grouse estate landlords must be borne in mind, too, they say. On the cruelty side, some would question whether the concept of killing any creature, largely for the fun of it, should hold a place in a civilized society.

In decline?

In truth, there's not been much to make 12 August glorious in recent years. Declining numbers of birds – too much shooting, say opponents; a parasite problem, respond the other side, defensively – have seen the day go off with more of a whimper than a bang of late. But you get the feeling that, even though restrictions have been placed on other forms of hunting, this is one activity that is unlikely to be phased out very soon.

Acknowledging the local importance of the Glorious Twelfth is a seasonal ale from Theakston. The brewery's home is in the attractive market town of Masham, close to the North Yorkshire Moors and within gunshot echo of August's first blasts. The beer is dedicated in name to the beater – perhaps suggesting it's the ideal way to wash away the thirst of a hot, active day among the heather and gorse – but it stands alone as a very pleasant summery drink.

Protesters may shun Grouse Beater because of the name, but they'd be missing out. Attractively golden in the glass, the beer has a powerful floral aroma, laced with juicy citrus notes, which reveal the often-overlooked versatility of the Fuggle hop, which is added here dry to the finished beer. The taste is equally flowery, with a peachy character and more juicy citrus. The finish is not as full as many beers but that's okay when you're just looking for something summery, refreshing – and appropriately glorious.

Births Robert Southey (poet), 1774; Cecil B de Mille (film director), 1881; Pete Sampras (tennis player), 1971

Deaths William Blake (artist and poet), 1827; Thomas Mann (writer), 1955; Henry Fonda (actor), 1982

Events Isaac Singer patents his sewing machine, 1851; IBM introduces its personal computer, 1981

Golden Ale

Left Hand Juju Ginger

Source Left Hand Brewing Co., Longmont, Colorado **Strength** 4% **Website** lefthandbrewing.com

It's a club with an illustrious membership list. US Presidents Gerald Ford, Ronald Reagan, George Bush and Bill Clinton; Queen Victoria, Prince Charles and Prince William; Lewis Carroll, Mark Twain and HG Wells from the literary world; Leonardo da Vinci, Michelangelo and Raphael representing art. The organization in question is The Left-Handers Club, formed in 1990 to provide a voice for the 10%, or thereabouts, of the world's population that is left-handed.

The Left-Handers Club is more than just a friendly association. It also performs a useful role in flagging up matters of concern to those who are left leaning: the issue of household devices, for instance, such as scissors, knives, can openers and even power tools, which are often tricky or dangerous for left-handers to use. It also researches into the phenomenon of 'sinistrality', provides advice to parents of left-handed children, and, as part of its remit, has a bit of fun every year with its Left-Handers' Day, which falls on 13 August. The first event was staged in 1992, and it is now marked around the world, with events such as left-versus right-hand sports games, left-handed tea parties and other such profile-raising stunts.

We can do our bit for the cause by choosing a beer from the Left Hand Brewing Company. This business was founded in Longmont, Colorado, in 1993, initially as the Indian Peaks Brewing Company. However, before a drop of beer had even been brewed, the business was forced to change its name. Another brewery was using 'Indian Peaks' for part of its beer range, and so Left Hand was adopted as the company title instead. The new name was derived from an Arapahoe Indian chief whose tribe used to winter in the area. His name was Niwot, meaning Left Hand.

Out of the ordinary

Probably the best-known beer in the Left Hand portfolio is Sawtooth Ale, a nutty amber ESB-style brew, but the range extends to nine regular beers, plus a host of seasonals. The selection for today is one of the company's earliest creations and is available on both sides of the Atlantic. It is also something out of the ordinary, as left-handers may well consider themselves to be. The defining feature is the inclusion of crushed fresh ginger root. Pale, Munich, Vienna and light crystal malts go into the mash tun, with Cascade, Saaz and American Golding hops added in the copper, but with the ginger replacing some of the hop input.

Home-made ginger beer finds echoes in the nose of this golden ale, as an earthy spiciness runs alongside the malt aromas. The taste is crisp, clean and pleasantly bitter. There's a hoppy edge and, of course, a warming bite of ginger, but it's all deftly done so that the ginger is subtle and supportive rather than bold and boisterous. The spice comes through yet again in the dry and bitter finish, making it mildly warming.

The name Juju comes from African culture and implies a magical property. I wouldn't go that far but this is an unusual, highly refreshing beer, perfect for a summer's day like today. Raise the glass in your left hand and enjoy.

Births John Logie Baird (inventor), 1888; Alfred Hitchcock (film director), 1899; Alan Shearer (footballer), 1970

Deaths Florence Nightingale (nurse), 1910; HG Wells (writer), 1946; Henry Williamson (writer), 1977

Events Chinese Communist Party announces plans for a cultural revolution, the 'New Leap Forward', 1966; East Berlin sealed off from the West, 1961

Spiced Ale

Duvel-Moortgat Duvel

Source Brouwerij Moortgat, Breendonk-Puurs **Strength** 8.5% **Website** duvel.be

Following on from 18 July, where we encountered brewing saint Arnold of Metz, we now find ourselves in the company of yet another St Arnold, who is also a patron of brewers. The one celebrated on this day is St Arnold (alternatively known as St Arnulf) of Soissons.

Arnold's biography tells us that he was born into a noble French family and served in the army with distinction before turning to God in a big way. Around the year 1060, he became part of a Benedictine order, then squirrelled himself away as a hermit for three years. He was called back to the abbey to become its abbot, a promotion Arnold was keen to refuse. But orders are orders – especially when a wolf blocks your escape route, as reportedly happened to Arnold – and abbot he became. Arnold then progressed up the ecclesiastical ladder, eventually becoming – with equal reluctance – Bishop of Soissons, a town between Paris and Reims. His tenure didn't last long. When another bishop muscled in on his territory, Arnold saw his chance, handed in his resignation and scooted off to Flanders to set up his own abbey in Oudenburg, near Ostend.

Beer not water

The Belgians need little excuse to quaff a beer or two, and perhaps Arnold was partly responsible for this admirable affection for ale. Recognizing that beer was far safer to drink than untreated water, he advised his flock to make it their daily tipple. He wouldn't have known that it was the boiling part of the brewing process that made beer so healthy by killing off most of the germs, but he did know that fewer people died after drinking beer than drinking the fetid local water.

It seems a touch blasphemous to celebrate a saint's day with a devil of a beer, but one would hope that Arnold wouldn't mind that much, considering it still keeps Flemish folk off the water. Duvel ('Devil' in Dutch) is one of Belgium's best-known beery exports. It's also a trendsetter. The Moortgat brewery at Puurs, just south of Antwerp, coined a new beer style when it created this pale golden beer at the end of the 1960s.

The use of a Scottish ale yeast provided a novel twist, enhanced by a delicate hopping from Czech Saaz and Slovenian Styrian Goldings. A long maturation at the brewery paved the way for a smooth, refined glass of ale that throws up a rocky, foaming head when poured into the specially designed tulip glass. It proved that beer didn't have to be dark to be packed with flavour – although Duvel, in fact, started life as a brown beer – and it paved the way for unwary drinkers to fall into the trap of thinking this is just another easy-drinking blonde. Only when they try to stand up do they realize how strong it is. The light body and zesty fruitiness, with more than a touch of pear, really make it dangerously drinkable for its strength. It's not called Devil for nothing.

Births John Galsworthy (writer), 1867; Steve Martin (comedian and actor), 1945; Halle Berry (actress), 1966

Deaths Bertold Brecht (writer), 1956; JB Priestley (writer), 1984; Enzo Ferrari (motor car pioneer), 1988

Events Cologne cathedral completed after six centuries' work, 1880; cricketer Donald Bradman plays his final test innings, 1948; UK troops deployed in Northern Ireland, 1969

Hogs Back BSA

Source Hogs Back Brewery Ltd, Tongham, Surrey **Strength** 4.5% **Website** hogsback.co.uk

Three months after the German surrender in Europe on 8 May 1945 – thereafter dubbed VE (Victory in Europe) Day – the dying embers of World War II were still glowing in the Far East. Japan, the last standing member of the Fascist Axis alliance, fought on. However, things changed dramatically in August, when the US unleashed its new weapon, the atomic bomb, with devastating results. Within days, Japanese Emperor Hirohito had agreed to a surrender, and the war, after six bloody years, was finally at an end.

Nowhere was VJ (Victory in Japan) Day – as 15 August became known – more welcome than in the minds of the Allied soldiers, sailors, airmen and civilians who had suffered at the hands of their enemies in the Far East. Many of these were honoured in 1951 when the Burma Star Association was founded in memory of service personnel who endured the conflict in Burma as the Japanese advanced across the region. Thirty-two thousand servicemen lost their lives during this brutal campaign. Can there be a more fitting drink to raise in respectful memory of those who gave everything than a beer that generates funds to help support the Association?

Respectful beer

BSA (Burma Star Ale) is a malty, spicy, lightly fruity, copper-red ale with a dry, hoppy finish, featuring Fuggle and Golding hops and a grist of three malts, pale, crystal and chocolate. It was created in 1995 by Hogs Back

Brewery, of Tongham, Surrey, to mark the 50th anniversary of VJ Day and was repackaged six years later for the 50th anniversary of the founding of the Burma Star Association (a donation is made to the Association from sales of the beer). One of the parents of the brewery's founders actually served in the Burma Star movement, and he is pictured on the label of the bottle, which also recalls the famous and moving statement that is the motto of the Association:

When you go home tell them of
us and say –
For your tomorrow we gave our
today.

The image of beer is often much maligned but it proves here yet again that it can be a force for harmony and respect in society, reiterating these poignant words at a time when World War II and the sacrifices made by millions are fading from the consciousness of a public that sets more store by the ignorant antics of publicity-crazed 'celebrities' and the banality of reality TV. Here, as elsewhere in this book, memories of otherwise-forgotten heroes and events have been kept alive by their simple commemoration in the name of a beer. And none deserve prolonged fame more than those who knew the horror of the war in the Far East.

Births Napoleon Bonaparte (Emperor of France), 1769; Sir Walter Scott (writer), 1771; Princess Anne, 1950

Deaths Roland (warrior), 778; Macbeth (King of Scotland), 1057

Events Panama Canal formally opened, 1914; India becomes independent, 1947

ABOVE: AMERICAN SAILOR AND NURSE CELEBRATING VJ DAY IN TIMES SQUARE, NEW YORK

Best Bitter

Schöfferhofer Hefeweissbier

Source Binding Brauerei, Frankfurt **Strength** 5% **Website** schoefferhofer.de

There are a lot of things known about the King of Rock 'n' Roll, including most of his dietary preferences, but whether or not Elvis enjoyed a good pint is not so easy to discover. However, his sudden, premature death in Memphis, Tennessee, on this day in 1977, does give us an opportunity to explore any connections he may have with the world of beer and allow us to draw a few, perhaps rather shaky, conclusions.

Given his upbringing in the religious South, it's not certain that Elvis would have tasted much beer before he embarked on his showbusiness journey, and what would have been available would have been very drab in those days before craft brewing in the US. But what about when he was conscripted into the US Army? Did he drink beer then? Considering that he was posted to Germany, one of the world's most beer-entrenched countries, there must have been a good chance. He certainly became acquainted with German beer culture, indirectly at least, as in his 1960 film *GI Blues*, Elvis sang *Wooden Heart*, which went on to become a massive hit in both the UK and the US. The words were new and rather schmaltzy, but the tune was old and well worn. The Germans had been using it as a drinking song for decades.

German selection

So what beer would Elvis have had the opportunity to taste while on his travels? Well, he was based in the town of Friedberg, not far from Frankfurt. Taking advantage of a loophole in the rules that allowed a serviceman to live off base if he was looking after his family, he shipped over some relatives and bought a house in the town of Bad Neuheim. Considering that the German beer market is highly fragmented, with national brewers today still holding only a small market share, and nearly every town, even the size of Bad Neuheim, boasting at least one brewery, Presley would have had the pick of a number of small brewery beers. Even if these breweries still exist, however, their beers will be hard to come by, so if you're a huge Elvis fan and can't let this day pass without raising a glass to the big man, perhaps Schöfferhofer Hefeweissbier will hit the spot.

This traditional wheat beer, loaded with banana and clove spiciness from the action of the yeast, is no longer brewed at its original home in Kassel, but has been kept in the region Elvis knew well by its current owner Binding. It's been quite easy to get hold of for many years, making it one of the early ambassadors of the weissbier style outside Germany – a mellow, easy-drinking and refreshing beer with an increasingly bitter, fruity finish. Take this opportunity to pour yourself a glass. Because it's meant to be naturally cloudy, it doesn't even matter if it's 'All Shook Up'.

Births TE Lawrence (of Arabia: writer and soldier), 1888; Trevor McDonald (broadcaster), 1939; Madonna (singer and actress), 1958

Deaths Babe Ruth (baseball player), 1948; Bela Lugosi (actor), 1956; Stewart Granger (actor), 1993

Events London's Tate Gallery opens to the public, 1897; Cyprus gains independence from the UK, 1960

Wheat Beer

Moorhouse's Pendle Witches Brew

Source Moorhouse's, Burnley, Lancashire **Strength** 5.1% **Website** moorhouses.co.uk

For 29 February, this book reports the shocking story of the so-called witches of Salem, Massachusetts. For 17 August, attention turns to a similarly appalling tale set this side of the Atlantic, 80 years earlier.

The legend of the witches of Pendle Hill, just outside Burnley, begins on 18 March 1612, when a poor girl named Alizon Device, travelling on the road to Colne, had an altercation with a peddler. She cursed him, only to see him almost instantly overwhelmed by a seizure, akin to a stroke. In her confusion and fear, Alizon confessed that she had cursed the man to his son, who promptly informed the authorities. The king at the time, James I, had launched a mission to eradicate Britain of witchcraft, hence it is little wonder that the local aristocracy, responsible for meting out justice locally, should be keen to act and curry favour with their monarch. So it was that they vigorously pursued Alizon, her family and her associates.

Hauled before a magistrate, Alizon again confessed her 'crime'. Her mother and brother were also interviewed and, under pressure, confirmed the suspicion that witchcraft ran in the family. Accusation then flew at another local family, the Chattoxes, who also became embroiled in the sorry tale. The matriarchs of both families – reputedly in their 80s, frightened and probably suffering from dementia – deepened the misery by providing testimonies that implicated the whole clan, including themselves. With the accused all locked away to await trial, their supporters did themselves no favours at all by holding a meeting to discuss their plight. The gathering was denounced as a witches' coven, and they, too, were arrested.

The trial

The trial began on 17 August, with no legal representation for the accused. Testimony for the prosecution came from witnesses as young as nine, as well as from the panic-stricken, bewildered defendants themselves. By the end of the day, three women had been found guilty. When the whole ordeal had been concluded, two local men and seven local women (including Alizon Device) had been convicted and sentenced to hang. One of the old ladies died in prison before she could be tried.

Today, the truth behind the story of the Pendle Witches is impossible to ascertain, except for the fact that justice could not possibly have been done.

Moorhouse's Brewery in Burnley, Lancashire, has been brewing a beer called Pendle Witches Brew since the early 1980s. It is a dark golden, strong ale that falls the sweet side of bittersweet. Creamy malt is well to the fore, along with an apricot fruitiness, with a gentle hop tang in the background that develops more strongly in the sweetish finish. It is a very pleasant, well-balanced drinking experience that contrasts dramatically with the grim events it recalls in its name.

Births Davy Crockett (frontiersman), 1786; George Melly (jazz musician), 1926; Robert de Niro (actor), 1943; Thierry Henry (footballer), 1977

Deaths Ira Gershwin (lyricist), 1983; Rudolf Hess (politician and war criminal), 1987

Events Indonesia declares independence, 1945; US President Bill Clinton admits having an affair with intern Monica Lewinsky, 1998

Golden Ale

Maisel's Weisse

Source Brauerei Gebr. Maisel KG, Bayreuth **Strength** 5.4% **Website** maisel.com

While the summer for rock music fans is built around Glastonbury, the Isle of Wight, Reading and other major open-air festivals, lovers of the classics have their own little circuit at this time of year. They include the Royal Albert Hall for the Promenade concerts, Verona's Arena, a Roman amphitheatre, for opera, and the Festspielhaus in Bayreuth, northern Bavaria, which is home to an annual showcase for the works of 19th-century composer Richard Wagner.

Wagner is celebrated for his larger-than-life music, for dramatic, grand-scale retellings of classic German folklore, and for ambitious orchestration. His influence extends even beyond the classical world – into the rock fables of Jim Steinman and Meatloaf, for example. To say the least, his music was colourful, but then so, it seems, was his life.

Colourful life

Wagner was born in Leipzig in 1813. From an early age, music became his passion and, on leaving university, he took various jobs – as the musical director of theatres in German provincial cities and further afield, and as a journalist in Paris, for instance – in a bid to keep his debts at bay while trying to get his compositions accepted. Involvement in left-wing politics during the turbulent 1840s didn't help his cause, and he was forced to travel around Europe after being exiled from Germany. Extra-marital affairs and scandals contrived to ensure Wagner was never out of the spotlight throughout his later years. Nevertheless, he was committed to his music and, finally, fulfilled a long-cherished ambition to see his (subsequently) most famous work, *The Ring of the Nibelung*, performed in totality when he opened his own theatre in the city of Bayreuth in 1876. Wagner died just seven years later, but his music lives on – despite being, unfortunately, appropriated as a patriotic weapon by the Nazis – and so does the Wagner Festival, held in that same theatre.

Tickets for the event, which runs across the whole of August every year, are notoriously hard to obtain, so you may wish to create your own little piece of Bayreuth by slotting in a CD of *The Ring*, *The Flying Dutchman*, *Parsifal* or one of Wagner's other works, turning up the volume and opening a bottle of the city's beer as the perfect accompaniment. As in most German towns, there is more than one brewery in Bayreuth, but the best known is Maisel's, a business founded by brothers Hans and Eberhard Maisel in 1887, shortly after Wagner's death. Their most famous beer is Maisel's Weisse, a fine example of the weissbier style, featuring vanilla, banana and pink bubblegum in the aroma, a drying lemon and apple fruitiness with a touch of sourness in the taste, and a mellow, gently bitter finish. Nicely chilled, it'll make a great refresher for a warm August day.

Births Roman Polanski (film director), 1933; Robert Redford (actor and film director), 1936; William Rushton (satirist), 1937

Deaths Genghis Khan (warrior), 1227; Honoré de Balzac (writer), 1850

Events Lester Piggott, aged just 12, rides his first winner, 1948; South Africa banned from the Olympic Games over apartheid, 1964

White Beer

Ringwood Fortyniner

Source Ringwood Brewery, Ringwood, Hampshire **Strength** 4.9% **Website** ringwoodbrewery.co.uk

One of the largest instances of human migration was stimulated on this day in 1848, when the *New York Herald* reported that gold had been discovered in California. Thousands of East Coast Americans, and even foreigners, who saw this as the ultimate 'get-rich-quick' opportunity, threw in their jobs and headed west. By the time many of them got there – and the journey was so arduous that many didn't – the best pickings had been had. A lucky few did, indeed, get rich, but many more were no better off when the Gold Rush ended around 1856.

It all started in January 1848, when construction work was underway for a new lumber mill, owned by pioneer John Sutter. One of Sutter's foremen spotted shiny metal pieces in the local river and took them to his boss. Sutter had the material tested and found it to be gold, but he tried to keep the discovery secret, knowing that his plans for a major agricultural business would be devastated if word of easy riches reached the streets. His subterfuge failed, however, and despite early scepticism about the find, California soon went gold crazy. When the news reached the eastern seaboard on this day in 1848, the rest of America flipped. By the following year, some 90,000 immigrants had flocked to the gold fields, threatening the way of life of local Native American residents and the delicate Californian environment, and putting pressure on basic infrastructure. Within a few more years, their number had swollen to 300,000. These hopeful prospectors were colloquially dubbed 'fortyniners', after the year in which they arrived, and they are remembered in a beer from Ringwood Brewery.

Hampshire gold

Ringwood has proved to be a little gold mine in itself. Founded in 1978, the Hampshire microbrewery grew rapidly in the hands of brothers David and Nigel Welsh, soon surpassing in size many long-established regional brewers. In 2007, David decided to retire, and the business was sold to Marston's, which has kept the New Forest brewery open and added Ringwood's excellent range of beers to its large portfolio.

Fortyniner was one of the company's first ever beers, its name a play on the 1049 original gravity figure, the measure of fermentable sugars in a brew before fermentation begins. It also, appropriately, has 4.9% ABV, and is available in both cask- and bottle-conditioned versions. Brewed with Maris Otter pale malt, crystal malt and chocolate malt, Fortyniner is generously seasoned with Challenger, Progress and Golding hops. There's a glint of gold in the glass, as you'd expect, and the aroma is filled with luscious orangey hop notes. Malt and oranges lead in the mouth, with bitterness edging out sweetness as the hops kick in. As befits a beer of this strength, there's plenty of body, too, but this is an easy-drinking ale with a dry, hoppy, orange peel finish.

ABOVE: CALIFORNIA GOLD RUSH MINERS

Births Coco Chanel (fashion designer), 1883; Bernard Levin (writer and broadcaster), 1928; Bill Clinton (US President), 1946

Deaths James Watt (inventor), 1819; Groucho Marx (actor and comedian), 1977; Mo Mowlam (politician), 2005

Events Coronation of King Edward I, 1274; Soviet President Mikhail Gorbachev overthrown in a short-lived coup, 1991

Strong Ale

St Bernardus Tripel

Source Brouwerij St. Bernard, Watou **Strength** 8% **Website** sintbernardus.be

Born in 1090, in Fontaines, near Dijon, our saint for today – St Bernard – was one of his era's great religious characters, an abbot and theologian who influenced not only his contemporaries but also the course of religion in the centuries to come. Bernard's background was aristocratic and, normally, he would have entered the military when of age. Physically, however, he was deemed unfit and so a life in the Church beckoned instead. His aim was to join an abbey and he eventually did so, when he became part of the first Cistercian order, a new movement that aimed to restore the fiercely tough discipline of the early Benedictine monks. When the order expanded, Bernard became abbot of its offshoot abbey at Clairvaux. His influence grew steadily, until Bernard was treated as a key consultant in major Church decisions and recognized as a peacemaker in European affairs. Crucially, it was Bernard who repositioned the Virgin Mary in the centre of the Church's thinking. He died in 1153 and was canonized only 21 years later.

Cheese & beer

Beers that bear the St Bernardus name in Belgium are produced by a brewery in the village of Watou, near Poperinge, close to the border with France. There is no direct connection with the saint, but the name does refer to a refuge built in his honour by a group of monks who moved here from an abbey in northern France because of religious repression. They returned home in the 1930s, and the Refuge Notre Dame de St Bernard, as they called it, became a private cheese farm, taking on the business that the monks had developed for the upkeep of their home. When the nearby Trappist abbey of St Sixtus at Westvleteren decided to expand and commercialize its beer production, the farm also became a brewery. For 60 years, it brewed Westvleteren beers under licence. However, the agreement was terminated in 1992, with Westvelteren taking all production back inside the abbey walls after it was declared that only beers brewed by monks themselves could be labelled 'Trappist'.

Undaunted, the Watou brewers decided to carry on production under the St Bernardus name, with due reference to the old refuge. A new beer introduced at the time was St Bernardus Tripel. Golden in colour, it is defiantly potent yet remarkably easy to drink, with a mostly sweet taste, balanced by bitter orange flavours from the ample hops. Spicy and yeasty in true Belgian fashion, it leaves a dry, gently warming finish of zesty bitter orange, with a sugary note at the back of the throat. On the whole, it's a rather mellow expression of the tripel style, one to enjoy on more occasions than just the feast day of its namesake.

Births Isaac Hayes (soul musician), 1942; Robert Plant (rock singer), 1948; David Walliams (comedian), 1971

Deaths William Booth (Salvation Army founder), 1912; Fred Hoyle (astronomer), 2001

Events Premiere of Tchaikovsky's *1812 Overture*, 1882; last joint recording session by the Beatles, 1969

Tripel

Exmoor Gold

Source Exmoor Ales, Wiveliscombe, Somerset **Strength** 4.5% **Website** exmoorales.co.uk

Cask ale had a bad year in 1995. A few torrid months of warm weather jammed the brakes on the ale expansion that had taken place after the introduction of the guest beer law a few years earlier. In the process, it exposed the distribution network that brought the beers into the pub. Refrigerated drays were few and far between, and the so-called warehouses used by some middlemen were shown up to be no more than basic sheds exposed to all elements. The ale was cooking before it reached the pub. The heatwave also turned the spotlight on inadequate pub cellars. Drinkers deserted cask ale in droves and, as they switched to chilled, pasteurized keg lagers and the new, equally cold nitrokeg ales, sales of real ale plummeted, down 7–10% on the year.

Since that time, major improvements have been made to the distribution chain, but there has been a more profound change, too, with the whole concept of cask ale for summer coming under review. Brewers finally grasped that when the temperature's up, folk need to cool down, but their response was not simply to write off the summer period and abandon ale production in favour of lager. Instead, they turned their minds to developing a style of ale that offered an alternative to the established brown bitter.

To compete with lager brands, they resolved that this new style had to be pale. They achieved this by buying in best-quality pale ale malt, and the paler, the better. Crystal malt, so often used to provide the rich russet colour of a British ale, was mostly cast aside. Strength-wise, there was some conformity about hitting the 4–4.5% mark, ensuring the beer had enough body to make it satisfying but taking on board the fact that, because it's summer, customers will probably want to drink more than one or two pints. But it's in the hop department that the major changes were rung, with the fruitiest hops pushed into the spotlight. All this, combined with cooler serving temperatures in the pub, saw the widespread development of the summer ale.

Ahead of the game

But, while most brewers of summer ales are relatively new to the concept, there are a few that have always been ahead of the game. Hop Back Summer Lightning has been mentioned elsewhere (see 24 January). It was first produced in the late 1980s, not long after its equally blond near-neighbour Tanglefoot, from Hall & Woodhouse. Also early into the market for golden, refreshing ales was Exmoor Gold from Wiveliscombe, Somerset.

Exmoor was one of the new wave of microbreweries that sprang up in the late 1970s and early 1980s. It's now a sizeable regional brewery. Exmoor Gold first arrived in 1986. It is brewed simply from pale malt and laced with four different hops – Challenger, Golding, Fuggle and Styrian Golding. Honeyed malt with a little lemon tartness is what strikes you in the aroma, and the same honeyed texture, with traces of butterscotch, washes over the tongue. But this is not a sweet beer. Bitterness just has the edge, thanks to hops that also bring a spicy zing and a gentle lemon sharpness, before a dry and malty, honeyed finish in which bitterness gradually takes over. In cask, it is satisfying and refreshing, as a summer ale should be, with a strength of 4.5%. There's also a 5% bottled version, on which the above tasting notes are based. Both are available year-round.

Births William 'Count' Basie (jazz musician), 1904; Kenny Rogers (country singer), 1938; Joe Strummer (rock musician), 1952

Deaths Leon Trotsky (revolutionary), 1940; Ettore Bugatti (car manufacturer), 1947; Robert Moog (electronic music pioneer), 2005

Events Theft of the *Mona Lisa* by a worker at the Louvre museum, 1911; the new Shakespeare Globe Theatre in London opens, 1996

Golden Ale

241

Greene King Old Speckled Hen

Source Greene King, Bury St Edmunds, Suffolk **Strength** 4.5% **Website** oldspeckledhen.co.uk

William Morris – entrepreneur, motor magnate and philanthropist – was quite an achiever. Born in Worcester in 1877, he moved to Oxford when he was three. As a teenager, he took a job in a bicycle repair shop, and within months had branched out on his own, building new models as well as fixing broken bikes. The business developed into motorcycles and, eventually, into cars. Morris was soon in production on a major scale, using land vacated by a military training college at Cowley, to the south of the city.

After World War I, Morris's business expanded rapidly, as he brought Ford-style mass production to Britain; at the height of its success, his firm was building half of the new cars sold. By the time Morris died, he had been elevated to the peerage, adopting the title of Lord Nuffield. He had no heir and was happy to distribute his vast wealth to good causes through his Nuffield Foundation, also founding Nuffield College at Oxford.

The brands that made Morris great were the Morris Minor – a popular, affordable car for the working man – and the MG, a sportier range of motors for the more affluent. The MG letters stand for Morris Garages, after the Oxford distributor of Morris's cars, which was also owned by William Morris and which developed a line in modifying Morris vehicles for a more sporty look. The first MG rolled out in 1924. One of the most interesting MGs ever built is now celebrated in the name of one of Britain's best-selling ales, which uses the distinctively octagonal MG badge as part of its brand image.

Curious prototype

Old Speckled Hen is brewed by Greene King in Bury St Edmunds, but its original home was at Morland Brewery, Abingdon, where MG acquired a new factory in 1929. A curious-looking prototype car was brought to Abingdon as part of the move and turned a few heads with its gold paintwork stippled with black. Locals called it the 'old speckled 'un', which evolved into the name seen on the beer when it was first produced in 1979 to mark 50 years of MG arriving in town. Initially, Old Speckled Hen was regularly available only in bottle but, in 1991, a cask version was introduced as Morland began to broaden its portfolio. Unusually for a regional brewer, small advertisements were placed in the national press, and the beer became a huge success, drinkers falling for the sweet, malty, estery fruit flavours that became its hallmark.

When Greene King closed Morland in 2000, they took the beer to Suffolk, and continued to plough in marketing money to make the beer a national brand. But, in 2006, its strength was deemed too high for today's drinker and the ABV of the cask version was slashed from 5.2% to 4.5%. Inevitably, today's Old Speckled Hen has lost the depth of the original, but you can still buy a bottle at the original strength. Either form is pleasant enough, however, to mark the day on which the influential Mr Morris passed away in 1963.

Births Ray Bradbury (writer), 1920; Steve Davis (snooker player), 1957; Tori Amos (singer-songwriter), 1963

Deaths Michael Collins (revolutionary), 1922; Jacob Bronowski (scientist and broadcaster), 1974; Jomo Kenyatta (politician), 1978

Events Battle of Bosworth Field, 1485; the Red Cross founded, 1864; first broadcast of *Match of the Day*, 1964

Best Bitter

ABOVE: A CLASSIC MORRIS CAR, THE MORRIS MINOR

Traditional Scottish Ales William Wallace

Source Traditional Scottish Ales, Stirling **Strength** 4.5% **Website** traditionalscottishales.co.uk

Traditional Scottish Ales, an amalgamation of three breweries – Bridge of Allan, Trossachs Craft and City of Stirling – in 2005, operates from a brewhouse in Stirling. It specializes in beers that glorify the proud history of Scotland, one of which is the obvious choice for 23 August – the day that freedom fighter William Wallace met a bloody end at the hands of his mortal enemies, the English.

Wallace was born around 1270, most likely in Renfrewshire. He gained a reputation as a rebel when he struck out against the bullying English, who had taken over Scotland in 1296 and imposed unpopular high taxes. When he murdered an English sheriff in 1297, his stock rose and he found himself thrust forward as one of the leaders of the Scottish uprising against King Edward I. The rebellion came to a head with the Battle of Stirling Bridge later the same year (see 11 September), which gave the Scots a decisive victory. It was a personal triumph for Wallace, who was swept up to the position of national leader. However, the English were not beaten, and rallied to inflict a revenge defeat at the Battle of Falkirk in 1298. While many of the Scottish nobles who reclaimed control of Scottish affairs from Wallace in the aftermath of the battle ultimately bent themselves to English rule and recognized Edward as their superior, Wallace always refused. Thus he became known as an outlaw and a traitor, and, when captured near Glasgow in 1305, he was taken to London for a show trial. There, in the absence of defence lawyers and even a jury, he was sentenced to death and subjected to a horrific execution that involved a dragging through the streets of the city, hanging, disembowelling and decapitation.

Folklore figure

Such a martyrdom inevitably increased empathy among Scots for this fallen hero. His story became the subject of romanticized folklore and was enhanced yet again in 1995 when Hollywood took an interest. His portrayal by Mel Gibson in the blockbuster film *Braveheart* carried the name of William Wallace forward to a new generation.

The copper-coloured beer that Traditional Scottish Ales brews in his memory has a distinctly Scottish accent, in the form of a dominant malty presence. It was first brewed in 2006 and is derived from a malt grist of pale, crystal, chocolate and caramalt, with a little wheat. First Gold hops are used for both bitterness and aroma.

There are hints of chocolate in the nutty aroma, while the taste is bittersweet and crisp, with a pleasantly sharp tart note – it's rather unusual for such a malty beer to be so refreshing. The finish, meanwhile, is dry, malty, nutty and enjoyably bitter. Try it on draught or in bottle.

Births Keith Moon (rock musician), 1947; Willy Russell (playwright), 1947; Shelley Long (actress), 1949

Deaths Rudolph Valentino (actor), 1926; Oscar Hammerstein II (lyricist), 1960

Events Len Hutton scores 364 against Australia at The Oval, 1938; citizens of Latvia, Lithuania and Estonia join hands in a human chain to demand independence from the USSR, 1989

80/-

243

Weissbier Etalon

Source Ridna Marka, Kiev **Strength** 5% **Website** etalon-beer.com.ua

It's been more than a decade since Ukraine achieved independence from the Soviet Union, and it's not been an easy period. The economy has ebbed and flowed, internal politics have been marred by accusations of ballot rigging and the poisoning of opponents, and former partner Russia is still casting jealous glances over the eastern border. Ukrainians do not take their independence for granted. It was hard won, even if the transition from Russian satellite to sovereign nation was ultimately peaceful, and they intend to keep it that way, making overtures to the EU and NATO for membership as a safeguard. It was on 24 August 1991 that Ukraine followed other Eastern Bloc states and asserted the right to self-rule, and the date is still marked with parades and ceremonies across the country.

As an outsider, I am indebted to the website ehow.com for suggestions of what can be done to commemorate the occasion from a distance. The site offers a five-point plan for making the most of Ukraine's most important day, beginning with cooking Ukrainian dishes for the family and ending with entertaining friends with Ukrainian folk music. In between, it advises reading up on the history of the country, drawing the flag and teaching your kids the value of independence. Sucking eggs with your Ukrainian grandmother strangely doesn't appear on the list. Neither does finding a bottle of Ukraine beer and downing it with celebratory gusto. For such invaluable advice, the book you're reading remains the most vital source.

German lessons

The most widely travelled Ukrainian beer in recent times is undoubtedly Weissbier Etalon. It wasn't even born when Ukraine raised its two digits of independence to the Russians, emerging from the fermentation vessels for the first time in 2003. The Radomyshl brewery is just outside the capital, Kiev, and draws on Ukraine's plentiful natural resources of barley and hops – the country was, after all, known as the bread basket of the Soviet Union. Part of the Ridna Marka drinks group today, Radomyshl operates a sparkling new £15 million brewhouse alongside the original one, which dates from 1886.

In charge of affairs is a German brewmaster. He produces other beers, too, but it is the Weissbier that turns all the heads. Its label looks remarkably like the label for Erdinger Weissbier, and the similarities don't end there – this is a beer born in Bavaria, learning all the lessons that wheat beer producers there have been teaching for centuries. It's a very fine beer, packed full of the bubblegum, banana, green apple, clove and vanilla notes that characterize this rather peculiar beer style. Like all great weissbiers, with its subdued bitterness and fresh, fruity flavours, it has appeal way beyond the world of beer, perfect for handing round when you're serving Ukrainian food or cranking up the volume on the traditional folk music CD.

Births Yasser Arafat (politician), 1929; Jean-Michel Jarre (musician), 1948; Stephen Fry (actor and comedian), 1957

Deaths Pliny the Elder (writer), 79; Captain Thomas Blood (adventurer), 1680

Events Mount Vesuvius erupts, destroying Pompeii, Herculaneum and Stabiae, 79

Wheat Beer

Wood's Shropshire Lad

Source The Wood Brewery Ltd, Wistanstow, Shropshire **Strength** 4.5% **Website** woodbrewery.co.uk

Wood Brewery's bottled ale Shropshire Lad is a tribute to the local poet AE Housman, whose own work of the same title was published in 1896. *A Shropshire Lad* is a cycle of poems nostalgically extolling life in the county from the standpoint of a soldier or a farm boy. Among its verses, it proffers the line 'Ale man, ale's the stuff to drink', which reveals Housman to be a lover of beer. The quote now graces the label of Wood's fine ale, which was introduced in 1996 to mark the centenary of Housman's opus. However, the beer, with its crisp, fruity nature, and skilful balance of pale and dark malts, and Fuggle and Golding hops, could equally have been dedicated to another local boy come good – the very first man to swim the English Channel, a feat achieved on this day in 1875.

Matthew Webb was born in Dawley, Shropshire, in 1848. He showed his swimming prowess at an early age, building up his muscles and his dogged determination by battling with the heavy currents on the River Severn. Careerwise, he entered the Merchant Navy, where his swimming strength earned him yet more admirers. On one occasion, he received a £100 reward for diving into the middle of the Atlantic Ocean in a fruitless attempt to save the life of a man overboard.

Time & tide

When Webb learned of a failed effort to swim the English Channel in 1873, he set his mind to taking the record for himself. He resigned from the position of steam ship captain, and trained long and hard for the daunting task ahead. He first set off on 12 August 1875, and was well into his swim before deteriorating weather conditions forced a return to base. Twelve days later Webb was back. On 24 August, he dived into the water at Dover and began his crossing. At first, the tide was on his side and carried him out into the Channel. By the time he was approaching the French shore, however, the tide was against him and he was forced to swim along the coast for hours, waiting for the chance to fight his way to shore. It eventually came when he waded through the waves to set foot on the beach at Calais at 10.41 am on 25 August. His effort had lasted nearly 22 hours and it is estimated that he swam around 64km (40 miles). Strong ale, it was reported, was one of the drinks that kept his spirits alive during the ordeal.

Webb returned to Shropshire a genuine local hero. His celebrity thereafter ensured that exhibition swimming became his new profession. It also led to his untimely death. The Shropshire Lad accepted one challenge too many when he agreed to try to swim beneath Niagara Falls in July 1883. The whirlpool generated by the ferocious cascade was simply too powerful. Webb was swept under and his body was recovered downstream four days later.

Births Sean Connery (actor), 1930; Frederick Forsyth (writer), 1938; Elvis Costello (rock musician), 1954

Deaths Henry Morgan (privateer), 1688; Sir William Herschel (astronomer), 1822; Michael Faraday (scientist), 1867

Events City of New Orleans founded, 1718; Paris liberated by the Allies, 1944

Best Bitter

ABOVE: MATTHEW WEBB, THE FIRST MAN TO SWIM THE ENGLISH CHANNEL

St Austell Black Prince

Source St Austell Brewery, St Austell, Cornwall   **Strength** 4%   **Website** staustellbrewery.co.uk

'**O**ne of St Austell's best-kept secrets,' declares the brewery's own website about this delicious dark ale. Hopefully, it won't be a secret for much longer and availability will be extended beyond Cornwall and selected beer festivals so that 26 August can be marked more widely with a very appropriate drink.

The connection with today relates to the Battle of Crécy, the occasion of the first English victory during the Hundred Years' War. This interminable conflict stemmed from King Edward III's dashed hopes of becoming King of France. Being beaten to the throne by Philip VI, he set about claiming the land by force, launching distraction raids on towns and villages in the north of the country to humiliate and undermine his rival. In 1346, following one such foray, the English found themselves grossly outnumbered and cornered in a small village near Abbeville called Crécy, but as the vastly superior French army approached, Edward marshalled his forces very effectively to create a strong defence. Helped by shambolic organization on the part of the enemy, his brave but seemingly inadequate troops fought off the attack and claimed an unlikely victory. It was the longbowmen that Edward had recruited from all over England and Wales who were the heroes of the hour, their relentless torrent of arrows cutting down the advancing foe.

Duke of Cornwall

Also singled out for praise was the king's own son, Edward, Prince of Wales, later known as the Black Prince, allegedly from the colour of his armour. He was just 16 at the time but had a great military career ahead of him, going on to secure further victories in this bitter struggle with the French. At the age of 45, Edward pre-deceased his father and so never ascended to the English throne. He was, however, father of the future King Richard II.

Among Edward's other titles was that of Duke of Cornwall, which leads us back to the beer that shares his name. Effectively, Black Prince, is an upscaled mild. Indeed, its origins lie in a beer called XXXX Mild that St Austell sold for many, many years. New head brewer Roger Ryman set about improving the recipe in 2003, increasing the strength along the way from 3.6 to 4%. Pale, crystal and black malts now provide the malt grist, with Fuggle and Golding hops adding the spice. Appropriately dark in colour, with ruby highlights, the beer has a welcoming caramel nose and more soft caramel and creamy notes in the mouth. Pleasantly fruity, it ends dry, with lingering caramel again and a gentle bitterness.

Births Robert Walpole (politician), 1676; John Buchan (writer), 1875; Macaulay Culkin (actor), 1980

Deaths Ralph Vaughan Williams (composer), 1958; Charles Lindbergh (aviator), 1974; Clyde Walcott (cricketer), 2006

Events Volcanic island Krakatoa erupts, 1883; Albino Luciani becomes Pope John Paul I, 1978; the Rugby Union world turns fully professional, 1995

Mild

InBev Mackeson

Source InBev, Tennent's Wellpark Brewery, Glasgow **Strength** 3% **Website** None

Sir Francis Chichester was one of the icons of the 1960s. Like the Beatles, Harold Wilson, George Best and Twiggy, he was a new British hero, albeit an unlikely one at the age of 65 – all thanks to a mammoth, ground-breaking sea journey that started on this day in 1966.

Chichester was born in Devon in 1901. On leaving school, he headed off to New Zealand to make his fortune. This he achieved through investment in a combination of businesses, including aviation. Flying was soon his first love, and by piloting himself from Britain to Australia, he became only the second man to do so. In the post-war years, Chichester turned his attentions to sailing, taking to the high seas in his racing yachts *Gypsy Moth II* and *Gypsy Moth III*, and claiming transatlantic titles and records before embarking on his greatest venture in his best-known boat, *Gypsy Moth IV*. Catching the wind at Plymouth on 27 August 1966, Chichester sailed south to Sydney, where he broke his journey 107 days later. He returned to Plymouth in a further 119 days, so becoming the first man to solo circumnavigate the globe with only one port of call. Chichester arrived home to a flotilla of admiring boats, a vast, cheering crowd and, when he then sailed on to the capital, the fanfares of Swinging London. The journey had gripped the public's imagination so much that the Queen knighted him within weeks.

Forgotten favourite

Francis Chichester died in 1972. His sailing achievements have inevitably been surpassed by new ocean heroes, and the heady days of his triumphant return have slipped from the minds of the British public. But they are worth marking, nonetheless, as a milestone during that tumultuous decade.

When asked what helped him relax out on the wild and unpredictable ocean, Chichester confessed to a love of beer. His preferred tipple, he revealed, was Mackeson – another '60s icon that has rather faded from memory. At only 3% ABV, Mackeson would seem the perfect drink for circumstances when you need to unwind a little and yet keep your wits about you.

Mackeson is the best-known surviving milk stout. This doesn't mean it contains milk, but it does contain milk sugar, or lactose, which bolsters the body of the beer without making it too strong (brewer's yeast cannot ferment lactose). What you get is a rich, creamy sweetness to marry with chocolate and coffee notes from dark malts. It's a travesty that this beer has been allowed to dwindle because first Whitbread and now InBev have failed to invest in the product. It used to be a handy fall-back in pubs where the draught beer was not up to scratch, but few pubs stock it these days. Cans from the supermarket are the easiest to acquire, which doesn't sound like a great recommendation, but, if you haven't tried Mackeson for a while, it's still well worth sampling.

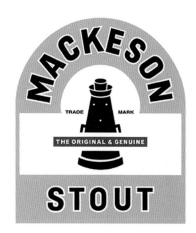

Births Donald Bradman (cricketer), 1908; Lyndon B Johnson (US President), 1908; Mother Teresa (missionary), 1910

Deaths Titian (artist), 1576; Brian Epstein (music agent), 1967; Earl Mountbatten (last viceroy of India), 1979

Events Volcanic island Krakatoa erupts, 1883; BBC Radio 5 goes on air, 1990

Milk Stout

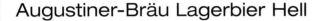

Augustiner-Bräu Lagerbier Hell

Source Augustiner-Bräu Wagner KG, Munich **Strength** 5.2% **Website** augustiner-braeu.de

Among the numerous patron saints of beer and brewing, St Augustine of Hippo stands alone. Whereas others owe their association with the industry to sensibly advocating beer consumption in the days when most drinking water was full of bugs, or by performing dramatic beery miracles, Augustine joins this particular club by simply having enjoyed a pint or two in his time.

Augustine was one of the great converts to Christianity, a hugely influential figure who began life in rather different circumstances. He was born in what is today Algeria, the son of a Catholic mother, but he dabbled with numerous ideologies before turning to Christ. In those pre-Christian days, Augustine made the most of his youth, fathering a son, indulging in affairs with various women and, yes, it seems, kissing the barmaid's apron, to revive that handy old euphemism, on a fairly regular basis. 'Grant me chastity and continence,' he was said to have urged God on his way to his conversion, 'but not yet'.

It was while living in Milan that his spiritual journey reached its Catholic conclusion. There, Augustine abandoned his hedonistic past and began a new life in the cause of Christ. In the years that followed, he became a bedrock of the fledgling Church. He returned to Algeria, became bishop of the city of Hippo (today's Annaba), and is now considered one of the fathers of Christianity. He died on 28 August 430, aged 75.

In his honour, a monastic order came into being. Following the example of Augustine (in his later life), the Augustinian brotherhood gradually spread throughout the world, and it is to them that we can give thanks for the development of one of Germany's most loved breweries.

Monks' place

In 1294, the Augustinians set up court in Munich and, naturally enough for the times, began brewing beer for their own consumption. Brewing records don't exist for the early years, but it is known that a brewery was up and running here in 1328. The monks eventually gave up the brewery in 1803, when Napoleon secularized the monastery, and the business, known as Augustiner-Bräu, is now in private hands. The original site has long been abandoned, and the brewery now sits on the city's Landsberger Strasse, with a pub alongside. However, the best place to sample the beers is at Augustiner's showpiece pub-restaurant in the heart of Munich's central pedestrianized area.

Augustiner turns out some thoroughly enjoyable beers, one of which, of course, lends itself perfectly to today's celebration. Lagerbier Hell, at 5.2% ABV, is the brewery's take on Munich's standard pale lager style. It pours a thin-looking, watery gold, but is far more substantial in its taste, which is crisp and bittersweet with a drying hop note. In keeping with the style, hops are nicely restrained, making this a handsomely delicate yet very satisfying drop of heavenly beer.

Births Johann Wolfgang von Goethe, 1749; John Betjeman (poet), 1906; LeAnn Rimes (country singer), 1982

Deaths John Huston (film director), 1987

Events Martin Luther King makes his 'I have a dream' civil rights speech in Washington, 1963; Sunday trading made legal in the UK, 1994; Kelly Holmes wins her second gold medal at the Athens Olympics, 2004

Pale Lager

Schöfferhofer Kristallweizen

Source Binding Brauerei, Frankfurt **Strength** 5% **Website** schoefferhofer.de

Now here's an odd anniversary. There aren't many meals that can claim a precise date of origin, but Chop Suey is one. It was on 29 August 1896, it is said, that this novel blend of Chinese and American food first saw the light of day.

The inspiration was said to have been the visit of the Chinese Ambassador, Li Hung Chang, to New York. On this occasion, diplomacy extended right into the kitchen, when the chef decided to combine elements of the two nations' diets to serve at an official dinner. A hot-potch of stir-fried vegetables and pieces of meat in a Chinese sauce was the result and Chop Suey – meaning 'mixed pieces' – was born. Since that day, it has featured, in one form or another – there is no set recipe – on Chinese restaurant menus the world over.

As ever, such a fanciful tale needs to be taken with a generous pinch of salt or perhaps a liberal splash of soy sauce. It's more likely that the visit of the ambassador saw a surge of interest in Chinese cooking and led to restaurants developing new dishes like this that would satisfy the locals' taste for the exotic while not straying too far from what they knew and trusted. Alternatively, and even more feasibly, the dish could have been just a popular way of using up left-overs among low-paid Chinese immigrants in the US.

Sweet & sour

There is no evidence – reliable or otherwise – to suggest that any particular beer was promoted as the perfect partner for a Chop Suey, but trial and error has revealed that Chinese food does perform spectacularly well with certain beer styles. An oriental lager is usually competent, as long as there's enough body to deal with strong spices, and Harbin, a Chinese pilsner clone that is now part of the Anheuser-Busch portfolio, is not at all a bad option. But there's more enjoyment to be had by pouring a glass of a German wheat beer to sip with your take-away.

Weissbier is extremely versatile as a table beer – think of those complex fruit and spice flavours that marry perfectly with components in the cooking – and a fine companion to a Chop Suey would be something like Schöfferhofer Kristallweizen. This is an easy-drinking, filtered beer that's been seen on the international stage for many years, and is now owned by the multinational food group Dr Oetker. It's not the most exuberant of weissbiers but it still has all the qualities you're looking for when pairing with Chinese food, with banana, lemon and spice flavours in perfect balance. It also offers plenty of lively carbonation to cut through any grease and those thick, starchy sauces. And if you add sweet and sour to your Chop Suey, the match is even more dynamic. After all, the weissbier is the beer world's own sweet and sour creation.

Births Ingrid Bergman (actress), 1915; Richard Attenborough (actor and film director), 1923; Michael Jackson (pop musician), 1958

Deaths Brigham Young (religious leader), 1877; Ingrid Bergman (actress), 1982; Lee Marvin (actor), 1987

Events The Beatles' last official concert, at Candlestick Park, San Francisco, 1966; Hurricane Katrina hits New Orleans, with devastating effect, 2005

Wheat Beer

ABOVE: CHINESE NOODLE CHEF IN FRONT OF HIS RESTAURANT

City of Cambridge Atom Splitter

Source City of Cambridge Brewery Co. Ltd, Cambridge, Cambridgeshire   **Strength** 4.7%
Website cambridge-brewery.co.uk

In 1997, former Bass, Carlsberg, Greene King and Eldridge Pope executive Steve Draper took the plunge and set up his own business in a small industrial unit in a quiet corner of Cambridge. When I first visited, I found it to be one of the best organized little breweries I'd seen for some time. The beers were good, too.

A few years later, Steve had outgrown the original premises and moved out of the city to a new rural site halfway towards Ely. I called again and was this time impressed by the steps he was taking to make his output environmentally friendly, including using natural reed beds as a method of treating waste from the brewery. His beers were still good.

Even though it's actually no longer in the urban area, his City of Cambridge Brewery retains a close affinity with its birthplace. Most of the beers are named after the city's places, people and traditions, and one of them honours today's birthday hero.

In the field of atomic physics, no star shines brighter than Ernest Rutherford's. Born on this day in 1871, near Nelson, New Zealand, Rutherford gained three degrees in his homeland before accepting a scholarship for post-graduate research in physics at Cambridge University in 1895. After three years, he left to take up a professorship at McGill University in Montreal, where his research was to earn him the Nobel Prize for Chemistry. Rutherford returned to the UK in 1907, when he was offered a chair in physics at

Manchester University. Here, his pioneering work in nuclear physics was to surpass even the mighty Nobel honour when, in 1917, he became the first person to 'split the atom' – an achievement in scientific history akin to Darwin's theory of evolution or Einstein's theory of relativity.

Cambridge connections

Cambridge was to feature prominently in Rutherford's life yet again, however, when he became Professor of Physics and director of the esteemed Cavendish Laboratory. Under his auspices, the unit became a world centre for research into radioactivity. He was elevated to the peerage in 1931, as Baron Rutherford of Nelson, and died six years later, due to complications following a hernia operation.

The beer Steve Draper named for this great scientist was originally called Rutherford IPA. This was dismissed at the time but has returned as the title of another beer in the Cambridge stable. Steve settled instead on Atom Splitter as a fitting label, although, confusingly, it has also been sold under other names, including Atomic Ale and, for St George's Day, as Patron Saint. The beer falls into the stronger end of the premium ale sector, weighing in at 4.7% ABV, and is available both cask and bottle conditioned. The single hop is First Gold, the enormously successful dwarf hop that was developed in the 1990s, and it exhibits a lemon-orange citrus

fruitiness when showcased against the complex but well-balanced grain bill of Maris Otter pale malt, crystal malt, caramalt and roasted barley. Amber in colour, the beer is a fine mix of malt and fruit flavours, with a clean, dry, pleasantly bitter finish.

Births Samuel Whitbread (brewer), 1720; John Peel (broadcaster), 1939; Jean-Claude Killy (skier), 1943

Deaths Lindsay Anderson (film director), 1994; Charles Bronson (actor), 2003; Michael Jackson (beer writer), 2007

Events Hong Kong liberated after Japanese occupation, 1945

Strong Ale

Žatec

Source Žatec Brewery, Žatec **Strength** 4.6% **Website** zatec-brewery.com

The ancient town of Žatec (roughly pronounced 'Shatets') stands nobly on a hilltop 64km (40 miles) northwest of Prague, master of all it surveys. Most of what it surveys are hopgardens. This is the heartland of the Czech hop industry, the area that gave the world the fragrant Žatec hop, used so widely in the best pilsner beers. It's a shame, then, that we mostly know it by its German name of Saaz.

Not surprisingly, the people of Žatec make the most of their hop culture. The town is home to a fascinating hop museum, which not only charts the progress of hop growing around the world, but also shows how cultivation locally has changed over the centuries. But the main hop celebration takes place every year at the end of August/start of September, with a weekend festival dedicated to the humble little green flower that brightens up the life of so many of us.

The Žatec Hop Festival, or Docesna, was inaugurated in 1957. Today, it is a damned good excuse for a knees-up, with feasting, dancing and live music adding to the fun. There's a chance to visit the hop fields and try your hand at harvesting, if you're really keen, otherwise you can take a ride on the fun fair, watch the crowning of the Hop King and Queen, or stop for a pint or two at the bustling beer festival.

Brewing revival

Central to events is the town's own brewery. It's home is in the old castle, and for 200 years it has given work and pleasure to local residents in equal measure. Under the Communists, its role was secure, as breweries in Czechoslovakia were allowed to sell only regionally, safeguarding both local flavours and local jobs. But 40 years of state control also meant underfunding. As the decades rolled by, so the brewery became more and more dilapidated. In 1995, a local investor took over the business but failed to inject either capital or life. Žatec, like so many Czech breweries, was going nowhere, unless it was into oblivion. Its saviour proved to be Rolf Munding, a British businessman of Scandinavian descent. Rolf has invested money and, more importantly, breathed new life into the brewery, and his reward has come with a selection of new beers that are keeping locals happy and engaging the interest of the wider world.

The beer that Rolf focuses on is the '11 degree', as the Czechs describe that middle-strength band falling around 4.5% ABV. The beer is pasteurized for export, but is naturally carbonated by its own yeast and remains a delicate golden creation, lagered for 45 days. Fine hop resins, plus unusual light banana notes and a touch of toffee, fill the aroma. In the taste, juicy, sweet malt takes the lead, with a floral hop note soon fighting its way through. Banana and lemon fruitiness is ever present, running on into the refined, bittersweet finish that becomes increasingly hoppy and tangy – a final reminder for drinkers of this beer's illustrious provenance.

If you can't join the 20,000 visitors to the Docesna, be there in spirit at least, with a glass of this classy beer.

Births Caligula (Roman emperor), 12; Bernard Lovell (astronomer), 1913; Van Morrison (rock musician), 1945

Deaths John Bunyan (writer), 1688; Henry Moore (sculptor), 1986; Diana, Princess of Wales, 1997

Events Garfield Sobers hits six sixes in an over against Glamorgan bowler Malcolm Nash, 1968; Soviet troops withdraw from Germany and Central Europe, 1994

Pale Lager

Brakspear Triple

Source Brakspear, Witney, Oxfordshire **Strength** 7.2% **Website** brakspear-beers.co.uk

Nicholas Breakspear is a stalwart of pub quizzes. Along with the title of the Beatles' first number 1 and the capital of Mongolia, his identity is one of those questions that always crops up. His fame in this context relates to his unique position: the only Englishman ever to have been Pope.

Nicholas was born near St Albans around 1100. His father became a monk at the local abbey, but Nicholas was denied permission to do the same and told to go off and further his education. In defiance, he headed for France and joined a monastery there instead. His dedication was noted, and Breakspear eventually became abbot, and a tough, demanding one at that. His rigorous reforming manner saw him called to Rome to answer for his behaviour, only to find when he got there that the existing Pope, Eugene III, rather approved of his diligence. Thus it was that Nicholas continued his meteoric rise through the ranks and, when Eugene's successor, Anastasius IV, died in 1154, it was Breakspear who became Pontiff, adopting the name of Adrian IV.

The family brewery

Somewhere among the splits and forks of Nicholas's family tree we arrive at Robert Brakspear, 18th-century father figure of a brewing enterprise that still bears his name. Brakspear's became world famous as 'the Henley Brewery', sitting contentedly on the banks of the Thames in the Oxfordshire rowing town. Sadly, it was swept aside by the glint of gold, when, in 2002, its directors decided to sell the brewery for redevelopment. Money talks louder than ever in today's brewing industry, and even if there were a Brakspear Pope today, it's unlikely that an appeal from Rome would have changed the minds of those who had their eyes on the family silver.

Thankfully, the Brakspear name lives on, rescued by the people who run Wychwood Brewery and finding a new home in a brewhouse constructed alongside Wychwood at Witney. There's also a bit of a bonus resulting from these dramatic changes. Some new beers have been added to the range, one of which is the excellent Triple. The name is derived from the fact that the beer is hopped three times (once with Northdowns and twice with Cascades) and is also thrice fermented – in the fermenting vessel, in the maturation tank, and in the bottle – but there's a neat link back to the holy days of the Brakspear clan, too: tripel is, of course, a style of beer brewed by monks in Belgium. You wouldn't say that Brakspear Triple has much in common with a Trappist tripel, which is usually pale and hoppy, but there is some symmetry in the substantial strength of the beer and the fact that it is now attractively served in a chalice-style glass.

Enjoy the satisfying, malty flavours and the full, tangy, tropical fruit notes as you ponder who won the FA Cup in 1954 or try to recall the chemical symbol for tin.

Births Rocky Marciano (boxer), 1923; Barry Gibb (pop musician), 1946; Ruud Gullit (footballer), 1962

Deaths King Louis XIV of France, 1715; Brian Moore (football commentator), 2001

Events Germany invades Poland, beginning World War II, 1939; Bobby Fischer beats Boris Spassky to become World Chess Champion, 1972

Strong Ale

Wychwood Hobgoblin

Source The Wychwood Brewery Co. Ltd, Witney, Oxfordshire **Strength** 5.2% **Website** wychwood.co.uk

Beer and literature: a perfect combination. Whether it's a good book with a good beer, the inspiration found in beer by an author, or perhaps the respite that beer provides after a gruelling day at the typewriter, the relaxing, mind-freeing, restorative qualities of ale have been well documented. One of Oxford's most famous pubs stands testimony to the enjoyment received from our favourite drink by one of the world's most celebrated authors, John Ronald Reuel Tolkien, who died this day in 1973.

Tolkien was professor of English at Merton College, Oxford, and shared the love of a good pint with a number of fellow academics. The Eagle and Child in the city centre was a popular rendezvous for his group of local literati. Here, for 16 years from 1933, the city's most fertile imaginations met twice a week, taking over the back room for a pint and an intellectual chinwag. Collectively, these bibulous bibliophiles were known as the Inklings and among their number was CS Lewis, creator of the magical world of Narnia.

Tolkien's own magical world provides yet more evidence of the pleasure the author took from a glass of ale. In his grand opus, *The Lord of the Rings*, set in Middle Earth, no fewer than seven different inns are mentioned, and the hobbits who are the heroes of his tale are always ultra-keen to grab the handle of a foaming jug of ale whenever one is presented.

Supernatural supping

The brewing world has changed considerably since Tolkien's day. He never, for example, had the satisfaction of sampling beers from Wychwood Brewery, founded at Witney, just a few miles from Oxford, ten years after the author's death. More's the pity, as the brewery trades heavily on imagery drawn from a similar world of elves, imps, wizards and witches. Its prize beer brand is called Hobgoblin, a creature described in the works of Tolkien as a larger version of a goblin or orc. The 5.2% ale (4.5% in cask form) pours a rich red-brown colour and is sweet and nutty, with chocolate and soft toffee notes throughout, plus a drying hoppiness for balance.

The Wychwood website reveals that the beer was created by founder brewer Chris Moss in 1988, for the marriage of the daughter of a nearby publican. A local artist, charmed by the beer, decided to illustrate the character of the drink in a sketch featuring a mischievous creature. The name Hobgoblin stuck and, soon, other beers in a similar vein arrived in the brewery's portfolio. Even the brewery's own name was changed, from the original Glenny Brewery, to build on mystical associations with nearby Wychwood Forest, said to have been the home of many of these supernatural creatures.

Births Billy Preston (rock musician), 1946; Jimmy Connors (tennis player), 1952; Lennox Lewis (boxer), 1965

Deaths Thomas Telford (civil engineer), 1834; Roy Castle (entertainer), 1994; Christiaan Barnard (heart surgeon), 2001

Events Start of the Great Fire of London, 1666; first edition of *The Economist* published, 1843

ABOVE: HEROIC HOBBITS IN THE FILM VERSION OF TOLKIEN'S *THE LORD OF THE RINGS*

Strong Ale

Hopdaemon Leviathan

Source Hopdaemon Brewery Co., Newnham, Kent **Strength** 6% **Website** hopdaemon.com

Offer most people today the chance of a back-breaking 'holiday' in Kent, bringing in the hop harvest, and they'll laugh in your face. Yet, until the days of mechanization, the chance of a month in the fresh, country air was too good to refuse for the working classes trapped in the smoggy streets of London. A week on the Costa del Sol may now be more the average person's cup of September tea, but for the Cockney hordes that made the short journey down the A2, time spent among friends and family in the Garden of England was vacation enough.

Kent, along with Herefordshire and Worcestershire, remains one of the main areas of hop growing in England. The wondrous, pungent, resin-loaded plant has been cultivated here for centuries. It used to be a labour-intensive product. When harvest time came, the precious green cones needed to be gathered in swiftly. Kent, itself, never had enough hands and so the call went up to the city for workers to come and strip the fields of their emerald bounty.

Londoners arrived in hordes. They made it their annual excursion, whole families setting up temporary home in the farmland camps and working together from dawn till dusk, plucking the hop flowers from the bines. The piecework nature of the job meant that some earned more money than they could back in the Smoke, but most were happy just to savour the change of scenery and enjoy the camaraderie of the experience.

Beast of a beer

With the arrival of mechanical hop picking in the 1950s, the annual Cockney invasion came to an end. However, its legacy is still celebrated in an annual festival staged at Faversham, usually over the first weekend in September. Launched in 1991, this is an opportunity to revisit the boisterous spirit of the hop-picking days, with singing, dancing, street entertainers, musicians, a 'hoppers' ball' and, of course, gallons of Kentish ale. At the heart of the celebrations is Faversham's own brewery, Shepherd Neame, but beers from this historic business are featured elsewhere in these pages. Consequently, the choice of beer for today goes to one of Shep's smaller rivals.

Hopdaemon Brewery was founded by New Zealander Tonie Prins, near Canterbury, in 2001. He has since moved to larger premises in Newnham. The hopdaemon in the name is an imaginary sprite that, according to Tonie, lives among the local hopgardens.

Tonie's beers, as befits his origins, have a decidedly New World character, loaded with hops that do not simply impart bitterness but also launch a bombardment of fruit onto the tongue. This is exemplified in Leviathan, his 6% 'beast of a beer', named after the giant sea monster mentioned in the Bible. The malt grist is complex, packed with pale, crystal, chocolate and caramalt varieties, plus a little wheat malt, with Fuggle and Bramling Cross hops working their magic in the copper. The beer glows

red in colour, and has hints of pineapple and lemon showing through the dark malt in the nose. Juicy, fruity hops skip and jump over the palate, merging with estery fermentation flavours to provide pineapple and pepper notes that offset the smooth sweet malt. The dry finish is fruity and hoppy, too.

The hop pickers of old would surely have been delighted to see the fruits of their finger-numbing, limb-stretching, dry, dusty labour put to such excellent use.

Births Ferdinand Porsche (motor car designer), 1875; Pauline Collins (actress), 1940; Charlie Sheen (actor), 1965

Deaths Oliver Cromwell (Lord Protector of England), 1658; Frank Capra (film director), 1991; Billy Wright (footballer), 1994

Events Coronation of King Richard I, 1189; World War II breaks out after Germany invades Poland, 1939; US TV premiere of the cop show *Starsky and Hutch*, 1975

Strong Ale

La Choulette Ambrée

Source Brasserie Artisanale La Choulette, Hordain **Strength** 8% **Website** lachoulette.com

From the annals of detective fiction, a handful of names leap out. Sir Arthur Conan Doyle and Agatha Christie probably lead the pack, but comfortable in their company is the prolific Georges Simenon, who died on this day in 1989.

Simenon was born in Liège, Belgium, in 1903. He moved to Paris in 1922, to try to forge a career as a writer, eventually finding success in 1931 when he introduced a character that was to become internationally famous. Pipe-smoking Inspector Jules Maigret of the Police Judiciare was a hit on the written page and even more so on the small screen, played initially in the 1960s by Rupert Davies and, in a 1990s revival, by Michael Gambon.

Maigret has been recognized as the leading exponent of psychological detective work. Rather than relying on scientific deduction or forensic evidence to secure a conviction, the French inspector solves his puzzles by breaking down the motives and the character of his suspects. He is a keen observer of class and of the mores that accompany each stratum of society, and one of his key indicators of personality is the sort of drink a person takes. Significantly, beer is Maigret's own tipple of choice, often enjoyed at his favourite local, the Brasserie Dauphine.

The bar is said to be situated close to the Palais de Justice, where Maigret works, and alongside the River Seine, which the detective watches flow serenely by as he sups his beer. If Maigret were to return to Paris today, he'd find the beer scene a lot more cosmopolitan than it was during his day. While Kronenbourg dominates most bar counters, Belgian beers have taken over much of the city's more selective outlets, with Leffe the main beneficiary. Some of France's more interesting beers also find their way onto the drinking stage, including bières de garde from Northern France. One of these is certainly worth seeking out for today's commemoration.

Aged for pleasure

The beer comes from the town of Hordain, near Cambrai, from a small brewery that goes by the name of La Choulette, after a primitive form of golf that is played in this part of the world. The business was founded in 1977, when Alphonse Dhaussy took over a failing 19th-century brewery. One of the first beers that he launched was La Choulette Ambrée. Alphonse's son, Alain, who runs the brewery today, still brews this, among a dozen or so regular beers.

Ambrée is a top-fermented beer that enjoys four months of conditioning at the brewery before it is filtered for the bottle and for draught sales. Its attractive, deep amber colour reflects the dark, aromatic malts that go into the mash tun, as does the sweet, nutty, caramel-laced taste. At 8% ABV, this is a sipping beer rather than one to quaff, and that gives you plenty of time to draw out the fruity notes (red berries or prunes?) and savour the spicy warmth of the brew before the drying, lingering, malt and fruit finish.

You can just picture Maigret at his favourite window table, puffing on his pipe, raising a glass of La Choulette to his lips like an early-day Inspector Morse, and allowing the world he is observing to bring him the clues that will help him nail his latest culprit.

Births Dawn Fraser (swimmer), 1937; Tom Watson (golfer), 1949; Beyoncé Knowles (pop singer), 1981

Deaths Edvard Grieg (composer), 1907; Albert Schweitzer (doctor, musician and missionary), 1965; Steve Irwin (naturalist), 2006

Events The Forth Road Bridge opens, 1964; Mark Spitz claims a record seventh swimming gold medal at the Munich Olympic Games, 1972

Bière de Garde

Van Steenberge Bruegel

Source Brouwerij Van Steenberge, Ertvelde **Strength** 5.2% **Website** vansteenberge.com

If you want a colourful insight into the life of common Flemish people in the 16th century, it is to Pieter Bruegel that you turn. Bruegel – also known as Bruegel the Elder – has been described as the most original of Flemish artists from that era, and his legacy is a collection of vibrant paintings that depict simple country folk active and busy, enjoying their everyday lives and the added excitement of holidays. It is from this that Bruegel has earned the nickname of 'Peasant Bruegel', although it is often mistakenly assumed that this was because of the circumstances of his birth.

In fact, Bruegel was born near Breda, sometime between 1525 and 1530. He studied in Antwerp before making his own mark in the world of art, later travelling around France and Italy, absorbing influences, before settling in Brussels, where he began to turn out the artworks he is known for today. He died on this day in 1569, bestowing to the world not only a memorable oeuvre of art but also two sons, who followed him into the trade, with no little success themselves.

While Bruegel, like many of his contemporaries, also mastered religious painting, it is his depiction of common folk that is most acclaimed. Among his most celebrated works are *Netherlandish Proverbs*, an intriguing depiction of more than 100 proverbs in the setting of a Flemish village, and *Peasant Wedding*, which shows his familiar subjects in celebratory mood. They have an air of cartoon about them, with an earthy vulgarity that echoes the times in which he lived. Significantly, mugs of ale are seldom far from the elbows of his characters.

Peasant brew

A detail from another of Bruegel's great works, *The Peasant Dance*, features on the label of a beer brewed in his honour by Van Steenberge, a family-run brewery in the village of Ertvelde, near Ghent. The painting was finished around the year 1568 and now hangs in the Kunsthistoriches Museum in Vienna; the beer is an amber ale, with malt, toffee and gentle butterscotch in the aroma, along with a yeasty spiciness and a floral hop note. Much the same flavours recur in the taste, which also has a drying backnote, while the finish is dry, malty and increasingly bitter.

The brewery describes it as 'the best amber beer of Belgium'. That may be going a bit too far, considering the fierce local competition, but it's certainly a fine ale and a generous tribute to an influential Flemish master.

Births Raquel Welch (actress), 1940; Freddie Mercury (rock musician), 1946; Mark Ramprakash (cricketer), 1969

Deaths Douglas Bader (aviator), 1982; Mother Teresa (missionary), 1997; Georg Solti (orchestral conductor), 1997

Events First episode of the BBC comedy series *Porridge* broadcast, 1974; deep-space probe *Voyager I* launched, 1977

Strong Ale

Woodlands Old Willow

Source Woodlands Brewing Co., Wrenbury, Cheshire **Strength** 4.1% **Website** woodlandsbrewery.co.uk

The intrigued spectators who made the journey to Kennington on this day in 1880 could not have known what they were starting. For three consecutive early September days that year, the London suburb's Oval stadium was the venue for the first ever test match on English soil. The opponents were what have become known now as the old enemy – Australia – and the event proved such a success that the longevity of international cricket was assured.

This wasn't the first time that the two teams had met, however. Three years earlier, representative sides had gone head to head in Australia, with the home team winning by 45 runs. This second time around, England gained a five-wicket revenge, thanks largely to a mighty innings of 152 from the legendary WG Grace. Grace was joined in the England team by two of his brothers, EM and GF Grace – the latter catching pneumonia and dying only two weeks later – and some blue blood, too, in the forms of the Honorable Alfred Lyttelton and skipper Lord Harris. Australia's captain, WL Murdoch, for once outperformed Grace with 153 not out in the second innings, but it wasn't enough to save the match.

Two years later the first proper test series was inaugurated between the two nations, and with England's defeat a *Sporting Times* columnist satirically declared that English cricket had died, the body had been cremated and the ashes were on their way to Australia. Unwittingly, the first Ashes series had been played. Later the charred remains of what appears to have been a bail or a ball were placed in a pot as an appropriate trophy and have been used as the prize ever since.

Historic soulmates

Beer and cricket are excellent soulmates, as Roger Protz's fine book *The Beer Lover's Guide to Cricket* handsomely reveals. A few pints at the boundary's edge are one of life's greatest pleasures but the partnership runs deeper than that. The game actually sprang to life at a pub – The Bat & Ball at Hambledon, Hampshire – and some of the leading exponents of the game have been lovers of a good pint, from fast-bowling ace Fred Trueman to today's front-line attack of Andrew Flintoff and Matthew Hoggard. This most gentlemanly of games has also been recognized in the names of various fine beers, including today's selection, Old Willow from Woodlands Brewery in Cheshire.

Woodlands was founded in 2004, when it acquired brewing equipment from the short-lived Khean Brewery. Khean had named all its beers after cricketing terms, including Caught Behind and Fine Leg, and, with a nod to the former business, Old Willow was included in the Woodlands range. It's brewed with a mix of Maris Otter and Golden Promise pale malts, plus a dash of crystal malt to deepen the golden colour. Three strains of hops – Cascade, Challenger and Target – add zest to the palate, making this a crisp, bittersweet, highly quaffable ale with citrus notes to the fore and hops lingering in the dry, clean aftertaste.

Births John Dalton (scientist), 1766; Greg Rusedski (tennis player), 1973; Tim Henman (tennis player), 1974

Deaths Gertrude Lawrence (actress), 1952; Len Hutton (cricketer), 1990

Events *The Mayflower* sets sail from Plymouth, 1620; funeral of Diana, Princess of Wales, 1997

Golden Ale

Blythe Old Horny

Source Blythe Brewery, Hamstall Ridware, Staffordshire **Strength** 4.6% **Website** blythebrewery.co.uk

The Monday following the first Sunday after 4 September (still with me?) is known as Wakes Monday. On Wakes Monday (the actual date varies obviously), the place to be is the Staffordshire village of Abbots Bromley, where they've been conducting a strange but fun ritual for nearly 800 years.

It all started in 1226, at the village's Barthelmy Fair (the celebration of St Bartholomew's Day, 24 August). As a special treat for the abbots of Burton, the locals performed a novel 'horn dance', wearing sets of deer antlers. Now, at 8am on Wakes Monday, today's generation of Horn Dancers congregate at St Nicholas's church in the village, to collect the horns that are mounted, for safe keeping, on the walls. Setting the horns on their shoulders, they set off for a tiring day of performance, one that will take them on a circuit of around 16km (10 miles), visiting pubs and farms.

The unit comprises 12 characters, some of which will be familiar to fans of morris dancing. There are six deer men, a jester, a hobby horse, a bowman and Maid Marian. Music is provided by melodeon- and triangle-players. The horns are said to be more than 1,000 years old and range in weight from just over 7kg (16lb) to just over 11kg (25lb), so this is quite a physical undertaking. Other 'fair'-type activities also take place, with craft stalls laid out to attract browsing visitors, who come from all over the world for the spectacle. Needless to say, a few beers are sunk during the course of the festivities.

Autumn brew

Celebrating this eccentric but typically English event is the local Blythe Brewery, founded by Robert and Jennie Greenway in 2003. Their base is on a farm in the village of Hamstall Ridware, 6.5km (4 miles) from Abbots Bromley, and it's an idyllic place to work. There are one or two other businesses on the site, but there is very little traffic, and the River Blythe – hence the brewery name – meanders lazily through the meadows that run up behind the brewhouse. The Greenways' regular autumn brew is a 4.6% ale called Old Horny. It features an image of the Horn Dance on the pump clip/label and is brewed with a trio of hops – Challenger, Golding and Styrian Golding – that spice up a cereal grist comprised of pale, crystal and black malts, with some torrefied wheat. Amber in colour, Old Horny offers light citrus fruit and malt in the nose, followed by a crisp and bitter taste, supported by sweetish malt. The finish is rather bitter and dry, as hops take over from the lingering malt. Like all Blythe beers, it's a good, satisfying drink, just the ticket, one would imagine, after an exhausting day under the horns.

Births Queen Elizabeth I, 1533; Anthony Quayle (actor), 1913; Buddy Holly (rock 'n' roll musician), 1936

Deaths Keith Moon (rock musician), 1978; Katrin Cartlidge (actress), 2002

Events Grace Darling and her father rescue a shipwrecked crew off the Northumberland coast, 1838; start of the Blitz bombing campaign on London by Germany, 1940

Best Bitter

Hampshire Lionheart

Source Hampshire Brewery, Romsey, Hampshire **Strength** 4.5% **Website** hampshirebrewery.com

Hampshire Brewery has generated a whole range of beers named after famous British kings. They include beers for Alfred the Great and Arthur Pendragon, the father of King Arthur. Some of these feature in this book and the one most appropriate to 8 September is Lionheart, a golden best bitter dedicated to the king who was born on this day.

Richard I was born in Oxfordshire in 1157, the son of King Henry II and Eleanor of Aquitaine. He succeeded his elder brother, Henry, to the throne in 1183, and immediately began preparations to lead a Crusade to the Holy Lands, attempting to free Jerusalem of Muslim control. It was the start of almost permanent absenteeism from the throne. In fact, out of the ten years he was king, Richard spent only around five months in England. Having a French mother endowed him with strong ties to life across the Channel, especially when he also inherited lands there from his father, while a two-year imprisonment in Austria also helped keep him away.

In battle to the end

The legend of Robin Hood is closely tied into Richard's story. It is said that Robin and his Merry Men needed to look after the poor and victimized when good King Richard was away and his cruel brother John was put in charge. Even though in real life John did try to steal Richard's throne, he was eventually forgiven and was made his brother's heir, coming to the throne on Richard's death in 1199. Richard's skill and courage in battle had earned him the nickname of Lionheart, or *Coeur de Lion* in French, but even these couldn't save him when he was fatally wounded by an arrow during the siege of a castle in France.

Hampshire Brewery has been in operation since 1992. It began life in Andover, but, growing quickly, moved to new premises in Romsey in 1997. Romsey was once home of the well-known Strong's Brewery, which was closed by Whitbread, so the company has brought brewing back to the once-proud beer town. Hampshire's Lionheart depicts the celebrated 12th-century warrior on its colourful label and combines pale malt and lager malt to achieve that appealing golden glow in the glass. A light toffee note emerges in the mouth, contrasted by a lemon accent from a blend of Northdown, First Gold and Perle hops. It's a refreshing and satisfying combination.

Births Antonin Dvorak (composer), 1841; Harry Secombe (comedian and singer), 1921; Peter Sellers (comedian), 1925

Deaths Richard Strauss (composer), 1949; Zero Mostel (actor), 1977; Leni Riefenstahl (film director), 2003

Events Queen Elizabeth II opens the Severn Bridge, 1966; US President Gerald Ford pardons ex-President Nixon for any offences he may have committed against the US while holding office, 1974

Golden Ale

Deschutes Hop Henge Imperial IPA

Source Deschutes Brewery, Bend, Oregon **Strength** 8.1% **Website** deschutesbrewery.com

When revolution came to France at the end of the 18th century, part of the plan to establish a new order involved introducing an alternative calendar, one that would diminish the power of the Pope, who had created the existing Gregorian way of counting down the year. The revolutionaries, however, were also metric minded and sought to simplify life by partially decimalizing the breakdown of days, inventing a system based on 12 months, each comprised of three ten-day weeks. To balance out the solar year, five days (or six in leap years) were tagged onto the end.

In the new calendar – which was introduced in 1793 but abandoned in 1806 – months were grouped by season and named after the weather likely to prevail at that time. Saints' days were ruthlessly cast aside and replaced with days dedicated to things that really mattered to the working man, be they tools, animals, plants or minerals. Hence, the second day of Nivôse ('Snow Month') was dedicated to Houille, or coal; the fifth day of Pluviôse ('Rain') to the Taureau, or bull; and the tenth day of Messidor ('Harvest') to the Faucille, or sickle.

With beer an important part of the daily diet, it's not surprising to find references to the brewing world in the Revolutionary Calendar. Consequently, the 29th day of Vendémiaire ('Vintage') is Orge, or barley, and the 23rd day of Fructidor ('Fruit') is dedicated to the Houblon, or hop. The latter date translates in our present calendar as 9 September, so we really need a hop celebration to mark the occasion.

Hop worship

As tempting as it is to look to France, there is only one place where hops are placed on the same pedestal as saints, and that is in the US. The beer revolution there has been as radical as the political one in France, if happily less bloody. Craft brewers have cheerfully guillotined the old rules for selling bland beer and have introduced a new order based on the cult of the hop, which is now being taken to higher levels with 'extreme' beers that pack in more of the pungent, tangy, fruity little green flowers than ever before.

A good example is provided by Hop Henge from Deschutes Brewery in Oregon. The brewers have had a bit of fun with the name of this mighty ale – even once building a fake Stonehenge out of hop pockets – but they are deadly serious when it comes to brewing it. The amber-red beer is loaded with Centennial, Cascade and Northern Brewer hops, so many that a rock-solid foundation of pale and crystal malts is needed to keep them in balance. Hop Henge used to weigh in at 7% ABV but has now been boosted to 8.1% to cope better with a bitterness level that has been recorded at a remarkable 95 IBUs (a standard British bitter clocks up around 30).

If today calls for a houblon fix, Deschutes is definitely your dealer.

Births Otis Redding (soul musician), 1941; Hugh Grant (actor), 1960; Natasha Kaplinksi (broadcaster), 1972

Deaths William the Conqueror (King of England), 1087; Henri de Toulouse Lautrec (artist), 1901; Chairman Mao Tse-tung (revolutionary), 1976

Events Battle of Flodden Field, 1513; California joins the United States of America, 1850

Imperial IPA

Wolf Granny Wouldn't Like It!!!

Source The Wolf Brewery, Besthorpe, Norfolk **Strength** 4.8% **Website** wolfbrewery.com

On the face of it, today's celebration is just another schmaltzy American creation, something that's not even noted on this side of the Atlantic. Grandparents' Day, however, does have a moral root, as its founder, West Virginian housewife Marian McQuade, explained when she started campaigning for it back in 1970.

To Mrs McQuade, the neglect by young people of the wisdom and knowledge of their elderly relatives was a crime. Men and women in their later years have a lot to impart to society, she claimed, and so she urged the younger generations to cherish their elders. It was a quid pro quo arrangement, too. The grandparents stood to gain from the closer contact and attention of their families. Even elderly folk without families were covered, with a suggested scheme for adopting foster grandparents.

McQuade, a mother of 15 children – the unkind may say she had a vested interest in the idea – took her proposal to the West Virginia state government with rapid success, and proceeded to lobby politicians across the US. Within eight years, she had achieved her goal, when President Jimmy Carter signed an annual Grandparents' Day celebration into law. It was to take place on the first Sunday after Labor Day (first Monday in September), an appropriately autumnal date for those in the autumn of their lives.

Howlin' good beer

As a bit of fun for the occasion, you could send your grandmother a bottle of beer from Wolf Brewery. Wolf was founded in Attleborough, Norfolk, in 1996, and changed ownership in 2007, when it moved to new, larger premises. All the brewery's beers are themed around wolves/dogs, and the motto is 'Howlin' good beer!', with which plenty of drinkers in East Anglia concur. The beer highlighted for today is called Granny Wouldn't Like It!!!, but it would be worth seeing if she did.

The pump clip/label depicts the scene from Little Red Riding Hood, when the young heroine discovers a wolf dressed up as her grandmother, all ready to gobble her up. However, fairy tale artwork and gimmicky name do little to reflect the interesting profile of this amber-red strong ale. With pale, crystal, chocolate and wheat malts in the mash tun, there's plenty of body to this beer, providing roasted notes in the taste and finish, while Golding and Challenger hops supply a peppery balance and some vinous fruit.

If Granny doesn't like it after all, then give it to Grandad, who will be sure to tell you all about the beers he enjoyed when he was a lad. You see: the grey generation do have important things to pass on.

Births Arnold Palmer (golfer), 1929; Colin Firth (actor), 1960; Guy Ritchie (film director), 1968

Deaths Jock Stein (football manager), 1985; Anita Roddick (retailer), 2007; Jane Wyman (actress), 2007

Events American Express launches its credit card service in the UK, 1963; cult TV series *The X-Files* debuts in the US, 1993

Strong Ale

261

Traditional Scottish Ales Stirling Brig

Source Traditional Scottish Ales, Stirling **Strength** 4.8% **Website** traditionalscottishales.co.uk

As mentioned elsewhere in this book, Traditional Scottish Ales is a craft brewery that specializes in producing beers to commemorate momentous occasions in Scottish history. It is to this Stirling-based brewery that we turn once again today, to remember the significant events of 11 September 1297.

As outlined in the entry for 23 August, 1297 was a big year for the Scots as they looked to seize back their country from the rule of heavy-taxing English king Edward I. Leading the opposition was William Wallace, in partnership with fellow rebel Andrew Murray. Jointly they commanded Scottish resistance at the Battle of Stirling Bridge on this day, as Edward's men surged north in a bid to quell the uprising.

The confrontation took place close to Stirling Castle, literally at a small bridge that crossed the River Forth. It was a strategic position, the gateway to the north through which the English needed to pass to assert their authority. To the east, the river opened out and was too wide to cross; to the west, the land was marshy and difficult to negotiate. Everything depended on a tiny wooden bridge across which just two men on horseback could move at one time.

In charge of the English forces was John de Warenne, the Earl of Surrey and Edward's local governor. Having arrived at the scene and assessed the situation, he delayed his crossing of the bridge in the expectation that the Scots, massively outnumbered, would prefer to surrender rather than face certain defeat. He was wrong and was eventually forced to take his men across the bridge in preparation for an assault. Wallace and Murray waited for half the English army to arrive slowly on the north bank before launching a fierce attack. The English were trapped with their backs to the river, and only a few escaped. The others were massacred, left to die after Warenne tore down the bridge to prevent the Scots from crossing south.

Andrew Murray suffered fatal wounds in the battle, but Wallace emerged triumphant, effectively installed as the leader of the rebellious nation.

700th anniversary

Traditional Scottish Ales' Stirling Brig was first brewed in 1997 to mark the 700th anniversary of the battle. It's an 80/- in style, which, for readers unaccustomed to Scottish beers, equates to a best bitter, but usually with a notably malty character (Scotland has always grown barley but, historically, hops have been scarce). A former gold medal winner in the Society of Independent Brewers' Scottish beer competition, Stirling Brig is brewed from Maris Otter pale malt, crystal malt and chocolate malt, plus a little wheat. Golding hops are used for gentle bitterness, with First Gold employed later in the copper boil for aroma. The deep red beer is malty and chocolaty throughout, with hints of bramble in the biscuity nose, and winey dried fruit and nuts adding some complexity on the palate. With its dry, malty finish, it won't even leave a bitter taste in the mouth of English drinkers.

Births DH Lawrence (writer), 1885; Franz Beckenbauer (footballer), 1945; Harry Connick Jr (singer), 1967

Deaths Nikita Kruschev (politician), 1971; Peter Tosh (reggae musician), 1987; Jessica Tandy (actress), 1994

Events Dissident Bulgarian writer and broadcaster Georgi Markov dies after being 'stabbed by a poisoned umbrella' in London, 1978; the 9/11 terrorist strikes on mainland US, 2001

80/-

St Bernardus Grottenbier

Source Brouwerij St. Bernard, Watou **Strength** 6.5% **Website** sintbernardus.be

It sounds like the opening scene for a Scooby-Doo adventure, but when, in 1940, four teenage boys and a dog went for a ramble in the forests near Périgueux in south-central France, they stumbled upon something of great historical significance. Exploring an area where a large pine tree had fallen, the dog tumbled into a hole and, in so doing, unearthed a crevice that led deep underground. Working their way through the succession of chambers, the boys realized they had discovered something special. The walls of the caves were vividly decorated with paintings of animals that dated back to pre-historic times. Raging bulls, galloping horses and wiry stags seemed to blink in the new light brought by the first visitors for thousands of years. It was a troglodyte Tate Gallery, a Guggenheim grotto that graphically provided an insight into the lives of the early dwellers of these parts.

It didn't take long for the teenagers' discovery to become major news. Soon the world of archaeology was on their doorstep – despite the restrictions of the war. The caves at Lascaux were opened to the public and tourists flocked in. But, where man treads there is so often destruction, and deterioration set in, caused by exhaled carbon dioxide and other human factors. While this has been successfully treated and limited, the caves now remain closed, although a facsimile of the main halls has been created just 200m (220 yards) away, so that the magnitude of the teenagers' discovery can be properly appreciated.

The cave man

What we need to mark this important find is a beer brewed in a cave. We can't quite do that, but there is a beer that's matured in a cave. Grottenbier was the creation of Pierre Celis, the man who revived the Belgian white beer style and founded Hoegaarden back in the 1960s. He'd long harboured the idea of conditioning a beer in the same way as champagne, which, for Pierre, meant using caves where the dank atmosphere would lend a different quality to the process than a simply chilled brewery cellar. He also planned to 'riddle' the beer like champagne, inverting the bottle and turning it daily by hand to condense the sediment in the neck and then freezing the collar so that the plug of ice containing the sediment could be removed. Other brewers have since taken up this concept, but when Pierre finally realized his plan in the late 1990s, he backed away from the idea, in favour of leaving the yeast in the bottle. But the beer is still cave-matured and turned regularly in a champagne rack.

As Celis no longer has his own brewery, the beer is brewed for him by St Bernardus in Belgium. Dark malts feature heavily in the recipe as do some mysterious spices. After primary fermentation, the beer is bottled and taken to caves along the Belgian/Dutch border where it is matured. The finished article is chestnut in colour, with a spicy, slightly sour, creamy malt aroma. Peppery spice leads the way on the palate with vaguely liquorice notes and a full, smooth, sweet maltiness. There's just a little citrus, too, that points the finger in the direction of coriander, which may also be responsible for the prolonged, peppery finish. The natural conditioning produces a wonderfully light, mouth-filling texture, keeping the beer lively and complex.

Spectacular discoveries are still being made in caves, it seems.

Births Maurice Chevalier (actor and singer), 1888; Jesse Owens (athlete), 1913; Barry White (soul musician), 1944

Deaths Steve Biko (political activist), 1977; Jeremy Brett (actor), 1995; Johnny Cash (country musician), 2003

Events John F Kennedy marries Jacqueline Bouvier, 1953; England wins The Ashes in cricket, 2005

Spiced Ale

ABOVE: PAINTINGS IN THE CAVES AT LASCAUX

Westerham General Wolfe 1759 Maple Ale

Source Westerham Brewing Co., Edenbridge, Kent   **Strength** 4.3%   **Website** westerhambrewery.co.uk

The name of today's beer provides plenty of clues to both its inspiration and content. It's a fruity autumn bitter from Kent, dedicated to a local soldier who became a hero of the old British Empire.

James Wolfe was born in Westerham in 1727 and served in numerous military campaigns at an early age, with commendable efforts in the Jacobite uprising in Scotland, where he fought against Bonnie Prince Charlie at Falkirk and Culloden, and in the War of the Austrian Succession. However, it is on the other side of the Atlantic that he gained iconic status. Pitched into the Seven Years' War, Wolfe won great praise for his role in the siege of the French fort Louisbourg in modern-day Nova Scotia, which saw him being given command of British forces aiming to conquer the city of Quebec. This Wolfe duly achieved, against the odds, when he cleverly arranged for his men to scale sheer cliffs and take the defending French by surprise. In the ensuing battle on the Plains of Abraham, the enemy was routed, Quebec was taken but, sadly, Wolfe was mortally wounded. He died on 13 September 1759.

Local heroes

Westerham Brewery pays handsome tribute to one local war hero in the shape of its British Bulldog (see 10 May) and it does the same here to General Wolfe with this transatlantic ale. The North American connections come not only from the Quebec campaign. They stem from Westerham's Canadian brewer Anthony Richardson and also from the use of pertinent ingredients in the beer, namely the Bramling Cross hop – which, the brewery reveals, is a close relative of a wild hop from Manitoba – and a subtle splash of Canada's most famous culinary export, maple syrup.

Although the beer is only available in draught form, it can be purchased from the brewery in 5-litre mini-casks, which provide the full flavours of real ale for home consumption. The beer pours orange-amber in colour – 'the colour of turning maple leaves', say the brewers – and has a perfumed, floral aroma of toffeeish malt, orchard fruits, bitter oranges and blackcurrants. The taste is firmly bitter, but very fruity, with juicy blackcurrants and more orchard fruits doing Wolfe-style battle with toffee-malt, grassy hop resins and the scented floral contribution of the maple syrup, which, happily, doesn't make the beer too sweet. With roasted malt emerging in the finish, this is a chunky, bitter beer, as robust and assertive as the military man it commemorates.

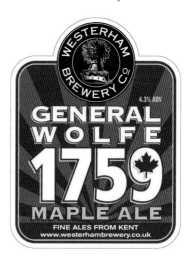

Births JB Priestley (writer), 1894; Shane Warne (cricketer), 1969; Goran Ivanisevic (tennis player), 1971

Deaths Joe Pasternak (film director), 1991; George Wallace (politician), 1998; Dorothy McGuire (actress), 2001

Events Israel and the PLO agree a peace deal in Washington that sees limited autonomy handed to the Palestinians, 1993; Iain Duncan Smith becomes leader of the Conservative Party, 2001

Best Bitter

Brakspear Oxford Gold

Source Brakspear, Witney, Oxfordshire **Strength** 4.6% **Website** brakspear-beers.co.uk

There can be few initiatives as eye-catching as the recent trend towards organic farming. With increased concern over the use of pesticides, the sustainability of crops and healthy living generally, bodies such as the Soil Association in the UK have been converting huge numbers of consumers to organic products.

Part of the Soil Association's success story is its annual Organic Fortnight, two weeks of organic celebration around this time every September. Events such as organic breakfasts are staged, special markets are held, and the Organic Market Report is published to highlight the state of the industry.

The brewing industry has been battling to keep pace with the new interest in organic goods. For most brewers, organic beer forms just one small part of their range. Other brewers such as Atlantic, Black Isle, Butts, Little Valley, North Yorkshire, Organic (naturally), Marble and Spectrum in the UK, have gone the whole hog and converted their entire output to organic. It's not an easy choice, however. To be certified as organic and display the all-important logo, breweries need to register and pay a substantial fee to a ratifying body, such as the Soil Association. They are then inspected and quizzed about the provenance of their ingredients, with paperwork closely analyzed and storage arrangements checked to make sure that organic items are not housed with non-organic. The whole brewing process needs to be organic, too,

which has implications when adjusting the mineral content of the water and when clarifying the beer.

Another issue for brewers is the availability of ingredients. There are only limited supplies of organic barley and organic hops, and some need to be ordered from as far away as New Zealand. The quality of the ingredients also varies. Whereas most hop farmers, for instance, can be generally confident about the quality of their hops, those growing organic hops are, by definition, reliant on the quirks of nature for a bountiful, healthy crop.

Praise & support

So the brewers who have committed to organic production not only need praise but support. I suggest we take the opportunity of Organic Fortnight to sample as many organic beers as we can get hold of. At the very least, we should make sure that today, as a representative day of the fortnight, is an organic beer day.

One of the most widely available organic beers comes from Oxfordshire. Brakspear Live Organic was first launched in 2000, when the brewery was still at Henley-on-Thames. It was but one of four organic beers produced by Brakspear at the time but was the only one carried over when the Brakspear beers finally found a new home in Witney. In 2007, the name was changed to Oxford Gold. The beer is brewed from organic pale and crystal malts and seasoned with organic hops: Hallertau from

Germany, Golding from Belgium and English Target. The beer is bottle conditioned and packaged for Brakspear by Fuller's.

Copper in colour, the beer offers a zesty aroma of bitter oranges, pears and apples. The taste is crisp and bittersweet with an oily marmalade note from the hops and a background pear fruitiness, plus a dash of pepper. Dry, lightly roasted malt leads into the finish, but hoppy bitterness builds nicely and oranges linger.

Under its previous name, the beer was the winner of the first ever Organic Beer Challenge, staged in 2000. The name may now be different but it's still a champion ale.

Births Peter Scott (naturalist), 1909; Jack Hawkins (actor), 1910; Ray Wilkins (footballer), 1956

Deaths Dante Alighieri (poet), 1321; Duke of Wellington (soldier and Prime Minister), 1852; Grace Kelly (actress), 1982

Events Britain adopts the Gregorian calendar, 1752; OPEC, the association of oil exporting countries, established, 1960

Best Bitter

Shepherd Neame Spitfire

Source Shepherd Neame, Faversham, Kent **Strength** 4.5% **Website** shepherdneame.co.uk

'The Battle of France is over… the Battle of Britain is about to begin': prescient words from British Prime Minister Winston Churchill on 18 June 1940. The premier was reflecting on the rapid progress made by the Nazis following their invasion of Poland in September 1939, and the relative ease with which Norway, Denmark, the Netherlands, Belgium and France had fallen to the enemy advance. Churchill knew that Britain lay next in Hitler's sights.

It is often erroneously believed that the Battle of Britain took place on a single day, a misconception perhaps fuelled by the naming of 15 September as Battle of Britain Day. In fact, the onslaught took place over more than three months, beginning 10 July 1940 and ending 31 October, although this September day can be seen as the day when the battle really came to a head.

The Battle of Britain remains the only major wartime battle fought solely in the air. Hitler knew that, in order to get his convoys across the English Channel, the Royal Air Force needed to be neutralized. Hence, he sent forth the Luftwaffe with the express aim of destroying Britain's air defences. The RAF was not prepared. It had suffered major losses in the campaign to save France and now needed to rapidly train a new corps of fighter pilots and acquire new aircraft. Fortunately, Hitler decided to consolidate his position across the Channel first, giving Britain's airmen time to reorganize. When the first wave of attacks finally arrived, the RAF had just enough men and machines in place to fight them off. And so it continued throughout the summer. Despite being heavily outnumbered, the RAF kept the Germans at bay until, on 15 September, Hitler sent over what seemed to one observer as 'the whole bloody Luftwaffe'. Britain's pilots, aided by refugee airmen from occupied countries, doggedly saw off the attack. Although the Battle of Britain was to continue for another six weeks, and German bombing of Britain until 1944, after this day Hitler realized that his planned invasion of Britain was in trouble.

Wartime icon

The Battle of Britain created many heroes, some who survived with bitter memories and many who took to the skies but never returned. They became known as 'the Few'. The Battle also created a new wartime icon in the form of the Spitfire, Reginald Mitchell's highly manoeuverable fighter that, along with the Hurricane, outperformed the Germans' much-vaunted Messerschmitts.

The aircraft is remembered today in the title of one of Britain's most popular ales. Spitfire is brewed at Shepherd Neame in Kent, beneath skies once darkened by wartime rage. It is a highly quaffable best bitter made from pale and crystal malts, and Target, Admiral and East Kent Golding hops, which generate a lasting hoppy finish. The beer was first produced in 1990 for the 50th anniversary of the Battle of Britain and, like the aircraft with which it shares its name, it is perfectly balanced.

Births Agatha Christie (writer), 1890; Oliver Stone (film director), 1946; Prince Harry, 1984

Deaths Isambard Kingdom Brunel, 1859; Johnny Ramone (rock musician), 2004; Raymond Baxter (broadcaster), 2006

Events *The Sun* newspaper replaces *The Daily Herald*, 1964; the US loses golf's Ryder Cup for the first time since 1957 when beaten by Europe, 1985

Best Bitter

Casta Milenia

Source Cervéceria Cuauhtémoc-Moctezuma, Monterrey   **Strength** 8%   **Website** ccm.com.mx

ABOVE: THE YELLOW CITY IZAMAL, YUCATAN

The Mexicans celebrate 16 September as their independence day, but that date really only commemorates the start of the movement for independence from Spain, back in 1810. The liberty of the nation was actually not acquired until 24 August, 11 years later.

Spain had been the colonial power in Mexico for some 300 years. Making a stand for the downtrodden locals was one Father Hidalgo y Costilla, the outspoken priest of a small parish known as Dolores. Hidalgo began plotting insurrection with a group of like-minded local intellectuals, and an uprising was precipitated when the home of one of his associates was raided and a stash of weapons uncovered. Hidalgo was alerted and, rather than retreat into hiding, he issued a rallying call to his flock. On 16 September 1810, the Cry of Dolores, as it has become known, urged Mexicans to rise up and claim their land for themselves. The response was positive.

Hidalgo's followers rapidly grew in number and hit the road. He had the opportunity to take Mexico City but feared that, if victorious, his army would lack discipline, with regrettable consequences for law and order. He pulled back, and the steam ran out of his campaign. In July the following year, Hidalgo was executed by his enemies, but his call to arms had ensured that the movement towards independence was unstoppable. Still, it took another ten years for the Spanish to accept that they were not welcome in Mexico. Eventually, on 24 August 1821, Spanish officials conceded defeat by signing the Treaty of Cordoba, that granted Mexico its freedom.

Mexican rebels

On the face of it, it would seem there are very few Mexican beers that could do justice to such an important celebration. Most are of the thin, golden, stick-a-slice-of-lime-in-the-neck-to-provide-some-flavour type of lager that simply holds no appeal for discerning beer drinkers. Scratching

beneath the surface, however, reveals a clutch of handsome beers from the FEMSA drinks group, which also produces Sol and Dos Equis. The Casta brand is a cut above the company's other beer provision. That's because it was produced by an independent brewery until that was taken over and closed in 2005, with production transferred to another centre. In the selection, there's a golden ale called Dorada, a pale ale confusingly called Bruna, a dark beer called Morena and a wheat beer called Triguera, but the big beer to wheel out today is called Milenia.

At 8% ABV, it's a Belgian-style creation, featuring pale and roasted malts along with hops from the UK and the Czech Republic. The taste is sweetish and lightly warming, with hints of liquorice in the bitterness, a faintly orange fruitiness and plenty of spicy malt character. The finish is quite dry with more spicy, bitter flavours. As if made for this particular day, Milenia is packaged in champagne fashion – bottle conditioned and closed with a cork and cradle.

Births BB King (blues musician), 1925; Russ Abbot (comedian), 1947; Neville Southall (footballer), 1958

Deaths Gabriel Fahrenheit (scientist), 1736; Marc Bolan (rock musician), 1977; Maria Callas (opera singer), 1977

Events Argentine President Juan Peron overthrown in a coup, 1955; the pound forced out of the European Exchange Rate Mechanism on 'Black Wednesday', 1992

Strong Ale

Silenrieux Joseph

Source Brasserie de Silenrieux, Silenrieux **Strength** 5.4% **Website** http://users.belgacom.net/gc195540

Brewers latch onto patron saints with unseemly eagerness. Perhaps it is the suggestion of vice that hangs around their product that prompts them to look for a holy sponsor. Several brewing saints are featured in this book, and another has pride of place for today, the day she died in 1179.

The saint in question is Hildegard of Bingen, a truly remarkable woman from the Rhineland, who was born in the year 1098 and sent to a convent at the age of eight. Thereafter, she dedicated her whole life to the church as an abbess in the Benedictine order, becoming known as a visionary and an oracle. In the 12th century, it was highly unusual for a woman to have power and influence but Hildegard had both, built on a reputation as a great healer and source of wisdom, as well as a lady of culture – she was an accomplished poet and an inspirational musician who left a legacy of melodic songs. Amazingly, in an era when lives rarely extended beyond 40 years, she lived to be more than 80.

The importance of Hildegard for brewers lies in the fact that she encouraged her followers to drink beer, realizing that it was safer than polluted water, and also because she was the first person to extol the use of hops in beer, again no doubt for their health and preservational qualities. This was all part of Hildegard's promotion of a balanced lifestyle and a healthy diet, in which mind, body and spirit all played a part in a person's well-being.

Alternative cereal

Interestingly, one food product that she advocated strongly was spelt. This cousin of wheat is little known these days but references to it can be found in the Bible and, as Hildegard suggested, it is now acknowledged to have great dietary benefits. Like many cereals, it can, of course, be used for making beer. It is one of the four grains in Gulpener Korenwolf, for example (see 11 December), but one of the best beers to be based on it comes from Belgium.

The Silenrieux brewery was founded in 1991, in the French-speaking south of the country, between Beaumont and Philippeville. The beer they call Joseph is openly declared as 'spelt beer'. It is in the witbier style, typically hazy yellow in the glass, and including spices instead of hoppiness for balance. The aroma presents sweet and sour lemons, spices and a faintly nutty, bready cereal note. In the mouth, the beer is lively and refreshingly bittersweet, with spritzy citrus notes, a soft dryness and gentle herbs. Once again, nutty cereals – no doubt the spelt showing through – provide a light backdrop. It's a clean and classy, bottle-conditioned beer that retains your interest right through to the bittersweet, slightly chewy, faintly nutty, drying finish in which sweet lemon flavours linger.

You have to be careful about labelling a beer as a health drink but, as this one draws together two nutritious foods that she rated highly, the wise Hildegard would surely have nodded her approval to Joseph.

Births Stirling Moss (racing driver), 1929; Desmond Lynam (broadcaster), 1942; Anastacia (pop singer), 1973

Deaths William Fox Talbot (photographer), 1877; Laura Ashley (fashion designer), 1985; Spiro Agnew (politician), 1996

Events First episode of *M*A*S*H* screened in the US, 1972; Israel and Egypt sign the Camp David Accords, 1978

Wheat Beer

Whim Dr Johnson's Definitive

Source Whim Ales, Hartington, Derbyshire **Strength** 5% **Website** None

'The tavern chair is the throne of human felicity,' declared Dr Johnson, a little pompously perhaps, but I think we all know what he meant. Johnson, as well as being a man of letters, compiler of the first *Dictionary of the English Language*, political pamphleteer, editor of Shakespeare and early travel writer, was, it is well documented, partial to a good pint.

Samuel Johnson was born in Lichfield, Staffordshire, on this day in 1709. As the son of a bookseller, he was always likely to forge a literary future, despite being only partially sighted. But his early studies at Oxford were disrupted by poverty and he left before graduating to become a teacher.

Eventually, he found his forte in writing, working in London. He engaged himself in hack journalism, put together acclaimed parliamentary reports and then spent eight years compiling the dictionary that raised his profile as one of the era's great literati. In 1773, he took himself off on a tour of Scotland with his friend James Boswell, who became a close enough companion to be able to publish his biography in 1791. Among Boswell's anecdotes from his time in Johnson's company were numerous tales that reveal the great man's love of a good beer and of the public house in particular. 'There is no private house, (said he), in which people can enjoy themselves so well, as at a capital tavern,' recalled Boswell with due reference to Johnson's keenness to hit the bar.

Definitive tribute

Johnson's enthusiasm for fine ale is echoed on the label of a beer from Broughton Ales in Derbyshire. Whim was founded in 1993 and has created in Dr Johnson's Definitive a dark red-amber beer that it thinks would have found favour with the good doctor, who was born only a short coach ride from the Peak District farm that Whim calls home. 'How do you define a "quality dark ale"?,' says the label. 'There is surely no gentleman better qualified to address this compelling matter than the most learned Doctor Samuel Johnson.' Unfortunately, the text goes little further towards enlightening us about the man and his drinking preferences, apart from a mention of his bibulous travels with Boswell, so the beer is allowed to do the rest of the talking.

Dr Johnson's Definitive is a richly malty brew, offering hints of bourbon biscuit in the sweet, dark malt flavours that dominate the taste, with just a little fruity tartness to sharpen it up and a spicy warmth that continues with lingering malt into the hoppy, bitter finish. In style, it's clearly closer to the tipples that Johnson admired in the 17th century than most beers today.

Births Greta Garbo (actress), 1905; Mo Mowlam (politician), 1949; Lance Armstrong (cyclist), 1971

Deaths Sean O'Casey (writer), 1964; Jimi Hendrix (rock musician), 1970; Jimmy Witherspoon (blues musician), 1997

Events *The New York Times* first published, 1851; citizens of Wales vote to establish the Welsh Assembly, 1997

Strong Ale

ABOVE: DR SAMUEL JOHNSON, MAN OF LETTERS AND ENTHUSIASTIC ALE DRINKER

Glastonbury Golden Chalice

Source Glastonbury Ales, Somerton, Somerset **Strength** 4.8% **Website** glastonburyales.com

September 1970 proved to be a significant month for rock music. In the space of two remarkable days, it lost a hero and gained a festival. On 18 September, Jimi Hendrix was found dead; the next day Glastonbury welcomed its first bands on stage.

It cost just £1 to attend that original, rather modest, event deep in the Somerset countryside. Farmer Michael Eavis, inspired by a blues festival at nearby Shepton Mallet, was the brains behind the project, throwing open his land to acts like Marc Bolan and Al Stewart, and startling his cattle in the process. Around 1,500 fans made the journey and they were rewarded with free milk from Eavis's farm.

The following year, the event switched to the summer solstice, where it has remained, more or less, ever since. As years rolled by, extra land was acquired, crowds swelled accordingly – they now top 150,000 – and organizations such as CND, Greenpeace and Oxfam benefited enormously from the proceeds. The biggest names in rock history have graced its various stages and tents, from Bob Dylan and Paul McCartney to Oasis and The Killers.

With sideshows and family-related attractions thrown in, Glastonbury has turned into something of a carnival. Yet it's remarkable and, frankly quite baffling, why a festival staged every year at the end of June should consistently turn into a mud bath. Wellies and waterproofs are now standard equipment among attendees, along with an industrial-strength pump to dry out their tents. Perhaps they ought to move it back to September.

Legendary pint

There are mystical souls who will suggest to you that it's something to do with the geography and aura of the area. This is the land, legend has it, of King Arthur, of ladies in lakes and swords stuck in big stones. The Glastonbury area is crossed by ley lines, the experts say – sources of magical energy that run between structures of archaeological interest, including Glastonbury Tor.

The myths and legends of Glastonbury are also recalled in the names of beers from Glastonbury Ales, a five-barrel microbrewery founded in 2002. Despite the fact that the music festival has a multinational brewery sponsor – exemplifying the event's drift away from its simple, hippy past – Glastonbury's beers have also been available on site, along with other small brewery products, much to the relief of thirsty, if rather damp, real ale drinkers.

To mark the occasion of the first ever Glastonbury event, grab yourself a pint of the brewery's 4.8% strong, straw-coloured ale. It goes by the name of Golden Chalice, latching onto the rumour that the Holy Grail was brought to Glastonbury after the Last Supper and is still buried beneath Glastonbury Tor. British Challenger and American Mount Hood hops provide the seasoning and ensure the beer has a hoppy, fruity taste and – unlike most visitors to the festival – a clean finish.

Births Brian Epstein (music agent), 1934; Twiggy (model and actress), 1949; Jarvis Cocker (rock musician), 1963

Deaths James Garfield (US President), 1881; Thomas John Barnardo (philanthropist), 1905; Italo Calvino (writer), 1985

Events First episode of *Fawlty Towers* broadcast, 1975; mummified corpse from c.3300 BC discovered in the Alps and nicknamed Ötzi the Iceman, 1991

Golden Ale

ABOVE: A MUDDY SCENE AT THE GLASTONBURY FESTIVAL IN 2005

Hacker-Pschorr Oktoberfest Märzen

Source Hacker-Pschorr, Munich **Strength** 5.8% **Website** hacker-pschorr.de

In Germany, they're now well into their March beer season. Yes, I know it's September, but this is how it works there.

Märzen (March) beers have a history that goes back to before the industrial age. In those pre-refrigeration days, brewers couldn't produce beer in warm weather because fermentation was unreliable to say the least. It meant that they brewed a stock of beer in late winter/early spring and stored it in ice-filled caves for drinking later in the year. It's a process that gave rise to the idea of lagering and is similar in some respects to the culture of saison and bière de garde beers in Belgium and France (see 23 July). When the new brewing season arrived, complete with freshly harvested barley and hops, it was time to drink up the stocks of the old beer, so Märzen beers flowed freely in September.

As reported on 12 October, Märzen beers have been associated traditionally with the Oktoberfest, although the event has become so commercial and international that these days most Oktoberfestbiers are like mainstream lagers, golden in colour. The traditional Märzen is stronger than a hell or pilsner lager, but not quite as potent as a bock. Munich malt is used in the recipe alongside pale malt, turning out a beer with a rich copper/amber colour and a malty, nutty aroma and flavour. Hops have a lower profile. That's certainly the case with the example selected for today, which comes from the Munich brewery of Hacker-Pschorr.

Two become one

The brewery that became Hacker-Pschorr was founded in 1417, the strange name coming from the later marriage of Joseph Pschorr into the brewing Hacker family. Pschorr then built a second brewery, running separate Hacker and Pschorr enterprises that were carried on by his two sons after his death. Hacker-Pschorr eventually came together in 1971, later merged with local rival Paulaner and is now part of the Heineken group. The original breweries have closed and all beers are brewed at Paulaner. Its Märzen is one of the more widely available outside of Germany and it hints at the history of the style with the full name of Oktoberfest Märzen.

The beer comes in a swing-stoppered bottle and has a full, biscuity aroma of nutty malt. Smooth rich malt is the main feature in the sweetish taste, with a raisin fruitiness and plenty of body. The finish is dry, bittersweet and malty, with some lingering raisin. There's simply no substitute for making the pilgrimage to Bavaria and drinking this beer fresh from the tap, but the bottled version does at least give a flavour of what's going on there at this time of year.

Births Jelly Roll Morton (jazz musician), 1885; Kenneth More (actor), 1914; Sophia Loren (actress), 1934

Deaths Jean Sibelius (composer), 1957; Jim Croce (singer-songwriter), 1973; Brian Clough (football manager), 2004

Events First Cannes Film Festival, 1946; launch of the liner *Queen Elizabeth II*, 1967

Märzen

Ridgeway Ivanhoe

Source Ridgeway Brewing, South Stoke, Oxfordshire **Strength** 5.2% **Website** None

'I wish I could be like David Watts,' warbled The Kinks and, later, The Jam, in a despairingly envious song about the cultured boy at school who was good at simply everything. One can only assume that, had there been a similar rivalry among the literati of the 19th century, the same sentiments would have been expressed about Sir Walter Scott.

Scott has become renowned as the master of the historic novel, a writer whose work sold by the wagonload, even when he wrote it anonymously. In his prose period, Scott rattled up nearly 30 novels, turning out books based on Scottish legends that went on to inspire the Brontës, George Eliot, Mrs Gaskell and others. His novels and short stories were, however, only a second thought. He first caught the eye as a poet and wasn't half bad. Indeed, he was offered the position of Poet Laureate, but magnanimously turned it down and suggested Southey for the job instead.

The multi-talented Scott was born in Edinburgh in 1771. At first, literature was no more than a sideline as he set out to build a future in law. He studied at Edinburgh University, was called to the Bar in 1792 and worked his way up to becoming Sheriff-Depute of Selkirkshire. By 1805, his interests had diversified and he had become a partner in the printing business of James Ballantyne. Ballantyne's brother was to publish Scott's forthcoming novels, beginning with *Waverley* in 1814, but Scott's connection to this business was to prove personally destructive. When the company failed and left him insolvent, he held himself responsible to creditors and worked relentlessly for the rest of his life to sort out the debts. The pressure ultimately took its toll on his health and he died on 21 September 1832.

Saxons & Normans

Scott's best-known novel was his first work to switch the action away from his native Scotland and towards England instead. *Ivanhoe* is set in the 12th century and chooses as its backdrop the conflict between the Saxons and Normans that rumbled on through those primitive years. It tells of the gallant Wilfred of Ivanhoe, who fights on the side of King Richard when the dastardly John usurps the English throne, all the while pursuing his forbidden love, Rowena, and stalling the advances of a beautiful and virtuous Jewish girl named Rebecca. The book was a massive hit, selling out its print run of 10,000 copies in just two weeks.

To celebrate Scott's life and achievements, we are able to call upon a similarly classy beer from Ridgeway Brewing in Oxfordshire. The brewery has picked up the name of Ivanhoe for a bottle-conditioned strong ale that features some chocolate malt alongside pale malt, to give a smooth nutty base and a barley-sugar-type sweetness, with Golding and Admiral hops adding a lightly fruity, floral flourish. Ivanhoe was originally designed as a British-style beer for the Swedish market, such is the association of Scott's opus with the spirit of old England – and the renown of the author beyond these shores.

Strong Ale

Births HG Wells (writer), 1866; Gustav Holst (composer), 1874; Stephen King (writer), 1947

Deaths Virgil (poet), 19 BC; Arthur Schopenhauer (philosopher), 1860; Florence Griffith Joyner (athlete), 1998

Events JRR Tolkien's *The Hobbit* published, 1937; Malta becomes independent, 1964

Huyghe Delirium Tremens

Source Brouwerij Huyghe, Melle **Strength** 8.5% **Website** delirium.be

It seems at first glance like just another of those Internet-promoted non-events – a flimsy excuse to get punters to download clip art and e-cards – but Elephant Appreciation Day is now being exploited for more important, conservation reasons.

This bizarre celebration was the brainchild of one Wayne Hepburn, boss of an American graphics company. The legend has it that having bought his daughter a gift of a paperweight featuring a parade of elephants, he started putting together a collection of other elephant paraphernalia, along the way developing an interest in the real-life creature. It turned into a jumbo-sized hobby, a love of the greatly abused grey giants.

Hepburn's business, Mission Media, launched the first Elephant Appreciation Day in 1996 because, among other things, the elephant 'is most undeservedly threatened with extinction' and 'is entertaining and amusing'. The initiative has been latched on to by charities such as America's In Defense of Animals, which is using 22 September to ask the public to consider the fate of maltreated elephants.

It's no joke

You could ponder the fate of this noble beast over a glass of Carlsberg's Elephant Beer, a strong lager from Denmark, or you could opt for a Belgian beer that also sees the elephant as a fun figure. The beer is called Delirium Tremens, which suggests it's a bit of a joke before you even open the porcelain-effect bottle. On the label you'll find little pink elephants, the unwritten message being that if you drink too much of a beer as strong as this (8.5%), then don't be surprised if you start seeing strange things. It's all very odd really because this is a seriously good beer. It may be strong but it's not for park-bench consumption: this is a connoisseur's drink with complex estery fruit in the nose – banana, peach and pear – over creamy pale malt. Considering its potency, it's frighteningly easy to drink, a bittersweet, fruity, citrus-sharp, golden ale with a light spiciness, an airy texture and a clean balance of flavours. Not surprisingly, the finish is warming with a bitter fruit character.

The beer is described as 'triple fermented', and is the result of the action of three different yeasts. It was created on Boxing Day 1989, which seems as good a day as any to come up with a beer that derives its name from the after-effects of over-indulgence.

Such has been the success of the beer that the brewery's (Huyghe) website is simply known as www.delirium.be. The name has also been lent to a bar in Brussels that offers one of the world's largest beer selections – an elephantine list of more than 2,000 beers listed in a folder the size of a Freemans catalogue and stored in glass-fronted coolers along the side of the bar.

Pink elephants, however, are just part of the Huyghe story. The brewery produces probably the biggest range of beers in Belgium, some of them bizarre to say the least, including a peppermint-flavoured ale and beers containing various fruit extracts, honey and spices. In pachyderm terminology, they're the sort of beers that, once tasted, you never forget.

Births Anne of Cleves (fourth wife of King Henry VIII), 1515; Michael Faraday (scientist), 1791; Billie Piper (singer and actress), 1982

Deaths Irving Berlin (composer), 1989; George C Scott (actor), 1999; Marcel Marceau (mime artist), 2007

Events Start of Independent Television (ITV) in Britain, 1955; Iran-Iraq war breaks out, 1980

Strong Ale

ABOVE: SOUTH AFRICAN ELEPHANT

Fuller's Red Fox

Source Fuller, Smith & Turner, Chiswick, London **Strength** 4.3% **Website** fullers.co.uk

Technically, an equinox is a point where the sun is directly positioned above the equator, so creating a 'night equal' to the amount of daylight. The autumn equinox takes place on or around 23 September in the northern hemisphere, and around 20 March in the southern hemisphere. Followers of pagan rituals know the occasion as Mabon, and use it for ceremonies that reflect on the bounteous summer just gone and the impending darkness of winter. But for most people, the equinox is just annual formalization of the fact that the nights are getting longer and the days shorter. It's the time of year when the harvest needs to be gathered in, as nature battens down the hatches ready for winter.

Nature's colours

The tendency among brewers is to create autumnal ales that echo the patterns of nature outside. That's why so many of them have russet or chestnut-brown colours, in sympathy with the warm shades of fallen leaves. It's the darker malts that produce these, and they can also introduce a touch of nut and toffee, linking flavours with the toffee apples and chestnuts often seen over Halloween and Bonfire Night.

Fuller's autumn seasonal beer is part of this tradition. It was created in 1997, and these days is sold around September every year in cask form, with a filtered bottled version available for a longer period. They call it Red Fox, not because there's a charming rustic tale behind it but simply because when the brewers saw the welcoming tawny colour they looked for a name that would sum it up. Having considered several 'Red' options, Red Fox proved to be the favourite. To achieve the rich, warming hue, they take pale malt created from spring barley and marry it with crystal malt in the mash tun. Also at this stage toasted oats are added. The single hop is Challenger, with more than half the amount added late in the copper boil.

Malty sweetness is the first thing that strikes you in the aroma, but with a creamy, nutty oat character pushing through. The oats really have an impact in the mouth, doing just as the brewers hope and bringing creamy notes to the texture and taste, blending perfectly with nutty malt sweetness and a good, firm hoppy balance. The finish is equally well balanced – dry, creamy and wonderfully biscuity, with a good smack of hops.

No one particularly looks forward to seeing the nights draw in and the air turn chill, but happily the brewing industry does its best to lighten the mood by releasing some distinctive autumnal beers, and this is one of the best.

Births Mickey Rooney (actor), 1920; Ray Charles (soul musician), 1930; Bruce Springsteen (rock musician), 1949

Deaths Wilkie Collins (writer), 1889; Sigmund Freud (psychiatrist), 1939; Bob Fosse (dancer and choreographer), 1987

Events Planet Neptune discovered, 1846; rower Steve Redgrave wins his fifth Olympic gold medal, 2000

Best Bitter

Anchor Old Foghorn

Source Anchor Brewing Company, San Francisco, California **Strength** 8.8% **Website** anchorbrewing.com

Fritz Maytag is a member of the wealthy Maytag washing machine dynasty, but he didn't make his name in laundrettes. Fritz is celebrated by beer lovers worldwide as the saviour of one of America's great brewing styles and for proving that, in an era when light lager was sweeping all before it, great-tasting beer had a future in the US.

Some people call Fritz the first American craft brewer. He was certainly ahead of the game. It was a visit to a bar in San Francisco that changed his life and, consequently, that of a generation of American beer drinkers. Maytag popped into the Old Spaghetti Factory, a bohemian restaurant that was one of the few remaining stockists of Anchor Steam Beer, the city's historic brew (see 19 January). Licensee Fred Kuh, noting Fritz's interest in the beer, recommended he race down to the brewery and take a look around, as it was unlikely to be there for much longer. Fritz took the bait and when he looked into what was going on at Anchor found that the business was in dire straits, with a bank balance of only $128. For a few thousand dollars,

he was able to purchase 51% of the company on this day in 1965, but this was only a prelude to the many thousands more he needed to invest to return the brewery to success.

Maytag set about cleaning up the act (and the brewery itself). With new equipment and new business disciplines, he once again made Anchor a going, and growing, concern, becoming the sole owner in 1969. Eventually, its small premises were no longer big enough and a new home, in a former coffee roasting house high on one of the city's many hills, was acquired in 1979. That's where Anchor still resides today, a magnet for beer lovers from all over the world who have been drawn to San Francisco by the siren call of Anchor Steam Beer.

Mighty brew

Maytag's pre-eminence in US craft brewing circles stems not just from the resurrection of this 19th-century beer classic, however. He was the first of the current crop of brewers to broaden his range. In 1972, he introduced Anchor Porter. In 1975, Liberty Ale, with its rich American hop accent, and the Christmas ale came on stream, encouraging the thousands of craft brewers who have transformed the American brewing scene in his wake to experiment.

In the same year, Fritz added Old Foghorn to the Anchor selection. This is a barley wine, inspired by a beer that Maytag discovered on a visit to Britain, but given an American accent through the inclusion of Cascade

hops, which are also used to dry-hop the beer. Only the first runnings from the mash tun are used to make the beer, so it takes three mashes to get enough wort to produce one batch.

Old Foghorn is a mighty brew. There's plenty of malt, as you'd expect, to get the beer up to this strength, but that's amply countered by a good smack of hops. The aroma is nutmeg-spicy and malty with softly citrus hops and raisins. The taste is smooth, sumptuous, creamy-sweet and nicely warming with a lovely contrast from the fruity hops. Sweetness lingers in the dry, malty finish until bitterness gradually makes its way through. As for the name, well that's a reference to the hooters sounded to keep ships off the rocks of San Francisco Bay.

Births F Scott Fitzgerald (writer), 1896; Jim Henson (puppeteer), 1936; Gerry Marsden (pop musician), 1942; Jack Dee (comedian), 1962

Deaths Pope Innocent II, 1143; Dr Seuss (writer), 1991

Events First running of the St Leger classic horse race at Doncaster, 1776; Honda Motor Company established in Japan, 1948

Barley Wine

Lees Harvest Ale

Source JW Lees & Co. (Brewers), Manchester **Strength** 11.5% **Website** jwlees.co.uk

The idea of giving thanks to God for the bounty of the harvest has, of course, been taken to a new level in the US, where Thanksgiving Day is an official national holiday (see 25 November). In the UK, although churches and schools annually organize harvest ceremonies, there is no fixed date in the calendar on which they are held. Generally, these events are staged close to, or on, the Sunday that follows the harvest moon, which is the full moon of September, generally appearing at the time of the autumn equinox – roughly, we could say, on the 25th of the month.

Britons have offered gratitude to the deities for abundant crops since pagan times, when the tradition came into play of making a corn dolly out of the last sheaf of cut corn as a tribute to the goddess of the grain. The modern-day Christian aspect of the festival can be tracked down more or less to one man, the Reverend Robert Hawker, who, in 1843, invited parishioners to celebrate the safe gathering-in of the year's harvest with a service at his church in Morwenstow, Cornwall.

Harvest supping

Beer drinkers may like to drink their own toast to the bounty of the fields around this time of year – if there were no barley or hops harvested, we'd all have a pretty glum time of it in the following 12 months – and there's a perfect beer with which to do so. Its origins lie in a brewers' dinner in Blackpool in 1986, at which guests were bemoaning the takeover of the brewing world by lager. Giles Dennis, head brewer at Lees in Manchester, decided to do something about it by brewing a really special British ale. The result was a barley wine that is created fresh each year in October from new-season malted barley and East Kent Golding hops. Harvest Ale, as it became known, enjoys a long copper boil, extending up to three hours. Fermentation takes a week and a half, and then the beer is conditioned at the brewery for a month. Around 30 barrels are brewed each year, with around ten barrels of this going into casks for sale in the US, and at a few selected Lees pubs. The rest is bottled. The beer is not bottle conditioned, but it certainly improves with age, thanks to its heady 11.5% ABV and full malty complexion. Each bottle carries a vintage date, so, if you have the self-restraint to keep some bottles back, you can try various vintages to see how they have matured.

When young, the beer typically has a big fruity aroma of tart red berries, oranges and sultanas, although each year brings something new to the harvest table. There are hop resins, too, plus creamy malt and perhaps also a winey note. The taste can be syrupy-sweet, packed with more creamy malt and orange and sultana notes, perhaps maybe some strawberry, while the finish tends to be warm and smooth, with lingering sweet malt, some hop spice and yet more fruit. Over time, the sweetness fades and more of a fortified wine nature can be discerned. Indeed, young or old, this beer has the strength and complexity to be served daintily in sherry schooners, but you may well find that one small glass is not enough. Shine on harvest moon.

Births Ronnie Barker (actor and writer), 1929; Felicity Kendal (actress), 1946; Will Smith (actor), 1968

Deaths Johann Strauss Sr (composer), 1849; John Bonham (rock musician), 1980; Walter Pidgeon (actor), 1984

Events Battle of Stamford Bridge, 1066; first edition of the political debate *Question Time* broadcast, 1979

Barley Wine

Green Man Best Bitter

Source Green Man Brewery, Dunedin **Strength** 4.5% **Website** greenmanbrewery.co.nz

Having selected an Australian beer for the commemoration of ANZAC Day (see 25 April), I need to redress the balance and make sure a New Zealand beer also features in this book. Today provides the opportunity.

It was on 26 September 1907 that New Zealand ceased to be a colony of the British Empire and officially became a dominion. The difference between a colony and a dominion is negligible – nothing actually changed in the way the country was administered – but it was a move that helped raise national pride.

Initially, Dominion Day was celebrated fervently in some parts of the country, with parades, fairs and ceremonies, but attempts to install this as a formal public holiday came to nothing. Indeed, the term dominion itself is not used any more, and the UK no longer has any legislative rights over New Zealand. In hindsight, however, Dominion Day can be seen as a stepping stone between colony status and independent recognition, promoting nationhood in the people's mindset.

Progressive beers

New Zealand is also progressing very nicely in beer terms. Victim of the pan-global bland lager epidemic for so long, the country is now home to a number of enterprising microbreweries, the first of which, McCashin's, opened in the early 1980s. Mac's, as it is familiarly known, is still running but the brewery selected for today was only set up in 2006. It is already making a name for itself, however, both through the quality of its beers and the way in which it operates.

The business is Green Man Brewery, based in Dunedin. As its name suggests, this is an environmentally-conscious concern. Its bottles are recycled and reused, and its beers are organic. They are also brewed to the strictures of Germany's Reinheitsgebot beer purity law and are acceptable to vegans. The range extends from Green Man Lager, the first ever brew, to a Dark Mild, and takes in specials such as Green Man Strong. This novel creation starts life as a doppelbock, which is then matured for three months in former whisky casks. The resulting elixir is then blended with Best Bitter to produce a complex oaky, creamy, bittersweet drink with a softly warming fruitiness. The beer for today's commemoration, however, is Best Bitter in its natural form.

Packed with pilsner, Munich and Carafa malts, and balanced by Pacific Gem, Hallertau and Saaz hops, this robust ale is filtered but not pasteurized. Spicy, sappy hops and nutty malt feature in the aroma, with more tart, sappy notes providing a refreshing edge in the taste, backed by a pleasant sweetness from the malt. The full, satisfying finish is bitter, nutty, hoppy and dry with hops that linger and linger.

The ingredients may not be British but the brewery describes Best Bitter as a 'taste of Old England' – ironic, perhaps, considering the nature of today's commemoration.

Births TS Eliot (writer and poet), 1888; Anne Robinson (journalist and TV presenter), 1944; Olivia Newton John (singer and actress), 1948

Deaths Daniel Boone (frontiersman), 1820; Levi Strauss (clothing manufacturer), 1902; Robert Palmer (rock musician), 2003

Events Coronation of King William II, 1087; Francis Drake completes his circumnavigation of the world, 1580

Best Bitter

Samuel Adams Triple Bock

Source The Boston Beer Co., Boston, Massachusetts **Strength** 18% **Website** samueladams.com

America's most successful craft brewery is called The Boston Beer Company. Most people don't know it by that name, however. They just call it Samuel Adams, after the labels on the beers.

Boston Beer was founded by Jim Koch in 1984. His first brew – based on a recipe belonging to his great-great-grandfather – was an immediate smash, an amber lager that he initially brewed in his kitchen and then scaled up to be touted around stores and bars and turned into a commercial success. He named the beer Samuel Adams Boston Lager, latching on to a famous figure in American history.

Samuel Adams was himself born into a brewing family, but he made his name as a politician and patriot, a man who roused public sentiment against the insensitive British. He was born in Boston on this day in 1722 and graduated 18 years later from Harvard University. His professional career had its ups and downs – mostly downs, it has to be said – before he turned to politics and became a member of the Massachusetts legislature. Increasingly, he found himself at odds with the British and their heavy-handed treatment of the colonists in America. He was one of the founders of the rebellious group known as the Sons of Liberty, which was behind the act of defiance that became known as the Boston Tea Party (see 16 December). Adams emerged onto the national stage and was one of the signatories of the American Declaration of Independence in 1776. He served as Governor of Massachusetts between 1793 and 1797, and died in 1803. His second cousin, John Adams, was the second US President.

Stretching the definition

The name of Samuel Adams has since been extended across Boston Beer's range of products, including to the beer selected for today. Triple Bock was first brewed in 1994, and has been produced only a couple of times since, although bottles remain – ageing beautifully – in circulation. Some drinkers may not recognize this as a beer, in fact, as it emerges from the bottle at a whopping 18% ABV. It is brewed from pale and caramel malts, German Tettnang hops and a little maple syrup, and then matured in oak whiskey barrels.

The bottle is distinctive and, being bright blue in colour, shaped like a neat little vase and stoppered with a chunky black cork, should give notice that the contents are something rather different. If the bottle doesn't do the trick, then one glance at the impenetrable deep ruby-brown colour or one sniff of the intense aroma should help. The nose is immediately heady, alcoholic, oaky, malty and laced with dried fruits such as raisins and sultanas. It's spicy, too, with traces of treacle, liquorice and even Marmite. On the palate, Triple Bock has virtually no carbonation, giving a soft, silky mouthfeel as a backdrop to sweet caramel, creamy dried fruit, a peppery warmth, soft powdery chocolate and a bitter, cedary note. Elements of all the above linger on into the warming finish, but basically every sip unearths something new.

The brewery claims that Triple Bock 'stretches the definition of beer' and, to back this up, says it has 'the depth and complexity of a fine cognac', and should be 'sipped from a small crystal glass in a two-ounce serving'.

Births William Conrad (actor), 1920; Peter Bonetti (footballer), 1941; Alvin Stardust (singer), 1942

Deaths Edgar Degas (painter), 1917; Engelbert Humperdinck (composer), 1921 Gracie Fields (singer), 1979

Events Lancaster, Pennsylvania, becomes US capital for one day, 1777; The Stockton & Darlington Railway opens, 1825; hippy musical *Hair* opens in London, 1968

BOCK

ABOVE: SAMUEL ADAMS, AMERICAN POLITICIAN AND PATRIOT

Guinness Foreign Extra Stout

Source Diageo **Strength** 7.5% **Website** guinness.com

Wish a happy birthday today to one of the greatest names in the history of brewing.

Arthur Guinness was born in County Kildare on 28 September 1725 – at least that's what is sometimes reported, although no hard evidence seems to exist to pinpoint this exact date. Some sources give 24 September; others commit to earlier in that year. Happily, other details of his early life are a bit more reliable. Arthur's father, a land steward, used to brew for workers on the local archbishop's estate and, when the archibishop bequeathed Arthur the princely sum of £100 in his will, he knew just what to do with it: he opened his own brewery about 16km (10 miles) from Dublin. That was in 1756. Three years later, Arthur left the brewery to his brother and headed into the city to make his fortune.

Guinness already had a shrewd business brain, as is evident from the deal he put together to take a 9,000-year lease on a run-down brewery at St James's Gate, for a low rent that also – vitally – included the rights to free water. His business acumen was also obvious in the way in which he latched onto the latest brewing craze – porter from London that was taking Dublin by storm. Guinness not only brewed his own equivalent, he rapidly made the style his own, even abandoning in 1799 all other ales in favour of this new dark style of beer. Arthur died only four years later, but he had already laid the foundations for a business that is almost as internationally known today as McDonald's.

Irish stout

An extension of Guinness's standard porter was the stronger or 'stout' porter, which soon became abbreviated to stout. The dry, heavily roasted note associated with the Irish stout style was actually developed by Arthur's son (also called Arthur), as a cost-cutting measure. With the British government of the late 19th century heavily taxing malt, he decided to include a proportion of unmalted roasted barley to the mash to save money.

Guinness Original, as the company's standard stout is called today, is served in several ways. You can buy it nitrogenated on draught – cold or extra cold – nitrogenated in cans, or normally carbonated in bottles. The last is infinitely preferable, despite no longer being bottle conditioned. However, for a beer that truly celebrates the success and influence of Arthur Guinness, you should reach for Guinness Foreign Extra Stout. This mighty, 7.5% beer is a real treat and dates from the original Arthur's last days at the brewery. Made in Dublin by blending stout that has been aged in wooden casks for a few months with younger stout, FES has a full chocolaty, coffeeish taste, beautifully offset by a vinous, woody edge from the soured 'stale' beer at its core. This beer is brewed to slightly different recipes and strengths around the world. All are well worth sampling.

Births Marcello Mastroianni (actor), 1924; Brigitte Bardot (actress), 1934; Helen Shapiro (singer), 1946

Deaths Louis Pasteur (scientist), 1895; Harpo Marx (comedian), 1964; Pope John Paul I, 1978; Miles Davis (jazz musician), 1991

Events Radio Times first published, 1923; Arsene Wenger becomes manager of Arsenal FC, 1996

Imperial Stout

City of Cambridge Mich'aelmas

Source City of Cambridge Brewery Co. Ltd, Cambridge, Cambridgeshire **Strength** 4.4%
Website cambridge-brewery.co.uk

The feast of St Michael and All Angels – commonly known as Michaelmas – falls on 29 September. In Christian history, Michael – often depicted as ready for righteous battle – was one of the archangels close to God, indeed the angel who threw the rebellious Lucifer out of Heaven. It is this action that is said to be behind the folk warning that blackberries should not be picked after Michaelmas. Apparently, Lucifer crash-landed in a bramble bush and cursed the fruit accordingly. In practical terms, this may have something to do with the fact that Michaelmas also traditionally marks the end of the harvest season, and blackberries, among other crops, are soon past their best.

Among his patronages, Michael is the saint of seafarers, which makes today rather appropriate as it is also the birthday of Horatio Nelson in 1758. Michaelmas is associated with geese, too. It's the traditional bird eaten at this time of year, thanks, some sources say, to Queen Elizabeth I, who was dining on goose when news of the victory over the Spanish Armada came through and so declared that she would in future eat goose to celebrate this momentous day. The bird is also celebrated in traditional goose fairs around England, the most famous of which still takes place shortly after Michaelmas in Nottingham. This is now dominated by a giant fun fair, but still attracts thousands of visitors each year.

Geese & scholars

Our beer for today would probably be an ideal accompaniment for a goose dinner, given its malty, nutty, sweetish qualities that would marry beautifully with the rich, buttery flavours of the goose, with the natural carbonation of the beer cutting admirably through the fattiness of the bird. The copper-coloured, 4.4% brew is simply called Mich'aelmas – and comes from City of Cambridge Brewery. It is, in fact, a blend of the company's Parkers Porter and Boathouse Bitter. Consequently, the malts used are pale, crystal and caramalt, with some roasted barley, while the hops are First Gold and Cascade. The brewery originally produced it as a Christmas ale, but then decided to bring it forward in the year to not only tie in with Michaelmas itself, but also Michaelmas term, as the autumn period of study at Cambridge University is known. The aroma is malty, biscuity, chocolaty and nutty, preparing you for more of the same in the taste, which, despite the full malty complexion, remains crisp, with a drying backnote. Roasted malt flavours come through more in the finish, which is pleasantly bitter and dry. The beer is available in cask form from September to December, and bottle conditioned for a while longer.

Births Horatio Nelson (military commander), 1758; Lech Walesa (trade unionist and politician), 1943; Sebastian Coe (athlete and politician), 1956

Deaths Emile Zola (writer), 1902; WH Auden (poet), 1973; Leslie Crowther (comedian), 1996

Events The BBC Third Programme radio network goes on the air, 1946; John Paul II becomes the first Pope to visit Ireland, 1979

Best Bitter

ABOVE: ARCHANGEL ST MICHAEL

Samuel Adams Boston Lager

Source The Boston Beer Co., Boston, Massachusetts **Strength** 4.75% **Website** samueladams.com

The pub is a staple of TV comedy. There aren't many sitcoms that haven't featured a Nag's Head, a Royal Oak or a Hare and Hounds somewhere along the way, and there have been other series wholly set within the walls of a boozer. One of the earliest examples was *Not on Your Nellie* – starring Hylda Baker as landlady of The Brown Cow – while recently *Time Gentlemen Please*, *The World of Pub* and *Early Doors* have developed the concept even further. There's no questioning the king of the pub comedies, however, and that's a programme that began on this day in 1982.

Cheers was set in a basement bar of the same name in Boston, Massachusetts, with the action centring on the pitiful lives of its staff and regulars. Owner of Cheers was Sam 'Mayday' Malone, one-time

ABOVE: THE CAST OF *CHEERS*

pitcher for the Boston Red Sox and a reformed alcoholic whose main pastime was chasing women. He met his match when academic researcher Diane Chambers entered the bar and took a job as a waitress. Also on the team were sharp-tongued waitress Carla Tortelli and confused bartender Coach, later replaced by dim country boy Woody. Completing one of TV's biggest bunch of losers were the bar's regular customers, forever playing practical jokes and indulging in petty rivalries. Accountant Norm was the ringleader, supported by know-it-all mailman Cliff and pompous psychiatrist Frasier. Life in the *Cheers* bar never amounted to much, but it was great fun all the same.

Boston beer

From appearances, the beer in the *Cheers* bar never amounted to much either. Golden, highly agitated and frothy, it was slung along the bar when called for, and downed with a flourish, but seldom was a comment made about the flavour. Perhaps if *Cheers* had started a little later in the 1980s, it could have made more of the growing craft beer revolution in the US, and particularly in Boston where a home-brewer named Jim Koch was soon joining *Cheers* in putting the city on the American brewing map.

Koch founded a business called The Boston Beer Company in 1985. His first beer was based on a Vienna-style, amber-coloured lager that he cooked up in his own kitchen from

a recipe belonging to his great-great grandfather. He named it after a local patriot (see 27 September) and Samuel Adams Boston Lager was born.

For an America brought up on the sort of wishy-washy suds served up by Sam Malone, Boston Lager was a revelation. It wasn't the first new, full-flavoured beer by any means, but Koch's marketing nous ensured that the beer hit the ground running and was soon on the tips of beer drinkers' tongues across the country. It's a beer that always takes the uninitiated by surprise, by its colour and by its taste of rich, biscuity malt and tangy, citrus hops. To the inexperienced, it comes across as an ale, rather than a lager, and therein, it seems, lies part of the appeal.

These days Boston Lager is a national brand in the US. You can buy it in airports and gas stations, you can find it in corporate hotel lounges, and it's commonly consumed in good, old-fashioned neighbourhood bars, some of which still bear a striking resemblance to Cheers.

Births Buddy Rich (jazz musician), 1917; Truman Capote (writer), 1924; Marc Bolan (rock musician), 1947

Deaths James Brindley (engineer), 1772; James Dean (actor), 1955; Simone Signoret (actress), 1985

Events Premiere in Vienna of Mozart's *The Magic Flute*, 1791; BBC Radio 1 begins broadcasting, 1967; Muhammad Ali defeats Joe Frazier in the 'Thriller in Manilla', 1975

Vienna-style Lager

Little Valley Stoodley Stout

Source Little Valley Brewery, Hebden Bridge, West Yorkshire **Strength** 4.8%
Website littlevalleybrewery.co.uk

In 1977, the North American Vegetarian Society declared 1 October to be World Vegetarian Day. The date was adopted by the International Vegetarian Union a year later and has been celebrated by those who advocate meat-free diets every year since. The aim of the celebration is to raise awareness of the benefits of vegetarianism for personal health, for combatting famine, for preserving resources and ecosystems, and for animal welfare, and the occasion is marked by special dinners, cooking demonstrations and educational fairs.

For vegetarians, real ale would seem to present little in the way of problem drinking. Brewed from simple, non-animal products like barley malt, wheat, hops and water, there is nothing to fear for the vegan in the ingredient list (unless, of course, the beer contains honey). But there is one part of the brewing process that presents an obstacle. It is the fining stage, when beer is clarified so that it looks bright in the glass. This is usually achieved by adding a substance called isinglass to the cask that, almost magnetically, draws clumps of yeast in suspension to the bottom, so that the beer pours clear. Isinglass, however, is made from the swim bladder of a tropical fish, and therein lies the difficulty.

This shouldn't mean that vegetarians should give up on tasty real ale and opt instead for filtered lager or keg beer, however, as there are ways in which cask beer can be served without using isinglass. Some brewers use an alternative, animal-free source of finings, and others simply don't bother with any finings. They just allow the sediment to settle out over time. It can mean that the beer in the glass is sometimes hazy, but that shouldn't affect the taste.

Green ticks

When it comes to bottle-conditioned beers, which have yeast in the bottle, vegetarians again need to choose carefully. Some beers still incorporate isinglass at some stage, although there is a growing band of brewers that now forgo this method of clearing the beer altogether. One such brewer is Little Valley, based at Hebden Bridge in Yorkshire. It was opened in 2005 by Wim van der Spek, a Dutch brewer who had previously worked at Black Isle Brewery. All his beers are organic and approved by the Vegan Society (look for the green tick).

The beer selected from Wim's range for today is Stoodley Stout, a full-bodied, dark ale that takes its name from a local hill famous for the Crimean War monument that stands on the top. Pale malt, crystal malt and chocolate malt are blended with oats for a smoother texture, with Pacific Gem hops from New Zealand married with First Gold UK hops for balance. The beer is deep ruby in colour and is deliciously biscuity and bittersweet, with coffee and plain chocolate flavours, rounded off by a bitter, roasted grain finish. It's isinglass-free and highly enjoyable.

Other vegetarian bottle-conditioned beers to try today include brews from Atlantic, Bazens', Black Isle, Cropton, Durham, Frog Island, Hobsons, Hoggleys, Isle of Skye, Jolly Brewer, King, Old Chimneys, Organic, Pitfield, Purple Moose, St Austell, Spinning Dog, Tunnel and Vale.

Births Jimmy Carter (US President), 1924; Richard Harris (actor), 1930; Harry Hill (comedian), 1964

Deaths Richard Avedon (photographer), 2004; Al Oerter (athlete), 2007; Ned Sherrin (broadcaster), 2007

Events Disney World opens in Florida, 1971; Muhammad Ali defeats Joe Frazier in the 'Thrilla in Manilla', 1975

Stout

ABOVE: AUTUMN VEGETABLES

Wold Top Wolds Way

Source Wold Top Brewery, Wold Newton, East Yorkshire　**Strength** 3.6%　**Website** woldtopbrewery.co.uk

It's no coincidence that many members of the Ramblers' Association are also members of CAMRA. There's a glorious symbiosis between the two interest groups built around the fact that there's nothing better after a long, thirst-generating walk through the countryside than a refreshing and satisfying pint of well-kept real ale.

Wold Top Brewery recognized this when it introduced a beer to celebrate the 25th anniversary of the launching of the Wolds Way long-distance trail.

The Wolds Way runs through some of Yorkshire's most appealing scenery. It starts near the Humber Bridge, at Hessle, and meanders north and east for a total of 127km (79 miles) through rolling hillside, dry valleys, peaceful woodlands and picturesque villages. It takes around five days to a week to complete if you take time to savour the scenery or a pint or two at some of the many pubs en route, and winds up at Filey Brigg, just south of Scarborough, where it joins up with another majestic walk, the Cleveland Way. The hike is easily navigable and not particularly demanding, which means it holds plenty of appeal for the novice rambler as well as those with feet hardened to trail walking. It was cleverly pieced together by the Ramblers' Association first, and then adopted by the Countryside Commission as its tenth National Trail in 1982.

Healthy associations

Wold Top Brewery was founded by Tom and Gill Mellor in 2003, in a converted farm granary just a few miles off the trail, close to its northern finish. It is certainly not the first brewery to trade on the associations between good walking and good beer – Pilgrim Brewery in Surrey celebrates the nearby Pilgrim's Way, and Ridgeway Brewing in Oxfordshire reflects the proximity of that ancient track. But the ale that Wold Top created for the Wolds Way celebrations is just the sort of beer you'd hope to find at one of the wayside pubs: crisp, full of flavour, refreshing and, crucially, not too strong.

The quality starts with the ingredients. The barley used in Wold Top's beers is home grown and water is sourced from the farm's own borehole. Golding and Cascade are the hops, bringing lots of bitter citrus flavours in the mouth. Tart lemon notes waft around and continue into the dry, bitter and temptingly moreish finish. Available in cask form or filtered for the bottle, it's a golden ale for a silver anniversary, tempting enough to make even couch potatoes reach for their walking boots.

Births Mohandas K Gandhi (politician), 1869; Groucho Marx (comedian), 1890; Sting (rock musician), 1951

Deaths Rock Hudson (actor), 1985; Alec Issigonis (motor car designer), 1988; Gene Autry (singing cowboy), 1998

Events Italy invades Abyssinia, 1935; *Peanuts* comic strip by Charles M Schulz first published, 1950; Neil Kinnock becomes leader of the Labour Party, 1983

Golden Ale

Bitburger Pils

Source Bitburger Braugruppe GmbH, Bitburg **Strength** 4.8% **Website** bitburger.com

The Germans celebrate their national day on 3 October. This is the day that the country was formally reunified in 1990, less than a year after the collapse of the Berlin Wall and the East's slip from the grasp of the Soviet Union.

For some Germans, 'celebrate' is not perhaps the right verb to use. The absorption of decaying, former-Communist East Germany into lively, prosperous West Germany has not been comfortable, for either side. Citizens of the old East have found it difficult to come to terms with the dynamics of a western economy and it's taken time for infrastructure to be remodelled to give them a chance to compete in a 'free market'. Inevitably, there's also been a labour drain, as workers in areas of high unemployment have decamped to western cities. For the West, re-equipping the East, providing welfare for its unemployed and investing in modernization has proved costly, helping to undermine Germany's former position as a highly efficient and successful economy. Those who were 'liberated' by the reunification and those who bore the cost of it both have reason to be uncomfortable about 3 October. Nevertheless, after more than 40 years of brutally enforced division, reunification has a massive symbolic and political value that can't simply be explained in terms of Marks or Euros, which is why this day is important to the restored nation.

Access to the East has also meant renewed interest in East German beer. Western breweries have looked closely at their struggling counterparts in the old Soviet Bloc, and some have invested there and improved resources. One such investor is Bitburger, a family-owned business in the Eifel region of Germany, near the Luxembourg border. They saw potential in the Köstritzer Brewery near Weimar, and have turned around its fortunes (see 22 March). Bitburger also has the answer if you're looking for a beer to celebrate Germany's national day, as its popular and high-quality Pils is about as close to a national beer you can find in a country where localism still thrives.

'Bitte ein Bit'

Marketed with the slogan 'Bitte ein Bit' ('a Bit please'), the beer has its origins in the small settlement of Bitburg in 1817. Today, it flows from a state-of-the-art brewhouse on the fringe of town where quality malt is steeped in naturally soft well water and seasoned with hops grown in two areas. Some come from the Hallertau region and some are cultivated locally. Production takes around 60 days on average, allowing up to ten days for primary fermentation, another week for secondary fermentation, and the rest of the time for a long, cold lagering. What emerges is a crisp, super-clean pilsner, with a soft malty underbelly and a notably bitter, dry, herbal-hoppy overlay.

Making this beer even more enjoyable is the fact that it is left unpasteurized. Only canned beer gets the heat treatment; kegged beer and bottles are just filtered, which is a cause for celebration in itself.

Births James Herriot (vet and writer), 1916; Gore Vidal (writer), 1925; Eddie Cochran (rock 'n' roll musician), 1938

Deaths St Francis of Assisi, 1226; Woody Guthrie (folk musician), 1967; Ronnie Barker (actor, comedian and writer), 2005

Events Siege at London's Spaghetti House restaurant ends after five days, 1975; OJ Simpson acquitted of murdering his former wife, 1995

Pilsner

ABOVE: THE BITBURGER STATE-OF-THE-ART BREWHOUSE

Franziskaner Hefeweissbier

Source Spaten-Franziskaner-Bräu, Munich **Strength** 5% **Website** franziskaner.com

It was animals, not ale, that made St Francis famous. Unlike fellow saints Arnold, Augustine, Veronus and others, Francis has little or no direct connection with the world of beer. However, his name has long been associated with a Munich brewery.

St Francis was born in the central Italian town of Assisi around 1181. His father was a successful cloth merchant, and so Francis wanted for little in his youth. Indeed, he was quite profligate at first, and harboured dreams of military glory, before a dramatic conversion to the Church signalled an end to his days of material wealth. He began by giving away clothes and money to beggars but then, after a major falling out with his father, Francis stripped himself bare, returning all the clothes his father had paid for, and embarked decisively on a life of chastity and poverty. All trappings of comfort were eschewed in his quest for communion with nature and God, and his preachings became legendary. Stories were told of how Francis even talked to the birds and tamed a wild wolf, all in the course of bringing peace and contentment to the world.

Spreading the word

Francis died on 3 October 1226 and the day after has been declared his feast day. He is buried beneath the awesome two-storey cathedral that today dominates Assisi. This monumental tribute was raised by his close followers – brothers in faith who adopted Francis's simple mode of dress and unworldly lifestyle. Indeed, so inspiring was his message that the Franciscan fraternity grew rapidly, spreading around Europe. One offshoot of the order made its home in Munich, and the legacy of this particular group of monks remains in the form of the Franziskaner brewery, a private concern founded across the street from the abbey in 1363. Franziskaner moved to a new location in the city in the 19th century and became linked to the Spaten brewery. It is now owned by InBev but remains true to the style of beer on which its fortunes were founded. Wheat beer is Franziskaner's forte and this is available in both filtered form (Kristall-klar) and with yeast. It is the latter, the Hefeweissbier, that is today's recommendation.

Franziskaner Hefeweissbier has played on an international stage for many years, helping to introduce the world's drinking public to this offbeat type of beer. It pours a hazy yellow colour, topped by a big, fluffy head of foam. Subtle spices and soft banana notes are lifted to the nose and, when you taste the beer, it is immediately pleasantly chewy with more light spices and delicate sour fruits like lemon, orange and green apple. It's not the most demanding or challenging of weissbiers, but it's certainly refreshing. And, as St Francis knew only too well, sometimes the simplest treats are the most enjoyable.

Births Buster Keaton (actor), 1895; Charlton Heston (actor), 1924; Ann Widdecombe (politician), 1947

Deaths Josiah Wedgwood (potter), 1795; Conrad Hilton (hotel magnate), 1979; Freddy Heineken (brewery executive), 2002

Events Sarcophagus of Tutankhamen discovered in Egypt by Howard Carter, 1924; first Open University broadcasts, 1971; Charles Schulz pens his last *Peanuts* comic strip, 2000

Wheat Beer

Black Sheep Monty Python's Holy Grail

Source The Black Sheep Brewery, Masham, North Yorkshire **Strength** 4.7%
Website blacksheepbrewery.com

It's October 1969 and late on a Sunday night. On BBC 1, in a slot normally reserved for religious programming, the rousing notes of Sousa's *Liberty Bell* ring out. The largely unknown Michael Palin fills the screen with his trouser legs rolled up and a knotted handkerchief on his head. The similarly obscure Terry Jones appears dressed as a nagging housewife, while Graham Chapman tries to bring order in the guise of a starchy, but rather silly, army officer. John Cleese – possibly familiar from *The Frost Report* – sits behind a desk, which may be on a beach, as po-faced as a BBC announcer can be, while anarchy rules all around him – perhaps instigated by Eric Idle as a seedy little salesman – and images from classical art are transformed into manic cartoons in the hands of American illustrator Terry Gilliam. Welcome to the brave new world of *Monty Python's Flying Circus*.

Confused? You bet viewers were. But they were also enthralled. What they were watching was a comedy series that was to change the face of TV comedy for ever. Although

essentially a sketch show, *Monty Python* was never just that. There were odd moments of clever satire, and whole hours of simple stupidity. Erudite in-jokes were dropped in among scenes of childish slapstick, but all the time the boundaries of taste and acceptability were being challenged, as the Oxbridge-educated team rewrote the rules of TV comedy. Everyone has their favourite *Python* moment, but who can forget such ridiculous items as *The Argument Clinic*, *The Ministry of Silly Walks*, *The Fish-Slapping Dance*, *The Lumberjack Song* or *The Dead Parrot*?

Branching out

Once viewers had grasped the concept, *Monty Python* soon transferred to a more amenable time and channel, finding a new home on BBC 2. In all, it ran for four series but its work still wasn't done, as a succession of records, stage shows and films pointed *Python* towards new media. One of these films was a spoof on Arthurian legend, and is celebrated in the name of a beer from Black Sheep Brewery in Yorkshire.

Monty Python and the Holy Grail was released in 1975. It featured Graham Chapman as King Arthur and the rest of the troupe as assorted knights, cheerfully debunking the myths of the Dark Ages. The bright copper beer with the same name was commissioned by the *Python* team for their 30th anniversary in 1999, and they receive a royalty from every case sold – a procedure

commonly known as the 'Python Pension Plan'. Brewed from Maris Otter pale malt, crystal malt, torrefied wheat and demerara sugar, and seasoned with Whitbread Golding Variety hops, it has a distinct elderflower and melon aroma, with just a hint of Spam. There's more Spam on the palate, along with a slightly perfumed estery note that gives a suggestion of almonds, but, as you'd expect from Black Sheep, this is a generally hoppy and bitter ale. The finish, too, is hoppy, bitter and very dry, with only the merest hint of Spam.

Want to know the secret of the beer's success? It's because, as the label reveals, it is 'tempered over burning witches'.

Births Vaclav Havel (writer and politician), 1936; Steve Miller (rock musician), 1943; Kate Winslet (actress), 1975

Deaths Leonard Rossiter (actor), 1954; Dennis Quilley (actor), 2003

Events The start of the Jarrow March, 1936; The Beatles release their first single, *Love Me Do*, 1962

Strong Ale

Wylam Rocket

Source Wylam Brewery, Heddon on the Wall, Northumberland **Strength** 5%
Website wylambrew.co.uk

It's often wrongly assumed that George Stephenson's *Rocket* was the first steam locomotive. In fact, there had been plenty of successful steam engines before *Rocket* came on the scene, and Richard Trevithick had constructed the first engine to run on tracks a quarter of a century before *Rocket* was built. But the fact that *Rocket* is so well known largely stems from events that began on this day in 1829.

George Stephenson was born in Wylam, near Newcastle-upon-Tyne, in 1781. He worked initially in the collieries, where he learned how the primitive engines in use operated. Promoted to enginewright, he developed his first locomotive in 1814. Stephenson later worked for the Stockton to Darlington Railway, where he pioneered new track technology and introduced an engine named *Locomotion*, and later became chief engineer for the fledgling Liverpool and Manchester Railway.

Show-stopping run

The directors of the Liverpool railway were split between using a stationary engine or a locomotive to move the vehicles on the new track, so trials were arranged to prove the value of the latter. Five engines took part, with rules laid down regarding their weight (maximum 6 tons) and the speed they needed to reach (at least 10 mph), among other issues. The engines were asked to run along the length of the Rainhill track 20 times, thus covering approximately the distance between Liverpool and Manchester. More than 10,000 people came along to see the spectacle on the first day. In the trials, there were impressive performances from engines named *Sans Pareil* and *Novelty*, but it was *Rocket*, built by George and his son, Robert, that stole the show, being the only locomotive not to break down. It won the directors' £500 prize. Despite its triumph, however, the railway ultimately selected *Sans Pareil* as the locomotive that would work the line.

The original *Rocket* can be seen today in the Science Museum in London, and is also celebrated by a brewery based close to Stephenson's home town. Wylam Brewery was set up in 2000, using an old farm dairy as a base. The company expanded well in its early years and moved into new premises on the farm site in 2006, with capacity raised to 20 barrels at a time. The beer named in Stephenson's honour briefly outlines the story of the Rainhill trials on its label.

Rocket is an exceptionally good, strong copper-coloured bitter with lots of malty, nutty, chocolaty flavours from the Maris Otter pale malt, the amber malt and the pinch of roasted barley, yet it's still enjoyably crisp thanks to its generous seasoning of Bramling Cross and Centennial hops. At 5% ABV, it's a big, satisfying robust ale, with wonderful balance. If they held a Rainhill challenge for beers named after locomotives, this one would stand an excellent chance of repeating its namesake's success.

WYLAM

Best Bitter   Alc. 5% vol.

Rocket

George Stephenson was born in Wylam. He designed and built the locomotive Rocket in 1829 for the Rainhill speed trials. It hauled the first rail passengers in the world on the Liverpool and Manchester railway.

Wylam Brewery Ltd
Heddon-on-the-Wall Northumberland NE15 0EZ
Tel: 01661 853377   www.wylambrew.co.uk

Births Richie Benaud (cricketer and broadcaster), 1930; Britt Ekland (actress), 1942; Ricky Hatton (boxer), 1978

Deaths Alfred, Lord Tennyson (poet), 1892; Nelson Riddle (bandleader), 1985; Bette Davis (actress), 1989

Events Opening of the Moulin-Rouge music hall in Paris, 1889; actress Elizabeth Taylor marries her eighth husband, Larry Fortensky, 1991

Strong Ale

Budweiser Budvar

Source Bud ě jovický Budvar, n.p., Česk é Bud ě jovice **Strength** 5% **Website** budvar.cz

Much has been reported about the relentless trademark conflict between the two Budweiser beers. Legal disputes have been running for years between Anheuser-Busch, American owner of the internationally famous light lager called simply Budweiser, and Budweiser Budvar, a brewery in the Czech town of Česk é Bud ě jovice. It all boils down to the right to use the name Budweiser. In some countries, the Americans have won, giving them the right to sell Budweiser under that name and prohibiting the Czechs from doing the same. In the US and Italy, for example, Budvar is now marketed under the name of Czechvar. In other countries, it has been the Czechs who have been the victors, forcing a change of name of the American beer to the abbreviated Bud. The battle rages on.

The Czech brewery, however, is no stranger to such disputes. In fact, it was out of a bitter rivalry that the business was born. Česk é Bud ě jovice is a town in the south of the Czech Republic, not far from the Austrian border. In the 19th century, it was heavily populated by Germans and seen very much as a German town. The town name was even known by its German title, Budweis – hence the origin of the term Budweiser, meaning 'from the town of Budweis'.

The fight back

By the end of the 19th century, however, the Czechs began to fight back. Deprived of a significant voice in local politics – despite making up a greater percentage of the population than German inhabitants – they recognized the need for more financial and commercial muscle to challenge the unfair status quo, and Czech banks and factories were founded to rival dominant German concerns. An obvious progression – for a country where beer was an important part of everyday life – was to establish a Czech brewery in competition to the German business that dominated the local brewing scene. So it was that the Czech Joint Stock Brewery was formed, taking investment from Czech citizens and building on assurances from the Czech-owned bars and restaurants that they would take the new beer in preference to the German, as long as it was of good quality.

They weren't to be disappointed. On 7 October 1895, the first beer was

brewed at what has now become known as Budweiser Budvar. To ensure the beer was of top quality when it went on sale, it underwent a long period of maturation after fermentation. Not a drop reached the outside world until Christmas. So Budvar was born and with it its now-famous reputation for extensive conditioning.

Today, Budvar is still cold-conditioned, in fact for a full 90 days – a lagering period that rounds off all the rough edges and produces one of the world's smoothest and best-balanced beers. Other Czech breweries have changed their methods of fermentation and cut down the conditioning time, but Budvar makes great play of its adherence to tradition. The long-awaited result is a delicate balance of ripe sweet malt and gently tangy hops, with a herbal, vanilla-like finish that defines the Budweiser drinking experience.

Births Desmond Tutu (clergyman and peace campaigner), 1931; Clive James (writer and broadcaster), 1939; Jayne Torvill (ice dancer), 1957

Deaths Edgar Allan Poe (writer), 1849; Clarence Birdseye (frozen food pioneer), 1956; Mario Lanza (singer and actor), 1959

Events Captain Cook discovers New Zealand, 1769; the German Democratic Republic (East Germany) established, 1949; *The Independent* newspaper first published, 1986

Pale Lager

St-Sylvestre Gavroche

Source Brasserie de St-Sylvestre, St-Sylvestre-Cappel **Strength** 8.5% **Website** brasserie-st-sylvestre.com

Les Misérables is one of the theatre world's great success stories. It began on 8 October 1985 at London's Barbican Theatre to only mixed reviews from critics. However, the public response was rapturous and, two months later, the show transferred to the West End, taking up residence at the Palace Theatre. It was soon playing all over the world, translated into 21 languages and notching up theatrical records along the way. Around 40,000 performances have now taken place and more than 50 million people have seen the show, which has picked up more than 50 major awards.

Among the original cast that October night were Alun Armstrong, Michael Ball and, in the chorus, Caroline Quentin. The show was written by Alain Boublil, Claude-Michel Schönberg and Herbert Kretzmer, produced by Cameron Mackintosh and directed by Trevor Nunn and John Caird. The tale is romantic and dramatic, based on the novel of the same name by French poet and author Victor Hugo and set amid the turmoil of early 19th-century France, as the hero, a reformed criminal named Valjean, makes his way through a world filled with injustice, duplicity and revolution.

The urchin's beer

As well as on the stage, Hugo's classic story is celebrated in the name of one of France's top beers. The St-Sylvestre Brewery is based in the town of St-Sylvestre-Cappel, in Flanders, close to the Belgian border. It has been run by the Ricour family since 1920, and in 1997 they launched a new beer entitled Gavroche, after the lively, warm-hearted street urchin who is one of the most colourful characters in Hugo's book.

'Gavroche was a whirlwind… He troubled the loungers, he excited the idle, he reanimated the weary, provoked the thoughtful, kept some in cheerfulness…,' so the author describes him. 'Boisterous', 'nimble' and 'vivacious' are other adjectives that Hugo applies to the little Artful Dodger. With a touch of poetic licence, and a short flight of fancy, such a depiction could also be applied to the beer that shares his name.

Gavroche is bottle conditioned and, if poured with care, glints in the glass the colour of burnished copper. It has a wonderfully fruity aroma, sweet and juicy, with pineapple notes and a little biscuity malt. The taste is surprisingly delicate for such a powerful beer, offering a complex mix of sweetness, estery fruit and a little hop, before winding down with a bittersweet malt and hop finish.

It's a beer that certainly provokes the thoughtful and keeps more than a few drinkers cheerful.

Births Ray Reardon (snooker player), 1932; Jesse Jackson (politician), 1941; Sigourney Weaver (actress), 1949

Deaths Henry Fielding (author), 1754; Clement Atlee (politician), 1967; Willy Brandt (politician), 1992

Events London's Post Office Tower opened, 1965; LBC, Britain's first commercial radio station, begins broadcasting, 1973

Strong Ale

289

Goose Island India Pale Ale

Source Goose Island Beer Co., Chicago, Illinois **Strength** 5.9% **Website** gooseisland.com

Sometime after 9pm on Sunday, 8 October 1871, a fire broke out in a barn behind a house on the west side of Chicago. It quickly ran out of control, crossed the river and spread into the business district. From there, the fire grew in intensity and, as Sunday turned into Monday, was blown across town – Chicago is not known as the Windy City for nothing. Thankfully, wet weather helped fire fighters to slow the conflagration eventually, but by the end of 9 October, the city had been devastated. It is estimated that around 300 citizens lost their lives, and around 90,000 were made homeless. Fortunately, Chicago is a resilient city and was quickly back on its feet. By 1875 much of the conurbation had been rebuilt.

It is inevitable that a number of breweries would have been affected by this tragedy. According to local brewer Greg Hall, there were around 50 breweries in the city by the turn of the 20th century. Greg is a member of the family that runs Goose Island Brewery – part of the team that restored brewing to Chicago after later devastation of a rather different kind.

Black market blues

Goose Island – named after a district of the city – was set up in 1988 as a brewpub, in what used to be a car wash. By that time, local brewing had been completely wiped out – not, it has to be said, by the Great Fire or its consequences, but by the aftermath of Prohibition. Unlike in other cities, the breweries here did not all disappear when alcohol production was banned by the US Government in 1920. Thanks to the involvement of Al Capone and his gangster cronies, businesses surreptitiously brewed on, supplying illicit drink to the black market. It was a situation that ultimately proved to be the undoing of brewing in Chicago. 'At the end of Prohibition, there were still 30 breweries in the city,' Greg told me, 'but, because the pie was carved up so many ways, the breweries had trouble growing.' 'St Louis had only two,' he added, hinting at the reason for Anheuser-Busch's rapid expansion and eventual domination of the US beer market.

The last surviving Chicago brewery closed in 1977, but Greg and his colleagues have picked up the baton with gusto. Today, they run two brewpubs and a microbrewery, where they produce one of America's finest ales. India Pale Ale opens with one of the world's great beer aromas, with big, juicy, fruity hops leaping out of the glass. The palate is sweet and just as juicy, balanced by zingy, fruity resins from a clever mix of Styrian Golding, Fuggle, Cascade and Centennial hops, which linger and linger in the pronounced aftertaste. It is an outstanding pale beer, a hop showcase that has put Chicago well and truly back on the brewing map of the world, echoing the remarkable revival that the city enjoyed after the terrible events of 8 and 9 October 1871.

Births Jacques Tati (actor and film director), 1908; John Lennon (rock musician), 1940; Steve Ovett (athlete), 1955

Deaths Che Guevara (revolutionary), 1967; Jacques Brel (singer-songwriter), 1978; Jackie Milburn (footballer), 1988

Events Uganda becomes independent, 1962; the musical *The Phantom of the Opera* premieres in London, 1986

IPA

Jacobsen Bramley Wit

Source Carlsberg, Jacobsen Brewhouse, Valby **Strength** 4.6% **Website** carlsberg.co.uk

Every artist knows how hard it is to follow success. Be it in literature, art, music or film, the second and subsequent attempts at a masterpiece invariably suffer in comparison with a massive initial breakthrough. One artist who knew that more than anyone was Orson Welles, who died on this day in 1985.

Welles was born in Kenosha, Wisconsin, in 1915, and trained as a stage actor before becoming a radio producer. In 1938, he made radio history when his dramatization of HG Wells's *War of the Worlds* proved so realistic that it sent America into a panic, and the fame this brought helped Welles to break into the world of cinema.

In 1941, he wrote, produced, directed and starred in his first feature film. Relating the controversial story of a newspaper baron (based on William Randolph Hearst), *Citizen Kane* was a revelation. Critics gushed over it, and Welles was feted as the future of cinema. The film has since been voted the best of all time, but for Welles it was the proverbial hard act to follow. Many of his subsequent contributions would have crowned many a directorial career – *The Magnificent Ambersons*, *The Lady from Shanghai* and *Macbeth*, to name but three – but, after *Kane*, they lacked lustre, leading numerous authorities to declare that Welles never really lived up to his potential. But when you start with nigh-on perfection, there's very little room for improvement.

Inspired marketing

Welles did enjoy another moment of high fame, however, as the voice of one of the most famous beer advertisements ever broadcast. It was inspired marketing on the part of Carlsberg when it signed up Welles to intone authoratively that most memorable of commercial lines: 'Probably the best lager in the world.' Welles may have been of considerable stature (both physically and artistically), but not many beer aficionados would easily recognize his particular description of Carlsberg. That said, the company does have a number of beers in its stable worthy of drinking today in memory of the lost genius.

As explained on 30 April, the company has opened up a microbrewery on the site of its original brewhouse and here it produces a selection of beers that are considerably more interesting than the standard Carlsberg fare. One, Saaz Blonde, was covered earlier. Another is an intriguing brew called Bramley Wit. It's a variation on the Belgian witbier style – a wheat beer laced with fruit and spices. In this case, as the name suggests, the fruit is apple, and a fresh, bready aroma of apple pie and coriander leads the way. There's more apple pie in the taste, along with a mild clove bitterness and gently spicy, orange-citrus flavours from the coriander, while the finish is dry, chewy and softly bitter with light lingering fruit.

Probably the best witbier in the world? I don't think so, but it's certainly a pleasant drink. Full marks to Carlsberg for adventure.

Births Giuseppe Verdi (composer), 1813; Harold Pinter (playwright), 1930; Chris Tarrant (broadcaster), 1946

Deaths Ralph Richardson (actor), 1983; Yul Brynner (actor), 1985; Christopher Reeve (actor), 2004

Events US President Woodrow Wilson ceremonially demolishes a dike to complete the construction of the Panama Canal, 1913; Sir John Betjeman becomes Poet Laureate, 1972

Wheat Beer

Oakleaf Heart of Oak

Source The Oakleaf Brewing Co. Ltd, Gosport, Hampshire **Strength** 4.5% **Website** oakleafbrewing.co.uk

An estimated television audience of more than 60 million watched as the wreck of the *Mary Rose* was carefully raised from the seabed on 11 October 1982. It was the first time the ship had seen daylight for 437 years, and her constitution seemed delicate and fragile. Good thing, then, that she had a heart of oak.

The *Mary Rose* was jointly named after King Henry VIII's sister and his Tudor emblem, and was launched in 1511. The event was akin to the unveiling of a new supersonic jet fighter at the time, as this was a warship built for speed and one of the first vessels capable of firing a broadside. The ship went on to fight in three wars against France before sinking, mysteriously, in Portsmouth harbour in 1545, as the English fleet once again took to the sea to chase off the old enemy.

The wreck of the ship remained hidden until 1971, when divers unearthed its frame from the mud of the Solent. Thousands of artefacts were brought to the surface but the ship itself remained stubbornly in Davy Jones's locker. Finally, employing a cradle device that gently lifted the wreck from its watery grave, the *Mary Rose* returned to fresh air. Now preserved at Portsmouth's Historic Dockyard, the ship is constantly sprayed with a mix of water and wax that will hopefully seal the oak timbers and preserve them from rotting.

Rousing & robust

Oak and the Royal Navy go hand in hand. The finest vessels over the years have been largely constructed of this reliable material, and the force's own theme tune is even named after it. 'Heart of Oak' was composed by 18th-century composer Dr William Boyce, with words added by actor David Garrick. It's the rousing march heard during major ceremonial events and is recalled in the name of a beer from Oakleaf Brewery.

If there's one brewery that has the right to brew beer with naval connections it is Oakleaf. The brewery sits right on the edge of Gosport harbour, just across the water from the Historic Dockyard and with a view out to the bustling Solent. It was founded by father-in-law/son-in-law Dave Pickersgill and Ed Anderson in 2000, and Heart of Oak was added to their extensive range of cask- and bottle-conditioned beers in 2005, to commemorate the 200th anniversary of the Battle of Trafalgar.

This is a notably bitter ale, red in colour and full of body, thanks to the inclusion of crystal and chocolate malts in the grist, and abundantly hoppy, courtesy of the Cascade, Brewer's Gold and Bramling Cross hops in the copper. Considering how luscious these hops can be, surprisingly this is not a fruity beer. There is a little estery orchard fruit floating around but the hops express themselves instead in a solid, uncompromising bitterness. What we have here is something as sturdy as King Henry's old flagship, with as dry a finish as the *Mary Rose* will acquire in due course.

Births HJ Heinz (food manufacturer), 1844; Bobby Charlton (footballer), 1937; Dawn French (comedian), 1957

Deaths Chico Marx (comedian), 1961; Edith Piaf (singer and actress), 1963; Donald Dewar (politician), 2000

Events First edition of sports programme *Grandstand* broadcast, 1958; US President Reagan and Soviet premier Gorbachev hold a missile reform summit in Reykjavik, Iceland, 1986

Best Bitter

ABOVE: THE TUDOR WARSHIP *MARY ROSE* BEING RAISED FROM THE SEABED AT PORTSMOUTH

Spaten Oktoberfestbier

Source Spaten-Franziskaner-Bräu, Munich **Strength** 5.9% **Website** spatenusa.com

Call it by its German name, Die Wiesn, and you'll get blank looks, even among hardened beer drinkers. Mention Oktoberfest and everyone understands what you mean. It's that orgy of beer consumption that takes place every autumn in Munich, where brass bands provide a rousing score as deceptively muscular waitresses barge their way through swaying crowds to bang foaming glasses down on long wooden tables.

It's a colourful picture, full of cheer, but in recent decades the Oktoberfest has lost some of its sheen for beer connoisseurs. The traditional darker style of beer known as Märzen is rarely sold here now, as pale lager – the internationally dominant beer style – has been introduced to cater for foreign visitors. Quantity rather than quality is on the minds of most drinkers, with predictable consequences.

Staggering statistics

Oktoberfest kicked off on this day in 1810, as a celebration of the wedding of Crown Prince Ludwig of Bavaria and Princess Theresa of Saxony. It wasn't a beer festival as such at the time, just a general knees-up, concluding with a horserace five days later. The festival now runs a little earlier in the year, beginning in late September. It is still staged at the same location, however, a massive showground known as the Theresienwiese after Ludwig's fair bride. Organizers these days welcome a staggering (in every sense) 6.5 million visitors each year, who

cram themselves into 14 enormous, wooden-framed tents, each serving beer from a Munich-based brewery. Around 100 oxen are roasted, more than 300,000 sausages are consumed and nearly half a million chickens find their way to the table as typically heavy Bavarian fare is dished out at a prodigious rate. Something like 7 million litres of beer are quaffed, making this a serious binge.

Finding a hotel room in the city, if you haven't booked well in advance, is all but impossible. As an alternative, stay home, turn on some cheesy oompah music, roast yourself a knuckle of pork and open a bottle of a beer that is brewed to mark this larger-than-life celebration. There are several Oktoberfest beers in circulation, but a good choice is the one from Spaten.

Spaten was founded in 1397 and for many years was in the hands of the highly influential Sedlmayer family of brewers. It merged with wheat beer specialists Franziskaner in 1922 and with Löwenbrau in 1997. Today, it is part of the InBev empire. Its

Oktoberfestbier was first produced in 1872 and is today as pale as the other lagers that dominate the event. There is a more traditional Oktoberfestbier in the Spaten stable. It's called Oktoberfest Ur-Märzen, but it's not so easy to find. Nevertheless, the regular Oktoberfest beer is smooth, well rounded and enjoyable. It pours a golden colour and has a sherbety hop nose, followed by a clean, malty flavour and more spritzy hops. Considering the strength runs to 5.9%, it's a remarkably easy-drinking beer – it needs to be, I suppose, if all those visitors are to happily sink a litre or two.

Births James Ramsay MacDonald (Prime Minister), 1866; Luciano Pavarotti (operatic singer), 1935; Angela Rippon (newsreader and presenter), 1944

Deaths Elizabeth Fry (prison reformer), 1845; Edith Cavell (nurse), 1915; John Denver (singer-songwriter), 1997

Events The IRA bombs Brighton's Grand Hotel, 1984; Bali nightclub bombings, 2002

Oktoberfestbier

Meantime India Pale Ale

Source The Meantime Brewing Co. Ltd, London **Strength** 7.5% **Website** meantimebrewing.com

Our beer for today is a traditional and authentic India pale ale. It has been carefully re-created by the Meantime brewery in Greenwich and is a stunning beer in every sense, from its elegant champagne-bottle packaging to its full, hoppy flavour.

The history of the IPA style has been well documented, and tales of ships carrying casks of strong beer from England to the Indian subcontinent have been repeated time and again (including elsewhere in this book). Perhaps not explored as part of this beery archaeology are the more mundane aspects of contemporary seafaring life, one of which – navigation – certainly has a bearing on today's choice of beer.

In this age of satellites, we take for granted the ease with which vessels can find their position on the big, wide, featureless ocean, but going back a couple of centuries, in order to work out where, exactly, their ships lay, British sailors needed to employ a more basic technique. It was based on using a fixed reference point. That reference point was the Greenwich Meridian, the imaginary line of longitude that ran north to south through the Royal Observatory in south London. By keeping one watch always set to Greenwich Mean Time (the time in Greenwich), and comparing its reading to the position of the sun above the ship, they could cleverly calculate where exactly in the world they happened to be.

Convincing majority

Seamen from other countries used their own native meridians for their readings but, gradually, the Greenwich Meridian became the most favoured. When the US called the world together to agree finally on a standard meridian for naval use, at a convention held in Washington on this day in 1884, it was Greenwich that had the nod. Only San Domingo – modern-day Haiti – voted against, and Brazil and France abstained. Indeed, many defiant French sailors shrugged their Gallic shoulders and continued to use the French meridian for decades afterwards, but even so there was a convincing majority to establish the dividing point of the eastern and western hemispheres in London. It also meant that Greenwich Mean Time became the point from which all other time zones took their lead.

There are two breweries that trade successfully on the back of this international renown. The Zerodegrees brewpub chain began life close to the path of the meridian in Blackheath in 2000, but its near-neighbour Meantime's beers are more widely available and make today's selection easy.

Meantime's India Pale Ale was introduced in 2005, after considerable research into the origins of this beer style. It is brewed from juicy Maris Otter pale malt and seasoned with the rounded bitterness of Fuggle hops, with the smoky orange tang of Goldings employed for a rich, sensuous aroma. The beer is packed with tangy, peppery hop flavours and lots of bitter citrus fruit, all firmly supported by ripe, abundant malt. The beer conditions naturally in the bottle and pours at around 7.5% ABV – potent and heady yet perfectly true to style, as those early seafarers would no doubt have confirmed.

Births Margaret Thatcher (Prime Minister), 1925; Paul Simon (singer-songwriter), 1941; Edwina Currie (politician and broadcaster), 1946

Deaths Claudius (Roman Emperor), 54; Henry Irving (actor), 1905; Ed Sullivan (broadcaster), 1974

Events The cornerstone of the White House in Washington laid, 1792; Damon Hill wins the Formula 1 motor racing championship, 1996

IPA

Cottage Norman's Conquest

Source Cottage Brewing Co., Lovington, Somerset **Strength** 7% **Website** cottagebrewing.co.uk

There are a number of beery options with which to mark one of the most significant dates in British history. William the Conqueror's defeat of Harold at the Battle of Hastings on this day has been recalled in the names of beers such as 1066, brewed by Hampshire Brewery, and 1066 Country Bitter by White Brewing, based very close to the site of that historical conflict. But the honours, on this occasion, go to a former CAMRA Champion Beer of Britain.

The Battle of Hastings on this day in 1066 was the culmination of William of Normandy's long-planned invasion of England. His objective was to take the crown, a title once possibly promised him by his cousin, King Edward the Confessor, but one that had in the meantime passed to Harold, Earl of Wessex. William played a waiting game, letting other would-be invaders have first crack at England so that Harold's forces would be stretched and his soldiers tired. It worked. When Harold was forced to march north to dispatch the Viking king Harald Hardrada at Stamford Bridge near York, William, seizing his chance, invaded the south coast and raided local settlements to draw Harold into a fight. Less than three weeks after the difficult battle in Yorkshire, Harold's men found themselves squaring up to a new, well-prepared enemy on a field just outside the town of Hastings.

At first, the battle seemed to go Harold's way. His men repelled assault after assault from the Normans. Eventually, however, the numbers took their toll and the English were overrun. Harold, as depicted in the illustration of the battle on the Bayeux Tapestry, took an arrow in the eye and was then mown down. William claimed the battle and with it the English throne, being crowned in Westminster Abbey on Christmas Day the same year.

Inspired title

Cottage Brewery is not local to Hastings. It is based in Somerset and most of its beers take their names from steam locomotives. Norman's Conquest is an exception, however, drawn from the name of the brewery founder, Chris Norman, but depicting a character, possibly a refugee from the Bayeux Tapestry, on its label. Considering the beer's early success, in the 1995 Champion Beer of Britain contest, it was a very inspired title.

Also appropriate to the beer's identity is its original gravity – the reading taken before fermentation begins, which tells the brewer how much sugar there is in the wort – which, in this case, is 1066. When brewed out, this brings the beer up to a formidable 7% ABV, but it wasn't just the strength that turned the heads of the judges at CAMRA's most important beer competition. They also appreciated the vinous fruitiness of this rich, dark ale and the sweetish, roasted malt flavours that linger on in the finish – all skilfully conjured out of a mix of pale, crystal and chocolate malts, spiced with Challenger hops.

Births Dwight D Eisenhower (soldier and US President), 1890; Roger Moore (actor), 1927; Cliff Richard (pop musician), 1940

Deaths Errol Flynn (actor), 1959; Bing Crosby (actor and singer), 1977; Leonard Bernstein (composer), 1990

Events AA Milne's *Winnie the Pooh* published, 1926; US President Jimmy Carter legalizes home brewing, 1978

Old Ale

ABOVE: A RE-ENACTMENT OF THE BATTLE OF HASTINGS IN 2006

Brewster's Mata Hari

Source Brewster's Brewing Company, Grantham, Lincolnshire **Strength** 4.8% **Website** brewsters.co.uk

A brewster is a name for a female brewer – traditionally the member of the household who made the beer while the husband was out at work. The brewer in Brewster's Brewing Company is Sara Barton, who worked for Courage, brewing major international beer brands, before setting up her own business in her native Vale of Belvoir, Leicestershire, in 1998. The brewery moved to Grantham, Lincolnshire, in 2006.

Sara produces a wide range of regularly available cask beers, plus a selection of special ales dedicated to 'Wicked Women'. These have included beers named after Jezebel, Salome, Nell Gwynne and Mata Hari, the notorious female spy from World War I, who was executed for her alleged crimes on this day in 1917.

Mata Hari was born Margaretha Geertruida Zelle in Leeuwarden, The Netherlands, in 1876, the daughter of a hat maker. Her turbulent marriage to a Scottish-Dutch army officer named MacLeod broke down acrimoniously, after which she embarked on a career as a dancer, adopting the stage name of Mata Hari, also working, it seems, as a prostitute. It's certainly true that she had many lovers – some in very high places – which drew her into intrigue during the war years, especially as she continued to travel brassily throughout Europe. Her flighty reputation, you could say, was carried before her.

Double agent

The beer that bears her name is created from pale and crystal malts, with three strains of hops – Northdown, Progress and Fuggle. A bottle-conditioned version has been produced in conjunction with The Beer Counter, a contract brewing and packaging business run by former Brakspear head brewer Peter Scholey, and this has been sold in the US as well as in the UK. However, it looks like sales for the foreseeable future may be confined to cask. It's a nicely balanced premium ale, with a light amber colour. Nutty malt is washed over by juicy fruit salad flavours, with a drying backnote from the hops and the crystal malt.

Mata Hari's sad demise came when she was accused by France – on flimsy grounds provided by British intelligence – of betraying secrets to the Germans. In response, she revealed that she was working as a double agent. Evidence unearthed in later years seems to support this, but at the time such claims were conveniently ignored. Consequently, after her sudden arrest in February 1917 and subsequent trial, she was brought before a firing squad in Paris and executed on 15 October the same year. Although the name Mata Hari has become synonymous with female espionage, and the sultry seduction often linked to this activity, some now claim that she was simply the result of extreme spy paranoia in France and the need to find an easy victim to prove that the authorities were in control. Perhaps she was not such a Wicked Woman after all.

Births Virgil (poet), 70 BC; PG Wodehouse (writer), 1881; Chris de Burgh (singer-songwriter), 1948; Sarah Ferguson, Duchess of York, 1959

Deaths Cole Porter (songwriter), 1964

Events Nikita Kruschev steps down as Soviet Premier, 1964; Sir Menzies Campbell resigns as leader of the Liberal Democrats, 2007

Strong Ale

Mighty Oak Oscar Wilde Mild

Source Mighty Oak Brewing Company, Maldon, Essex **Strength** 3.7% **Website** mightyoakbrewery.co.uk

The world of literature is well endowed with flamboyant, eccentric characters, and one of the most outrageous entered the world on this day in 1854.

Oscar Wilde was born in Dublin, the son of a noted surgeon and his writer wife. He studied at Trinity College in his home city, before moving onto Magdalene College, Oxford, where his literary talents were acknowledged with an academic prize. While his subsequent personal life proved highly controversial, attracting plenty of attention and hostile gossip – with which Wilde was happy to play along – his career advanced nicely and, over a period of some 20 years, he successfully married poetry and prose with drama. His greatest works included the novel *The Picture of Dorian Gray*, the plays *Lady Windermere's Fan* and *The Importance of Being Earnest*, and the poem *The Ballad of Reading Gaol*, which was written after a two-year incarceration (with hard labour) for homosexual activity. Wilde had been a true celebrity of his era, a reckless non-conformist in prim-and-proper times, but he never recovered his earlier social acceptance after his time in prison. On release, he moved to Paris, adopting a pseudonym, and there he died, three years later, in 1900.

Champion pig's ear

The other thing that Wilde has become famous for is his acerbic wit. 'Work is the curse of the drinking classes', he once quipped, and these words now appear on the pump clip of a beer that also shares his name from the Mighty Oak brewery in Maldon, Essex. Oscar Wilde Mild was first brewed in 1999 for CAMRA's May Mild Month promotion but, when the first batch of beer claimed the Beer of the Festival title at the local Ongar Beer Festival, it had to be made part of the regular range. Pale, crystal and black malts combine to provide a deep mahogany colour with red highlights, a soft mouthfeel and a pleasant coffee accent to the nose, taste and drying finish, with bittersweet notes encouraged by the presence of Challenger hops.

It sounds as if Oscar Wilde is well-established cockney rhyming slang for mild – just as pig's ear stands for beer – but it's not the case. Brewery founder John Boyce merely suggested that this was so, in a light-hearted sort of way, when he named the beer. But considering it was judged CAMRA's overall Best Mild in 2006, who's to say that 'a pint of Oscar' won't become the new way of asking for a beer like this in the London area before too long.

'Moderation is a fatal thing – nothing succeeds like excess,' Wilde once jested. I would never suggest taking that approach with beer, but it's certainly tempting with a brew like this.

ABOVE: OSCAR WILDE

Births Eugene O'Neill (writer), 1888; Angela Lansbury (actress), 1925; Peter Bowles (actor), 1936

Deaths Marie Antoinette (Queen of France), 1793; Gene Krupa (jazz drummer), 1973

Events First edition of *Blue Peter* broadcast, 1958; Karol Wojtyla becomes Pope John Paul II, 1978; hurricane force winds strike southern England, 1987

Mild

Fuller's London Porter

Source Fuller, Smith & Turner, Chiswick, London **Strength** 5.4% **Website** fullers.co.uk

One of the greatest tragedies associated with the world of brewing happened on this day. On the face of it, the event sounds vaguely ridiculous, even rather innocuous in a cartoon-like way. But it was no laughing matter. This was a disaster on a large scale, one long in the making and revolving around the production of porter. It was the result of brewer one-upmanship taken to absurd new levels.

It's hard to believe today but porter was by far the most popular drink in London in the 19th century. It also had economic advantages for brewers. Being strong, robust and dark, it could be brewed in bulk for economies of scale and stored for months in giant wooden casks, maturing well where more delicate beers would have deteriorated.

Tragic waste

Such was the demand for porter that brewers began building larger and larger tuns in which to store it. They boasted about the size of their latest additions, even holding celebratory dinners inside them to show how big they were. Then, on 17 October 1814, tragedy struck. A porter tun at Meux's central London brewery burst its sides. The delicious but deadly contents rushed into the open, sending a deluge of beer down Tottenham Court Road. Estimates of the quantity vary but it seems that more than 3,500 barrels of beer gushed forth. Walls were demolished, eight people lost their lives, homes were ruined and a business was shaken to the core.

Jokes about neighbours dying happy soon wore thin when the extent of the disaster became clear.

The catastrophe wasn't the death-knell for porter, however. Porter did fade later, but the rise of pale ale was partly responsible for that, coupled with wartime restrictions on the use of energy to produce dark malts. As the 20th century ticked by, porter gradually disappeared from view. It survived largely in name only, etched into the frosted glass of many pub windows. By the 1970s, very few people even knew what porter was.

It was thanks to the smaller brewers of Britain that porter bounced back. The likes of Burton Bridge, Larkins and Nethergate began reviving this rich, nutritious beer in the 1980s, and soon bigger brewers began to realize its potential. Fuller's introduced its London Porter in 1995. Head brewer Reg Drury dusted down the company's ancient brewing books and came up with a 19th-century recipe that combined pale and brown malts for a coffee dryness. Reg added a little crystal malt to fill out the palate and some chocolate malt for a deeper colour. With a generous but balanced seasoning of Fuggle hops, it is a magnificent beer, especially if you can track it down on draught. But even in its bottled form it is a treat – creamy, chocolaty, coffee-accented and deeply satisfying.

On this evidence, it's easy to see why this type of beer was once the capital's most popular drink and why brewers competed so vigorously to supply it to the people.

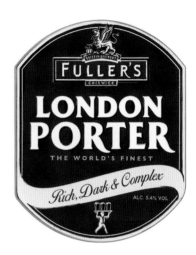

Births Arthur Miller (playwright), 1915; Harry Carpenter (sports presenter), 1925; Eminem (rap artist), 1972

Deaths Frédéric Chopin (composer), 1849; Joan Hickson (actress), 1998

Events First staging of The Open golf championship, at Prestwick, 1860; Mother Teresa of Calcutta awarded the Nobel Peace Prize, 1979

Porter

Dogfish Head Raison D'Etre

Source Dogfish Head Craft Brewery, Milton, Delaware **Strength** 8% **Website** dogfish.com

The Great American Beer Festival is now one of the big 'musts' of the annual brewing calendar, usually taking place over a weekend in the middle of October.

The festival was first staged in the town of Boulder, in the foothills of the Rockies, in 1982. Only 40 beers from 22 breweries were on show, and just 800 punters showed up. Since 1984, the event has been held in Denver, attracting more than 40,000 visitors annually. The GABF is a whoop and holler festival. The crowds are boisterous and it's not easy to find a quiet corner.

You could say the same about the beer selection. As you tour the bars, you simply never know what you're going to find next – especially with more than 1,600 beers to choose from. It's easy to be knocked senseless by the range and flavours of beers on show here. Whereas in Britain the defeatist response to falling beer sales is generally increased blandness – through ever duller, middle-of-the-road brands or plummeting serving temperatures – in America, they drive on regardless, with hops and malt cherished in the way new beers are invented. They don't just brew hoppy IPAs in America: they brew double IPAs, with even more hops. They fiddle about with wood ageing, far more than brewers in the UK. They dip into unusual ingredients. Grab a taster of Lemongrass Pils, Smokin' Mesquite Ale or Wake-n-Bake Coffee Oatmeal Imperial Stout, if you want to know what I mean.

Devil-may-care attitude

A visit to Denver at this time of year is a pilgrimage every beer lover should make at least once. But, if you can't get there – and it's not a cheap option, to be frank – then perhaps I can point you in the direction of a beer that sums up the devil-may-care attitude of many US brewers represented at the festival. I've plumped for a beer from Delaware, from the same Dogfish Head brewery featured later, for 7 December. As mentioned then, brewer Sam Calagione likes to push the envelope and he's done so again with today's choice, a beer with a French name but a truly American pioneering spirit. It's called Raison D'Etre, and the label declares it to be 'brewed with Belgian beer sugars, green raisins and a sense of purpose'. It's also fermented with a Belgian ale yeast.

To say it's a complex beer would be an understatement. The aroma alone takes some evaluation: malty and creamy at first, with a lactose-like note often found on milk stouts. Then there's gentle vinous fruit that eventually gives way to bitter oranges and a whiff of Darjeeling tea. In the sweet taste, there's a slightly wild Belgian character that makes it spicy and fruity, while the smooth, creamy malt base provides a good foundation for peppery, citrus hops, as well as more winey fruit. The spicy, hoppy and dry finish, with lingering vine fruits, is surprisingly subtle, mellow and rather moreish.

While some US beers are perhaps a little over-egged for easy drinking, this one is all too quaffable for its

ABV. But, if you want something even bigger and bolder, to see what American brewers can really do, Dogfish also produces an 18% version called Raison D'Extra.

Births Canaletto (artist), 1697; Chuck Berry (rock 'n' roll musician), 1926; Martina Navratilova (tennis player), 1956

Deaths Thomas Edison (inventor), 1931; Red Rum (racehorse), 1995; Johnny Haynes (footballer), 2005

Events Harold Macmillan resigns as Prime Minister, 1963; Bob Beamon breaks the world long jump record at the Mexico Olympics, 1968

Strong Ale

ABOVE: GREAT AMERICAN BEER FESTIVAL-GOERS GET INTO THE SPIRIT

Hepworth Pullman

Source Hepworth & Co., Horsham, West Sussex **Strength** 4.2% **Website** hepworthbrewery.co.uk

It's sad to report that the day a prominent person dies is a day of celebration for others, but that would have been the case back in 1897, when railway pioneer George Pullman went to meet his maker.

Pullman was born near Buffalo, New York, in 1831. He trained first as a cabinet maker and later made a name for himself as an engineer – raising sinking buildings. In the 1850s, when Chicago was installing a sewage system, it was Pullman who came up with a smooth and efficient method of lifting whole structures above the new pipes. The money he earned from this enterprise he channelled into establishing his own factory to build carriages for railroad trains.

Pullman was all too aware of the discomforts of rail travel up to that point and saw a gap in the market for a revolutionary kind of carriage, one that offered a touch of luxury. He developed an elegant new sleeping car and fitted it out with crisp, clean bedding, and he made advances with dining cars, too, serving high-quality food and making it, at last, a pleasure to undertake a long rail journey.

Pullman was also a shrewd businessman. He never sold his rail cars: he simply leased them out to railroad lines and took a cut from the premium they charged passengers. He also knew a PR opportunity when it presented itself. When Abraham Lincoln's body was transported to his funeral by train, Pullman made sure one of his cars was part of the procession, thereby guaranteeing his company maximum exposure.

Model town

Sadly, Pullman's eye for business was not so focused when it came to looking after his staff. It started well enough. He built a whole town in Illinois to house his workers, a self-contained, exceptionally well-serviced settlement that was both comfortable and convenient. This model town was somewhat egocentrically named after Pullman himself and, it has to be said, wouldn't be the sort of place readers of this book would wish to live, as he declared it to be 'dry'. The other drawback was that houses were leased, rather than sold, to employees, with rent taken directly from salaries, and when economic troubles appeared on the horizon, this proved to be a flashpoint. With business tight, Pullman cut his workers wages, but foolishly didn't reduce the rent. The anti-union boss refused to negotiate, and industrial action was the consequence. It led to a national rail strike in 1894 that was only broken when its leaders were jailed, troops took over trains and police began shooting strikers. Pullman, who had simply closed his factory and walked away from the turmoil, became a figure of hate, especially when he refused to reinstate striking workers once the business reopened. On his death a few years later, his family buried him in a specially fortified grave to deter those who might have considered posthumous revenge.

Pullman's human legacy may have been dreadful, but industrially the man shook up the transport industry,

and it is in him that the comforts of travel today have their origin. That is recognized in a premium ale from Hepworth & Co., a brewery housed in premises known as The Beer Station, adjacent to the railway line in Horsham, Sussex. Pullman is bitter, crisp and fruity, with Admiral hops in the copper and locally grown Goldings added late for aroma. A 'First Class Ale', they call it.

Births Michael Gambon (actor), 1940; Philip Pullman (writer), 1946; Sam Allardyce (football manager), 1954

Deaths King John, 1216; Ernest Rutherford (physicist), 1937; Jacqueline du Pré (cellist), 1987

Events Napoleon begins retreat from Moscow, 1812; beatification by Pope John Paul II of Mother Teresa of Calcutta, 2003

Best Bitter

Teignworthy Edwin Tucker's Maris Otter

Source Teignworthy Brewery, Newton Abbot, Devon **Strength** 5.5% **Website** teignworthybrewery.com

For 9 September, this book celebrates Houblon Day, the day of the hop in the strange but rather fascinating calendar installed by the revolutionary government of France in the 18th century. The calendar, as you would expect from a vehicle designed to celebrate items important to the working man, also had a day set aside for Orge, or barley. That was the 29th day of Vendémiaire ('Vintage'), which, in today's money, is the equivalent of 20 October.

There are plenty of malty beers with which to mark this day but surprisingly very few that are actually named after a type of barley. Hops seem to fare much better in this respect. However, there is one beer that certainly fits the bill. Deep in the West Country, Tucker's Maltings has been providing top-quality malt for brewers for nearly 150 years. After its origins as a seed merchant in 1862, the business expanded considerably when it opened its state-of-the-art floor maltings at Newton Abbot in 1900. That's still where Tucker's operates today, taking fine barley and skilfully malting it for the brewer. Capitalizing on its geography, Tucker's has also become a major tourist attraction, offering tours in summer that reveal the secrets of malt production to holidaying families.

Two other features make Tucker's a bit special. The first is an on-site brewery, Teignworthy, which is not owned by Tucker's but leases parts of the rambling old premises. Seeing the steam rise from the copper and sensing the rich, malty wort in the air certainly brings to life the visitor experience. The second is an excellent bottled beer shop, offering hundreds of great beers, and in doing so graphically concluding the complex field-to-glass barley cycle.

Premium barley

The brewery and the shop also happily work in tandem. Beers commissioned by Tucker's are brewed by Teignworthy for sale in the shop, and these generally follow a historical theme. Old recipes for largely forgotten beer styles have been re-created to underline the authenticity and heritage of the Tucker's business. Significantly for today, there has also been a beer named in honour of the brewer's favourite malting barley.

Edwin Tucker's Maris Otter celebrates a strain of barley that many brewers swear by for its reliability. Not so long ago, Maris Otter was heading for extinction, as larger maltings met demands from big breweries for more economical malt made from other strains of barley. It was largely the British craft brewers who kept Maris Otter alive, happy to pay a premium for farmers to continue to grow it. Maris Otter production still only amounts to small beer, but its future seems assured, especially as brewers are increasingly turning their attention to quality over convenience in a bid to halt declining beer sales.

Edwin Tucker's Maris Otter is suitably rich and malty, with hops – even though four varieties are blended into the brew – kept largely in check until the bittersweet finish. Instead, countering the malt in the mouth are fruity fermentation flavours with traces of pear drop and lemon to the fore. At 5.5% ABV, it's a substantial and satisfying beer with which to thank the French for taking time to recognize the true value of barley to everyday life.

Births Christopher Wren (architect), 1632; Tom Petty (rock musician), 1950; Ian Rush (footballer), 1961

Deaths Richard Burton (explorer), 1890; Herbert Hoover (US President), 1964; Burt Lancaster (actor), 1994

Events Jacqueline Kennedy marries Aristotle Onassis, 1968; opening of Sydney Opera House, 1973

Strong Ale

301

Freeminer Trafalgar

Source Freeminer Brewery Ltd, Cinderford, Forest of Dean, Gloucestershire **Strength** 6%
Website freeminer.com

As a national celebration in the UK, 21 October had somewhat faded from memory until the year 2005. Nelson's famous victory at the Battle of Trafalgar in 1805 was a cause for common rejoicing throughout the Victorian age but the occasion became less significant as new wars arrived to occupy the minds of the population – and bring home the true misery of bloody conflict. By the time of the battle's 200th anniversary, there weren't many people who could actually pinpoint the date of Britain's greatest naval victory and, despite the flag waving and fanfares that marked the bicentenary in 2005, there are still whole swathes of the nation for whom 21 October means nothing.

That may be a mixed blessing. On the one hand, the glorification of war is always a rather uncomfortable concept. On the other, the 7,700 men who lost their lives on this gory day deserve some remembrance, especially if, as historians have it, by their bravery they helped thwart the greatest threat to Britain's security for more than 200 years.

The context was this. Napoleon, rampant on the continent, saw the wrecking of the British fleet as a way of both preparing for an invasion and of curbing British domination of the waterways, freeing up the seas for the French. Nelson, as head of the Royal Navy, considered attack the best form of defence, so while the French fleet and their Spanish allies harboured at Cadiz, he put in place the traditional British tactic of a blockade, waiting to pounce as soon as the enemy made their move. That came on this day, off the headland of Cape Trafalgar, and Nelson's strategy was decisive.

Doing his duty

Taking his own flagship, *Victory*, first into the fray, he hounded and destroyed the flagship of his opposite number, Admiral Villeneuve. Nelson knew that, through this unconventional tactic, he could render the enemy leaderless and confused, and that his skilled officers would be able to mop up the rest of the opposition. And that's how it turned out, even with the mortal wounding of Nelson. 'England expects that every man will do his duty,' the admiral had dictated as a

rallying call to his men that morning. By the time he breathed his last at around 4.30 in the afternoon, Nelson had certainly done his. Not only had he trashed the enemy fleet, so crushing Napoleon's hopes of invasion, he had also set the scene for British domination of the high seas that was to last a century.

While others have let Trafalgar slip their minds, the brewing industry has done its best to ensure that the day is not forgotten. Commemorative ales have been produced by numerous breweries and the one selected for today is called simply Trafalgar. Its label depicts historic warships in full sail, but there is a little secret behind the name. When it was first created, this traditional IPA was named not after Nelson's last stand but after a coal mine in the Forest of Dean. The brewery is Freeminer, which has been operating in Gloucestershire since 1992. Its beers are notably hoppy, and Trafalgar especially so, packed to the gunwales with tangy, lip-smacking Goldings. At 6%, it's a full-bodied, chunky, fruity beer, worth seeking out today or any other day.

Births Dizzy Gillespie (jazz musician), 1917; Leonard Rossiter (actor), 1926; Geoffrey Boycott (cricketer), 1940; Peter Mandelson (politician), 1953

Deaths Jack Kerouac (writer), 1969; François Truffaut (film director), 1984

Events Aberfan coal tip disaster, with the loss of 144 lives, 1966

IPA

Theakston Old Peculier

Source T&R Theakston Ltd, Masham, North Yorkshire **Strength** 5.6% **Website** theakstons.co.uk

This day in 2003 was a big day for supporters of independent breweries. After 16 years of being part of one of the country's biggest brewing companies, the small but distinctive Theakston brewery in Masham, North Yorkshire, returned to private ownership. Even better, it came back into the hands of the Theakston family.

There aren't many stories like this in the world of British brewing. The trend has always been one of take-over and closure. Very few small breweries that have entered the jaws of a brewing whale have ever been spat back out, so full marks to the powers that be for making a very welcome exception on this occasion.

Theakston was one of the iconic breweries during CAMRA's formative years. In the early 1970s, as breweries either closed or dumped all their traditional cask-conditioned ales in favour of horrible, gassy keg beers, a handful of small, authentic producers stood tall. They included Marston's, Wadworth, Young's, Ruddles… and Theakston.

Being swallowed

Theakston started life way back in 1827, when Robert Theakston, in partnership with John Wood, opened a brewery at Masham's Black Bull pub. Business was good and by 1875 a new purpose-built brewery had been constructed in the town. Over the years, the family concern developed an excellent reputation for its beers, but perhaps it became the architect of its own downfall.

As demand for Theakston beers continued to grow in the 1970s, the company looked to expand. It took over a brewery in Carlisle that had been owned by the Government since World War I, and for a while brewed Theakston beers at two sites. But being bigger meant that you were easier to spot by other predators. In 1984, the whole business was taken over by Matthew Brown, a Blackburn brewery, and that, in turn, was swallowed up by Scottish & Newcastle three years later. The Carlisle and Blackburn breweries soon disappeared, but the Masham brewery remained open, some say as a small real ale 'fig leaf' to cover S&N's embarrassment at diverting most of its attention to the production of Foster's and Kronenbourg. Happily, thanks to S&N's decision to sell the business back to its founding family, Theakston has moved a long way to re-establishing its individuality.

The jewel in the crown of Theakston is, and always has been, the beer they call Old Peculier. It's a dark old ale combining complex vinous flavours, rich sweet malt, a touch of caramel and fine balancing hops – Challenger, Target and Fuggle – that add a hint of blackcurrant. It takes its peculiar name from the ecclesiastic court, or peculier, that was established in Masham in the Middle Ages and still meets, ceremonially, in the town.

Old Peculier is one of Britain's classic beers, a glass of which – preferably the cask version – makes the perfect toast to the renewed health of a great brewing survivor.

Births Franz Liszt (composer), 1811; Doris Lessing (writer), 1919; Derek Jacobi (actor), 1938

Deaths Paul Cézanne (artist), 1906; Pablo Casals (cellist), 1973; Kingsley Amis (writer), 1995

Events Dr Crippen convicted of murdering his wife, 1910; Michael Schumacher retires from Formula 1 motor racing, 2006

Old Ale

Why Not Cavalier Red

Source The Why Not Brewery, Norwich, Norfolk **Strength** 4.7% **Website** thewhynotbrewery.co.uk

It is October 1642 and civil war is about to erupt in England. Parliament has made a stand against Charles I and now the King is on the warpath. Advancing south from Shrewsbury, his aim is to take control of the capital. Resistance is met, however, in Warwickshire, where the Parliamentary army, under the control of the Earl of Essex, blocks his path. On a Sunday afternoon, in open fields near the village of Kineton, battle is engaged.

With around 14,000 men on either side, it is considered that this could be the confrontation to decide once and for all the dispute between King and Parliament, but that doesn't turn out to be the case. After a couple of hours of bloody conflict in which about 1,500 men lose their lives, night brings the engagement to a close. The Battle of Edgehill, the first battle of the English Civil War, is over.

At the time, Edgehill was generally seen to be an honourable draw, but experts, with the benefit of hindsight, claim it was the King and his Cavaliers who gained the advantage. The Roundheads retreated to Warwick, leaving the Royalists to march on Oxford – which was to be the King's headquarters throughout the conflict – where he was in control, for the time being at least, of the road to London.

Royal ale

Most of the beers that recall the English Civil War do so from a Parliamentary perspective. Cromwell, his Roundheads and the New Model Army are well represented on the shelves of specialist beer shops. To

redress the balance, and reflect the success of the King's forces on this day in 1642, we need to find a beer with Royalist connections. It comes from a tiny brewery in Norwich and it's called Cavalier Red.

The Why Not Brewery is run on a part-time basis by Colin Emms, who started brewing professionally in 2005. His beers carry the slogan: 'Fancy a beer? Why not!', which, I suppose, provides the rationale behind the rather odd brewery name. Colin's beers are mostly produced in bottled form, for sale at East Anglian farmers' markets, although some cask beer is available for beer festivals and to order. Cavalier Red is a strong bitter with a red-tawny hue and is one of the first beers Colin brewed.

Created from Maris Otter pale malt, crystal malt and chocolate malt, and seasoned with Golding and Fuggle hops, the beer conditions in the bottle and has light fruit cocktail notes in the

aroma, along with creamy malt. Creamy malt also leads on the palate, but with a firm, bitter, fruity, hoppy balance, plus a little nut and caramel. The finish is hoppy and bitter with lingering creaminess.

Overall, this is a fine, satisfying English ale but, if your sympathies are simply too republican to allow Cavalier Red near your lips, you can always opt for Why Not's Roundhead Porter (4.5% ABV) instead.

Births Johnny Carson (broadcaster), 1925; Pelé (footballer), 1940; Ang Lee (film director), 1954

Deaths WG Grace (cricketer), 1915; Zane Grey (writer), 1939; Al Jolson (actor and singer), 1950

Events First meeting of the Parliament of Great Britain, 1707; beginning of the ultimately unsuccessful Hungarian uprising against the Soviet Union, 1956

Strong Ale

ABOVE: ATTACK ON A ROYALIST BAGGAGE TRAIN AT EDGEHILL

Samuel Adams Black Lager

Source The Boston Beer Co., Boston, Massachusetts **Strength** 4.9% **Website** samueladams.com

The end of the Roaring Twenties, the start of the Great Depression – call it what you will, but Thursday 24 October 1929 was a disastrous day for the American economy.

In the post World War I years, America – to borrow a phrase coined later by Harold Macmillan – had never had it so good. The manufacturing world had really taken off, inspired by Henry Ford and his production line innovations, and US businesses were booming. Dividends rose steadily and share prices climbed accordingly. It seemed that there could be no end to the nation's increasing prosperity.

All this optimism came to a sudden and abrupt halt on this day in 1929. The day began with share disposals on the New York Stock Exchange that turned into panic selling when the tickertape system for recording prices fell an hour and a half behind. In a normal day, the stock exchange would have expected around four million transactions; on what became known as Black Thursday, there were nearly 13 million. Fortunately, the ship was steadied a little by the intervention of the major finance houses, which meant that, even though the market fell by 9% that day, the Friday that followed remained relatively calm. Unfortunately, panic returned on 'Black Monday', three days later, when the tickertape again ran hopelessly behind and prices fell by a further 13%. The market headed into almost terminal decline on 'Black Tuesday', by the end of which US share prices had plummeted another 12%. All confidence in the financial

markets disappeared. Fortunes were lost, and men, faced with financial ruin, took their own lives. The market was not to recover to 1929 levels for more than two decades. In the meantime, America collapsed into depression, with unemployment at record levels and economic light not even a pinprick at the end of a very long tunnel.

Uplifting experience

There had been no war, natural disaster or political crisis – or even good reason, economists claim, for such a decline in share prices: the country had been torn apart by the simple loss of confidence witnessed on Black Thursday and the days that followed. The day has since lent its unfortunate nickname to other days of financial crisis around the world, so it's not a particularly cheerful day to celebrate. But we can make it a bit brighter with an American beer that may be equally dark in nature but is always an uplifting experience.

The beer in question comes from the Boston Beer Company. Among its extensive range of Samuel Adams beers is a lager first brewed in 2004 in the tradition of the East German schwarzbier. These 'black beers' are brewed with plenty of roasted malts to give them not only their dark lustre but also complex toasted flavours. Samuel Adams Black Lager is no exception and includes Munich malt plus a trademarked, husk-free German malt called Carafa, that ensures the beer doesn't become too dry. The name says black but the beer

pours a deep ruby-red. Biscuity chocolate notes fill the aroma and continue into the bittersweet, nutty, caramel-accented taste and the drying finish. The hopping, with German Spalt, is light.

Beers like this work well because they provide all the dark malt flavours of a stout combined with the crispness and cleanness of a well-lagered beer. This one also proves that you can have a Black Thursday without getting depressed.

Births Bill Wyman (rock musician), 1936; Kevin Kline (actor), 1947; Wayne Rooney (footballer), 1985

Deaths Jane Seymour (third wife of King Henry VIII), 1537; Christian Dior (fashion designer), 1957; Rosa Parks (civil rights activist), 2005

Events James Hunt becomes Formula 1 world champion, 1976; last commercial flight of *Concorde*, 2003

Dark Lager

Greene King The Tanner's Jack

Source Greene King, Bury St Edmunds, Suffolk   **Strength** 4.4%   **Website** greeneking.co.uk

The late, great Ronnie Barker, it has been revealed, used to warm up *The Two Ronnies*' studio audiences by getting them to yell out answers to some very provocative questions. The first would be: 'What do you call men who mend shoes?' To which, the audience would warmly respond: 'Cobblers!'. Barker then followed up with similar questions that prompted the raucous replies of 'Knockers!' and 'Bullocks!'. It was wonderfully effective audience participation, drawing heavily on the school of saucy seaside postcards that the comedian himself loved so much.

Anyway, I digress, as Barker's on-screen partner, Ronnie Corbett, was wont to confess in his little monologues from the big chair. The purpose of this little aside is to introduce St Crispin's Day, the day devoted to the memory of the patron saint of – altogether now! – cobblers.

Crispin was born in Rome in the third century and was possibly the brother of a fellow Christian named Crispinian. In those dark, dangerous times for early Christians, the future saints funded their evangelical work by making shoes. Not surprisingly, Crispin's legacy is celebrated in the town of Northampton – England's shoemaking capital – where the local Frog Island Brewery produces a cask beer called simply Shoemaker. However, being in cask only, it's less easy to get hold of than the beer highlighted for today, so the attention switches to another of Crispin's trade associations.

Leather bondage

As well as being the saint of you know what, Crispin is also the patron of tanners, the men who turned animal hides into leather, ready for shoe- and other garment-manufacturing. They did this by soaking the hides in a bath of oak or hemlock bark, or, even worse, urine and dung. It was a smelly and unpleasant job, so some compensation came in the form of their daily ale, which the tanners drank from a leather tankard known as a jack. In those days, leather was much cheaper and easier to obtain than glass or pewter, and it was just as efficient at holding beer, so the tanner's jack became a familiar sight in places where the industry was prevalent – such as in Abingdon in Oxfordshire.

This Thames-side market town was also, for nearly 300 years, a major brewing centre, the home of Morland Brewery, until it was acquired and closed by Greene King in 2000. Greene King has maintained several of the Morland brands and now brews them at Bury St Edmunds. Among them is The Tanner's Jack, a premium bitter introduced in the mid-1990s to celebrate Abingdon's strong associations with the leather industry.

A combination of pale, crystal and amber malts in the mash tun, The Tanner's Jack presents an attractive amber colour in the glass. The bittering hops are First Gold and Challenger, with a little Admiral also early in the copper, and more First Gold and Challenger, plus Fuggle, added late for aroma. The result is a beautifully balanced, bittersweet beer that nicely combines fat, juicy barley sugar flavours and almost liquorice-like hop notes, with a little apricot fruitiness and toffee behind. Drink it from the cask, from the bottle or, for even greater authenticity, from a tanner's jack.

Births Johann Strauss, the Younger (composer), 1825; Georges Bizet (composer), 1838; Pablo Picasso (artist), 1881

Deaths Geoffrey Chaucer (poet), 1400; Vincent Price (actor), 1993; John Peel (broadcaster), 2004

Events Battle of Agincourt, 1415; Charge of the Light Brigade during the Crimean War, 1854

Best Bitter

306

Hirter Privat Pils

Source Brauerei Hirt, Friesach **Strength** 5.2% **Website** hirterbier.at

Following the Anschluss ('union') of 1938, through which a newly fascist Austria had annexed itself to Germany, the two countries had fought side by side during World War II. With the Nazis' defeat, Austria was occupied by Allied forces, including Russia, which was keen to maintain influence in this part of central Europe. A struggle for power ensued but, with the fate of Germany dominating the talks tables, it took ten years before the future direction of Austria was finally agreed by world powers. Eventually, the Russians made a tactical, negotiated withdrawal, leaving Austria a neutral country in the western sector. Soviet forces moved out of the country in September 1955, with western troops leaving shortly afterwards. On 26 October that year, Austria was finally able to re-assert its sovereignty and the date has been marked since as the country's national day.

Today, 26 October is when shops are closed and much of the population enthusiastically takes itself off on long walks. It's become a sort of unofficial fitness day, and consequently not such a boozy occasion as the national day in other countries, but inevitably a stein or two of beer is happily tucked away, too, especially if the long country walk has built up a thirst.

Bohemian influence

Austria's beer culture has suffered in the same way as its long-hoped-for independence – overshadowed by Germany – but it broadly shares the beery preferences of its larger neighbour. You can find weissbiers and other more exotic styles, but pilsner is particularly popular, with some Austrian brewers emulating this firmly hoppy, notably bitter style that is associated with German brewing. Others take the mellower approach. Typical of this subtler attitude is Privat Pils from Hirt brewery, based in the town of Friesach, near Klagenfurt, in the southern province of Carinthia (Kärnten), which borders Slovenia and Italy.

Hirt claims to have origins back in 1270 and to be, therefore, one of the oldest breweries in Austria. As far as its main beer is concerned, it declares the influence to be Bohemia, rather than Germany, and the taste bears this out. Hirter Privat Pils has plenty of creamy, sweet, malty body, which provides a bed for a good (but not over-the-top) smack of tangy, herbal Czech Saaz and German Hallertauer Perle hops. The beer is not pasteurized, which ensures good natural flavours and none of the cooked-in staleness you often find from big brewery beers. As a result, it's a fine, refreshing beer to mark this historic day.

Births Bob Hoskins (actor), 1942; Hillary Rodham Clinton (politician), 1947; Andrew Motion (poet), 1952

Deaths King Alfred the Great, 899; William Hogarth (artist), 1764; Alma Cogan (singer), 1966

Events Football Association founded, 1863; Gunfight at the OK Corral, Tombstone, Arizona, 1881; the Beatles collect MBEs from The Queen, 1965

ABOVE: HALLSTÄTTER SEE, A POPULAR SPOT WITH AUSTRIAN OUTDOOR ENTHUSIASTS

Pilsner

Fuller's Vintage Ale

Source Fuller, Smith & Turner, Chiswick, London **Strength** 8.5% **Website** fullers.co.uk

Dates commemorated in this book relate to events with which fine beers have a connection. Today's celebration, however, ignores the outside world and confines itself purely to beer per se, marking the time of year when one of Britain's finest ales makes its annual bow. It all began In 1997 when Fuller's released the first edition of its Vintage Ale.

Vintage Ale is a bottle-conditioned version of the company's pasteurized barley wine Golden Pride. I've sampled the two 8.5% ABV beers side by side and, while I'm always impressed with the full, rich flavours of Golden Pride, the complexity and easy-drinking nature of Vintage Ale takes it into a new league. It's a brilliant example of natural conditioning in the bottle.

Vintage Ale is brewed in late spring/early summer. After primary fermentation, it spends up to eight weeks in conditioning tanks before being filtered and then reseeded with fresh Fuller's yeast. It's bottled in late June/early July and given time to settle before going on sale in the autumn (the precise date changes annually). The number of bottles available each year has varied, but it is now up to 150,000, with each one attractively packaged in an individually numbered presentation box graced with the signature of Fuller's head brewer, John Keeling.

Initially, the beer was used as a showcase for the champion strains of barley for that year, blended with award-winning hops, but that no longer applies. To celebrate the Queen's Golden Jubilee in 2002, that year's beer had a golden theme, incorporating Golden Promise malt and Golding hops. The 2007 version, in contrast, features Maris Otter pale malt and Fuggle, Target and Super Styrian hops.

Vertical tastings

To show how the ageing process has changed the character of Vintage Ale over time, Fuller's has hosted a couple of 'vertical tastings' in recent years. This involves sampling a little of each vintage. Generally, as the beer ages, it becomes a touch darker, the hop presence subsides, and fortified wine notes grow. These tastings don't quite allow precise conclusions to be drawn, because the ale's ingredients change year by year, but what they do prove is that this beer – and other similarly strong bottle-conditioned beers – can not only survive for years in bottle, but actually improve as it matures. When the first edition was released in 1997, it was given a best before date of only three years down the line. At the Fuller's most recent tasting, it was ten years old and still in fine order.

Picking out some other highlights of that ten-year tasting, the 2000, 1999 and 1998 beers were fantastic survivors. They'd become mellow, a touch drier and marginally stronger, with the yeast eating away at the sugars, but they were still beers that would grace the podium at any beer competition. Additionally, the 2002 brew had retained a deeper malt presence than other beers, and the added sweetness marked it out for me as the most complete of the selection.

What we have here, I suppose, is the ultimate rainy-day beer. It's sorely tempting to drink it all when it's fresh and exciting off the production line, but it really does pay to be prudent and tuck some bottles away for future benefit.

Births James Cook (explorer), 1728; Theodore Roosevelt (US President), 1858; John Cleese (actor and writer), 1939

Deaths James M Cain (writer), 1977; Xavier Cugat (bandleader), 1990

Events The 'Big Bang' deregulation of UK financial markets, 1986; Gerhard Schröder becomes Chancellor of Germany, 1998

Barley Wine

Van Honsebrouck Brigand

Source Van Honsebrouck, Ingelmunster **Strength** 9% **Website** vanhonsebrouck.be

The small town of Ingelmunster, just north of the Belgian city of Kortrijk, has a notable place in the history of the French Revolution. Here, the locals defiantly stood up to Napoleon and the changes he was bringing to their everyday lives. In particular, they opposed his policy of conscription into the French army.

Consider the local men's position. Being forced to fight in unwanted, far-off battles is horrific enough. Being forced to do so in the army of an oppressor is far worse. Consequently, a small war was waged by locals against the occupying forces. It was called the Farmers' War and the reluctant conscripts – or brigands, as they were labelled by the French – were at the heart of it. After various skirmishes and acts of rebellion, matters came to a head on Sunday 28 October 1798, when a band of brigands came face to face with a French infantry company that was heading from Brugge to Kortrijk. It turned out to be a bloody encounter, with dozens killed. The brigands' revolt, however, was short-lived, although Brigandszondag, or Brigands' Sunday as that fateful day has become known, is still remembered in the name of a beer from the local brewery.

Cause without a rebel

The Van Honsebrouck family started brewing here in 1900 and, in 1986, bought the town's famous 18th-century castle, as their home. The castle's roots go back even further, to the 7th century, when an abbey is believed to have stood here. Today, the Van Honsebroucks produce examples of almost every beer style for which Belgium is famous, from lambics to oak-aged fruit beers, and including strong ales under the Kasteel name. Brigand is one of their most popular beers. It used to be an amber ale but the recipe has changed in recent years and it is now a beer in the Duvel mould, although not quite as subtle.

Sitting lively and golden in the glass, it presents a spicy, bready, malty aroma laced with bitter oranges and tropical fruit. As befits a beer of 9% ABV, the taste is warming and peppery, with more bitter orange flavours but estery fruit happily kept well in check. On the whole, it's sweetish and rather perfumed, and it fills the mouth with prickly carbonation. When it comes to the finish, Brigand is bittersweet and again lightly scented, with lingering fruit and a moreish drying quality.

It's not quite what you'd call a rebel in beer terms, but it's very enjoyable nonetheless.

Births David Dimbleby (broadcaster), 1938; Hank Marvin (guitarist), 1941; Bill Gates (computer pioneer), 1955

Deaths Ted Hughes (poet), 1998; Trevor Berbick (boxer), 2006

Events The Statue of Liberty dedicated by US President Grover Cleveland, 1886; Cuban Missile Crisis ends when Russia orders withdrawal of missiles, 1962

Blonde Beer

Greene King Hen's Tooth

Source Greene King, Bury St Edmunds, Suffolk **Strength** 6.5% **Website** greeneking.co.uk

'**A**rtists in brewing' was the slogan used by the much-missed Morland Brewery in Abingdon, Oxfordshire. It was a message reinforced by colourful plaques set into the walls of Morland's many homely pubs, each depicting an artist at work, eyeing up his subject with palette and beer glass in hand. But the use of this strapline and imagery wasn't merely marketing or a fanciful boast. Not only did Morland brew some excellent beer, it also claimed a famous artist in the founding family.

George Morland was born in London in 1763, the son of painter Henry Robert Morland. It seems his talents were apparent from an early age. The gifted youngster was exhibited at the Royal Academy by the time he was ten, and seemed to have the artistic world at his feet. However, despite undertaking an apprenticeship with his father, George was never disciplined enough to exploit his skills fully. In fact, you could say that he became an artist of an altogether different sort. Although he earned considerable sums of money by selling his paintings – which were often sentimental, soft-focus images of animals, inns and other country scenes – such was his love of life that the alcoholic, womanizing Morland was perennially in debt. Tragically, it was in this impecunious state that he died on this day in 1804.

Rare survivor

The story of Morland Brewery is no happier. It was set up by John Morland, said to be a relative of George's, in the Berkshire Downs village of West Ilsley in 1711 and moved to a new site in Abingdon in 1887. There, Morland brewed until its regrettable demise in 2000, the victim of a take-over and closure by the ever-expanding Greene King. Morland's beers did not always find favour. The Original Bitter, for instance, was uncompromisingly bitter, but it had its dedicated following. For many years, the business just traded on this session beer, augmented by a dark mild and a slightly sweeter best bitter, until, in the last days of its independence, it branched out into more exotic wares. The popular bottled ale Old Speckled Hen was launched as a draught ale, with phenomenal success, and on its coat-tails Morland added a bottle-conditioned beer to its range. This was christened Hen's Tooth because, the management said, beers of such strength that were not too heavy or chewy were 'as rare as a hen's tooth'. The beer was an immediate hit, with listings in major supermarket chains. That was, undoubtedly, a factor that encouraged Greene King to keep this beer alive after the Abingdon brewery was closed.

Today Hen's Tooth is brewed at Greene King's HQ in Bury St Edmunds and then tankered to Hepworth & Co. in Horsham for the special bottling process that involves adjusting the yeast count and the amount of sugars in order to ensure a good secondary fermentation in the bottle. It's a beer with plenty of character, an appealing dark amber in colour with a fruity, malty, herbal aroma. The taste is sweet and a little nutty, loaded with ripe, juicy malt and ample Challenger and Golding hops, with another dimension added by fruity fermentation flavours like pear drops and pineapple. Multifaceted and complex, Hen's Tooth is a fine example of the brewer's art.

Births Robert Hardy (actor), 1925; Winona Ryder (actress), 1971; Michael Vaughan (cricketer), 1974

Deaths Walter Raleigh (explorer), 1618; Joseph Pulitzer (newspaper publisher), 1911; Woody Herman (jazz musician), 1987

Events John Glenn becomes the oldest man in space, aged 77, 1998; Iain Duncan Smith resigns as leader of the Conservative Party, 2003

Strong Ale

Old Chimneys Good King Henry Special Reserve

Source Old Chimneys Brewery, Market Weston, Diss, Norfolk **Strength** 11%
Website oldchimneysbrewery.com

Alan Thomson is not one to shout about his talents. At his Old Chimneys brewery, on the border of Norfolk and Suffolk, he just gets on with creating excellent ales, one of which is today's selection. It is an imperial Russian stout, aged over oak, and, even if it had no connection with our highlighted event, it would be a wonderful tipple to keep out the draughts of a cold October evening.

The name of the beer is Good King Henry Special Reserve. It sounds right royal but, in fact, is named after a vegetable. This leafy green plant is also sometimes called Lincolnshire spinach, poor man's asparagus or other names but is primarily known by its regal title. This, it seems, comes from England's own Good King Henry, who, in most critics' books, was not King Henry VIII but his father, Henry VII, the founder of the Tudor dynasty.

When Henry VII came to the throne, England was in a state of turmoil. It was the end of the Wars of the Roses, the battle for the crown between the houses of Lancaster and York that had divided the country. Henry, from the Lancaster side, may have been the victor, but he acted quickly to stabilize the situation, marrying Elizabeth of York shortly after his coronation on this day in 1485.

Anniversary brew

Henry's legacy was considerable. Not only did he quell the in-fighting, he made the country more prosperous. By taxing the barons, who had unsettled the nation, he reduced their influence and bolstered the royal coffers at the same time. He established peace with France and, by marrying his son Arthur to Catherine of Aragon, fostered good relations with Spain. On his death in 1509, the country was in decent shape.

The beer that borrows Henry's nickname was first brewed to a strength of 9.6% ABV. It wasn't aged over oak but it was still a very fine imperial stout. In 2005, however, Alan Thomson decided to create something special for the brewery's tenth anniversary and hit upon the idea of making Henry a little stouter and maturing the beer in a cask with oak granules. The beer was then given an extra 18 months to develop in the bottle before going on sale.

This stunning beer is created from pale, crystal and wheat malts, roasted barley and Fuggle and Challenger hops. It pours a near-black colour and attracts the drinker with a rich aroma of treacle and molasses, backed by oaky vanilla. In the mouth, it is full, sweet and creamy, rich in malt, vinous and warming, with a pleasant bitter balance. The finish is bittersweet, and leaves mellow caramel and roasted barley on the palate. Good King Henry Special Reserve is brewed only in small batches, but is definitely one to lay your hands on if at all possible.

Births Henry Winkler (actor), 1945; Diego Maradona (footballer), 1960; Courtney Walsh (cricketer), 1962

Deaths Henri Dunant (Red Cross founder), 1910; Andrew Bonar Law (Prime Minister), 1923; Barnes Wallace (inventor), 1979

Events Orson Welles panics America with his realistic radio broadcast of HG Wells's *War of the Worlds*, 1938; the Government announces plans to allow women to sit in the House of Lords, 1957

Imperial Stout

Moorhouse's Black Cat

Source Moorhouse's, Burnley, Lancashire **Strength** 3.4% **Website** moorhouses.co.uk

We already know, from the entry for 17 August, that the Pendle Hill area near Burnley, Lancashire, has a macabre reputation for things that go bump in the night. Local brewery Moorhouse's capitalizes on this with its strong ale called Pendle Witches Brew and builds further on the occult with another beer, this time a highly quaffable dark mild that they call Black Cat. On a day like today, when witches are said to be out and about, it's a very appropriate tipple.

Hallowe'en is derived from the ancient Celtic festival of Samhain, which marked the end of the bountiful days of harvest-time and the beginning of dark, cold, barren winter. It was the time of year, pagans believed, that evil spirits were afoot and so bonfires were lit and feasting arranged to provide last-minute cheer. The Christian church knows Hallowe'en as All Hallows Eve, the day before All Saints' Day. This, too, was originally marked with bonfires and festivities, in this case to celebrate the temporary release of penitent souls from Purgatory. The two traditions have been blended over time to create today's odd mix of fun, fear and supernatural suspicion.

Feline friend

Numerous beers have been created to cash in on this atmospheric time of year. Pitfield has brewed a Pumpkin Porter, for example, while Rogue Ales' Dead Guy Ale from Oregon has a glow-in-the-dark bottle label. None has received quite the acclaim of Moorhouse's Black Cat, however,

which is named after the witch's sinister feline friend. This beer was added to the brewery's portfolio in the late 1980s, but it wasn't an instant success. Indeed, as recently as the late 1990s, its future looked bleak. 'It nearly used up one of its lives,' the brewers once quipped. 'We were down to three barrels a week.' A major rethink was required and the solution was found by raising the alcohol a little, adding a touch more bitterness, and making the beer darker. Pale malt, mixed with a little crystal and some chocolate malt, now provides the cereal base, with a touch of torrefied wheat to develop a good head and some invert sugar. Fuggle hops supply the gentle bitterness, and a few spoonfuls of molasses enhance the taste. There may be another special ingredient in the brew, too, but the Burnley lads won't let that particular cat out of the bag. The result is a beautifully balanced beer that looks stunning in the glass and is equally delightful on the tongue – crisp, fruity, with a pleasantly dry, roasted finish with just a hint of liquorice. But you don't need to take my word for it: just look at the awards it's won, including CAMRA's supreme Champion Beer of Britain in 2000. Judges that year agreed it was a little drop of black magic.

Births John Keats (poet), 1795; Jimmy Savile (broadcaster), 1926; Peter Jackson (film director), 1961

Deaths Harry Houdini (escapologist), 1926; Federico Fellini (film director), 1993; River Phoenix (actor), 1993

Events Martin Luther nails 95 theses to the door of a Wittenberg church, thus starting the Protestant Reformation, 1517; the UK's first zebra crossing comes into use, 1951

Westvleteren 12

Source De Sint-Sixtusabdij van Westvleteren, Westvleteren **Strength** 10.2% **Website** sintsixtus.be

The Trappist monks that brew in Belgium and Holland have remarkable self-restraint. One wonders how, with so much outstanding beer wafting beneath their noses, they are not tempted to take a glass more often but, in most of the seven monasteries that comprise this select group, the brothers tend to reserve their beer allowance for high days and holidays. It is to be hoped that 1 November, being All Saints' Day, gives them a very good reason for lifting the cap off one of their wondrous beers.

This day of the year was set aside by Pope Gregory IV in 837 for the remembrance of all the saints and martyrs in the history of Christianity. In firmly Catholic countries, the day is well observed, with families making pilgrimages to their loved ones' tombs. The day after All Saints' Day is designated All Souls' Day. This is when attention turns from the already blessed to those who have departed and may still be in need of assistance on the road to Heaven. It's all part of the tradition of praying for souls trapped in Purgatory, the place between Hell and Heaven where lesser sinners do penance while awaiting admission to Paradise. The prayers of the living can help these stranded souls climb the ladder.

Rare treat

The beer selected for today is appropriately religious. It comes from the smallest Trappist brotherhood, at the abbey of Saint Sixtus at Westvleteren, not far from Ypres and its sombre World War I battlefields. In the 1940s, the brothers entered into an arrangement to have their beers also brewed by a commercial brewery now known as St Bernardus (see 20 August). However, when the licence expired in 1992, brewing was brought back wholly into the abbey. The downside is that brewing capacity is obviously less than before, and supplies to the outside world are strictly rationed. You can buy it by the case from the abbey itself (when supplies are available), and also in the café/visitor centre across the road. Otherwise, you're in the hands of those who have queued up themselves to acquire the beer and have managed to put some on wider sale.

On the plus side, when you do have the opportunity to lay hands on a bottle of Westvleteren beer, you know you have to appreciate it as a rare treat, and a special day in the religious calendar would seem like just the occasion to do that.

The Westveleren monks produce three beers, each identified by a number. The one chosen for today is the top of the range, number 12, and is also known as Abt, or Abbot. It comes with a yellow cap but no label, and was voted by the ratebeer.com website as the 'best beer in the world' in 2005. It's hard to argue with

that finding. Here we have a full-bodied ale of 10.2% ABV, a nourishing combination of malts, sugars and hops that demands respect from the first sip. The ruby colour results only from the inclusion of dark candy sugar; there are no dark malts used. The aroma has malt and a rhubarb-like tartness. On the palate, the malty flavours, dried fruit and delicate spice are well supported by creamy nut and herbs, before a drying, malty and herbal finish that starts bittersweet and gradually becomes more bitter. But this is a beer not to be judged with one sip, or perhaps even one bottle: it's that complex. How the monks manage to keep their distance is beyond me.

Births LS Lowry (artist), 1887; Gary Player (golfer), 1935; Mark Hughes (footballer and manager), 1963

Deaths Ezra Pound (poet), 1972; King Vidor (film director), 1982; Phil Silvers (actor and comedian), 1985

Events The first Premium Bonds go on sale in the UK, 1956; S4C, Channel 4 for Wales, begins broadcasting, 1982

Trappist Ale

Mauldons Black Adder

Source Mauldons, Sudbury, Suffolk **Strength** 5.3% **Website** mauldons.co.uk

Champion namesake

There is a beer called Black Adder. It first appeared in 1988, when the series was in its prime, although its creators at Mauldons brewery in Sudbury, Suffolk, have since claimed that the beer was actually named after a local vicar. Whatever the origin, it's certainly a fitting name for a beer that is both dark and has an alcoholic bite.

Mauldons has changed hands in recent years, and moved to a new, larger brewery, but Black Adder is central to the image of the business, thanks to the day in 1991 when it claimed CAMRA's top beer accolade – Champion Beer of Britain.

Brewed from pale, crystal and black malts, and dosed with Fuggle hops, the near-black ale features coffeeish dark malt in the aroma, followed by a complex taste of mellow dark malt and chocolate, before an increasingly bitter, roasted grain finish. It's been described as a stout, but it could easily be classed as a strong mild. Either way, it's a supremely easy-to-drink beer that consistently proves that there's more to it than a gimmicky name.

When it began in 1983, *The Black Adder* (sic) was not a success. Richard Curtis and Rowan Atkinson's period sitcom, set during the Wars of the Roses and featuring a cringing, devious but feeble-minded duke played by Atkinson, failed to attract the size of audience to justify its BBC budget. But, somehow, the series was given a reprieve. Ben Elton replaced Atkinson as writer, leaving the latter free to provide some of his most memorable comedy performances in front of the camera, and the action moved indoors to studio sets where costs could be kept under closer scrutiny. The new combination was a winner. Set in the Tudor age, it saw a descendant of the original duke, one Edmund Blackadder, a weasely, ruthless sycophant in the court of Queen Elizabeth, being hindered and frustrated by his dozy manservant Baldrick, played by Tony Robinson.

Thus the premise had been set for future manifestations of Blackadder the blackguard, and the next series saw a further descendant fight the same battles for social standing and wealth, this time in the Georgian era. For its final series, *Blackadder* was taken to the trenches of World War I, with survival the main priority for the scheming lead man. It was a brave setting for a comedy, perhaps taking courage from the success of *M*A*S*H*, which found laughs amid the blood and guts of the Korean War. Wisely, the writers trod a fine line, never belittling the courageous men sacrificed to the mud and gore of the front line, and instead taking the rise out of the public school imbeciles who barked out insane orders from the comfort of the rear. When the final episode went out, on this day in 1989, the producers had one final tribute to pay. As Blackadder and his close colleagues reluctantly went over the top to what they knew was instant death, the action was frozen and subtly over-faded with a field of red poppies. It was as if to say, we've had a laugh but we always knew who the heroes were.

Births Daniel Boone (frontiersman), 1734; Marie Antoinette (Queen of France), 1755; kd lang (singer-songwriter), 1961

Deaths George Bernard Shaw (writer), 1950; Hal Roach (film producer and director), 1992; Eva Cassidy (singer), 1996

Events The BBC launches the world's first regular high-definition television service, 1936; M1 motorway officially opened, 1959; Channel 4 takes to the air, 1982

Stout

ABOVE: TONY ROBINSON AND ROWAN ATKINSON AS BALDRICK AND BLACKADDER IN *BLACKADDER GOES FORTH*

Harviestoun Old Engine Oil

Source Harviestoun Brewery, Alva, Clackmannanshire **Strength** 6% **Website** harviestounbrewery.co.uk

For a country still crippled by the debts of the post-war years, 3 November 1975 was a red letter day. Britain, dogged by inflation, industrial disputes and international creditors, was given a chance to build a new financial footing in the 1970s when oil was struck in the North Sea, and it was on this day that the first pipeline to bring in the bounty was officially opened.

At a lavish ceremony held in the small town of Dyce, on the outskirts of Aberdeen, The Queen pressed a button to send the first wave of black gold rushing down a 209-km (130-mile) BP line that connected the Forties oilfield to the refineries at Grangemouth, via the appropriately named Cruden Bay. While the British oil legacy was never large enough to allow the country to challenge the supremacy of major oil producing nations, it nevertheless boosted the UK's finances substantially, for which governments of all political shades rendered a hearty thanks. Britain even became a net oil and gas exporter. North Sea output began a slow decline in 2001 but reserves should yield some value to the British economy for decades to come.

Today, there's another kind of viscous liquid flowing out of Scotland, precious in its own way. It's a beer called, somewhat unflatteringly, Old Engine Oil from the Harviestoun Brewery in Alva, near Stirling. Harviestoun was founded in 1985 by former Ford motor company executive Ken Brooker. He sold the business to Caledonian in 2006 but secured some major triumphs in his time at the brewery, including CAMRA's Champion Beer of Britain title with his hoppy session ale Bitter & Twisted.

Rising to the challenge

Ken was also highly successful in the Tesco Beer Challenge, a competition that aimed to find new beers for the supermarket giant to stock. One year, Ken took up the challenge to create a new winter beer and conjured up a deep ruby-brown old ale that reminded him in appearance of the sort of lubricants he worked with during his Dagenham days. So Old Engine Oil he called it. The beer won, of course, and the name stuck, although not really doing justice to the beer inside the bottle, which has a biscuity roasted barley aroma and a rich, sweet taste laced with roasted grains. There's an airy texture in the mouth and an appropriately oily slickness, thanks in part to the inclusion of malted oats in the mash tun, while four different types of hops – Galena and Willamette from the US and Fuggle and Golding from the UK – provide a subtle balance without ever trying to steal the show. It all wraps up with a drying, chocolaty finish, making this a perfect after-dinner beer, or one to try with puddings. Harviestoun has also released versions of Old Engine Oil aged in whisky casks and named Ola Dubh. In motoring terms, it's simply sump-tuous.

Births Jeremy Brett (actor), 1933; Lulu (pop singer), 1948; Larry Holmes (boxer), 1949

Deaths Annie Oakley (sharpshooter), 1926; Henri Matisse (artist), 1954; Lonnie Donegan (skiffle musician), 2002

Events The first Act of Supremacy sees Henry VIII become head of the English Church, 1534; the first animal, a dog named Laika, launched into space, 1957

Old Ale

Baltika No. 4

Source Baltika, St Petersburg **Strength** 5.6% **Website** baltikabeer.com

Russia's Unity Day is the newest public holiday featured in this book. It was only inaugurated in 2005 but one already wonders how long it may continue, given its rather inauspicious start.

The Russian government created Unity Day ostensibly as a means of bringing the people of the country together. Its origins, they claimed, date back to the year 1612, when Russians of all backgrounds banded together to drive out the Polish army, which had captured Moscow. Those were dark years in Russia, and the expulsion of the invaders was a turning point in bringing back better times.

Much of the action in 1612 seems to have taken place at the end of October, so quite why 4 November was ever chosen to mark this feat remains a mystery. Indeed, historians have gone on record to state that 4 November has no significance whatsoever. The key point seems to be that the new public holiday replaced another holiday on 7 November that celebrated the Bolshevik Revolution – the authorities wanted to extract Communist associations from this time of year but didn't want to deprive the people of their day off work. But when the first Unity Day approached, it seemed the people didn't really care what the celebration was all about, as long as they didn't have to go to their offices or factories.

Vienna original

Unfortunately, in the years since its inauguration, Unity Day has become an ideal opportunity for radical groups to protest, with immigrants a popular target. Marches and rallies held by racists, anti-Semites and ultra-nationalists have drawn criticism from the likes of Amnesty International, and Unity Day has turned into a public soapbox of a rather distasteful kind.

One thing that does bring people together, though, is a glass of beer, and if you fancy uniting with the more tolerant people of Russia today, I can recommend a beer from the Baltika brewery. As discussed in the entry for 9 February, this modern brewing group is part of Baltic Beverages Holding, a division of Carlsberg. They have driven forward exports of beer from Russia, with Baltika No. 3 Classic the market leader. One stop up in the Baltika numbered range is No. 4 Original, a red-coloured beer, created in 1994. It is brewed using pale and caramel malts, as well as malted rye, at the company's St Petersburg brewery. It is seasoned with Magnum hops and weighs in at 5.6% ABV.

No. 4 is an extremely enjoyable lager in the Vienna style, with an aroma that is malty and creamy, smoky and toffeeish. There's more smoky malt and toffee in the complex taste, along with gentle raisin and sultana notes and some chocolate. The finish is dry, malty, smoky, softly chocolaty and gently bitter, with a developing tang of hops. In short, it's a fine autumnal beer, in both colour and character.

Births Walter Cronkite (journalist), 1916; Freddy Heineken (brewery executive), 1923; Loretta Swit (actress), 1937

Deaths Felix Mendelssohn (composer), 1847; Wilfred Owen (poet), 1918; Malcolm Marshall (cricketer), 1999

Events Floods devastate the Italian city of Florence, 1966; Ronald Reagan elected US President, 1980

Vienna-style Lager

Harvey's Bonfire Boy

Source Harvey & Son, Lewes, East Sussex **Strength** 5.8% **Website** harveysonline.co.uk

The story behind the infamous Gunpowder Plot needs little explanation here. The tale of how a group of Catholic conspirators tried to blow up the Houses of Parliament during their state opening by the religiously suppressive King James I has been well aired, and with it the tale of Guido 'Guy' Fawkes, who was caught red-handed with the explosives. Imprisoned in the Tower of London, Fawkes was tortured into confession and into revealing the names of his accomplices, who were hastily rounded up and paid the price for their subversion with some brutal executions. Fawkes himself was hanged, drawn and quartered. When bonfire celebrations began a year later, on the orders of King James, it was an effigy of the Pope that sat atop the rising flames. Since the 19th century, the Pope has been tactfully replaced with a dummy of Fawkes.

Sussex celebrations

There is nowhere in Britain where bonfire celebrations are more elaborate than at Lewes in East Sussex. This historic market town has been marking the foiling of the Gunpowder Plot for more than 150 years in dramatic style, and still burns an effigy of 16th-century Pope Paul V alongside the familiar 'guy'. Six bonfire societies host the event, arranging barrel racing down the high street, torch-lit, costumed processions and a flurry of fizz-bang fireworks. It's become quite a privilege to witness the event, as the town is closed off for the day, and public transport and parking are at a premium. Indeed, visitors are often advised to stay away.

Marking the event is a beer from the town's brewery. Harvey's is even more a part of Lewes than the bonfire celebrations, having been based here, alongside the River Ouse, since 1790. Its Bonfire Boy is a strong, malty, warming ale that really hits the spot at this time of year. It is brewed from a grist of Maris Otter pale malt, crystal malt and black malt, with four types of hops – Fuggle, Golding, Progress and Bramling Cross – for balance. Its amber-ruby hue reflects the colour of a November sky licked by angry flames, and the abundant malt shows its presence in a sugary sweet taste balanced by the bitter, smoky notes of roasted grain. To add a further dimension, zesty orange notes bounce around the palate, dodging light alcohol vapours like a jumping jack, and there are pruney dried fruit notes, too. When it comes to the finish, the sweetness persists but hops fight their way through as the beer begins to dry. With such a complex blend of sweet and smoky flavours, it's not surprising to learn that Bonfire Boy was voted The Ultimate BBQ Beer in the 2002 Beauty of Hops awards.

Available both in bottle and on draught, the beer also has a poignancy for the brewery itself. In July 1996, Harvey's was very nearly consumed by fire, and its shop and offices were destroyed. As a tribute to the emergency services who saved the site, Bonfire Boy – originally named Firecracker – was added to the company's range of seasonal beers.

Births Roy Rogers (actor and singer), 1911; Lester Piggott (jockey), 1935; Art Garfunkel (singer), 1941

Deaths Mack Sennett (film director and producer), 1960; Jacques Tati (actor and film director), 1982; Robert Maxwell (newspaper magnate), 1991

Events Britain and France defeat Russia at the Crimean Battle of Inkerman, 1854; George Foreman becomes the oldest world heavyweight boxing champion, 1994

Strong Ale

Caracole Saxo

Source Brasserie Caracole, Falmignoul **Strength** 7.5% **Website** brasserie-caracole.be

To the list of famous Belgians we can add Antoine Joseph Sax – Adolphe to his friends. This is the man who invented an instrument that changed the sound of brass music, the man without whom jazz and rock 'n' roll would never have sounded the same.

Sax was born on this day in 1814 in the town of Dinant. The son of a musical instrument maker, he started developing new instruments himself at an early age. One of his first successes was the bass clarinet, which, up to that point, had existed only in very unreliable forms. He then moved to Paris, where his glory years were to ensue, as he worked on new forms of brass instruments and, ultimately, developed his range of what became known as saxophones. These were horns that combined the reedy tone of a woodwind instrument with the power of the brass section, features that collectively produced a sound that was previously unheard in orchestral circles – except, perhaps, when the entire wind section had been out for a few pints and a curry the night before.

Jazz greats

Strangely, even though a composer as illustrious as Hector Berlioz sang the new instrument's praises, it never really caught on for orchestral work. Instead, the saxophone found its métier later, in the worlds of jazz and big band, when, in the hands of such greats as Woody Herman, Stan Getz and John Coltrane, its vibrant, rasping tones engaged a new generation of music lovers. It was the same story in the 1950s, when the backing groups of the great rock 'n' roll singers relied heavily on blasts of Sax's robust creation for their depth of sound. Phil Spector blew it on into the 1960s and since then the sax has retained a mesmeric hold on popular music.

But while the saxophone remains one of the coolest instruments to play, its creator has been somewhat forgotten in recent times. He died in 1894 in poverty. Even though he had patented his designs, commercially they weren't a success, as other instrument makers muscled in on his work. His memory has gradually slipped from public consciousness, which is why it's good to welcome to this book a beer simply called Saxo, brewed by the Caracole brewery, which is based not far from where the inventor was born. More about the brewery can be read in the entry for 2 July.

Saxo is a strong, satisfying golden ale, first produced in 1992 but renamed a year later in honour of Monsieur Sax. The malt used is pilsner with a little wheat also in the mash. In the copper, the hops are Saaz, and there's also a little pinch of coriander. The aroma is packed with estery fruit notes – lemon, melon and pineapple – with a typically Belgian yeasty spiciness for contrast. In the mouth, it is bittersweet and ultra-smooth, loaded with fruit and balanced by a clove-like, herbal bitterness that has a snatch of coriander. The finish is bittersweet and slightly chewy, but with fruit and cloves lingering very pleasantly. The beer is also available in an organic version – look for the word 'Bio' on the label.

Births John Philip Sousa (composer), 1854; Frank Carson (comedian), 1926; Nigel Havers (actor), 1949

Deaths Pyotr Ilyich Tchaikovsky (composer), 1893; Fred Dibnah (steeplejack), 2004; Hilda Braid (actress), 2007

Events Abraham Lincoln becomes US President, 1860; Australian voters reject a proposal for the country to become a republic, 1999

Spiced Ale

Kaltenberg König Ludwig Dunkel

Source König Ludwig Schlossbraueri, Kaltenberg **Strength** 5.1% **Website** kaltenberg.de

There aren't many breweries run by a prince. In fact, there's probably only one: Kaltenberg. In charge of this internationally known Bavarian business is His Royal Highness Prince Luitpold, a softly spoken, intelligent man who lives in a fairy-tale castle. It sounds like a romantic and soft lifestyle, but the castle is also one of the brewery sites, and Luitpold is no pampered figurehead. The days of royalty are long gone in Bavaria, and Luitpold, like most of us, works for a living.

Kaltenberg's home is a 17th-century construction, on the site of earlier castles, close to the town of Geltendorf, some 48km (30 miles) west of Munich. Remodelled in neo-Gothic fashion in the 19th century, it's quite a complex today, with a restaurant, pub, beer garden, gift shop and function rooms. It even has a stadium where, for three weekends every July, a medieval jousting tournament attracts thousands of visitors (see 12 July).

This was where Prince Luitpold grew up, long after his ancestors had given up their throne. That happened at the end of World War I – indeed, on this day in 1918, when the last king, Ludwig III, fled Munich in the face of popular unrest – but the family still hold titles and, whatever the problems of the past, are well regarded by their fellow citizens.

Dark arts

Luitpold is a great grandson of that last king, and he's been running the brewery since the mid-1970s. At the time, the business had begun to stagnate. From success in the 1960s, it seems that Kaltenberg lost the plot with the changing times of the new decade. Luitpold's solution, unusually, was to take a step backwards. While other brewers were heavily promoting pils or hell (standard Bavarian lager), his plan was to specialize and move strongly into dark lager, the beer that used to command the largest volumes way back in the 1920s. Thus Kaltenberg developed the König Ludwig (King Ludwig) Dunkel brand, building on the royal name and tradition. Today, it is the biggest selling dark beer in Germany, and enjoys a 50 per cent market share in dark beer in Bavaria.

König Ludwig is a fascinating red-coloured beer made from Munich malt, pilsner malt and a touch of roasted barley. It's hopped with Hallertauer Magnum and Tradition hops, and relishes four weeks of conditioning in the chilly cellars beneath the famous castle. Interestingly, the brewery also adds a second yeast culture that brings a slightly sour, lactic edge to balance out the sweetness of the malt.

From all of the above, you'll gather that this is quite a complex dark lager. It begins with the slightly sour, creamy and smoky aroma of dark malt. These malt flavours go on to dominate the taste, with a little peppery warmth, some dried fruit and hints of chocolate throughout. Roasted grain pushes through in the finish and a hoppy dryness lingers.

The monarchy may no longer exist but you can still drink royally in Bavaria.

Births Marie Curie (scientist), 1867; Billy Graham (evangelist), 1918; Joni Mitchell (singer-songwriter), 1943

Deaths Gene Tunney (boxer), 1978; Steve McQueen (actor), 1980; Howard Keel (actor), 2004

Events Disputed US Presidential election sees George W Bush claim victory, 2000; Belgium's Sabena Airlines goes bust, 2001

Dark Lager

Augustiner Edelstoff

Source Augustiner-Bräu Wagner KG, Munich **Strength** 5.6% **Website** augustiner-braeu.de

The story of Adolf Hitler's meteoric rise to power in 1920s Germany is punctuated by numerous events that took place in the beer halls of Munich. One of these has its anniversary today, an occasion that so nearly saw Hitler's career ended as swiftly as it had begun.

Hitler had served in the Bavarian army during World War I and was appalled at the 'dishonour' that had been brought on the German nation through the Treaty of Versailles. Taking this and similar disillusionments in German society, he cleverly whipped up support for a new political party, the National Socialist Workers' Party, or Nazis, as members became known. Although this had only been founded in 1919, by 1923 Hitler erroneously believed he had the groundswell of support to challenge for power. Bursting into a political meeting at the Bürgerbräu Keller beer hall in Munich, Hitler's army of thugs took senior Bavarian ministers hostage and placed their deluded leader in charge. The next day, the Nazis looked to build on their success with plans to advance on the German national government in Berlin. They marched through the Munich streets, but were intercepted by police still loyal to the elected government. A stand-off ensued, shots were fired and Hitler fled the scene. Most of his supporters followed and the beer hall putsch, as it has become known, was over.

Hitler's career should have ended there and then, and we could have heartily raised a glass to celebrate this swift demise, but he was allowed to turn his subsequent trial into a political showcase. When he was found guilty, his sympathetic jailers gave him only five years. In the end, he spent only a matter of months behind bars, just long enough to write his personal political manifesto, *Mein Kampf*, and set the scene for a rapid return to frontline politics on his release, with brutal consequences that need no further explanation here.

Precious substance

The Bürgerbräu Keller no longer exists. It was badly damaged by a bomb intended for Hitler in 1939. Although it was rebuilt, it was eventually demolished in the post-war years. Thankfully, numerous beer halls in the city have survived and are worth celebrating as beacons of conviviality, despite their chequered history. Pour yourself a glass of an authentic Bavarian beer and imagine yourself ensconced in the sociable glow of one of these beery wonders, with their long tables, hearty food and boisterous company.

One of the best, centrally located halls is owned by the Augustiner Brewery. Augustiner Hell is featured for 28 August, but another from the range would go down rather well today, especially with its extra little bit of warming strength as autumn grows cooler. The beer is called Edelstoff, and it's in a style that the Germans call export, which means it's fuller than a hell lager but is by no means as hoppy as a pils. Such technicalities are beautifully illustrated

in Edelstoff, which is full-bodied and sweet with just a counterbalance of hops that add a lemony sharpness before a bittersweet, drying and hoppy finish. Appropriately the name translates as 'precious substance'.

Births Margaret Mitchell (writer), 1900; Ken Dodd (comedian), 1927; Richard Curtis (screenwriter), 1956; Brett Lee (cricketer), 1976

Deaths John Milton (poet), 1674; 'Doc' Holliday (gunfighter), 1887

Events The Louvre museum opens in Paris, 1793; Wilhelm Röntgen discovers x-rays, 1895; *Rupert Bear* cartoon first appears in the *Daily Express*, 1920

Pale Lager

ABOVE: ADOLF HITLER WITH MUSSOLINI

Otley O8

Source Otley Brewing Company, Pontypridd, Glamorgan **Strength** 8% **Website** otleybrewing.co.uk

Has there ever been a better description of the joys of drinking beer than that delivered by Dylan Thomas in his short story *Old Garbo*? You can almost savour the ale with him as he revels in the glory of a good pint.

'I liked the taste of the beer,' he says, 'its live, white lather, its brass-bright depth, the sudden world through the wet brown walls of the glass, the tilted rush to the lips and the slow swallowing down to the lapping belly, the salt on the tongue, the foam at the corners.'

Sadly, those who have to point fingers will say that Thomas enjoyed too much of a good thing, that beer was his downfall. It's true that alcohol did play a large part in his early demise – he was just 39 when a drinking spree in New York led to his collapse – but the finger should perhaps be more pertinently pointed at spirits, rather than the beer he had supped – in both moderation and excess – over the course of his short but flamboyant life.

Thomas was born in Swansea in 1914. He was educated at Swansea Grammar School where his dad was an English teacher, and he followed his schooling with a brief sojourn in local journalism. His first book of poetry was published in 1934, and he headed for London in the same year, beginning work for the BBC as a writer of documentaries. Vibrant prose and dramatic works ensued, as did performances in front of the microphone as a radio actor, and a pint glass was rarely far from his lips. From first-hand accounts, Thomas was a showman, taking advantage of the glow gleaned from a few beers to warm to his pub audience. As in his poetry and prose, he always entertained and inspired with the colour of his wit and verbal ostentation.

Poetic justice

If the life of someone so naturally gifted is to be toasted, it cannot be with anything other than beer, and good beer at that. A Welsh beer would be even more appropriate, which is why today's bibulous offering is a former CAMRA Champion Beer of Wales. It's not a beer that Thomas ever had the chance to drink – the brewery wasn't even founded until 52 years after his death – but it's one you can't help feeling would find favour in his eager hands.

The Otley Brewery has its roots in a pub called The Otley Arms at Treforest, near Pontypridd. The business began with Alf Otley, who entered the pub trade in the 1950s. His family still runs The Otley Arms and, between various members of the clan, now operates two other pubs in the area as well. In 2005, they decided to start making beer, too.

All of the names of the beers trade on the letter O, for Otley. They include O1, a pale golden bitter, and Dark-O, a mild. The star of the show, however, is O8, which in November 2006 claimed the Champion Beer of Wales crown. It's a fruity, 8% barley wine, packing sweet sultana and earthy hop resin flavours, with a lingering orange note in the finish, courtesy of Progress and Bramling Cross hops.

I can't get anywhere close to the poetry in Dylan Thomas's words when it comes to describing such a beer, so I'll leave you to seek out a pint or a bottle and let the muse of beer speak for itself.

Births King Edward VII, 1841; Tom Weiskopf (golfer), 1942; Bryn Terfel (opera singer), 1965

Deaths James Ramsay MacDonald (Prime Minister), 1937; Neville Chamberlain (Prime Minister), 1940; Charles de Gaulle (President of France), 1970

Events Medici family rule in Florence comes to an end, 1494; capital punishment abolished in the UK, 1965; first edition of *Rolling Stone* magazine, 1967

Barley Wine

Fuller's 1845

Source Fuller, Smith & Turner, Chiswick, London   **Strength** 6.3%   **Website** fullers.co.uk

In the small park in the middle of London's Leicester Square, there's a bust on display of William Hogarth, celebrated 17th-century artist. Hogarth used to live in this area but it's easy to overlook the monument unless you know it's there. Further west in London, there's a memorial to the painter that's less easy to ignore. Just try leaving the city on the A4. When you reach Chiswick, you'll have to negotiate the notoriously busy Hogarth Roundabout. It's not a particularly eye-pleasing tribute to the great man, but it certainly keeps his name alive.

This major traffic intersection owes its dedication to Hogarth to the fact that, when tired of life in the centre of London, the artist decamped to Chiswick. Hogarth was born in London on 10 November 1697, and his first work was as an engraver for books and other printed materials. He progressed into portrait painting, but then took the road into satire. His most memorable works appear today almost like early cartoons, the subject matter being the ridiculous and troubling things he spotted in everyday life. *A Harlot's Progress* is a sad reflection on the life of a country girl who turns to prostitution in the city; its counterbalance is *A Rake's Progress*, revealing the ultimate misery of a wealthy young man who blows his inheritance and his health on a diet of drink and women. Hogarth's most stinging attacks, however, came upon gin, the prevalent drink of the working classes. Not for nothing has this spirit acquired the nickname of 'mother's

ruin': one glance at the chaotically colourful painting Hogarth entitled *Gin Lane* reveals how much harm this poison was doing to contemporary British life. In contrast, his *Beer Street* offers a much rosier perspective on society. Here, people are drinking beer, and they are happy, healthy and industrious. Thus we can celebrate Hogarth as an early promoter of the great long drink that many of us love and responsibly enjoy.

Historic re-creation

Hogarth died in 1764 and is buried in a Chiswick graveyard. It would be wonderful to pick up a beer named in his honour but, strangely, there isn't one currently around. The next best thing is to return to the Hogarth Roundabout, the area where he spent his last years. Alongside the dual carriageway there stands the Griffin Brewery, home these days of Fuller's. Beer has been brewed here since the 16th century, so it's likely that Hogarth supped a pint or two of its output in his time. Fuller, Smith & Turner took over in 1845, a fact that is celebrated in the name of one of its most popular beers.

1845 is a strong, dark ale that was first created in 1995, to mark 150 years of the Fuller's business. Head brewer Reg Drury aimed to re-create the sort of beer that would have been drunk in those Victorian times and so included amber malt in the mash tun, along with pale and crystal malts. The hops he selected were Goldings. Enjoying a thorough secondary fermentation in the bottle, 1845 offers

a fruity, malty nose, balanced by hints of sherry and hop. The taste is also malty and fruity, but quickly tempered by hop bitterness, before a dry, malty, hoppy and almost liquorice-like, bitter finish. It is truly complex and even if Hogarth never drank a beer exactly like this, it's a brew of which he would have surely approved.

Births Oliver Goldsmith (writer), 1728; Richard Burton (actor), 1925; Tim Rice (lyricist), 1944

Deaths Arthur Rimbaud (poet), 1891; Leonid Brezhnev (politician), 1982; Ken Kesey (writer), 2001

Events Stanley meets Livingstone, 1871; Hirohito becomes Emperor of Japan, 1928; first edition of *Sesame Street* broadcast in the US, 1969

Strong Ale

Pilsner Urquell

Source Plzensky Prazdroj, Pilsen **Strength** 4.4% **Website** pilsner-urquell.com

There have been few more significant days in the history of beer production than 11 November 1842, the day that pilsner was born.

The name pilsner comes from the German term meaning 'from Pilsen', referring to the town in the Czech Republic, 96km (60 miles) southwest of Prague. It was here that a beer revolution took place when the world's first golden lager was produced. The story begins with the independent brewers of Pilsen – some 250 of them. There was no major brewing business in town: licences were simply issued to individuals to brew beer on a small scale. This meant that beer locally was often dearer than beer imported from other areas because there were no economies of scale. It also meant that there was often bad beer. In short, beer in Pilsen was poor and expensive.

The answer lay, it was agreed, in brewers banding together to set up a new town brewery, from which they would all benefit as shareholders. In 1839, work began on the site, and the brewery was finally commissioned in autumn 1842. In search of a brewmaster, officials employed a brewer from Vilshofen in Bavaria named Josef Groll. Groll was in his late twenties and a notably gruff, rude man, but he knew his stuff. Given free rein, he set about creating Pilsen's new beer, abandoning the town's tradition of brewing top-fermenting dark ales and importing a Bavarian technique he had learned for bottom fermentation, with beers conditioned at low temperatures for several weeks. Crucially, he brought with him a strain of yeast that allowed this method of fermentation to take place, and also the idea of using paler-coloured malts that had recently been made available through the advances of the Industrial Revolution. On 11 November, the beer was deemed ready for sale. Locals were astonished. Gone were the opaque, chewy ales they had grown up with; in their place, a crisp, soft-textured, bittersweet, hoppy and highly refreshing golden beer that immediately won them over.

Lasting legacy

Groll was brewmaster in Pilsen for only three years, but his legacy was immediate. Word of this wondrous new golden beer spread rapidly across Europe. Copies were made and pilsner became all the rage. Its expansion has hardly slowed since, and it's the dominant beer style of the world today, even if many of the beers that claim to be pilsners have little in common with Groll's invention, apart from colour.

The beer that Groll created is still sold today. Its name is Pilsner Urquell, which means 'original source pilsner'. The brewery still stands, too, although it is now owned by the international group SABMiller. However, the way the beer has been produced has changed somewhat in recent decades, with the old conditioning cellars beneath the brewery, where the beer used to age in wood for two or three months, now rendered redundant by less romantic stainless steel tanks up above.

Conditioning is now down to around 30 days. 'We have better control and we don't need longer,' is the word from the brewers, but traditionalists disagree. The beer was better, they say, when it was given time to express itself. It was less bitter, not so dry and had more malty complexity.

Pilsner Urquell is still a fine beer nonetheless, rich in buttery malt and vanilla flavours and offset beautifully by the herbal tang of local Saaz hops. It's easy to see how, when all was dark and depressing, this ray of sunshine changed the world.

Births Fyodor Dostoyevsky (writer), 1821; June Whitfield (actress), 1925; Asafa Powell (athlete), 1982

Deaths Ned Kelly (outlaw), 1880; Jerome Kern (songwriter), 1945; Yasser Arafat (Palestinian leader), 2004

Events Armistice signed to end World War I, 1918; first edition of *Panorama* broadcast, 1953; Rhodesia declares itself independent of Britain, 1965

Pilsner

Batemans Dark Lord

Source Batemans Brewery, Wainfleet, Lincolnshire **Strength** 5% **Website** bateman.co.uk

Known widely as 'Black Tom' because of his dark complexion, Thomas Fairfax was one of the most skilful commanders of the English Civil War. He was born near Otley, Yorkshire, in 1612 and in his early years was a keen supporter of King Charles I. Indeed, after studying at Cambridge University, he served with the king's forces, and was knighted for his services. But Fairfax also believed in the power of Parliament and when civil war broke out, unlike most of his Yorkshire associates, he joined the side fighting against the king.

He proved to be a shrewd commander, playing a significant part in victories at Gainsborough, Nantwich, Selby and Marston Moor. When Parliament developed a new highly organized army in 1645, it was Fairfax who was placed in charge. The New Model Army, as it was called, never lost a single battle with Black Tom at its helm (see 10 July). Eventually, however, Fairfax could not reconcile his political views with his respect for royalty. He opposed the execution of King Charles I and, when he was asked to lead an attack against the Scots who had rallied to the cause of King Charles II, he refused, and stepped away from the action. After supporting the restoration of the monarchy, he retired from public life and died on this day in 1671.

Winceby winner

Fairfax is remembered in the name of a rich, ruby ale from Batemans in Wainfleet. It's called Dark Lord in his honour, and features his image on the label. The beer links to the Battle of Winceby that took place close to the Royalist stronghold of Bolingbroke Castle, Lincolnshire, in October 1643. It was a battle that lasted minutes rather than hours but it ended conclusively in favour of the Parliamentarians and helped destroy the Royalist hold on the county. Significantly, it was during this battle that Fairfax first teamed up with a rising Parliamentarian officer named Oliver Cromwell.

Dark Lord is a porter, brewed using a high proportion of crystal malt alongside pale malt and roasted barley, with hop character added through Goldings and Challengers. The aroma is creamy and malty, laced with caramel and raisins, with plain chocolate pushing through and a hint of liquorice emerging, too. The same creamy richness dominates the palate, with a silky-smooth chocolate flavour leading the way, rounding off dry, bitter, malty and increasingly hoppy. According to Batemans, it's the sort of beer that was 'drunk in the local taverns by knighted gentry celebrating their victories'. But I think today will do just as well.

Births Auguste Rodin (sculptor), 1840; Grace Kelly (actress), 1929; Neil Young (rock musician), 1945

Deaths King Cnut, 1035; Elizabeth Gaskell (writer), 1865; Percival Lowell (astronomer), 1916

Events Yuri Andropov succeeds Leonid Brezhnev as General Secretary of the Soviet Communist Party, 1983; first episode of *Absolutely Fabulous* broadcast, 1992

Porter

Williams Bros Fraoch

Source Williams Bros Brewing Co., Alloa, Clackmannanshire **Strength** 5% **Website** fraoch.com

In 1986, home-brewing supplier Bruce Williams was handed a translation of a 16th-century Gaelic recipe for beer. This simple transaction was to change his life. The recipe was for heather ale, a long-forgotten brew spiced with the flowers of wild Scottish heather, the sort of beer that had once been enjoyed by the Picts who inhabited this part of Britain.

With the arrival of hops into brewing, the use of such ingredients as wild herbs and flowers fell away, and heather ale disappeared from sight – if not from memory, as can be seen in a poem by Robert Louis Stevenson, who was born in Edinburgh on this day in 1850.

Stevenson was a sickly child and his health failed to improve as he grew up. He was expected to follow his father into the engineering trade but he was forced to give up his studies and turn to law instead. Literature was his first love, however, and while travelling the world in search of a climate that would be beneficial to his health, he expanded his writing work that was later to culminate in classic novels such as *Treasure Island*, *Kidnapped* and *The Strange Case of Dr Jekyll and Mr Hyde*. His poetry was less celebrated but, as mentioned above, it does have a relevance for today's choice of beer.

Tale of torture

In his *c.*1880 work *Heather Ale: A Galloway Legend*, Stevenson weaves a tale of a warrior king who so much wanted to taste this fabled drink that he tortured two Pictish dwarfs in order to obtain the recipe. He was outsmarted, however, by his victims, who took the secret with them to the grave.

From the bonny bells of heather
They brewed a drink long-syne,
Was sweeter far than honey,
Was stronger far than wine.

So begins Stevenson's ode to a lost beverage, but it doesn't sound like this was the basis for the beer that Bruce Williams finally created, which is certainly not that sweet and weighs in at only 5% ABV. Fraoch (named after the Gaelic for heather) first went on commercial sale in 1992, when a small batch was brewed under Bruce's supervision at the now-defunct West Highland Brewery in Argyll.

Fraoch has a distinctively perfumed, floral and slightly gingery aroma and taste, with light earthy notes and a faint hoppiness on top of a toffeeish sweetness. There's also an unusual but pleasant minty coolness in the background. To achieve this effect, the hot wort is infused with heather flowers before fermentation. Also added is the herb sweet gale (bog myrtle), which presumably is responsible for the spicy flavours. Despite its highly floral character, Fraoch is still very much a beer, which no doubt ensured it enjoyed a flying start. Indeed, it was so successful that Bruce soon needed to transfer production to the long-established Maclay's in Alloa. When Maclay's closed, brewing resumed at Bruce's own plant based near Glasgow, and

today Fraoch is brewed at the new Williams Bros brewery that Bruce runs with his sibling Scott in Alloa.

You could say that Fraoch has been around the block a bit in its short life – it's travelled almost as much as Stevenson – but when you've been lying dormant for centuries, it's probably good to be active again.

Births Adrienne Corri (actress), 1933; George Carey (Archbishop of Canterbury), 1935; Whoopi Goldberg (actress and comedian), 1955

Deaths Gioacchino Rossini (composer), 1868; Vittorio De Sica (actor and film director), 1974

Events *Mariner 9* becomes the first space probe to orbit another planet when it reaches Mars, 1971; Washington's Vietnam Veterans Memorial dedicated, 1982

Spiced Ale

Duchy Originals Winter Ale

Source The Wychwood Brewery Co., Witney, Oxfordshire **Strength** 6.2% **Website** duchyoriginals.com

Born on this day in 1948, The Queen's eldest son has always been seen as quirky and independently minded within the royal circle, particularly when it comes to environmental issues. Not so long ago, much humour was generated by his admission that he talked to his plants as a means of stimulating their growth, and his concerns over the protection of the planet were similarly dismissed as flaky until climate change became an acknowledged fact. As the green lobby grows ever more powerful, he's developed into something of a father figure in the movement, feted by the likes of former US Vice President Al Gore.

Prince Charles has also proved a catalyst for positive change in the brewing world. As the figurehead of the 'Pub is the Hub' initiative, which aims to preserve community locals by encouraging them to take on extra services or empowering customer buy-outs, he has shown that there is an alternative to soulless villages where the only pub is now an expensive private residence for outsiders.

Charles also deserves a birthday toast for his encouragement of organic brewing. In 1992, the Prince set up the business Duchy Organics, using his alternative title of Duke of Cornwall as a guarantee of quality. His aim was to demonstrate that food of the highest standard could still be produced even while working in harmony with nature and the environment. Based on experiences at the farm on his Gloucestershire estate, the business offers a trading name for

goods generated from organic and sustainable farming by reliable producers all over the UK. The first product was an oaten biscuit, made in Scotland from cereals grown on the Prince's farm, and ground at a local mill. The range now extends to cover sausages, chutneys, cakes, soups and even supermarket ready-meals. As well as ploughing a furrow for sustainable farming, the Duchy Originals range also generates a profit, which is channelled into good causes by one of The Prince's charities. To date, more than £6 million has been raised.

Organic trio

There are now three beers in the Duchy Originals range, produced for the company by Wychwood Brewery in Oxfordshire. The first offering was Duchy Orginals Organic Ale, a 5% brew made from Plumage Archer, a rather forgotten variety of barley grown on the Prince's farm, and organic First Gold hops. This was followed by a bottle-conditioned, fruity Summer Ale – combining the same barley with some wheat malt and organic Fuggle, Golding and Target hops – and also by today's beer selection.

Like the other Duchy beers, Duchy Originals Winter Ale is based on Plumage Archer barley, but organic oats and rye from the Gloucestershire estate are included, too. The hops are similarly organic: the First Golds come from Herefordshire and Worcestershire, and Target is sourced from Kent. The beer has an unexpectedly peppery aroma, with orange and lemon leading over softly

nutty malt. In the mouth, perfumed hop notes come to the fore, outpointing chocolate and toffee flavours from the malt, with roasted grain taking over in the otherwise hoppy, bitter finish. It's a very complex old ale, with bags of character – just right for a royal toast, or if your leanings are more republican, simply perfect for warding off the chills of a dark November evening.

Births Claude Monet (artist), 1840; Bernard Hinault (cyclist), 1954; Condoleezza Rice (US Secretary of State), 1954

Deaths Nell Gwyn (actress), 1687; Tony Richardson (film director), 1991; Charlotte Coleman (actress), 2001

Events The BBC begins daily radio broadcasts, 1922; first UK records chart published in the *New Musical Express*, 1952; Princess Anne marries Captain Mark Phillips, 1973

Strong Ale

ABOVE: PRINCE CHARLES ENJOYING A PINT

Sierra Nevada Pale Ale

Source Sierra Nevada Brewing Co., Chico, California **Strength** 5.6% **Website** sierranevada.com

Chico is a university town 265km (165 miles) northeast of San Francisco with a population of around 100,000. It's not the sort of place you'd feel would excite an overseas visitor but it attracted me for two things. The first was a rumour of a quirky local law that rigidly imposes a $500 fine on anyone exploding a nuclear bomb in the vicinity. The second was its brewery, the highly regarded Sierra Nevada Brewing Company.

The nuclear bomb bit has turned out to be something of an urban myth. True, the municipality has expressed its outrage at nuclear proliferation by banning all production and testing of such bombs in the area, but it was simply a manipulation of the facts by a satirical journalist that resulted in the rather ridiculous idea of fining anyone who fired one up. The brewery, on the other, is not so much myth as the stuff of legend.

Quality in, quality out

Sierra Nevada was once described by Michael Jackson as 'the Château Latour among American micros'. The enterprise was started in 1979 by homebrewing partners Ken Grossman and Paul Camusi, and their first brew went into the mash tun on this day in 1980. From the start, the emphasis was placed firmly on quality ingredients in and quality products out. Even though their original brew kit was a cobbled-together mélange of second-hand equipment of which Heath Robinson would have been proud, their beers, with the accent firmly on the hop, oozed class from the outset.

The company has grown somewhat, over the course of 30 years. In 1989, it moved to larger premises and a purpose-built new home. In 1997, it tagged on a second brewhouse, to keep up with demand that had already started to grow way beyond the boundaries of California – today, Sierra Nevada produces in the region of half a million barrels of beer a year. That's roughly the annual output of British regionals Fuller's, Hall & Woodhouse, Everards and Sharp's all put together. Strangely, it is still often described as a craft brewery, which is testimony to its commitment to outstanding beer.

Sierra Nevada Pale Ale, born today in 1980, has long been acknowledged as the archetypal American pale ale, skilfully brewed from two-row barley malt, caramel malt and dextrin malt, with whole Perle and Magnum hops for bitterness, and Cascade to finish. At 5.6% ABV, it has a rich copper colour and a full mouthfeel, with a sound, malty base overlaid with juicy grapefruit and lime flavours courtesy of pungent, resin-like hops. Sold throughout the world in bottle-conditioned format, Pale Ale is beautifully fresh and has a nicely spritzy natural effervescence. It's the beer that has placed American craft brewing – and the sleepy town of Chico – well and truly on the map.

Births William Pitt 'the Elder' (Prime Minister), 1708; William Herschel (astronomer), 1738; Petula Clark (singer), 1932

Deaths Johannes Kepler (astronomer), 1630; Tyrone Power (actor), 1958

Events First meeting of the League of Nations, 1920; Margaret Thatcher and Irish premier Garret FitzGerald sign the Anglo-Irish Agreement, 1985

Pale Ale

Hofbräu Kaltenhausen Edelweiss Weissbier

Source Hofbräu Kaltenhausen, Kaltenhausen **Strength** 5.5% **Website** edelweissbier.at

Just think: if it hadn't been for events taking place on this day in 1959, there would be a gaping hole in the BBC TV schedules every Christmas. It was on 16 November that Rodgers and Hammerstein's musical *The Sound of Music* enjoyed its premiere, and the audience, in turn, enjoyed it so much that it ran for 1,443 performances. Then, of course, it simply had to be transferred to the big screen, where, with Julie Andrews and Christopher Plummer in the lead roles, it was a box office smash.

The film eventually gained a British television premiere in 1978, and has been repeated countless times since, with its army of armchair fans never tiring of the tuneful tale of a wayward nun who becomes governess to a large, unruly family, teaches them all to sing and warms the heart of their icy father. Throw in some stunning shots of alpine meadows, add a little Nazi menace, and the story was always likely to be a hit.

The Sound of Music was based on the life of Maria von Trapp. Her autobiographical book, *The Story of the Trapp Family Singers*, was set to music by Richard Rodgers and Oscar Hammerstein II, with the libretto written by Howard Lindsay and Russel Crouse. When the curtain went up on Broadway in 1959, it was Mary Martin (mother of *Dallas* star Larry Hagman) who was cast as Maria, playing opposite Theodore Bikel as Captain von Trapp. One of the songs gives us our lead for a beer for today.

Sung by the Captain, *Edelweiss* is an ode to the little white alpine flower of the same name, the national flower of Austria. Don't ask Austrians to sing it to you, though: the film wasn't even shown in the country's cinemas (don't mention the war!), and although *Edelweiss* has the air of an old alpine folk song, it was actually a new composition for the musical.

Blossom of snow

There is one Edelweiss that the Austrians know rather well, however, and do appreciate. It's a wheat beer from the Hofbräu Kaltenhausen brewery, the oldest brewery in the Salzburg area, with origins dating back to the 15th century. The brewery has been producing wheat beers for more than 300 years, although this one was only introduced in 1986. Edelweiss is brewed from alpine water and is presented cloudy and yellow in colour, with a big, rocky foam head, thanks to its lively carbonation. The spicy aroma offers a distinct tinned pears note, and the same fruit pushes through in the taste, which is refreshingly tart and spiked with a little herbal/clove bitterness. There are more pears in the drying, bready, herbal finish.

The brewery these days is part of the Heineken group and, while that may have a consolidation downside, it does at least mean that Edelweiss can now be enjoyed on draught many miles from its alpine home, as well as in bottle. Beerwise, when I'm thirsty, it's one of my favourite things.

Births Willie Carson (jockey), 1942; Griff Rhys Jones (comedian and presenter), 1953; Frank Bruno (boxer), 1961

Deaths Clark Gable (actor), 1960; Arthur Askey (comedian), 1982; Milton Friedman (economist), 2006

Events Anthony Blunt is named as the 'fourth man' in the Philby, Burgess and Maclean spy ring, 1979; Dennis Potter's *The Singing Detective* debuts on British TV, 1986

Wheat Beer

Riva Vondel

Source Liefmans Breweries, Dentergem **Strength** 8.5% **Website** liefmans.be

Beer is a great educator, as hopefully this book has proved. By the simple action of placing a portrait on a label, or even just naming a beer in honour of a historical figure, brewers set the grey matter working.

The beer for today is a case in point. It's called Vondel and features on its bottle the image of a balding man with wispy side hair and a rather demonic moustache and beard. The V of 'Vondel' is artistically shaped to include an old-fashioned quill, and the rest of the name is scrawled with an artistic flourish, which all suggests that the man in the frame was actually a writer of some renown. A little research proves that that was indeed the case. It doesn't take long to discover that Vondel is the most important poet in the history of The Netherlands.

Joost van den Vondel was born in Cologne on this day in 1587. His parents were Dutch and it was back to The Netherlands that he moved when he took over the family hosiery business in Amsterdam. His leisure hours, however, he devoted to literature, writing satirical verse and drama in the Greek classic mould, with religion at the heart of his output – he was a prominent convert to Catholicism at a time of religious intolerance. Vondel's writings were to be highly influential among German poets in the 17th century, and today he is honoured by having the largest park in Amsterdam named after him.

Give us a clue

Apart from teasing us with his portrait and name, the beer label gives no further clues about this great man, but it does tell us that the beer is a Flemish Brown Ale in style.

It actually pours red in colour, suggesting a mash tun loaded with dark malts. Further evidence of this comes in the aroma, which is malty and creamy, with a hazelnut richness. There's also a fruity note, with strawberry perhaps the closest comparison to be drawn, and this continues in the creamy, sweet, malty, nutty taste, perhaps with some sultana and little bursts of clementine. It's surprisingly light-drinking for a brown ale, and complex, too, thanks to the bottle conditioning, rounding off with a gum-tingling, sweet, malty finish that has a bitter orange note. The beer is a product of the Riva Brewery, part of the Liefmans group, which looked likely to be sold to another Belgian brewery (probably Duvel-Moortgat) after going into liquidation at the end of 2007. 'A poem on the tongue,' the brewers call it, but it's a World Beer Cup gold medallist, so don't just take their word for it.

Births Peter Cook (comedian), 1937; Martin Scorsese (film director), 1942; Jonathan Ross (broadcaster), 1960

Deaths Queen Mary I, 1558; Auguste Rodin (sculptor), 1917; Ferenc Puskas (footballer), 2006

Events Sir Walter Raleigh tried for treason, 1603; Arnold Schwarzenegger inaugurated as Governor of California, 2003

Strong Ale

ABOVE: DUTCH POET JOOST VAN DEN VONDEL

Wadworth Malt 'n' Hops

Source Wadworth & Co., Devizes, Wiltshire   **Strength** 4.5%   **Website** wadworth.co.uk

Forget wine: the Beaujolais Nouveau of beers has arrived. Intriguingly, more and more brewers are turning their hands to beers brewed with green hops – hops from the new harvest that have been plucked fresh off the bine and tossed straight into the copper. And, unlike the often overrated French wines that emerge with great fanfares on or around 18 November, these topical ales are usually packed with flavour.

At the Talbot pub, the home of Teme Valley Brewery in Knightwick, Worcestershire – right in the heart of the local hop gardens – they showcase this novel beer style with a green beer festival on the second weekend in October every year. There are usually around a dozen green-hop beers on show, with brewers such as Breconshire, Hanby, Oakleaf and Wye Valley all contributing, and Teme Valley providing five or so of its own, each brewed with a different green hop. However, probably the most practised exponent of green-hop beer brewing is Wadworth, which has produced its beer Malt 'n' Hops annually since the early 1990s.

Culinary terms

Malt 'n' Hops is seasoned mostly with conventional Goldings that are cut and dried from the new season crop, but a dose of sappy green hops – gathered from the fields that very day – is added late to the copper. The same hops then linger in the hop back as the wort is being run off from the copper, introducing a resin-like, strongly citrus flavour and aroma.

The green hops only go into the brew late and are not used throughout the beer as they would be simply too overpowering. Former Wadworth brewing director Trevor Holmes once described the process to me in culinary terms. 'It's like when you make a curry: you have to have the right balance of herbs and spices. The green hops bring a lot of flavours that would normally be driven off when they are dried in the kiln. These may be undesirable flavours for some brewers, but in moderation they work for us.' The hops complement a grist comprised almost entirely of pale ale malt, with just a hint of crystal for colour.

After a week's brewing and fermentation, plus another couple of weeks for conditioning, Malt 'n' Hops goes on sale towards the end of September. A second batch is now usually brewed towards the end of the harvest period, which means that the beer tends to be available right up to the time when that other Beaujolais Nouveau finally arrives. It's always available in bottle, too, so, if you are little late getting hold of the cask version, you still can cherish that fresh-picked flavour and those tart, sappy citrus notes throughout the late autumn.

Births WS Gilbert (librettist), 1836; Alec Issigonis (car designer), 1906; Johnny Mercer (lyricist), 1909

Deaths Marcel Proust (writer), 1922; Ted Heath (bandleader), 1969; James Coburn (actor), 2002

Events William Caxton prints the first book in England, 1477; end of the Battle of the Somme during World War I, after more than four months' fighting, 1916

Jennings World's Biggest Liar

Source Jennings Brewery, Cockermouth, Cumbria **Strength** 4.3% **Website** jenningsbrewery.co.uk

Did you know that the Lake District was not formed by glacial or volcanic activity but by large moles and eels? Were you aware that turnips grown locally were as big as sheds?

Both these facts are true, according to some of the people who visit the Bridge Inn at Santon Bridge around this time in November. You see, this hospitable Cumbrian pub – a ramblers' haven perched at the foot of Wasdale, by the side of a babbling river – has become a magnet for lovers of a tall story. It all started with one Will Ritson, a 19th-century publican whose flair for the outrageous fib has been celebrated here since 1974 in the World's Biggest Liar competition. The event is widely anticipated and hotly contested, with entrants called upon to spin a yarn or two in front of an audience of 120 gullible drinkers and a clued-up judging panel. Each contestant is allowed five minutes to charm the crowd, without the aid of props. The competition is even attracting professional performers. In 2006, comedian Sue Perkins – throwing herself into the competition as part of a Radio 4 documentary she was making – stole the show with her mendacious insistence that it was flatulent sheep in the Lake District that were creating the hole in the ozone layer. 'Muttons of mass destruction,' she called them. However, the rules of the contest, it seems (unless this is another lie), include a clause prohibiting politicians and lawyers from taking part, because they are 'too practised in the art'.

Mendaciously malty

In 2007, Jennings, owners of the pub and sponsors of the growing event, realized its marketing potential by releasing a new beer for the occasion. World's Biggest Liar is now available in the autumn in cask form, and for longer periods in bottle. Brewed from Maris Otter pale malt, plus crystal, amber and chocolate malts, with Fuggle, Challenger and Golding hops for bitterness, it is a fine amber ale of 4.3% ABV, with a strong malt presence throughout. Toffee notes and hints of chocolate fill the aroma, with a more roasted edge joining toffee in the mouth, along with a crisp bitterness for balance. The beer finishes dry, malty and bitter, as hops come through more and more.

But Jennings is not the first brewer to support the event. Up the valley from the pub is the Wasdale Head Inn, with its Great Gable microbrewery. Owner Howard Christie has won the title himself, as have brewery workers Abrie Kruger (the South African being the first overseas winner) and Mike Naylor (who also claimed to be a South African who had read *Teach Yourself Cumbrian* to be able to address the audience). And, believe it or not, for several years now, Great Gable has been brewing its own commemorative seasonal ale, called simply Liar!

Births Calvin Klein (fashion designer), 1942; Meg Ryan (actress), 1961; Jodie Foster (actress), 1962

Deaths Franz Schubert (composer), 1828; Basil Spence (architect), 1976

Events The Gettysburg Address delivered by President Abraham Lincoln, 1863; the first National Lottery draw in the UK, 1994

Best Bitter

Greene King Abbot Ale

Source Greene King, Bury St Edmunds, Suffolk **Strength** 5% **Website** abbotale.co.uk

This day in November marks the anniversary of the death of St Edmund, the man after whom the Suffolk town of Bury St Edmunds is named. Some say the year was 870, others say it was 869 – typical of the mystery that surrounds the life of this extraordinary man. What does appear clear is that Edmund was a local ruler – King of East Anglia, effectively – ascending to the throne when aged just 14, having been born in Germany.

Edmund, we believe, took his royal responsibilities seriously. He was a model ruler and a pious man whose Christian values eventually led to his sad demise. When the Danes invaded this part of England, Edmund was presented with the chance to surrender, but he felt that the terms were too cruel for his people. Seriously outnumbered, he knew he couldn't win any battle, so he simply disbanded his own forces to avoid

senseless bloodshed and walked away. His enemies caught up with him, however, and inflicted upon him a savage and cruel slow death, in which he was beaten with cudgels, whipped, shot at with arrows and finally beheaded. Later, Edmund's supporters retrieved his remains and buried them with reverence. His reputation as a martyr grew to the point where, before the installation of St George, he was known as the patron saint of England.

Bury highs & lows

Edmund's body was later moved to what is today Bury St Edmunds, and a Benedictine abbey developed around his tomb. It grew into one of the most important abbeys in Europe during the Middle Ages, although it fell into ruin after Henry VIII dissolved the monasteries in the 16th century. Only the gardens of the abbey remain today, but Bury has developed into a pleasant and popular market town, with two industries that act as its heartbeat. The first is the production of sugar by the Silver Spoon company; the second is brewing.

Mention the name Bury St Edmunds to many beer lovers today and you'll receive a scowl in return. Sadly, the rapid expansion of the town's major brewer, Greene King, into a national company, and the take-over and closure of breweries like Morland, Ridleys and Hardys and Hansons, has led to Bury beers swamping much of England and destroying drinkers' choice. It is a shame that this once popular regional

brewery has advanced in this way, as it still keeps a focus on traditional ale and has some excellent beers in its portfolio. Indeed, the company's flagship ale is one of the best.

Abbot Ale has been somewhat devalued by its omnipresence, but, when served in top condition, it is a beautifully balanced, complex beer with glorious, crisp, fruity flavours. Brewed from pale, crystal and amber malts for substantial body, and skilfully seasoned with Challenger and Fuggle hops, Abbot delivers a satisfying 5% ABV and combines hop fruitiness with gentle tropical notes derived from fermentation.

While Greene King are no saints in the eyes of some beer connoisseurs, this is the obvious beer to turn to for today's commemoration.

Births Alistair Cooke (broadcaster), 1908; Robert Kennedy (politician), 1925; Bo Derek (actress), 1956

Deaths Leo Tolstoy (writer), 1910; General Francisco Franco (dictator), 1975; Robert Altman (film director), 2006

Events Nuremburg war trials begin, 1945; marriage of the Queen (then Princess Elizabeth) and Prince Phillip, 1947; fire badly damages Windsor Castle, 1992

Strong Ale

Weltenburger Kloster Asam Bock

Source Weltenburger Kloster, Kelheim **Strength** 6.9% **Website** weltenburger.de

Despite his Roman-sounding name, St Columbanus is one of Ireland's saints. Born in Leinster in 543, he turned his back on the material world at a young age and joined religious orders in his native country, before hearing the call to missionary work overseas. For many years, Columbanus lived in France, setting up a small chain of abbeys where his simple lifestyle and close observance of Christian principles could be followed by his growing band of brothers. Later in life, a dispute with local rulers meant he was forced to move on. A boat that was due to carry him back to Ireland ran into a storm and returned to port, and so the wandering preacher and his adherents travelled to Germany instead and thence to Italy, where he was to die in 615. His day is celebrated mostly on 21 November, although in Ireland they remember him three days later.

Columbanus is listed among the small group of 'beer saints', for the miracles he performed involving our favourite drink. It was said that he was able to multiply bread and beer so that it fed his growing band of followers, and also that he once ruptured a barrel of ale that was dedicated to a pagan deity simply by breathing on it.

One minor miracle that has resulted from Columbanus's life, if not directly from the saint himself, is the stunning abbey at Weltenburg, near Regensburg in northern Bavaria. The abbey occupies a striking position on a wide bend of the River Danube. It

has been here since the early 7th century, when it was constructed by Eustasius, one of Columbanus's earliest disciples. The abbey was later acquired by Benedictine monks and they live here still, sharing the summer months with some 750,000 tourists, who are attracted not only by the fantastically ornate baroque church, which is the abbey's centrepiece, but also by the fact that the abbey still brews its own beer.

Since 1973, the brewery, which shows up in historic records as early as 1050, has been licensed out to a local brewer. Regensburg's Brauerei Bischofshof therefore runs the operation on a commercial footing, although it's not quite as materialistic as it sounds, as Bischofshof itself is owned by the Bishop of Regensburg.

Dark delights

They specialize in dark beers at Weltenburger, beers that are strong and substantial. Visitors consume them with relish in the abbey's own pub and beer garden, and some are also bottled. To confuse the issue a little, lighter-coloured beers labelled Weltenburger Marke are separately brewed at Bischofshof. These are still extremely good but look for the words Weltenburger Kloster when hunting the authentic abbey beers, such as Asam Bock, the beer choice for today.

This beer is brewed from a mix of pale and dark malts, with the hops remaining a closely guarded secret, except to say that they are sourced from the nearby Hallertau region. On first sip, the beer seems to lack a little

subtlety and balance. However, the initial sweetness is gradually countered by pruney fruit, nutty dark malt and various shades of chocolate, to complete a beer of real character and depth. The strength – 6.9% – is evident in the pleasing tingle of warmth, and hops emerge more strongly in the finish.

Asam Bock is a full-value, nourishing strong lager that is conditioned for a full 12 weeks at the abbey. It fits well into the monastic brewing tradition – even one that probably dates back 14 centuries.

Births Voltaire (philosopher), 1694; Goldie Hawn (actress), 1945; Björk (pop musician), 1965

Deaths Henry Purcell (composer), 1695; Max Baer (boxer), 1959; Quentin Crisp (writer), 1999

Events TV soap *Dallas* finally reveals 'Who shot JR?', 1980; proceedings in the House of Commons first televised, 1989

Bock

Adnams Bitter

Source Adnams plc, Southwold, Suffolk **Strength** 3.7% **Website** adnams.co.uk

The sleepy Suffolk coastline is an area of marshy creeks, wildlife reserves, pleasant beaches and unspoilt fishing towns. Music and beer have their parts to play, too, and join together harmoniously for today's celebration.

North of the port of Felixstowe, there are two coastal towns that stand out in this part of the world. The first is Southwold, home of Adnams Brewery; the second is Aldeburgh, where the county's most famous musical son, Benjamin Britten, made his home.

Britten was born in Lowestoft in 1913. His talents, obvious from an early age, took him to the Royal College of Music, where he completed his formal studies. After a period spent composing incidental music for films, he emigrated to the US in the early years of World War II, but was nostalgically drawn back to the quiet loveliness of his home county three years later. It was here that he developed his most famous works in the decades that followed. These include the operas *Peter Grimes*, *Billy Budd*, *Gloriana*, *A Midsummer Night's Dream* and *Death in Venice*.

Making music with hops

Britten often worked closely with the operatic tenor Peter Pears, and with him dreamt up the idea of staging an annual music festival in Aldeburgh. The event started in 1948 and transferred to a new venue, with a beery connection, in 1967 – a spectacular new concert hall created in the shell of the maltings at nearby Snape. Britten died in 1976. He is remembered by the unusual sculpture of a scallop shell on Aldeburgh beach, donated to the town by local artist Maggi Hambling and The Adnams Charity, a benevolent body set up by the brewery in 1990 to contribute to society within 40km (25 miles) of Southwold.

This all seems rather appropriate, as Adnams beers are as much a part of the fabric of Suffolk as Britten's music. The beer they now call simply 'The Bitter' is one of the brewing world's greatest compositions. Head brewer Mike Powell-Evans likes to describe hops in musical terms, assigning high and low notes to the little green flowers depending on their robust flavours or delicate nuances within a beer. In Adnams Bitter, he has scored a masterpiece, a highly quaffable session ale with a pitch-perfect balance of malt and hops. The clear high notes of Goldings and the bass baritone of Fuggles provide the vocal lead, according to Powell-Evans, with First Gold as the chorus, pulling everything together.

There's another feature of Adnams Bitter that can't be overlooked. It's that little whiff of Suffolk sea air that invades every glass, making it the closest you can get to a bracing walk in this stress-relieving, largely unspoilt part of England.

Births Thomas Cook (tourism pioneer), 1808; George Eliot (writer), 1819; Hoagy Carmichael (songwriter), 1899; Peter Hall (theatrical director), 1930

Deaths John F Kennedy (US President), 1963; CS Lewis (writer), 1963; Mae West (actress), 1980

Events Margaret Thatcher resigns as Prime Minister, 1990; England wins the Rugby World Cup, 2003; Angela Merkel becomes Germany's first female Chancellor, 2005

Okells Dr Okells IPA

Source Okells Ltd, Douglas **Strength** 4.5% **Website** okells.co.uk

If Prohibition proved one thing, it was that if you wanted a drink badly enough, you could usually get one. The US Government's ban on the production, sale and transportation of alcohol was intended to set America on a better social footing, eradicating workplace accidents and keeping the country responsible and prudent. In reality, it was easily undermined, usually by gangsters and racketeers who commissioned illicit brews and smuggled in liquor from other countries. But there was another branch of American society that was also hindering the country from staying dry, and that was the nation's medical fraternity.

Legal loophole

A loophole in the 18th Amendment to the US constitution, which introduced Prohibition to America in 1920, allowed doctors to prescribe alcohol as they would any other medication. In a country where strong spirits were traditionally considered effective methods of seeing off colds and other ailments, this should not be surprising. Even today, the benefits of alcohol – when taken in moderation – are recognized by physicians as ways of easing stress or reducing heart disease, for instance.

The anti-alcohol brigade didn't see things the same way. Their hard-won victory for enforced abstinence looked set to be eradicated by doctors liberally handing out prescriptions for booze. According to a feature in *Smithsonian* magazine, it was even suggested that drug stores should be able to supply beer over the counter, alongside the soft drinks they sold to children. The erstwhile triumphant temperance lobby hit the roof, forcing the Government to reconsider the doctors' exemption. Consequently, on 23 November 1921, prescriptions of wine and liquor were made subject to new limitations, and it became illegal for doctors to prescribe beer.

Had the same restrictions been imposed 70 years earlier across the Atlantic on the Isle of Man, they would certainly have caused a panic at a brewery in Douglas. Okells, the island's major producer, was founded here in 1850 by one Dr William Okell, so through his rare combination of training and profession, Prohibition would have come as a double whammy.

The good doctor's name has been revived in recent years as Okells has expanded its range of beers, with an eye on exporting to the wider British market. One of the newcomers is Dr Okell's IPA (4.5%), a thoroughly modern, spritzy golden ale, brimful of pungent, citrus hops. Six varieties of hop, in fact, are blended to achieve the zesty flavours, and in such quantity that the brewhouse whirlpool can't cope unless the beer is brewed in smaller batches than other Okells beers. The medical properties of hops continue to be examined by researchers, with promising results, but it would be too much to boast that a pint of Dr Okell's IPA is going to greatly enhance your health. Still, if you prescribe yourself a glass today, you may well find it's quite a tonic.

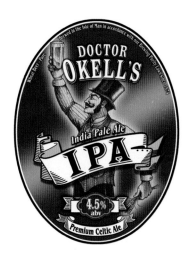

Births Billy the Kid (outlaw), 1859; Boris Karloff (actor), 1887; Lew Hoad (tennis player), 1934

Deaths Merle Oberon (actress), 1979; Roald Dahl (writer), 1990; Nick Clarke (broadcaster), 2006

Events First episode of *Doctor Who* broadcast, 1963; southern Italy rocked by an earthquake, 1980

Golden Ale

Hook Norton Old Hooky

Source Hook Norton Brewery, Hook Norton, Oxfordshire **Strength** 4.6%
Website hooknortonbrewery.co.uk

There's a touch of Brigadoon about Hook Norton Brewery. As you meander through the pretty Oxfordshire village it calls home, you'd hardly know the brewery was there. In fact, you almost begin to doubt whether it really exists. It's not until you crest the brow of the lane that leads to where farmer John Harris founded the business in 1849 that this magnificent brewhouse is revealed in all its Victorian glory.

John Harris was a farmer. He expanded his interests when he acquired a farm in Hook Norton that also included a maltings. He probably began brewing there almost as soon as he took over, but, like most brewers in those days, his output would have been on a small scale and largely for his own use. It wasn't until 1856 that he began brewing on a commercial basis and, according to the earliest brewing book kept at Hook Norton, his first brew went in on this day that year.

The recipe was for a beer known as Mild XXX. It included 18 bushels of pale malt and 18lb of hops, and was the start of something big. The business was well established by the time of Harris's death in 1887, and it has remained in his family's hands ever since. John's great-great-grandson, James Clarke, is the present managing director.

A new brewery was constructed in 1899. It was six storeys high in the tower tradition, which allowed the brewing process to begin at the top and continue by gravity feed through lower levels until finished beer rolled out on the ground floor. Steam power raised the water and grains to the top level so production could begin. Remarkably, the same steam engine is still in use today. Perhaps this should not be so surprising, though, as Hook Norton still brews in largely the same way as it did more than 100 years ago. Worn-out bits and pieces of kit have been replaced over the decades, and there's been expansion here and there, but essentially the brewery is working evidence of how breweries used to be run in Victorian times.

The old & the new

What is not so old-fashioned is the range of beers, which has broadened considerably in recent years. Hooky's beers remain exceptionally popular in both the company's own 40 or so pubs and in the free trade, and the business has also targeted the off-trade with a range of colourful, informatively labelled bottled beers, several of which successfully follow the trend for easy-drinking, golden ales.

To mark today's anniversary, however, the beer selected belongs to the old Hook Norton school, even though it's been around for only just over 30 years. Old Hooky was first brewed to celebrate The Queen's Silver Jubilee in 1977, and is a satisfying, full-bodied beer in the strong bitter tradition. The recipe's a tad more complicated than the one for Mild XXX, but includes all the features you'd expect in a pint of

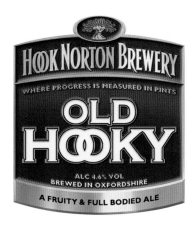

copper-coloured English ale. Pale and crystal malt supply the barley notes with a little wheat malt to enhance the drinkability. Fuggle, Golding and Challenger hops then provide fruit and a robust bitter balance.

It's the beer with which to toast this wonderful brewery's long and successful history – and, hopefully, its long and successful future. It would be a crime to see a treasure like this disappear permanently into the Oxfordshire mist.

Births Henri de Toulouse-Lautrec (artist), 1864; Billy Connolly (comedian and actor), 1942; Ian Botham (cricketer), 1955

Deaths John Knox (religious reformer), 1572; George Raft (actor), 1980; Freddie Mercury (rock star), 1991

Events Darwin's *On the Origin of Species* published, 1859; flexible licensing hours introduced in the UK, 2005

Best Bitter

Deschutes The Abyss

Source Deschutes Brewery, Bend, Oregon **Strength** 11% **Website** deschutesbrewery.com

The precise date varies from year to year but we can't let Thanksgiving pass without finding an outstanding American beer with which to mark this historic festival.

The first Thanksgiving is said to have taken place in 1621, when settlers from the *Mayflower* joined with local native Americans to give thanks for their first harvest. The concept evolved over time and was formally installed in the calendar by President Lincoln in 1863. These days the occasion is celebrated on the fourth Thursday of November and is as important a holiday in the US as Christmas.

As at Christmas, turkey is the festive bird, served with all the trimmings as part of an all-embracing family celebration. The right sort of beer to serve with turkey is something a little darker than normal, with a raised malt character. The light caramel notes seem to bring out the bird's gamey flavours. In American terms, we could be looking at an amber ale or amber lager, or perhaps an American take on an Oktoberfestbier. I've decided, though, to look beyond simple beer and food matching, as this is such an important day for Americans. There are plenty of outstanding US beers to choose from, courtesy of the craft brewing revolution, but I've settled on a beer that claimed the top prize in the International Beer Challenge in 2007, which I helped judge.

Satanic yet divine

It comes from Deschutes Brewery in Bend, Oregon. They've gained a fine reputation over the years – and numerous awards – for their excellent bottled beers, but today's selection moves them into a new league. The beer is called The Abyss and, although it sounds vaguely satanic, it is divine. It's an imperial stout but one that has had a few twists and turns added during the production process to create a beer of remarkable character. The key twist is the ageing in French oak and Bourbon casks, which adds astonishing complexity.

The Abyss lives up to its name with broodingly dark brown appearance in the glass, topped by a lively foam the colour of a smoky bar-room ceiling. The nose is biscuity, slightly vinous and packed with the aromas of chocolate, orange and liquorice. Then there's the taste, loaded with oily chocolate flavours, nuts, coffee, hints of orange cream, a tinge of liquorice and an oaky dryness. It's super-smooth, with the sumptuousness of a chocolate truffle, only more bitter. There's more dark chocolate, coffee and oak in the warming, drying finish that follows, but you could drink this beer all night (slowly!) and keep finding new flavours. I can't think of a better way to round off a Thanksgiving meal, perhaps sipped sagely with a slice of traditional pumpkin pie.

One of my fellow judges in the International Beer Challenge that year was Glenn Payne, formerly beer buyer for Safeway supermarkets in the UK. He hit the nail on the head when he declared that, 'as a celebration of the brewer's craft, The Abyss would be hard to better'. That's something for which we should give thanks, too.

Births Andrew Carnegie (industrialist and philanthropist), 1835; Pope John XXIII, 1881; Joe DiMaggio (baseball player), 1914

Deaths U Thant (UN Secretary-General), 1974; George Best (footballer), 2005

Events First performance of Agatha Christie's long-running play *The Mousetrap*, 1952; Band Aid record *Do They Know It's Christmas?* for Ethiopia famine relief, 1984

Cask-aged Beer

ABOVE: THE FIRST THANKSGIVING, IN 1621

Samuel Smith Winter Welcome

Source Samuel Smith, Tadcaster, Yorkshire **Strength** 6% **Website** None

Winter doesn't officially begin until 21 December in the northern hemisphere, but try telling brewers that. They rightly recognize that, when the weather turns this cold and the nights become this long, it's time they produced some compensating beers.

So what constitutes a winter ale? The short answer is that there is no specific winter style. Old ales and barley wines tend to arrive at this time of the year, but so does a host of other beers that are simply wintry by connotation. There are, however, a number of similarities among the most popular examples.

Most notably there is the strength, which is generally about 5% ABV and above. Tied in with this is a chunky malt presence. You do, after all, need to include plenty of malt sugars so the yeast can raise the alcohol to this level. Also, unlike in summer ales where very pale malt is the key, the biscuity, nutty, toffeeish richness of crystal and other darker malts comes into its own in winter. Hops, however, tend to be the poor relation, generally used to provide a comfortable balance, taking the edge off that initial sweetness, and also bringing a touch of fruit. The other source of fruit is the fermentation process, creating chemical compounds called esters, which introduce pronounced exotic aromas and flavours, such as banana and pineapple. There may be spices in the beer, too, but spiced beers are treated in this book as a different style (see 20 December).

Dickensian desire

Ultimately, what brewers have tried to do over the years is give drinkers the sort of ale that keeps out the draughts and chills, beer with plenty of nourishing body and a gentle alcoholic glow to ensure a little inner warmth. To a degree, they exploit a cosiness factor, an almost Dickensian desire among the public to hole up somewhere warm when the freeze descends, to draw the curtains and flip the cap off a beer that will make them glad they don't have to venture outside.

If you do make the effort to savour the log fire down at the pub, you can find such treats as Wadworth's Old Father Timer, Highgate Old Ale and Young's Winter Warmer on draught. These beers are also available in bottle, to enjoy at home, along with today's selection, the appropriately named Winter Welcome Ale from Samuel Smith in Tadcaster, North Yorkshire. This beer is particularly popular in the US – as, indeed, are all Sam's bottled beers, courtesy of effective distribution by a company called Merchant du Vin. In the UK, this copper-coloured strong ale needs to be pursued in independent off-licences, as the strangely reticent, and very private, brewery doesn't deal with supermarkets. Smooth, creamy malt and raisin-toffee are the key features, with light bitter oranges showing up against the background sweetness. While there's more raisin and toffee in the finish, a dry bitterness is the final impression as the hops come through more and more.

The picture on the label tends to change from year to year but always featured is a quotation from Shakespeare. It's the same line that adorns the facade of The Vine pub, home of Bathams Brewery in Brierley Hill in the West Midlands, and it comes from *The Two Gentlemen of Verona*: 'Blessing of your heart you brew good ale.' That's a seasonal message of gratitude we drinkers should send to brewers everywhere.

Births Charles Forte (hotelier), 1908; Pat Phoenix (actress), 1923; Tina Turner (rock singer), 1939

Deaths Tommy Dorsey (bandleader), 1956; Michael Bentine (comedian), 1996

Events Brinks Mat gold bullion robbery at London's Heathrow Airport, 1983; Tony Blair becomes the first UK Prime Minister to address the Irish parliament, 1998

Strong Ale

Thwaites Flying Shuttle

Source Thwaites Brewery, Blackburn, Lancashire **Strength** 4.9% **Website** thwaitesbeers.co.uk

On 1 August, we celebrated Yorkshire Day. It would remiss of us, to say the least, not to draw attention to Lancashire Day, which, since 1996, has been commemorated on 27 November.

Lancashire Day is at the forefront of a long-running campaign by a body known as The Friends of Real Lancashire, whose aim is to restore the historic boundaries of the county. In 1974, in a shake-up of local authority areas, much of Lancashire was hived off into the new metropolitan districts of Greater Manchester, Cumbria and Merseyside, with some slipping away into Cheshire, too. Even though some of those districts have themselves now been abolished, erosion of traditional Lancastrian identity has continued, say campaigners, and it's time to put Lancashire back on the map, both figuratively and literally.

The choice of 27 November for the celebration of all things Lancastrian was not arbitrary. On this day in 1295, King Edward I called to Westminster the county's first elected representatives. They sat in what became known as the Model Parliament and thus played a major role in establishing parliamentary democracy in Britain. Events staged annually now include local brass band concerts, dialect literature readings, pie suppers, quizzes, lectures, Lancashire beer festivals and even George Formby and Gracie Fields tribute nights. The 'Lancashire Day Proclamation' is read out in towns and cities around the county, once again laying claim to lost regions.

Kay's contraption

Supporting the campaign is Daniel Thwaites. The Blackburn brewer has been brewing in the county since 1807. In its bicentennial year of 2007, it introduced a new beer to highlight Lancashire Day. It takes its name from the device developed by John Kay in 1733, an invention that changed the face of weaving in Britain and put Lancashire firmly centre stage during the Industrial Revolution. Kay's creation was the flying shuttle, a simple bit of kit that took the labour out of weaving large pieces of fabric, speeding up the process and enabling single operators to take the place of two or more.

Thwaites Flying Shuttle is a blend of 90% Pearl pale malt and 10% crystal malt, hence its attractive ruby colour. The hops used are Golding, Fuggle, Challenger and Whitbread Golding Variety. There are lots of powdery milk chocolate notes in the nose, along with nuts and a suggestion of dried fruit. The taste is smooth and richly malty, with more nuts, chocolate and toffee. It's mostly sweet, with just some bitter highlights. The same deep malty flavours carry on into the drying finish, which gets increasingly bitter. The label declares that it's a beer 'crafted to restore vigour after a hard day's work', and the abundant malty sugars would certainly do that.

As Thwaites suggests, it's a beer that can do justice to the Lancastrian dishes that may be on the menu today, from strong Lancashire cheese to Lancashire hot pot. The brewery has even come up with a recipe for hot pot that includes this particular beer.

Births Ernie Wise (comedian), 1925; Bruce Lee (martial arts expert and actor), 1940; Jimi Hendrix (rock musician), 1942

Deaths Horace (poet), 8 BC; Ross McWhirter (statistician), 1975; Alan Freeman (broadcaster), 2006

Events The Liverpool branch of the Labour Party suspended by the national leadership over allegations of infiltration by the Militant Tendency, 1985

Strong Ale

Wells Satanic Mills

Source Wells & Young's Brewing Company, Bedford **Strength** 5% **Website** charleswells.co.uk

Gifted but insane – that was the general view of William Blake among many of his contemporaries. The 18th-century artist and poet certainly was a talented and rather eccentric soul, but to put a kinder interpretation on his life, it may simply have been that his genius was not properly recognized while he lived.

Blake was born on 28 November 1757, the son of a London hosier. He was given no formal schooling but sent as an apprentice to an engraver. This he made his profession, turning also to painting, becoming a member of the Royal Academy and furthering his name among the artists and literati of the time. Poetry added a second string to his bow and he combined the two arts to produce engraved copies of his own verse. After a turbulent professional and personal life, he died in relative obscurity in 1827.

While Blake's artworks – inspired by Gothic and Renaissance masters – are less easy to identify, there are two poems that are widely associated with him. The first is *The Tyger*, an exploration of the good and evil that God placed on this Earth; the second is the preface to his epic poem *Milton*, which – set to music by Hubert Parry in 1916 – has become adopted as an alternative English national anthem. 'And did those feet' begins what has become known as *Jerusalem*, as Blake calls for a new beginning for the country. This should not be surprising, as he was a known supporter of the French Revolution and an associate of radical thinkers like Thomas Paine.

The national pint

Blake's rousing words have been picked up by Wells & Young's brewery, which has spent a small fortune positioning its Bombardier bitter as the 'Drink of England'. To boost its patriotic identity, the company has now expanded the Bombardier range to include two beers inspired by lines from Blake's *Jerusalem*. One is a blonde ale called Burning Gold ('Bring me my bow of burning gold'); the other is a stout called Satanic Mills ('And was Jerusalem builded here/ Among these dark Satanic mills?'). Both, like the original Bombardier, are sold in pint bottles.

Satanic Mills is brewed from a grist of pale and chocolate malts, and is seasoned with Fuggle and Golding hops – as English as you can get in these cosmopolitan brewing days. It pours a deep brown colour and presents a slightly smoky, biscuity aroma of dark chocolate and coffee. There's more bitter chocolate and coffee in the taste, but also sweet caramel notes beneath to make it very easy to drink. Roasted grain arrives on the swallow, leaving lingering coffee and chocolate flavours as the beer dries and bitterness increases.

If your 'arrows of desire' are aimed in the direction of a decent pint today, then dark Satanic Mills provides the perfect target.

Births Friedrich Engels (philosopher), 1820; Randy Newman (singer-songwriter), 1943; Martin Clunes (actor), 1961

Deaths Gian Lorenzo Bernini (artist), 1680; Enrico Fermi (physicist), 1954; Enid Blyton (writer), 1968

Events William Shakespeare marries Anne Hathaway, 1582; Lady Astor becomes first female British MP, 1919; John Major becomes Prime Minister, 1990

Stout

Bernard Sváteční Ležák

Source Rodinny Pivovar Bernard, Humpolec **Strength** 5% **Website** bernard.cz

Often seen topping 'greatest hits' polls, Queen's *Bohemian Rhapsody* broke all the rules of chart singles. It absurdly introduced an element of opera to a pop song; its running time extended well beyond five minutes, when everyone knew that a chart hit needed to last only three; it introduced what has become known as the first pop video; and, from the time it topped the charts on this day in 1975, it held the UK number one spot for a remarkable nine weeks – the longest period at the top since Paul Anka's *Diana*, way back in 1957. The track then went on to become the first number 1 to top the charts on its re-issue, 16 years later. Put simply, you could say that it was a record breaker.

Queen's arty lead singer Freddie Mercury had always been a lover of opera and stunned fellow band members when he suggested a detour from their standard repertoire of heavy rock, putting together a song that included a memorable multitracked classical section in the middle. When the tape finished spinning, the song lasted nearly six minutes. Record executives urged the band to cut it back, to ensure radio airplay, but they refused and, with the help of early exposure from DJ Kenny Everett, released the single to a somewhat confused, but hugely impressed, audience. In those days, records rarely shot straight to number 1, and *Bohemian Rhapsody* was no exception. It charted first at 17, climbed to 9 one week later, but then rocketed to the top, aided by a novel video produced so that the band didn't have to perform the impossible song on stage. This was not really the first pop video – films had been made for pop songs since the 1960s – but it did launch a new era in such promotion. The track lingered in the charts for 17 weeks in all and then was re-issued shortly after Mercury's premature death in 1991, notching up five more weeks as Britain's biggest selling single.

Geographical mystery

There is a narrative, of sorts, running through the song, but what it's actually all about remains a mystery. The title was also enigmatic. The rhapsody bit was straightforward, but not many teenagers in 1975 knew where Bohemia was. That's not such a problem for beer lovers, who can point their pint glasses towards the Czech Republic and tell you that Bohemia is the home of some of the world's finest beers. This is the land where pilsner originated, and ever since the fall of the Iron Curtain, enthusiasts have been flocking here to sample beers of outstanding quality and heritage. There's no mention of beer in Freddie's mercurial composition, but for a Bohemian rhapsody of a different kind with which to mark its rise to the top, take a look at the Bernard brewery. Launched in 1991 in the historic town of Humpolec, 80km (50 miles) southeast of Prague, its speciality is unpasteurized beer, which ensures a fresher taste than you find in many Czech lagers. The beer selected for today goes a step further. Sváteční Ležák is not just unpasteurized, it is also bottle conditioned, delivering full, complex, buttery malt and herbal hop flavours and leaving behind a natural sediment in the tall impressive bottle. Being as close as you can get to a drink in a Czech pub, it offers an unusual opportunity to enjoy unprocessed Bohemian beer fresh off the yeast. Flick off the swing-stopper today and discover a beer that is breaking almost as many rules as Queen's magnum opus.

Births Busby Berkeley (choreographer), 1895; Jacques Chirac (President of France), 1932; Ryan Giggs (footballer), 1973

Deaths Cardinal Thomas Wolsey, 1530; Giacomo Puccini (composer), 1924; George Harrison (rock musician), 2001

Events Florence Nightingale becomes the first female recipient of the Order of Merit, 1907

Pilsner

ABOVE: FREDDIE MERCURY, LEAD SINGER OF QUEEN, IN CONCERT AT HYDE PARK, 1976

Belhaven St Andrew's Ale

Source Belhaven Brewery, Dunbar, East Lothian **Strength** 4.6% **Website** belhaven.co.uk

'Homage to the home of golf from the home of good beer,' declares the Belhaven website about St Andrew's Ale. The Dunbar brewery – some 48km (30 miles) east of Edinburgh and now part of the Greene King empire – has been turning out fine ales since the year 1719, but St Andrew's Ale was only added to the range in 1992. The strapline that they've tied to it suggests that the inspiration was the championship golf course further up the eastern Scottish coast, but surely at the outset it must have been Scotland's patron saint – whose feast day falls on 30 November – who gave rise to this beer?

Fisher of men

St Andrew is one of the better-known saints, given the fact that he was one of Christ's original 12 disciples. The younger brother of fellow apostle Simon Peter, Andrew was born on the shores of Lake Galilee and, like his brother, was a fisherman before being converted to Christ's cause. As with many early Christian leaders, he paid a cruel price for his steadfastness in his faith and his missionary work. He was executed at Patras, Greece, crucified on an X-shaped cross, an echo of which can be found in the saltire cross that graces the flag of Scotland, one of the countries of which he is patron. It is said that the saint chose this unusual-shaped cross as he didn't consider himself worthy of the same execution as Christ.

Most of the remains of St Andrew are today preserved in the cathedral at Amalfi on the southern Italian coast, but it is said that at one point they were taken to Scotland by St Rule, who founded the town of St Andrews where he landed. Another tale has it that Bishop Acca of Hexham brought them along. A few of the saint's relics have now been returned to Scotland as a gesture by the Roman Catholic Church and are displayed in St Mary's Cathedral in Edinburgh.

Helping Scots celebrate the memory of their patron saint, St Andrew's Ale is brewed from Optic pale malt, crystal malt and just a hint of black malt for colour. The hops are Challenger for bitterness and Golding and Fuggle added late for aroma. The result is a nicely balanced beer with a copper hue that has rich malt and sultana fruitiness in the aroma. Creamy malt and dried fruits continue in the bittersweet taste, which also has a light citrus tingle, before roasted malt comes through early in the drying, hoppy finish.

Births Mark Twain (writer), 1835; Winston Churchill (Prime Minister), 1874; Gary Lineker (footballer and broadcaster), 1960

Deaths Oscar Wilde (writer), 1900; Terence Rattigan (writer), 1977; Evel Knievel (daredevil), 2007

Events London's Crystal Palace burns down, 1936; the coronation stone of Scotland, the Stone of Scone, returned to Edinburgh after 700 years in England, 1996

80/-

ABOVE: SCOTS EMBRACE THE EMBLEM OF THEIR PATRON SAINT

Ursus Black

Source Ursus Breweries, Buzau   **Strength** 6%   **Website** ursus.ro

Considering its position as a bulwark between the Balkans, Europe and Russia, it's perhaps not surprising that Romania has suffered more than most countries over the centuries. As megalomaniacs and dictators have sought eternal fame by trashing their neighbours and plundering their wealth, Romania has been knocked around more than a punchbag in a boxing gym.

In the 20th century alone, the country has seen more trouble than any nation has the right to. After forging itself into a larger mass in the wake of World War I, with the addition of the historically close provinces of Transylvania, Bessarabia and Bucovina, it fell under the gaze of Hitler, who threatened to tear it apart again, unless Germany was granted a monopoly on valuable Romanian exports. Soon the Nazis took over here, too, until, with the tide turning, they were booted out in 1944 when Romania sided instead with the Soviets, a move that was to cost them dear when peace finally ensued. Under the Communists, and particular under the brutally egocentric Nicolae Ceausescu, Romania became a pauper on the world stage. With Ceausescu's overthrow and hasty execution in 1989, Romania had a chance to start again, albeit from a very disadvantaged position. One of the first moves of the new regime was to legislate for a new national day, to give pride back to the country. Previously, 23 August was the day marked for national celebrations, that being the date in 1944 when the Nazis were turfed out. As Romania defiantly broke free of the shadow of the Soviet Union, its leaders looked to a more propitious time as a reason for national bonding. They referred back to 1918 when, in the Great Union, those provinces came together to make Romania the country it is today.

Black to the future

Little was known about Romanian brewing during the Cold War, and not much has leaked forth since, but one of the country's most highly regarded beers is called Ursus Black. The Ursus brewery, in the town of Buzau, about 80km (50 miles) northeast of the capital, Bucharest, has a history dating back 130 years. It is now part of the SABMiller group, which has invested heavily in the business. Ursus Black, which was introduced in 2000, still takes a bit of tracking down, but this may all change as interest in dark lagers increases, for that's the style of beer we have here.

The deep ruby beer includes chocolate malt and Hallertauer Magnum hops, and presents an aroma filled with creamy coffee and caramel, with a slightly sour note similar to that found in a milk stout. It is crisp and bittersweet in the mouth, with creamy dark chocolate, more coffee and spicy alcohol vapours, plus a drying backnote. The finish begins subtly, but builds in bitterness as more coffee, plain chocolate and vaguely liquorice elements come into play.

No doubt several bottles of this hearty lager are sunk with relish each 1 December, not just for national pride but also because it does a rather good job of keeping out the winter cold.

Births Marie Tussaud (waxworks pioneer), 1761; Woody Allen (comedian and film director), 1935; Lee Trevino (golfer), 1939

Deaths Lorenzo Ghiberti (artist), 1455; David Ben-Gurion (politician), 1973; Stéphane Grappelli (violinist), 1997

Events The Ford Motor Company introduces the first moving assembly line, 1913; Alabama seamstress Rosa Parks refuses to relinquish her bus seat to a white man, sparking civil rights demonstrations, 1955

Dark Lager

343

Brauhaus Schweinfurt Advents-Bier

Source Brauhaus Schweinfurt, Schweinfurt **Strength** 5.4% **Website** brauhaus-schweinfurt.de

The start of December coincides with the religious season known as Advent. This is a four-week holy preamble to Christmas and marks the beginning of the Christian year. Unfortunately, it's mostly known these days for the largely irrelevant, chocolate-filled calendars that excite children in the run-up to the big day.

The term Advent is derived from the Latin for 'arrival', with due reference to the birth of Christ. It officially begins on the closest Sunday to the last day of November, allowing church services to take place over four Sundays before Christmas Day. Advent ends at midnight on Christmas Eve. At each Sunday service, a new candle is lit on the traditional Advent wreath. The candles represent, in order, Hope, Peace, Love and Joy. A fifth candle, for the arrival of Christ – the Light of the World – is lit on Christmas Day.

Christmas export

In early Christian times, the season ran for a much longer time, starting on 11 November, St Martin's Day. The beer selected to note the period also arrives earlier. It comes from a small Bavarian brewery called Brauhaus Schweinfurt, which was founded in the town of Schweinfurt, about 48km (30 miles) northwest of Bamberg, in 1858. In 1912, a new brewery was constructed to meet demand, and a year later it merged with a local rival. Today, the brewery produces a wide range of beers, reflecting most of the popular German beer styles, including a pilsner, a weissbier, a dark wheat beer and an export. Its Advents-bier is also described as an export in style, which generally implies it is maltier than, and not as dry as, a pilsner. The beer is available between October and December and is also sold outside of Germany.

When you splash the beer into your glass, the pale golden colour is somewhat deceptive. It implies it's going to be light in flavour, but the truth is rather different. From the first sniff of the fresh, floral, lemony, herbal aroma, you know this beer is not going to disappoint. Sweet malt is the first impression in the mouth but this is soon countered by a generous helping of dry, herbal hops. The body, as you'd expect from an export, is full, and there are pleasant suggestions of lemon floating around the palate. The finish is dry, hoppy and bitter, and lingers nicely. Why let the kids have all the Advent fun?

Births Maria Callas (opera singer), 1923; Gianni Versace (fashion designer), 1946; Monica Seles (tennis player), 1973

Deaths Marquis de Sade (writer), 1814; Marty Feldman (comedian and writer), 1982; Philip Larkin (poet), 1985

Events Napoleon crowned Emperor of France, 1804; 'Rogue Trader' Nick Leeson jailed for six-and-a-half years, 1995

Pale Lager

Felinfoel Double Dragon

Source The Felinfoel Brewery Company, Felinfoel **Strength** 4.2% **Website** felinfoel-brewery.com

In the entry for 24 January, the world of canned beer was explored to mark the anniversary of the first example back in 1935. We're celebrating canned beer again today, but it's really the technological achievement of a small Welsh family brewery that's in the spotlight, rather than the liquid packed inside a tin.

Although America's CanCo company, together with the Krueger Brewery of New Jersey, was the first in the world to produce canned beer, little Felinfoel, a brewery close to Llanelli in South Wales, almost beat them to it.

Felinfoel's home area used to be a blue-collar heartland, with tin-plate manufacturing a major employer in the early 20th century. Family connections brought the two trades of brewing and metal together, and led to close collaboration on the novel project. In conjunction with the Metal Box company in London, they found a way to prevent cans from bursting under the pressure of the beer and – they believed – to prevent the metal tainting the beer inside. Consquently, in December 1935, Europe's first canned beer made its debut.

The first cans were secured with a crown cork (what we call today a standard bottle top) and looked more like tins of Brasso polish than beer. Interestingly, however, those first cans held beer that was not pasteurized, something Felinfoel was extremely bullish about, drawing attention to the fact that it was proper beer, not processed, inside. Unfortunately, despite an initial flurry of excitement surrounding the new product, canned beer was slow to take off, and Felinfoel's influential role in developing what is today an enormous market has been largely forgotten.

Double take

Felinfoel beer can still be found in cans but it's the cask version that's to be recommended. The brewery's best-known ale is Double Dragon, once an obvious contender to be national ale of Wales, but now somewhat overshadowed by the more thrusting ales from Brains and the various winners of CAMRA's Champion Beer of Wales contest. Nevertheless, Double Dragon is a tasty best bitter with a fine balance of malt and hops that is manifested in an enjoyable, fruity toffee taste.

Sadly, at the time of writing this book, the Felinfoel website was rather ambiguous about this long-established beer, describing it as, 'The full drinking premium Welsh ale, malty and subtly hopped with a rich colour and a smooth balanced character, developed by the brewing expertise of five generations of the founding family.' So far, so good. It was the next sentence that was the killer: 'Available in smooth with all the advantages of cream flow dispense.' In other words, we're really proud of this beer but you can also have it pasteurized, nitrogenated and stripped of all character.

That's some way to treat your flagship product – and quite a reversal from the days when the company led the world technologically but still believed in the integrity of its products.

Births Andy Williams (singer), 1928; Ozzy Osbourne (rock musician), 1948; Franz Klammer (skier), 1953

Deaths Robert Louis Stevenson (writer), 1894; Pierre Auguste Renoir (artist), 1919; Madeline Kahn (actress), 1999

Events First successful human heart transplant, conducted by Christiaan Barnard, 1967; gas leak at the Union Carbide chemical plant near Bhopal, India, resulting in thousands of deaths, 1984

Best Bitter

Wolf Cavell Ale

Source The Wolf Brewery, Besthorpe, Norfolk **Strength** 3.7% **Website** wolfbrewery.com

'**P**atriotism is not enough,' reads the famous quotation attributed to World War I heroine Edith Cavell. A dedicated nurse and humanitarian, Cavell had made a significant contribution to her own nation's defence but, by making this statement on the eve of her execution at the hands of the Germans, she recognized that magnanimity needed to be extended beyond her friends and allies. 'I must have no hatred or bitterness towards anyone,' she stated, which is an astonishingly gracious declaration to make, given the shocking circumstances in which Edith was soon to meet her death.

Edith Cavell was born in Swardeston, just south of Norwich, on 4 December 1865, the daughter of a local vicar. She worked initially as a governess, spending five years in Brussels, but soon found her vocation in nursing, when she was called home to care for her sick father. In 1895, she decided to formalize her knowledge of medicine and trained at the London Hospital. She then worked for various institutions around the country before returning to Brussels, where she was placed in charge of a nursing training school. When war broke out and Belgium was invaded, she remained at her post in what soon became a Red Cross hospital, insisting that her nurses treat all prisoners equally – be they friend or foe. Soon, however, she also began to work with the local resistance, secretly helping soldiers return to Britain. When the hospital was infiltrated by a collaborator, Edith was questioned and tricked into confessing her role in the scheme. For her actions, she was sentenced to death. In the early hours of 12 October 1915, Edith and four colleagues were placed before a firing squad.

A reluctant martyr

The execution of a virtuous middle-aged woman, a nurse who had cared for all sides, proved to be a massive propaganda own goal for the Germans. It brought condemnation from all over the globe, and was said to have hastened America's arrival into the war. When news of her death broke in Britain, army recruitment doubled. Edith never wanted to become a martyr – she even suggested that her death sentence had been quite just – but her brutal slaying was an important milestone in the course of the hostilities.

Edith was initially buried close to the spot where she died but, after the war, her body was transferred back to Norfolk where her name is honoured today by a local brewery. Wolf Brewery was founded in Attleborough in 1996 and changed hands in 2006, moving at the same time to new, larger premises on the fringe of the same town. Its Edith Cavell beer was first brewed specifically for The Beehive pub in Norwich, the meeting place of the Edith Cavell Lodge of the Royal Antediluvian Order of Buffaloes. The beer is now more widely available, including in bottle. Pale and crystal malts join with wheat malt in the mash tun, with Fuggle and Challenger hops adding the fruit and bitterness. The result is an enjoyable, fruity, softly bitter amber beer with a dry, bitter finish.

Births Ronnie Corbett (comedian), 1930; Jeff Bridges (actor), 1949; Pamela Stephenson (actress and psychologist), 1949

Deaths Thomas Hobbes (philosopher), 1679; Benjamin Britten (composer), 1976; Frank Zappa (rock musician), 1993

Events Nicholas Breakspear becomes the first English pope, 1154; first edition of *The Observer* newspaper, 1791

Sierra Nevada Celebration Ale

Source Sierra Nevada Brewing Co., Chico, California **Strength** 6.8% **Website** sierranevada.com

In 1933, 5 December was a big day for American beer lovers. This was the date that the 21st amendment to the US Constitution was ratified, thereby bringing an end to the ghastly period of Prohibition. After nearly 14 years, it was once again legal to produce, sell and buy beer.

From the time the US legislature ratified the 18th Amendment in 1919, rendering the manufacture, sale or transportation of intoxicating liquors, within, into or out of the country a criminal offence, America's brewers ran into a wall. They either shut up shop or, to keep their heads above water, diversified into 'near beer', soft drinks or related products such as baker's yeast and malted milk.

Prohibition came about when temperance bodies took advantage of restrictions that had been imposed on alcohol supply during World War I to persuade politicians to go one step further and ban it altogether. It turned out to be a disaster for the country. While once-legal, commercial brewers twiddled their thumbs, illegal home-brewers, smugglers and racketeers had a field day. However, with the depression of the late 1920s gathering speed, the country grew tired of deprivation, crime and unemployment. They wanted their brewers, farmers and transport industry back at work, and Franklin D Roosevelt provided it, winning a landslide presidential election victory on a ticket that promised the repeal of Prohibition. By the end of 1933, America was mostly wet again.

Nevertheless, the devastation of the US brewing industry was obvious. Before Prohibition, the US could boast 1,568 brewers; on resumption of legal brewing, the initial number of companies able to pick up production was a mere 31. With demand legally restored, that number was able to grow to 756 within a year.

Californian celebration

The ideal way to celebrate this momentous day would be to hop on a plane to San Francisco, where on 2nd Street, you can raise a glass or two in the 21st Amendment Brewery and Restaurant. If that's out of the question, I recommend Sierra Nevada's Celebration Ale. This is the Christmas seasonal brew from a brewery in Chico, northern California, that started out as a microbrewery in 1980 but is now bigger than most of the UK's long-established regionals. It's a fine example of the balanced use of pungent American hops. There are three types in all, the three Cs: Chinook, Centennial and Cascade. The result is a beer brim-full of grapefruit notes that are kept in balance by the sort of full maltiness you need to bring a beer up to 6.8%. Being bottle conditioned, you can pick it up internationally, and some UK supermarkets now stock it in winter. Had it been around 70-odd years ago, it would, in itself, have been a good enough reason to repeal Prohibition.

Births George Armstrong Custer (US General), 1839; Walt Disney (film producer), 1901; Otto Preminger (film director), 1906; Little Richard (rock 'n' roll musician), 1932

Deaths Wolfgang Amadeus Mozart (composer), 1791; Claude Monet (artist), 1926

Events UK's first motorway opens (Preston Bypass), 1958; Margaret Thatcher defeats Sir Anthony Meyer in a challenge for the leadership of the Conservative Party, 1989

Strong Ale

Eggenberg Samichlaus

Source Brauerei Schloss Eggenberg, Vorchdorf **Strength** 14% **Website** schlosseggenberg.at

At the Eggenberg family brewery in Austria, they take 6 December very seriously. This is the day when the brewery's most famous beer is produced.

The Eggenberg brewery enjoys a most envious setting, based in a lake and mountain paradise between Salzburg and Vienna. From the brewhouse, the vista is one of snowy peaks and lush green meadows. The brewery itself is a mix of clinically modern and charmingly antique, with the oldest parts contained in a country house, complete with chapel. The business is run by the Stöhr family, as it has been for 200 years, whose enthusiasm has made the company Austria's leading producer of specialist beers. Among Eggenberg's oddities are a whisky malt beer (see 17 June) and a beer made with locally grown 'harmless' hemp. But one beer stands out, a beer initially produced in another country, an alpine climb away over the *Sound of Music* mountains.

Samichlaus was created in 1979 by the Swiss brewer Hürlimann. Its scientists had long been known as yeast specialists and they took their work to new extremes by developing a beer yeast that could ferment to higher than normal strengths. Standard beer yeast usually gives up the ghost when it has created around 11–12% alcohol, overwhelmed by its own inebriating output. The Hürlimann special yeast fought on, however, and produced a beer at 14%, strong enough to win a place in the *Guinness Book of Records*.

Special dark lager

Rather than squander their achievement on a stupid beer for park bench consumption, the brewery applied it to a special dark lager for Christmas. They called it Samichlaus, the Swiss German for Santa Claus, and decided to brew it once annually on 6 December, St Nicholas's Day. They set it aside for ten months to mature and bottled it the following October. The beer then went on sale the next 6 December.

Unfortunately, in 1997, Hürlimann was taken over by Swiss rival Feldschlössen, and Samichlaus production ground to a halt. It's not often in history that the Austrians have ridden to the rescue of the Swiss (ask William Tell), but they did so in this case. Eggenberg Brewery secured the rights to brew and market the beer in 1999, and the first Austrian version emerged a year later.

The Stöhrs have modified the Samichlaus recipe a little, and now use crystal clear mountain spring water in the brew, but, being wise men from the East, they still return to Switzerland for the special yeast that achieves this Christmas miracle. The beer ferments for up to three weeks and still enjoys ten lazy months of cold conditioning. When you take the first sip, it washes over the tongue like a warming, ultra-smooth sherry. Break one open and you'll slide effortlessly into the Christmas spirit.

Births Ira Gershwin (lyricist), 1896; Dave Brubeck (jazz musician), 1920; Andrew Flintoff (cricketer), 1977

Deaths Jefferson Davis (US Confederate President), 1889; Roy Orbison (pop musician), 1988

Events David Lloyd George becomes Prime Minister, 1916; Irish Free State declared, 1921; David Cameron becomes leader of the Conservative Party, 2005

BOCK

Dogfish Head 90 Minute Imperial IPA

Source Dogfish Head Craft Brewery, Milton, Delaware **Strength** 9% **Website** dogfish.com

Although celebrated in the title of a punningly awful song by Perry Como, Delaware is an often neglected state of America. Dwarfed by its near neighbours Maryland and Virginia, and minuscule in comparison with Alaska, Texas and California, this triangular area of Atlantic shoreline tends to be passed through, or more likely over, by foreign tourists, and unfairly so, as this is a land of historic import. The state nickname is 'The First State', a reference to the events of this day in 1787 when Delaware became the first of the 13 original American states to ratify the Constitution. It may be small and tucked out of the way, but it was a part of the US before any other state.

Delaware has a number of other nicknames, too. 'Uncle Sam's Pocket Handkerchief' is either cruelly dismissive or genially endearing, in a pat on the head sort of way, while 'The Blue Hen State' refers to the Revolutionary Wars, when Delaware soldiers identified themselves with the local bird of the same name that was known for its fighting prowess. 'The Diamond State', Thomas Jefferson called it, noting that its strategic position on the eastern seaboard made it small but valuable, and his elevated opinion of the state is echoed in the modern nickname of 'Small Wonder', a description coined to celebrate the state's beauty and its size-defying contribution to the nation's culture and economy.

Extreme beers

Helping Delaware punch above its weight is a microbrewery with a global reputation. Dogfish Head was founded in the town of Milton only in 1995, but has already acquired cult status among beer nuts. The inspiration is founder Sam Calagione, a man who knows no fear when it comes to loading the mash tun and copper. It is Sam who has been chief architect of the move towards 'extreme beers', beers that go way beyond the accepted boundaries of taste to pack in excessive amounts of flavour. Typical of Sam's boldness is his series of IPAs. It begins with a 60 Minute IPA (6%) – its name is derived from the length of the copper boil. Hops are the crucial ingredient, as you'd hope in an IPA, and here they are not simply added in two or three charges but constantly as the boil continues. The same pattern is followed for the two other IPAs.

120 Minute IPA is a Goliath of a beer, pounding out at 20% ABV and brewed only in small batches. Less frightening, but equally demanding of respect, is today's choice of beer, 90 Minute Imperial IPA. A mere 9% in alcohol, it tastes sweet and nicely warming at first, but then immediately hoppy, tangy and spicy. Malt flavours struggle to fight their way through, but there is a touch of toffee, along with some red berries and juicy citrus notes. The mouthfeel is rich and creamy, spiked all the time by the peppery hops, but the alcohol remains under control with none of the coarseness and distracting vapours you find in inferior strong ales.

There are some truly outstanding IPAs available today in the US, but this is one of the very best, and yet another reason for not ignoring the small, but perfectly formed, First State.

Births Gian Lorenzo Bernini (artist and architect), 1598; Tom Waits (singer-songwriter), 1949; John Terry (footballer), 1980

Deaths Cicero (orator), 43 BC; Robert Graves (writer), 1985; Billy Bremner (footballer), 1997

Events Royal Opera House, Covent Garden, opens, 1732; Japanese air force attacks US naval base at Pearl Harbor, Hawaii, 1941

Imperial IPA

349

Achel Blonde

Source Sint Benedictus Abdij De Achelse Kluis, Hamont-Achel **Strength** 8% **Website** achelsekluis.org

For years, there were only six genuine Trappist monastery breweries in Belgium and Holland. In 1998, a seventh was added, when the brotherhood at Achel – just on the Belgian side of the Dutch border, near Eindhoven – added a small brewhouse to its facilities.

Of course, this wasn't the first brewery on the site. Like nearly all abbeys, Achel had brewed in the past, but the last beer production here had been in 1914. The invading Germans stole the equipment. The abbey itself has its origins back in the 17th century, when it sprang into existence as a colony of hermits. The brotherhood was evicted during Napoleon's sweep across the continent but was restored when monks from the Westmalle monastery set up home here in the 1840s.

After World War II, the abbey was partly rebuilt, and agriculture and traditional crafts became the economic mainstays of life. The fraternity's website relates the various trades that contributed to the monks' income. It mentions a bakery, cheese-making, cabinet-work and a printing office, as well as 'forgery' and a 'bras shop', although I suspect the last two are mistranslations. In 1989, most of the land was sold off to form a nature reserve, giving the brotherhood the financial resources to consider installing its own brewery.

Brewing renaissance

The revival of brewing was overseen by Brother Thomas, the recently retired brewing monk from Westmalle. Also involved at some stage was veteran brewer Brother Antoine from another Trappist settlement, Rochefort. The brewery took a little time to find its feet and its direction – initially only weaker beers were produced, all for draught consumption – but it seems well on course now, with a range of bottle-conditioned strong ales also part of the package.

The selection includes both blonde and brown ales, and the one chosen to mark today's event is probably the most easily discovered. Achel Blonde, at 8% ABV, is in the tripel style and pours a dark golden colour. The aroma is filled with juicy melon and oranges, with typically spicy Belgian monastic beer notes and even a little bubblegum. The taste is also spicy and yeasty, sweet and warming, with an orange fruitiness and a delicate hop bitter note. Those juicy oranges run on into the finish, which remains sweet but becomes drier as bitterness develops.

Achel Blonde tastes great from the bottle but there's something special about savouring a beer on draught at source. This is possible if you visit the pleasant café at Achel abbey, which offers a viewing window onto the brewery.

Births Mary, Queen of Scots, 1542; Sammy Davis Jr (actor and singer), 1925; Jim Morrison (rock musician), 1943

Deaths Golda Meir (politician), 1978; John Lennon (rock musician), 1980

Events Brunel's Clifton Suspension Bridge in Bristol opens, 1864; war declared on Japan by Britain and the US, 1941; the Soviet Union dissolved, 1991

Farsons Lacto

Source Simonds Farsons Cisk plc, Mriehel **Strength** 3.8% **Website** farsons.com

Raise a glass today to the world's longest-running prime-time soap opera. At 7pm on 9 December 1960, the sounds of a mournful cornet played into British living rooms, and the equally gloomy roofscape of industrial Manchester flickered into view as the title sequence for the first *Coronation Street* began to run. Thirty minutes later, viewers had been introduced to a dour but sparky group of residents who were to dominate their TV screens for the next half-century.

In its early days, *Coronation Street* played like a kitchen-sink drama – domestic conflict in a grim northern town – but it quickly mellowed into a semi-sitcom, adding moments of high farce to its quarrels, street-fights and moments of deep sentimentality. It was a winning mixture.

The series was born in the days when working-class neighbourhoods had a pub on nearly every corner, where the pay packet would be emptied and the grime and grit of the day washed away with a pint or two of honest, local bitter (in this case, Newton & Ridley's). But the pub was not just a second home for the grafters. It was a community centre. Even the local old maids congregrated there. Their den was the snug, now – as in so many real-life pubs – sadly long gone. In this quiet corner, away from the bustle of the public bar, the tittle-tattling trio of Ena Sharples, Minnie Caldwell and Martha Longhurst spent their evening hours, contentedly sipping bottle after bottle of milk stout.

A forgotten beer

Like the snug, milk stout belongs to another era. This style of beer was so named not because it contains milk, but because it contains lactose – or milk sugar. The lactose is added to the mash tun and, because it cannot be fermented by brewers' yeast, adds body-building sugars to the beer while keeping the strength respectfully on the low side. As delicious as it is, this dark, creamy treat went rapidly out of fashion in the 1960s and, if it weren't for the ladies in the snug bar of the Rovers Return, it may well have been forgotten even sooner.

In their memory, I suggest opening a bottle of Lacto. This comes from the Farsons brewery in Malta (see 15 April and 13 December) and, appropriately, is described as a milk stout. It drinks like one, too, with dark, sweet malty flavours and a rich creamy note, but the brewery admits it's a bit of a cheat. It's actually the company's Simonds Hop Leaf Bitter, darkened with caramel and dosed with lactose and a mix of B vitamins, which in the past encouraged the custom of invalids. It is an enjoyable creation, though, especially as a sweetish finish to a meal. With milk stouts now so few and far between, Ena, Minnie and Martha would surely have approved.

Births John Milton (poet), 1608; Judi Dench (actress), 1934; Donny Osmond (singer), 1962

Deaths Anthony van Dyck (artist), 1641; Edith Sitwell (poet), 1964; Danny Blanchflower (footballer), 1993

Events England cricket captain Mike Gatting angrily rows on field with umpire Shakoor Rana, 1987; Lech Walesa elected President of Poland, 1990

ABOVE: THE ROVERS RETURN, SECOND HOME TO THE RESIDENTS OF *CORONATION STREET*

Milk Stout

Pietra Ambrée

Source Brasserie Pietra, Furiani, Corsica **Strength** 6% **Website** brasseriepietra.com

As an island nation, with a mountainous terrain unfriendly to farming, the Corsicans learnt the hard way to be self-sufficient. Starvation was always a possibility until the 15th century, when citizens were urged to plant harvestable trees. Olives, mulberries and cherries were part of the solution, but it was the chestnut that took hold and became the island's leading source of sustenance. Its fruit not only fed the locals but also nourished the pigs they reared and the horses they rode. Ground into flour, it was the basis for bread and cakes, and even its wood came in handy for making furniture. The chestnut tree may no longer be essential to the national diet, but it still holds a symbolism that the people won't let die. The Chestnut Festival is proof.

The Fiera di Castagna is staged this time in December every year, in the village of Bocognano, between the western port of Ajaccio and the inland town of Corte. Initially, this was very much a local celebration, with a healthy interchange of farming news one of the main sources of entertainment. Today, it's an international event, as around 30,000 tourists descend on the village for a weekend of fun in honour of the mighty chestnut, with local craft and food stands vying for attention, offering every possible culinary use for the humble local product, from jams to liqueurs. Not surprisingly, a Corsican brewery has joined the party, producing a beer that includes in its recipe the island's prized crop.

Nutty nuance

This brewery was founded in 1996 by husband and wife Dominique and Armelle Sialelli. They were living in Paris and looking to return to Dominique's Corsican homeland. But they needed to create the right sort of business that would allow them to do so. The Sialellis wanted to make the chestnut central to their plans and spent a couple of years working out how best to incorporate the nut in their new beer. The conclusion was that it should go in flour form in the mash tun. They called the beer – and the brewery – Pietra, after Dominique's home town of Pietraserena. The range has now expanded to include a blonde lager called Serena and a wheat beer called Colomba, neither of which are chestnut inspired.

Pietra is an amber-coloured lager, and the nose is malty but rather subtle. Chestnuts are just about noticeable through the light, perfumed floral aroma and the hint of tart citrus fruit. In the malty, creamy, drying taste, spicy warmth adds depth, and mellow nut flavours linger in the background. Hop does a fine balancing job without ever taking over, and there's just a suggestion of apple from the fermentation. As befits a beer of this magnitude, the finish is pleasantly warming. It's also increasingly bitter, with malt continuing to provide fullness and, of course, a softly nutty note always in evidence.

These characteristics make it ideal for beer and food matching, with dishes such as chicken and turkey benefiting from the nutty nuance.

Births Dorothy Lamour (actress), 1914; Clive Anderson (comedian and TV presenter), 1952; Kenneth Branagh (actor and director), 1960

Deaths Alfred Nobel (industrialist), 1896; Otis Redding (soul musician), 1967; Richard Pryor (actor and comedian), 2005

Events The world's first traffic lights go into use, close to London's Houses of Parliament, 1868; awarding of the first Nobel Prizes, 1901

Vienna-style Lager

Gulpener Korenwolf

Source Gulpener Bierbrouwerij, Gulpen **Strength** 5% **Website** korenwolf.co.uk

It's hard to overplay the significance of 11 December in European life. On this day in 1991, the leaders of the European Community countries brought to a close 31 hours of intense negotiation and argument, thrashing out a new treaty that would allow for the transition of what was previously a trading organization into a political body. The Maastricht Treaty, as it became known, was to turn the EC into the EU.

Masterminding proceedings was EC President Jacques Delors. On the agenda were issues such as the social chapter and political and monetary union, and they were controversial to say the least. European leaders knew that their political futures were in the balance if they handled things badly, and UK Prime Minister John Major faced open revolt in his own Conservative Party if he gave too much away. *The Sun* summed up the right-wing position in Britain: 'Up Yours Delors!' was its typically hysterical front-page headline.

Ultimately, Major secured an opt-out from both the social chapter (although this was later signed up to by Tony Blair's Labour government) and monetary union, and pronounced himself satisfied when the summit concluded. The treaty still had hurdles to clear – the Danes rejected it at first, and there were other close shaves in France and Germany – but it was eventually signed in February 1992 and came into effect in November 1993.

The venue for this hugely significant summit was the small, unassuming town of Maastricht, one of the prettiest communities in the Netherlands. It sits right at the south of the country, in a narrow finger of Dutchness that plugs the gap – like the boy with the dike – between the Belgian and German borders. It's an old Roman settlement that was later favoured by the Holy Roman Emperor Charlemagne, when he made his base at nearby Aachen and endowed the town with Romanesque churches that can still be visited today.

The corn wolf

On the beer front, the area is best known through the Gulpener Brewery, sited about 16km (10 miles) away in the town of Gulpen. Considering their geographical position, the brewers here have a fittingly cosmopolitan attitude to their work. They don't just brew pilsner or ale, but almost a little bit of everything, including abbey, fruit and sour beers. Their most famous beer is called Korenwolf, an unusual witbier that is imported into the UK by Coors. Unlike standard Belgian-style wheat beers that are made only with barley malt and wheat, Korenwolf also includes rye and a second type of wheat called spelt. Together, these cereals provide a lightly grainy, sweetish base for the typical citrus-and-spice seasoning of beers of this style, which is enhanced by a little flutter of elderflower. It's a quenching, quaffable beer that also lends itself beautifully to the dining table, especially alongside seafood dishes.

The name Korenwolf sounds rather dramatic when translated literally into English as 'corn wolf', and that's part of the charm of the beer, for the creature referred to is the hamster, which runs free in this part of the Netherlands. Look for the cute picture on the label.

'Freddie Starr ate my hamster!' bellowed another of *The Sun*'s infamous front pages. Now, if it had reported that the comedian had drunk the hamster, that would have been a rather different matter.

Births Hector Berlioz (composer), 1803; Alexander Solzhenitsyn (writer), 1918

Deaths Sam Cooke (soul musician), 1964; Willie Rushton (writer and comedian), 1996

Events King Edward VIII abdicates the throne, 1936; *Apollo XVII*, the last manned lunar mission, lands on the moon, 1972; boxer Muhammad Ali defeated by Trevor Berbick in his last fight, 1981

Wheat Beer

East African Breweries Tusker Lager

Source East African Breweries, Nairobi **Strength** 4.2% **Website** eabl.com

Africa, as we all know, is a troubled continent. But one of the most politically stable of its countries has been Kenya. Sadly, recent times have shown that here, too, crisis lurks only around the corner. Allegations of rigged elections in December 2007 led to unrest on the streets, a succession of horrific murders and a state of emergency. National day celebrations earlier in the month were quickly forgotten amid scenes of carnage.

Jamhuri Day – to give it its proper local title, after the Swahili word for republic – was instituted in 1964, to celebrate both the independence gained by Kenya from the United Kingdom the previous year and the declaration of the country as a republic. Celebrated with family feasts, parades and speeches, it's a day when Kenyans traditionally have come together. It can only be hoped that it will serve this purpose again in future.

There is only one beer to drink on Jamhuri Day. It comes from the country's East African Breweries, which was founded in 1922. Its beer range includes some interesting items, including an Allsopps lager, which brings back memories of the famous Burton ale brewery of the same name. The company also brews Guinness under licence. The main product, however, is called Tusker. This accounts for nearly a third of all beer drunk in the country and is the biggest beer brand in East Africa. It is also exported to the UK, North America and Japan.

Tusker is a clean, pale golden lager with a grainy, mildly herbal aroma. Refreshing light lemon notes work alongside delicate malty sweetness in the mouth, with hops way down the pecking order. The dry finish is equally gentle, with only a soft bitterness. It's never going to please drinkers who thrive on robust beers with great depth of character, but it's certainly nicely balanced and, fresh off the line, is probably an ideal thirst quencher under the blistering equatorial sun.

The beer takes its unusual name from an elephant that tragically killed the brewery founder George Hurst, while he was on a hunting expedition in 1923. The beer pre-dates his demise, but was renamed in his memory. Among other cereals, it contains malt from barley grown in the Kenyan Rift Valley. There is also a stronger (5%), premium version known as Tusker Malt, which is an all-malt brew, but much harder to get hold of.

Births Frank Sinatra (singer and actor), 1915; John Osborne (playwright), 1929; Bill Nighy (actor), 1949

Deaths Robert Browning (poet), 1889; Douglas Fairbanks (actor), 1939; Joseph Heller (writer), 1999

Events An IRA siege in London's Balcombe Street ends peacefully after six days, 1975; the Clapham rail disaster claims 35 lives, 1988

Pale Lager

ABOVE: ELEPHANT IN KENYA'S MASAI MARA

Farsons Hopleaf Extra

Source Simonds Farsons Cisk plc, Mriehel **Strength** 5% **Website** hopleafbeer.com

Older beer lovers may well remember a brewery in Reading, Berkshire, called Simonds. It was founded in the late 18th century and taken over by Courage in 1960. The historic brewery in the centre of town was unceremoniously demolished at the turn of the 1980s and usurped by a state-of-the-art facility, close to the M4 motorway, a modern brewery that has itself now been earmarked for closure. But while Courage rapidly and conveniently confined the name of Simonds and its hop leaf logo to history, there has remained one place where you can still drink Simonds beer. It's on a small Mediterranean island with strong British connections – connections that came to a formal end on this day in 1974.

It was in 1880 that Simonds began to put the malt into Malta. In the days of the British Empire, UK troops were stationed on this strategically important island or used it as a staging post. Spotting the market for good old British ale, Simonds set up an office, importing casks and bottles of beer to quench the thirsts of soldiers and sailors. In 1929, Simonds became even more integrated into the island's community when it merged its local interests with a Maltese brewer named Farrugia & Sons, commonly known as Farsons. In the post-war years, a new brewhouse was constructed, in striking art deco style. At the same time, a third brewer joined the business. The Malta Export Brewery had been founded with the assistance of Munich brewery Augustiner, so its beers had a distinctive Germanic character, and the twin portfolio of ales and lagers that resulted has continued to be popular on the island.

Changing times

Malta is a tiny country in a state of flux. In 1964, it secured independence from the UK but continued to be a member of the Commonwealth, with Queen Elizabeth II still the head of state. In 1974, however, the country became a republic. It remains part of the Commonwealth but now has a president overseeing affairs. This peaceful transition is celebrated each 13 December with military parades in the capital, Valetta, ceremonies to honour local worthies, and horse races at Marsa in the south of the island. You can join in the fun by opening a bottle of Hopleaf Extra, a 5% bitter that was a finalist in the Tesco Beer Awards in 2006 and which is based on the original Simonds recipes. Surprisingly, for a beer of such a vintage, it pours a bright golden colour – proof that golden ales were around long before the current trend started. In keeping with its name, the beer is crisp, toffeeish and hoppy, brewed with British malt and hops.

Malta joined the EU in 2004 and building work is taking place all over the island. It's a similar story at Farsons, where a new brewhouse is being constructed. However, unlike at Reading, the attractive and historic brewing vessels are not being trashed: they will hold their place as part of Maltese brewing history when the current brewhouse is converted to a museum.

Births Dick van Dyke (actor), 1925; Steve Buscemi (actor), 1957; Jamie Foxx (actor), 1967

Deaths Donatello (artist), 1466; Samuel Johnson (writer and lexicographer), 1784; Lew Grade (entertainment impresario), 1998

Events Battle of the River Plate, 1939; Al Gore concedes defeat in the controversial presidential election won by George W Bush, 2004

Golden Ale

Fuller's Jack Frost

Source Fuller, Smith & Turner, Chiswick, London **Strength** 4.5% **Website** fullers.co.uk

In 2003, London decided to take a step back in time. In centuries past, when winters were severe, the city used to host an annual frost fair, when traders set up stalls on the frozen River Thames and sold their wares to partying citizens. Stands provided hot and cold drinks – including ale – and pies, buns, nuts, gingerbread and fruit were all available to soak them up. With the river no longer icing over, the fairs ended in 1814, but Southwark Council has now brought back the spectacle in a modern format.

Each year, over a weekend in the middle of December, the Bankside Frost Fair takes place on the south bank of the Thames, alongside the Tate Modern art gallery and the re-creation of Shakespeare's Globe Theatre. The event echoes the spirit of the old festivities, with attractions such as a lantern parade, a boat race, husky dog sleigh rides, ice sculpting, street theatre, arts and crafts workshops, and festive sing-alongs, as well as offering a chance for some late Christmas shopping courtesy of market traders. One particular element of the original fair has not been brought back, however. Bear baiting, thankfully, is not the done thing these days. The event is free to attend, with any monies raised going to charity.

Fruity surprise

If you can't make it to London, have your own frost fair with a winter ale from Fuller's. Jack Frost is a copper-red ale brewed using pale and crystal malts and Northdown and First Gold hops, with an interesting novel ingredient – blackberries. The aroma is full of juicy fruit and toffee, with just a hint of tea. If you didn't know it was blackberry, it would be hard to pinpoint the fruit specifically, but you'd certainly spot that there were dark berries present. In the palate, there's more toffeeish malt, juicy berries and tea, all wrapped up in a well-judged level of hop and bitterness. The finish is dry and fruity with some lingering malty sweetness, although hops soon take over.

The use of the fruit in this beer is very clever: it enhances the natural beer flavours rather than dominates them, which means this is still very much a beer for beer drinkers, rather than a drink for those who don't really like beer. You can usually try it hand-pulled in Fuller's pubs at this time of the year, or settle for a very good bottled version if that's not possible.

Births Nostradamus (astrologer), 1503; King George VI, 1895; Michael Owen (footballer), 1979

Deaths George Washington (US President), 1799; Prince Albert (consort), 1861; Stanley Baldwin (Prime Minister), 1947

Events First trials of the Montgolfier Brothers' pioneering hot-air balloon, 1782; Roald Amundsen and his team become the first persons to reach the South Pole, 1911

Best Bitter

Alcazar Maple Magic

Source Alcazar Brewery, Old Basford, Nottinghamshire **Strength** 5.5% **Website** alcazarbrewery.co.uk

In a quest to build a stronger national identity, Canada adopted a new flag on this day in 1964. Previously, the flag flown to represent the country had been the Union flag or various versions of the naval Red Ensign, with a Canadian crest added. It was time to find a fresh design, said those arguing for a change, especially with the centennial of the establishment of the Canadian Confederation looming in 1967. A national debate ensued and various options were considered. Heraldic experts were consulted and much thought went into finding an emblem that summed up the geography and history of the country.

The red-and-white traditional colours of the nation – declared by King George V in 1921 – were maintained and a prominent symbol associated with the world's second largest country was selected. The maple tree grows assiduously across Canada and its syrup is one of the country's important exports. The distinctive leaf of the tree, already used as a symbol by the nation's athletes, therefore, won the debate. On 15 December 1964, the lower house of Canada's parliament voted in favour of accepting a design that placed the maple leaf centre stage. Three days later, the upper chamber consented, and on 15 February the next year, the Red Ensign was lowered for the last time and replaced by what has become internationally known as Canada's official flag.

Canadian porter

The maple remains a potent symbol of Canadian identity. There's even a Canadian brewer working in the UK who has named a beer after it. David Allen is the owner of the rather un-Canadian sounding Alcazar Brewery in Nottingham. Set up behind the Fox & Crown pub in the suburb of Old Basford in 1999, the 12-barrel brewery now offers a range of beers with connections to local folk hero Robin Hood and Sherwood Forest (see 27 July), but still finds time to show off David's Canadian roots – at least at this time of the year. One of Alcazar's regular winter offerings is called Maple Magic. It's a porter brewed from pale, crystal, amber and chocolate malts, plus some roasted barley. Four hops add to the complexity – Fuggle, Golding, Challenger and Northdown – and a mix of seasonal spices (nutmeg, cinnamon and cloves) takes the beer off in the direction of Christmas cake and such festive confections. Significantly, as the name implies, there's also a lacing of maple syrup, and the end result is a deep ruby beer with dark malt and sweet spice flavours throughout, rounding off with a dry, coffeeish, spicy, bitter finish.

The beer has also been sold in bottle, so should be available at other times of the year, too, if you feel the need to go Canadian.

Births Henri Becquerel (physicist), 1852; Harold Abrahams (athlete), 1899; Frankie Dettori (jockey), 1970

Deaths Fats Waller (jazz musician), 1943; Charles Laughton (actor), 1962; Walt Disney (animator), 1966

Events Prime Minister John Major and Irish Premier Albert Reynolds issue the Downing Street Declaration, paving the way for peace talks in Northern Ireland, 1993

ABOVE: CANADA'S MAPLE LEAF FLAG

Porter

357

Hogs Back TEA

Source Hogs Back Brewery, Tongham, Surrey **Strength** 4.2% **Website** hogsback.co.uk

'No taxation without representation,' was a rallying cry heard among New England colonists prior to the American War of Independence. It was a matter of principle. Why should they continue to pay taxes and duties to the English crown when they had no say in how it was being spent? On the evening of 16 December 1773, the grievance came to a head.

Inflaming the situation was the favouritism being shown to the East India Company. This global trader was in severe financial difficulty and, to help it survive, the British Parliament had introduced The Tea Act, which allowed it to transport tea to America, tax-free. There – even after the imposition of local duties – it could be sold at a lower price than that offered by American merchants, who were obviously appalled. On the back of a series of tax penalties suffered by the colonies – on sugar, coffee, paper and wine, for instance – this came as a bitter blow.

Opposition to the Government and the East India Company stiffened across the American colonies, but it was in Boston that things came to a head. When three ships laden with tea docked in the city's harbour, an opportunity was spotted to make a stand. The ships were blockaded by citizens who refused them permission to unload and demanded that they leave the harbour. But the British Governor refused to let the vessels sail until the locals had paid duty on the tea. With stalemate achieved, it was time for drastic action.

On the night of 16 December, a group of patriots known as the Sons of Liberty launched an attack on the three ships. Thinly disguised as Mohawk Indians, around 150 men stole aboard and hacked apart 342 tea chests, depositing the contents into the water. A huge crowd watched in admiration as crate after crate was submerged. I suppose that's what's called harbouring a grudge.

A catalyst for war

There was an understandable backlash, and the furious British retaliated by limiting the powers of self-government for colonialists even further. These, in turn, raised the hackles of the local patriots. Thus, the Boston Tea Party, as it became known, proved to be one of the catalysts for the forthcoming War of Independence.

As part of the growing protest against the British, the American colonists boycotted the drinking of tea. No doubt they found an able replacement in beer. In the UK, you can now enjoy both at the same time, thanks to a brew called TEA from Hogs Back Brewery in Surrey.

It should be stated that there is no tea in this particular beer, although I have come across a tea-flavoured lambic beer from Belgium, which, you'll be relieved to hear, does not feature in this book. Hogs Back's TEA was voted CAMRA's Champion Best Bitter in 2000 and its name is a play on the British obsession with a cuppa. The letters apparently stand for Traditional English Ale and that's exactly what it is – tea-brown in colour and admirably balancing the nutty flavours of pale and crystal malt with the smoky orange fruitiness of Fuggle and, particularly, Golding hops. It's as British a beer as you're likely to find – and the Americans appreciate it, too.

Births Jane Austen (writer), 1775; Noel Coward (actor, writer and composer), 1899; Arthur C Clarke (writer), 1917

Deaths Camille Saint-Saëns (composer), 1921; William Somerset Maugham (writer), 1965

Events Oliver Cromwell becomes Lord Protector of England, 1653; MPs vote to abolish hanging in the UK, 1969

Best Bitter

Wychwood Bah Humbug!

Source The Wychwood Brewery Co. Ltd, Witney, Oxfordshire **Strength** 5% **Website** wychwood.co.uk

Christmas wouldn't be Christmas without a dollop of Dickens, largely thanks to the publication on this day in 1843 of his famous seasonal short story, *A Christmas Carol*.

The story is so well known that it hardly needs recounting, but here are the highlights anyway. The tale centres on one Ebenezer Scrooge, a man so miserly that he detests this season of goodwill. Scrooge's character is radically transformed the night before Christmas, when his sleep is disturbed by the ghosts of his former business partner, Jacob Marley, and of Christmas Past, Christmas Present and Christmas Yet to Come, which show him the miserable fate that awaits him if he perseveres with his mean-mindedness. The world sees a new Scrooge the next morning as he strives to repair his avaricious ways.

Inevitably, just as film makers and television producers have eagerly latched onto *A Christmas Carol* for festive treats – memories of Alastair Sim, George C Scott, Bill Murray and even Rowan Atkinson, as Ebenezer Blackadder, come to mind – brewers have also taken full advantage of Dickens's unforgettable creation when choosing appropriate names for their Christmas beers. Currently in circulation at this time of the year are ales called Old Scrooge from the Three Tuns in Shropshire, and Marley's Ghost from Archers in Wiltshire, for instance. Also to be found is Bah Humbug!, a winter warmer produced by Wychwood Brewery in Oxfordshire, which takes its name from Scrooge's dismissive remark about the whole Christmas celebration. Wychwood is not the only brewery to seize on this nifty name: there have also been Bah Humbugs from Blindmans, Mauldons, Ossett and Wizard breweries in the UK.

Seasonal spice

Wychwood's typically colourful label depicts the old curmudgeon dressed in nightshirt and nightcap, holding a candle and being pursued by one of the ghosts that manage to turn around his life. A spring barley named Cocktail provides the pale malt for this seasonal brew, with some crystal malt thrown in to deepen the colour to a rich copper-red. The hops in the copper are Challenger, but the interesting ingredient is cinnamon essence, which is added during the cold conditioning, providing a light spicy note and helping the beer marry nicely with holiday treats like Christmas cake, mince pies and plum pudding. A soft and mellow aroma of cinnamon and toffee, with light banana and a touch of marzipan, leads into a perfumed spicy taste, with banana and creamy malt flavours, plus hints of sultana. Cinnamon and marzipan continue in the slightly chewy, dry, bitter finish. This is not going to be a beer for every palate, but it's certainly a bit of festive fun. It was first bottled in 2003, and may also be found on draught. An export version is brewed to a slightly stronger (6% ABV) and, to my mind, even more successful, recipe.

Births Tommy Steele (singer and actor), 1936; Paul Rodgers (rock musician), 1949; Paula Radcliffe (athlete), 1973

Deaths Simón Bolívar (statesman and liberator), 1830; Lord Kelvin (physicist), 1907; Dorothy L Sayers (writer), 1957

Events The Wright Brothers make the first recorded powered flight, 1903; *The Simpsons* cartoon series premieres on US TV, 1989

ABOVE: THE GHOST OF CHRISTMAS PRESENT APPEARS TO SCROOGE IN *A CHRISTMAS CAROL*

Spiced Ale

Sierra Nevada Bigfoot Barleywine Style Ale

Source Sierra Nevada Brewing Co., Chico, California **Strength** 9.6% **Website** sierranevada.com

The mother of all deceptions? In archaeological terms, quite possibly. On this day in 1912, newspapers all over the world ran a story that evidence had been unearthed to support Charles Darwin's theory that man was descended from the ape. Four decades later, it turned out that the real monkeys in the story were the experts who fell for this elaborate hoax.

The tale of Piltdown Man begins with amateur archaeologist Charles Dawson. Dawson claimed that, in a gravel pit near Piltdown, Sussex, he had found the skull of an ancient human. He reported the find to Sir Arthur Smith Woodward of the British Museum. Woodward joined Dawson in further searches of the site, where they discovered an intriguing jawbone. Using this and other supportive finds as a basis, Woodward declared that what had been revealed was a 'missing link' between man and his primate forebears. The historic creature was dubbed Piltdown Man.

Experts elsewhere in the world remained suspicious of the claim, but it wasn't until 1953 that, with the help of new dating technology, Piltdown Man was proved to be a fake. It turned out that the cranium was human and only around 500 years old – not the one million years suggested earlier. The convincing jawbone, it transpired, was that of an orang utan.

With the truth exposed, attention switched to finding the perpetrator of the hoax, with eyes firmly on Dawson, but with other figures, including Sherlock Holmes creator Sir Arthur Conan Doyle, who was a keen archaeologist and lived locally, also implicated. No one, however, has been blamed officially for embarrassing the nation's archaeological experts.

Californian links

Evidence of other missing links – some still living, it is claimed – has been presented elsewhere in the world, too, with the Yeti or Abominable Snowman of the Himalayas the best known. In the Pacific North West of America, there have been numerous 'sightings' of a giant ape-like creature, possibly 2.1m (7ft) or more tall. It has been given the name of Sasquatch or Bigfoot, and was captured on film in 1967 by documentary makers Roger Patterson and Robert Gimlin. The authenticity of the footage continues to divide analysts.

Such is the legend of Bigfoot that it is even celebrated in one of America's finest beers. This comes from Sierra Nevada Brewery, whose home at Chico in northern California is right in the heart of Sasquatch territory. The gorilla-like creature is seen lurking in the woods on the label. A barley wine in style, the beer, which conditions in the bottle, is skilfully constructed from pale and caramel malts, and abundantly seasoned with American hops. Chinooks go into the copper first for bitterness, joined later for extra aroma by Cascades and Centennials. The hopping is not finished, however. More of all three hop strains are used to dry-hop the beer after fermentation. The beer pours a deep copper-red in colour. A sweet fruity aroma packs in juicy citrus notes, California raisins, plums, strawberries and a lush creamy maltiness with a hint of chocolate. There are more red berries and citrus fruits in the taste, which is powerful and full bodied, with rich malt and plenty of sweetness but a fine bitter counterbalance, too, from the generous hopping. The finish is full and malty yet loaded with bitter hops. It's a genuine monster of a beer that begs to be taken seriously.

Births Keith Richards (rock musician), 1943; Stephen Spielberg (film director), 1947; Brad Pitt (actor), 1963

Deaths Antonio Stradivari (violin maker), 1737; Kirsty MacColl (singer-songwriter), 2000; Joseph Barbera (animator), 2006

Events End of the Battle of Verdun, the longest battle of World War I, 1916; capital punishment for the crime of murder abolished in the UK, 1969

Oulton Gone Fishing

Source Oulton Ales, Lowestoft, Suffolk　**Strength** 5%　**Website** oultonales.co.uk

Fishermen, raise your glasses to one that got away on this day in 1683. The man in question is Izaak Walton, born in Stafford in 1593. The son of an alehouse keeper, he lived until he was 90, which was quite remarkable for the time. When he was born, Queen Elizabeth was on the throne; by the time he passed away, the English Civil War and the Great Fire of London had both come and long gone.

Professionally, Walton was a draper, having served an apprenticeship as a teenager in London, where he later set up in business. But literature was his great love. In his time, he wrote a number of biographies, including one of his friend, the poet John Donne, but he is best remembered for his classic treatise on the art of coarse fishing, which he entitled *The Compleat Angler* and which was first published in 1653.

If you've never read the book, it's easy to assume that this is no more than a practical guide to fishing. In fact, it's a lot more than that, being a rambling, whimsical collection of folklore, complete with descriptions of country life (including inns), songs, poems and quotations from classical writers – all of which cover up the author's technical angling inadequacies, which he himself was content to acknowledge. Indeed, the section on fly-fishing that was added to later editions was written by his friend Charles Cotton, with whom Walton spent many hours fishing on the River Dove in Staffordshire and Derbyshire.

Time to think & drink

Walton was spot on in the subtitle he gave to the book, *The Contemplative Man's Recreation*. For him and thousands of other fishermen, it's not so much the sport as the time to think that is the real pleasure. And it's even better if you have a glass of good ale to hand. The perfect choice would be Barbus Barbus from Butts Brewery in Berkshire, but that's already been featured on 16 June. An alternative, not just because of its name but also because it's a fine beer, is Gone Fishing from Oulton Ales.

Wayne and Rosemary Moore run Oulton Ales. They produce various beers with nautical connections, and Gone Fishing was added to their selection in 2002. Brewed with Maris Otter pale malt, caramalt, crystal malt and chocolate malt, it's an amber-red-coloured beer. The hops are purely Fuggle, which gives the lie to the idea that this great British bittering hop needs to be used alongside an aroma hop to create a great beer. Bitter oranges, toffee and raisins feature in the nose, with more oranges and toffee in the malty, bitter taste.

As Oulton is located near Lowestoft in coastal Suffolk, there's a strong possibility that the sort of fishing alluded to in the name is sea rather than coarse, but it would be a perfect beer with which to round off a day either on the riverbank or on the ocean.

Births Edith Piaf (singer), 1915; Gordon Jackson (actor), 1923; Ricky Ponting (cricketer), 1974

Deaths Emily Brontë (writer), 1848; Stella Gibbons (writer), 1989; Marcello Mastroianni (actor), 1996

Events Coronation of King Henry II, 1154; Britain agrees to return Hong Kong to China, 1984

Strong Ale

361

Anchor Christmas Ale

Source Anchor Brewing Company, San Francisco, California **Strength** 5.5% **Website** anchorbrewing.com

Three days ago, this book recommended a beer to mark the first publication of Charles Dickens's *A Christmas Carol*. Wychwood's Bah Humbug! is a spiced ale, laced with cinnamon. It's a good time now, with the festive season upon us, to look more closely at the tradition of brewing beers that contain spices, as there are quite a few in production at this time of year.

The whole concept of throwing spices into a beer – usually during the copper boil – dates back to the pre-hop era, when brewers needed flavourings that would stop the sweetness of the malt from being too cloying, or perhaps to disguise the fact that beer, all too often, turned sour very quickly. In Belgium, spiced beers remain common, as illustrated by the number of wheat beers that are spiked with coriander and citrus peel. Elsewhere in the world, however, spiced ale is not so obvious and, while there are year-round exceptions such as Nethergate's Umbel Ale, which includes coriander, they tend to reach the public around Christmas. This may be because a little spicy warmth helps keep out the winter cold or because spices also feature in traditional Christmas fare – the plum pudding or the Christmas cake, for instance. Brewers creating such yuletide treats include Samuel Adams, with its cinnamon-, orange peel- and ginger-infused Old Fezziwig Ale, and St Peter's, whose Spiced Ale includes cinnamon, apple and nutmeg.

Their special ale

Another brewery that has made an annual feature out of the idea is Anchor in San Francisco. Every year since 1975, the brewery has produced a spiced ale for Christmas, but it is never the same spiced ale. The label, usually carrying the words 'Our Special Ale', has a different design every year and carries a picture of a different species of tree each time – a symbol of the winter solstice when the Earth, 'with its seasons, appears born anew', according to the brewery. The recipe is always different, too, with the ingredients a closely guarded secret. As well as spices – perhaps cinnamon, nutmeg, ginger, juniper or clove – other natural flavourings may be added. The beer is presented in a vintage-dated bottle, so that you can – if you have enough willpower – keep some back to compare with future releases.

All this means that providing meaningful tasting notes is a little on the tricky side, but you can expect something rich and malty that leaves a golden glow inside. Sometimes there's a spruce note; at other times a touch of perfume. There could be vanilla, or maybe lemon, and perhaps coffee or chocolate. The strength varies, too, but usually hits around 5.5%. Enjoy the anticipation. The beer is also available on draught in the US between November and January.

Births Geoffrey Howe (politician), 1926; Uri Geller (psychic entertainer), 1946; Jenny Agutter (actress), 1952

Deaths James Hilton (writer), 1954; John Steinbeck (writer), 1968; Bobby Darin (singer), 1973

Events Cardiff becomes capital of Wales, 1955; Queen Elizabeth II becomes the oldest reigning UK monarch, 2007

Spiced Ale

Hop Back Entire Stout

Source Hop Back Brewery, Sailsbury, Wiltshire **Strength** 4.5% **Website** hopback.co.uk

Thanks to the likes of Jeffrey Archer, Ann Widdecombe and Edwina Currie, we have become rather accustomed to politicians writing blockbuster novels. But the concept is not a new one. Benjamin Disraeli, who was born on this day in 1804, beat them to it. Before he entered the House of Commons, the future Earl of Beaconsfield had built a significant career in literature, with successful works such as *Vivian Grey*, *Henrietta Temple*, *Coningsby* and *Sybil* pre-empting a life in politics.

Disraeli was born in London, the son of writer Isaac Disraeli. His family was Jewish, but he followed an Anglican upbringing, which allowed him, eventually, to take his place in Parliament in 1837 – Jews were not enfranchised at the time. His political leanings were conservative, but with an agenda for social reform, and he eventually became a Tory Prime Minister, developing a close relationship with Queen Victoria while earning himself a great rival in the shape of Liberal leader William Gladstone, a man who finally ousted him from Number 10. But Disraeli even had detractors in the world of literature. 'Trashy' was the word Wordsworth, perhaps unfairly, used to describe his writing – strangely, the same adjective often used to describe politicians' departures into the world of thrillers and romances today.

Bon viveur

Disraeli died in 1881. He had cut a colourful figure as a fine orator and a man of wit. In his private life, he was known as a bon viveur and gourmand, and it seems that oysters were a particular favourite – although these would not have been seen as extravagant during his time, when, dredged from the Thames estuary, they were a cheap, everyday staple for working Londoners. On one famous occasion, it was widely reported that Disraeli rounded off a hard day in the political office with a hearty supper of oysters and Guinness – the classic seafood combination.

With Guinness no longer conditioned in the bottle, some of the complexity of the Irish beer has been lost, so if stout and oysters seems the appropriate way of marking Disraeli's birth, it's worth scouting around for alternatives. Wye Valley's

Dorothy Goodbody's Wholesome Stout would be a perfect match, but we featured that 11 months ago, on 21 January, so I would turn today to Hop Back's Entire Stout.

Brewed in deepest Wiltshire, this is a class act and winner of several major awards. Chocolate malt, roasted barley and a little wheat crystal malt join pale malt in the mash tun, giving rich coffee and caramel flavours and a dry roasted finish, with added robustness coming from the infusion of Challenger and Golding hops in the copper. With the roasted character, firm bitterness and peppery dryness to balance the briny ocean notes of the oyster, it would have been as welcome in Victorian times as it is today.

Births Samuel L Jackson (actor), 1948; Chris Evert (tennis player), 1954; Kiefer Sutherland (actor), 1966

Deaths Giovanni Boccaccio (writer), 1375; F Scott Fitzgerald (writer), 1940; George S Patton (soldier), 1945

Events Premiere of Disney's *Snow White and the Seven Dwarfs*, 1937; Charles de Gaulle elected President of France, 1958; Pan Am flight 103 explodes over the Scottish town of Lockerbie, 1988

Stout

ABOVE: BENJAMIN DISRAELI, PRIME MINISTER AND A FAN OF STOUT AND OYSTERS

Coniston Old Man Ale

Source Coniston Brewing Co., Coniston, Cumbria   **Strength** 4.8%   **Website** conistonbrewery.com

'Once upon a time there were four little Rabbits, and their names were Flopsy, Mopsy, Cottontail and Peter.' It's not a very promising opening line to a literary career that was to generate millions of pounds and an equivalent number of readers, but that's how Beatrix Potter made her first mark on the world of publishing.

The line comes from *The Tale of Peter Rabbit*, a story Potter initially penned for the sick child of her former nanny. From this you can gather that she grew up in a prosperous family. Potter was born in Kensington, London, in 1866 and, despite (or perhaps because of) the affluence of her parents, her childhood appears to have been dull and lonely. Her younger brother was sent away to school, but Potter remained at home to be educated by governesses, from whom she picked up the literary and artistic skills she used to find her own way in the world.

Although initially rejected by a number of publishers, *The Tale of Peter Rabbit* was eventually released in 1902, to instant success. Potter followed it with *The Tale of Squirrel Nutkin* and then *The Tailor of Gloucester*, eventually compiling a series of 23 children's stories, which she also illustrated. Among the famous characters she created were Mrs Tiggy-Winkle, Jemima Puddle-Duck and Jeremy Fisher.

Out of the proceeds of her considerable wealth, Potter purchased Hill Top Farm in the Lake District village of Near Sawrey. She fell in love with the area, setting many of her subsequent tales there. Her later years, however, were spent muck-deep in agricultural pursuits, most notably in the rearing of the endangered local Herdwick sheep. She died on 22 December 1943, leaving her property – some 4,000 acres – to the National Trust.

Local landmark

Her story has been related recently in the film *Miss Potter*, starring Renée Zellweger, and anyone visiting Cumbria in the wake of the film's release is likely to be as engaged by the Lake District scenery as the late author herself. Near Sawrey sits on the small, but perfectly formed, Esthwaite Water, with Grizedale Forest behind and then, towering above, the famous Old Man of Coniston. This impressive 792m- (2,600ft-) high fell is not only a prominent local landmark but also features in the name of a popular cask and bottled ale brewed by Coniston Brewery, which sits right at its foot.

The cask version of Old Man Ale is the weaker of the two, at 4.2%, with the bottle-conditioned equivalent (produced under contract for Coniston by The Beer Counter/Ridgeway Brewery) packing a bit more punch at 4.8%. Both are brewed from the same ingredients: Maris Otter pale malt, crystal malt and roasted barley in the mash tun, producing a rich, ruby colour and a toffeeish, chocolaty, dark malt flavour; Challenger and Mount Hood hops in the copper bringing a wonderful orangey fruitiness to the aroma and taste. It's not clear whether Miss Potter was ever a beer lover, but she would surely have given her approval to such a traditional, agricultural product that also celebrates the beauty of her adopted home.

Births Noel Edmonds (broadcaster), 1948; Maurice and Robin Gibb (pop musicians), 1949; Ralph Fiennes (actor), 1962

Deaths George Eliot (writer), 1880; Richard Dimbleby (broadcaster), 1965; Joe Strummer (rock musician), 2002

Events Coronation of King Stephen, 1135; the Brandenberg Gate, between East and West Berlin, opened for the first time in almost 30 years, 1989

Strong Ale

Wells Bombardier

Source Wells & Young's Brewing Company, Bedford   **Strength** 4.3%   **Website** wellsandyoungs.co.uk

Bear with me on this one. I'm about to spin you a story about a beer that has no actual connection with today's commemoration.

This day in December is the birthday of J Arthur Rank, the man who led the British film industry in its 20th-century battle with the might of Hollywood. Rank was born in Hull, East Yorkshire, in 1888 and, having failed in the flour-milling trade, found his way into the cinema by showing religious films in church halls. In a very short space of time, he had established a network of film studios and cinemas that was larger than any of his Hollywood rivals, producing work by directors such as David Lean, Sidney Gilliat and Frank Launder, and introducing many household names who learned their acting trade in the Rank 'charm school', such as Christopher Lee and Diana Dors. The Rank 'gong' introduction to each film was internationally known. By the time he died in 1972, J Arthur had been elevated to the peerage as Baron Rank of Sutton Scotney.

Boxing clever

What has all this to do with Bombardier Bitter? The answer, as already declared, is actually nothing at all. However, a story grew up over the years that the most famous man to beat that gong at the start of Rank films was a member of the Charles Wells brewing dynasty. His name was William Thomas Wells (1889–1967), a heavyweight boxer from East London. In 1911, he became one of the first boxers to win a Lonsdale Belt, for successfully defending his British championship on two occasions. He went by the professional name of 'Bombardier' Billy Wells and it was widely assumed that he was the Bombardier referred to in the name of the beer. Wells & Young's now denies this, referring instead to the military rank, rather than the cinematic Rank, as the origin of the beer's name.

Still, it's always good to sink a pint of Bombardier, be it on draught at the pub or on draught at home. By the latter, I refer to the highly effective mini-casks that Charles Wells pioneered in the early 2000s. These giant cans hold more than eight pints of real ale – real because it still contains living yeast and, just like the real ale in the pub cellar, continues to ferment so that the flavours in your glass are fresh and complex.

Bombardier is brewed from pale and crystal malts, hence the attractive dark copper colour, and Challenger and Golding hops. The taste has plenty of malt character but also a keen hoppy, fruity accent. Overall, it's a satisfying best bitter with nothing Rank about it.

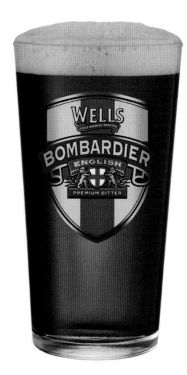

Births Richard Arkwright (inventor), 1732; Joseph Smith (Mormon founder), 1805; Helmut Schmidt (politician), 1918

Deaths Peggy Guggenheim (art collector), 1979; Victor Borge (musician and comedian), 2000; Charlie Drake (comedian), 2006

Events Vincent Van Gogh cuts off part of his left ear, 1888; Agatha Christie's *The Mousetrap* breaks the record for the longest-running stage play, 1970

Best Bitter

De Dolle Brouwers Stille Nacht

Source De Dolle Brouwers, Esen **Strength** 12% **Website** dedollebrouwers.be

If ever there were a perfect counterpoint to the madness of war, Christmas Eve 1914 provided it. The story of how Allied and German soldiers downed their weapons and brokered an unofficial Christmas truce has been widely aired but, nevertheless, it does more than most historical tales to reinforce this time of year as the season of peace and goodwill.

World War I had started in earnest in August 1914. By December that year, thousands of lives had already been lost, and for the soldiers on both sides of the front line, life was testing, to say the least. Dug deep into the Flanders mud, keeping company with rats and shaking with the cold, these men waited in trepidation for the shells to fall, or until they heard the vacuous calls of the generals to 'go over the top'. The war was progressing nowhere, and the enemy, in some places, was bogged down less than a hundred yards away.

As darkness fell on 24 December, the mood changed dramatically. It started on the German side. Among their Christmas 'treats', the Germans had been sent small Christmas trees and candles. They decided to share them with their adversaries, raising them above the trenches. At first the Allies were bemused, even more so when the enemy began singing a song whose words they couldn't understand but whose tune was all too familiar. The carol was 'Stille Nacht' ('Silent Night'). Soon, some brave German souls climbed out of their hiding places. The Allies reciprocated. Hands were shaken, sentiments were exchanged about the misery of the war, and small tokens of friendship passed between them as the spirit of Christmas descended onto the battlefield.

The respite from the conflict gave both sides a chance to bury fallen men whose bodies had been trapped in no man's land. It also provided an opportunity for lighter antics, including a now-famous game of football between the two sides. Inevitably, the generals were not amused and, after a few, all-too-brief, days of calm, gunshot again filled the air and the shelling recommenced.

Time for reflection

The beer selected for today is strong enough to send the drinker into a reflective mood, and a little thought about the sacrifices made by those engaged in that brutal war is not inappropriate at this time of plenty. The beer is also relevant in other ways. It is brewed near Diksmuide, Flanders, close to the scene of the carnage, and it goes by the name of Stille Nacht.

De Dolle Brouwers – 'the Mad Brewers' – is a family business that started life in 1980 when it took over a struggling brewery that had been founded in the early 19th century. Its beers are noted for their originality and high quality, and Stille Nacht is one of the best, a sublime example of the brewers' art, constructed from pale malt and candy sugar, and laced with Nugget hops from the nearby hop gardens at Poperinge. Golden and naturally effervescent, it presents

a spicy, smoothly malty aroma that is packed with the zest of oranges. The same crisp, citrus notes take the lead in the taste, which is nicely warming, and the body is surprisingly light for the strength. The bittersweet, drying, almost burning finish marks this out as a beer with huge character and yet one that is not too demanding. There can be few better ways in which to slip reverently into a Christmas frame of mind.

Births King John, 1166; Howard Hughes (film producer and aviator), 1905; Caroline Aherne (actress and writer), 1963

Deaths Vasco da Gama (explorer), 1524; William Makepeace Thackeray (writer), 1863; Peter Lawford (actor), 1984

Events Premiere of the carol *Stille Nacht*, in a church near Salzburg, 1818; *Apollo 8* becomes the first manned spacecraft to orbit the moon, 1968

Strong Ale

Bosteels Deus Brut des Flandres

Source Brouwerij Bosteels, Buggenhout **Strength** 11.5% **Website** bestbelgianspecialbeers.be

This must be the hardest day of the year on which to decide what to drink. Everyone tends to spoil themselves and raid the supermarket for quality provisions, so the beer cupboard's probably full of interesting items. There's a temptation to recommend a beer that will do a terrific job alongside the turkey – you need something malty, and a Belgian brown ale or a dubbel is just the ticket – but on the basis that Christmas is a time for sharing, I've gone for a big bottle of bubbly that makes a perfect accompaniment for a festive brunch or a sparkling aperitif to thrust into the hands of your guests as they arrive.

The beer comes from Belgium and, rather fittingly, goes by the name of Deus, meaning God. The subtitle is Brut des Flandres, or Flanders Dry in the language of wine. Earlier in the book, we noted Champagne Day (4 August) by featuring a fascinating beer from Brazil called Lust. With Deus we focus more on virtues than sins, but there are strong similarities between the beers.

Deus is brewed by Bosteels, a seventh-generation family brewery founded in 1791 that is better known for its amber ale, Kwak, and the widely exported Tripel Karmeliet. The beer is brewed, from very pale malt and 'aromatic hops', in the small town of Buggenhout, about 48km (30 miles) east of Ghent, and undergoes two fermentations at the brewery. There is a third fermentation, however, and this takes place in the bottle. Echoing the method of producing sparkling wine, the large bottles are filled with beer primed with live yeast and new fermentable sugars, and shipped to the Champagne region of France for a long period of maturation. The beer is then inverted to allow the yeast to sink into the neck of the bottle, which is then frozen to remove an icy plug of beer that contains all the sediment. Topped with a cork, the beer – taking 12 months to produce from start to finish – is then ready for sale.

Deus, like Lust and the original Belgian Champagne beer, Malheur (also brewed in Buggenhout), needs to be served icy cold, so stick your bottle in the fridge well before you plan to open it (the brewery recommends six to 12 hours). Then remove the metal foil, loosen the wire cradle, gentle prise free the cork and pour watchfully into tall, fluted glasses, taking care that the bubbles don't foam over the top. Of course, you can always shake it up, Formula 1 fashion, but that would be a waste, especially as Deus is not cheap.

An appealing golden colour in the glass, with champagne-like bubbles lifting a spicy, fruity aroma to the nose, Deus is a fairly sweet beer with a peppery warmth. The bubbles are impossible to ignore, and bounce around flavours of creamy pale malt, vanilla, herbs and a pleasant grapey sourness. Sweetness still reigns when it comes to the finish, but a champagne-like dryness fights its way through. It's a clean, surprising beer – not for all beer lovers perhaps, but a novel choice for special occasions like today.

Births Humphrey Bogart (actor), 1899; Lew Grade (TV executive), 1906; Annie Lennox (rock singer), 1954

Deaths WC Fields (actor), 1946; Charlie Chaplin (actor and director), 1977; Dean Martin (actor and singer), 1995

Events Coronation of William the Conqueror, 1066; Mikhail Gorbachev resigns as President of the Soviet Union, 1991

Champagne-style Beer

Weihenstephaner Pilsner

Source Bavarian State Brewery, Freising **Strength** 5.1% **Website** brauerei-weihenstephan.de

When, in school, we sang about Good King Wenceslas looking out on the feast of Stephen, I was always impressed by the fact that this chap named Stephen had so much to eat that even a king needed to take a peek. It all became clearer once it was explained to me that the reference was to a date not a dinner.

The confusion probably stemmed from the fact that the feast of Stephen, or St Stephen's Day, is rarely mentioned these days, overshadowed by the British holiday Boxing Day that is celebrated on the same date.

St Stephen was one of the early deacons of the Christian church, charged with the distribution of alms to the needy. He was born a Jew, possibly of Greek descent (his name comes from the Greek word for 'crown'), and he paid the price for his religious conversion by being stoned to death by those with whom he had once joined in prayer. Thus Stephen became the first Christian martyr. It is said that Saul of Tarsus, the future St Paul, was one of the men present at his execution.

Holy Stephen

For a beer to mark the feast of Stephen, we return to a brewery that we visited for 19 April. As mentioned then, Weihenstephan, based in Freising, just north of Munich, claims to be the oldest brewery in the world, dating from the year 1040. It's also a brewery with a strong religious background, as it started out as an abbey in the eighth century. More importantly,

for today, the name Weihenstephan translates as 'Holy Stephen' after the hill named after the saint on which the brewery stands.

Weihenstephan is rare in being owned by the Bavarian state. It is also part of a university and brewing school, so students have access to the brewhouse, although all the commercial brews are professionally made. Its speciality is weissbier, as discussed in the earlier entry, but it also turns out some other fine beers, including hell, bock and dunkel beers, plus a pilsner that would make a fine palate sharpener before a Boxing Day lunch of cold meats and pickles.

Pale golden in colour, this clean, crisp beer has a surprisingly fruity aroma – suggestions of melon, peach and pear to me. Tastewise, it's fairly sweet for this style of beer but, as you'd expect, does have an overlay of firm, tangy Hallertauer hops, which continue through into the long, drying, herbal finish. The brewery describes its pilsner as 'a cut above the ordinary', and that's certainly something beer connoisseurs are looking for at this time of the year. It may take a bit of finding, as exports from the brewery major on wheat beers, but it's well worth the effort.

Births Thomas Gray (poet), 1716; Charles Babbage (mathematician), 1791; Mao Tse-tung (politician), 1893

Deaths Harry S Truman (US President), 1972; Nigel Hawthorn (actor), 2001; Gerald Ford (US President), 2006

Events Marie and Pierre Curie announce their discovery of radium, 1898; an Indian Ocean tsunami claims hundreds of thousands of lives, 2004

Pilsner

Alhambra Mezquita

Source Grupo Cervezas Alhambra, Cordoba **Strength** 7.2% **Website** cervezasalhambra.es

There's not much written about Spanish beer, a fact that says a lot about brewery output in the country in recent decades. But today marks a momentous occasion in Spanish history, so it's worth hunting for a beer with which to celebrate it.

On 27 December 1978, Spain finally emerged from under the clouds of dictatorship and entered once again the sunny domain of democracy. The transition was a long time coming. The Spanish Civil War of the late 1930s had torn the country apart after elections that had given power to a left-wing coalition had raised the hackles of the rich and powerful members of the Spanish Establishment. Landowners, the Church, monarchists and the military joined together to form a powerful right-wing response. Bloodshed followed when army chief General Francisco Franco led these 'Nationalist' forces against the ruling Republicans. Aided by the might of Nazi Germany and Fascist Italy, who feared the rise of communism in Western Europe, Franco and his right-wingers ultimately overwhelmed the Republican forces, whose outside help consisted largely of volunteers from the International Brigade.

When the war ended, so did democracy in Spain. Franco was installed as leader, confirming himself President for life in 1947. When he died, he nominated Prince Juan Carlos as his successor, returning the country to a monarchy. The new head of state had a different view on how the country should be run, however,

and this led to the drawing up of a new constitution – promulgated on this day in 1978 – that finally ended the dictatorship, with Juan Carlos, as non-ruling king, ceding power back to the people.

Exports & bocks

Despite the suppression of political dissent under Franco, Spain was never totally shunned by the western world, which was quietly content that communism wasn't taking a hold there. But, since the return of democracy, Spain has enjoyed a full partnership with the international community, joining both NATO and the EU.

Benefiting from new commercial openings are some of the country's breweries, including the producer of today's selection. Cervezas Alhambras was founded in Granada in 1925, its name an allusion to the stunning Moorish palace that brings thousands of tourists to the Andalusian city every year. In its lifetime, the business has been part of both the Damm and Cruzcampo groups, but in 1995 was bought by private investors, who sold out to the Mahou-San Miguel group in 2006. Seven years earlier, it had expanded by buying Cordoba's Compania Andaluza de Cervezas, and it is this part that is home to Mezquita, today's beer, a copper-red bock with a brain-lightening ABV of 7.2%.

Spain does have this strange tradition of brewing German export and bock clones, turning out rich, malty, very potent lagers that don't seem quite right in a country where

the heat of the sun is often intoxication enough. But December's a cool time to do justice to Mezquita, which is named after Cordoba's majestic ancient mosque.

The beer is brewed from pilsner and caramel malts, with Nugget the main hop strain. It is lagered for 25 days and opens up with rich toffee and a little spice in the aroma. Toffee and malt dominate the taste, with a reasonable bitter/hoppy counterbalance and spicy alcohol always present. Bitterness builds in the finish but creamy malt persists. By the standards of other countries, it is perhaps somewhat understated, but for a taste of what goes on in Spanish brewing, it's a good bet. Lay out a few plates of tapas and enjoy a little winter sunshine.

Births Johannes Kepler (astronomer), 1571; Louis Pasteur (scientist), 1822; Gérard Depardieu (actor), 1948

Deaths Gustave Eiffel (architect), 1923; Hoagy Carmichael (composer), 1981; Benazir Bhutto (politician), 2007

Events Charles Darwin begins the voyage that inspires his theories on evolution, 1831; foundation of the World Bank, 1945

Bock

Schneider Aventinus

Source G. Schneider & Sohn, Kelheim **Strength** 8.2% **Website** schneider-weisse.de

If you haven't overindulged at Christmas and are still in the mood for something special, then set some time aside today to open a weizenbock.

The German tradition of brewing strong lagers to greet the oncoming seasons has been explored in detail on other pages in this book, with days devoted to both the doppelbock (see 21 March) and the maibock (13 May), for instance. There is, however, another sort of bock beer that we haven't yet explored. and a lazy day in cold December seems just about the right time to do so.

The style of beer in question is called the weizenbock, essentially a scaled-up wheat beer. Such beers are strong and nourishing but also pack in the most amazing flavours. Before we focus on the one selected for today, it's worth highlighting a couple of other examples that are well worth seeking out.

The first is called Pikantus, a 7.3% ABV creation from Erdinger, the wheat beer specialists based in the town of Erding on the outskirts of Munich. This is fairly sweet and mildly spicy with almond and raisin notes. The second beer comes from the other side of the world, from the Eisenbahn brewery in Brazil. The guys over there have enormous fun emulating great beer styles from both Europe and the Americas, and they do so with great success, as proven yet again with their chocolaty, toffeeish, sweet and creamy Weizenbock (8%).

Complex creation

By far the best known of the weizenbock beers, however, comes from Schneider, another wheat beer specialist, based in Kelheim, north of Munich. The brewery has already featured in this book with its classic Schneider Weisse (see 18 May). Here, its stronger offering, Aventinus, takes centre stage. This 8.2% beer was first brewed in 1907. Its name comes from Aventinstrasse, the road on which the original brewery in Munich stood, although the label carries a picture of Johannes Aventinus, a 16th-century Bavarian historian. As well as the trademark high proportion of wheat, the brewers throw some dark malt into the grist. Typically, the hops, from the local Hallertauer fields, are kept firmly in check. The beer is fermented in open vessels, then conditions in the bottle for three weeks before going on sale.

A darkish chestnut-brown colour, with a white head, this is an extremely complex creation. Marzipan, bananas, raisins and lemon all feature in the aroma, with more banana and lemon in the spicy, vinous taste. Light bitterness carries through into the long-lasting finish. But, frankly, everyone who tastes Aventinus finds something different, be it chocolate, figs, cloves or prunes.

Weizenbocks like Aventinus work brilliantly with all kinds of foods, from their native Bavarian partner, pork, to rich fruity desserts. If you have a little Christmas pudding left over, here's the perfect drinking companion.

Births Woodrow Wilson (US President), 1856; Denzel Washington (actor), 1954; Nigel Kennedy (violinist), 1956

Deaths Rob Roy (outlaw), 1734; Maurice Ravel (composer), 1937; Sam Peckinpah (film director), 1984

Events Westminster Abbey consecrated and opened, 1065; the Tay Railway Bridge collapses, 1879

Bohemia Regent Prezident

Source Bohemia Regent, Třeboň **Strength** 6% **Website** pivovar-regent.cz

As the 1980s drew to a close, communism and totalitarianism in Eastern and Central Europe were in rapid decline. In some countries, the uprising against the Soviet Union and its puppet leaders was brutal; in others, it was gentler. In Czechoslovakia, the transition was so subtle that they called it the Velvet Revolution, and the transformation of the country to a Western-style democracy took a major step forward on this day in 1989 when Vaclav Havel was elected the country's new president.

Havel was born in 1936 into a bourgeois family that owned Prague's Lucerna Ballroom. He worked in a brewery in his younger years, but after the war it was literature and drama that gave him a home, as well as scope to indulge his ever-political mind. As one of Czechoslovakia's foremost playwrights, he found himself in a unique position to criticize its Communist leaders, with the result that he spent several years as a political prisoner. So troublesome did Havel prove to be that the state even offered him the chance to emigrate to the US. He declined. When the anti-communist movement came to a head, Havel was favourite to take over as the country's new leader. He remained president until 1992, when, with the country agreeing to split into the two new states of the Czech and Slovak Republics, he resigned in protest. Havel, however, was soon coaxed back into the top job, becoming the first president of the Czech Republic in 1993, a position he held for ten years.

Man of the people

Despite his intellectual and privileged upbringing, Havel has often been seen by outsiders as a man of the people, perhaps because of his clear pleasure at drinking beer, which, of course, is part and parcel of daily Czech life. On one occasion, he absconded from a function during a visit to the US in order to grab a beer and watch a music concert. On another occasion, he personally took visiting US President Bill Clinton to his Prague local, U Zlatého Tigra (the Golden Tiger), for a pint. Consequently, it would be remiss of us not to note this important day in Czech history with a glass of the local brew.

For this our direction turns to the south of Prague, to the city of Třeboň that has been home to the Regent brewery since 1379, when it was founded by Augustinian monks. The current brewhouse dates from the late 19th century, and the company has been in private hands since the fall of the communist state. Regent is perhaps best known for its fine dark lager, but there's only one beer we can seriously choose for today. It's called, simply, Prezident. This 6% strong, golden pilsner was introduced in autumn 2000 in honour of the brewery's new owner, a Mr Stasek, although the brewery concedes that the nominal link with Vaclav Havel was also in their minds. It is brewed from local pale malt and Saaz hops, is lagered for three months, and has a full, bittersweet taste, with a herbal hop edge and then a squeeze of lemon on the swallow. There's a rather creamy texture throughout. A strong beer for a real connoisseur is how the brewery describes it. Clearly one for Mr President, then.

Births William Ewart Gladstone (Prime Minister), 1809; Jon Voight (actor), 1938; Marianne Faithfull (singer), 1946

Deaths Thomas Becket (Archbishop of Canterbury), 1170; Harold Macmillan (Prime Minister), 1986; Bob Monkhouse (comedian), 2003

Events Texas becomes part of the US, 1845; the UK Sex Discrimination Act comes into force, 1975

Pilsner

ABOVE: VACLAV HAVEL

Burton Bridge Empire Pale Ale

Source Burton Bridge Brewery, Burton-upon-Trent, Staffordshire **Strength** 7.5%
Website burtonbridgebrewery.co.uk

This day in December marks the birthday of Rudyard Kipling, a man who brought exotic tales of the Indian subcontinent to the wider world.

Kipling was born in Bombay, the son of British author and illustrator John Lockwood Kipling. He attended school in England, but was far happier back in the warmth of India, to which he returned when beginning work as a journalist in 1882. Gradually, Kipling built up an impressive portfolio of prose and poetry, writing material for local publications, which brought him fame when he moved back to England seven years later.

Undoubtedly, Kipling's most famous works were those he compiled for children – the *Just So Stories*, *Kim* and, especially, *Jungle Book*, which reached a universal audience when it was given the Disney treatment 35 years after the author's death in 1932. Otherwise, Kipling has become known as 'the Bard of the Empire'. His depiction of life in the Raj brought home the colour of the times, varying between a cynicism of the regime and, later, a celebration of it, which brought attacks from anti-imperialists and liberals. On the other hand, the poems that he wrote about ordinary British soldiers show an empathy with the lot of the young serviceman abroad. In his poem *The Young British Soldier*, he offers advice to new recruits. Take the chores as they come, he says, and enjoy the reward of a beer afterwards.

If you're cast for fatigue by a
* sergeant unkind,*
Don't grouse like a woman nor
* crack on nor blind;*
Be handy and civil, and then
* you will find*
That it's beer for the young
* British soldier.*
Beer, beer, beer for the soldier…

Like Kipling's words, the brewing industry also keeps alive the spirit of that era, eagerly turning back the clock and replicating the sort of beer that was once an important part of British life in the subcontinent. The story of India pale ale has been recounted elsewhere in this book. Suffice to say here that one of the earliest revivals of the style came, very appropriately, from Burton-upon-Trent.

Every picture…

It was from Burton that IPAs flowed regularly in the 19th century, beginning their long and arduous journey to the ports of India. In 1996, Burton Bridge Brewery, a craft brewery situated next to the River Trent, launched Empire Pale Ale. The wordless label said nothing about the beer, but its image said everything. It featured a Victorian army officer in full regalia alongside a cricketer from the same era, both posing patriotically in front of an unfurled Union flag, crates of Empire Pale Ale at their feet, and tankards of foaming beer in their hands. Here, we had two sides of the service coin: men on- and off-duty, with beer playing an important role in both.

In keeping with the style of original and authentic IPAs, Empire Pale Ale packs as much punch as a steamy Madras, pounding out a daunting 7.5% ABV. The extract of pale malt is enhanced with invert sugar to provide plenty for the yeast to chew on, and Challenger and Styrian Golding hops ensure a fruity, spicy, bitter bite. After the first fermentation at the brewery, the beer is conditioned in cask for six months, and is dry-hopped with more Styrian Goldings before being bottled. Malt figures abundantly in the taste, as you'd expect, but so do hops, bringing tangy bitter orange flavours that carry on right through into the warming, gum-tingling finish.

Births Del Shannon (pop singer), 1934; Gordon Banks (footballer), 1937; Tiger Woods (golfer), 1975

Deaths Sonny Liston (boxer), 1970; Richard Rodgers (composer), 1979; Artie Shaw (bandleader), 2004

Events USSR established, 1922; astronomer Edwin Hubble declares the existence of other galaxies apart from our own, 1924

IPA

St-Sylvestre Trois Monts

Source Brasserie de St-Sylvestre, St-Sylvestre-Cappel   **Strength** 8.5%   **Website** brasserie-st-sylvestre.com

It's the last day of the year and we all want something a little bit special with which to see in the next 12 months. If you're planning on knocking back more than a few beers, then today's selection may prove too potent. But if you're just looking for a quality product to sup at midnight, there's a very suitable beer from northern France that hits the spot.

Trois Monts is not just a fine beer, it also has a significance in that it is brewed in a village named after the saint whose feast day falls on 31 December. St Sylvester was born in Rome, probably in the late third century. He rose through the ranks of early Christians to the point where, on the death of Pope Miltiades, he was selected as his successor. It was during Sylvester's 21-year papacy that the Emperor Constantine converted to Christianity, thereby turning an erstwhile persecuted religion into an accepted faith.

Sylvester died in 335. The village that shares his name dates back to at least the 11th century, and was previously known as Hillewaerts Cappel. It became St-Sylvestre-Cappel in 1538. The little community is located just south of Dunkirk, in Flanders hop-growing country close to the Belgian border, and is best known today for its brewery, a business that has blossomed in the hands of the latest generation of the Ricour family.

Ale success

During the post-war years, the St-Sylvestre Brewery had followed the wider trend of international brewing and converted from ale production to lager. It didn't do much for the company's fortunes. It remained small and local, with beers that hardly stood out against the major brands. When brothers François and Serge joined the business in 1983, the decision was taken to resume ale brewing and to look to expand distribution. It's been a success.

Trois Monts – named after three small hills close to the village – was introduced in 1985. It's a pale golden ale in the bière de garde tradition, which means that it is matured at the brewery before being filtered for the bottle. It is a surprisingly delicate beer, extremely easy to drink for its strength. Smooth, sweet pale malt, a fruity acidic zing and a perfumed, spicy warmth are the main features, with a drying, spicy, delicately hoppy finish to round off.

Trois Monts is presented in a tall corked bottle, fixed with a strange metal band that can be a little tricky to remove. The label describes the beer as 'Bière Spéciale Dégustation' – a special beer to savour – and proffers the friendly advice, 'A consommer avec modération' – in other words, take it easy. On New Year's Eve, that may prove difficult, but you've been warned!

Births Charles Edward Stuart (claimant to the British throne), 1720; Alex Ferguson (football manager), 1941; Ben Kingsley (actor), 1943

Deaths John Flamsteed (astronomer), 1719; Malcolm Campbell (speed-record challenger), 1948; Ricky Nelson (pop singer), 1985

Events The farthing coin goes out of circulation, 1960; the three-day week imposed in the UK in response to energy shortages, 1973

Bière de Garde

ABOVE: ST SYLVESTER

The Wonders of Brewing

Brewing is a magical process, presided over by magicians. Anyone who can take simple ingredients such as grains of barley, hop flowers and water and turn them into such a beguiling product as beer is clearly someone special. It's hard to do justice to the skills of a brewer when prosaically describing the brewing process but it's useful to set out, in basic terms, how beer is made, so that at least there's some explanation of how the various flavours described in this book arrive in your glass. For further details, readers can also check the Glossary on pages 376–7.

Malt & mash

The process of brewing begins with malt. Malt is barley grain that has been partially germinated, to help release starches and enzymes needed for the brewing process, and then kilned to prevent further germination. The degree of kilning also dictates the character of the malt; the more 'baked' the malt, the darker the colour and the more roasted the taste. Some malts are toasted dark for bitter, coffeeish flavours; others are just lightly crisped for a sweeter, nuttier taste. At the brewery, the malt is crushed and then combined in a vessel called a mash tun with hot water (known as 'liquor' in the trade), which has usually been treated to adjust its chemical balance. At lager breweries, a mash converter is generally used instead of a mash tun. This may be part of a decoction system, which involves pumping part of the liquid to and from a separate vessel and exposing it to a higher temperature to help enzymes in the malt convert the starches into fermentable sugars, because lager malt, traditionally, is not as refined as that used in ale production.

Hopping abroad

In both ale and lager processes, the result is a thick, sugary liquid called wort. This is run off from the mash tun and diverted into a boiler known as a copper. Here the wort is boiled up with hops, which add bitterness and sometimes herbal, spicy, citrus or floral characters. Like malts, hops come in many varieties. Some are very bitter; others milder. Some make themselves known in the aroma; others are expressed in the taste. Hops also act as a preservative. They can be added as whole hop flowers or as compressed pellets. Some brewers use hop oils (concentrated extract), but these can be astringent. The hops are added at various stages of the boil.

Fermentation time

After an hour or two in the copper, the hops are strained out and the wort is run off and cooled, before being pumped into a fermenting vessel, where yeast is added ('pitched'). Yeast is a single-celled fungus that turns the sugars in the wort into alcohol and carbon dioxide (the gas that gives beer its natural effervescence). Each yeast, however, also has its own character, which is harnessed and preserved by brewery chemists. Many breweries use the same yeast for decades.

During the first few days of fermentation, the yeast works furiously with the wort, growing quickly and covering the top with a thick, bubbly layer of foam. Most

is skimmed off, but some sinks into the brew and continues to work, eating up the sugars and generating more carbon dioxide and alcohol. Lager beers are known as 'bottom fermenting', because the yeast they use sinks to the bottom of the wort, rather than lying on the top. They also ferment at a lower temperature than ale. A few days later, this 'primary fermentation' is deemed over. Ales may then be transferred to a conditioning tank, where the yeast continues to round off the rough edges before the beer is ready for packaging. Lagers, ideally, should be transferred to a lagering tank where the beer will sit for weeks, perhaps months, at near-freezing temperatures to bring the beer slowly to crisp, clean perfection.

Ready for sale

The next stage of the brewing process depends on the sort of packaging the beer requires. If ale is to be sold as a living product, it is racked into casks where yeast continues to ripen and mature the beer right up to the point of sale. This produces 'cask-conditioned' beer, or 'real ale'. A similar process is employed to produce 'bottle-conditioned' beer, or 'real ale in a bottle', which, like the draught equivalent, contains living yeast and needs to be poured with a little caution to prevent this sediment from entering the glass.

Lagers tend to be filtered, or at least drawn off their yeast. If sold locally, in places like Germany and the Czech Republic, they may be served without being pasteurized.

Most bottled beers – ales and lagers – are filtered and many, regrettably, are pasteurized, too, which can spoil the flavour, especially if the beer is delicate or light-coloured. Bottled beers that are 'sterile filtered', but not pasteurized, are fresher-tasting than pasteurized beers, but they do not acquire the complexity of bottle-conditioned beers. Filtered and pasteurized draught beers are known as 'keg beers', or 'nitrokeg beers', depending on which gas is used to pump them to the bar and give these dull, dead beers some artificial life.

For more information about draught and bottled real ale, see CAMRA's *Good Beer Guide* and *Good Bottled Beer Guide*.

ABOVE: SIERRA NEVADA'S GLEAMING COPPER KETTLES

A Beer a Day

Glossary

ABV: Alcohol by Volume – the percentage of alcohol in a beer.

Abbey beer: a beer brewed in the style of monastic beers by commercial companies. Only authentic Trappist monasteries have the right to call their beers 'Trappist'; others producing beers in similar style under licence from a clerical order have adopted the term 'Abbey'.

Adjuncts: materials like cereals and sugars that are added to malted barley in the mash, often to create a cheaper brew but sometimes for special flavours or effects.

Aftertaste/afterpalate: *see* Finish.

Ale: a top-fermenting beer (the yeast mostly sits on top during fermentation).

Alpha acid: the bittering component of a hop; the higher the alpha acid content, the fewer hops needed for bitterness.

Aroma: the perfumes given off by a beer.

Barley: the cereal from which malt is made, occasionally used in its unmalted form in brewing, primarily to add colour.

Barley wine: a very strong, sweetish ale.

Bitter: a well-hopped ale.

Body: the fullness of the beer, generally indicative of the malt content.

Bottle-conditioned: beer that undergoes a secondary fermentation in the bottle ('real ale in a bottle').

Brewery-conditioned: beer with a fermentation completed at the brewery and usually pasteurized.

Bright: filtered (often pasteurized) beer.

Burtonize: to adjust the salts in brewing water to emulate the natural, hard waters of Burton-upon-Trent.

Carbon dioxide: a gas created by yeast during fermentation and vital to the drinkability of a beer; *see also* Condition.

Cask: container for unpasteurized beer.

Cask-conditioned: beer given a secondary fermentation in a cask ('real ale').

Condition: the amount of dissolved carbon dioxide in a beer. Too much and the beer is gassy; too little and it is flat.

Decoction: a continental mashing system in which parts of the extract are moved into a second vessel and subjected to a higher temperature, before being returned to the original vessel. The aim is better starch conversion into sugar.

Dry hopping: the process of adding hops to a beer after it has been brewed, usually in the cask or in a conditioning tank prior to bottling, in order to enhance the hop character and aroma.

Dubbel: a Trappist or Abbey 'double' ale of about 7% ABV, generally dark brown and malty, with low hop character. Tripel ('triple') beers are stronger (around 8–9%), fruity and often pale in colour.

80/-: *see* Shilling system.

Esters: organic compounds comprised of an alcohol and an acid, produced during fermentation. These have unusual – often fruity – aromas and flavours.

Filtered: a beer with its yeast and other sediment extracted; sterile-filtered beer has passed through a very fine filter.

Finings: a glutinous liquid that attracts yeast particles and draws them to the bottom of a cask (or a conditioning tank in the case of many bottled beers), leaving the beer clear. Finings are usually made from the swim-bladder of a tropical fish. Also known as isinglass.

Finish: the lingering taste in the mouth after swallowing beer.

Framboise/frambozen: *see* Kriek.

Green beer: beer not fully matured.

Green hops: hops picked fresh from the vine and used without undergoing the traditional drying process that allows them to be stored for months. Green hops provide a pungent, sappy character.

Grist: crushed malt ready for mashing. The term also refers to a mix of cereals, or hops, used in the brew.

Gueuze: *see* Lambic.

Hop: fast-growing plant, a relative of the nettle and cannabis. Its flowers are used to provide bitterness and other flavours in beer. Hops also help preserve beer.

Isinglass: *see* Finings.

Keg: a pressurized container for storing usually pasteurized beer. Brewery-conditioned beers, or 'keg' beers, need gas pressure to give them artificial fizz.

Kräusen: to add a small quantity of partially fermented wort to a beer in order to provide fresh sugars for the yeast to continue fermentation. It helps generate extra condition.

Kriek: a Belgian lambic beer undergoing a secondary fermentation with the addition of cherries or cherry juice. Similar beers incorporate raspberries ('framboise'/'frambozen') and other fruits. *See also* Lambic.

Lager: a bottom-fermented beer (the yeast sinks to the bottom of the wort during fermentation) that is matured for several weeks (months in the best instances) at low temperatures.

Lambic: a Belgian wheat beer fermented by wild yeasts and aged in casks. Blended lambic is known as gueuze. *See also* Kriek.

Late hopping: the process of adding hops late to the copper boil, to compensate for any aroma that may have been lost from hops used earlier in the boil.

Malt: barley that has been partially germinated to release vital starches and enzymes for brewing, then kilned to arrest germination and provide various flavours.

Malt extract: commercially produced concentrated wort, used by some brewers to save mashing, or to supplement their own wort.

Mash: the infusion of malt and water in the mash tun, which extracts fermentable materials from the grain.

Mild: a lightly hopped, usually lowish-strength ale, often dark in colour.

Mouthfeel: the texture and body.

Nose: *see* Aroma.

OG: Original Gravity – a reading taken before fermentation to gauge the amount of fermentable material in a beer. The higher the OG, the more fermentables and the greater the likely strength of the finished brew.

Old ale: a strong, dark beer; traditionally, a beer set aside to mature.

Original gravity: *see* OG.

Oxidation: the deterioration in beer caused by oxygen, usually manifested in a wet paper or cardboard taste.

Palate: the sense of taste.

Parti-gyle: method of brewing more than one beer at the same time, using one standard brew that is then adapted – often by adding water to change the strength, or by using the first runnings from the mash tun to make a heavy beer, and later runnings for a lighter beer.

Pasteurized: beer that has been heat treated to kill off remaining yeast cells and prevent further fermentation.

Porter: a lighter-bodied predecessor of stout, usually dry, with some sweetness.

Rack: to run beer from a tank or a cask.

Real ale: an unpasteurized, unfiltered beer that continues to ferment in the vessel from which it is dispensed ('cask-conditioned' or 'bottle-conditioned').

Sediment: solids in beer, primarily yeast but also possibly some proteins.

Shilling system: a Scottish system of branding beers according to style and strength, derived from Victorian times when the number of shillings stated referred to the gross price payable by

the publican on each barrel. 60/-, or light, is the Scottish equivalent of a mild; 70/-, or heavy, is a Scottish bitter; and 80/-, or export, is a stronger beer again.

Single-varietal: a beer using just one strain of hops or one type of malt.

Sterile-filtered: *see* Filtered.

Stock ale: a very strong beer intended to be kept and matured for several months.

Stout: traditionally, a strongish beer, usually dark in colour and tasting dry and bitter, often with roasted barley flavour.

Sunstruck: beer that has been over-exposed to bright light. This can cause a chemical reaction, leading to unsavoury aromas and flavours.

Trappist ale: *see* Abbey beer.

Tripel: *see* Dubbel.

Weissbier: a Bavarian style of wheat beer, known for its fruit-and-spices character. Hefeweissbiers are naturally cloudy; kristalweissbiers are filtered to be clear. Also called weizenbiers.

Wheat beer: a style of beer originating in Germany and Belgium, brewed with a high percentage of wheat and often served cloudy with yeast in suspension.

Witbier: a Belgian-style, spiced wheat beer; also known as bière blanche.

Wort: the unfermented sweet liquid produced by mashing malt and water.

Yeast: a single-celled micro-organism that turns sugar in wort into alcohol and carbon dioxide.

Index

Books for Beer Lovers

CAMRA Books, the publishing arm of the Campaign for Real Ale, is the leading publisher of books on beer and pubs. Key titles include:

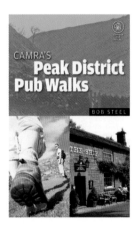

300 BEERS TO TRY BEFORE YOU DIE!
Roger Protz

300 beers from around the world, handpicked by award-winning journalist, author and broadcaster Roger Protz to try before you die! A comprehensive portfolio of top beers from the smallest microbreweries in the United States to family-run British breweries and the world's largest brands. This book is indispensable for both beer novices and aficionados alike.

£14.99 ISBN 978 1 85249 213 7

GOOD BEER GUIDE
Editor: Roger Protz

The *Good Beer Guide* is the only guide you will ever need to find the right pint, in the right place, every time. It's the original and best independent guide to around 4,500 pubs and more than 600 breweries throughout the UK. In 2002 it was named as one of the *Guardian* newspaper's books of the year and the *Sun* newspaper rated the 2004 edition in the top 20 books of all time! This annual publication is a comprehensive guide to the best real ale pubs in the UK, researched and written exclusively by CAMRA members and fully updated every year.

£14.99 ISBN 978 1 85249 231 1

PEAK DISTRICT PUB WALKS
Bob Steel

A practical, pocket-sized travellers guide to some of the best pubs and best walking in the Peak District, the book features 25 walks, as well as cycle routes and local attractions, helping you see the best of Britain's oldest national park, while never straying too far from a decent pint. This book also explores some of the region's fascinating industrial heritage and has useful information about local transport and accommodation. Each route has been selected for its inspiring landscape, historic interest and beer – with the walks taking you on a tour of the best real-ale pubs the area has to offer.

£9.99 ISBN 978 1 85249 246 5

CAMRA
BOOKS

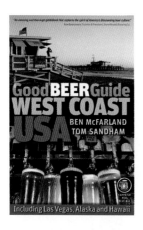

GOOD BEER GUIDE WEST COAST USA
Ben McFarland & Tom Sandham

Taking in the whole western seaboard of the USA, as well as Las Vegas, Alaska and Hawaii, this is a lively, comprehensive and entertaining tour that unveils some of the most exhilarating beers, breweries and bars on the planet. It is the definitive, totally independent guide to understanding and discovering the heart of America's thriving craft beer scene, and an essential companion for any beer drinker visiting West Coast America or seeking out American beer in the UK. Written with verve and insight by two respected young beer journalists, *Good Beer Guide USA* is a must – not just for those who find themselves on the West Coast, but for all discerning beer enthusiasts and barflies everywhere.

£14.99 ISBN 978 1 85249 244 1

100 BELGIAN BEERS TO TRY BEFORE YOU DIE!
Tim Webb & Joris Pattyn

100 Belgian Beers to Try Before You Die! showcases 100 of the best Belgian beers as chosen by internationally known beer writers Tim Webb and Joris Pattyn. Organised by brewery, each entry includes a history of the brewery, tasting notes for the beers, visitor information and the authors' verdict.

Lavishly illustrated throughout with photography of the beers themselves, where and how they are brewed, Belgian beer bars and some of the characters involved in Belgian brewing, the book encourages both connoisseurs and newcomers to Belgian beer to sample them for themselves, both in Belgium and at home.

£12.99 ISBN 978 1 85249 248 9

THE BOOK OF BEER KNOWLEDGE
Jeff Evans

A unique collection of entertaining trivia and essential wisdom, this is the perfect gift for beer lovers everywhere. Fully revised and updated, it includes more than 200 entries covering everything from fictional 'celebrity landlords' of soap pubs to the harsh facts detailing the world's biggest brewers; from bizarre beer names to the serious subject of fermentation.

£9.99 ISBN 978 1 85249 198 7

Order these and other CAMRA books online at **www.camra.org.uk/ books**, ask your local bookstore, or contact: CAMRA, 230 Hatfield Road, St Albans, AL1 4LW.
Telephone 01727 867201

A Beer a Day

It takes all sorts to Campaign for Real Ale

CAMRA, the Campaign for Real Ale, is an independent not-for-profit, volunteer-led consumer group. We actively campaign for full pints and more flexible licensing hours, as well as protecting the 'local' pub and lobbying government to champion pub-goers' rights.

CAMRA has 90,000 members from all ages and backgrounds, brought together by a common belief in the issues that CAMRA deals with and their love of good quality British beer. From just £20 a year – that's less than a pint a month – you can join CAMRA and enjoy the following benefits:

A monthly colour newspaper informing you about beer and pub news and detailing events and beer festivals around the country.

Free or reduced entry to over 140 national, regional and local beer festivals.

Money off many of our publications including the *Good Beer Guide* and the *Good Bottled Beer Guide*.

Access to a members-only section of our national website, **www.camra.org.uk**, which gives up-to-the-minute news stories and includes a special offer section with regular features saving money on beer and trips away.

The opportunity to campaign to save pubs under threat of closure, for pubs to be open when people want to drink and a reduction in beer duty that will help Britain's brewing industry survive.

Log onto **www.camra.org.uk** for CAMRA membership information.

Do you feel passionately about your pint? Then why not join CAMRA?

Just fill in the application form (or a photocopy of it) and the Direct Debit form on the next page to receive three months' membership FREE!*

If you wish to join but do not want to pay by Direct Debit, please fill in the application form below and send a cheque, payable to CAMRA, to: CAMRA, 230 Hatfield Road, St Albans, Hertfordshire, AL1 4LW. Please note that non Direct Debit payments will incur a £2 surcharge. Figures are given below.

Please tick appropriate box

	Direct Debit	Non DD
☐ Single membership (UK & EU)	£20	£22
☐ Concessionary membership (under 26 or 60 and over)	£11	£13
☐ Joint membership	£25	£27
☐ Concessionary joint membership	£14	£16

Life membership information is available on request.

Title _____ Surname _____

Forename(s) _____

Address _____

_____ Postcode _____

Date of Birth _____ Email address _____

Signature _____

Partner's details (for Joint Membership)

Title _____ Surname _____

Forename(s) _____

Date of Birth _____ Email address _____

CAMRA will occasionally send you e-mails related to your membership. We will also allow your local branch access to your e-mail if you would like to opt-out of contact from your local branch please tick here ☐ (at no point will your details be released to a third party)

Find out more about CAMRA at **www.camra.org.uk** Telephone 01727 867201

*Three months free is only available the first time a member pays by DD

A Beer a Day

Instruction to your Bank or Building Society to pay by Direct Debit

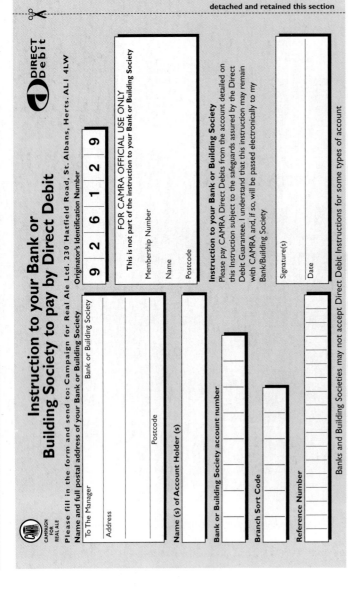

Please fill in the form and send to: Campaign for Real Ale Ltd. 230 Hatfield Road, St. Albans, Herts. AL1 4LW

Name and full postal address of your Bank or Building Society

To The Manager   Bank or Building Society

Address

Postcode

Name (s) of Account Holder (s)

Bank or Building Society account number

Branch Sort Code

Reference Number

Banks and Building Societies may not accept Direct Debit Instructions for some types of account

Originator's Identification Number

| 9 | 2 | 6 | 1 | 2 | 9 |

FOR CAMRA OFFICIAL USE ONLY
This is not part of the instruction to your **Bank or Building Society**

Membership Number

Name

Postcode

Instruction to your Bank or Building Society

Please pay CAMRA Direct Debits from the account detailed on this Instruction subject to the safeguards assured by the Direct Debit Guarantee. I understand that this instruction may remain with CAMRA and, if so, will be passed electronically to my Bank/Building Society

Signature(s)

Date

This Guarantee should be detached and retained by the payer.

The Direct Debit Guarantee

- This Guarantee is offered by all Banks and Building Societies that take part in the Direct Debit Scheme. The efficiency and security of the Scheme is monitored and protected by your own Bank or Building Society.

- If the amounts to be paid or the payment dates change CAMRA will notify you 10 working days in advance of your account being debited or as otherwise agreed.

- If an error is made by CAMRA or your Bank or Building Society, you are guaranteed a full and immediate refund from your branch of the amount paid.

- You can cancel a Direct Debit at any time by writing to your Bank or Building Society. Please also send a copy of your letter to us.

detached and retained this section